To my mother

CONTENTS

PREFACE **vii**

ACKNOWLEDGMENTS **viii**

INTRODUCTION **ix**

THE AMERICAN ETHNIC COOKBOOK FOR
  STUDENTS 1
Acadians (Cajuns) 1
African-Americans 5
Albanian-Americans 9
Amish 10
Anglo-Americans (English) 12
Apache 15
Arab-Americans (Lebanese and Syrians) 17
Armenian-Americans 19
Asian Indian-Americans 22
Assyrian- and Chaldean-Americans
    (Mesopotamians) 25
Australian- and New Zealander-
    Americans 27
Austrian-Americans 29
Bahamian-Americans 32
Barbadan-Americans 34
Basque-Americans 35
Belgian-Americans 38
Belorussian-Americans 41
Black Muslims 42
Brazilian-Americans 44
Bulgarian-Americans, Macedonian-Americans,
    and Vlachs (Arumanians) 46
Cambodian-Americans 49
Cane River Creoles 50
Cape Verdean-Americans 54
Carpatho-Rusyn-Americans (Ruskins,
    Rusnyaks, Ruthenians, Lemkians) 56

Cherokee 59
Chickasaw 61
Chinese-Americans 63
Chitimacha Tribe of Louisiana 67
Choctaw 69
Colombian-Americans 70
Cornish-Americans 72
Creek Indians of Oklahoma 74
Creoles (Louisiana) 76
Croatian-Americans 79
Cuban-Americans 82
Czech-Americans 84
Danish-Americans 88
Dominican-Americans 90
Dutch-Americans 93
Ecuadorian-Americans 96
Egyptian-Americans 98
English Canadian-Americans 99
Eskimos (Inuit) and Aleuts 101
Estonian-Americans 103
Ethiopian- and Eritrean-Americans 104
Filipino-Americans 106
Finnish-Americans 108
Franco-Americans 111
French Canadian-Americans 113
German-Americans 115
Germans from Russia 119
Greek-Americans 122
Guamians (Chamoros) 125
Guatemalan-Americans 126
Gullah (Geechee and Sea Islanders) 127
Guyanese-Americans (and Indo-
    Caribbeans) 129
Gypsy-Americans (Romanichals, Travellers,
    and Roma) 131

Haitian-Americans   134
Hawaiians   136
Hmong-Americans   137
Honduran- and Garifuna-Americans   139
Hopi   141
Hungarian-Americans   142
Icelandic-Americans   145
Irish-Americans   148
Iroquois   151
Italian-Americans   153
Jamaican-Americans   157
Japanese-Americans   159
Jewish-Americans   161
Korean-Americans   164
Laotian-Americans   166
Latvian-Americans   169
Lithuanian-Americans   171
Lumbee Indians of North Carolina   173
Melungeons   175
Mexican-Americans (Chicanos)   178
Moravians   182
Mormons   184
Narragansett   187
Navajo (Diné or Dineh)   189
New Mexico Hispanics   192
Nicaraguan-Americans   195
Nigerian-Americans   197
Norwegian-Americans   200
Ojibway (Chippewa, Ojibwe, and
    Ojibwa)   202
Okinawan-Americans   204
Pakistani-Americans   206
Panamanian-Americans   208
Pennsylvania Dutch   210
Persian-Americans (Iranians)   213
Peruvian-Americans   216
Pima and Papago (Tohono O'odham)   218
Polish-Americans   220
Portuguese-Americans   224
Potawatomi   226
Pueblo Indians (Eastern)   228
Puerto Ricans   230

Romanian-Americans   232
Russian-Americans   234
Salvadoran-Americans   237
Samoan-Americans   240
Scotch-Irish   241
Scottish-Americans   244
Seminole and Miccosukee   247
Serbian-Americans (including
    Montenegrins)   249
Shawnee   251
Sioux (Dakota, Lakhota, and Nakota)   252
Slovak-Americans   256
Slovene-Americans   258
Spanish-Americans   261
Swedish-Americans   264
Swiss-Americans   268
Texas Wends   269
Thai-Americans   271
Tlingit and Haida   272
Trinidadian-Americans (and Indo-
    Caribbeans)   274
Turkish-Americans   276
Ukrainian-Americans   278
Vietnamese-Americans   280
Wampanoag   285
Welsh-Americans   287
Zuni   288

APPENDIX 1: HOW TO KNEAD   291

APPENDIX 2: THEY ALL STUFFED
    CABBAGE   293

APPENDIX 3: THEY ALL FRIED BEAN
    CAKES   295

APPENDIX 4: THEY ALL FRIED
    DOUGH   296

ANNOTATED BIBLIOGRAPHY   299

INDEX OF RECIPES BY STATES   305

INDEX   311

PREFACE

This is not a book about recipes. This is a book about people's stories. In particular, it is a book about belonging to a group, about cooking and eating foods that remind ethnic Americans where they came from, who they are, and how they can be Americans without losing touch with their ethnic heritage.

This book focuses on foods that have been used to express ethnic identity in the United States. These are not authentic foreign dishes. They are not necessarily dishes ethnic Americans eat every day or even every year. They are dishes that people use to remember another time and place. They are dishes people use to share feelings with a group that has a common history, and, frequently, a common national origin, culture, religion, or language.

Foreign recipes are inevitably changed by being transplanted to the United States, and all ethnic recipes change as the ethnic group and its identity change. The old theory that the United States is a "melting pot" in which ethnicity eventually blends out of existence is no longer widely accepted. The "Roots" phenomenon of the 1970s and 1980s produced many Americans whose sense of belonging to an ethnic group spans many generations in the United States. As you will see in this book, new ethnic groups have formed in the United States, from the Pennsylvania Dutch in the 1760s to the Black Muslims in the 1960s. The ethnic foods of Native Americans also changed over their long history before contact with Europeans, and continue to change today.

The American Ethnic Cookbook for Students includes almost 400 recipes from members of 122 ethnic groups living in all 50 states and the District of Columbia. Because almost all the recipes were written by individual members of the ethnic group, they are often more representative than typical. I have tried to select recipes that tell how dishes have changed, about the subgroups within ethnic groups, about different kinds of meals and occasions, about different times in American history, about ethnicity in different regions of the United States, and about cooks both skilled and precise, clever or experienced, desperate and creative.

These recipes were collected as a resource for ethnic understanding, and for school projects in social studies, American history, modern languages, local history, culinary arts, and literacy. The sources included existing school projects in all those areas, church and community cookbooks, surveys of national and regional cooking, historical and commemorative cookbooks, family cookbooks, political cookbooks, and my own recipe archives as a food journalist of almost 30 years. For many small ethnic groups, Indian tribes, and recent immigrants, the Internet has become a crucial tool for preserving and exchanging recipes.

This book is intended to supplement *The Multicultural Cookbook for Students* by Carol Lisa Albyn and Lois Sinaiko Webb, as well as Ms. Webb's *Holidays of the World Cookbook for Students* and *Multicultural Cookbook for Celebra-*

tions, Life Cycle Events, and Rites of Passage. Readers will gain a great deal by comparing the worldwide recipes in those books with the foods developed by immigrants in the United States. *The American Ethnic Cookbook for Students* also contains foods of 21 Native American groups; of ethnic groups that formed in the United States; of ethno-religious groups with various national origins; and of immigrant groups that were also minorities in their countries of origin, such as Jewish-Americans, Carpatho-Rusyn-Americans, Hmong-Americans, Gypsy-Americans, or Okinawan-Americans.

Recipes were selected to represent the many ways ethnic cooking changes in the course of ethnic history. Some, like Swedish meatballs, are now widely used in the general community. Others are known only within the ethnic group. Some recipes in this book represent individual inventions within ethnic traditions. In a few cases, the author of the recipe is not herself or himself a descendent of the ethnic group, but acquired the recipe with membership by marriage or church affiliation.

Home cooks will find this a very good cookbook. Ethnic cooking by definition is nostalgic and old-fashioned, but the dishes that have survived the American "melting pot" are useful, adaptable, and delicious. A lot of cooks stirred a lot of pots to create these dishes.

Each section includes a short history of the ethnic group and an estimate of their current numbers. The book includes almost every immigrant group with more than 100,000 descendants now in the U.S., as well as the 10 largest Indian tribes. It also contains a sampling of smaller groups and tribes, if only to illustrate that small ethnic groups also survive. Some groups have been radically transformed. One common phenomenon is for a group to form in the United States out of what had been ethnically diverse or even mutually hostile groups in their homeland.

Two to six recipes are provided for each group, and each recipe includes a note about where it came from and how it has been used or changed. The Introduction contains some general rules of how ethnic recipes develop, a section on "Getting Started in Ethnography," and another on

"Getting Started in the Kitchen." In a departure from the previous Oryx cookbooks mentioned above, I have used **bold-face type** to indicate the names of ethnic groups with related foods, and of related recipes elsewhere in the book. Appendix 1 is a description of how I knead dough. Also, certain recipes are repeated among many ethnic groups. Rather than repeat these recipes, the various names and some identifying details are summarized in Appendixes 2, 3, and 4, with tables called "They All Stuffed Cabbage," "They All Fried Bean Cakes," and "They All Fried Dough." The book also contains an annotated bibliography of some of the most useful sources employed in compiling this volume.

ACKNOWLEDGMENTS

A special thanks to my wife, Virginia Vogel Zanger, whose work in bilingual and multicultural education has opened many worlds to me over the last 25 years.

I wish to thank Donna Sanzone, my editor at Oryx, and our mutual friend Evan Levinson for matching me up with a book I was born to write. In all matters of food, I am influenced by my late father, Martin Zanger, and my maternal grandmother, Malvina Kurtz. My cooking priorities benefited from an early reading of the work of John and Karen Hess, and the continuing influences of John Thorne and Chris Kimball. In the study of cultures, my beacon has been Dr. Carmen Judith Nine-Court. This book owes much to many discussions with Dr. Judith A. Birnbaum. Illustrator Judy Love added to everything she touched, and especially the Cornish Rope. Individual cooks are too many to mention, but I especially appreciated the immediate and patient aid of Dr. Ian F. Hancock on Gypsy-Americans, Linda Griggs on Melungeons, Katherine Balthazzar Heitzmann on the Cane River Creoles, Mary Chitwood of the Lumbee Indians of North Carolina, and Stands Alone in the Moon Wilson-McSwain (Cherokee and Shawnee).

And because, as Woody Guthrie sang, "My father's own father, he waded that river."

INTRODUCTION

How Ethnic Recipes Change

Ethnic recipes change as ethnic identity changes.

All U.S. immigrant groups have followed the same general course of adjustment to their new country—an adjustment that also includes a modification of cooking styles. (Exceptions to the pattern are discussed below.)

Listed below are 10 specific kinds of changes that mark the Americanization of an ethnic recipe:

1. What Chef Louis Szamarathy has called the "passion for ease of preparation"—reduction of cooking time and complexity of preparation.

2. Pre-portioning into portable and hand-size forms like sandwiches, pasties, or cookies.

3. Combining ingredients into one-pot dinners.

4. Use of labor-saving machines.

5. Substitution of baking powder for yeast, and increased sugar in baked goods.

6. Increased amount of meat, especially beef, and substitution of beef for other meats.

7. Substitution of American foodstuffs, specifically corn, chili peppers, beans, and squash.

8. Increased use of tomatoes and substitution of canned tomatoes for other acidic ingredients such as vinegar, lemons, or yogurt in sauces, soups, and stews.

9. Increased use of potatoes and substitution of potatoes for other carbohydrate foods.

10. Substitution of canned or otherwise packaged foods for whole-food ingredients.

These changes made ethnic foods faster to cook and easier to eat, more suited to the rhythm of American life, but the dishes did not necessarily become less ethnic, or even more like each other. Although many ethnic foods are lost, the ones that fit into the American pattern have become more popular and more complicated, and have developed new variations. Jewish-American bagels have not only become softer and easier to eat, they have also become much larger and have developed flavors. The first flavors were taken over from other Jewish-American breads—egg, rye, sesame seed, poppy seed, onion. The second wave of flavors compressed even more ethnic content into a single product—garlic, cheese, and the "everything" bagel with all kinds of seeds. Today, there are "post-ethnic" flavors like blueberry, jalapeño, and honey-wheat. This trend may be the end of the bagel as a Jewish-American food. Or it may be that Jewish-American identity will come to include blueberry bagels that will seem exotic to Jews in France or Israel.

THE IMMIGRANTS' COOKING

When immigrants first arrive, foreign recipes do not quickly change because the group must struggle to survive under new conditions. Many familiar foods are simply not available, and some recipes are lost. Other recipes survive because they can be made to work with simple ingredient substitutions. Some immigrant groups consisted mostly of male workers at first, and had no ethnic foods until women arrived and set up boardinghouses on an ethnic basis. Even then, the range of recipes was greatly reduced.

This pattern of briefly dropping ethnic foods on arrival, then briefly reverting to foreign foods has held through the four periods of immigration described by historians. For "Old Stock" (pre-1776) immigrants, there was also a dislocation in time and social class as they moved from settled European countries to frontier subsistence. For "Old Immigrants" (1820-1860), those who pioneered farmland experienced that kind of dislocation, while those who moved to American cities often increased their wages and were able to exchange their traditional recipes for diets with more meat. "New Immigrants" (1880-1924) came to more concentrated urban neighborhoods where they could more quickly organize supplies of their old foods. After a shorter survival period, their foods reverted to a traditional diet, and more of their old-country recipes survived. This pattern has accelerated with "Recent Immigrants" (since 1965) who are sometimes able to set up import networks within months. This is more true, for example, of Nigerian-Americans than of Hmong-Americans, but the acceleration is there for all.

IMMIGRANTS COOK "AMERICAN"

After the brief revival of foreign foods, the immigrant groups became more settled and began to adopt specific American foods. The definition of an ethnic group changed as people resorted themselves. Generally, ethnic groups in America were more inclusive than they had been in Europe because people from different regions were thrown together in American settlements. But some groups divided further in the United States, where they were free to express differences. Most workday food became "American"—which might include a dish of another ethnic group that fit the new lifestyle. This was how Cornish pasties were adopted by miners of many backgrounds. Ethnic foods were used more on Sundays and major religious holidays. As the group members became financially established, holiday foods like Christmas puddings or cookies moved onto the Sunday table, increasingly as ethnic rather than religious foods. At the same time, Sunday dinners often became more elaborate, and recipes began to merge. Soups and stews literally developed more and more ingredients. A clear soup like the Belgian-American booyah became a thick multi-ingredient stew over the course of the twentieth century.

Second-generation immigrants were usually encouraged to be "more American" than their parents, and in some groups tried to eat "American food" everywhere except at home. As members of this generation moved into their own homes, their recipes became less ethnic, and the Sunday ethnic food festival became a visit to parents. The daily menu might support the "melting pot" theory, and some second-generation ethnic Americans tried to melt as fast as they could. Groups strongly identified with a particular church have often retained more ethnic identity in the second generation.

ETHNIC GRANDCHILDREN

The third generation, which often marks the end of the foreign language for immigrants, frequently has meant a revival of ethnic foods. The Sunday visits to grandparents are supplemented with visits to ethnic restaurants. Again, this pattern developed somewhat more slowly among "old immigrants" and much more rapidly among "recent immigrants." But as a generalization, the third generation revived the ethnic recipes, with a limited selection, and often in different forms. For example, the third generation of Belgian-Americans took that bouillon out of the home and into church basements and taverns where booyah is now a dish made by groups of men for fundraising occasions a few times a year, or for Green Bay Packer football weekends. Groups of women make traditional Belgian pies (which would have been purchased from a bakery in Belgium, but are otherwise unchanged).

Another way ethnic food has changed by the third generation is that is has remained the same, while the food of the home country has changed. Norwegian-American men began making lutefisk, a Christmas dish of dried fish in nineteenth-century Norway, for large-group events in social halls. And they still do. But back in Norway, people have stopped eating lutefisk because improved transportation supplies fresh fish in the winter.

About 4,000 Puerto Ricans migrated to Hawaii in 1899 to work on the plantations. They took with them flour-based dumplings called *surrulos*. When Dr. Carmen Judith Nine-Court visited Hawaii's Puerto Rican community in 1989, people were still doing dances that only a few old people knew in Puerto Rico. The band played the old songs, but no one knew the words, and few people spoke much Spanish. But her biggest surprise was the *surrulos*. Because corn meal came to Puerto Rico shortly after 1899, *surrulitos* are now corn cakes stuffed with cheese. Moreover, *surrulitos* are now fried in Puerto Rico, but are still boiled among the Puerto Rican families in Hawaii.

What is revived in the third generation is often not the same ethnic group as the one rejected by the second generation. For example, immigrant Sicilians, Venetians, and Romans had Italian-American grandchildren. Over three generations, an Italian-American identity had united descendents of various Italian provinces. More subtly, southern Italians who emigrated to the U.S. in 1910 might have had grandchildren who loved to make northern Italian food out of a cookbook by the 1960s.

In a few cases, acceptance of an ethnic food by the general community has led the original group to give up a food. African-Americans brought peanut soup to Virginia, where it became a favorite of George Washington. But these days the usual cooks of peanut soup in Virginia are Anglo-Americans in historical societies. You also don't see too many Mexican-Americans at chili bake-offs these days, although Mexican-Americans in San Antonio had a near-monopoly on chili con carne into the early years of the twentieth century.

Sometimes a dish migrates from one ethnic group to another, taking on new meanings. Tea cakes came over from England with founding-stock English settlers. After the Civil War, southerners began to think of tea cakes as a symbol of Anglo-American gentility, and northerners lost interest in them. But from the 1900s to the 1960s, African-Americans migrating from the South to northern cities began to cherish tea cakes as a symbol of how far they had come, from being the cooks of those tea cakes in the Old South, to where they could serve them to their own guests.

EXCEPTIONS TO THE IMMIGRANT PATTERN

NATIVE AMERICANS

Native Americans are obviously not immigrants. Although they had moved around the continent before contact with Europeans, and some tribes have moved from Canada to Mexico since contact, Native Americans did not leave a place with one language and culture and move to a place with another language and culture. Some of the tribes have moved through many different climate zones in a few hundred years, and have lost recipes by doing so because they lost access to necessary ingredients. Relatively settled groups like the Eastern Pueblo Indians, the Hopi, and the Zuni have a lot of recipes because they have lived in the same places for many centuries, and have learned how to use more species of plants and animals. More isolated or migratory groups may be very adaptable, like the Apache, but they tend to have fewer traditional recipes.

At every stage of Native American history, people have revived their sense of Indian identity by camping out and researching wild foods, fish, and game. The consistent strains that run through the cooking of more than 100 Indian tribes today are a love of hunting and of gathering native plants; cooking with the corn, beans, and squash that were farmed all over North America; and a set of "Indian foods" from the

Pan-Indian movement of the twentieth century (such as fry bread, buffalo steaks, and wild rice). The Pan-Indian movement argued that Indian ways are the common heritage of all Native Americans, and began the inter-tribal pow-wows. Many tribes have food traditions from more recent history—if the tribe was forced into a new region, if girls were taught European cooking in boarding schools, if people developed ways to cook the foods distributed on reservations, or if other ethnic groups married into the tribe. Food writers of Native background such as E. Barrie Kavasch and Dale Carson are creating new ethnic dishes every year. As with many ethnic Americans, Indian descendants may eat like non-Indian neighbors most of the year, but still treasure certain traditional dishes at certain times.

AFRICAN-AMERICANS

The vast majority of African-Americans are descendents of involuntary immigrants who came to America as slaves. The earliest arrivals were able to hang on to their ethnic African identities (which were once called "tribal" instead of "ethnic") more than scholars initially recognized. In the 1960s and 1970s, a Pan-African movement developed, like the Pan-Indian movement described above. Pan-Africanist Maulana Ron Karenga proposed the celebration of Kwaanza, which includes a concluding feast of heritage foods from Africa or the Caribbean. Today, a given black family's ethnic foods may include African-influenced southern dishes such as sweet-potato pie, old Anglo-American dishes such as tea cakes, dishes of Afro-Caribbean immigrant groups, and contemporary African foods explored during Kwanzaa Karamu feasts.

JAPANESE- AND CHINESE-AMERICANS

These groups began as voluntary immigrants, but were then limited by harsh laws against new immigrants, female immigrants, property ownership, and access to public facilities. Eight full decades passed from the first Chinese Exclusion Acts to the end of Japanese internment after World War II, and full equality under law was not achieved until the 1960s. One unusual consequence was that Chinese- and Japanese-American foods have been conservative, remaining at the level of simple ingredient substitutions more than 100 years after the first generation of immigrants. The notable exception is in Hawaii, which early on developed an Asian-American majority, and a more typical immigrant pattern of mutually influenced ethnic American foods.

MULTIRACIAL GROUPS

Because a uniquely American description of "race" by color defined slavery, it came to define all American understanding of ethnicity. The 40 or more races of European racial theory became "white," all others became "black," "Indian," "Mexican" (later "Hispanic"), or "Asian." Multiracial groups just didn't fit, and efforts were made to force them into one category or another. This made some groups very conservative about their food, like the Chinese- and Japanese-Americans, and left other groups with many layers of food customs, like African-American or Native American groups.

Some multiracial ethnic groups in this book are the Lumbee Indians of North Carolina, the Melungeons, Cape Verdean-Americans, and Cane River Creoles. Although these groups are variously defined as immigrants, an Indian tribe, African-Americans, "whites," or a "tri-racial isolate," there is a surprising amount of intermarriage between these dispersed groups, and many people in them would reject all the larger categories and define themselves as group members and Americans.

IS EVERY FOOD ETHNIC?

Whole lists of foods are seldom identified with any ethnic group, including dishes invented in restaurants in the United States, such as vichyssoise, Boston cream pie, Carpetbag steak, or Cincinnati chili. Individual Mexicans or Mexican-Americans invented Caesar salad, and fried corn chips, and we may call nachos "Mexican food," but they have never been a point of ethnic identification for Mexican Americans

Many American ethnic recipes are shared among different groups. Sometimes it seems like they all stuff cabbage (see Appendix 2), they all fry bean cakes (see Appendix 3), they all crimp pasties, they all bake coffeecake, they all fry dough (see Appendix 4), and they all boil dumplings.

Some dishes from "Founding Stock" groups have been in general use for so long that they no longer have any ethnic content, and lots of dishes never did. Hamburgers have a German name and vaguely German antecedents, but have never been a German-American food. Chowder and barbecue have had so many hands in the pot they cannot be called ethnic recipes.

WHAT IF SOMEONE DOESN'T FEEL ETHNIC?

Americans who don't think they are ethnic are part of a very large group. The 1990 census ancestry survey projected about 12.4 million Americans who would have listed their ancestry as "American," 1.8 million as "white," and 643,000 as "United States." More than 20 million Americans wouldn't have written anything on the survey.

Many Americans simply don't think of themselves as part of any group with a common history, religion, national origin, or language. They know their ancestry but they don't eat foods identified with it. At some periods of American culture, this lack of an ethnic consciousness was posed as the ideal consciousness toward which all ethnic-Americans should work. Individuals may drop their ethnic identification for a time, and may or may not return to it later on.

In this book, you can get an idea of how Americans who are ethnically involved view their ethnicity, and what they might eat to express it. Many school units on understanding other groups start with a family tree exercise to get people thinking about ethnicity. But it also works the other way. Studying other ethnic groups often stimulates people to think about themselves differently. For many Americans, the televised mini-series based on Alex Haley's *Roots* set off a process of ethnic identification that had nothing to do with the particular experiences of Haley's ancestors. Just watching the drama of ethnic identification over so many generations of an African-American family stirred up a lot of stories about how families of many diverse backgrounds had struggled in America.

MULTI-ETHNIC IDENTITY

About one-third of the people who reported a "first ancestry" on the 1990 census survey also reported a "second ancestry." We can guess that a decent fraction would have reported third and fourth ancestries if they had been given a chance. My own grandparents were born in four different countries, and many people can trace their genealogy back to six or eight or twelve ethnic groups. People like to cook and eat different kinds of food, and good ethnic cooks are likely to enjoy many kinds of food. Back when women did all the cooking in American homes, they not only cooked dishes from their own backgrounds, but also learned dishes familiar to their husbands' families. My Jewish-American friend Helen Strahinich makes a walnut roll she learned from her Italian-American mother-in-law, who learned it from her Croatian-American in-laws. But it's still a Croatian-American dessert. While cooks like to joke that their family's favorite dish is "Irish spaghetti" or "Polish lasagna" or "Cajun matzo balls," I can think of few recipes that actually carry a dual-ethnic identity, and none that are made regularly by more than one person to express a three-way ethnic identity.

HOW LARGE ARE ETHNIC GROUPS?

Since ethnic identification over the history of the United States has sometimes been dangerous, and sometimes a matter of choice, there are no definitive counts of the size of various groups. For political and cultural reasons, groups have been counted differently. As an extreme example, African-Americans have generally been counted to include anyone with one great-grandparent of African descent, regardless of national origin. Some immigrant groups have been counted by last names, which would include people with anywhere from one to eight great-grandparents in the group. Until recently, Native American groups were counted by tribal enrollments of federally recognized Indian nations, which required residence and active involvement.

To count ethnic Americans for this book, I relied on the 1990 census ancestry survey. Since this was voluntary, it is at least a measure of how many people feel that they are part of an ethnic group. Although the sum of first and second ancestry projections is larger than the actual population, it seems to accord with people's sense of having several ethnic loyalties. However, these numbers present several problems. For one thing, it is a survey. The numbers are projections based on the sample number of people who actually filled out the questionnaire. It is likely to be more accurate about larger groups than smaller ones.

Secondly, the Bureau of the Census is prevented by law from keeping statistics on religious affiliation. So answers of "Jewish" or "Mormon" or "Black Muslim" were not tabulated, even if people wrote that in. If I had written in "East European Jewish" as my ancestry, that apparently would have appeared on the survey among the projected 466,718 Americans who listed "European" as their ancestry. Not all national-origin answers are tabulated. The 1980 survey didn't accept Czechoslovakian, British, or Scotch-Irish as answers. So the 10 million Scottish-Americans in the 1980 census became the 5.6 million Scotch-Irish and 5.4 million Scottish-Americans in 1990. In 1980, the census listed 1.8 million Americans of Czech ancestry and 777,000 Americans of Slovak ancestry, but in 1990 the survey projected only 1.3 million Czech-Americans, 315,000 Czechoslovakian-Americans, and 1.9 million Slovak-Americans.

Thirdly, ethnic affiliation is not only voluntary, but subject to some change. The 1990 survey shows much lower numbers for Germans from Russia than surveys in 1970 and 1980. The 1990 numbers for German and Cherokee ancestry are much higher. There hasn't been a population explosion in German-American and Cherokee neighborhoods! In all likelihood, Germans from Russia have either stopped thinking of themselves so much as ethnic Americans or feel more like German-Americans than they used to. The increasing interest in genealogy may have renewed interest in Cherokee or German ancestors. Or German descendents may be feeling less embarrassment about World War II. A recent poll of students in southern states noted that more now mention being descended from Na-

tive Americans than being descended from Confederate soldiers. This is a change in attitudes, not facts, but the facts of ethnic membership are often determined by attitude.

The ancestry survey is still keyed to race, with the result that ethnic groups within the African-American community are not recorded well, Native American groups are undercounted, and mixed-race groups are often ignored, although the 1970 census actually counted people in 200 groups of "tri-racial-isolates."

For Native American tribes, I have generally used the 1990 Census of Population Characteristics of American Indians by Tribe and Language (July 1994, Census Publication CP-3-7). It seems to be based on a combination of tribal enrollments and ancestry surveys, lists some state-recognized tribes, and gives higher numbers than previous government publications. For ethnoreligious groups, such as Moravians or Black Muslims, I have generally used published estimates based on church enrollment.

GETTING STARTED IN ETHNOGRAPHY

Cooking and eating the foods that are used to express ethnic identity in the United States are great ways to learn about how other people see themselves as both Americans and members of one or more ethnic groups. The information in this book is only a starting point for your own investigations. To learn more about ethnic cooking, it is important (1) to know your own background, (2) to ask other people questions, (3) to keep careful records, (4) to verify facts, (5) to try things for yourself, (6) to exchange information with other researchers, and (7) to ask other people more questions.

ETHNIC IDENTITY

If you ask people what foods express ethnic identity in their family, some people will answer, "None. I'm a white-bread American and just because I eat pizza doesn't make me Italian any more than going into the garage makes me a car." That's not a wrong answer. There are no wrong answers to questions about your identity. Your identity is what you think it is, and sometimes what other people around you think it is.

But, as you know, white bread wasn't invented in your house. The wheat was bred from various weeds in the ancient Middle East. The grinding technology and the use of yeast began in South Asia and North Africa. And the methods of refining white flour were developed in Europe. The first people in the United States to grow wheat were not the Jamestown settlers or the Pilgrims, but the Zuni and Pima Indians of Arizona and New Mexico, who got it from Spanish missionaries. If there were such an ethnic group as Whitebread-Americans, they would have a very mixed background! Immigrant foods will not seem so strange when you understand how your ancestors had to change their foods when they first came to the United States.

SAMPLE QUESTIONS

Some sample questions to ask include the following: When do you make this food? When did your mother make this food? What is ethnic about it? How has the recipe changed from the way it was before? What do you change when you make it from the way you learned it? Are there any ways to do it more easily? Are there any ways to do it better if you have more time?

Although the information in this book comes from hundreds of community cookbooks and Internet sites, it is a tiny piece of ethnic cooking in the U.S. There are many things still to be learned. And because ethnic food is still changing, no one will ever know everything about the cooking of even one ethnic group.

FIELD NOTES

One of the best ways to learn about any kind of cooking is to keep "lab notes" as you go along. How long did the dish actually cook "until done?" How many lemons did you have to squeeze to make a half cup of juice? If you are fortunate enough to help in the kitchen with an ethnic cook, take notes on the recipes—and not just the list of ingredients, but the order in which they are put together and the techniques of cutting or cooking. A recipe is only a blueprint. It may make a lot of difference whether the salt is added at the beginning or the end. It's hard to remember cooking details that might turn out

to be important. Taking notes also trains us to notice things and ask more questions.

POLITICS AND RELIGION

Is it bad manners to talk about religion or politics? Sometimes it is, although it's hard to understand ethnicity without religion or politics. Language and national origin are two more touchy subjects. But hardly anyone minds talking about food. Every ethnic group has special foods eaten as part of their culture, and most have special foods that *aren't* eaten—at least some of the time—as part of their culture.

VERIFY FACTS AND ACCEPT OPINIONS

To understand how foods have changed, you can look in cookbooks about foreign foods. There are also ethnic encyclopedias, books about ethnic history, and books about food history. Not everyone is sure or objective about facts, but people usually are telling the truth about their opinions. So if you learn from an ethnic cook that red peppers taste better than green peppers, you have to decide if this is a fact or an opinion. If it's a fact, you should check it in printed sources. Or you could set up a blindfold test to see if your classmates can tell the difference between red and green peppers. If it's an opinion, you should record it as an opinion of an ethnic cook. You should also check your own opinion and record that. For example: "One veteran cook of southern Italian background told me that in her group, red peppers are considered tastier than green peppers. When she gave me some of each to try, I thought the red peppers were sweeter, but I don't like sweet vegetables, so I preferred the green peppers. I will ask my grandmother if she preferred green peppers, too. Maybe this is part of my own culture."

EXCHANGE INFORMATION

A good way to obtain information is to exchange it with other researchers. What do your classmates think about red peppers versus green peppers? What does a Jamaican-American cook think? If you want to know what a Jewish-American male cook thinks, you can e-mail me at mark@ethnicook.com (I like red peppers). I'm also interested in learning more ethnic American recipes being used right now, and I'm especially interested in learning about mistakes in this book. I have a place on my Web site <http://www.ethnicook.com> where you can leave me ethnic recipes or questions, and read what other people have posted. You can publish the recipes you find in a pamphlet or on the Internet. Help other scholars by writing exactly where you got the recipe.

Ask More Questions

There are still many mysteries to be solved about ethnic cooking in the United States. Why is German-American oatmeal scrapple called "goetta" in Cincinnati? Why did clam chowder start being made with milk and potatoes in the 1840s? Who invented chili con carne? How is Indo-Caribbean food different from South Asian Indian food in New York City? Do any other Icelandic-Americans remember creamed potatoes? Some of the hardest questions are things about our own ethnic foods that we might not notice because they are just part of the scenery, such as, Is it still white bread if it has sesame seeds on it?

Getting Started in the Kitchen

This recipes in this book assume that you are cooking in a kitchen with measuring cups, measuring spoons, salt, pepper, water, a set of saucepans with lids, one or more frying pans, a stove, an oven, knives, work surfaces, a cutting board, and a few other basics. Nevertheless, you should begin by reading the recipe all the way through several times to make sure you have everything you need, and know what you have to do. Because this book includes many unfamiliar ways of cooking, you should assemble all the equipment and ingredients in plain sight before you begin.

Before we start the safety warnings, I want to emphasize that you should relax and have fun in the kitchen. It's only food. If the dish doesn't come out right the first time, this is not an ethnic slur. You might have made a mistake. The oven temperature might be off. You should cook with other people. Not only do professional cooking students always cook with an experienced professional to answer questions, but many expert ethnic cooks like to work in a group. That way, they can compare techniques and discuss problems (and gossip and have a good time). If the recipe contains a warning, or if any step is new to you, go over your plans with an adult cook. I have tried to avoid difficult and dangerous steps as much as possible, but some important ethnic dishes involve deep-fat frying or candy-making, and should be supervised.

Fire Safety

Always have a fire extinguisher rated with A, B, and C numbers handy. Grease fires can actually be spread by water. In an emergency where you do not have a fire extinguisher, do not hesitate to call the fire department. With fire, a few minutes can make a big difference. To prevent kitchen fires, be most careful with hot oil, which can flash up. Never turn your back on a pan of hot oil. Never try to move a pan with hot oil in it. Turn off the heat and let it cool down. This book attempts to minimize deep-fat frying, and generally suggests doing so in saucepans with high sides. It is much safer to deep-fry chicken in a soup pot than in a frying pan. Don't answer the telephone while cooking. Don't leave wooden or plastic utensils on or near the stovetop.

Burn Safety

Besides avoiding kitchen fires, you can avoid burning yourself by being extra careful with hot oil, hot sugar mixtures, boiling soup, and when opening covered pots of steaming food. Keep dry oven mitts or pot holders handy. Don't adjust the shelves in hot ovens, or reach into a hot oven when you can use tongs or a wooden pothook instead.

Knife Safety

Keep knives sharp so they don't slip on hard foods. If you find yourself sawing or forcing a knife through food, stop to sharpen the knife or ask for help. The most common cutting accidents involve round foods like bagels, onions, winter squash, crusty loaves of bread, and carrots. The food rolls under the knife and the knife comes down on a finger. Stabilize round foods by cutting a slice from one side and setting them on that flat side. All other knife rules are based on keeping the cutting edge foremost in your mind: Don't push foods under a moving knife; only move the knife. Don't put down a knife anywhere near the edge of a working surface. Don't put anything else on top of a knife, ever. Don't carry a knife and anything else at the same time. When you finish a cutting step, wash the knife and put it back in a block. If you drop a knife, move your feet—don't try to catch it.

HOT PEPPER SAFETY

Hot peppers carry most of their heat in oils that are hard to remove from hands, and easy to transfer to eyes and other sensitive parts. You can avoid many problems by wearing gloves or plastic bags over your hands while handling hot peppers, even just one small one. Washing hands after working with hot peppers does not remove all the burning oils, but it does remove some. If you do touch your eyes, splash them with a lot of cold running water.

FOOD-BORNE ILLNESS

Don't cook for other people when sick. Wash your hands frequently. Most food poisoning is caused by bacteria on the surface of uncooked protein foods such as chicken and then *transferred* to cooked protein foods—which are then held at room temperature. The key is to clean up right away after working with raw chicken or other meats or uncooked sausages. Wash your hands before working with other foods, especially foods that aren't going to be cooked through for at least five minutes. If you are unsure how to handle any food, or if you think the food has spoiled, ask an adult.

DON'T BURN FOOD

Burning food isn't usually dangerous, just frustrating. Most pots of burned food belong to cooks who were distracted. As a beginner, don't answer the telephone or leave the kitchen while cooking. Food burns because too much heat is being transferred too rapidly across too small an area. Too much food in a small pot doesn't circulate well, so only a little of it is getting all the heat. Once it starts to burn on the inside of the pot, the food will stick and circulate less, and burn more. Use a larger pot, so the heat is spread

across a larger bottom, and the food can be stirred around more easily. Pots that are not covered cool off on top, but burn on the bottom. A covered pot with lower heat is more efficient and cooks more uniformly. (Sometimes instructions are not to cover a pot so a food will become more concentrated, or so that it simmers at a slightly lower temperature.) Heavier pots transfer heat more evenly than light-gauge pots. Stickier foods are more likely to burn—clear soups simmer safely for hours while starchy porridges have to be stirred constantly. Sugared foods burn quickly.

If your food does burn on the bottom, you can save most of a soup or stew by pouring it into another pot without stirring. Usually the burned food and the burned taste will stay stuck to the pot.

A WARNING FOR GOOD COOKS

Because the object of most projects that use this book is to understand ethnic cooking as it is, you should try to make the recipe exactly as written, even if you know a better way. The results of the ethnic technique may be a pleasant surprise (they often surprised me), but in any case, they are what the original ethnic cooks intended to communicate. This is actually a more serious warning than the one, below, about changing the ingredients because professionally trained cooking writers have so often changed the techniques in ethnic recipes. For example, most ethnic American stews are cooked in one pot for convenience, which blends the flavors. Almost all trained chefs will cook the ingredients individually because this is how restaurant kitchens are organized, and the resulting dish is *completely different* despite starting from the exact same list of ingredients.

PERSONAL DISTASTE

Because the object of this book is to increase understanding, you should try to taste at least a little bit of anything you make. I have not searched out weird and disgusting foods, but we each have our own ideas of taste. The recipes in this book are exactly as made by individual ethnic cooks so that you can get as close as possible to their food experiences. If your culture is not one that uses a lot of pepper, and the recipe is very spicy, try to make at least a sample of the highly spiced dish to get an idea of the difference between cultural norms. In fact, individuals have different tolerances for hot pepper, and some people in, say, India or Jamaica, don't cook spicy food. But a lot of the taste for hot pepper *is* cultural, as shown by the way many ethnic groups have embraced chili peppers in the American South and Southwest, although there may be little pepper in traditional Spanish, French, Navaho, or Scotch-Irish cooking. In general, you should avoid substituting ingredients even when you think it would taste better with something different. In fact, you should especially avoid trying to make the recipes taste better because this almost always means using the taste rules of your own culture.

RELIGIOUS AND OTHER TABOOS

No one using this book should feel under any pressure to eat something that would normally break a food rule of their own group. Observant Jews and Muslims should feel free to substitute for pork products. Traditional-minded Navajo should feel free to substitute for seafood. Members of the Hmong Vang families who try to avoid foods with bones should feel free to substitute foods without bones. Vegetarians may have to do some research outside the book. Ask creative adult cooks in your group how they might make such a "foreign" recipe, and they may have good suggestions. Some of my observant Jewish relatives use soy-based false bacon, and others use salad oil and a drop of liquid smoke seasoning. I have generally avoided recipes with alcohol or caffeine. Again, committed Mormons, Christian Scientists, and recovering alcoholics will get the best advice from adult cooks in their own group on how to substitute vanilla sugar for vanilla extract and so on.

FOR INTERNET USERS: WWW.ETHNICOOK.COM

This book has a Web site, where you can find additional recipes. You can also leave questions, comments, or corrections for the author, and check back for answers. The Web site has links to other sources of ethnic recipes and some completed student projects. There are even some hints about my next book, *The American Historical Cookbook for Students*.

THE AMERICAN ETHNIC COOKBOOK FOR STUDENTS

ABURESHE

See ALBANIAN-AMERICANS; ITALIAN-AMERICANS

ACADIANS (CAJUNS)

Although Cajun-style cooking is well-known today, the Cajun (or Acadian) people were, until recently, a little-known group of white Louisiana sharecroppers. Their history in North America goes back almost 400 years. The original Acadians were French Catholic peasants who in the early seventeenth century came from the northwestern provinces of Normandy and Brittany to settle around the Bay of Fundy in areas that now comprise the Canadian provinces of Nova Scotia and New Brunswick. The Acadians called their successful farming settlement "La Cadie" or "Acadie," perhaps taking the name from the mythical Greek paradise of Arcadia. They were probably the first European settlers of North America to view themselves as a people distinct from their country of origin. When Great Britain took over the government of the region in 1713, they forced the Acadians to swear loyalty to the British crown or emigrate to the French colony of Quebec.

On September 15, 1755, the British called all Acadians to meet in their churches, where some 6,000 to 8,000 people were ordered to board ships for transportation to British colonies to the south. The population of 15,000 was split up at bayonet point, without regard to family ties. The Acadians came to call this event "El Grand Derangement," the "great trouble." Thousands fled into the wintry forests of New Brunswick, where many died. Thousands more died of smallpox in the crowded ships. Three years later, a second mass deportation sent many Acadians back to France. In all, as many as half the Acadians died during the deportations. Some survivors reached the Madawaska region of Canada and northern Maine, where 50,000 or more of their descendants live today. Those who boarded the ships got a poor reception in the Protestant English colonies on the East Coast, and over about 30 years worked their way to Louisiana, which was under Catholic Spanish rule from 1762 to 1800.

In Louisiana, the Acadian refugees were encouraged to settle in swampy and prairie areas, where some Acadian families prospered in cattle raising. Large extended families with strong ties and isolated settlements with their own Catholic parochial schools helped Acadians maintain their language and culture after Louisiana became part of the United States in 1803. Louisiana's new Protestant, English-speaking majority viewed the Acadians as backward and began calling them "Cajuns." When Catholic immigrants from Germany, Italy, and Croatia settled in Acadian areas in the nineteenth century, they learned Acadian French and Acadian cooking and became "Cajuns" too. Although African-Americans in Cajun areas took on some aspects of Cajun culture, they were still preceived as a distinct group called "Creoles."

After the end of the Civil War in 1865, a few wealthy Cajuns joined the white Creole elite (the descendents of the French settlers who had dominated Louisiana society before 1803) or the English-speaking majority, but most continued as subsistence farmers, trappers, and fishers. In the twentieth century, cotton and rice planters and oil companies pushed many Cajun families off their farms, but most remained in rural areas as sharecroppers. Since the 1940s, many Cajuns have worked for high wages in the oil industry, dispersing the Cajun population into Texas and Alabama, but also enabling some families to buy their own farms. Although many younger Cajuns have lost their language and some of their traditional culture, the rising national popularity of Cajun food and music has inspired a revival of Cajun identity over the last few decades.

Originally, Acadian food was probably as bland and filling as the **French Canadian-American** dishes eaten by the descendants of Acadians living today in Maine. Much of it was boiled, as are a few traditional Cajun dishes even today. The Cajuns have also stuck with yellow cornmeal for their cornbread, although most southerners prefer white cornbread. Eventually, the Cajuns learned to love the Creole seasonings of New Orleans, but used ingredients that were available in the countryside, such as bayou crawfish instead of ocean shrimp. One of the most interesting things about the Cajun cooking recently popularized by New Orleans chef Paul Prudhomme is that this white ethnic group now identifies with spicy food. In fact, Cajun cooking today seems to exaggerate the most African features of Louisiana Creole food: use of hot chile peppers, use of the strongly browned roux (a mixture of flour and fat) that suggests African palm oil, use of okra and filé powder to thicken soups and stews, frequent use of deep-fat frying, and preparation of African-named dishes like gumbo and coush-coush (see **Creoles [Louisiana]**). During the century following the Civil War, Cajuns likely learned some of these tastes from rural white Creoles and from African-Creole sharecroppers. Another possibility is that as recent arrivals Cajuns in the early nineteenth century may have been more open to Native American and Spanish influences than white Creoles. The remaining northern French influences in Cajun cooking are the extensive use of stocks and the reliance on butter and lard.

SHRIMP JAMBALAYA

Although most cookbooks state that jambalaya is a combination of the French or Spanish words for ham (*jambon, jamón*) and either the Spanish word *paella* or an African expression for rice, food historian Karen Hess has found references to a rice pilaf called "jambalaia" in nineteenth-century Provençal French, where the word was thought to be of Arabic origin. Hess also points out that many early recipes for Jambalaya have no ham. In any case, jambalaya was a Creole dish embraced by the Cajun community. The following recipe, from Mrs. Donald Labbe, appeared in *Talk About Good*, published in 1967 by the Service League of Lafayette, Louisiana. The recipe is typically Cajun in that it uses a tomato sauce and a brown roux.

Yield: serves 4

3 tablespoons shortening
2 tablespoons flour
1 1/2 cups chopped onions (one large onion)
1/2 cup chopped green peppers (one small)
1 cup chopped celery
1 clove garlic

salt to taste

red pepper to taste

2 pounds raw peeled shrimp (or frozen cooked shrimp)

1 can whole tomatoes

1 small can tomato sauce

2 cups raw rice

1 bunch scallions or green onions

1/2 bunch parsley

Equipment: Heavy pot with tight lid

1. Heat shortening in a heavy pot, add flour and let it cook slowly until golden brown, stirring constantly. (If the roux burns, it will ruin the flavor and you will have to start over. Long, slow browning is the key to Louisiana cooking of any kind.)

2. Halve, peel, and chop the onion.

3. Core, seed, and dice the green pepper.

4. Dice the celery.

5. Peel and mince the garlic.

6. Add vegetables to roux, stir well, and cook slowly until transparent, cooking often, and covering pot.

7. Add tomatoes and tomato sauce and let cook slowly until oil rises to top.

8. Stir in raw rice, raw shrimp, and 2 1/2 cups water.

9. Bring to a boil, reduce heat, and cook covered until rice is tender. Add more oil and water if mixture appears too dry.

10. Slice scallions into thin rounds.

11. Mince parsley.

12. If using frozen cooked shrimp, add when rice is nearly done, so shrimp should be thawed and warmed up, but don't overcook or allow to become stiff.

13. Stir in parsley and scallions.

Serve hot.

CATFISH COURTBOUILLON

In France, a "court bouillon" is a clear broth in which fish are poached. The Louisiana Creoles—possibly influenced by **Croatian-American** fishermen—made this into a thickened tomato sauce, and applied it to redfish and red snapper. The Cajuns, dependent on what they could catch in ponds and bayous, applied it to catfish. This simple recipe is from Wildridge Doucet of Sulfur, Louisiana, as collected in *The County Fair Cookbook* by Lynn Stallworth and Rod Kennedy, Jr. I have seen other Cajun recipes that include a dark roux and six or more herbs and spices, more like the jambalaya recipe, above.

Yield: serves 4-6 as a main dish

2 pounds catfish fillets

2 tablespoons vegetable oil

1 cup chopped onion

10 large cloves garlic

1 16-ounce can tomato sauce

1 cup chopped scallions (green onions)

1 tablespoon Tobasco (red pepper sauce), or to taste

salt and freshly ground black pepper to taste

Equipment: Large skillet with a cover

1. Peel and chop garlic cloves.

2. Halve, peel, and chop onion.

3. In a large skillet, heat the oil over moderate heat.

4. When a bit of onion sizzles, put in the catfish.

5. Add chopped onion, garlic, and tomato sauce to the pan. Lower heat, cover, and simmer gently for 10 minutes.

6. Cut roots off scallions and chop into fine rings.

7. Add Tabasco, salt, and pepper to taste.

8. Stir in the scallions and Tobasco, taking care not to break up the catfish fillets.

9. Cover again and simmer for 20 minutes longer.

Serve over rice.

PLOGUE

"Plogue" is the pronunciation of "ployes," an Acadian-French term from Maine for these buckwheat flatbreads. The term probably comes from the French verb for "bend" or "fold." Buckwheat crepes are still eaten in the Normandy and Brittany regions of France, the areas from which many Acadians came originally, but those crepes aren't called ployes or eaten as a separate bread. The following recipe is one of four in *Nothing Went to Waste/Rien N'Etait Gaspille*, a bilingual cookbook by Betty A. Lausier Lindsay that was published in 1981 by the National Materials Development Center for French & Creole of Manchester, New Hampshire.

 1/2 cup pure buckwheat flour (or buckwheat grains)
 1/2 cup unbleached white flour
 2 teaspoons baking powder
 1/4 teaspoon baking soda
 frozen lard or margarine to grease frying pan
 butter to spread on pancakes

Equipment: Blender (if needed) to grind buckwheat, heavy skillet

 1. "If pure buckwheat flour is not available, use dry buckwheat grains, 1/2 cup in blender makes enough flour."

 2. Mix dry ingredients together.

 3. Add one cup cold water to form a paste.

 4. Add one cup hot (not boiling) water to form a thin batter.

 5. Grease pan using a frozen piece of lard or frozen margarine.

 6. Pour into skillet in thin layers (spread thinner with a spoon if necessary).

 7. Cook one side only until the top appears dry and full of holes.

Serve at any meal as a bread substitute. "You butter it, roll it up, and eat it with your fingers." Ployes are also dipped in molasses or maple syrup, or spread with a potted pork pate called "cretons."

SMOTHERED POTATOES

Although the shrimp and crawfish etouffée are well known outside Louisiana, Cajun families use this technique on many meats and vegetables. This simple dish comes from Ralph and Mary Ann Prudhomme's *The Prudhomme Family Cookbook*, a collection of country recipes from the 13 brothers and sisters of the famous New Orleans chef, Paul Prudhomme. Because most of the siblings are older, the book is a rare source for everyday Cajun recipes from the Great Depression.

Yield: 8-10 side dish servings (or sandwich fillings)
 1/3 cup vegetable oil
 3 pounds potatoes
 1 1/2 cups chopped onions (from 3 medium onions)
 2 teaspoons salt
 1/2 teaspoon black pepper
 1/2 teaspoon minced garlic (from one clove)
 1 1/2 cups stock or water
 1/2 cup finely chopped green onions (or scallions) from one bunch

Equipment: Very large heavy skillet with cover, flexible spatula to scrape skillet

 1. Peel potatoes. Slice 1/4-inch thick, and cut into "about one-inch squares."

 2. Peel and mince garlic. Halve, peel, and chop onions very fine. (Wear swim goggles to avoid tears.)

 3. Heat oil in skillet over high heat about one minute.

 4. Add potatoes, onions, salt, black pepper, garlic, and white pepper, stirring well.

 5. Cook about 10 minutes, letting mixture stick and brown (but not burn) on the bottom, then scraping pan and stirring well. "It's this sticking process that makes these potatoes special, so be sure to let the mixture stick before you stir." (If you do scorch some, you can rescue the dish by pouring it into another pan, without scraping. The burned parts will stick in the first pan.)

6. Reduce heat to low, cover and cook until mixture is mottled brown throughout, about 20 minutes, stirring and scraping only occasionally.

7. Add 1/2 cup of the stock or water and scrape pan bottom well; cook covered about 5 minutes, stirring only once or twice.

8. Repeat with another 1/2 cup of stock or water, "breaking up half of the potato pieces, if not already broken up, so the potatoes are half creamed, half lumpy."

9. Chop the tops only of the green onions.

10. Add the last 1/2 cup of stock and the green onions, and cook another 5 minutes, stirring and scraping occasionally.

Serve immediately as a side dish, or in rolls to make a sandwich.

AFRICAN-AMERICANS

The 30 million African-Americans living today in the United States are mostly descended from about 500,000 Africans transported to North America as slaves prior to the legal end of the U.S. slave trade in 1807. This multi-ethnic population included people from all over West and Central Africa to modern-day Angola, with some East Africans and slaves from Madagascar. Recent scholarship has only added to the complexity, suggesting that up to 5 percent of the slaves may have been Muslims, that some numbers of European Gypsies were sold into slavery in the Americas, and that Afro-Indian and tri-racial groups were more extensive than previously recorded. In addition, the African-American community has generally welcomed Afro-Caribbean immigrants, African immigrants, and Afro-Indian groups like the Lumbee, the Garifuna, and the Seminole (*see* **Honduran- and Garifuna-Americans, Lumbee Indians**, and **Seminole and Miccosukee**).

Not only did African-Americans introduce the New World to many basic foods, such as okra, yams, and sesame seeds, they also transmitted many Arab, Iberian, and South American foods and cooking techniques that had been previously introduced to West Africa, such as deep-fat frying, rice, cassava, coconut palms (from Asia), peanuts, chile peppers, plantains, and sweet potatoes. Because Africans had more experience with hot-climate farming and produce than their French or English masters, and were plantation cooks during and after slavery, they developed much of what is now thought of as southern regional cooking. When millions of African-Americans migrated to northern industrial cities in the twentieth century, southern-style food became a way to celebrate African-American identity.

In addition to "soul food," an African-American cuisine found throughout the country, there are at least two other ethnically distinct African-American cuisines, both of which are discussed separately in this book: **Creoles (Louisiana)** and **Gullah (Geechee and Sea Islanders)**. The **Cane River Creoles**, a specific group of Louisiana Creoles, are also discussed separately.

In recent times, African-Americans have embraced cuisines from all over the "African Diaspora," including **Bahamian-, Barbadan-, Ethiopian- and Eritrean-, Jamaican-, Nigerian-, Panamanian-, and Trinidadian-American** foods. Dishes from many of these cuisines are made especially for the December 31 feast at the end of Kwanzaa, a holiday developed in 1966 by the Pan-Africanist leader Maulana Ron Karenga (see the discussion of Pan-Africanism in the Introduction). Alex Haley's book *Roots*, about the history of his African-American family, set off an ethnic revival among all Americans when it was made into a television series in the 1970s. In recent years, the African-American community has become increasingly concerned with health-food regimes, including that of the **Black Muslims**, a uniquely American ethno-religious group.

BAKED GRITS

Author Jessica Harris says that cheese grits are the universal African-American recipe. They may echo the rich West African sourdough mushes (compare with **Barbadan-American** coo-coo). This recipe is from *Spoonbread and Strawberry Wine* by Norma Jean and Carole Darden, who use it to remember their Aunt Norma Duncan Darden. Aunt Norma served these grits with scrambled pork brains at come-as-you-are breakfast parties.

Yield: serves 6
   3 cups cooked grits (from one cup dry)
   2 tablespoons butter
   2 eggs
   1 1/2 cups evaporated milk (12-ounce can)
   1 3/4 cups grated cheddar cheese
   1/2 teaspoon paprika
   1 or 2 dashes cayenne pepper

Equipment: Potato masher if using leftover grits, two mixing bowls, oven-proof casserole dish, oven mitts

   1. If not starting from leftover grits, make grits according to package directions. If starting from leftover grits, mash thoroughly.

   2. Melt butter, add to milk.

   3. Beat eggs, mix with milk and butter.

   4. Work liquid mixture into grits.

   5. Mix in 1 1/2 cups of the grated cheese, the paprika, and the cayenne, if using.

   6. Preheat oven to 425 degrees.

   7. Butter the casserole dish and spread in the grits mixture.

   8. Bake in the oven for 25 minutes or until brown (time varies with the size and shape of the casserole).

   9. Remove from oven and sprinkle with the remaining grated cheese and a little more paprika.

   10. Return to oven and cook until topping has melted.

Serve as a breakfast dish or side dish.

MARINATED PORK CHOPS

At first taste, this dish of pickled pork and smothered onions resembles a number of salads and main dishes throughout the South. However, the long marinating in vinegar and onions links it specifically with Spain and Portugal, and the use of vinegar pickling to preserve meat and fish. It is thus a first cousin of chicken adobo (found in the **Filipino-Americans** chapter). This Iberian influence had already reached West Africa before American slavery, and may have been reinforced by Spanish colonial rule in Florida and Louisiana, or by Caribbean trade with southern U.S. cities. The recipe, by the late Betty Shorter, is found in the Dorchester [MA] *International Cookbook*.

NOTE: Requires marinating overnight.

Yield: "serves 2-6 depending on appetite"
   6 pork chops
   1/2 teaspoon pepper
   2 large onions
   4 cloves garlic
   1/2 teaspoon cloves
   1/2 tablespoon salt
   2 cups vinegar
   1/2 cup brown sugar
   1/4 cup oil
   1 green pepper
   1 tablespoon cornstarch
   1/2 teaspoon salt
   1 cup water

Equipment: Blender, tongs, paper towels, spatter screen pot cover (optional), flat whisk or sieve

   1. Halve, peel, and chop coarsely one onion.

   2. Arrange chops in the marinating bowl.

   3. Puree next 7 ingredients (but save the other onion) in blender.

   4. Pour marinade over chops, lifting so all sides are in contact with marinade.

   5. Marinate overnight in a refrigerator.

   6. Pat chops dry with paper towels.

7. Halve, peel, and slice the second onion into thick, round slices.

8. Core the green pepper and slice the same way.

9. Heat oil in frying pan or pans and brown chops on both sides.

10. After chops have been turned once, put sliced onion and green pepper on top of them, cover the frying pan or pans, and sauté on lowered heat for 25 minutes.

11. If there is no burned residue in the pan, make a gravy by removing chops and vegetables from the pan, stirring cornstarch and salt into water, and pouring the mixture into the pan.

12. Over low heat, scrape up browned (but not burnt) residue with a wooden spoon.

13. Cook gravy until thickened, whisk or strain to remove any lumps.

Serve with rice.

GUILT-FREE COLLARD GREENS (AND POT LIKKER)

Slow-cooked greens are still a vitamin- and mineral-rich "sauce" with grain mushes throughout Africa. Greens stewed with cheap smoked pork hocks and other minor cuts of pork became an important survival food during slavery times, and were popular with both white and black southerners thereafter. Ronnie Carlow, who contributed this recipe to an "African American Recipe Page" on the Internet, has reduced the fat and salt by using smoked turkey parts instead of pork hocks or bacon, but keeps the traditional flavor.

Yield: easily serves 4 to 6 adults
   1 bunch of collards, washed and finely cut (stems can be left off or on)
   1 pound smoked turkey necks or wings
   2 to 3 cloves of garlic (optional)
   small yellow onion (optional)
   1 small green pepper (optional)
   non-stick food spray

Equipment: Large cooking pot with a lid

1. In a large cooking pot with a tight fitting lid, boil the smoked turkey meat in water to cover. Usually smoked turkey is already cooked, but you should cook it more to achieve desired tenderness. This usually takes at least 1 hour.

2. Meanwhile, chop collard greens. Stems can be left off or on. Wash greens using a great deal of water—the final water the greens are washed in should show little green color.

3. Set greens aside and peel onion and garlic and dice fine.

4. Remove the stem, pith, and seeds of the green pepper and dice fine.

5. When turkey meat is tender, remove meat and broth from pot and reserve in separate bowls.

6. Allow turkey to cool and remove bones.

7. Dry out the pot and sauté the onions, garlic, and green pepper using a small amount of non-stick food spray.

6. When vegetables turn slightly transparent, add greens and stir fry for about 2 to 3 minutes.

7. Gradually add the water the turkey was cooked in and the turkey meat. Allow greens to cook until tender, with lid tightly on pot.

8. Check and stir greens regularly to ensure a sufficient amount of water remains in pot.

Serve with hot sauce to taste. Serve the nutritious cooking liquid as "pot likker," in mugs as a hot drink or soup. Cornbread goes with either greens or pot likker.

SWEET POTATO PIE

In West Africa, yams were and are a staple food. Sweet potato pie is thus an African-American classic. This recipe by Christina Wilson, a retired school teacher, appeared in *Mama Cooked 'n' Said*, a project of the Winter Park Historical Society and the Seniors First Program at Westside Community Center in Winter Park, Florida.

   2 cups sweet potatoes

4 eggs

1/3 cup margarine or butter

1 cup brown sugar

1/2 teaspoon cinnamon

1/2 teaspoon ginger

1/2 cup milk

1/2 teaspoon salt

1/3 cup sugar

1 9-inch unbaked pie shell

1. Cook and mash sweet potatoes to get 2 cups. (Two medium sweet potatoes and 10 minutes in the microwave should be about right.)

2. Heat oven to 375 degrees.

3. Mix sweet potatoes, egg, margarine, sugar, and salt.

4. Add spices and milk.

5. Pour into unbaked pie shell.

6. Bake for 15 minutes, then lower oven temperature to 350 degrees and bake for 20 minutes.

WHITE POTATO PIE

Although less common that sweet potato pie, white potato pie recipes also recur throughout African-American cooking. This one was collected from Mrs. N.P. Bradford of Little Rock, Arkansas, by Freda De Knight for her 1948 book, *A Date with a Dish.*

Yield: one pie, serving 6 to 8

unbaked 8-inch pie shell

2 cups mashed white potatoes

1/3 tablespoon butter

1/2 teaspoon salt

2 cups milk

3 eggs

1 tablespoon orange juice

1 teaspoon cinnamon

1/2 teaspoon nutmeg

1 teaspoon mace

1 cup sugar

1 teaspoon grated orange peel

Equipment: Zester or grater

1. Mash potatoes with butter and salt.

2. Beat the eggs slightly.

3. Add sugar, eggs, spices, and milk to potatoes.

4. Grate orange peel with zester or grater.

5. Add orange peel and juice to potato mixture.

6. Pour into unbaked pie shell.

7. Bake until firm, about 40 minutes.

NECK BONES AND RICE

This recipe is from Mary Day Nowden of Alabama, grandmother of Mary Carter Smith, one of three authors of *The Griots Cookbook,* a 1985 fund-raiser for the radio station at Morgan State, a historically black college in Maryland.

Yield: Serves 4

2 pounds pork neck bones

1 tablespoon salt

1 teaspoon pepper

2 medium onions (chopped coarsely)

2 cups rice

1. Purchase or have butcher cut neck bones into pieces approximately 4 inches by 2 inches each.

2. Wash neck bones thoroughly. Remove any white marrow between bones on flat side.

3. In a large pot, barely cover the neck bones with cold water. Heat to boiling.

4. Halve, peel, and coarsely chop onions.

5. Add onions, salt, and pepper to the stew.

6. When stew comes to a boil, reduce heat and simmer until just done.

7. Drain liquid and reserve it for use later.

8. Rinse rice.

9. Put 4 cups of reserved liquid in pot with meat and rice, and cook until rice is tender. If rice looks too dry later, add more liquid from broth you saved. Stir enough to keep rice from sticking.

ALBANIAN-AMERICANS

Although the 1990 census recorded fewer than 50,000 Americans of Albanian ancestry, other estimates are higher, the disagreement perhaps arising from the complexities of Albanian ethnicity. The present country of Albania is home to about 60 percent of Europe's Albanians, who are divided between the majority southern group, known as "Tosks," and the northerners, known as "Ghegs." (Albania also has small numbers of Vlachs, Gypsies, and Greeks.) Most Albanians in Yugoslavia and Macedonia are Ghegs, while the "Abureshe," descendants of refugees from the Turkish conquest of the Balkans, live in villages in Italy and Sicily and speak dialects of Tosk. Although most Albanians in the Balkan countries are Muslims, they are divided into two competing sects. Some Tosks (and many of the first wave of Albanians in the U.S.) are Eastern Orthodox Christians, but the Abureshe and some Ghegs are Roman Catholics, like many Albanians who came to the U.S. after World War II, when Albania became a Communist dictatorship. The first Albanians came to Boston and New England in the 1880s, before Albania became independent of Turkish rule in 1912. Another early community was in the Bronx, New York. Greater Detroit contains the third, and perhaps most diverse, Albanian-American community.

Albanians are also a significant component of the Sicilian communities in New Orleans and Wisconsin, and Catholic Albanians have often joined **Italian-American** communities, while Orthodox Christian Albanians have sometimes joined **Greek-American** communities.

Albanian-American food is seldom served in restaurants, although some Albanians have been successful restaurant owners. Dishes you may encounter are meat and vegetables pies, stuffed flatbreads, forms of baklava and moussaka, an egg lemon soup, and a yogurt-vegetable soup called tarator.

HAMBURG WITH POTATO (ALBANIAN MOUSSAKA)

This recipe was contributed by Carolyn Corriveau to *Favorite Recipes of Fifty Years*, a cookbook compiled by the United Methodist Women of Wesley United Methodist Church, Worcester, Massachusetts, perhaps in the late 1970s.

Yield: serves 6

1 1/2 pounds ground beef
3 onions
1/2 teaspoon paprika
salt to taste
1/2 cup tomato sauce
6 potatoes
2 tablespoons butter or shortening
3 eggs
2 cups milk

Equipment: 9 by 13-inch cake pan or lasagna pan

1. Halve, peel, and chop onions.

2. In a large skillet, brown meat, onions, paprika, and salt together for 20 minutes.

3. Peel and slice potatoes into round slices.

4. Fry sliced potatoes "lightly" in shortening or butter and set aside.

5. Add tomato sauce to meat mixture and simmer an additional 5 minutes.

6. In pan, alternate layers starting with meat and ending with potatoes on top.

7. Crack eggs individually into a cup, then combine in a mixing bowl and beat.

8. Add milk to eggs and blend well.

9. Pour over casserole and bake for 30 to 40 minutes in a 350-degree oven.

BOAT (ALBANIAN)

This recipe was called in to a radio show by a friend of the daughter of an Albanian immigrant, Mrs. Magdalini Costa, and appears in Dave

Maynard's *Secret Family Recipe Cookbook*. Despite the American ingredients, this dish is recognizable as a version of the meat-stuffed pies called boureg in Albania. When Albanians settled in Italy and Sicily, they began using baker's loaves. In some Sicilian villages, the bakers began making special hollow loaves to be filled and made into hot or cold sandwiches. Sicilian-Albanians who moved to New Orleans began selling a round loaf called "muffaletta," with cold cuts and an olive spread, and this creation is now the popular Italian sandwich in New Orleans. Vienna bread is a flattened loaf of white bread with sesame seeds, also sold as "scali" or Italian bread. Any unsliced white bread will work.

1 unsliced Vienna bread
2 tablespoons butter or margarine
1 large onion
1 cup shredded lettuce
1 large tomato (or one cup of canned, chopped tomatoes)
1 pound hamburger
1/2 teaspoon salt
1/4 teaspoon pepper
oregano to taste

Equipment: Frying pan with lid, baking pan, aluminum foil

1. Refrigerate bread for a few hours to make it dry out so that it is easier to handle, then slice off the top.

2. Scoop out the inside, and set the top and bottom crusts aside.

3. Halve, peel, and chop the onion; shred the lettuce; and chop the tomato.

4. Melt the butter in a frying pan, add onion, and stir to sauté under cover until soft.

5. Add hamburger, break up, and cook until done.

6. Add lettuce and tomato and cook for a few minutes to blend.

7. Add seasonings, stir well, and cover to simmer for 5 minutes.

8. Cut up the inside of the bread into small cubes.

9. Remove hamburger mixture from heat, and add the bread to absorb all liquid.

10. Set Vienna bread shell on baking pan.

11. Pack mixture into the Vienna bread shell, and place top back on loaf.

12. Cover assembled loaf with aluminum foil, and bake at 400 degrees for 20-25 minutes.

13. Remove from oven, cut into slices.

Serve with a crisp salad.

ALEUTS

See ESKIMOS (INUIT) AND ALEUTS

AMERICAN INDIANS

See UNDER NAMES OF INDIVIDUAL TRIBAL NATIONS

AMISH

The Amish are an ethno-religious group that began in Holland and Germany in 1693 when Jakob Ammann proposed more stringent beliefs within the Mennonite movement, a Protestant sect that had arisen in Switzerland in the sixteenth century. The Amish and other Mennonites were persecuted in France, southwestern Germany, and Switzerland, and began arriving in the English colony of Pennsylvania between 1727 and 1790. With other German-speaking Protestants, they formed the **Pennsylvania Dutch** ethnic group. The Amish can be seen as a conservative group within the Pennsylvania Dutch because they still speak the Pennsylfaanisch dialect at home and in church sermons, and their original settlements were in the heart of the Pennsylvania Dutch homeland. By spreading westward and northward to Ontario, Canada, the Amish also followed the general direction of the Pennsylvania Dutch "diaspora."

By some estimates, the 150,000 Amish are only 8 to 10 percent of the Pennsylvania Dutch community, and their small settlements have always been somewhat self-contained. Only about 150 family names are found among all the Amish. Although they have accepted converts, the great majority of the Amish are descended from fewer than 4,000 immigrants who arrived before 1860. Large families are customary, and 80 percent of Amish children eventually make the required adult decision to join the sect. The Amish are known for their old-fashioned clothing, beards, and horse-drawn carriages. Amish children leave school after the elementary grades to work with their families on farms and in home workshops. Amish foodways begin with a selection of Pennsylvania Dutch specialties, but the continuing farm-based self-sufficiency of the Amish has caused their cooking to diverge from Pennsylvania practices. Although they avoid mass media, automobiles, and electric appliances, the Amish are not trying to live in the eighteenth or nineteenth centuries. They enjoy selected modern diversions like jigsaw puzzles and card games. Familiar with Pennsylvania Dutch foods, the Amish also enjoy spaghetti, pizza, and store-bought breakfast cereals, and in many areas cook with velveeta cheese, miniature marshmallows, and canned mushroom soup.

Peanut Butter Spread (Amish Church)

The Amish don't build churches, but rotate meetings every Sunday in the home or barn of a church "district" of 15 to 25 families. One Sunday a lengthy worship service will be followed by a business meeting, socializing, and a light lunch served by the host family. On the alternate week, Sunday school will be held, also with food. One variety of distinctly Amish ethnic dishes are the recipes used to cater these Sunday services. This recipe comes from the 1992 *Down Home Cookin'* by Abe and Edna Miller of Fredericksburg, Ohio.

2 1/2 cups brown sugar
1/2 cup Karo green label (light corn syrup)
1 1/4 teaspoons maple flavoring
1 1/2 pounds smooth or crunch peanut butter
1/2 quart marshmallow topping

1. Bring 1 1/4 cups of water to a boil.

2. Mix with brown sugar and corn syrup to dissolve.

3. Add maple flavoring, peanut butter, and marshmallow topping, and stir to a smooth spread.

Serve with thick slices of homemade bread, home-canned strawberry preserves, and home-canned pickled beets.

Yummasetti

This apparently middle-American hot dish is popular in Amish communities across the United States. Some recipes layer the spaghetti mixture with cheese. Although there is a strong Pennsylvania Dutch focus on casserole dishes, and the wordplay of the name Yummasetti is typical of German speakers, the history of this dish is a good subject for further research. Given their avoidance of mass media, the Amish probably didn't get this dish from a magazine, but may have swapped it with a non-Amish neighbor or invented it, and then spread it from one Amish family to another. The recipe comes from Susan Beachy of Kalona, Iowa, via Susan Puckett's A Cook's Tour of Iowa (1988).

Yield: "12-16 servings"
  1 pound spaghetti
  1 stick butter
  1 large onion
  3 pounds ground beef
  1 pint peas (or one pound frozen)
  2 10 3/4-ounce cans cream of mushroom
    soup
  1 10 3/4-ounce can cream of celery soup
  1 cup sour cream
  1/2 loaf bread

Equipment: Turkey roaster (this is a large recipe)

1. Cook spaghetti according to package directions and drain.

2. Butter the bread lightly, reserving two tablespoons of the butter.

3. Toast the bread on the wire racks of an oven.

4. Halve, peel, and chop the onion.

5. Heat the two tablespoons of butter in a large skillet; add the chopped onion and sauté slowly until soft.

6. Let the toast cool, then break it into crumbs.

7. Add ground beef to the skillet and break it up. Cook until meat is no longer pink.

8. Drain off excess fat.

9. Preheat oven to 350 degrees.

10. Mix all ingredients except the crumbs in a large bowl.

11. Pour mixture into casserole, and top with the bread crumbs.

12. Bake uncovered in preheated oven for 45 minutes.

ANGLO-AMERICANS (ENGLISH)

Because the United States began with the independence of the 13 British colonies, Anglo-Americans have seldom seen themselves as an ethnic group. This perception has been less true of other British Isles groups, such as **Cornish-Americans, Scottish-Americans, Scotch-Irish (Appalachian),** and **Welsh-Americans.** Although recent immigrants often feel English as well as American, they do not usually group together in particular neighborhoods, form mutual aid societies, or even gather around Episcopal, Methodist, Congregationalist, Unitarian, or Quaker churches—Protestant denominations that began in England or are offshoots from the Anglican Church. (Another tiny Anglo-American sect, the Shakers, influenced American food by growing and selling fresh and dried herbs.) For the 1990 census, only 34 million Americans listed English or British ancestry.

Anglo-Americans were greatly divided by the American Revolution, and many thousands loyal to the king moved to Canada or back to Great Britain. Although tensions between the United States and Great Britain continued through the War of 1812 and well into the nineteenth century, immigrants from England were readily accepted into a country founded on English institutions and culture.

Many American foodways come directly from the English immigrants, including the preference for roast meats (especially beef), boiled vegetables, and white bread. The American love of rich and sweet desserts can be traced to British puddings. Although we use the expression "as American as apple pie," that dessert is English and the only American thing about it is the round pie tin with sloping sides, designed for more even cooking in smaller ovens. Some other English foods in general American use are sandwiches, custard desserts, trifle, meat and eggs for breakfast (a tradition reinforced by **Irish-American** and **German-American** breakfast practices), lamb chops with mint jelly, roast beef with Yorkshire pudding, hot cross buns, raisin bread, and many sweet puddings. Another list of American foods came from English versions of foods acquired from the British trading empire in Asia, such as ketchup (from a Malaysian soy sauce) and chow-chow (from a Singaporean pickle).

One of the few ways Anglo-American families express themselves as an ethnic group is in preserving historic houses and villages from English colonial times and re-enacting colonial life or Revolutionary War battles. This tradition goes back at least to the first Founder's Day dinner in Plymouth, Massachusetts, in 1754. Leading citizens of what was then an English colony considered the lives and ate the foods (including a succotash) of their pioneering English ancestors. Founder's Day was a predecessor to our national holiday of Thanksgiving, proclaimed by President Abraham Lincoln in 1864 to reinforce the Anglo-American identity of the then-warring northern and southern states.

RHODE ISLAND JOHNNY CAKE

Although now unknown in England, Johnny cakes comprise a variety of corn cakes and griddle breads made in the U.S. and Australia since the early eighteenth century. This 1886 recipe appeared on the box for Kenyon's Johnny Cake Meal (Kenyon Corn Meal Company, 21 Glen Rock Road, Usquepaugh, RI 02892; 401-783-4054). It makes a browned Johnny Cake with a soft center, typical of eastern Rhode Island and southern Massachusetts. Unlike most northern corn meal, Rhode Island Johnny cake meal is white, made from Narragansett white cap corn. The Johnny cakes made by **Narragansett** Indians are richer and typical of western Rhode Island Johnny cakes. Both kinds are more like pancakes than cornbread.

Yield: 8-10 pancakes as a breakfast or side dish
   1 cup white corn meal
   1/2 teaspoon salt
   1 teaspoon sugar

1. Bring 1 1/4 cups water to a boil.

2. Blend dry ingredients.

3. Mix with water to a thick batter

4. Drop by tablespoons on "any type well greased fry pan or griddle. Medium hot—380 degrees for electric fry pans."

5. "Do not touch or turn over for 6 minutes."

6. "At 6 minutes turn over and cook for about 5 minutes."

7. For optional thin, crisp style, thin batter with 1/2 cup more water or milk.

Serve with butter and maple syrup, or under "your favorite newburg, creamed chipped beef, creamed cod, or as dumplings in stew."

CUSTARD JOHNNYCAKE

What Johnnycakes (as they are often spelled outside Rhode Island) have in common is that they are made from cornmeal, were originally flatbreads, and were originally cooked next to an open fire or in a skillet rather than in an oven. Food historian Karen Hess is probably correct in tracing them to the flat "bannocks" of the British Isles, via the northern English versions called "jannock" and "jonikin." Compare this and the previous recipe to **Wampanoag** bannocks, **Irish-American** soda bread, and **Narragansett** Johnnycakes, as well as to **Scottish-American** scones and **Welsh-American** Welsh cakes. This recipe is from *Yankee Hill-Country Cooking* by Beatrice Vaughan (1963). The dish was also known as spider corn cake because it used to be cooked in a large fireplace with a three-legged cast-iron skillet called a "spider." It will be heavier than modern cornbread.

   1 1/2 cups cornmeal
   1/2 cup flour
   2 tablespoons sugar
   1 teaspoon baking powder
   1 teaspoon baking soda
   1 teaspoon salt
   2 eggs
   1 cup buttermilk
   2 cups milk
   3 tablespoons butter, melted

Equipment: 10-inch round cake pan or cast-iron skillet

1. Grease cake pan or skillet with shortening.

2. Sift dry ingredients together.

3. Beat eggs and stir in one cup of the milk and the buttermilk.

4. Combine egg mixture and dry ingredients.

5. Add melted butter.

6. Pour mixture into the greased pan.

7. Without tipping the pan or stirring the batter, pour the remaining cup of milk into the center of the batter.

8. Do not stir (really!).

9. Bake in a 400-degree oven for 30 minutes.

Serve hot in pie-shaped pieces, with butter.

CONNECTICUT KEDGEREE

Kedgeree comes from "khichri," an Asian Indian gruel of rice and lentils often flavored with vegetables and spices. During the British colonial period in India, kedgeree became popular as a hash or pilaf with rice, eggs, and leftover fish, and went home as such to England where it is still flavored with commercial curry powder. The Anglo-American version has lost the lentils and the curry powder and added milk. So what began as a foreign dish in British cooking became an Anglo-American ethnic dish. This recipe from *The New England Yankee Cookbook* (1939) by Imogene Walcott, is attributed to Mrs. Evan J. David of Westport, Connecticut, and states that the original recipe used summer savory and thyme.

Yield: serves 5
   2 cups rice cooked (from one cup raw rice)
   4 hard-boiled eggs
   2 cups cooked white fish, flaked
   1/2 cup "top milk" (substitute half-and-half)
   2 tablespoons minced parsley
   pepper, salt

Equipment: Double boiler
   1. Cook rice according to package directions.

   2. Chop eggs fine.

   3. Mince parsley.

   4. Mix all ingredients in top of double boiler.

   5. Heat water in lower part of double boiler to boiling. Heat up kedgeree.

Serve as a brunch dish on toast or dried rusks (zwieback).

QUICK SALLY LUNN

This is one of four recipes for Sally Lunn (and another for Sally Lunn muffins) in *Virginia Cookery, Past and Present* (1957) by the Woman's Auxiliary of Olivet Episcopal Church, Franconia, Virginia. The recipe is attributed to Mrs. E.H. Selden, Women's Auxiliary, Christ Episcopal Church, Unit 1, Smithfield, Virginia. The original may have been a French egg bread called a *soleil et lune* ("sun and moon") or *solimeme*. In England, Sally Lunns are associated with the seaside resort of Bath, and a story about a baker named Sally Lunn. In the United States, this sweet loaf is a popular tea cake or dessert throughout the South. Most Sally Lunns are made with yeast, but this one is a quick bread using baking powder. The traditional shape was a round cake pan with medium-high sides, but tube pans and muffin tins are widely used.

Yield: large cake or about 16 muffins
   4 cups flour
   4 eggs
   1 pint milk
   1 tablespoon sugar
   2 tablespoons butter
   1 teaspoon salt
   2 teaspoons baking powder
   solid shortening to grease pan

Equipment: Large tube cake pan or muffin tins, toothpick or wire cake tester to test cake
   1. Sift together flour, baking power, salt, and sugar.

   2. In another bowl, beat eggs until very light.

   3. Melt butter.

   4. Add milk to flour mixture, then eggs, then melted butter.

   5. Grease a large tube pan or muffin tins.

   6. Mix all together, stir well, and bake in a 425-degree oven for about half an hour, or a 350-

degree oven for as much as 50 minutes for the larger cake.

7. Test with a toothpick or wire cake tester.

Serve hot at the table, with butter or jam. Leftover Sally Lunn makes fine toast, French toast, or bread pudding.

YORKSHIRE PUDDING

Yorkshire pudding is still commonly served with roast beef in England, and the combination is one of the identifiably Anglo-American foods still served in the eastern U.S. It was originally made in the drip pan underneath a spit-roasted joint of beef. The beef drippings coming down from above gave it the flavor of the roast, so it stretched the meat. The name may have been a British ethnic joke about poverty and thrift, like "Welsh rabbit." When stoves with ovens became common in the nineteenth century, Yorkshire pudding began to be made separately from the roast, even in muffin tins. This recipe is from the 1948 *Massachusetts Cooking Rules Old and New* by the Women's Republican Club of Massachusetts; it was submitted by Mrs. J. Verity Smith.

CAUTION: Recipe uses hot meat drippings.

Yield: serves 8-14
  1 cup flour
  1 1/2 cups milk
  2 eggs
  1 teaspoon salt
  3 tablespoons "beef or lamb dripping"

Equipment: 8 by 14-inch baking pan or muffin tins, basting brush (optional)

1. Mix flour and salt with half the milk to make a smooth paste.

2. "Break eggs into the batter and mix well."

3. Add the remaining milk and mix.

4. Spread drippings in baking pan or muffin tins, and put into a 450-degree oven to heat up.

5. When pan is sizzling hot, pour in batter and bake 25 minutes. (Some older recipes suggest basting with more drippings. This is about the time needed for a roast to rest and firm up for carving.)

Serve with roast beef or lamb.

APACHE

The Apache are the seventh largest Indian tribe in the U.S., with about 53,000 members and descendants on the 1990 census. Apache is a Pueblo Indian word for "enemy." The Apache language is most closely related to **Navajo,** and scholars believe both groups arrived in the American Southwest more than 500 years ago, well after the foundation of such Pueblo peoples as the **Hopi** and **Zuni** (*see also* **Pueblo Indians [Eastern]**). The Apache hunted and foraged over much of Arizona and New Mexico, and have a romantic image as hunters and trackers. Perhaps the best-known Apache is the great war chief, Geronimo (1829-1909). Over the last few centuries, the Apache retreated from the plains under pressure from the Comanches, adapted to desert environments, and effectively maintained their way of life despite Mexican and U.S. interference. About 1886, after some 20 years of war with whites, most Apache tried to succeed on reservations; they had some success in the cattle business and, more recently, with hunting and fishing resorts.

ACORN STEW

This recipe is from a Web page project by "Mr. Alvarez's fifth grade class on the Ft. Apache Indian Reservation." The students were all members of the White Mountain Apache Tribe. If you are using acorns other than from Arizona white oak or gambel's oak, use Steps 1 through 5 of the Acorn bread recipe, below.

Yield: 10-12 small bowls

 2 1/2 to 3 pounds round steak (or elk or deer meat), cut into bite-size pieces

 sweet acorns (enough to make 3/4 cup of acorn flour)

 1 teaspoon salt

Equipment: Nutcracker and nutpicks to shell acorns, food processor or blender or metal-burr grinder to grind acorns, wooden bowl

1. Cook beef in about 1 quart of water. Let it simmer for about 3 hours or until meat is well done.

2. Shell acorns and grind them into very fine flour until you have approximately 3/4 cup of flour.

3. Salt meat to taste.

4. Strain the broth from the meat (it will be used later).

5. Shred the meat and, placing it in a wooden bowl, mix it with the acorn flour. (*Note:* Steel utensils or a steel bowl will discolor the flour, usually turning it black.)

6. Pour hot broth over the mixture and stir. It is now ready to serve in individual bowls.

Serve with fry bread.

ACORN BREAD

This recipe appeared in *American Indian Food and Lore* by Carolyn Niethammer. It has been widely republished, and is more precise than most Apache recipes, but seems to represent an authentic style of modern Apache baking. I have developed the first five steps using New England red oak acorns, which are large and easy to shell, but very bitter and astringent. Native Americans developed several technologies for washing the bitter tannins (similar to those in tea) out of acorns, such as sinking baskets of acorns in running streams and pouring boiling water over acorns on sand.

Yield: 16 2-inch squares

 1 cup acorn meal (from 2-4 cups acorns)

 1/2 cup cornmeal

 1/2 cup whole wheat flour

 3 tablespoons salad oil

 1 teaspoon salt

 1 tablespoon baking powder

 1/4 cup honey

 1 egg

 1 cup milk

Equipment: 8 by 8-inch brownie pan, food processor or blender, wire cake tester or toothpick

1. Shell acorns with a nut-cracker and nut pick, discarding any with worms.

2. Chop nuts to a coarse meal in food processor.

3. Soak nuts in boiling water for 30 minutes. Drain water, which will be reddish-brown.

4. Taste a little of the meal. If it is still bitter and astringent, repeat Step 3.

5. When nuts lose their bitter taste, spread meal out on a baking sheet and put it into a 300-degree oven, so that the meal dries out and toasts slightly, being careful not to let the meal burn. (You can skip this step, but it adds flavor.)

6. Measure one cup meal and combine with cornmeal, flour, salt, and baking powder.

7. Combine honey, beaten egg, and milk.

8. Add milk mixture to dry ingredients and mix until all dry ingredients are moistened.

9. Grease the 8 by 8 pan and pour in the batter. Level off with a spatula if necessary.

10. Pour into greased 8 by 8 pan and bake at 350 degrees for 20 to 30 minutes.

11. Test for doneness with a wire cake tester or toothpick.

Serve cut into squares.

BLACK WALNUT CORN BREAD

This recipe appeared in *American Indian Food and Lore* by Carolyn Niethammer, and derives from her research in academic sources or from her Apache informant, Daisy Johnson. Black walnuts are sweeter and oilier than European walnuts. Pecans are a fair substitute.

Yield: a small loaf, slices for 4-6
  6 ears fresh corn on the cob, with husks
  pinch of salt
  1/2 cup black walnut meats

Equipment: Food grinder or blender or food processor, small loaf pan

1. Peel corn, saving husks in a plastic bag so they won't dry out.

2. With a sharp knife, cut kernels off corn.

3. Put the corn through a food grinder or blender, saving all the milky juice.

4. Line a small metal bread pan with the corn husks, reserving some husks for the top.

5. Chop or grind the black walnut meats.

6. Combine the ground corn, corn juice, salt, and the walnuts.

7. Pour mixture on top of corn husks.

8. Cover with some of the remaining corn husks.

9. Bake at 350 degrees for about one hour. Check occasionally to prevent overbaking because some corn is juicier than others.

ARAB-AMERICANS (LEBANESE AND SYRIANS)

Neither "Arab-Americans" nor "Lebanese" nor "Syrians" are entirely comfortable or fully accurate terms for the roughly two million Americans whose families emigrated from areas in the modern countries of Lebanon, Syria, Israel, Jordan, the Palestinian Authority, and parts of Iraq. Until the end of World War I, this area was the province of Greater Syria in the Ottoman (Turkish) Empire, but, before 1900, U.S. immigration authorities listed immigrants from the region as Arabs or Turks, and, from 1900 to 1930, as Syrians. Most of these immigrants described themselves as Syrians, although about half came from what is now Lebanon, and many were Palestinians. About 90 percent of the "new immigrant" generation (i.e., those coming to the U.S. between the 1880s and the 1920s) were Christians of several denominations, although only Lebanon ever had a Christian majority. (A few non-Arab immigrants from Greater Syria joined the **Armenian-American** or **Jewish-American** communities.) After the formation of Israel as a Jewish state, and the increasing hostility of Syria toward Israel, Arab-Americans were more likely to describe themselves as Lebanese or "Christian Arabs" or "from the Middle East." In 1965, when immigration quotas increased, a new wave of Arab immigration began; this movement has been more balanced toward Muslims and more inclusive of other parts of the Arab world. The ethnic revival of the 1980s affected all American ethnic groups, but Arab-Americans in particular became more willing to describe themselves as such, even as the outbreak of civil war in Lebanon, the invasions of Lebanon by Israel and Syria, and the beginning of the Palestinian "intifadeh" resistance intensified political passions in the Middle East.

Although some Arab-American cookbooks stress the author's family origins (and some do not), there has been no apparent effort in the United States to differentiate the regional cuisines. Of "recent immigrants" from the Arab world (those arriving since 1965), only **Egyptian-Americans** have so far expressed a distinct public identity. New York, New England, and New Jersey were early centers for Arab-Americans. Greater Detroit early attracted Muslim Arabs from many countries, as well as **Assyrian- and Chaldean-Americans** from Iraq.

Tiny Kibbee Balls

Kibbee, a mixture of bulgur wheat and ground lamb, is used in a variety of ways in the Middle East. (Bulgur wheat is pre-cooked somewhat like converted rice; ordinary cracked wheat will not work the same way.) Some forms of kibbee are used as one of the tests of a young woman's skill in cooking. This recipe appeared in *Arabic Cooking in America* (1972, revised 1977) by Yvonne Homsey, Mary Maloof, and Evelyn Menconi, who are of mostly Palestinian background. These small balls might go into stew or sauce, but are well adapted to the American appetizer course, or a similar course called "mezza" in Arabic. The lamb should be lean leg or shoulder meat.

1 1/2 pounds ground lamb
1/2 pound "fine burghul (#1)" (bulgur wheat)
1 small onion (optional)
pine nuts (optional)
oil for frying
salt, pepper, and allspice to taste

1. Soak burghul 15 minutes in cold water.

2. If using onion, halve, peel, and mince fine.

3. Squeeze handfuls of burghul to remove water. Put all the dried burghul into a bowl.

4. Mix lamb, burghul, onion (if using), salt, pepper, and allspice.

5. Shape into tiny balls. (Balls may be stuffed with a few pine nuts.)

6. Heat a thin coating of oil in a heavy frying pan and fry balls in batches, rolling them around to brown thoroughly.

Serve hot. May be frozen and reheated in a covered baking dish. "[C]an be served uncooked on a platter. May be garnished with a tablespoon of oil, chopped onion, or a dash of cinnamon, or all three."

Kibbee

In this recipe by Bubba Mohamed, whose father came to Mississippi to run a store, the traditional lamb has been replaced by beef, and the pine nuts and spice are gone. The recipe appeared in *The Share-Cropper*, published by the Central Delta Academy PTO in Inverness, Mississippi, and was reprinted in *A Gracious Plenty: Recipes and Recollections from the American South* by John T. Edge.

1 cup bulgur wheat
1 pound lean round steak, ground twice
1 onion
1/2 cup vegetable oil
salt and pepper to taste
fresh parsley, fresh mint, or olives for garnish

Equipment: Blender or food processor to puree onion

1. Soak the wheat in cold water for 45 minutes.

2. Pour off some of the water, and squeeze handfuls of the wheat to get out the rest.

3. Halve, peel, and cut the onions into pieces so you can puree it in the blender or food processor with the oil.

4. In a bowl, mix the wheat, beef, onion, oil, salt, and pepper.

5. Form into patties or balls (or a flat meatloaf in a brownie or lasagna pan). Traditional recipes would make the loaf in two layers with pine nuts in the middle, or into cakes in a long oval shape.

6. "Or mold on a platter and eat uncooked." (This raw-meat kibbee was traditionally made with lamb liver.)

7. "Fry or bake."

Tabouli

Tabouli is a nutritious salad of wheat and herbs. This recipe comes from *It Happened in the Kitchen: Recipes for Food and Thought* by Rose B. and Nathra Nader, Lebanese immigrants who were the parents of consumer advocate Ralph Nader.

Yield: serves 10
3 bunches parsley
2-3 bunches scallions

4 tablespoons dried mint or 4 sprigs of fresh
  mint
1/2 cup olive oil (or to taste)
1 cup fine burghul #1 (bulgur wheat)
5 tomatoes
8 lemons
1 head Romaine lettuce (or more as needed)

1. Wash burghul. (Coarser-grain burghul will have to be soaked for 15-20 minutes.)

2. Wash hands and rinse thoroughly. Squeeze water out of burghul by handfuls, and place in a large bowl.

3. Cut off stems of parsley with fingers, leaving the leaves.

4. Wash parsley in a bowl of water, rinsing and draining until all sand has disappeared. Drain well.

5. Pick leaves of mint stems (if using fresh mint). Wash fresh mint.

6. Mince parsley and mint fine, using a knife. "If you use a machine chopper, try to leave the parsley partly not mashed."

7. Trim and mince scallions.

8. Mince 3 tomatoes.

9. Combine burghul and herbs, scallions, and minced tomatoes.

10. Juice lemons and add the lemon juice "until tart taste has been achieved."

11. Add olive oil to taste (usually about as much as lemon juice).

12. Season with salt and pepper.

13. Wash lettuce and separate leaves. Drain well.

14. Slice the last 2 tomatoes thinly.

15. On a platter, place a bed of lettuce and put the tabouli over it. Decorate the top with thin slices of tomato and small pieces of lettuce all the way around the platter so that these can be used with each serving.

ARMENIAN-AMERICANS

The 1990 census ancestry survey projects 308,000 Armenian-Americans, most descended from refugees who fled the Turkish oppression of 1900 to 1924. The ancient Armenian homeland was then already divided among Turkey, Iran, and Russia, and the mass murders and forced relocations of 1915, in particular, are often compared to the Nazi Holocaust. The 1990 figure shows a decrease from estimates in the 1970s, and seems low in light of the large communities around Boston, Los Angeles, and Fresno, California (immortalized by writer William Soroyan), and the strong community identity of Armenian-Americans. Another group of Armenians came to the United States in the 1960s, 1970s, and 1980s from Soviet Armenia and from many countries in the Middle East. The present country of Armenia has been independent of the former Soviet Union since 1991; it has generally good relations with the United States and the Armenian-American community. An ongoing problem is sporadic war with Azerbaijan over the Ngorno-Karabach region.

Armenians have kept their culture for more than 2,500 years, and were traders throughout the Middle East. Their cooking has acquired a lot from fine Turkish and Iranian cuisine, and Armenian-Americans are great compilers of church cookbooks. One of my favorite ethnic cookbooks, *Rose Baboian's Armenian-American Cookbook* (1964), includes charts of quantity cooking for church fairs.

ARMENIAN BEAN SALAD

Contributed by Sona Ekizian to the *Church of the Messiah Centennial Cookbook* published in Auburndale, Massachusetts, in 1971, this easy salad is called "fassoulia piaz" in both Armenian and Turkish.

Yield: serves 6

    1 can Progresso cannellini beans (white kidney beans)
    1/2 cup finely chopped parsley
    1/2 cup finely chopped scallions ("or onions")
    1/2 lemon
    1 clove garlic (optional)
    vinegar
    olive oil

1. Wash out beans in a colander.

2. Chop the parsley and scallions or onions.

3. Mix together in a bowl; squeeze on lemon juice.

4. Add vinegar and olive oil "to taste." (Start with 2 tablespoons of the oil and a dash of vinegar.)

5. "Mix all together early in day and refrigerate."

Serve as an appetizer or as a side dish with a light entree.

LEMON YOGURT CAKE

This cake comes from a 1946 *Delaware Armenian Women's Cookbook*, via Burt Greene's 1981 *Honest American Fare*. At the time, yogurt was not widely available, and Armenian families generally made their own.

Yield: 12-15 thin slices

    1 cup unsalted butter (2 sticks), softened
    1 1/2 cups sugar
    4 eggs
    1 tablespoon grated lemon rind
    1 teaspoon vanilla extract
    2 1/2 cups sifted all purpose flour
    1 teaspoon baking powder
    1 teaspoon baking soda
    1/2 teaspoon salt
    1 cup plain yogurt
    3/4 cup finely ground almonds
    1/2 cup lemon juice (fresh best, from 2-3 lemons)

Equipment: Tube pan or angel cake pan, whisk or hand beater, grater for lemon rind, juicer for fresh lemon juice (if using), flour sifter, toothpick or wire cake tester

1. Preheat oven to 350 degrees.

2. Butter and flour a 9-inch tube pan or angel cake pan.

3. Beat the butter in a large bowl until light and fluffy.

4. Slowly beat in one cup of sugar.

5. Beat in eggs, one at a time.

6. Grate lemon to get lemon rind; beat in lemon rind and vanilla.

7. Sift the flour with baking powder and salt.

8. Add flour mixture to the batter in three parts, alternating with three parts of yogurt.

9. Fold in ground almonds.

10. Pour into tube pan or angel cake pan.

11. Bake about one hour, or until a toothpick or wire cake tester comes out clean.

12. Cool on a wire rack 5 minutes.

13. Meanwhile, juice lemons or measure out bottled lemon juice.

14. Heat lemon juice in a small saucepan with remaining 1/2 cup sugar until sugar dissolves.

15. Slowly pour mixture over cake, allowing mixture to soak in.

16. Cool cake completely in pan before unmolding.

Serve in thin slices.

Armenian Nutmeg Cake

Somewhat similar in technique to the lemon yogurt cake, above, this recipe comes from *Add a Pinch of New England*, published in the early 1960s by the ladies of Grace Church, North Attleboro, Massachusetts. Yogurt was still hard to come by, so the original recipe called for "Mazoon (or yogurt)." The frosting is completely American and may have been added by the donor.

Yield: 8-10 squares
- 1/4 cup (1/2 stick) butter
- 1/4 cup shortening
- 1 1/2 cups sugar
- 3 beaten eggs
- 2 cups flour
- 1/2 teaspoon salt
- 1 teaspoon baking powder
- 1 teaspoon baking soda
- 2 teaspoons nutmeg
- 1 teaspoon vanilla extract
- 1 cup yogurt

For frosting:
- 10 tablespoons (one and one-quarter sticks) melted butter
- 1/2 cup brown sugar
- 1/4 cup cream
- 1/2 teaspoon vanilla extract
- 1 cup shredded coconut

Equipment: Square baking pan (or use tube pan or angel cake pan), whisk or hand mixer, toothpick or wire cake tester, flexible spatula to frost cake

1. Butter and flour baking pan.

2. Recipe says "Mix first 10 ingredients together, then fold in the mazoon [yogurt] gently." For a lighter cake, follow Steps 2-9 of the lemon yogurt cake recipe, above.

3. Bake in a square pan for 40 minutes in a 350-degree oven. (It will take a little longer in the tube pan.)

4. After the cake is baked, mix together the frosting ingredients.

5. Ice the cake.

6. Brown lightly under broiler (optional).

Serve cut into squares.

Tan

Tan (or tahn) is a drink of thinned yogurt like Asian-Indian "lassi." This recipe comes from *Rose Baboian's Armenian-American Cookbook* (1964), published in Boston. Although Armenian-Americans produce many cookbooks, Mrs. Baboian's stands out as a model of American ethnic food writing because she recorded many traditions, provided explicit instructions, and even anticipated such developments as chocolate yogurt!

- 1 1/2-2 cups madzoon (whole milk yogurt)
- 1/2 to 1 1/2 teaspoons sugar
- 1/4 teaspoon salt
- 4-6 ice cubes

Equipment: Egg beater

1. Beat yogurt with egg beater.

2. Beat in 4 cups cold water, the sugar, and the salt.

3. Add the ice cubes and let stand 5-10 minutes, or until tan is cold.

Serve with spiced meat dishes.

Prinzov Pilaf

This classic Armenian pilaf recipe comes from *Adventures in Armenian Cooking*, published in 1973 by St. Gregory's Armenian Apostolic Church of Indian Orchard, Massachusetts. This entire book was published on the Internet at <www.cilicia.com>.

Yield: serves 4
- 1/2 stick butter
- 1/4 cup curled vermicelli noodles, crumbled (or broken up thin spaghetti)

1 cup long-grain white rice
3 cups chicken broth
a few sliced almonds or pine nuts (optional)

Equipment: Covered skillet

1. Crumble the vermicelli into short lengths, about 3/4 inch or less.

2. Melt butter in a skillet with a good cover and brown the vermicelli and nuts, if using.

3. Add rice and stir until well coated.

4. Add broth and salt and pepper to taste. Bring to boil.

5. Stir once and simmer for 15-20 minutes, until broth is absorbed and rice is soft.

6. Let rice set covered but off the heat for about 20 minutes before serving.

Serve as a side dish or turkey stuffing.

ASIAN INDIAN-AMERICANS

About one million Asian Indians live in the United States, almost all of them "recent immigrants" since 1965. Although outsiders view all Asian Indians (as well as **Pakistani-Americans,** Bangladeshis, Sri Lankans, and Indo-Caribbeans from Guyana and Trinidad) as "Indian," India is one of the most multi-cultural countries in the world. Indian society is divided primarily by languages (more than 600), and also by religion, region, and vestiges of the ancient caste system. An estimated half of the Asian Indians in the U.S. are Gujaratis from western India, although they are only about 5 percent of the population of India itself. Patel is a common Gujarati name, and also the name of a subcaste in Gujarat. Some U.S. Gujaratis relocated here after political instability affected their communities in East Africa and Fiji. Another large group of Asian Indians are Indo-Caribbeans descended from Asians who came to Guyana and Trinidad as contract laborers in the nineteenth century. Other visible sub-groups are the Punjabis, the Sikhs (a religious group, also from Punjab), the Bengalis (including some Hindus from Bangladesh), the Tamils (some of whom are from Sri Lanka), and smaller groups of Biharis, Malayam-speakers, Telegu-speakers, Sindhis, Jains (a conservative religious group), and Maharashtrans.

Indian food is also much more diverse than the typical Indian restaurant menu, which is mostly meat dishes from northern India with a few dishes from elsewhere that were popular with British colonials before India became independent in 1947. Spices are important to all Indian cuisines, but they vary considerably from region to region, and even among families from the same city. Gujarati food, for example, is almost entirely vegetarian, frequently steamed, and many dishes have a sophisticated but mild palate of spices. Because of computer communications, the Indian community in the U.S. is exchanging regional recipes and obtaining Indian spices and ingredients. Indo-American food will probably become different from any particular ethnic cuisine of India within a generation. But no one can predict how fast and in what ways it will become Americanized. None of the following dishes are yet characteristic of the whole Indo-American community, but they are good, practical dishes that might become popular.

STUFFED GREEN PEPPERS

This recipe was contributed to *Green Mountain Favorites*, a recent fundraising cookbook for the American Red Cross, Northern Vermont Chapter, by Pam Rao of Shelburne, Vermont.

Yield: serves 4-6 as a vegetarian entree or side dish

4-6 large peppers
1 cup cooked rice
1/2 teaspoon turmeric
1/2 teaspoon curry powder

1 teaspoon salt
2 firm tomatoes
2 ounces butter
1 teaspoon ground black pepper
1/2 teaspoon coriander powder
4 hard cooked eggs

Equipment: Large pot, baking pan, small pan for cold water, mixing bowl

1. Bring a large pot of salted water to a boil.

2. Immerse tomatoes for a minute to loosen skins, then place in cold water.

3. Put green peppers in boiling water for 10 minutes.

4. Peel tomatoes and chop.

5. Chop the eggs.

6. Melt the butter.

7. Mix together tomatoes, eggs, butter, and the rest of the ingredients.

8. Remove peppers from boiling water.

9. Carefully cut the tops off the peppers. Dip in cold water as necessary to handle.

10. Remove the seeds and pith from the peppers.

11. Stuff the peppers with the stuffing mixture.

12. Replace the tops, and bake in a buttered baking dish at 375 degrees for 30-45 minutes.

SHEERA

Also from *Green Mountain Favorites*, this western Indian dish was contributed by Nirmala Karmath. This recipe for sheera (sometimes spelled "shira") has no milk and is more like fudge, though other recipes I have seen are for a milk pudding.

Yield: 20 pieces of fudge-like confection
  3/4 cup Cream of Wheat (farina)
  3 tablespoons butter (unsalted)
  3/4 cup boiling water
  1 pinch saffron

1 tablespoon raisins
1 cup sugar
1/2 teaspoon cardamom powder

Equipment: Small saucepan, pie plate, wooden spoon to stir

1. In a small saucepan, melt one tablespoon of butter.

2. Add Cream of Wheat and fry briefly.

3. Add boiling water, cover and cook over low heat until soft.

4. Add saffron, raisins, and sugar.

5. Stir until it thickens.

6. Add the rest of the butter and stir until it forms a ball.

7. Remove from heat and mix in cardamom powder.

8. Transfer to pie plate, smooth out.

9. When cool, cut into 20 pieces.

Serve as a dessert or snack.

PEANUT POTATOES

This recipe was collected from Maharashtrans in Chicago for the *Chicago Tribune's Ethnic Chicago Cookbook* by writer Colleen Taylor Sen.

CAUTION: Hot oil used.

Yield: serves 4 as a vegetarian entree or side dish
  1 1/2 pounds small to medium red potatoes
  2 tablespoons vegetable oil
  1 inch-long piece of fresh ginger root
  1 teaspoon cumin seeds
  1/4 cup roasted unsalted peanuts (measured ground)
  1 tablespoon ground coriander
  1 teaspoon ground cumin
  1/2 teaspoon salt
  1/4 teaspoon ground red pepper
  grated fresh coconut for garnish (optional)
  chopped cilantro for garnish

Equipment: Medium saucepan, large nonstick skillet, blender or food processor to grind peanuts, coconut grater if using fresh coconut garnish, screen to cover frying pan (optional)

1. Boil potatoes in water (enough to cover) until tender, about 15 minutes.

2. Peel and mince ginger by slicing off thin slices, thin sticks, and tiny dice. Grate coconut for garnish (optional). Chop cilantro for garnish.

3. Grind peanuts to a powder in a food processor or blender. Measure 1/4 cup.

4. Drain and cool potatoes.

5. When potatoes are cool enough to handle, rub off skins and cut into 1 1/2-inch cubes.

6. Heat oil in nonstick skillet over medium heat.

7. Add ginger and cumin seeds; fry until seeds stop crackling, 2-3 minutes. (If you have a screen to cover the frying pan, seeds can't pop out.)

8. Add potato cubes.

9. Turn a few times to brown all sides, perhaps 5 minutes in all.

10. Add ground peanuts, coriander, cumin, salt, and red pepper.

11. Cook, tossing gently, another 2 minutes, then remove from heat.

12. Garnish with cilantro or cilantro and coconut.

Serve with flatbreads or salad, or as a side dish.

BAKED YOGURT

This Bengali-American recipe was contributed by Anil B. Mukherjee to the *National Institutes of Health First Cookbook*, compiled in 1976 by the Recreation and Welfare Association of the National Institutes of Health in Bethesda, Maryland. The recipe is somewhat tricky because too much heat or low-fat yogurt will lead to a curdled, cheesy pudding. Also, don't halve the recipe without reducing heat. In India, it would be more usual to thicken yogurt by draining it.

In western India, a related dish called shrikand is flavored with saffron.

3 cups plain whole-milk yogurt
1 small can sweetened condensed milk
rose water (optional)

Equipment: Whisk, large Pyrex or stoneware casserole, aluminum foil

1. Preheat oven to 450 degrees.

2. Mix yogurt with condensed milk to a smooth liquid so that no curds of yogurt remain.

3. Pour yogurt mixture into casserole and cover tightly with aluminum foil.

4. Bake 20-25 minutes.

5. Remove from oven, remove foil, and let cool until tray can be touched.

6. Refrigerate one hour before serving. (It can be frozen or refrigerated longer, but may "weep.")

7. "Rose water could be sprinkled on the yogurt for flavor."

Serve like a pudding, but in smaller portions because it is very sweet and rich.

NUKED RICE

This recipe was contributed by Sanjiv Singh of Carnegie Mellon University to the online *Pittsburgh Dinner Co-Op Cookbook*, a collection of recipes by a group of cooks who meet regularly. According to Mr. Singh, who is from northern India, "[s]ince I discovered I could cook edible rice in the microwave, this recipe has been getting a lot of use." Basmati is a converted, long-grain rice with a distinctive flavor. The recipe will work, however, with any long-grain white or converted rice.

Yield: serves 6
    2 cups basmati rice
    1 teaspoon cumin seeds
    1 teaspoon coriander powder
    1/2 teaspoon salt
    3 3/4 cups water

Equipment: Any microwave-safe casserole dish, sieve or colander to drain rice

1. Wash the rice in several changes of water and drain.

2. Put the rice in a microwave-safe dish and add 3 3/4 cups water.

3. Cook the rice in the microwave on high for 10 minutes without a cover.

4. Add the rest of the ingredients and stir.

5. Cook for another 6-8 minutes, until the water has evaporated.

ASSYRIAN- AND CHALDEAN-AMERICANS (MESOPOTAMIANS)

All these terms have been used to describe several groups of immigrants who speak modern dialects of the ancient Aramaic language, and who are members of four Christian denominations. They came to the United States from what is now northern Iraq and Iran, as well as from parts of Turkey, Syria, and Lebanon. Some other Iraqi-Americans, who are Muslims and speak Arabic but who have a similar cuisine, are also known as Mesopotamians, especially in the Detroit area.

The Assyrians were probably one ethnic group in the Middle East until the fifth century, when they followed two different Christian dissenters, Nestorius of Constantinople and Jacobus Baraldeus. In the last 500 years, some from each group have rejoined the Roman Catholic, Eastern Orthodox, and various Protestant denominations. The Catholic Church has added to the confusion by calling ex-Nestorian Catholics, "Chaldeans," and ex-Jacobite Catholics, "Syrian Catholics." Of perhaps 150,000 Assyrian-Americans, the largest communities are in Chicago (Nestorian), greater Detroit (mostly Chaldeans), New Jersey (where they call themselves "Syrian Arameans") and the ports of entry in New York and Boston. These communities were established at the end of the nineteenth century, with groups of refugees arriving after World War I, during the Kurd-Iraqi conflicts of the 1960s and 1970s, and since the recent upheavals in Iran and Iraq. As an ancient minority community, Assyrian-Americans have kept largely to themselves. The Gulf War brought them unwelcome attention, but also inspired some younger Assyrian-Americans to be more public about their ethnicity.

As lovingly described in David Benjamin Warda's *Assyrian Cookery* (Cincinnati, 1996), the cooking of Assyrian-Americans has been maintained in extended-family celebrations, and draws from the ancient complexity of Iraqi and Persian cooking, using many herbs and sweet-sour sauces.

LETTUCE LEAVES WITH HONEY, VINEGAR, AND MINT DIP

This recipe offers a different way to eat salad. David Warda's grandmother would set out a bowl of this dip and each guest would dip their lettuce leaves, fresh from the garden. The dip can also be used as a salad dressing, which would be the Americanization of this recipe.

Yield: serves 6
    lettuce leaves (start with a head of romaine)

1/2 cup vinegar
1/2 cup honey
1 tablespoon fresh mint or to taste

1. Trim, rinse, and drain lettuce leaves.

2. Mix together vinegar and honey

3. Remove fresh mint leaves from stems. Rinse, drain, and chop leaves.

4. Add mint to vinegar mixture.

Serve as a dip or salad dressing. You can store extra dip in a covered jar in the refrigerator.

FLAT EGG AND FRESH HERB PANCAKES

These pancakes are really omelets, and a good introduction to the fresh herbal flavors of Iraqi cooking. If you can't get all the fresh herbs, the dish will still work. "Butter oil" is butter that has been heated for two hours to develop a browned flavor, then clarified (skimmed and the browned solids poured off).

Yield: serves 2 or 3 as a breakfast dish
  6 large eggs
  1 tablespoon butter oil or olive oil
  homemade yogurt (or yogurt cheese, or
    plain whole milk yogurt)
  1 tablespoon fresh cilantro (or to taste)
  1 tablespoon flat leaf parsley (or to taste)
  1 tablespoon chives (or to taste)
  1 tablespoon fresh dill (or to taste)
  1 tablespoon fresh tarragon (or to taste)
  salt to taste

Equipment: Heavy frying pan with a cover, paper towels to dry herbs

  1. Remove sprigs and leaves from stems of fresh herbs.

  2. Rinse herbs, dry, and chop.

  3. Salt herbs directly.

  4. Heat butter oil or olive oil in a heavy-bottom pan, but keep the heat relatively low.

  5. Beat 6 eggs lightly with a fork.

  6. Pour eggs into the heated pan.

  7. Sprinkle chopped herbs evenly over the beaten eggs.

  8. Cover mixture and cook over medium-low heat until lid feels hot to the touch.

  9. Remove the lid and loosen the edges of the pancake with a knife.

  10. The top of the pancake should be soft to the touch; the bottom should be lightly browned and crispy.

  11. Carefully slide the pancake onto a plate.

Serve cut into wedges with yogurt.

ZAZICH

This recipe is one of a dozen or so posted by the Assyrian-American Association of Modesto, California, on their Web site at <www. aaamodesto. org>.

  16-ounce package small curd cottage cheese
  2 large packages (6- or 8-ounce cream
    cheese)
  2 heaping tablespoons butter
  1/3 cup fresh cilantro
  1 1/2 cups chopped fresh dill
  2 hot banana peppers

Equipment: Food processor

  1. Let cream cheese and butter soften to room temperature, then microwave (according to oven instructions).

  2. Chop cilantro and dill.

  3. Cut off the stems and slit open the peppers. Strip out the seeds and pith with a spoon.

  4. Slice the peppers into thin strips and then cut into fine dice.

  5. Blend ingredients in food processor, or with a pastry blender or large fork.

Serve as a dip or spread with flatbread or crackers.

BOOSHALA

This recipe was a request on the <aaamodesto. org> Web site. "It is a rich, and creamy soup that will warm your heart on a cold winter day." Evidently, Central California has a cold climate by Assyrian-American standards. An alternate recipe uses homemade soured milk and is thickened with leftover rice or bulgur wheat.

Yield: *serves 4 to 6*
  2 pounds yogurt (one-quart container)
  2 tablespoons cornstarch
  2 tablespoons vegetable oil
  1 bunch Swiss chard
  1 bunch coriander (cilantro)
  1 bunch green onions (scallions)
  1 head celery

3 hot green peppers
4 fresh mint leaves
1 teaspoon crushed oregano
2 cloves crushed garlic
1 teaspoon salt
1/2 teaspoon pepper
3 tablespoons lemon juice (or to taste)

Equipment: Whisk, garlic press, large soup pots

1. Use a whisk to stir the yogurt in its container to break up the large chunks and to make it smooth, then pour it into a large pot.

2. Rinse the yogurt container with 5 cups water, then add that to the pot.

3. Gently bring the yogurt to a boil with continuous stirring using the whisk; add a little more water if needed.

4. As yogurt comes to a boil, combine the cornstarch with 1/4 cup water, then add to the yogurt.

5. Keep stirring with the whisk without stopping until yogurt thickens. Remove from heat and set aside.

6. Wash and chop the Swiss chard.

7. Wash and chop the coriander.

8. Wash and chop the green onions and celery.

9. Cut tops off the hot pepper and slit down one side. Use a teaspoon to strip out the seeds and white pith.

10. Chop mint.

11. In a second soup pot, heat the vegetable oil.

12. To the hot oil, add the Swiss chard, coriander, green onions, celery, green peppers, and mint.

13. Sprinkle on the oregano. Squeeze on the cloves of garlic. Add salt and pepper.

14. Cook on medium heat until greens are wilted and greatly reduced in volume.

15. Combine the vegetables with the yogurt and cook on medium heat until meal time.

16. Just before serving, add the lemon juice by drops, stirring as you add.

Serve as a soup.

AUSTRALIAN- AND NEW ZEALANDER-AMERICANS

The 1990 ancestry survey projects about 60,000 Americans who claim ancestors from Australia or New Zealand, but the actual number is probably somewhat larger. Although Australian and New Zealander immigrants came to the U.S. in a steady stream, mostly to California, two sudden surges of immigration occurred. One surge accompanied the California Gold Rush of 1849, when a particularly rough district in San Francisco was known as "Sidneytown." Many of these Australian-Americans returned home for the Australian Gold Rush of 1852. The other surge was after World War II, when American GIs who had served in the South Pacific brought home "war brides" from Australia or New Zealand. Recent immigrants from Australia or New Zealand have been mostly professionals and technicians.

Like the United States and Canada, Australia and New Zealand are former British colonies as well as nations of immigrants that must deal with the claims of aboriginal peoples. Although Australian-Americans often joke about the bad food of their homeland, they also gather to make the meat pies, pavlovas (a meringue dessert), lamingtons (cookies), and other good things they miss.

New Zealand Bacon and Egg Pie

Jo Mason contributed this recipe to the *Easy Gourmet Guide* (1975), compiled by Planned Parenthood of Northern Nevada. I also consulted a recipe from Miss Barbara Graham in *The English Speaking Union International Cookbook* (1962), published by the Active Members Group, New York Branch. In the latter recipe, the eggs are beaten with milk and sliced tomatoes are added to the bottom of the pie.

pastry shells for a covered pie
8 slices bacon
"5 or 6 eggs"
1/2 medium onion
1/4 cup grated cheese

Equipment: Grater or food processor with grating blade

1. Fry bacon "until almost done but not crisp."

2. Cut bacon into pieces and sprinkle these on the bottom shell.

3. Grate cheese if necessary.

4. Peel the half onion and grate. (Wear swim goggles to avoid tears.)

5. Break eggs into shell without breaking yolks, if possible.

6. Sprinkle with cheese and onion.

7. Top with pastry and bake at 350 degrees until pastry is golden.

Serve hot or at room temperature the same day; do not refrigerate. Miss Graham recommends the recipe "for picnics, barbecues, and cocktail parties."

"Anzacs" Golden Crunch Cookies

These durable cookies were shipped by mail to Australian soldiers serving with the Australia-New Zealand Army Corps (ANZAC) during World War I. The troops were known as Anzacs. This recipe was submitted to *Star Recipes from the Maryland Science Center* (Baltimore, 1982) by Owen Phillips, who noted that "Anzacs (for those who haven't seen the movie *Gallipoli*), are supposed to be hard as nails, but really, they are sweet inside." You can substitute honey or molasses for King syrup, or the original "Golden Syrup" from a British-Isles import store or brewing supply store.

1 1/4 cups plain flour
1 1/4 cups sugar
1 1/4 cups rolled oats
1 1/4 cups grated coconut
4 ounces margarine
2 tablespoons King syrup
1 level tablespoon baking soda

1. Melt margarine, add 4 tablespoons boiling water, syrup, and baking soda.

2. Combine all dry ingredients in a bowl and mix well.

3. Pour in the margarine mixture and mix.

4. Grease a baking sheet.

5. Drop cookie mixture by tablespoonfuls onto baking sheet.

6. Bake at 350 degrees for 8-10 minutes.

Pikelets

Mrs. Phyllis Albertis submitted this recipe to *The English Speaking Union International Cookbook* (1962), published by the Active Members Group, New York Branch. The English Speaking Union (ESU) is an international club that arranges student exchanges and events for people from countries of the British Commonwealth and the U.S. Small crumpets are also known as pikelets in Wales.

2 eggs
2 tablespoons sugar
1 cup milk
1 teaspoon baking soda
1 1/2 cups flour
2 teaspoons cream of tartar (or 1 teaspoon baking powder)
2 tablespoons butter

1. Beat eggs and sugar together.

2. Dissolve baking soda in milk and beat into the egg mixture.

3. Sift flour with cream of tartar and mix into the egg mixture.

4. Melt butter and stir in quickly.

5. Heat griddle (not too hot), grease it, and drop mixture on with teaspoon.

6. Brown on both sides.

"Served hot, these are also fine for Sunday brunch."

AUSTRIAN-AMERICANS

According to the 1990 census, 864,000 Americans claim Austrian descent. The present country of Austria is much smaller than the Austro-Hungarian Empire of 1867-1918, when most Austrians came to the United States. Thus, many of the 1.8 million "Austrians" who entered the U.S. during that period have since chosen to be identified as **Jewish-Americans, German-Americans,** or members of up to a dozen other national groupings then part of the Austro-Hungarian Empire. Because Austria's capital, Vienna, is also a culinary capital, the U.S. has had many "Old Vienna" restaurants and many chefs attempting fancy Austrian cuisine.

SALZBURGER RAISIN BREAD

This kugelhof cake from Austria has come down from a community of Austrian Lutherans who settled near Savannah, Georgia, in 1734. The recipe is from JoAnne Morgan Conaway of Springfield, Georgia, who gave it to the *Southern Heritage Breads Cookbook* (1983). The loaf was then being called kogle loaf or just kogle. It was originally baked in a turban-shaped tube pan and probably also contained almonds. Ms. Conaway's recipe fills three loaf pans.

1 1/2 cups milk
1/2 cup butter or margarine, plus enough to grease loaf pans
1/2 cup sugar, plus one teaspoon to "proof" yeast
2 teaspoons salt
2 packages dry yeast
1 teaspoon sugar
2 eggs
7-8 cups all-purpose flour
2 1/2 cups raisins
butter or margarine melted to brush cakes
solid shortening to grease bowl

Equipment: 3 large loaf pans, pastry brush or clean new paint brush

1. Melt butter in milk with sugar and salt.

2. Cool to lukewarm (105-115 degrees).

3. Dissolve yeast and 1 teaspoon of sugar in a cup of warm water. Let stand 5 minutes or until bubbly.

4. Combine cooled milk mixture and yeast mixture in a large bowl.

5. Break each egg into a cup, then combine and beat them in one of the cups.

6. Stir eggs into milk mixture, then work in 5 cups of flour.

7. Dredge raisins in 1/4 cup of flour, stirring to coat well.

8. Add raisins to dough, mixing well.

9. Stir in enough of the remaining flour to form a firm dough.

10. Flour a board and turn out the dough.

11. Knead (see Appendix 1) seven or eight times, no more. Work into a ball.

12. Grease a bowl, and put in the dough, turning to grease the top of the dough.

13. Cover and let rise in a warm place, free from drafts, for 1 1/2 hours or until doubled in bulk.

14. "Punch dough down" to remove air bubbles. Cover and let rest 10 minutes.

15. Turn out onto the floured board. Divide dough into 3 equal portions.

16. Grease 3 large loaf pans. Shape each part of the dough into a loaf and put into the greased pans.

17. Cover with a clean kitchen towel and repeat rising 45 minutes or until doubled in bulk.

18. Bake 30 minutes at 350 degrees, or until loaves sound hollow when tapped.

19. Remove bread from pans immediately and cook on wire racks.

20. Melt butter and brush onto the top of each loaf.

GRAM'S GOULASH SOUP

This recipe comes from Penzey's 1999 holiday spice catalog and is described as Austrian-Hungarian. The name "goulash soup" is a direct translation from the German. A Hungarian recipe would always include caraway.

Yield: 12 large bowls
   2 pounds beef stew meat
   3 medium yellow onions
   7 average-sized white potatoes
   2 tablespoons vegetable oil
   2-3 tablespoons Hungarian sweet paprika
   1/8-1/4 teaspoon cayenne red pepper
   2 bay leaves
   1 tablespoon salt (or 2 tablespoons kosher
      flake salt)
   8-10 cups water
   freshly ground black pepper to taste

Equipment: Frying pan, soup pot

1. Halve, peel, and slice onions into thin rounds.

2. Cut beef into one-inch cubes.

3. Heat one tablespoon of the oil in a large frying pan.

4. Add onions and cook until browned, about 5 minutes.

5. Remove onions to a soup pot.

6. Add another tablespoon of the oil to the frying pan.

7. When oil is hot, add half the beef to brown for about 5 minutes. ("It doesn't have to be dark brown on all sides.")

8. Sprinkle on half the paprika and stir to "somewhat fry" the paprika for another minute.

9. Remove beef to soup pot, scraping to get the paprika bits.

10. Repeat Steps 6 through 8, this time adding the cayenne pepper with the paprika.

11. Use some of the water to get all the browned bits from the frying pan to the soup pot.

12. Add the water and bay leaves to the soup pot and simmer for one hour.

13. Peel and cut potatoes in chunks like the beef.

14. Add potatoes and salt to the soup.

15. Raise heat to medium and cook another 45 minutes.

16. Taste for salt, as potatoes absorb salt.

"Serve with a simple salad, and, this is very important, fresh crusty white bread or rolls, which, eaten Gram and Gramp's style, should just be broken up into the soup in bite-sized pieces, though you could serve it on the side with butter. Make sure there is a pepper grinder on the table, so each person can grind a generous amount of black pepper on top of their bowl."

OATMEAL SOUP

This recipe is based on what the Austrians called "false soup," which gave the illusion of meat without using any. The bouillon cubes are something of a cheat, but you'll be surprised at the depth of flavor in this simple soup, which Robert Bloch of Lenox, Massachusetts, contributed to *Cook It in Massachusetts* (1981), a fund-raiser for the American Cancer Society.

Yield: serves 6
   1/2 cup butter or margarine
   2 cups uncooked oats
   5 beef bouillon cubes

1. Melt butter or margarine in a large saucepan.

2. When it is melted (but not browned), add the oatmeal.

3. Stir the oatmeal while it is browning to prevent burning in the bottom of the pan.

4. After all the butter has been absorbed by the oatmeal, and the oatmeal starts to brown, stir in 6 cups of water.

5. Increase heat to bring soup to a boil.

6. Meanwhile, crumble the bouillon cubes into the mixture and stir until completely dissolved.

7. When soup boils, reduce heat and simmer for 10 minutes.

LINZER TORTE

This recipe, for one of the most famous of many Austrian pastries, comes from one of the most famous Austrian-Americans, Maria von Trapp. Her story is the basis of the musical "The Sound of Music." The recipe appeared in *Just Christmas*, published by the Junior League of the City of Washington in 1970. Ms. von Trapp measured her ingredients by weight in the European manner; I have added volume measurements.

Yield: serves 8
   5 ounces butter (1 1/4 sticks) and a little
      more to grease cookie sheet
   5 ounces sugar (3/4 cup)
   5 ounces grated hazelnuts (or ground
      almonds, 1 to 1 1/4 cups)
   5 ounces flour (1 cup unsifted)
   2 eggs
   "some clove powder, nutmeg, and cinnamon" (pinch each)

   grated lemon rind (1 teaspoon)
   a pinch of salt
   1 1/2 cups red currant jam (or raspberry)

Equipment: Grater, pastry blender or food processor, spatula, kitchen scale, pastry brush or clean and unused paint brush, low soufflé dish or small cake mold

1. Combine first 8 ingredients (except for one egg) in bowl of food processor, or cut in with a pastry blender in a large mixing bowl. Make smooth mixture, and refrigerate 1/2 hour. Lightly grease cookie sheet or cake mold.

2. Roll out half the mixture with a floured rolling pin (or between sheets of waxed paper) to fit the cake mold, or 1/2-inch-thick to make a 6-inch round. Put on cookie sheet. This dough is crumbly and breaks easily, but is easy to mend.

3. Beat second egg with a little water. Paint wash onto the circle of dough.

4. Leaving a 1/2-inch margin around the edge, spread on the jam.

5. Roll out the second half of the dough into a rectangle about 1/4-inch thick.

6. Cut dough into strips 1/4-inch thick. (You can lift them with a spatula dipped in flour.)

7. Use some of the strips to make a "curb" around the base of the torte on the margin. Press down so it is well attached.

8. On a floured board, lay out 6 or 10 strips of the dough so that you can have 2 strips that are the full diameter of the torte, and 4 that are a little less.

9. Lay out the 2 longest strips in a cross on top of the jam, but don't connect the ends. See illustrations.

10. Lay out 2 of the shorter strips across the long strip on top.

11. Fold back the long strip on the bottom, and lay out one of the shorter strips across the 2 other short strips.

12. Fold the long strip back over the crossing strip.

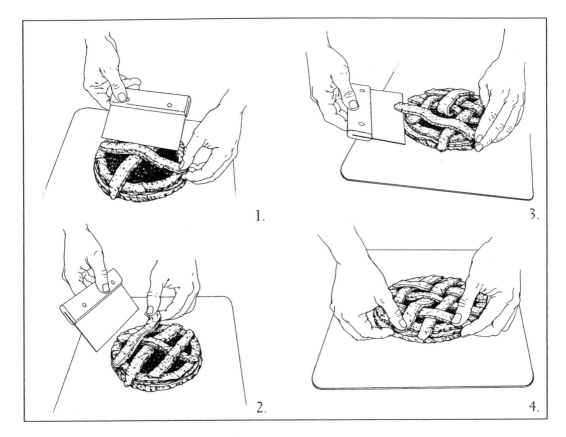

1.

3.

2.

4.

13. Fold back the long strip on the bottom the other way to make way for the last short strip across 2 short strips.

14. Fold the long strip back over the other crossing strip, and pinch to attach all the strips.

15. Brush the lattice with the egg wash.

16. Bake at 350 degrees for 60 or 70 minutes until golden brown.

Serve the next day.

BAHAMIAN-AMERICANS

According to the 1990 census, about 21,000 people of Bahamian ancestry live in the U.S., about one-third in Florida. However, in 1996, the Immigration and Naturalization Service (INS) estimated that there were also 90,000 "illegal aliens" from the Bahamas in the U.S., the eighth-largest such group. (The INS has since admitted that the Bahamas figures "appear to be too high.") In any case, Bahamian immigrants have played a part in all phases of American history and are a vibrant immigrant community today. Before the American Revolution, the Bahamas were owned by the proprietors of the Carolina colony, and thus many **Gullah** dishes, like hoppin' john, are still found in the Bahamas. Early settlers and slaves in South Carolina came from the Bahamas. An early voluntary settlement was a group of **African-American** fisherman who moved to Key West in the 1890s and contributed many dishes that are now in general use in the Florida Keys, such as conch chowder. Bahamian immigrants founded Coral Gables, Florida, and there is also a Bahamian-American component in the West Indian black community in New York City.

ESTHER'S AMERICAN CRAB AND RICE

This recipe is on the personal Internet page of Houston lawyer Martina Sherman-Cartwright, who grew up in Miami, the Bahamas, and England. She also has traditional Bahamian recipes for peas and rice, benne seed candy, and coconut candy, but I like this modernization of what is basically an African pilaf.

1 package shredded imitation crab legs
3 red peppers (fresh and finely chopped)
3 teaspoons salt
1 tablespoon tomato paste
1 teaspoon thyme (or 1/2 teaspoon dried thyme)
1/2 medium onion
1/2 cup of cut bacon (1/4 pound)
3 cups water
2 cups long-grain rice

Equipment: Soup pot with cover

1. Cut bacon into squares. Fry in a medium saucepan.

2. Halve and peel onion, and slice thinly into half rounds.

3. Add onions, thyme, salt, and pepper to bacon in the pan.

4. Sauté an additional 3-5 minutes.

5. Add tomato paste and sauté another 3 minutes.

6. If crab legs come "whole," cut into 2-inch lengths and shred.

7. Add crab legs to mixture, sauté for 2 more minutes.

8. Add 3 cups of water and bring to a boil.

9. Add rice. Reduce heat and boil "until water is 1/2 inch above rice (about five minutes)."

10. Reduce heat, cover tightly, and simmer until rice is cooked (about 15-20 minutes).

OLD SOUR

This Bahamian hot sauce survives under the same name in Key West, Florida. The recipe is from *Jane Nickerson's Florida Cookbook* (1983). The substitutions, in what has never been a fixed recipe in the Bahamas or Florida, are mine, with reference to other printed recipes. The main thing is that a flavor of lime and salt shouldn't be overpowered by the chile peppers. The sauce will get spicier as it ages. Red bird peppers are small hot chile peppers. You can substitute a few of any fresh whole red chile peppers, but ask about hotness.

2 cups key lime juice (substitute 1 1/2 cups fresh lime juice with 1/2 cup white vinegar)
1 tablespoon salt
12 red bird peppers

Equipment: Empty salad dressing bottles or glass jars

1. Strain lime juice.

2. Add one tablespoon salt and stir until dissolved.

3. Put a few peppers into clean bottles or jars, and fill with lime juice mixture. (You can slice chiles to make the sauce hotter.)

4. Cover tightly, but leave at room temperature, away from direct sunlight.

5. "Some say to keep the salted juice at room temperature for about three weeks without using it, then store in a cool place. Others insist the condiment can be used almost any time after it is made."

Serve with fried fish or shellfish, or as a hot sauce with any food.

BARBADAN-AMERICANS

Although the 1990 census estimated only 35,000 Barbadan-Americans, current numbers are probably much higher, even without counting the descendants of early settlers and African slaves who came to the British American colonies through Barbados. Beginning in the 1640s, Barbados became the first British Caribbean colony to produce sugar, as well as the sorting and training center for the British slave trade. After slavery was abolished in 1834, Barbados planters attempted to hold on to their workers over a four-year "apprenticeship" transition and a contract system that amounted to serfdom. Nevertheless, Barbadans began to migrate for higher wages to Panama, Trinidad, and British Guiana (now Guyana). By the 1900s, Barbadans were joining other West Indian blacks in New York City. Present-day Barbadans call themselves "Bajans," and come mostly to New York City. It is likely that two-thirds or more live in Brooklyn today. U.S. Representative Shirley Chisholm is the best-known Barbadan-American political leader.

COU COU OR TURN CORN

This old Barbados recipe combines the grain mashes of Africa with the molded cornmeal dishes of Brazil, and probably takes the name of North African cous-cous (which is also used in Cape Verde and Brazil). There is also a **Creole (Louisiana)** and Cajun version (*see* **Acadians [Cajuns]**), without the okra, called coush-coush. This particular recipe comes from New York actress and producer Cynthia Belgrave Farris via Vertamae Smart-Grosvenor's *Vibration Cooking, or Travel Notes of a Geechee Girl*.

1/2 cup sliced fresh okra (from 1/4 pound)
1 cup cornmeal
salt
butter to grease a mixing bowl

Equipment: Mixing bowl with a round bottom

1. Remove stems and tips from okra, slice thinly, and bring okra to a boil in 2 cups of water.

2. Mix cornmeal with 1/2 cup water, and cook over moderate heat until it thickens.

3. Add the okra and 1/2 cup of the okra water to the cornmeal, stirring with a wooden spoon.

4. Cook over low heat until done; the spoon will then come out clean. The mixture will be smooth but not sticky or pasty to the taste.

5. Grease mixing bowl with butter.

6. Put cornmeal in mixing bowl. Roll around the buttered bowl until it forms a ball that will hold its shape. You can also make two or more balls.

Serve in slices, with optional pat of butter.

EUNICE GRAY'S CODFISH CAKES

According to *The Brooklyn Cookbook*, by Lynn Stallworth and Rod Kennedy, Jr., Eunice Gray was born in Brooklyn and remembers the ticker tape parade for Charles Lindbergh in 1927 and her mother making codfish cakes on Saturdays "until we got Americanized, and then we had franks and beans on Saturday." Salt codfish was originally imported to Barbados from New England to feed slaves, but fried salt codfish cakes became popular all over the Caribbean. This detailed recipe gives a feeling of the high standards of craftsmanship of many West Indian immigrants.

CAUTION: Hot oil used and requires 12 hours to soak codfish.

Yield: 40 codfish cakes
　　1/2 pound dried boneless codfish
　　2 eggs
　　1/2 teaspoon paprika
　　1/2 teaspoon onion salt
　　1 stalk scallion
　　1/2 teaspoon black pepper

1/4 cup finely chopped onion, from a small onion

1/4 cup finely chopped green pepper from 1 medium pepper

1/2 cup flour

1 teaspoon baking powder

1/2 cup milk

vegetable oil for deep frying

Equipment: Heavy pot with high sides, skimmer, large bowl, paper towels to drain cakes

1. Soak the codfish for at least 12 hours, changing the water several times.

2. Place in a saucepan with cold water to cover by 3 inches and bring to a boil for 10 minutes.

3. Taste the fish. If too salty, repeat the boiling. The fish should shred easily.

4. When cool enough to handle, shred the fish with your fingers. "If the cod has any bones, be sure to pull them out."

5. Chop scallion, onion, green pepper, and tomato into very fine dice.

6. In a large bowl, combine eggs with the next 7 ingredients.

7. Sift the baking powder through the flour.

8. Add the flour mixture to the egg mixture. Add the milk and mix thoroughly.

9. Mix in the shredded codfish.

10. Heat 2 inches of oil in a deep pot until sizzling.

11. Drop tablespoon-sized portions of the fish mixture into the hot oil, about 5 at a time.

12. Fry on both sides for 2-3 minutes, until golden brown, and drain on paper towels.

Serve hot as an appetizer or party snack.

BASQUE-AMERICANS

The Basques are speakers of an ancient language, Euskera, which is unrelated to any other in Europe. Their homeland is about 100 square miles on the Atlantic coast of Spain and France. They are regionally divided into seven communities in Europe, and even in the United States there has often been only limited contact between French and Spanish (or Vizcayan) Basques. With a long tradition of seafaring, Basque fishermen may have visited the Americas before Columbus. Many Basques were members of Columbus' crews. Basques also have a long tradition of migration, and were among the leading Spanish settlers of Latin America. Recent immigrants to the U.S. from Latin America and the Caribbean sometimes have lengthy Basque names like Inchaustegui, Irrizarry, Urutia, or Echeveria. Several hundred Basques came to California during the Gold Rush in 1849, but more came as contract shepherds throughout the western states from the 1850s onward. They developed a successful method of moving sheep through different pastures over the course of a year that brought them into conflict with settled ranchers during the early years of the twentieth century. Despite isolated work with sheep in remote locations, Basque-Americans have held onto their culture by continuing the immigrant custom of boarding houses. "Basque hotels" were and are a mail drop, winter base, and family service center for shepherds. Several have become locally popular restaurants in parts of Idaho and Nevada that have few other ethnic restaurants. Today, 50,000 to 100,000 Basque descendants live in the United States, mostly in the Rocky Mountain states and California, with smaller communities of recent immigrants in Florida and Connecticut where Basques have come to play their national sport, jai alai.

Basque Soup

Former Nevada Senator and Governor Paul Laxalt contributed this recipe to the *Easy Gourmet Guide*, a 1975 fund-raiser for the Reno, Nevada, Planned Parenthood clinic; and to *The Republican Cookbook* (1969).

Yield: serves 10
- 3 pounds lean chuck
- 2 cans chicken broth
- 2 cans beef broth
- 2 cans (6-ounce size) V-8 juice
- 2 tablespoons salt
- 6 peppercorns
- 1 bay leaf
- 6 cloves
- 3 sprigs parsley
- 1 cinnamon stick
- 2 onions
- 4 carrots
- 3 stalks celery
- 2 cups cabbage
- 1 can chopped pimento

Equipment: Soup pot

1. Combine first 10 ingredients with 1 1/2 quarts water in a soup pot, bring to a boil.

2. Reduce heat and simmer, covered, for 1 1/2 hours.

3. Halve and peel onions, halve again to make quarters.

4. Peel and slice carrots into chunks.

5. Wash celery and cut into chunks.

6. Halve a small cabbage, then core and chop coarsely to make up 2 cups.

7. Add fresh vegetables and pimento to soup, cover and simmer 3/4 hour.

Serve "with vegetables and meat, or strain and add pasta."

Basque Beans or Sheepherder Beans

Anita Borghese collected this recipe from Jose Leniz, chief cook at the National Basque Festival in Elko, Nevada, for Borghese's *Foods from Harvest Festival and Folk Fairs* (Thomas Crowell, 1977). The original recipe was based on 250 pounds of beans at a time! Three pounds of dry beans is still a large pot, but it will give you a sense of the hearty, rather bland food of the Basque hotels. In the Basque homeland, the beans would be chickpeas. In parts of the U.S. with more acidic "soft" water, you may want to hold the can of tomatoes until Step 9, so that the beans cook fully.

NOTE: Beans must be soaked overnight.

Yield: serves 12
- 3 pounds dry pinto beans
- 1 or 2 slices bacon, chopped
- 1 medium onion, chopped
- 1/2 small green pepper, chopped
- 1 10-ounce can tomatoes
- 1 small ham hock (about 1/2 pound)
- 1 two-ounce piece salt pork
- 1 chorizo (or any garlic sausage such as kielbasa)
- 1 tablespoon salt (or to taste)

Equipment: Colander to drain beans, large pot to cook beans

1. Pick over the beans for stones or dirt, wash them in cold water, and place them in a large bowl. Cover with cold water and soak overnight.

2. Next day, chop the bacon, onion, and green pepper into small dice.

3. Slice sausage into thin rounds.

4. Fry the bacon, add the onions and green peppers, and sauté until lightly browned.

5. Add the tomatoes and simmer 15-20 minutes.

6. Drain the beans and place in a large pot. Add the tomato mixture, ham hock, salt pork, and chorizo.

7. Add cold water just to cover, and bring to a boil.

8. Reduce the heat and simmer 2 hours, partially covered, stirring occasionally.

9. Add salt and continue cooking another hour, stirring occasionally.

Serve with green salad and rolls.

WALNUT PUDDING

This recipe from the Boise Basque Museum was contributed by Maria Galdos Landeen. She notes that the bread crumbs are optional, but if you aren't using them, double the walnuts.

Yield: serves 6
   1 quart whole milk
   1 cup sugar
   1 cup ground walnuts
   1 cup bread crumbs

Equipment: Medium soup pot or kettle, stirring spoon, food processor (if grinding walnuts or bread crumbs), 6 bowls

1. If necessary, use food processor or blender to get the nuts and bread crumbs to a fine consistency.

2. Combine all ingredients in a medium-size kettle and bring to a boil over low heat, stirring constantly until the mixture thickens. ("This will scorch if not stirred.")

3. Pour into serving bowls and chill.

Serve as dessert.

WYOMING BASQUE POTATOES

This easy, flavorful recipe from a community cookbook is a good example of the kind of Basque cooking that has become popular outside the Basque community in the mountain states.

Yield: serves 8
   1 medium-sized onion
   1 small clove garlic
   2 tablespoons olive oil
   3/4 cup chopped parsley
   1/4 cup chopped pimento
   1 teaspoon salt
   1/8 teaspoon pepper
   1 envelope instant chicken broth or 1
      teaspoon granulated chicken bouillon
   6 medium-sized potatoes

Equipment: Garlic press, skillet, slotted spoon

1. Halve, peel, and chop onion to make about a half cup.

2. Peel garlic.

3. Heat oil in a skillet, crush garlic into the oil, add onion, and sauté until soft.

4. Chop parsley and pimento.

5. Dissolve chicken broth or bouillon in a cup of hot water.

6. Stir parsley, pimento, salt, and pepper into the skillet.

7. Add chicken broth. Remove from heat. Pour into a bowl.

8. Peel potatoes and slice thin.

9. Layer potato slices in skillet.

10. Pour broth and onion mixture over potatoes. Heat to boiling.

11. Reduce heat; cover and simmer 20 minutes, or until tender.

12. Remove potatoes with a slotted spoon to a heated serving dish.

13. Spoon remaining cooking liquid over potatoes.

BELGIAN-AMERICANS

About 250,000 Belgians have come to the United States since 1830, but only about 400,000 Americans listed Belgian (or Flemish) ancestry on the 1990 census. Belgium is itself a multi-ethnic country, divided between the French-speaking Walloons and the Dutch-speaking Flemish. In the nineteenth century, when Walloons dominated the country, more Belgian immigrants to the U.S. were Flemish and, despite religious differences, identified with **Dutch-Americans** who spoke their language. In the twentieth century, Belgium has been more united by the experience of German occupation in both World Wars, and more Belgian immigrants to the United States have been Walloons, who also settled in French-speaking communities in Canada. Those Walloons who subsequently moved to the United States from Canada were usually counted as **French Canadian-Americans**. Food is something Belgian ethnic groups don't divide up; most dishes have two names and are shared by all Belgians.

Belgian-Americans generally settled in the upper Midwest, first to find cheap farmland, later to get jobs in industry. The most visible and long-lasting Flemish settlements were in and around Detroit, Michigan, and South Bend, Indiana. Walloons settled more to the west of Lake Michigan, especially in northern Wisconsin, Michigan's Upper Peninsula, and Minnesota. The center of Belgian-American culture today is the four counties around Green Bay, Wisconsin, where about 50,000 residents identify themselves as Belgian descendants, and many restaurants serve booyah and "Belgian pies." This community was founded by a group of Walloon farmers who left the province of Brabant in eastern Belgium in the 1850s and settled briefly near Sheboygan, Wisconsin. A chance meeting with a Walloon priest from Door County (the small eastern Wisconsin peninsula that juts out into Lake Michigan) brought them north to Green Bay, where they were able to buy up about 80 percent of the farmland by 1860. An annual "Belgian Days" celebration is held every summer, and groups of men and women assemble to cook for a traditional pre-harvest festival called "Kermiss," which is held on successive weekends.

Some other Belgian-American recipes you may be able to collect are for Christmas cookies in waffle-like patterns, waffles, cabbage with sausage, fish soups, meat loaves, and fried potatoes with various dips.

CHICKEN BOOYAH

"Booyah" today is a hearty soup full of meat and vegetables, like Italian-American minestrone without the pasta. Around Green Bay, Wisconsin, a "booyah" is an event like a barbecue, and has a humorous culture like barbecue or chili cooking contests—there are "Booyah Kings," teams of assistants chopping vegetables, secret ingredients, and giant kettles handed down as heirlooms. Although "booyah" is a dialect pronunciation of the French word, bouillon, the soup now called booyah (and sometimes boulyaw) would not be recognizable as bouillon back in Brabant. In Belgium and in the early years in Wisconsin, booyah was a clear soup that made two meals for a thrifty family: one of the broth with rice on the side, and another of the boiled hen, perhaps cold the next day. The root vegetables may have come from memories of other Walloon soups, such as hochepot. In central Minnesota, a Polish-American soup called "bouja" is similar, except for a bag of pickling spices as flavoring. Another possibility is that the vegetables come from Brunswick stew, a hunter's dish that was popular all over the United States by the 1930s. The optional lemon is a good idea, and it would be fun to think it came from the thick Flemish chicken soup called waterzooi, perhaps once served in the Brussels airport to a Belgian-American visitor. So this dish has gone from family to festival, from female to male cooks, from thin to thick, and still is described proudly as "Belgian penicillin." The garnish these days is plenty of oyster crackers. This recipe is a fairly typical modern booyah, but the many individual variations include such items as canned beans, split peas, and "secret ingredients."

Yield: 8-10 quarts, 25 generous servings
  1 soup/stew hen, about 6 pounds
  1 1/2 pounds chuck roast or steak in one piece
  bay leaf
  1 tablespoon salt
  1 bunch celery chopped (2 1/2 cups)
  1 pound carrots chopped (about 4 large carrots)
  1 pound cabbage chopped (1/3 medium head)
  2 pounds potatoes diced (about 10-12 medium red bliss potatoes)
  2 pounds onions chopped (about 4-5 large onions)
  28-ounce can tomatoes
  1/2 pound green beans (or a 12-ounce can)
  1/2 pound corn cut off the cob (or a 12-ounce can)
  1/2 pound split peas or navy beans (or a 12-ounce can)
  juice of 2 lemons (optional)
  1 tablespoon soy sauce
  oyster crackers (substitute saltines)

Equipment: Two 8-quart "spaghetti pots," tongs to remove hen and beef, swim goggles for chopping onions (optional), turkey baster to recover broth from skimmed fat

1. Cut hen into quarters.

2. Put first 4 ingredients (and any dried peas or beans) in cold water just to cover, bring to a boil, and simmer for 2 to 3 hours, until hen meat comes off bones easily.

3. Remove meats from broth, and set aside to cool. Skim off fat. (You can recover any broth you skimmed off with a turkey baster.)

4. Add the next 6 ingredients and bring the broth back to a simmer for about an hour.

5. When the meats are cool, chop the beef and return to the broth.

6. Remove chicken meat from the bones, chop into 3/4-inch cubes, and return to the broth.

7. When potatoes are done, add green beans, corn, and any canned peas or beans, and cook until the beans are done.

8. Add the lemon juice and soy sauce, and serve.

Serve booyah with oyster crackers.

BELGIAN PIES

Belgian pies haven't changed as much as booyah, but the ritual around them has. In Belgium, there are still rice and prune tarts with cheese toppings, and using a buttery yeast dough (almost a French brioche dough) instead of pie pastry. The most obvious difference is that the Belgian tarts are made in a tart or quiche pan with straight sides, whereas Wisconsin Belgians have switched to American pie tins, or even flat rounds laid out on cookie sheets. Applesauce, raisin, poppy seed, and cherry—a major crop in Door County—are some other fillings. The pies are made in families, but more often as an annual event by mothers, daughters, and daughters-in-law for dessert at booyah suppers. The women make the toppings ahead of time or buy them from local stores.

Yield: 2 pies, one of each flavor, 12 servings
  2 teaspoons dry yeast
  3 medium eggs
  1 cup sugar
  1/4 cup light cream
  1/4 cup softened (not "soft") butter or margarine
  1 1/2 cups all-purpose flour
  shortening to grease pie pans
  1/4 cup cooked rice
  5 ounces milk
  few drops vanilla extract
  2 cups tightly packed prunes (or prunes and raisins)
  1 cup cottage cheese

Equipment: Pastry blender or large fork, 2 pie plates, double boiler for rice mixture, rolling pin

1. Dissolve yeast with 1 1/2 tablespoons sugar in 2 tablespoons of warm water, and wait until it froths up.

2. Beat 2 eggs briefly and combine with cream, yeast mixture, flour, and butter. Work with large fork until you have something like dough with only small flecks of butter.

3. Flour a clean surface and your hands, and knead (*see* Appendix 1) until you can roll the dough up into a slightly sticky, elastic dough ball, softer than bread dough.

4. Dust the dough ball with flour and let rise in a covered bowl until it looks almost doubled in size. (This step can be skipped.)

5. Knead dough a few times, if it has risen. Divide in half.

6. Flour the rolling pin, and roll out a circle of dough big enough to fit pie pan.

7. Roll the dough up on the rolling pin to carry it onto the pie plate. (Some old-time cooks just patted the dough into shape in the pans.)

8. Repeat for the other pie.

9. Make rice filling by combining cooked rice, 1/2 cup of the sugar, and one of the eggs in the top of a double boiler. Cook over simmering water until it thickens.

10. When rice filling is done, remove from heat and stir in vanilla extract.

11. Make prune filling by soaking prunes in hot water to cover and cooking until tender.

12. Remove any prune pits, drain, and save juice.

13. Mash prunes with 1/4 cup of sugar, adding only enough juice to make it spreadable. (Some cooks push it through a sieve or food mill.)

14. For cheese topping, beat together cheese, an egg, and a teaspoon of flour. Thin with a little milk or cream if necessary. It should spread but not pour. (You can make this in a blender or food processor.)

15. Spread the rice or prune fillings on the pie shells.

16. Spread the cheese topping on the rice and prune fillings.

17. Bake pies 15 minutes at 350 degrees.

Serve Belgian pies in thin wedges to show off the layered fillings.

FLEMISH BEEF AND BEER STEW

This Belgian dish is well known around the world as "carbonades de boeuf." This recipe is adapted from a cookbook printed by the Center for Belgian Culture in Moline, Illinois. The brown sugar and vinegar are simplified ways to recapture the sweet-and-sour qualities of Belgian ales when using milder American beer. (I have listed substitutes.)

Yield: 4-6 servings

2 pounds stew beef cut into 1-inch cubes
2 teaspoons salt
1/2 teaspoon black pepper
1/2 cup butter (substitute corn or canola oil)
1/4 cup all-purpose flour
2 medium onions
2 cloves garlic
2 cans beer (substitute 2 cups strong tea, quinine water, or water)
1 cup beef broth
2 tablespoons brown sugar
1/2 teaspoon thyme
1/2 teaspoon marjoram (substitute oregano or more thyme)
2 tablespoons fresh parsley, chopped
2 tablespoons vinegar

Equipment: Paper bag, skimmer, heavy skillet

1. Cut stew beef into 1-inch cubes.

2. Mix flour, salt, and pepper. Put mixture in paper bag and add beef cubes in groups. Toss to coat.

3. Heat half the butter or oil in a deep pot, and brown the coated beef cubes, not too many at once.

4. Remove browned cubes and add others until all have been browned.

5. Halve and peel onions, and slice into thin half-rounds. (Wear swim goggles to avoid tears.)

6. Peel and mince garlic.

7. In a heavy skillet, heat up the rest of the butter or oil, and sauté onions and garlic until brown but not burned.

8. When all the beef cubes are done, add onions and remaining flour to the big pot. Stir to cook the flour a little.

9. Stir in the rest of the beef cubes and all remaining ingredients except vinegar, scraping the bottom of the pan with the wooden spoon. Simmer uncovered until beef begins to soften and fall apart, about 2 hours.

10. Stir in vinegar.

Serve Flemish beef stew over noodles or rice.

BELORUSSIAN-AMERICANS

Although the 1990 census estimated only 4,000 Belorussian-Americans, estimates in the 1970s suggested that about 200,000 Americans identified themselves as Belorussian (or Byelorussian), and perhaps three times as many Americans had ancestors who once lived in Belorussia, a small country bordered by Lithuania, Poland, and Russia. Because most Belorussians came to the U. S. between 1880 and 1920 when the region was part of Russia, the majority identified with the **Polish-American, Russian-American, or Jewish-American** communities, depending on religious affiliation. In 1920, Belorussia was split between Poland and Communist Russia, and it all became part of the Soviet Union in 1939. These events produced a flow of refugees, and an increasing consciousness of Belorussian identity. The 1991 independence of Belorussia may also be a factor in raising this consciousness, although the independent Belorussian regime has been one of the most conservative and pro-Russian of the post-Soviet governments. Belorussian food most closely resembles that of **Lithuanian-Americans** and **Latvian-Americans,** with a number of Russian dishes reflecting the family experiences of more recent arrivals.

BELORUSSIAN MILK SOUP

This and the following recipe are from the Web site of Alex and Liliya Bederov, 1995 Belorussian immigrants to San Rafael, California.

4 cups milk
1 carrot
1 egg
1-1 1/2 cups flour
2 teaspoons sugar
1 tablespoon butter
salt

Equipment: Soup pot

1. Mix milk with 2 cups water in a soup pot, and bring slowly to a boil.

2. Peel and grate carrot, and add to soup with a pinch of salt.

3. Beat egg and mix with flour and a little water. "It should be as thick as sour cream."

4. When grated carrot is fully cooked, pour the egg-flour mix into the soup, little by little, mixing quickly.

5. Before serving, add sugar and butter.

Serve each bowl with a little melted butter floating on top.

APPLES BAKED WITH HONEY

4 "sour sweet" apples (Jonathan or Macoun)
2 tablespoons sugar
honey

Equipment: Shallow baking dish, paring knife

1. Wash apples, cut out the core (but do not cut all the way through the bottom), and fill the holes with 1 1/2 teaspoons sugar each.

2. Put apples in a shallow baking dish with 1 1/2 cups water.

3. Bake 30 minutes at 350 degrees. Check for doneness with the edge of a small paring knife.

4. Continue baking until done, often another 10-20 minutes.

"Before serving up, pour honey over the apples."

SAUERKRAUT SOUP

This recipe is from the 1972 *National Republican Heritage Groups Council World Cookbook*, edited by Peter J. T. Nelsen.

Yield: serves 6
  1/3 cup chopped onion (one small onion)
  3 tablespoons bacon fat
  1/2 clove garlic
  1/2 pound lean pork
  1 pound sauerkraut
  6 cups soup stock (substitute canned chicken broth)
  1 1/2 tablespoons butter
  1 1/2 tablespoons flour
  1 teaspoon sugar
  2 slices of ham or salami

Equipment: Soup pot

1. In a soup pot, sauté onion in bacon fat until golden brown.

2. Cut pork into 3/4-inch dice.

3. Mince garlic.

4. Add garlic and pork to onions.

5. Cover and cook over low heat for about 20 minutes.

6. Chop sauerkraut and add to pot, then add the stock.

7. Bring to a boil, then lower heat; partly cover the pot and simmer for about 45 minutes, until meat is soft.

8. In a skillet, melt the butter and stir in the flour.

9. Cook for a few minutes, then slowly stir in some of the hot soup.

10. Return this mixture to the kettle and stir into the main soup.

11. Add sugar.

12. Dice ham or salami into tiny squares.

13. Check to see if more salt and pepper are required.

Serve garnished with diced salami or ham.

BLACK MUSLIMS

The Nation of Islam, whose members are widely known as "Black Muslims," is not part of the worldwide Islamic movement, but was founded in Detroit by Wallace D. Fard in the 1930s as a way of life for African-Americans. The group became well known in the 1960s under Elijah Mohammed and Malcolm X, and claimed more than 2 million members at its peak. After Malcolm X left the group in 1963, and after Elijah Mohammed's death in 1965, some Black Muslim mosques moved away from the notion of racial separatism and joined traditional Islamic movements. The Nation of Islam reorganized under Louis Farrakhan and today has solidified as an alternative to Christianity in inner-city African-American neighborhoods.

Although the Nation of Islam's political teachings and style of dress are somewhat known through the media, less mention is made of Elijah Mohammed's two books on dietary regulations. Black Muslims are advised to eat only once a day. In addition to traditional Muslim rules against pork and alcohol, Black Muslims are advised against white bread, most dried beans, pie crust, corn bread (unless using a mixture with rye flour and cooked several times), and many other dishes familiar as "soul food."

BEAN PIE

The Delfonics, a Philadelphia soul music trio of the 1960s and 1970s, submitted this pie or casserole to *Cool Cooking: Recipes of Your Favorite Rock Stars* (Scholastic Books, 1972). They described it as a "special Muslim recipe." By using bread crumbs, it follows Elijah Mohammed's advice to cook bread two or more times before eating it. Similar pies were sold at stores set up in the 1970s by the Nation of Islam to raise funds, and are generally known as Muslim bean pies.

Yield: serves 6
   1 pound fresh green beans
   4 medium white onions
   2 medium green peppers
   salt and paprika
   1/2 stick butter
   1/2 cup bread crumbs

Equipment: Paring knife to prepare vegetables, covered Pyrex casserole or other baking dish

1. Dip green peppers in boiling water to loosen the skins.

2. Peel peppers, remove stem and seeds, and chop.

3. Wash and trim green beans.

4. Peel and chop onions.

5. Butter the baking dish.

6. Put a layer of green beans on the bottom of the pan.

7. Now put a layer of onions over that, and then a layer of green peppers.

8. Put on another layer of green beans, dot with butter, and sprinkle on salt and paprika.

9. Begin again with a layer of green beans, then onions, peppers, and green beans again.

10. Again dot with butter and sprinkle on salt and pepper.

11. Repeat until vegetables are used up, ending with green beans, butter, and salt and pepper.

12. Cover baking dish and bake at 350 degrees for 45 minutes.

13. Remove from oven, sprinkle with bread crumbs mixed with butter.

14. Replace in oven and bake 30 more minutes at 350 degrees.

MUHAMMAD SUPREME BEAN SOUP

Navy beans (small white beans) are one of the foods promoted in the Nation of Islam rules, and white bean soups were sold along with bean pies from the 1960s onward. This recipe was developed by Sister Wanda Muhammad of the University of Islam in Chicago, and appears in Joyce White's *Soul Food: Recipes and Reflections from African-American Churches* (1998).

NOTE: Beans need to be soaked overnight.

Yield: serves 8
   1 pound dried navy beans, soaked
   1 1/4 cups corn oil
   1/4 cup chopped parsley
   1 tablespoon paprika
   3 tablespoons tomato paste
   2 onions
   1 green or red pepper
   3/4 teaspoon freshly ground black pepper
   3 cloves garlic
   2 celery stalks
   1/2 teaspoon crushed red pepper
   1 1/2 teaspoons dried sage or rosemary
   1/2 pound chicken backs or necks, or
      smoked turkey wing (optional)
   3 carrots
   2 to 3 teaspoons salt

Equipment: 2 large soup pots, colander to drain beans

1. Soak beans for at least 8 hours or overnight. (You can also do a "quick soak" by bringing the beans to a boil in water for a few minutes, and soaking for an hour or more.)

2. Rinse the soaked beans well with cold water, drain, and set aside.

3. Peel and chop the onions; chop parsley; core and dice the green or red pepper; mince the garlic.

4. Dice the celery. Finely crush the sage or rosemary (rolling a glass jar over it on a cutting board works well).

5. Scrape the carrots and cut crosswise into 1-inch chunks.

6. Heat the oil in a large heavy pot.

7. Stir in onions, green or red pepper, garlic, celery, sage or rosemary, and parsley. Sauté for 5 minutes, stirring, or until onions are soft and translucent.

8. Stir into the pot the carrots and paprika, and heat 1 minute longer.

9. Add the tomato paste, 8 cups water, black pepper, crushed red pepper, chicken parts (or turkey wing, if desired), and soaked beans.

10. Bring to a boil, cover, reduce heat to simmer, and cook for 3 to 3 1/2 hours, or until the beans are tender and creamy.

11. Stir in salt and heat 10 minutes longer.

Brazilian-Americans

Most Brazilian-Americans are recent immigrants to the U.S. They may number about 500,000, including a substantial number of undocumented workers, who, since the 1980s, have fled an erratic Brazilian economy. New England, which already had **Portuguese-American** and **Cape Verdean-American** populations speaking Portuguese, has drawn many Brazilian immigrants. Other Brazilian-American population centers are New York and Miami. There is also a large Brazilian student population. Brazilian music and the Brazilian style of soccer are internationally respected. Brazilian food is a heady mixture of Native, African, and Iberian cooking, with characteristic salt-brined barbecue meats, and "feojada," the black-bean stew with many kinds of fresh and preserved meat.

Quindim

Cecilia Hoyt contributed this recipe to *Vermont Cooking from Bridgewater*, which was published in 1973 for the Bridgewater-Woodstock Restoration Society. I've also seen quindim served in individual cups or cupcakes.

Yield: serves 8
   5 eggs and 3 egg yolks
   4 tablespoons butter
   1 1/2 cups sugar
   1 coconut, grated (or small can coconut
      milk, or one cup grated coconut)

Equipment: Double boiler or mold that fits into shallow pan of water in the oven

1. Melt butter.

2. Separate 3 eggs by pouring from one half of the shell to the other over a cup. (If a yolk breaks, count that egg as one of the whole ones.)

3. In a large bowl, collect 3 yolks and 5 whole eggs, beat with sugar.

4. Stir in melted butter.

5. Stir in coconut milk or grated coconut.

6. Butter and sugar pudding mold, add quindim mixture, and place in shallow pan of water to bake in a 375-degree oven for 35 minutes. Or, bring water to a boil in a double boiler, add quindim mixture to the top of double boiler, and cook, stirring constantly, until it thickens.

7. Cool before serving.

Serve as dessert. Brazilian-Americans would serve this with strong black coffee.

CANJA (CHICKEN SOUP)

This recipe is from an online cookbook created by Daniel M. Queiroz, Adriana S. Franca, and Leandro S. Oliveira for the Brazilian Students Association at Purdue University <http://pasture.ecn.purdue.edu/~agenhtml/agenmc/brazil/recipes.html>. Compare this recipe to Cape Verdean canja, which is thicker.

Yield: 20 small bowls, or about 6 as a main dish
    half chicken (3-4 pounds)
    1 onion
    4 tomatoes (or 12-ounce can whole toma-
        toes)
    1 celery stalk (with leaves)
    fresh parsley, minced
    10 cups water
    3 carrots, sliced
    1/2 cup white rice (uncooked)
    salt and pepper to taste

Equipment: Tongs to remove chicken from soup, colander or food mill, large stock pot

1. Halve, peel, and chop onion.

2. If using fresh tomatoes, dip in boiling water for one minute; remove and cool to peel. Halve at the equator and squeeze out the seeds with your hand. If using canned tomatoes, squeeze out seeds.

3. Chop tomatoes roughly. Chop celery (including leaves). Mince parsley.

4. Place the chicken, onion, tomatoes, celery, parsley, and 8 cups water in a large stock pot.

5. Bring to a boil. Simmer for an hour over low heat.

6. Remove the chicken, cool, and strip the meat from the bones.

7. Discard the bones and chop the meat into chunks and reserve.

8. Force the cooking liquid through a colander or food mill.

9. Return the liquid to the stock pot. Add the chicken meat, rice, and 2 more cups water.

10. Bring to a boil. Cook for a half hour on low heat.

11. Peel and slice carrot into 1/4-inch slices. Add to soup.

12. When carrots are tender, soup is ready. Taste and add salt and pepper as necessary.

Serve hot.

COUVE À MINEIRA

Early Brazilian immigrants to Boston came from Minas Gerais, a cattle-raising province in the inland south. This recipe by Luiz F. Valente appeared in *Favorite Portuguese Recipes*, which was published about 1975 by the Portuguese American Federation, Inc. of Bristol, Rhode Island.

    1 bunch collard greens to make 4 cups
        shredded
    1/4 cup bacon fat

Equipment: Sharp knife, heavy saucepan with lid

1. Wash collard leaves.

2. With a sharp knife, shave down the stems, or cut the stems out.

3. Rolling 3 or 4 leaves together into a tight roll, make thin slices to shred the collards.

4. Boil a large pot of salted water. Plunge the kale into the water and drain immediately.

5. Heat bacon fat in a heavy saucepan with a lid. Put in shredded greens, and toss until they are all hot and mixed with fat.

6. Salt to taste.

Serve hot as a side dish with steak and rice for a Minas platter.

BRITISH-AMERICANS

See ANGLO-AMERICANS, CORNISH-AMERICANS, SCOTCH-IRISH (APPALACHIAN), SCOTTISH-AMERICANS, WELSH-AMERICANS

BULGARIAN-AMERICANS, MACEDONIAN-AMERICANS, AND VLACHS (ARUMANIANS)

The question of where Macedonia is and who is a Macedonian has been controversial for hundreds of years. Under Ottoman Turkish rule until 1913, Macedonians were Orthodox Christians who spoke a Slavic language and lived across the Balkans in areas that are now parts of five countries, only one of which is named Macedonia. Perhaps 50,000 to 100,000 Macedonians came to the United States after failed rebellions in the 1870s, in 1903, and during the Balkan War of 1913. In the latter conflict, the Turks were defeated, but Macedonia was divided into parts of Greece, Bulgaria, Serbia, (which became Yugoslavia), and Albania. However, most of the Macedonians who came to the United States were counted by the Immigration Service as Bulgarian, Greek, or Turkish immigrants, and indeed often joined those ethnic communities. Macedonians are thought to comprise more than two-thirds of the 70,000 Bulgarian-Americans. Some Macedonians have immigrated since 1913, especially from Greek Macedonia where the government has discouraged their language since the 1940s. Macedonians also have had problems as a minority ethnic group within Communist and post-Communist Bulgaria since the 1960s. The Macedonian Republic, which became independent of Yugoslavia in 1991, is only about two-thirds Macedonian, while tens of thousands of Macedonians remain as minorities in each of the neighboring countries.

The Vlachs, a small minority in today's Macedonia and Albania, speak a dialect of Romanian going back to ancient Roman times. A few thousand Vlach-Americans live in the United States, mostly in western Connecticut. Vlachs were active in the Macedonian revolts, but have formed their own small ethnic group in the United States.

Macedonians in the **Greek-American** community are active as restaurateurs, so their typical tomato sauces with cloves or allspice are known in the Greek restaurants of many cities. Some uniquely Macedonian-American recipes you may find are vegetarian soups, a variation of "Turkish delight" candy, and spinach pies. A Macedonian-American restaurateur invented "Cincinnati chili" as a diner version of chili con carne, but with Macedonian spices.

MACEDONIAN STYLE PEPPERS

Mary Ellen Matroyanis of Gary, Indiana, submitted this recipe to *Penelopian Culinary Favorites of the Hoosier District Members of Daughters of Penelope and Ahepa*, first published in 1964 and revised in 1974. Although this is a Greek-American source, the recipe is clearly Macedonian, and comparable with **Albanian-American** Albanian salad.

CAUTION: Wash hands after handling hot peppers and do not rub eyes or sensitive areas.

10-12 peppers (hot or sweet)
5 sprigs parsley
1/2 cup olive oil
1 teaspoon salt
2 tomatoes
2-3 cloves of garlic
2 tablespoons vinegar
1 small bunch fresh green onions (optional)

1. "Roast peppers on top of burners until skin is black." (Ms. Metroyanis would have done this with a long fork and gas stove, still an excellent method with small hot peppers. You can do this faster with bell peppers by cutting off the tops and bottoms of the peppers, then cutting down one side and removing pith and seeds. Unroll the cylinder that remains and flatten with your hands. You should have three flat pieces you can roast evenly and slowly on a roasting pan under a gas or electric broiler, or over a gas grill on medium heat.)

2. Put roast peppers while still hot in a closed paper bag to steam and loosen the skins.

3. Peel off skin and cut in 1-inch squares.

4. Chop parsley; peel and slice garlic.

5. Slice white part of green onions into small rings, the green part into 2-inch lengths.

6. Pour oil into a small bowl and add green onions, parsley, and garlic.

7. Cut up tomatoes into 1-inch chunks and mix with peppers.

8. Dissolve salt in vinegar.

9. Blend vinegar into oil mixture with a fork, and pour over tomatoes and peppers.

"This is usually eaten as a salad."

VLACH CHEESE CORN BREAD (PISPILITA)

Vicki Balamaci contributed this recipe to the Web site of the Vlach Farsarotul Society. It is an extremely ingenious use of American corn muffin mix to get something of the flavor of Romanian and Arumanian dishes of cornmeal mush and sharp cheese. Fresh from the oven, it is cheesier and somewhat sweet, like blintzes. When it cools down, it tastes more like cornbread and sharp cheese. Some other Vlach or Arumanian recipes you might find are for stuffed flatbreads. The original recipe was triple this size, and baked in a 9 by 13 cake pan.

Yield: one loaf, 8 squares
   1 box corn muffin mix
   3 1/3 tablespoons butter
   1/2 cup milk
   2 ounces of half-frozen cream cheese
   1 egg
   5 ounces cottage cheese
   3 ounces crumbled feta cheese (if you cannot get feta, substitute more cream cheese)
   Shortening to grease loaf pan

Equipment: Loaf pan

1. Measure and cut cream cheese; put in freezer for 15 minutes to make easier to cut.

2. Melt butter with low heat.

3. Cube half-frozen cream cheese into tiny cubes.

4. Mix egg; add cottage cheese and cubed cream cheese in one work bowl.

5. Grease loaf pan and sprinkle in 1/6 of the corn muffin mix (if it is lumpy, push it through a small sieve).

6. Dribble on some melted butter and then sprinkle some milk.

7. Sprinkle on another 1/6 of the muffin mix and dribble milk and butter as before. Don't worry if your cornbread layers seem uneven or lumpy; they will disappear in the finished cake.

8. Repeat to make a third layer.

9. Spread the filling over the third layer, then spread the crumbled feta cheese.

10. Add 3 more layers of corn muffin mix and dribbles of butter and milk.

11. Dribble a little extra butter over the top layer.

12. Bake at 350 degrees for 55 minutes or until golden brown.

13. Cool on a rack and cut into slices or squares.

"Best served warm."

Bulgarian Cucumber Soup

This recipe is from the 1972 *National Republican Heritage Groups Council World Cookbook*, edited by Peter J.T. Nelsen, with some details added from a recipe by Vera Zlidar found on the University of Pittsburgh Summer Languages Institute online cookbook. Ms. Zlidar's recipe is simpler, but has a lot more garlic, and she says this is the way it is in Macedonia now. The Republican version may be more in the style of Bulgaria proper, or of earlier times, or it may represent a common tendency of many immigrant groups to reduce garlic over several generations in the United States.

   1 clove garlic
   4 young (small, with few seeds) cucumbers
      (to make 1 1/2 cups diced)
   1 to 1 1/2 cups thick plain yogurt, or 1 cup
      sour cream
   1 teaspoon salt
   1/4 teaspoon pepper
   1/4 to 1 cup chopped walnuts
   2 tablespoons olive oil
   2 tablespoons chopped fresh dill

Equipment: Mortar and pestle, or garlic press

1. Peel and slice the cucumbers into sections, then 1/4-inch slices and sticks, working to 1/4-inch dice.

2. Peel garlic.

3. Pound garlic and salt in a mortar and pestle to a fine paste, or press garlic into a small cup and mix well with salt.

4. Mix all ingredients except yogurt and marinate for 2 to 6 hours. ("The fresh dill is the essential touch.")

5. When ready to serve, add yogurt.

6. "It should have the consistency of chilled borsch. If not thin enough, it can be thinned with a small amount of light stock."

Serve in soup bowls with an ice cube or two in each bowl.

Bulgarian Meatball Soup

This recipe comes from a cookbook of St. George's Bulgarian Eastern Orthodox Church in Los Angeles, as reprinted in 1992 in the *Los Angeles Times*, and posted online in the cookbook of the University of Pittsburgh Summer Languages Institute.

   1 pound ground beef
   1/2 bunch green onions (scallions)
   6 tablespoons uncooked rice
   1 green bell pepper
   1 teaspoon paprika
   2 carrots
   1 teaspoon dried savory
   3 tomatoes
   1 small yellow chile
   flour to roll meatballs, about 1/2 cup
   1/2 bunch parsley, minced
   1 egg
   2 beef bouillon cubes
   1 lemon (juice only)

Equipment: Large pot

1. Combine beef, rice, paprika, and savory. Season to taste with salt and pepper. (You can safely check seasoning by frying up a tiny piece.)

2. Mix lightly but thoroughly. Form into 1-inch balls, then roll in flour.

3. In a large pot, combine 6 cups water, bouillon cubes, 1 tablespoon salt, and 1 teaspoon pepper. Bring to a boil.

4. Trim and slice green onions. Add to soup.

5. Core, seed, and dice green pepper. Add to soup.

6. Peel carrots and slice thin. Add to soup.

7. Dip tomatoes in boiling water for one minute. Cool under running water and peel. Chop tomatoes and add to soup.

8. Reduce heat and simmer covered for 25 minutes.

9. Add meatballs and simmer 20 minutes more.

10. Slice the top off the yellow hot pepper. Slit down one side and scrape out seeds and pith with a teaspoon. Chop and add to soup along with rice.

11. Simmer an additional 40 minutes or until rice is cooked.

12. Mince parsley and add to soup during last 5 minutes of cooking time.

13. Taste and add more salt and pepper, if needed.

14. Juice lemon. Just before serving, beat egg with lemon juice.

15. Stir 1 to 2 tablespoons of hot soup into egg mixture, then stir egg mixture into soup.

16. Heat and stir until soup is thickened slightly, but do not allow to boil.

CAJUNS

See ACADIANS (CAJUNS)

CAMBODIAN-AMERICANS

Almost all the 147,000 Cambodian-Americans came as refugees between 1975 and 1990, with about half settling in California (especially around Long Beach), 14,000 in northern Massachusetts, 11,000 in Washington State, and smaller groups in Texas, Pennsylvania, and Rhode Island. In the late 1990s, reduced civil strife in Cambodia enabled some Cambodian-Americans to participate in rebuilding efforts there. Cambodian cooking is sophisticated, and it is likely that Cambodian-Americans will start more restaurants as their communities develop.

NGIOM

This fairly simple cole slaw, pronounced "nyome," was made for a program at the Boston Children's Museum by Dara Dong. More recent recipes call for basil and mint leaves. Salads are popular throughout Southeast Asia. Compare this recipe to **Hmong-American** Tomsun. Cellophane noodles (bean thread noodles) and fish sauce are sold at Asian markets and in special sections of many supermarkets.

8 ounces bean thread (cellophane noodles)
1 green cabbage
5 carrots
1-2 pounds cooked chicken, skin and bones removed
8 ounces chopped peanuts
1 cup fish sauce
5 tablespoons vinegar
3 tablespoons sugar

1 pinch monodosium glutamate (Accent, optional)

Equipment: Sharp knife or Asian cleaver and cutting board, food processor (optional), frying pan if roasting peanuts

1. To make chicken for this recipe, poach chicken breasts in water to cover for 40 minutes. Cool, remove bones and skin. You can save the water for a soup. You can also use leftover chicken.

2. Slice chicken into fine shreds.

3. Soak bean thread noodles in warm water for 10 minutes.

4. Shred cabbage by quartering the head, cutting out the core, and cutting thin slices across each quarter.

5. Shred carrots by peeling, cutting into 3-inch sections, halving the sections, cutting thin slices, then slicing shreds from the slices.

6. "Cambodian cooks usually prefer to buy raw peanuts and roast them in a frying pan without oil. Then grind them with a mortar and pestle." (Unsalted roast peanuts and food processor produces a similar texture.)

7. Mix together cabbage, carrots, chicken, and noodles.

8. Combine last 4 ingredients in a small bowl.

9. Pour dressing over salad and toss to mix.

10. Sprinkle ground peanuts on top.

Serve as a side dish, or with rice as a light lunch.

B'BAW POAT (CORN PUDDING)

This recipe is from *The Elephant Walk Cookbook* by Longteine De Monteiro and Katherine Neustadt. Mrs. De Monteiro is chef of three fine Cambodian restaurants in greater Boston. Although Cambodian corn is not as sweet as corn in the U.S., it is almost always eaten in desserts.

Yield: serves 4
　3 ears corn
　1 1/2 tablespoons small Asian tapioca pearls
　　or regular tapioca
　3/4 cup unsweetened coconut milk

5 tablespoons sugar
1/4 teaspoon salt

Equipment: Sharp knife, large saucepan, sieve

1. With a sharp knife, make several passes across the kernels of the corn until you're down to the bare cob, then scrape against the cob to get out the milky starch. You should have 2 1/2 to 3 cups.

2. Rinse the tapioca in a sieve. Place in a large saucepan with a cup of water and 1/2 cup of the coconut milk, and bring to a boil, stirring occasionally.

3. If using regular tapioca, follow package directions as to cooking time, but add the corn kernels during the last minutes of cooking the tapioca. If using small Asian tapioca pearls, add the corn now, reduce the heat to low, and simmer 15 minutes.

4. When tapioca starts to thicken and corn is tender, stir in sugar and salt.

5. Divide the pudding among 4 bowls.

6. Spoon a tablespoon of the remaining coconut milk into the middle of each bowl.

Serve warm.

CANADIAN-AMERICANS

See ENGLISH CANADIAN-AMERICANS, FRENCH CANADIAN-AMERICANS

CANE RIVER CREOLES

The section on **Creoles (Louisiana)** discusses some of the complexities of ethnicity in Afro-French Louisiana. The Cane River Creoles are today a few thousand people ("200 families" is their belief, but these are large families) notable for their cohesion as an ethnic group over 200 years of changing circumstances. Many still live along the Cane River, near Natchitoches (pronounced, NAK-a-dish), which is the oldest permanent settlement in Louisiana, five years older than New Orleans. Almost all Cane River Creoles are descended from one remarkable person, Marie Thérèze Coin-Coin (1742-1816?). She was born on the plantation of the commandant of the Natchitoches post, Sieur Louis Juchereau de St. Denis, and her original name may have been Kon-Kwe, which means "second daughter" in the Ewe language of what is now Togo and Ghana in Africa.

French settler Claude Thomas Pierre Metoyer met Marie in 1767, and leased her from St. Denis. They lived together openly until 1784, having 10 children, of whom 7 survived. Africans and French people were forbidden by law from getting married, but in remote Natchitotches, such common-law relationships were apparently respected. Metoyer was eventually censured by the Church for this illegal relationship, and he married a French woman in 1788. However, he purchased Coin-Coin's freedom, petitioned the king of Spain (which had since taken over Louisiana) for a land grant for her, and provided for their children in his will.

Freed slaves and their half-French descendants could not vote, but they could own property, including land and slaves. So Coin-Coin built up substantial land holdings for herself and her 7 surviving Metoyer children, as well as for 4 older children. On her first plantation, she had built a mansion in a unique style based on the thatched homes of West Africa. This "African House" and other plantation homes built by her descendants are now being restored by the National Park Service.

Cane River Creoles have remained a close-knit community, continuing to worship at St. Augustine Church, which they built in 1803; it is the oldest Catholic church built for people of color in the U.S. In the early generations, most married cousins, or New Orleans Creoles, because there were few other free people of color in the area. Later, they were able to intermarry with Mexicans, and people of Indian or Afro-Indian background.

Family land ownership was down below 8,000 acres by the beginning of the Civil War in 1861. After the Civil War, emancipation "placed all Negroes in the same class, a deprived one; virtually stripped the Creoles of Color of their free heritage and . . . all became 'former slaves,'" explains retired law professor Vanue B. Lacour. Carroll Jones (1815-1894), a skilled businessman who married into the Creole community, was able to consolidate some land that is still in Creole hands. Other Creoles became share-croppers on their former land.

Cane River Creoles have been somewhat isolated from other French-speaking Louisianians because Natchitoches is generally north of the areas of French and Cajun settlement. Older people spoke fluent French well into the 1950s. The group has always valued education, and provided professionals and leadership for their own community. They have also been able to use parochial schools and other Catholic institutions to insulate the group from some of the effects of racial segregation and economic change. According to Kathleen Balthazar Heitzmann, a Cane River Creole who is now a science teacher in upstate New York, "We lived in isolation for decades with our own school and church. I have older cousins (in their 80s now), who were unaware of racism until they left Cane River, pointing out just how isolated we were." But in all likelihood their survival as a small ethnic group owes more than a little to the character and self-sufficiency instilled in the early generations by Coin-Coin herself.

Cane River Creoles were the best cooks and often street vendors of the most famous dish of Natchitoches—meat pies. Cane River Creoles also have their own up-country spin on some familiar New Orleans Creole dishes, such as gumbo, and they enjoy the more general southern and "soul" food of northern Louisiana. They have precise ways—perhaps learned from **Choctaw** Indian relatives—of gathering sassafras leaves on August 15 and drying them in darkened rooms to make filé powder to thicken gumbos. A book about them is Gary B. Mills' *The Forgotten People: Cane River's Creoles of Color* (LSU Press, 1977). The recipes given here are from the Web site of Kathleen Balthazar Heitzmann and the forthcoming third edition of her *Cane River Genealogy: Balthazar, Jones, CoinCoin, Clifton, Metoyer, Delphin*.

MILDRED'S CREOLE MEAT PIES

Natchitoches meat pies are fried or baked turn-overs that were sold on the streets by Creole teenagers from the late 1800s though the early 1960s, with the shout "Hot-ta Meat Pies!" No one knows exactly how they got started, but the usual filling of pork and beef is like those of **Cajun** Christmas pork pies (and French Canadian tourtieres), while most deep-fat frying in the American South goes back to Africa. The turnover shape is like that of Latin-American "empanadas," and the spicy filling with garlic, peppers, and onions is Creole by any definition. This recipe comes from Mildred Metoyer Maury, now 86, who often made it for church suppers and community events. Her recipe, as told to Kathleen Balthazar Heitzmann, is all-beef and oven-baked. "She never uses a recipe, she just knows how to make them."

Yield: serves 15-20
  3 cups flour
  1 teaspoon salt
  2 teaspoons baking powder
  4 or 5 heaping tablespoons shortening
  3 eggs
  1/2 cup milk
  2 to 2 1/2 pounds ground beef
  1 large onion
  1/2 green pepper
  1 teaspoon garlic powder
  1 small can tomato sauce
  1 teaspoon dried parsley
  1 piece of green onion (scallion) cut up
  "Can include a dab of hot sauce or red
    pepper (to taste)"
  solid shortening to grease baking sheet (or
    vegetable oil to deep-fry the pies)

Equipment: Rolling pin, large fork or pastry blender, baking sheet

1. Put rolling pin in refrigerator to chill.

2. Using a large fork or pastry blender, mix the flour, baking powder, salt, and shortening "until crumbly."

3. Beat eggs with milk, then mix into the flour-shortening mixture to make a dough.

4. Form into a ball and refrigerate while making filling.

5. Brown meat in a deep pot or heavy skillet. Pour off excess grease.

6. Add tomato sauce, and cook about 10 minutes.

7. Dice green pepper. Halve, peel, and chop the onion.

8. Cut green onion or scallion into fine slices.

9. Add green pepper, onion, garlic powder, parsley, and green onion to meat mixture.

10. Taste, then add salt and pepper. If you include hot sauce or red pepper, add here (to taste).

11. Once meat has cooled, flour a board and rolling pin, and roll out the dough.

12. Cut into circles with a small saucer. Gather up scraps and roll out to make a few more.

13. Do not overload meat, use about 2 to 2 1/2 tablespoons of meat per pie.

14. Fold over dough and crimp the edges closed with a fork.

15. Preheat oven to 375 degrees.

16. Grease a baking sheet and lay out the pies neatly.

17. Bake about 10 minutes or until lightly or just slightly golden brown.

18. (For fried pies, brown in an inch of oil at 350 degrees in a deep pot, turning once.)

Serve with rice and salad, or with potato salad.

MILDRED'S CREOLE TEA CAKES

Tea cakes came to Natchitoches with the Anglo-American majority after the Louisiana Purchase in 1803, but there, as elsewhere in **African-American** cooking, they became a symbol of middle-class gentility. The recipe is from Mildred Ser.

  1 cup (2 sticks) butter
  2 cups sugar

4 eggs
6 tablespoons milk
2 teaspoons "real" vanilla extract
2 teaspoons nutmeg
4 cups flour
4 teaspoons baking powder
1/2 teaspoon salt
a little more butter to grease cookie sheet

Equipment: Flour sifter, pastry blender or large fork, cookie sheet

1. Preheat oven to 375 degrees. Let butter soften to near room temperature.

2. Lightly grease cookie sheet.

3. Beat 4 eggs in a cup by themselves.

4. Sift 4 cups flour with baking powder and salt.

5. Mash butter, adding sugar gradually, about 1/2 cup at a time, until mixture is well blended and light.

6. Mix in eggs, the sifted flour mixture, and the nutmeg and vanilla.

7. Stir until smooth.

8. "You will need to get two spoons to drop dough on cookie sheet because dough should be nice and thick." Take a tablespoon of cookie dough and place drop on cookie sheet. Use the other spoon to help get it onto the sheet.

9. Place sheet in oven and bake about 5-8 minutes, until edges around cookies are a light to golden brown. Center of tea cake will always be lighter than the edges, but will be fully baked.

Serve warm or at room temperature.

OKRA GUMBO

Most Cane River Creole gumbos use powdered sassafras leaves (filé), but some use the African ingredient known as okra to get the same thickening effect. This recipe is from Cassie Balthazar Pimentel, Mrs. Heitzmann's mother. After the Cane River was cut off from the Mississippi in the 1830s, people couldn't usually get fresh shrimp, so this recipe is intended for dried shrimp, which would also be used in similar soups in West Africa. It smells fishy but tastes good. A Cajun recipe would often call for crawfish. I have added some quantities.

Yield: 6 servings
    1 1/2 pounds fresh okra
    4 tablespoons vegetable oil to fry okra
    1/4–1/2 pound dried shrimp (or 1 pound fresh)
    1 large tomato
    1 medium onion
    2 cloves garlic
    1 tablespoon flour
    1 pound leftover chicken meat (optional)

Equipment: Skillet, soup pot or saucepan

1. Wash and towel-dry okra. Halve, peel, and chop onion. Peel and mince garlic.

2. Slice okra (remove tops and tips). Heat oil in skillet and fry okra, stirring constantly until it is browned and the seeds have turned pink (about 10 minutes).

3. Remove okra to a soup pot or saucepan, leaving the oil in the skillet

4. Fry onion in the skillet.

5. Remove onion to the soup pot.

6. Add flour to oil in skillet, stir constantly for several minutes.

7. Clean fresh or dried shrimp by removing any bits of shell and the dark vein along the back and put in pot.

8. (If using dried shrimp, remember that it is salty.) Add salt, pepper, garlic, and chicken.

9. Add about a quart of water and the flour mixture from the skillet. Stir and cook until shrimp are done, about 30 minutes.

10. Slice tomato and add to soup.

11. If too much fat, cool, refrigerate, and take off with spoon. "It tastes better the second day anyway."

Serve in soup bowls over hot white rice.

Cinnamon Praline Pecans

These Cane River Creole pralines "by Margot Coyote Moon and brought to us by Sharon Colas-Marquez" are sugar-coated nuts like the original French pralines. (The usual Louisiana pralines are candy with the texture and appearance of chewy cookies. They were developed by French settlers, but became a specialty of mixed-race Creole street vendors in New Orleans.)

2 pounds pecan or walnut halves
1 egg white, or equivalent pasteurized egg white product
1 cup sugar
1 teaspoon cinnamon
1 teaspoon salt (or a little less)
1/2 teaspoon cocoa (or more)
cayenne pepper to taste (if desired)
butter to grease baking dish

Equipment: 9 by 14 glass baking pan, spatula

1. Preheat oven to 325 degrees.

2. Beat egg white and one teaspoon water together.

3. Stir in pecans and toss quickly.

4. Mix together sugar, cinnamon, salt, and cocoa.

5. Pour over pecans and toss quickly.

6. Pour pecans into a greased baking pan.

7. Bake 45 minutes, stirring every 10 minutes.

8. Using spatula, loosen pecans immediately from the baking pan. Cool.

Serve as candy, and "can be stored up to two weeks in an airtight container."

Cape Verdean-Americans

Cape Verdeans are a Creole people from a small chain of islands 350 miles off West Africa. The islands were settled by Portugal in the fifteenth century as a refueling stop for their triangular slave trade involving Africa, Brazil, and Portugal. The islands were also a kind of experimental farm for New World crops introduced to Africa. When New England whaling ships began stopping at the Cape Verde islands, the first Cape Verdeans came to New Bedford, Massachusetts, in the 1790s. Cape Verdean immigration is difficult to track because Cape Verdeans were counted as Portuguese immigrants, if at all, until the islands' independence in 1975. Although the 1990 census counts only 51,000 Cape Verdean descendants in the U.S., earlier estimates of 300,000 to 400,000 are not unrealistic, given communities of 25,000 to 100,000 in Boston, New Bedford, Fall River, and Brockton alone. These figures suggest that there are now more Cape Verdeans in the United States than in Cape Verde. Over their long history in southern New England, Cape Verdeans have been only partially accepted into the **Portuguese-American** community, and their Catholic religion has kept them somewhat apart from other **African-Americans**. Anecdotally, I have noticed Cape Verdeans turning up in the family trees of many other mixed-race and Native American ethnics. A steady stream of immigrants and frequent contact with the islands have kept Cape Verdean culture and the Creolou language alive for more than 200 years in the United States.

Cachupa (Katxupa)

Cachupa is the national stew of Cape Verde. It can be anything from a simple succotash to an elaborate feast, and there are chicken and seafood versions as well. Leftover cachupa is refried for breakfast. I've seen it sold as mon chupa (the name used on the seaport island of Brava). This fairly fancy version was made by Nha Augustinha (Maria Augustina Faria Lima) of Gaithersburg, Maryland, for Smithsonian Folklife festivals in 1995 and 1997, and posted on the Smithsonian Web site. I have added substitutions and suggestions to make a simpler soup. You can also presoak the corn and beans to make cooking faster, but this is not the Cape Verdean method.

2 cups of cracked hominy or samp (or substitute 3 cans white or yellow hominy)

1 cup large dry lima beans (or one 16-ounce can)

1/2 cup dry stone beans (*feijao pedra*) (substitute a can of black beans)

1/4 cup dry red kidney beans

1 pound lean salt pork meat

1 split pig's foot (optional)

1/2 pound chorico sausage (or other smoked garlic sausage)

1 whole, uncut blood pudding sausage (optional)

1 small cabbage cut in quarters

1-2 cups big pieces of hard winter squash (if desired)

6 cloves garlic (or more to taste)

2 medium onions

2 seeded ripe tomatoes, or small can tomato paste

2 bay leaves

1 chicken bouillon cube (or substitute chicken stock for as much of the liquid as possible)

1/2 cup olive oil

Equipment: 10-quart or larger soup kettle

1. Wash all dry hominy. If you are using canned hominy, go on to Step 3.

2. In a heavy large kettle, boil dried corn for 10 minutes and carefully discard froth that collects on top.

3. Wash dried beans, and pick out any stones. If you are using canned beans, reserve until Step 6.

4. Add dry beans, 1 bay leaf, and 2 tablespoons of olive oil to corn and water in kettle. Bring to a boil. Lower heat enough to maintain a steady but slow boil.

5. Add salt pork. If you are using pig's feet, add at this time. Leave cover slightly ajar. Throughout cooking, make certain liquid covers the corn and beans. Use at least 4 quarts of water or stock.

6. After the mixture has boiled for the first hour, add any pork meat and sausage (and any canned beans or hominy). Cook partially covered at a gentle boil over low heat for an additional 1 1/2 hours.

7. Halve, peel, and chop onions. Peel and chop garlic.

8. Slowly sauté onions and garlic in the rest of the olive oil until soft.

9. Halve tomatoes and squeeze out the seeds.

10. Add seeded tomatoes or tomato paste and the second bay leaf to the onion mixture.

11. Add the mixture to the kettle when the cachupa has about one hour of cooking time left.

12. Correct seasoning by carefully adding salt and pepper to taste.

13. If adding squash, peel, seed, and cut into chunks. Add the squash when there is about 1/2 hour cooking time remaining. "Remember that squash will continue to cook even after the kettle has been removed from the heat."

14. For best results, let cachupa sit covered and off the flame for at least 20 minutes before serving. The spices and salt will be absorbed into the corn and beans and the "gravy" will take on its special texture.

To serve "arrange the meats and vegetables on a large platter and serve the corn and beans from a bowl. Some folks may want to individually drizzle a little Tabasco or piri-piri [hot pepper] sauce on top."

Jag (Jagacida)

Jagacida is a Cape Verdean Creole word for this dish of rice and beans. In New England, it is often called "jag." It is commonly sold at street fairs, county fairs, and Indian pow-wows in southern New England, usually with linguica, a Portuguese garlic sausage. This recipe from Mrs. Irene Reis is from the pamphlet *Cape Verdean Culture*, by Alcides da Graca, a teacher at New Bedford, Massachusetts, High School.

1 medium onion
2 tablespoons oil
3 cups rice
1 15-ounce can of lima or kidney beans
salt and pepper
2 teaspoons paprika
2 bay leaves
fresh parsley
4 tablespoons oil

Equipment: 2-quart covered saucepan

1. Halve, peel, and chop onion.

2. Heat oil in a 2-quart saucepan and sauté onions until golden brown.

3. Add 6 cups of water to onions and season (to taste) with salt, pepper, paprika, bay leaves, and parsley.

4. Bring to a boil and add 3 cups rice.

5. Lower heat, add beans (of choice), cover pan, and simmer for 25 minutes or until water is absorbed and rice is cooked.

6. Turn off stove and let stand about 15 minutes.

"Serve with chicken, linguica or other meats."

CANJA (KANJE)

Canja is a thick chicken-rice soup like the **Brazilian-American** canja or the **Puerto Rican** asopao. Cape Verde was both a station for the Portuguese slave trade, and an experimental area for Asian and African foods that were then established in Brazil. This soup is traditional for New Year's Eve and special family events, and was served at the 1995 Festival of American Folklife in Washington, DC. The recipe is archived at <http://www.umassd.edu/SpecialPrograms/caboverde/cvrecipes.html>. If you have a big enough pot, you can double the recipe.

1/2 chicken or hen
2 medium onions
3-4 chicken bouillon cubes
1 cup short-grain rice (may substitute long-grain)
3 tablespoons vegetable oil

Equipment: Deep soup pot

1. Halve, peel, and chop the onions.

2. In a deep soup pot, sauté onions in oil until translucent.

3. Cut the chicken into 5 or 6 pieces. Thus the breast should be cut in half or thirds.

4. Add chicken to onions.

5. Add water to cover (but at least 3 cups) and the bouillon cubes.

6. Bring back to a boil.

7. Add rice and reduce heat to a simmer.

8. Stir occasionally for 30-35 minutes to make a thick soup.

CARPATHO-RUSYN-AMERICANS (RUSKINS, RUSNYAKS, RUTHENIANS, LEMKIANS)

Carpatho-Rusyns are a Slavic people who came to the United States between 1880 and 1914 from villages in what is now the Slovak Republic, the Ukraine, the Czech Republic, southern Poland, and northern Hungary. In Europe, they were distinguished from their predominantly Roman Catholic neighbors by their language and their Byzantine Catholic or Eastern Orthodox religion. Because Carpatho-Rusyns have been a minority group in their homelands since the Middle Ages, the group has more than 20 names. Some divisions have persisted in the United States between those more oriented toward the Ukraine, toward Slovakia and the historic Hungarian empire, or toward southern Poland.

Although the 1990 census figures project only 11,000 people in the U.S. reporting Carpatho-Rusyn or Ruthenian ancestry, church membership figures suggest that about 600,000 to 800,000 descendants are still concentrated around coal-mining regions and steel-producing cities. Carpatho-Rusyns were prominent founders of the **Ukranian-American** communities of Chicago and Detroit. Although use of the Rusyn language seems to be declining, Americanized descendants are now reporting their ancestry in terms of national origin (Ukranian, Slovak etc.), while holding onto their Carpatho-Rusyn culture as a religious identity. A very good collection of traditional Carpatho-Rusyn recipes can be found on the Internet at <http://pages.prodigy.net/dkomar/ethnic_recipes.htm>; this collection was posted by the American Carpatho-Russian Citizens Club of Endicott, New York, which was established 1936. Carpatho-Rusyn-Americans also know most **Slovak-American** and Ukrainian-American recipes, such as borscht, pierogy, sauerkraut soup, meat pies, stuffed cabbage, and a list of treasured Christmas and Easter dishes. For this book, I have selected a few recipes that show how Carpatho-Rusyn cooks have kept their traditional foods on the weekday table despite changing American lifestyles.

MACHANKA (TOMATO GRAVY)

In the *St. Stephen's Byzantine Cookbook: 1892-1992 Leisenring, Pa.*, a volume compiled by the Centennial Committee of St. Stephen's Byzantine Catholic Church, Father Ed Pyo writes that "This recipe has been handed down through many generations of various Ruthenian-Slovak-Polish backgrounds." The St. Stephen's congregation also includes **Croatian-Americans** and others.

    1/4 pound sliced bacon
    3-4 tablespoons flour
    1 quart home canned tomatoes (or commercial canned whole tomatoes adding up to 32 ounces)
    stale bread

Equipment: Large skillet, bowls

1. Fry bacon in a large skillet until slightly crisp.

2. Tear or break up bread into bowls.

3. Add flour to bacon and drippings, stirring constantly to make a paste. Cook for a few minutes to remove raw-flour flavor.

4. Add tomatoes. Stir well until mixture thickens.

5. "Dilute with water to desired thick or thinness."

6. Serve over bread slices.

EASY BAKE PIEROGY

This recipe is from Jane Pyo also in the *St. Stephen's Byzantine Cookbook*. The book has several recipes for the usual boiled pierogy (or perohy). Baked turnovers are also common all over Eastern Europe, such as the Russian piroshky.

    1 cup instant mashed potato flakes
    1 can buttermilk biscuits
    1 teaspoon salt
    1/2 stick butter, plus one tablespoon
    4 ounces cheddar cheese
    1 onion
    solid shortening to grease baking sheet
    flour for rolling pin and board

Equipment: Baking sheet, whisk, rolling pin

1. Put 3/4 cup water, 1 tablespoon butter, the salt, and the cheddar cheese in a pot and bring to a boil.

2. When cheese has melted, add potato flakes and whip until mixture is smooth and creamy.

3. Allow filling to cool.

4. Open can of biscuits and separate.

5. Flour rolling surface and roll each biscuit into a 4-inch circle.

6. Grease baking sheet.

7. Place a heaping tablespoon of filling in each circle.

8. Fold in half and seal edges by crimping.

9. Place pierogy on greased cookie sheet.

10. Bake at 350 degrees for 10-12 minutes.

11. Halve, peel, and chop onion.

12. Sauté chopped onion in 1/2 stick of butter until onion is transparent.

13. Place baked pierogy on a serving plate, and pour sautéed onions on top.

PAGACH

This meatless meat pie was developed for Lent or the many Orthodox Christian meatless fast days. This recipe from Anita Kaschak is the easiest of several for stuffed breads to be found on the Citizen's Club Web site; the recipe was originally published in the 1984 *Favorite Recipes Collected by St. Mary's Ladies Guild* by St. Mary's Carpatho-Russian Orthodox Church of Endicott, New York. The fillings are the same ones used for pierogi (large ravioli): potatoes and cheese, sauerkraut and onion, or ricotta/cottage cheese and egg.

1 frozen bread dough (thawed)
flour for board and rolling pin
3 potatoes
1 medium onion
1/4 pound oleo (margarine)
1 tablespoon milk
5 ounces grated cheddar cheese
solid shortening to grease cookie sheet

Equipment: Rolling pin, grater, cookie sheet, heavy skillet

1. Peel potatoes.

2. Boil potatoes in 2 quarts of salted water until fork tender.

3. Halve, peel, and chop the onion.

4. In a heavy skillet, heat the oleo and fry the onion until golden.

5. Grate the cheese if necessary.

6. Cut bread dough in half.

7. On a floured board, roll out one-half and place on greased cookie sheet.

8. Drain and mash potatoes.

9. Mash in onions, cheese, milk, and salt and pepper.

10. Spread filling evenly over rolled-out dough, leaving a 3/4-inch margin all around.

11. Cover with the other half of the dough. Pinch edges together.

12. You can also make smaller squares called "baniki." A note on the Web site from Tom Pitel recalls that "his mother used to roll out the dough into a large square, spread out the [filling] mixture into the center, and then fold the edges of the dough back so that there was a small square of filling still exposed."

13. Bake at 350 degrees for 20-30 minutes, until golden brown.

Serve by cutting long slices across the bread.

CAYUGA

See IROQUOIS

CHALDEAN-AMERICANS

See ASSYRIAN- AND CHALDEAN-AMERICANS (MESOPOTAMIANS)

CHEROKEE

The 1990 census reports 369,000 Cherokee in the U.S., a figure that makes them the largest Indian tribe in the country. However, only about one-third of that number are enrolled with the three federally recognized Cherokee tribal governments or the State of Missouri-recognized Northern Cherokee Nation of the Old Louisiana Territory. This number is a tribute to the traditional Cherokee interest in education and technology, which helped many assimilate successfully into the United States, and which also makes Cherokee ancestry a point of pride for people of mixed ethnic background.

Like many Indian tribes, the Cherokee derived their name from how another tribe described them to European explorers. In this case, it was either the **Choctaw,** using their word for dog people or cave people, or the **Creek,** using their term for "people of different speech." The Cherokee generally accepted this name, rendered in their language as "Tsilagi," although some now prefer the phrase "Ani-Yun-Wiya," meaning "real people" or "original people." When they first encountered European explorers, the Cherokee were a powerful trading confederation controlling 40,000 square miles of the southern Appalachian mountains with seven well-marked trails. Most sided with the French in the French and Indian War, and with the British in the American Revolution. By this time, most of the Cherokee were successful farmers in northern Georgia, settled in log cabins, with some of their leaders living in fine southern mansions designed by colonial architects. They began to face forced removals as early as 1775, and were the intended victims of the 1830 Indian Removal Act, which was overturned by the U.S. Supreme Court. Despite this, the Cherokee were forced to sign the Treaty of New Echota in which they agreed to move west of the Mississippi, and in 1838, 20,000 Cherokees were herded into concentration camps in Tennessee to await boat transportation. When they petitioned to be allowed to march out, they were forced at gunpoint to march through the winter on what became known as the "Trail of Tears," because about 4,000 Cherokee died on the way. The survivors then fought a five-year civil war in northeastern Oklahoma over the treaty.

The Oklahoma Cherokee were also split by the Civil War, with most siding with the Confederacy and therefore suffering legal sanctions after the war. Oklahoma Cherokee did not become voting U.S. citizens until 1901. Nevertheless, they are now the most numerous Indian tribe in Oklahoma, Missouri, and North Carolina. The Cherokee had an advanced technology before contact, and were the first U.S. Indians to develop a system of writing, which was invented in 1821 by their chief Sequoyah. They had a written constitution by 1827, when a majority of the tribe was literate and prospering as farmers under a plan of Americanization. Cherokee farmers of the period even owned about 1,500 African slaves.

Today, the tribe continues to build a strong record in education and self-help. Their language is Iroquoian, which sets them somewhat apart from the other members of the "Five Civilized Tribes" in Oklahoma. Traditional Cherokee foods include a great variety of hominy dishes; corn breads; tamales and dumplings, some with beans; sweet potatoes; nut soups; and dried vegetable dishes.

BLUE DUMPLINGS

This recipe, a practical update of an old southern Indian dish, was contributed to the *Smithsonian Folklife Cookbook* by Clydia Nahwoosky of Norman, Oklahoma. These dumplings are flat noodles of wheat flour, like the dumplings in southern chicken and dumplings, whereas older Cherokee dumplings were made of cornmeal or hominy, with the ashes of bean vines used as a baking powder. Traditional dumplings were round; if some fell apart, that thickened the juice. Some southern tribes served blue dumplings at a wedding feast. You can make your own fruit juice by picking wild or domestic grapes, blackberries, or blueberries in season. Boil them with a little water until they release their juice, crush them with a potato masher, and strain out the seeds and skins. Some recipes add some grape juice and skins to the dumplings.

   1/4 teaspoon baking powder
   1/2 teaspoon salt
   2 tablespoons oil
   1/2 cup water
   1 1/2-2 cups flour
   1 quart unsweetened grape juice (or black-
      berry or blueberry)
   2 cups sugar

Equipment: Skimmer, large sieve if making fruit juice from wild grapes or berries

   1. Mix baking power, salt, oil, and water.

   2. Add flour, a little at a time, until a thick ball of dough forms, which is rather rubbery in consistency.

   3. Roll out onto a floured surface like a pie crust, until it is elastic and 1/8-inch thick.

   4. Bring juice and sugar to a boil for 4 minutes, until mixture begins to get sticky and almost jelly-like; stir occasionally

   5. Slice dough into narrow stripes about 1/2-inch wide and 4-6 inches long.

   6. Rapidly drop dough into boiling juice all at once, keeping dumplings apart.

   7. Boil for 2-3 minutes.

   8. Cover and set aside for about 30 minutes to cool and thicken.

Serve hot or cold with ice cream or whipped cream.

SUCCOTASH

The word "succotash" came from a settler's attempt to pronounce a New England Indian word, but the usual dish of stewed fresh corn and beans we eat today is southern, and might have been developed by Cherokee farmers. This recipe is from the September 19, 1999, issue of "Turtle Tracks," an online magazine for Native American youth at <http://www.turtletracks.org>. The author, "Momfeather" (M. Kaelbli Erickson of Omaha, Nebraska), describes the recipe as Cherokee, and the enrichment of nut butter is

like the pounded hickory nut balls the Cherokees stored to make rich soups.

   1 onion, chopped
   2 cups shelled lima beans (or 1 pound,
      frozen)
   1 green pepper, chopped
   2 cups yellow corn (or 1 pound frozen)
   3 tablespoons nut butter

Equipment: Food processor if you make nut butter from pecans, large covered kettle

   1. Halve, peel, and chop the onion.

   2. Slice off the top and bottom of the green pepper. Remove the stem from the top and chop. Chop the bottom. Core and seed the middle cylinder, remove the pith, and chop.

   3. You can make the nut butter from pecans (an American wild nut) in a food processor, or use purchased hazelnut butter or peanut butter.

   4. Simmer all ingredients together in a large covered kettle for 20 minutes.

Serve hot.

CHEROKEE HUCKLEBERRY BREAD

This is an Eastern Cherokee recipe from J. Ed Sharpe and Thomas B. Underwood's *American Indian Cooking & Herb Lore*, which was published in 1973 in Cherokee, North Carolina. The Eastern Band of Cherokee were not removed to Oklahoma because they had signed a separate treaty with the United States and owned an individual allotment of land, which they and some refugees from Georgia were able to expand over the nineteenth century. Compare this recipe to **Lumbee** blueberry sheet cake.

   2 cups self-rising flour (or 2 cups all-purpose
      flour and 1 1/2 teaspoons baking powder)
   1 cup sugar
   1 cup milk
   2 cups berries (huckleberries or blueberries)
   1 egg
   1 stick butter

1 teaspoon vanilla extract
shortening to grease loaf pan

Equipment: Pastry blender or a large fork, large loaf pan

1. Let butter soften 15 minutes at room temperature.

2. Cream butter and sugar together.

3. Stir in eggs.

4. If using all-purpose flour, mix in baking powder.

5. Add flour, milk, and vanilla to butter-sugar mixture.

6. Sprinkle a little more flour on the berries to prevent them from going to the bottom.

7. Add berries to mixture.

8. Grease loaf pan and pour in batter.

9. Bake in 350-degree oven approximately 40 minutes or until a toothpick comes out clean.

WILD ONIONS AND EGGS

The Oklahoma Cherokee used to hold a wild onion dinner in March. This dinner was a favorite of the part-Cherokee entertainer, Will Rogers. The wild onions used were ramps, which have a strong flavor of garlic. If you don't know where to get wild onions, try this recipe with a mixture of scallions and one minced garlic clove that has been poached in boiling water for a minute to take off some of the edge. This recipe comes from the 1932 *Indian Cook Book* of the Indian Women's Club of Tulsa, Oklahoma. The recipe was contributed by Mrs. Cherokee Adair Moore, with some details from more recent recipes.

4 handfuls of wild onions (or 4 bunches of scallions and one clove of garlic)
3 tablespoons bacon grease or oil
6 eggs

Equipment: Skillet with a cover

1. Wash the onions well and cut off roots and dead leaves.

2. If using garlic, poach and mince.

3. Chop onions into 1-inch lengths.

4. Put into a skillet with a tight cover.

5. Add salt and bacon grease and water to steam, perhaps a cup.

6. Cover pan tightly and simmer-steam 10 minutes.

7. Uncover and boil off water so the onions begin to fry, perhaps another 15 minutes.

8. Break eggs one at a time into a cup, then combine them in a bowl and stir well as though making scrambled eggs.

9. Scramble eggs into the pan with the onions.

Serve hot.

CHICANOS

See MEXICAN-AMERICANS

CHICKASAW

About 21,500 Chickasaw live in the U.S., making them the 12th largest American Indian tribe, but only the fourth largest of the "Five Civilized Tribes" of Oklahoma (the others being the **Cherokee, Creek, Choctaw,** and **Seminole**.) The Chickasaw language is closely related to Choctaw, and the two tribes probably lived together as one people before the Choctaw crossed the Mississippi into what are now the deep south states about 1,000 years ago. Around 1300, the Chickasaw followed the Choctaw, generally settling north of the larger Choctaw territory in areas that would become Tennessee, Kentucky, and northern Alabama and Mississippi. They retained control of the Chickasaw Bluffs overlooking the Mississippi River at Memphis, Tennessee, which eventually became a crucial point in the French-British colonial rivalry. The Chickasaw made an early alliance with the British, who armed them well. The Chickasaw were already a military society, and began to specialize in slave raids on other Indian tribes. Their early partners were Scottish slave traders from Charleston who both married into the tribe and invited a group of Chickasaw to settle in the Carolinas as protection against Spanish and French raids. Although the Carolina group lost its lands after supporting the British in the American Revolution, the Chickasaw never lost a major war until they sided with the Confederacy in the Civil War, and even then got off relatively well in negotiations.

The Chickasaw were generally free of missionaries until 1819. While the Cherokee resisted removal and suffered the disastrous "Trail of Tears," the Chickasaw negotiated a multi-million dollar settlement (most of which they never collected) and were allowed to delay removal until they found suitable land in Oklahoma. Thus, they arrived in 1837 relatively intact, with more than 1,000 African slaves. Although they had to lease land from the Choctaw (who had been their enemies), they were able to move to their own territory in 1854. The Chickasaw government was the last Confederate government to surrender, and the tribe retained its national government until 1906, when the last Indian governments were dissolved to make way for Oklahoma statehood. After the Civil War, the Union required Indian tribes that had held slaves to offer the former slaves tribal membership, and thousands of additional slaves traded to Texas by the Chickasaw also appeared with a claim upon the tribe. Eventually the Chickasaw lost all tribal lands but about 300 acres; however, they remained successful farmers and politicians in Oklahoma. The Chickasaw reorganized as a tribe in 1963.

Chickasaw traditional foods are similar to Choctaw foods, and all the southeastern tribes relocated to Oklahoma seem to have similar food traditions, especially concerning various products of corn.

PASHOFA

This pashofa recipe, which was made by Glenda A. Galvan of Ada, Oklahoma, for the 1976 Smithsonian Festival of American Folklife, is similar to that described by Mr. and Mrs. William Short of Davis, Oklahoma, for the 1956 *Oklahoma Indian Cookbook* by Mae Wadley Abbott. Ms. Galvan describes the dish as originally part of a three-day healing ceremony. Pashofa is rich and would have restored strength to all involved. It later became "the national dish" of the Chickasaw.

1 pound pearl hominy (cracked hulled corn or samp)
1 to 1 1/2 pounds lean pork meat

Equipment: Large pot, sieve or colander

1. Put 2-3 quarts water in large pot and bring to a boil.

2. Wash hominy in a sieve or colander under cold running water.

3. Cut pork into small pieces.

4. Add hominy and pork to the pot and bring back to a boil.

5. Lower heat and cook mixture for about 4 hours, or until mixture is soft and rich.

6. Add more water if necessary

"Do not salt until ready to serve individual portions." (*The Shorts liked a dash of red pepper as well.*)

PUMPKIN COOKIES

These nice old cookies are part of an online collection of recipes posted by the Chickasaw Nation Library at <www.chickasaw.net>. Use the small "sugar pumpkins" or winter squash because Halloween pumpkins have little taste. You can use canned pumpkin, but if it is "pumpkin pie filling," cut down on the spices.

Yield: about 36 cookies

1/2 cup shortening
1 1/2 cups cooked pumpkin
2 1/2 cups flour, less 2 teaspoons
4 teaspoons baking powder
1 cup raisins or dates
1 cup chopped nuts
1 teaspoon lemon extract
1 1/4 cups brown sugar
2 eggs
1/2 teaspoon salt
1/2 teaspoon nutmeg
1/4 teaspoon ginger
1/2 teaspoon cinnamon
solid shortening to grease cookie sheets

Equipment: 2 cookie sheets, pastry blender or large fork, carrot peeler

1. Peel pumpkin or winter squash with a carrot peeler, and steam in a little water until pumpkin can be mashed easily.

2. Pour off water, mash pumpkin, and measure the amount for the cookie recipe. Allow to cool.

3. Cream shortening and sugar with pastry blender or large fork.

4. Add eggs, pumpkin, and spices. Blend well.

5. Sift dry ingredients together and add to pumpkin mixture. Blend until smooth.

6. Stir in raisins, nuts, and lemon extract flavoring.

7. Grease cookie sheets with solid shortening.

8. Drop batter by teaspoons onto greased cookie sheets.

9. Bake at 400 degrees for 15 minutes.

CHINESE-AMERICANS

According to the 1990 census, 1.5 million Chinese-Americans and another 200,000 Taiwanese-Americans live in the U.S. This immigration has continued, and China (including Taiwan) was the fourth-largest source of immigrants arriving between 1981 and 1996. Chinese-Americans have been viewed by outsiders as a single ethnic group despite differing dialects and origins in different regions of China, Taiwan, Hong Kong, Vietnam, Singapore, or elsewhere in Asia. As a generalization, earlier immigrants were from South China, and some of their ethnic conflicts were seen from the outside as "tong wars." The students from Taiwan who came in the 1950s and 1960s were mostly of northern Chinese origin, but immigrants since 1965 come from many backgrounds, including more than 100,000 Chinese-Vietnamese "boat people." I once interviewed a successful Chinese-American grocer-restaurateur in Boston who had come to the United States from Malaysia, but who grew up in Vietnam, and considered himself "Chiu Chow"—a Chinese ethnicity based on the dialect spoken in the city of Swatow.

Chinese-Americans are the oldest large Asian-American ethnic group, with more than 300,000 immigrants arriving between 1850 and 1882, although legal restrictions limited the growth and development of the community until 1965. The Chinese-American contribution to building the railroads is well-remembered, but earlier immigrants had been gold miners, and by the 1880s most were farmers, factory workers, and miners. Almost all were male, intending to return to China, which many did.

California laws aimed at Chinese-Americans began with a special tax on Chinese miners in California in 1852, and the U.S. Congress excluded the immigration of laborers in 1882, and later excluded re-entry, and extended the ban to U.S. possessions. Violence against Chinese-Americans enforced their segregation into "Chinatowns" and, especially on the Pacific coast, they were segregated in schools and public accommodations as well. The Chinese Exclusion Acts were only repealed in 1943, as a wartime counter to Japanese propaganda. Immigration quotas were still low, although a few more Chinese women could come to the United States under family reunification provisions. In the late 1940s, many segregation laws in housing and the California ban on mixed marriages were overturned. But some state miscegenation laws remained until 1967, immigration quotas favored Europeans until 1965, and the United States did not recognize the Communist government of China from 1949 until 1973.

One of the most unusual features of Chinese-American food is that so little of it has developed in 150 years. Chinese chefs, mostly male, developed a series of dishes for American customers—such as chop suey, chow mein, large egg rolls, and so on—but never considered them to be real Chinese ethnic food. Within Chinese families, a few dishes have developed independently in the United States (and several more in Hawaii), but these dishes are not usually seen as authentically "Chinese" either.

Although chef Ken Hom wrote *Easy Family Recipes from a Chinese-American Childhood* (1997), Hom did not really think of himself as Chinese-American.

> Living in Chicago, America's most multicultural city, I might as well have been in Canton [China], because Chicago is also our most ethnically segregated city. Chicago's Chinatown was my turf, my familiar neighborhood. . . . The Chinatowns of America, which were "ghettos," were both forced upon the Chinese . . . and formed as a matter of choice. . . . I have discovered that my experiences in growing up are quite similar to those of almost every other Chinese-American I know. Social isolation tempered by extended-family ties, the tenacity of tradition, the central importance of traditional foods and family gatherings—these are part of the common ground shared by all Chinese in America.

Despite the title of his book, Hom tries to make the dishes more authentically Chinese, often with recipes he has gathered on trips to China as an adult.

Iceberg Lettuce-Egg Drop Soup

Chef Ken Hom got this family recipe from his friend Steve Wong, who grew up in Sacramento, California, where the Wong family sometimes used iceberg lettuce as a substitute for Chinese greens. Ironically, iceberg lettuce was originally developed in sixteenth-century Europe for soup, but most Americans use it for salads. Chinese sesame oil has a rich toasted flavor; there is no real substitute for it.

Yield: serves 4

  4 cups homemade chicken stock, or re-
    duced-salt canned broth
  1 egg
  2 teaspoons Asian sesame oil
  1 teaspoon sugar
  1 teaspoon salt
  1/4 teaspoon freshly ground white pepper
  1 tablespoon light soy sauce

  3 tablespoons finely chopped scallions or
    green onions, white part only
  3 tablespoons finely chopped green scallion
    tops (for garnish)
  1/2 pound iceberg lettuce, finely shredded
    (about 2 cups)

Equipment: Soup pot, small bowl and fork for mixing egg, knife to chop scallions and shred lettuce

  1. Chop 2 or 3 scallions, separating white and green portions.

  2. Cut lettuce in halves, take very thin slices to make shreds.

  3. Pour the chicken broth or stock into a pot and bring it to a simmer.

  4. Lightly beat the egg and then mix with the sesame oil in a small bowl.

  5. Add sugar, salt, pepper, and soy sauce to the simmering stock, and give it several good stirs.

6. Add white chopped scallions.

7. Drizzle in the egg mixture in a very slow, thin stream. Using a chopstick or fork, pull the egg slowly into strands. (Hom stirs in a figure-eight motion.)

8. Remove soup from heat and stir in the shredded lettuce.

Serve at once, sprinkling on the green scallion tops.

QUICK AND EASY CORN AND EGG

According to chef Ken Hom, sweet corn was unavailable in China until the 1950s, but has been popular with Chinese-Americans. In this recipe, his mother used sweet corn, where she might have used fresh shrimp, with scrambled eggs. American cooks had the same general idea 100 years earlier when they invented corn chowder. A western regional dish of oysters and eggs called "Hangtown Fry," which was associated with the gold mining camps, was probably a Chinese-American invention from the same Cantonese seafood omelet.

Yield: serves 4
  3 ears fresh corn, or 1 cup frozen or canned
    corn
  4 eggs
  1 teaspoon Asian sesame oil (optional, see
    note under previous recipe)
  pinch salt
  1 tablespoon butter
  2 teaspoons peanut oil (or other vegetable
    oil)
  1 teaspoon finely minced garlic
  1 teaspoon finely minced root ginger
  3 tablespoons finely chopped scallions
  1 teaspoon salt
  1/2 teaspoon ground black pepper

Equipment: 2 small bowls, wok or frying pan, spatula or souhok (Chinese wok spatula), knife for mincing seasonings, cutting board, cup to crack eggs

1. If using corn on the cob, husk it and cut off the kernels with a sharp knife. If using frozen corn, set aside in a small bowl to thaw.

2. Peel a large clove of garlic by twisting between your fingers to loosen the skin, then picking off the skin with fingernails or a sharp knife.

3. Mince garlic by cutting slices the long way, cutting those to shreds, and slicing tiny dice off the shreds. Rock a curved knife through the pile a few more times to get fine mince.

4. Cut a few thin slices from a piece of ginger root, cut off peel, and mince the same way.

5. Slice off 3 tablespoons of thin green scallion rings.

6. Mix garlic and ginger. Set aside mixture and scallions so they are ready to add to the wok or skillet. Measure out salt and pepper with scallions.

7. Crack each egg into a cup, use pieces of shell to pick out any bits of shell or red spots, and pour the egg into a small bowl. Repeat with the other 3 eggs.

8. Lightly beat eggs with a fork.

9. If you have an electric stove, set one burner for medium-high heat, and another for medium heat.

10. Set wok or skillet on medium-high heat.

11. Add butter and oil and toss with spatula to melt butter and coat pan.

12. Toss in ginger-garlic mixture. Let brown for a few seconds, and stir-fry for 10 seconds, tossing with spatula to prevent burning.

13. Add corn and stir-fry for 2 minutes.

14. Mix in the scallions, salt, and pepper.

15. Move to medium-heat burner, or turn down gas flame; add eggs and stir to scramble the eggs until set, about another 2 minutes.

16. If using sesame oil, drizzle on with last few stirs of the eggs before serving.

Serve hot with white rice.

TURKEY BONES AND RICE CHOWDER

One American food tradition that Chinese-Americans have taken up is turkey at Thanksgiving, although they may cook it with Chinese techniques or a Chinese-style stuffing. The bones are almost invariably made into a rice porridge like this one, known by the Cantonese name of "Jook" (or "Chuk") in Hawaii, and as "Turkey Shee-Fan" on the mainland. This recipe is from Mary Sia's *Chinese Cookbook*, first published in Hawaii in 1956. According to Ken Hom, "There was something comforting about shee-fan for Chinese-Americans, the way chicken soup is for Jewish-Americans."

Yield: serves 8
  1 cooked turkey carcass
  2 cups long-grain white rice
  3 teaspoons salt
  2 tablespoons soy sauce

Equipment: Soup pot, skimmer to remove bones, or second soup pot and colander

  1. Remove meat from turkey bones; save for sandwiches. Wash rice 4 times.

  2. Bring 14 cups water and carcass to a boil in a large pot.

  3. Lower heat to medium and simmer 20 minutes, then over low heat 50 minutes, "stirring occasionally after the first half hour to avoid burning."

  4. Remove bones.

  5. Add salt and soy sauce.

Serve with chopped cilantro, chopped scallions, and chopped peanuts for people to use as garnish.

CHINESE-STYLE CUCUMBER SALAD

Because there are few salads in classical Chinese cooking, this is one area where Chinese-American cooks freely mix ethnic flavors with American techniques. This recipe was contributed by Eleanor Chin of Boston to the *Cookbooklet* (Boston, 1985) compiled by Betsy Allen for the Children's Museum Staff. There is no real substitute for Chinese toasted sesame oil, but you could try the oil that forms on top of "natural" peanut butter.

Yield: serves 4 as a side-dish salad
  2 cucumbers
  2 tablespoons soy sauce
  2 tablespoons vinegar
  1 tablespoon sugar (or to taste)
  1 teaspoon Chinese sesame oil
  few drops hot chile oil or red pepper sauce to taste (optional)
  1-2 tablespoons sesame seeds

Equipment: Carrot peeler, paring knife

  1. Peel cucumbers.

  2. Slice into 1/4-inch rounds.

  3. Combine all other ingredients except sesame seeds in bowl.

  4. Mix in cucumber slices and marinate for 1 to 4 hours.

  5. Garnish with sesame seeds.

Serve as a side dish with soup or rice plates, or bring to pot-luck suppers.

SHOYU CHICKEN

The multi-ethnic mix of Hawaii encourages a lot of culinary mix-and-match, and this Chinese-American dish (despite the Japanese term for soy sauce, "shoyu") has become popular with all ethnic groups on the island. The original Chinese dish is sometimes called "master-sauce chicken," because leftover sauce can be chilled, skimmed, and added to the sauce for the next batch. This recipe is apparently from a 1988 book called *Popo's Kitchen*, by June Kam Tong, as posted by Nate Kaimuki on an exchange of Hawaiian recipes at <www.alohaworld.com>.

  1 3-pound fryer chicken
  1 cup shoyu (soy sauce)
  1/2 cup sugar

2 tablespoons honey
1/2 cup chicken broth
1 teaspoon hoisin sauce (optional)
1 whole star anise (or substitute 1/2 teaspoon anise seed or anise extract)
Chinese parsley (cilantro) for garnish
green onions (scallions) for garnish

Equipment: Chinese cleaver and rubber mallet to cut up cooked chicken

1. Steam chicken for 30 minutes in the half-cup of chicken broth.

2. Meanwhile, combine soy sauce, sugar, and honey and let simmer for 15 minutes.

3. Break up star anise (or one of the substitutes), and add to the sauce as it simmers.

4. Pour sauce into chicken pot and simmer chicken for 5 minutes on each side, until chicken is well coated with sauce.

5. Chop chicken into bite-size pieces (with bones) by using the cleaver and rubber mallet. (Don't swing cleaver wildly.)

Serve hot or cold arranged on a platter and garnished with chopped scallions and sprigs of cilantro. Shoyu chicken is especially good cold.

CHIPPEWA

See OJIBWAY (CHIPPEWA, OJIBWE, AND OJIBWA)

CHITIMACHA TRIBE OF LOUISIANA

The Chitimacha are about 900 survivors of a tribe that farmed the Mississippi Delta for many centuries before the arrival of Europeans. Their 260 remaining acres, occupied by 350 people, is the only federally recognized Indian reservation in Louisiana, although the state recognizes bands of Houma, Choctaw-Apache, and a few others. The Chitimacha were thought to have been wiped out by slaving raids and by a 12-year war with the French in the early 1700s. But two communities survived and established title to the present reservation with a land case in the mid-1800s. The recipes below and other information about the tribe come from their Web site at <www.chitimacha.com>.

MACQUE CHOUX

Macque choux is the French spelling of an Indian corn dish that has also been made by both **Cajuns** and Louisiana Creoles, who add tomatoes and sometimes beans and even chicken or other meats (see **Creoles** [Louisiana]). This detailed Chitimacha recipe is from Al LeBlanc.

12 ears fresh sweet corn
3 medium onions
1/4 cup vegetable oil
black pepper and salt
1 tablespoon brown sugar (if corn is not sweet enough)
cream or evaporated milk (optional)

Equipment: Sharp knife or corn stripper, heavy skillet or Dutch oven

1. Shuck and clean corn thoroughly.

2. Cut corn off cob using the "macque choux" method: a) Using a sharp knife, cut the first layer of corn about 1/8 inch (just taking the tops). b) Cut a second layer, getting very near the cob (not into it). c) Next, scrape the cob using the back of your knife to extract the rest of the pulp and "milk." "The cut of the corn is directly proportionate to the quality of the Macque Choux."

3. Cut the onions very fine by peeling, halving, slicing in 1/8-inch slices with the grain, and

finally an 1/8 inch across the grain, forming 1/8-inch dice. ("This is not so critical as the corn but try to keep it small.")

4. Mix the onions and corn thoroughly in a large bowl, seasoning with salt and black pepper to taste.

5. In a large black iron skillet or Dutch oven, heat the oil to frying temperature.

6. Add corn and onions all at once.

7. "You must cook this on a medium fire and keep well stirred for the next 45 minutes. It will brown to a nice golden brown and take on a slightly nutty flavor."

8. If the macque choux is not sweet, "then you can use a tablespoon or so of brown sugar to get it there."

9. You may also want to add a bit of cream (or canned evaporated milk) to give it a more creamy consistency.

Serve as a side dish.

CHITIMACHA BAKED DUCK

This recipe, which coincidentally resembles a Chinese-American technique for roasting turkey, is by Leroy and Dora Burgess. I have added some quantities. Don't throw away the stock you boiled the ducks in—it makes excellent soup.

1 or more wild or domestic ducks
salt and pepper
1 onion per duck
1 bell pepper per duck
3 stalks celery per duck
1 clove garlic (or more to taste)

Equipment: Pot that fits the number of ducks closely

1. Place cleaned ducks in large pot.

2. Halve and peel onion. Cut into big chunks.

3. Core pepper and cut into squares about the size of the onions.

4. Wash and chop celery into pieces about the same size.

5. Peel garlic and chop roughly.

6. Add salt and pepper, onion, bell pepper, celery, and garlic to pot.

7. Cover duck(s) with water and gently boil until tender.

8. Heat oven to 450 degrees.

9. Remove ducks from water and place in baking dish.

10. Put pats of margarine in and on the ducks.

11. Bake until brown, about 12 minutes.

CORN SOUP

This recipe is by Vickie Mora. The Chitimacha had access to salt deposits and may have been one of the few Native American tribes in the United States to use salt (rather than drying or smoking) as a preservative for game before contact with Europeans.

12-16 ears of corn
1/4 pound salt meat (substitute corned beef or lean salt pork)
1 can diced tomatoes (optional)
1 block margarine
2 onions

1. Melt margarine in pot.

2. Halve, peel, and chop onions. (Wear swim goggles to avoid tears.)

3. Sauté the onions for about 10 minutes.

4. Scrape the corn from the cobs.

5. Add the scraped corn to the pot and cook on a low fire for about 15 minutes.

6. Next add water to the corn to make a soup, and let it come to a boil.

7. Add the diced tomatoes to the soup.

8. If meat is salty, cover with water in another pot and bring to a boil.

9. Drain salt meat, cut into chunks, and add to soup.

10. Add salt and pepper to your desire.

CHOCTAW

Today, about 86,000 Choctaw live in the U.S., making them the fifth largest Indian tribe in the United States. When the French and Spanish settlers first encountered them, the Choctaw were about 20,000 strong, living in hundreds of villages in the deep South. Their oral history attaches them to a mound they call Nanih Nayih, which is thought to have been built about 500 B.C.E. In the colonial period, the Choctaw were caught between the English and French, and fought a civil war in 1747-1750 over how to align. The Choctaw language is closest to **Chickasaw,** and the tribes have many of the same traditional foods, although they were enemies for much of U.S. history. The Choctaw were the first Indians forcibly removed to Oklahoma in the early 1830s, and a Choctaw is believed to be the one who coined the phrase, "Trail of Tears." By 1834, 11,500 had been removed, but 5,000 remained in Mississippi, where a separate, state-recognized reservation remains today. The Oklahoma Choctaw were able to avoid taking sides in the Civil War, unlike many other Oklahoma Indians who were dragged into the Confederacy. Thus, the Choctaw Nation in southeastern Oklahoma had considerable power to tax non-Indian settlers and retain their own lands until the U.S. government dissolved the Indian government in 1893. The Choctaw ball game, "ishtaboli," involved whole villages over a vast playing field, and is still played as "Choctaw stickball."

Perhaps the most famous traditional Choctaw food is filé powder, made from the leaves of the sassafras tree, which became the thickener of many Louisiana **Creole** gumbos.

TONSHLA BONA

Tonshla bona is similar to the **Chickasaw** pashofa, but is not so rich, and in this recipe the hominy and pork are mostly cooked separately. The recipe comes from Mrs. Alice McCurtain Scott, daughter of the last elected governor of the nineteenth-century Choctaw Nation in Oklahoma. The recipe appeared in the 1956 *Oklahoma Indian Cook Book* by Mae Wadley Abbott. I have added quantities from other recipes. The Choctaw traditionally made Tonshla bona from a fresh hominy called tanfula. Whole frozen hominy or posole corn is the closest substitute, but Mrs. Scott was already using grits. Don't try this with instant grits.

2 pounds pork back bones, neckbones, or spareribs or chicken.

1 pound hominy grits (or 3 cans white hominy)

1. Make a stew of the pork bones or chicken in a large pot of water.

2. If using hominy grits, prepare according to package directions. For canned hominy, drain and add at Step 3.

3. Strain broth. Combine hominy with broth "and cook until the meat has seasoned the Tanfula."

4. "Though the Choctaws used no salt, the dish should be salted to taste for use today."

Another Choctaw pamphlet of 1955, by Amanda and Peter Hudson of Tuskahoma, Oklahoma, warned "Don't eat too much Tash-lubona as it will make you sick."

BANAHA (SHUCK BREAD)

This recipe is from *Spirit of the Harvest, North American Indian Cooking* by Beverly Cox and Martin Jacobs. The authors seem to be drawing on Mississippi Choctaw sources, but all Choctaw know this recipe for large, bland, unfilled tamales, which are closer in style to Cuban tamales than Mexican.

8 dried or fresh corn shucks

2 cups white cornmeal

1 teaspoon baking soda

1 teaspoon salt

1 cup partially cooked black-eyed peas or frozen black-eyed peas

1 stick butter for serving (optional)

1. If using dry black-eyed peas, cook according to package directions but stop when they are still a little chewy. Thaw frozen black-eyed peas.

2. Boil corn shucks about 10 minutes to soften. Drain and reserve.

3. Mix dry ingredients.

4. Add 1 1/2 cups boiling water and black-eyed peas.

5. When mixture is stiff enough to handle, form egg-shapes of about 4 tablespoons or more.

6. Set in the middle of a corn shuck, and roll, then fold up both ends and tie around the middle with a thin length of corn shuck. The old banaha were thinner at the middle than on the ends.

7. When all are ready, boil half a large pot of water.

8. Add tamales and cook 45-50 minutes.

Serve with a little butter or melted lard. Leftovers can be sliced and fried for breakfast.

Colombian-Americans

Although Colombian-Americans are probably the largest South American ethnic group in the United States, most have immigrated since 1980. Numbering about 500,000, including 75,000 to 100,000 "illegal immigrants," Colombian-Americans are estimated to be 9th largest group of undocumented residents in the U.S. Major communities are found in New York City, Miami, and Los Angeles. Colombia is a large, diverse country with a long history of democracy but also frequent and lengthy civil wars between historic "Liberal" and "Conservative" parties. One such period of civil strife, in 1948-58, drove hundreds of thousands of Colombians to neighboring Venezuela, Ecuador, and Panama. Since the 1970s, guerrilla war and organized crime problems have continued to plague the country.

Colombia is divided into regions by mountain ranges. Most Colombians in the United States identify with one of three large regions or their major cities—Bogota, Cali, or Medallin. As with many large groups of immigrants, Colombians in U.S. cities are learning about the foods of other regions of Colombia. Colombian food in general is a hearty, meat-and-potatoes cuisine without a lot of spice. Some Colombian dishes include avocado shakes, sancocho (stews of many roots and meats), and Caribbean-style seafood stews and coconut rice.

Arepas

Arepas are white corn cakes with a browned crust and soft, creamy insides. Some are made from fresh corn, some from dried corn, and some from precooked cornmeal, which is sold in Latin markets under brand names like Masarepa. Most are sautéed as in the recipe here, but they also can be charcoal-broiled. Some are stuffed with meat or cheese. In the United States, most Colombians make them the quickest way, from arepa flour. These superior New York street arepas are sold by a woman named Piedad who has been the subject of several stories by food-writer Jim Leff, and who gave her recipe to Anya von Bremzen for the book, *Fiesta*. The Latin American white cheese typically served with arepas is like a mild cheddar.

Yield: 8 arepas
  2 cups milk
  4 tablespoons (1/2 stick) unsalted butter, cut into pieces, plus more for serving
  1 1/2 cups white arepa flour (called Masarepa) or grits
  1 teaspoon salt
  1 1/2 tablespoons sugar
  1 cup grated mozzarella cheese

vegetable oil for the griddle
1 1/4 cups finely grated mild cheese for
  serving

Equipment: Small saucepan, sieve, 2 mixing
bowls, grater for cheese, blender (if using grits),
wax paper, spatula, griddle or heavy frying pan

1. If using grits, blend at a speed that keeps
them circulating through the blades for about 8
minutes to get a flour with the texture of fine
sand. Meanwhile, grate the cheese.

2. Meanwhile, in a small saucepan, bring 1 1/
2 cups milk to a boil.

3. Strain into a bowl and add 4 tablespoons
of butter. Let stand so the butter melts, while
you combine the dry ingredients.

4. In a large bowl, stir together the arepa flour
or blenderized grits, salt, sugar, and mozzarella.

5. Make a well in the center and pour in the
hot milk/butter mixture.

6. Stir this batter until there are no lumps.

7. If it is too thin to knead, add more arepa
flour or grits.

8. Knead the mixture (see kneading directions in Appendix 1) about 5 minutes, adding
the remaining 1/2 cup milk until you have a
smooth sticky dough.

9. Roll the dough between 2 pieces of wax
paper into a 1/2-inch-thick sheet.

10. With a cookie cutter or the rim of a mug
or glass, cut out 3-inch circles.

11. Re-roll the scraps and cut out more circles.
You should have 8.

12. Brush a griddle or heavy skillet lightly with
oil and preheat over medium-low heat.

13. Fry slowly as many arepas as will fit, until
they are golden and slightly crusty on the outside, about 4 minutes per side. If the heat is low
enough, they won't stick.

14. Keep the finished arepas warm in a low
oven.

*Serve by splitting the arepas like English muffins.
Brush them with butter and sprinkle on plenty of
cheese. The Arepa Lady fries them ahead, and
reheats them over a gas flame in her cart.*

SHORTCUT AREQUIPE

Arequipe is a thin custard that is cooked for
about five hours until the milk sugars turn into
caramel. It is then eaten as a pudding. This short-
cut version from a group of Colombian students
at the University of Colorado is similar to the
way Argentines make a similar caramelized milk
sweet called "dulce de leche."

CAUTION: Avoid puncturing hot can; hot
carmelized milk both burns and sticks to
skin. Follow direction to let can cool 30
minutes.

Yield: makes 4 small, rich portions
  1 can, sweetened condensed milk

Equipment: Deep saucepan or soup pot, can
opener

1. Put an unopened can of sweetened condensed milk on its side in a pot of hot tap water.
The water should fully cover the can.

2. Bring to a boil slowly.

3. Simmer slowly for 5 hours, adding water as
it evaporates to keep can fully under water.

4. Let can cool down for 30 minutes before
opening.

Serve as a sweet with coffee or for dessert.

COCONUT RICE

This African-influenced recipe from coastal
Columbia was submitted by Alba Orrega to *The
Melting Pot* (1974), a fund-raising cookbook for
English in Action, a volunteer tutoring program
in New York City.

Yield: serves 2-3
  2 tablespoons butter

1 1/2 tablespoons sugar
2 tablespoons flaked coconut
1 cup rice
1 teaspoon salt
1 small box raisins
Coca Cola

Equipment: Frying pan, large covered pot

1. Place butter, sugar, and coconut in a frying pan and cook on a low flame until brown.

2. Meanwhile, put rice, salt, and 2 cups water in a large pot over heat.

3. Add the browned coconut mixture and cook, stirring frequently, until water has almost evaporated.

4. Lower flame, and stir in raisins. Cover pot and cook for 10 minutes.

5. Stir again and cook another 10 minutes.

6. "If mixture is too dry, add a little coca cola."

Serve with fried plantains and grilled meats.

CORNISH-AMERICANS

Although Cornwall is a county of southwestern England, the Cornish people are related to the Bretons of northwestern France and to the people of Wales. Few Cornish-Americans so identified themselves on the 1990 census, even though about 100,000 Cornish immigrants came to the U.S. between 1860, when copper mining ceased in Cornwall, and the end of World War I in 1918. Because the Cornish language died out about 200 years ago, Cornish immigrants arrived speaking English with a West Country accent that was closer to American English than London speech. The first Cornish immigrants to get a job in the U.S. would recruit relatives, leading to their American nickname of "Cousin Jacks" for all Cornish-Americans. When they were joined by family, the women became "Cousin Jennies." The Methodist religion of Cornish-Americans was no barrier to their assimilation into American society. Most first-generation Cornish immigrants worked in the mines of Michigan and then on the Minnesota Iron Range, with a notable community in Butte, Montana. They brought their pasties to all three places, and Cornish pasties are still made by **Finnish-Americans** and other commercial bakers in Michigan and Minnesota.

CORNISH PASTIES

I have combined the pastry instructions of Jane Ann Nicholls Curto from Michigan with the filling recipe of Bill Paull of Butte, Montana—both complete recipes are available on the Internet at <www.sihope.com/~tipi/recipe.html>. Cornish pasties are surrounded by much lore and humor; they thrived in Cornish-American culture not only because they were "letters from 'ome" in Mr. Paull's phrase, but also because they were a practical lunch-box food. The variety of pasties in Cornwall were reduced to a beef-potato-turnip classic in the United States. Mrs. Curto uses rutabaga; Mr. Paull does not and uses more onion.

Yield: 4-5 pasties
  3 cups all-purpose unbleached flour
  1 teaspoon salt
  1 cup (minus one tablespoon) solid vegetable shortening (Crisco)
  3 tablespoons cold water
  2 1/2 pounds stew meat, round steak, flank steak, or chuck steak
  5 large potatoes
  2 large onions
  2 1/2 tablespoons chopped parsley
  1/2 teaspoon salt
  1/4 teaspoon pepper
  5-10 tablespoons butter
  solid shortening to grease baking sheets

Equipment: Baking sheets, rolling pin, long spatula, pastry blender or food processor (optional)

1. "Work the shortening into the flour and salt with fingertips" (or a pastry blender or food processor).

2. Gradually add 3 tablespoons cold water, gently mixing.

3. "Form the dough into a ball and divide in 4 (for a 12-inch pasty) or 5 (for an 8-inch one) pieces." Refrigerate until ready to roll.

4. Cut the stew meat into bite-sized chunks. (Mrs. Curto likes 1-inch strips).

5. Peel and slice potatoes into 1/4-inch slices.

6. Halve, peel, and dice onions.

7. Chop the parsley to get at least 2 1/2 table-spoons

8. Cut the butter into small pieces.

9. Flour a board and rolling pin; lightly grease baking sheet(s).

10. Gently roll the first pasty from the middle on a lightly floured surface to the (round) size desired. Trim the edges so that they are not scraggly. (Use the trimmings to mend any weak parts.)

11. Mr. Paull mixes his fillings together with salt and pepper, divides by the number of pasties, and tops each filling with butter. (Mrs. Curto layers each pasty with potato and turnip slices on the bottom, then meat, onion, parsley, and salt and pepper. She doesn't use butter.) In both cases, the idea is to have meat juices or butter on top melting down onto the other ingredients.

12. On one side of each circle, leaving an inch border, put in the filling.

13. Place bits of butter evenly on top of the pile of filling.

14. Moisten the edges of the pastry and bring the remaining portion of the pastry round over the top of the filling to form a large turnover. The folded-over pastry should meet the bottom part of the pastry just within the outside edge. Be careful no sharp edges of potato or onion

puncture the crust. (Mrs. Curto puts the filling in the middle of the round, and lifts 2 sides to the top.)

15. Crimp the lower pasty up around edge of the top to form the turnover making a tight envelope for the filling.

16. You can decorate the edge by pressing designs with the tines of a fork. One Cornish style that came to the U.S. is the "Cornish rope" made by crimping dough into long flutes between the thumb and forefinger of one hand, then folding the dough over to look like a twisted rope (see illustration).

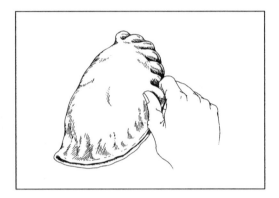

17. Make 3 or 4 small slits in the top of the pasty to allow the steam to escape during cooking.

18. Carefully transfer the pasties to a lightly greased baking sheet.

19. Bake at 425 degrees for 10 minutes.

20. Then turn oven down to 325 degrees and bake 50 minutes to an hour longer, until golden brown.

21. Remove pasties from baking sheet onto the plate with a long spatula.

22. If you are serving pasties immediately, you can get a little more juice by cutting a tiny hole, adding a teaspoon of boiling water, and covering for 10 minutes.

Mr. Paull remembers these as a Saturday ritual: "Uncle Howard used to dip his crust into his hot tea to soften it. Ketchup? Yes. . . . although this was never my thing. I used to drench my hot pasty with butter. Some like to smother them with gravy, but that's a sacrilege! Grandma Bysho would never approve such desecration. My favorite is still the second-day 'fried pasties.' You can also cut the pasty into halves and eat it like a sandwich."

SAFFRON BREAD (OR BUNS)

While many nationalities have pasties (or empanadas or meat pies), saffron bread is uniquely Cornish, going back to the times when saffron was grown in Cornwall, the only place where poor people used the world's most expensive spice to create the appearance of extra eggs in their bread! This recipe is from *Blue Ribbon Recipes: County Fair Winners* (1968). The recipe is from Mrs. Kenneth Alderton of Ishpeming, Michigan, who made the bread for the Marquette County Harvest Festival. I have added some details of procedure from a 1940 Michigan recipe in *America Cooks: Favorite Recipes from the 48 States* by Cora, Rose, and Bob Brown, and I also looked at the original Cornish saffron cake in Elizabeth David's *English Bread and Yeast Cookery*, a book every baker should own.

> 1 package saffron (1/16 ounce)
> 1/2 pound lard
> 1/4 cup butter
> 1 1/2 packages dry yeast
> 1 cup sugar
> 1/2 teaspoon nutmeg
> 2 teaspoons salt
> 1/2 pound raisins
> 1/2 pound currants
> 5 1/2 to 6 cups flour
> solid shortening to grease pans

Equipment: 2 large loaf pans, or a pair of 9 by 13-inch cake pans, oven thermometer

1. Soak saffron in 1/2 cup boiling water to make yellow saffron tea.

2. Melt lard and butter in large pan; cool to lukewarm. Combine with saffron tea.

3. Dissolve yeast in 1/2 cup lukewarm water; add another 1 1/4 cups of lukewarm water and mix well.

4. Add sugar, nutmeg, salt, raisins, and currants to saffron mixture.

5. When saffron mixture has cooled to lukewarm, add yeast mixture.

6. In a large mixing bowl, work the flour into the other ingredients to form a stiff dough.

7. Cover with a clean cloth and let stand in a warm place until doubled in bulk, an hour to an hour and one-half.

8. Knead (see Appendix 1) and shape into 2 balls.

9. Grease loaf pans or cake pans.

10. Shape into loaves and put into the loaf pans, or shape into small rolls or buns and put into cake pans.

11. Let rise for about 40 minutes.

12. Bake loaves 15 minutes at 250 degrees, 15 minutes at 275 degrees, and 15 minutes at 300 degrees. The small buns will be done more quickly; start with 15 minutes at 250 degrees and 15 minutes at 300 degrees.

Serve warm from the oven or reheated. This bread can be frozen.

CREEK INDIANS OF OKLAHOMA

The 1990 census lists 43,550 Creek Indians, mostly in Oklahoma, making them the third largest tribe in Oklahoma. The original Creek homeland stretched across the southern states, and, like the **Iroquois**, the Creek were a powerful trading federation of tribes. English settlers named them Creek Indians because their villages, some with temple mounds and carefully laid-out ball courts, were usually on stream banks. Their own name for themselves was Muskogee, which describes them as living on land that is sometimes flooded. In 1770, they were regarded as the most powerful and organized Indian tribe encountered by European settlers. Many died during their 1836 "Trail of Tears" removal to Oklahoma, and in the early years there. The Creeks were able to develop constitutional government for their nation in Oklahoma based on their old elected village council system, and generally held together despite internal differences over the Civil War, railroad development in Oklahoma, and land rights issues. Their national government was dissolved by federal law in 1906, and restored in the 1930s.

An important traditional Creek observance is the Green Corn Ceremony (Boskita) in early summer, which is a kind of Creek New Year, and still the time for stomp dancing. The Creeks have an advanced corn technology, and remember many traditional ways to prepare different mushes and drinks from hominy, roasted grits, and sourdough.

OSAFKEE

Osafkee is somewhere between a hot drink and a hot cereal. It is more usually called sofkee, and is still in daily use by Creeks and other tribes, including the Florida **Seminoles**. Mexican-Americans and Southwest tribes will recognize this recipe under the Aztec name of "atole." The nuts are a flavoring; daily osafkee would be just grits. Lilah D. Lindsay contributed this recipe to the *Indian Cook Book* (1933), compiled by the Indian Women's Club of Tulsa, Oklahoma. Mrs. Lindsay was president of the club, but the only member to contribute Creek recipes, including fresh and sour corn breads, dried beef hash, grape dumplings (see the **Cherokee** grape dumplings in this book), blue dumplings colored with bean vine ashes, and a beef-hominy soup like the **Chickasaw** pashofa. I have reduced the quantities by a factor of 12.

Yield: 7-8 mugs
   1 cup coarse hominy grits (or see instructions for fine grits)
   1/4 cup hickory nuts (or ground pecans from 1/2 cup pecan halves or 1/3 cup pieces)

Equipment: Cups, food processor

1. Simmer coarse grits in 7 cups of water for 3 hours. (If using fine grits, use 9 cups of water and cook for 30 minutes.) Stir frequently so the grits don't stick and burn.

2. Grind nuts in food processor.

3. Add nuts and cook another 15 minutes. (If the osafkee is too thick to drink from a mug, add a little cold water and stir well.)

Serve hot in mugs as a snack or hot beverage.

CREEK CORN PUDDING

This modern recipe is used for the mid-summer Green Corn Festival, known as the "Boskita." This corn custard recalls the creamy texture of dishes made from immature flour corn. The recipe is from *Spirit of the Harvest: North American Indian Cooking* by Beverly Cox and Martin Jacobs.

Yield: serves 6
   4 to 5 ears fresh corn, best if slightly under-ripe
   3 tablespoons unbleached flour
   3 eggs, beaten
   1 tablespoon sugar
   1 teaspoon salt
   1/4 teaspoon ground pepper (optional)
   dash of ground dried spice bush berries or allspice
   2 tablespoons butter
   2 cups milk

Equipment: Whisk, 2-quart baking dish or large loaf pan, larger oven-proof pan to hold baking dish or loaf pan in hot water

1. With a sharp knife, slit the rows of kernels down the length of the ears of corn.

2. Use the back of the knife in a downward pressing and scraping motion to remove pulp without getting whole kernels or hulls. You should have about 2 cups.

3. Preheat oven to 325 degrees.

4. In a large bowl, combine corn and flour.

5. Beat in eggs and seasonings.

6. In a saucepan, melt butter in milk over medium heat.

7. Whisk hot milk into corn mixture.

8. Butter a 2-quart baking dish or large loaf pan.

9. Pour mixture into baking dish.

10. Place dish in a pan of hot water and bake for 50 to 60 minutes, until custard has set.

"Serve as a side dish with meat or as a main course with a salad."

CREOLES (LOUISIANA)

The word Creole has been used in Louisiana for more than 200 years, and has meant different things at different times about people, food, and language. The word seems to have come from the Spanish "criollo," which meant a locally born person of European background. The children of European settlers almost immediately included some mixed-race people, who had a distinct legal status under Louisiana law, and were also Creoles. The word was reinforced in the early nineteenth century by the arrival in New Orleans of refugees from the Haitian slave revolts, who included French settlers, free "Creoles of color," and some African slaves, who introduced or reinforced the Dahomean-Fon Voodou religion. After the Louisiana Purchase in 1803, as Anglo-Americans became the majority in Louisiana, the word "Creole" was revived by the declining **Franco-American** elite to identify their branch of white society. "Creoles of color," such as the **Cane River Creoles**, continued to share the Creole dialect of French, the Catholic religion, and a nationally recognized style of cooking. Much of the finest Creole cooking in affluent homes was done by **African-American** slaves, and is still done by their descendants.

Over the 100 years following the end of the Civil War in 1865, many poor white Creoles in rural areas married into **Acadian (Cajun)** families, bringing their Creole recipes. European immigrants from Italy, Croatia, and Germany also became Cajuns. African-Americans and Creoles of color in rural Louisiana also took up Cajun music and dialect words, but are still today described as "Creoles," although their country cooking may be described as "Cajun." The cooking of New Orleans is generally described as "Creole," although it, too, may be cooked by European immigrants or by African-Americans of no French or Spanish background.

Cajun chef Paul Prudhomme has defined the cooking differences as follows:

Cajun is very old, French country cooking—a simple hearty fare. . . . Creole food, unlike Cajun, began in New Orleans and is a mixture of the traditions of French, Spanish, Italian, American Indian, African and other ethnic groups. Seven flags flew over New Orleans in the early days, and each time a new nation took over, many members of the deposed government would leave the city; most of their cooks and other servants stayed behind. . . . Those cooks, most of whom were black, would be hired by other families, often of a different nationality. . . . Over a period of time, they learned how to cook for a variety of nationalities, and they incorporated their own spicy, home-style way of cooking into the different cuisines of their employers. . . . Creole cooking is more sophisticated and complex than Cajun cooking—it's city cooking.

Today in homes, there is still a distinction between Cajun and Creole cooking; in restaurants, little distinction remains. That's why I've begun referring to the two together as one—Louisiana Cooking.

Some contemporary writers note that Creole cooking uses butter, cream, and tomatoes more than Cajun, and has more sweet desserts, while Cajun cooking uses more lard and spices.

Because this book is based on ethnic groups, I have assigned Louisiana recipes to the self-identified groups using them. For instance, this Creole (Louisiana) section contains dishes identified with French-speaking African-Americans, city or country, but almost anyone in Louisiana might cook or enjoy dishes that this book identifies as **Chitimacha**, Cane River Creole, Franco-American, Acadian (Cajun), or Creole. Louisiana food will likely continue to converge, blurring ethnic distinctions even more in a cuisine that has always benefited from cross-cultural exchanges. However, to the extent that the United States is moving away from a racial concept of ethnicity, there is a tendency for African-American ethnic groups to differentiate, thus building up a clearer Afro-Creole identity. For example, in the 1990s, a popular group of black-owned restaurants in New Orleans, The Praline Connection, promoted a style called "Creole soul food." Probably the most African-style dishes in the Creole repertory are the gumbos, since they use a browned roux to approximate the color and flavor of African dendé palm oil, mix meats and seafood, achieve a slimy texture with okra or filé powder, and are often served on rice.

GUMBO Z'HERBES

This is the only gumbo that uses neither okra nor filé (nor roux) for thickening. Although European cooking favors soups of spring greens, this dish has always been associated with African-American slave cooks, and was sometimes written as "gombo zhèbes" to imitate the African pronunciation of Creole French, without the 'r's. It was considered lucky to add more kinds of greens, or perhaps the number of friends you would make in the coming year would equal the number of types of greens used. This recipe is from *The Creole Feast* (1978) by Nathaniel Burton and Rudy Lombard, and loosely attributed to head chef Rosa Barganier of Corinne Dunbar's restaurant. "Precise measuring is never done in this gumbo." You can also use fewer kinds of greens.

Yield: serves 10-12
  1 bunch each of collard greens, turnip
    greens, mustard greens, spinach, water-
    cress, beet tops, carrot tops, radish tops,
    parsley, and chicory
  1/2 bunch green onions.
  1 head green cabbage
  1 pound boiled ham
  1 pound lean veal
  2 tablespoons shortening
  1 large white onion
  2 bay leaves
  4 springs thyme
  2 whole cloves
  2 whole allspice
  cayenne (red pepper) to taste

Equipment: Skillet, deep pot

  1. Wash all greens thoroughly and remove all stems, cores, or hard centers. Reserve a little parsley to make a tablespoon of chopped parsley for Step 8.

  2. Boil them all together in a gallon of water for about 2 hours.

  3. Strain the greens and save the water.

  4. Chop the greens finely.

  5. Dice ham and veal.

  6. Sauté ham and veal in shortening for about 10 minutes in a deep pot.

  7. Halve, peel, and chop the white onion.

  8. Chop a tablespoon of parsley.

  9. Add onion and chopped parsley to meat and sauté until onion is brown.

  10. Add greens and simmer 15 minutes.

  11. Add contents of skillet to water from the greens.

  12. Add bay leaves, thyme, cloves, allspice, salt, pepper, and cayenne.

  13. Cook over a low flame for 1 hour.

Red Beans (Mrs. Olivier's)

This is the famous red beans and rice, the New Orleans washday (Monday) stew made from Sunday's ham hock, the dish Louis Armstrong had in mind when he signed autographs, "red beans and ricely yours." The recipe is from the Web site of the French Quarter restaurant of the Olivier family at <www.olivierscreole.com>. If you can't find the bacon ends, use a pound of smoked ham hocks.

Yield: approximately 6 to 8 servings
  1 pound dried red beans
  3 quarts water
  1 yellow onion (chopped medium)
  1 rib celery (chopped fine)
  1/2 bunch green onions (chopped medium)
  1 green bell pepper (chopped fine)
  1 tablespoon garlic powder
  1 tablespoon salt
  1 teaspoon basil
  1/2 pound bacon ends (chopped coarsely)

1. Carefully sift beans and remove any small stones or dirt. Rinse dried beans thoroughly.

2. Place 3 quarts of water and the beans over low heat until beans have absorbed more than half the water.

3. Halve, peel, and chop the onion.

4. Chop the celery "fine." Trim and chop the green onions "medium."

5. Core the green pepper and remove seeds and pith. Chop fine.

6. When beans are nearly dry, add all ingredients except bacon. Cook approximately 3 1/2 hours, stirring occasionally to make sure beans do not adhere to bottom of pot.

7. Chop bacon ends "coarsely."

8. Add bacon and cook an additional 30 minutes.

Serve with rice.

Coush-Coush

This cornmeal mush is sometimes made with leftover cornbread. It is made by all ethnic groups in Louisiana, but the name points to Afro-Creole connections with Barbadan "coo-coo," and the cornmeal mushes of Brazil called "cuz-cuz," as well as the North African "cous-cous," which can be a grain (millet) as well as a pasta in the shape of that grain. This recipe is from Rebecca Henry of Opelousas, Louisiana, via Heidi Haughy Cusick's *Soul and Spice* (1995).

Yield: serves 6
  2 cups fine cornmeal or stone-ground cornmeal
  1 teaspoon salt
  1 teaspoon baking powder (optional)
  1/4 cup butter, bacon drippings, or vegetable oil

Equipment: Cast-iron or heavy non-stick skillet

1. In a bowl, stir together the cornmeal, salt, baking powder (if using), and 2 cups water. Mix well.

2. Melt the butter in the skillet.

3. Add the cornmeal mixture. Stir well, and reduce the heat to medium-low. Cover and cook, stirring often, for 20 minutes.

4. When a crust has formed on the bottom, stir and serve. "It will be very thick and clump together. Mash it down and then spoon it onto a plate."

Serve hot with cane syrup and sausage, or Creole tomato sauce, or with curdled milk "caille."

Turnips and Pork Ribs Etouffée

Etouffée means "smothered" in French, and this country dish of smothered turnips and ribs would not surprise any Cajun family, and would be only a little spicy for many **French Canadian-Americans**. The source of this recipe is *Cookin' with Queen Ida* by Queen Ida Guillory with Naomi

Wise. Queen Ida plays and sings a hybrid of blues and Cajun music called "zydeco," and grew up in Cajun country before her family moved to California in 1946, when she was 18. Her heritage is part **Cherokee** as well as African and French. According to Queen Ida, "[T]he mixture that I am is always referred to as Creole, not Cajun. . . although there is really very little difference between the cooking styles."

1/4 cup oil
2 pounds pork spareribs (or neck bones)
3 tablespoons chopped onion
1 teaspoon salt
1/2 teaspoon black pepper
1/2 teaspoon cayenne
2 pounds medium turnips
1 teaspoon sugar
2 tablespoons bacon fat (optional)

Equipment: Skillet with a tight lid.

1. If using spareribs, have them cut into 3-inch lengths and cut them apart into individual ribs.

2. Pare or peel turnips and slice 1/4-inch thick.

3. Heat the oil in a large skillet with a tight cover.

4. Over medium heat, brown the meat.

5. Chop enough onion to make up 3 tablespoons, and add to the meat with salt, pepper, and cayenne.

6. Stir in up to a cup of water to make a thin gravy.

7. Add the turnips, cover, and simmer slowly until meat is nearly tender, about 45 minutes. Only use enough water to keep the foods from sticking. The process is as much steaming as stewing.

8. Stir occasionally and add a little more water if necessary.

9. Add sugar to taste and cook a few minutes longer to blend flavors.

10. "Tilt the pot and with a large metal spoon skim excess fat from the surface (or refrigerate overnight, skim and reheat gently just until hot)."

11. Add bacon fat to flavor the dish, if desired; correct the seasonings and serve.

CROATIAN-AMERICANS

Although Croatia has been an independent country only since 1991, Croatian-Americans have so identified themselves since the first Dalmatian sailors settled in the English colonies and among the Spanish missions of California. Prior to 1815, much of coastal Croatia was part of the Republic of Venice, and so Dalmatian Croats were also known as Venetians. Inland Croatia was part of the Hungarian Empire from 1102 to 1918. The Dalmatian coast became part of Austria in 1815, and remained administratively separate from the rest of Croatia until 1918. Except for four years of independence under Axis control during World War II, Croatia spent most of the twentieth century as part of Yugoslavia. Croatians share the Catholic Church with Slovenia and Italy, but use the same Slavic language as Serbs (but write it with a different alphabet). Slavonians, not to be confused with **Slovene-Americans,** are from an inland province of Croatia that borders Serbia.

Tensions with Serbs, muted in the Communist Yugoslavia of 1945-1990, were sometimes a problem in American cities during and after World War II, and have twice in the 1990s erupted into civil wars in Croatia and neighboring Bosnia. Prior to 1860, about 20,000 Croatians had settled in the U.S., mostly sailors jumping ship in San Francisco and New Orleans. The latter community developed the local oyster industry, and some Croatians married into the **Acadian (Cajun)** community. The peak of Croatian immigration was about 400,000 who came between 1890 and 1914, with many becoming miners and steelworkers from West Virginia to Michigan, and westward. Industrial workers concentrated in Pennsylvania, and west to Cleveland and Chicago.

About 500,000 Americans claimed Croatian descent in 1990, but other estimates place the total as high as 2.5 million. Their foods are often generally similar to other Balkan ethnic groups, as well as to North Italian food and to the desserts of Austria and Hungary.

DALMATIAN BAKED FISH

This restaurant recipe, given as "Fisherman's Sauce" from Tadich Grill, appeared in *A Cook's Tour of San Francisco* (1963) by Doris Muscatine. The sauce was developed by Slavonian chefs in 1910, but the method of slow baking fish in a thick sauce came over with Dalmatian sailors in the Gold Rush days when Tadich Grill was founded. Dalmatian-style baked fish has continued as a local style in San Francisco. A Croatian fishing community around New Orleans made something similar of the **Creole** and Cajun Redfish courtbouillon.

Yield: serves 6
  3 ounces olive oil
  2 or 3 leeks
  1 bunch green onions
  1 quart solid pack tomatoes, squeezed, or
    well broken up
  1/2 cup chicken or beef broth (or water)
  about 3 pounds of halibut, sea bass, striped
    bass, or similar fish, whole or in slices or
    steaks
  salt and pepper

Equipment: Large baking dish, saucepan

1. Wash leeks thoroughly, and chop very fine.

2. Chop green onions into thin rings.

3. Heat oil in a saucepan and braise the chopped leeks and onions until well cooked, stirring so they do not burn.

4. Squeeze and break up tomatoes.

5. Add the tomatoes, and salt and pepper to taste to the leeks and green onions.

6. Cook 2 hours over a slow fire, stirring occasionally.

7. Add broth or water and simmer a few minutes more.

8. Heat oven to 400 degrees.

9. If using whole fish, cut slashes to the center so that it will absorb the juices. Cover bottom of baking dish with sauce and arrange fish on top.

10. Cook about 10 minutes to the pound, up to about 40 minutes altogether. Cook slices about 10 to 15 minutes. It is important to judge according to type and size of fish.

11. Test for doneness with a fork. "When done, meat should be moist but flaky." Today, many cooks stop cooking fish just before it flakes. Add remaining sauce over the top, and return to the oven for 5 minutes, or until heated through.

SPINACH PIE
(PITA SA SPINATOM)

A number of Croatian dishes are designed around dough stretched to the thinness of filo or strudel dough. Mira Tomas found a useful substitute in supermarket flour tortillas for this recipe, which was posted on the Web site of the Univerity of Pittsburgh Summer Language Institute. The filling, without the tortillas, can be cooked as a casserole similar to **Serbian-American** praesnaes.

Yield: serves 6 as a main dish, 12 as an appetizer
  12 large (burrito-size) tortillas
  2 cups chopped frozen spinach (or 1 pound
    fresh spinach)
  1 egg
  3 cups dry curd cottage cheese

1 cup sour cream
1/4 teaspoon salt
1/2 cup olive oil

Equipment: 9 by 12 baking pan or lasagna pan, pastry brush or clean new paint brush for oil

1. If using frozen spinach, thaw and drain. If using fresh spinach, boil a large pot of water. Push in the spinach for 3 minutes, then drain carefully, and chop on a board.

2. Pre-heat oven to 350 degrees.

3. Mix together cottage cheese, sour cream, beaten egg, and salt.

4. Mix in spinach.

5. Thinly oil a 9 by 12 baking pan.

6. Cover bottom of pan with a layer of tortillas.

7. Brush oil thinly on top of tortillas, then spread evenly with about 1/5 of the spinach mixture. (For all subsequent layers, tortillas must be brushed with oil on both sides.)

8. Repeat layering process with remaining ingredients. Tortillas must form the top layer.

9. Bake 45 minutes at 350 degrees.

10. Remove from oven, brush top with water and cover with a clean towel for 10 minutes, then serve.

Serve cut into squares or triangles. May also be eaten cold.

AJVAR

Also on the University of Pittsburgh Summer Language Institute Web site is this addictive spread. The recipe by Jane Rinear was taken from *Our Favorite Recipes*, published by the St. Anthony Croatian Catholic Church. Some gourmet stores carry a version imported from Bulgaria.

2 large eggplants
6 large red or green sweet peppers
1 garlic clove
juice of 1 lemon

1/2 cup oil, preferably olive oil
1 tablespoon minced parsley

Equipment: Juicer, stainless steel knives, glass dish

1. Core peppers. Bake eggplants and sweet peppers at 350 degrees until tender when pierced with a fork, about 30-50 minutes for eggplants depending on size.

2. Peel skin from hot vegetables and chop or mince the vegetables.

3. Season to taste with salt and pepper.

4. Mince parsley. Peel and mince garlic.

5. Stir in the garlic and lemon juice.

6. Gradually stir in as much of the oil as the vegetables will absorb. Mix well.

7. Pile into a glass dish and sprinkle with parsley.

Serve with bread and cheese, flatbread, or crackers.

ZGANCE (DEPRESSION DISH)

This is a kind of polenta (Italian cornmeal mush), a peasant food in Croatia, and a frequently used recipe in the Great Depression in the U.S. Mim Imblum submitted this recipe to the *St. Mary of Mt. Carmel Church Ethnic Cookbook* (1984).

1 tablespoon salt
1 1/2 cups yellow cornmeal
1/2 pound butter or oleo
2 large onions
1/2 pint sour cream

Equipment: Heavy and non-enamel pot, heavy skillet

1. "Boil 1 1/2 cups of water in a heavy pot, *not enamel*, add salt."

2. Slowly add cornmeal, over low heat, stirring constantly to prevent lumps and sticking to the pot.

3. Cook for 35 minutes. Keep cornmeal warm while preparing sauce.

4. Halve, peel, and chop the onions.

5. Heat butter in a heavy skillet and sauté onions until transparent.

6. Lower heat, add sour cream, and stir.

7. Cook slowly over low heat for 2 minutes until blended.

8. Pour cornmeal on warm platter.

9. Pour sauce on cornmeal and serve

CUBAN-AMERICANS

According to the 1990 census, 860,000 Americans consider themselves to be of Cuban descent. Although the great majority came after Fidel Castro took power in 1959, Cuban immigration began as early as 1831 with the establishment of cigar factories in Key West, Florida. By the time Cuba became independent of Spain in 1899, significant Cuban communities existed in Tampa and New York City. The recent expansion of the Cuban-American community has occurred in four phases. The first phase was an increase in the late 1950s, when the Batista dictatorship became increasingly corrupt and unpredictable. The second phase, with more than 150,000 departures, was from 1960 to 1963, beginning as the Castro government cracked down on private wealth, and ending after the U.S.-supported Bay of Pigs invasion lead to a suspension of air service. Air service resumed from 1966 to 1972, bringing another 250,000 people. Although most emigrants and refugees from Cuba came to Miami, a federal program helped almost 300,000 locate elsewhere in the United States and Puerto Rico in an effort to reduce the impact of this foreign group. Although Cuban-Americans succeeded in business and professional life, often in the Puerto Rican communities of eastern cities, most relocated themselves to Miami after a few years, setting a pattern of voluntary re-concentration that has held for all the U.S. government-assisted refugee groups since.

Cubans have continued to seek refuge and improved lives in the United States, but the most recent defined phase of Cuban immigration was the "Mariel boatlift" of 1980, in which another 125,000 Cubans were given permission to leave the island. Some tensions have arisen between this newer group and the established Cuban-American community, following a familiar pattern in which the newcomers are seen as significantly different from and embarrassing to the "pioneers." Although there was some publicity in 1980 about prisoners released into the Mariel group, the apparent demographic difference was that the new group had more Afro-Cubans than the disproportionately white refugees of 1960-72, and the new group arrived without possessions.

Cuban-American food has changed from what is eaten in Cuba, partially by retaining the cooking styles of the more abundant 1950s, partially by adaptation of modern American dietary ideas, and partially by adapting other cuisines current in Florida, where half of all Cuban-Americans now live. For example, Cuban restaurants in Miami often serve the **Nicaraguan-American** tres-leches cake. Some other Cuban-American dishes include caramel custard, moro (black beans and rice), Cuban sandwiches, arroz con pollo, and roast fresh ham. The older Cuban-American community in Key West has kept up a fried black-bean ball that may be related to the Nigerian accra. The communities in Tampa and Ybor City emphasize Spanish dishes like "yellow rice" and garbanzo bean soup.

BLACK BEAN SOUP

Black bean soup has been the best-known Cuban-American dish since the first Cuban immigrants arrived. Ironically, the eastern half of Cuba favors red beans, like the rest of the Caribbean. This recipe from Xaviar L. Suarez, the first Cuban-American mayor of Miami, appeared in the *The Mayor's Cookbook* (1987), edited by Thomas L. McClimon.

Yield: serves 8, or a half cup for 20

1 pound black beans
2/3 cup olive oil
1 large onion
4 cloves garlic
1 green bell pepper
4 teaspoons salt
2 teaspoons oregano
1/3 cup vinegar

1. Wash dried beans and soak in water with black pepper.

2. When beans are swollen, boil until soft (about 45 minutes).

3. Halve, peel, and chop the onion.

4. Peel and chop garlic.

5. Cut off the top and bottom of the green pepper, slit down one side, core and remove white pith. Cut into long slices, and cut across the slices to make dice.

6. In a pan, heat oil and sauté onion, garlic, and pepper. (This is the "sofrito" that flavors many Caribbean dishes.)

7. Put about 1 cup of the cooked beans into the pan with the onion and smash to a pulp.

8. Pour mixture back into simmering bean soup.

9. Add salt and oregano, and boil approximately another hour.

10. Add vinegar (which is added at the end because it prevents the beans from softening).

11. "Simmer for 1 more hour or so until it thickens."

"This soup is best served over white rice."

PICADILLO

Picadillo is a meat mixture like "Sloppy Joes." The recipe is from my friend Berta Berriz, and was published in *We're Cooking: The City Mission Society Real People's Cookbook* (1988). She writes, "Traditionally this dish is served over white rice with a fried egg on top, accompanied by sweet ripe fried plantains. In America, we use the picadillo to fill corn tortillas and garnish this with shredded lettuce, chopped tomatoes, green onions, hot peppers, grated Monterey Jack cheese, hot sauce." Thus Cuban food became Americanized by becoming part of a Mexican-American taco! Picadillo also makes the filling for a pasty like the **Cane River Creole** meat pie.

1/2 cup olive oil
6-8 cloves garlic
2 large onions
1 bunch parsley
2-3 tablespoons capers
1/2 cup stuffed green olives
4 or so bay leaves
4-5 tablespoons crushed cumin seeds
1 pound hamburger
1 16-ounce can tomatoes (or 2 diced fresh tomatoes)
1/2 cup wine vinegar
1 pinch cayenne pepper (hot red pepper)
1 can pimentos

1. Halve, peel, and chop the onions.

2. Peel and chop garlic.

3. Cut off the top and bottom of the peppers, slit down one side, and core and remove white pith. Cut into long slices, and cut across the slices to make dice.

4. Heat the olive oil in a large skillet and sauté the next 7 ingredients "until flavors are blended and onions are clear." This sofrito is more traditional and elaborate than the one described above.

5. Remove from pan and brown hamburger.

6. Drain off surplus fat and combine hamburger with sofrito.

7. Add vinegar, tomatoes, and cayenne.

8. Simmer for 30-45 minutes.

Serve over rice, decorated with sliced pimento.

PUFFED WHEAT BATIDO

Batidos are drinks made from fresh or frozen fruit, crushed ice, and a little milk and sugar. This unusual one reminds me of certain Spanish and Mexican oatmeal drinks. This recipe from the Mappy Restaurant in Miami appeared in *Miami Spice* by Steven Raichlin.

Yield: serves 1
  1 cup puffed wheat cereal
  1/2 cup milk
  1/2 cup crushed ice
  2 tablespoons sugar, or to taste
  pinch of salt

Equipment: Blender, food processor or ice crusher to make crushed ice

1. Combine all ingredients in a blender and purée until smooth.

Serve at once.

CZECH-AMERICANS

For the 1990 census, almost 1.3 million Americans claimed Czech ancestry. Czech immigration peaked in the early 1900s, but began in significant numbers before the Civil War, making the Czechs the first Slavic group to reach the United States, and the only one that arrived early enough to obtain significant farmland, especially in Nebraska, Texas, Iowa, Wisconsin, and Minnesota. Those who came later concentrated in cities, notably Chicago. As a group, Czech immigrants were somewhat slower to learn English and much slower to give up their own language than most other immigrants from Europe. One reason was that many had at least second-language fluency in German, which was widely used in some American cities before World War I. The history of their homeland helped prepare Czech-Americans to preserve their own culture while participating in a majority culture.

Czech-Americans speak almost the same home language as **Slovak-Americans,** and both groups are predominantly Catholic, but the two homelands were politically divided for much of European history, and divided again in 1991 by a vote for separation by what has become the Slovak Republic. The Czech kingdoms had been powerful in the late Middle Ages, but then suffered considerably in the Protestant Reformation and Counter-Reformation of the sixteenth and seventeenth centuries, when many battles were fought on Czech soil. The Czech homeland was part of German-speaking Austria when most of the immigrants came to the United States, and most were known as Bohemians and Moravians after the two largest provinces they left. German-speaking, Bohemians and Moravians generally identified with the **German-American** community. In the U.S. today, **Moravians** are members, from a variety of national backgrounds, of Protestant church denominations with historic roots in Moravia. After World War I, Czech-Americans worked with Slovak-Americans and **Carpatho-Rusyn-Americans** to persuade President Woodrow Wilson to support an independent Czechoslovakia. They often described themselves as Czechoslovakian-Americans, although the distinct Czech ethnic identity always remained. When Czechoslovakia was divided by German occupation forces in 1935, Czech- and Slovak-Americans generally rejected the Nazi puppet governments, supported the Allied war effort, and worked to re-establish a unitary country after the war. Neither the 1948 Communist coup d'etat nor the 1968 Soviet rejection of a liberalized Communism (under Slovak Alexander Dubcek) divided Czech-Americans from Slovak-Americans. The tensions that lead to the 1991 division of Czechoslovakia did not cause problems for these well-assimilated groups in the U.S.

Czech cooking benefited from the wide variety of surrounding cuisines, and most of all from the fancy cooking of Vienna. Czech-American cooking has a wonderful variety of soups, dumplings, stews, and, especially, pastries. If you talk to Czech-American cooks, you will hear about potato and plum dumplings; coffee breads called bobovka, houska, and vanocka; and a mushroom-barley pilaf called kuba.

VARMUZA

Varmuza was evidently a scrambled pancake dish like the **German-American** schman, but using mashed potatoes. It was adapted for cornmeal by the Sykora family of Oklahoma as early as the 1870s. It was recorded by Jerome and Earlene Sykora of Stillwater for Cleo Stiles Bryan's *Seems Like I Done It This A-Way*, which was published in 1976 and revised in 1980.

4 tablespoons bacon grease
3 green onions (scallions)
2 eggs
1/4 cup fine white cornmeal
2 cups milk
1/2 teaspoon salt

Equipment: Heavy skillet

1. Trim and chop green onions.

2. Heat grease in a heavy skillet, and fry onions "lightly."

3. Beat eggs and mix in cornmeal, milk, and salt.

4. Pour mixture into skillet of onions while they are still hot.

5. "Stir constantly until consistency of mashed potatoes."

MORKOVSKY SISTERS' KOLACHES

Kolaches are the best-known Czech-American food, popular in bakeries all up and down the central United States, and sold in many varieties at ethnic festivals. One way they have changed in the United States is to become larger and fluffier pastries. In addition to this "thumbprint" form, they are also made in squares. Several other ethnic groups from Central Europe make kolaches, but they are most strongly identified with Czech-Americans. This recipe from Rose Morkovsky Hauger and Ann Morkovsky Adams was featured in *Texas Monthly* magazine in November 1998. These sisters from San Antonio demonstrate kolaches at ethnic festivals in Texas. The fillings given are prune and cream cheese, but there are also cherry, cottage cheese, and poppy-seed fillings.

NOTE: Prunes should be soaked overnight.

Yield: about 48 kolaches
2 envelopes yeast
2 teaspoons salt
3 1/3 cups sugar
2 cups milk
1/4 cup oil
2 eggs, plus 2 yolks
9-10 cups flour
3 sticks butter
16-ounce package cream cheese
grated rind of one lemon
1 teaspoon vanilla
12-ounce package pitted prunes
1/2 teaspoon cinnamon
1/2 teaspoon grated lemon or orange peel

Equipment: Pastry brush, cookie sheets, pastry blender, grater, food processor (optional)

1. Put prunes in a small bowl, and cover with boiling water. Leave overnight, or at least 6 hours, to plump up.

2. Add yeast to 1 teaspoon of sugar in a small bowl. Combine 1/3 cup of sugar, the oil, and the salt in a mixing bowl.

3. Heat the milk to about 110 degrees (lukewarm).

4. Add 1/2 cup of milk to the yeast/sugar mixture and set aside.

5. Add the remaining milk to the mixing bowl and combine with the sugar, oil, and salt.

6. Begin adding the flour to the mixing bowl one cup at a time. By the time you have added the second cup, the yeast will have proofed (begun to foam up).

7. Add the yeast mixture to the flour mixture and combine.

8. Add a third cup of flour to the mixture and combine.

9. Beat the eggs, and, at this point, combine them into the flour mixture.

10. Begin adding the remaining flour 1/2 cup at a time, mixing after each addition. The dough is ready when "the dough chases the spoon around the bowl." This usually takes a total of about 5 1/2 cups of flour.

11. Cover the dough in the bowl and let it rise in a warm place until doubled, about 2 hours.

12. To make "posypka," cream together 2 sticks of butter, 2 cups of sugar, and 3 cups of flour until mixture resembles coarse crumbs.

13. To make cream cheese filling, take out cream cheese to soften it.

14. Grate lemon rind.

15. In a medium bowl, beat together cream cheese, lemon rind, 2 egg yolks, 1/2 cup sugar, and 1 teaspoon vanilla.

16. To make prune filling, drain liquid off soaked prunes and mash prunes thoroughly with a fork or run through a food processor.

17. Grate another 1/2 teaspoon of lemon or orange zest.

18. Add the zest, the cinnamon, and 1/2 cup sugar to the prune puree. Mix thoroughly.

19. When dough is almost doubled in bulk, melt the last stick of butter on the stovetop so that it is ready for spreading on the dough.

20. Grease the tops of 2 cookie sheets and preheat the oven to 350 degrees.

21. After the dough is doubled, punch it down into the bowl to eliminate large air bubbles.

22. Flour the work surface slightly.

23. With a tablespoon, scoop out balls of dough and drop onto work surface, maybe a dozen at a time.

24. Take each ball of dough to the palm of your hand and roll into a real ball. Place the balls on a cookie sheet in evenly spaced rows of 4 across and 6 down to make a pan of 24.

25. Brush the balls with melted butter. Let them proof (rise) maybe another 30 minutes.

26. Repeat the process to make the other 24 or so kolaches.

27. After they have risen, press down your thumb to make an indentation in the center of each ball and fill with approximately one heaping teaspoon of one of the fillings. Let them set another 10 minutes.

28. Sprinkle with posypka.

29. Bake the pans of kolaches about 20 minutes, but check after 15. They should be a light golden.

30. Brush the kolaches with melted butter when they come out of the oven and cool on wire racks.

MOLASSES COOKIES (MELASOVÉ CUKROVÍ)

This unusual cookie recipe was submitted by Ella Klechka for the Web site of the Caldwell, Texas, Czech festival at <www.rtis.com/reg/caldwell/czech>.

  1 cup lard plus a little more to grease baking sheet
  1/2 cup sugar
  1 cup molasses
  1 cup sour cream
  1/2 teaspoon salt
  1 teaspoon baking soda mixed with a little hot water
  2 eggs
  1/2 teaspoon caraway seed
  1 teaspoon ginger
  1/2 teaspoon cloves
  1/2 teaspoon cinnamon
  "flour enough to make thick dough" (about 4 cups)
  1 teaspoon nutmeg

Equipment: Round or fancy cookie cutter, cookie sheet, rolling pin

1. Mix baking soda with a little hot water, then add all ingredients except flour. Mix well. Add flour to get a stiff dough.

2. Knead dough (see Appendix 1) a little to get a smooth dough. Chill half hour or more.

3. Flour board and rolling pin, and roll out dough 1/4-inch thick.

4. Bake on ungreased cookie sheets at 350 degrees, 10-15 minutes, until just golden at the edges.

POPPY SEED CAKE

This cake is from a selection of recipes found in *Favorite Recipes of Nebraska Czechs*, which can be ordered from the Web site at <http://www.barnasdrug.com/recipes.html>.

1 cup poppy seed
1/3 cup honey
1 cup butter or margarine
1 1/2 cups sugar
4 eggs
1 cup sour cream
1 teaspoon vanilla
2 1/2 cups flour
1 teaspoon baking soda
scant 1 teaspoon baking soda
1 teaspoon salt

Equipment: Pastry blender or large fork, electric hand mixer or whisk to beat egg whites, wire rack, 9-inch tube-cake pan, flexible spatula to remove cake, small saucepan

1. In a small saucepan, cook poppy seed with honey and 1/4 cup water for 5-7 minutes. Cool.

2. With a pastry blender or a large fork, cream butter or margarine and sugar until light and fluffy.

3. Separate eggs by pouring back and forth between shells over a cup to catch whites. Keep yolks in a separate cup. (If you break an egg, put it in with the yolks and reduce sour cream slightly.)

4. Beat yolks. Add cooled poppy seed mixture and 1/4 of the egg yolks alternately to the butter and margarine mixture, beating well after each addition.

5. Blend in sour cream and vanilla.

6. Sift together flour, soda baking powder, and salt.

7. Gradually add poppy seed mixture, beating well.

8. Beat egg whites until stiff and fold into batter.

9. Lightly grease and flour the tube-cake pan.

10. Pour batter into tube pan.

11. Bake at 350 degrees for 1 hour and 15 minutes.

12. Cool in pan for 5 minutes.

13. Remove from pan and cool on a wire rack.

DAKOTA

See SIOUX

DALMATIANS

See CROATIAN-AMERICANS

DANISH-AMERICANS

More than 1.6 million Danish-Americans lived in the U.S. in 1990. They are generally regarded as one of the "new immigrant" groups that smoothly adopted to American life, perhaps because they were among the smallest and most scattered of the Scandanavian groups, and because they spoke a language related to English and also to German, which was spoken by a large fraction of Americans early in the twentieth century. Although Denmark did not colonize North America (leaving aside the Danes among the Vikings), about 500 Danes were the largest minority in Dutch New Netherlands (New York) in the 1640s. Ancestors of most Danish-Americans immigrated to the U.S. between 1860 and 1930. About 17,000 were recruited to Utah by Mormon missionaries, but most settled across the lower Midwest, concentrating in western Iowa. Some specifically Danish settlements were undertaken, the last and most lasting being Solvang, California, established in 1911. A few more Danes became U.S. citizens when the United States purchased the Danish Virgin Islands in 1917.

Danish-American food is similar to **German-American** food and something like **Swedish-American** food, but you will find lots of recipes for Danish Christmas cookies because it is a custom to have at least seven kinds! The Danish custom of eating six meals a day contributed to our coffee breaks and late-night snacks, and you may well encounter recipes for frikadeller (Danish meatballs), rodkal (the Danish version of red cabbage), or kringler (the original Danish pastries). You may notice old iron pans with large round dimples for making aebleskivers, a kind of spherical pancake.

RIS A LA MANDE

Alice Jorgensen Wood contributed this Americanized version of a Scandinavian rice porridge, like the Swedish risgrynsgröt, to a Seattle church cookbook in the early 1990s. Mrs. Wood uses cooked rice, skips the long cooking down to porridge, and usually substitutes canned cherry pie filling for the red "fruit soup" formerly used as a sauce. "This is served by the Danes for 'Jukeaften' (Christmas Eve) dinner with one blanched whole almond hidden in the serving bowl. When found, that person must hide it in his or her mouth until everyone has finished, and then will receive a prize (usually a marzipan pig). My Danish parents always served this, I have always served it, and now our daughter does every Christmas Eve. A fun tradition."

Yield: serves 6
  1 cup cooked rice
  1 cup whipped cream
  2 tablespoons sugar
  1 teaspoon vanilla extract
  1/2 cup chopped blanched almonds (and 1
    whole one)

1 can cherry pie filling for red fruit sauce
1. Mix first 5 ingredients well and chill.

Serve with a topping of cherry pie filling.

DANISH SWEET SOUP

Mrs. Richard Giles contributed this recipe to *Favorite Recipes from Our Best Cooks*, which was compiled in 1980 by the Marching Bears Booster Club of the Big Bear (California) High School Band. This kind of dried fruit soup is typical all over northern Europe, and was probably simplified to fit what "Grandma Christensen of Denmark" could find in South Dakota, where she came in 1867. Grandma Christensen would have used pearl tapioca or plain rice, cooked with the fruit, and would have soaked the prunes and raisins overnight so she could remove the seeds. Mrs. Giles adds that you "can add other pieces of dried fruit if you like. Also a package of Jell-O strawberry or cherry flavor."

Yield: serves 8 or more
  2 quarts water
  2 cups pitted prunes
  1 cup sugar

1 cup raisins
1 cup Minute Tapioca or Rice
juice of one lemon (1-3 tablespoons) or 1
    tablespoon vinegar

1. Let prunes and raisins simmer in 2 quarts of water until tender.

2. Add 1 cup instant tapioca or instant rice, and the lemon juice or vinegar.

3. Cook until smooth and add the sugar.

Serve hot as soup at the beginning of a meal or cold as pudding served with cream.

KRINGLE

This most famous Danish dessert comes in many forms, from Christmas wreath coffee cakes and rolled Yule logs to individual "Danish pastries." This recipe is for the most typical Danish-American homemade kringle, which is a flat, filled coffee cake, frosted, and cut into pieces. Yes, it is possible that kringle inspired the toaster tart. The recipe is from Mrs. Dorothea Ahlm, secretary of Pioneer Grange No. 792, in Warba, Minnesota. It was published in *The New Grange Cookbook: 900 Favorite Recipes from America's Farm Families* (1970).

NOTE: Recipe needs to be refrigerated overnight.

Yield: serves 10-16
    4 cups flour
    1 cup lard or shortening
    3 tablespoons sugar
    1 cup warm milk
    1 teaspoon vanilla
    1 teaspoon salt
    2 eggs
    1 yeast cake
    1 can pie filling (or cinnamon-sugar mix)
    2 cups confectioner's sugar
    solid shortening to grease baking sheets

Equipment: Pastry blender or large fork, 2 baking sheets, rolling pin

1. Cream together flour, lard, and sugar "as for pie crust."

2. Add milk, vanilla, salt, and beaten eggs.

3. Dissolve yeast cake in 1/2 cup lukewarm water.

4. Add yeast solution to flour mixture.

5. "Refrigerate overnight."

6. Divide dough into 4 parts.

7. Flour rolling pin and surface, and roll dough into a thin rectangle. Cut edges neatly and use to patch weak spots.

8. Place pie filling on one-half of the dough, leaving a half-inch margin.

9. Fold dough over and seal edges by crimping with a fork.

10. Grease baking sheets.

11. Place baking kringles on baking sheets and let rise until doubled in bulk.

12. Bake at 400 degrees for 20 minutes.

13. Mix confectioner's sugar with a small amount of water, just until it all melts.

14. Spread on top of the warm cakes with a spoon.

To serve, cut into pieces to show the filling.

DINEH

See NAVAJO

DOMINICAN-AMERICANS

According to the 1990 census, 520,000 Americans have roots in the Dominican Republic, almost all of whom came to the United States since the 1965 United States invasion. This immigration has continued, with 40,000 Dominicans immigrating in 1996 alone, the sixth largest group that year. A large population of Dominican-Americans lacks legal immigration papers, although federal statistics have confused them with people from the much-smaller island republic of Dominica, a former British colony. Dominicans are heavily concentrated in New York City, which is now the largest Dominican city in the world, with 600,000 to 800,000 people, including the largest foreign-language group in the New York schools. Large Dominican-American communities also exist in Boston and Miami, and Dominican workers live in Puerto Rico and the Virgin Islands.

Dominican food partakes of the French and Spanish colonial history of the Caribbean island of Hispaniola, which the Dominican Republic shares with Haiti; the island is today strongly Afro-Caribbean. Dominican food also shows a surprising number of survivals from the Taino Indians, who were the first Americans to trade foods with Columbus. The persistent sugar economy feeds a considerable Dominican sweet tooth, although the foods Dominican-Americans feel most strongly about are twice-fried plantains (tostones) and a thick stew of tropical roots and meats (sancocho).

CHICHARRONES DE POLLO

Chicharrones de pollo means "fried pork rinds of chicken," and the unusually small pieces and marinade with soy sauce, though distinctly Dominican, may reflect the influence of Chinese contract laborers. This dish has become well known in New York. This recipe combines several printed recipes and a New York Internet recipe.

CAUTION: Hot oil used.

Yield: serves 6-8 as an appetizer, with 24 or more pieces
  1 frying chicken
  1 teaspoon salt
  3 cloves garlic
  pinch of black pepper
  1/2 teaspoon paprika
  1 tablespoon soy sauce
  1 cup flour
  1/4 cup fresh lime juice, from 3-4 limes, plus
    2 more for garnish

Equipment: Garlic press, deep-fry thermometer, sharp chef's knife or cleaver and rubber mallet, wire rack, or paper towels, paper bag

1. Cut the chicken into very small pieces with a sharp chef's knife or a cleaver and rubber mallet. See illustration. Don't swing a cleaver wildly. Generally I have seen each wing segment cut in half, the drumsticks in 2 or 3 pieces, the breasts in at least 4 pieces, and the thighs in halves.

2. Juice limes and mix with soy sauce, 3/4 teaspoon of the salt, and pressed cloves of garlic. Mix up the chicken pieces with this marinade for about an hour.

3. In a paper bag, mix the flour, paprika, pepper, and the rest of the salt.

4. Put groups of chicken pieces in the bag and shake to coat.

5. Set the pieces on a wire rack to dry a little.

6. Heat oil in a deep-sided, heavy pot to 325 degrees.

7. Being careful not to splash hot oil, dip skimmer in oil, add a few pieces of chicken, and lower into the hot oil. Fry until golden, no more than 5 minutes per side. You may have to turn over some of the larger pieces.

8. Remove pieces that are done to a wire rack or to paper towns to drain. (If you are making a

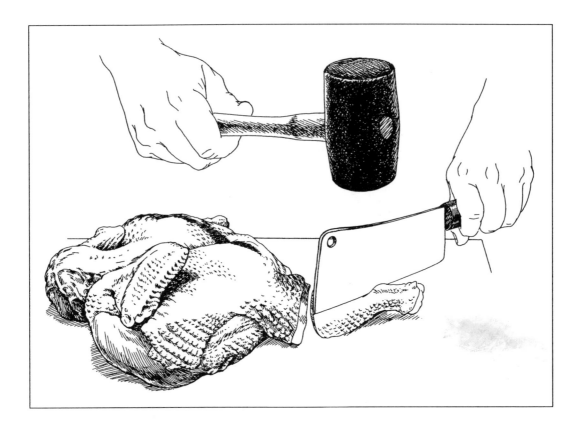

lot, you can keep them warm in a 200-degree oven.)

9. Cut 2 limes into wedges for a garnish.

Serve with beans and rice, or strips of fried plantain and wedges of lime.

Ceci's Dominican Coconut Fish Stew

We got this recipe from Consuelo Cecilia Inchaustegui Pluta, who was my wife's student at Brighton (Massachusetts) High School, came to live with us after college, married and became our downstairs tenant for a while, and remains our friend. There is no real substitute for the "ajies," which are small chile peppers with a lot of flavor and rather little heat. You can find them in Latin American groceries, sometimes spelled "achies." They were the first peppers given to Columbus, who wrote down "axi." In this dish, the other peppers will provide enough flavor.

Yield: serves 6

1 1/4 pounds fish fillets
2 tablespoons vegetable oil
4 garlic cloves
2 big sweet Italian frying peppers
7 ajies
2 green bell peppers
3 onions
4 sprigs cilantro (fresh coriander)
1 tablespoon tomato paste
juice of 1 lime
1/2 teaspoon oregano
1/4 teaspoon cumin
1/4 cup white wine (or water)
2 teaspoons soy sauce
3 large carrots
1 can unsweetened coconut milk
1 large can plum tomatoes
7 potatoes

Equipment: Garlic press, juicer, soup pot, skillet

1. Peel garlic cloves. Halve, peel, and chop onions. (Wear swim goggles to avoid tears.)

2. Cut the tops and bottoms off the bell peppers, slit down one side, and cut out the core and pith. Cut the pieces into strips, and the strips into squares.

3. Seed the frying peppers and cut into squares.

4. If you have ajíes, cut out the seeds and stems and mince them.

5. Heat oil in a soup pot, and begin frying the onions and peppers.

6. Press 2 cloves of garlic into the skillet.

7. Juice the limes.

8. When onions are almost done, add half the lime juice and all the tomato paste and mix well.

9. Chop the cilantro. Reserve half. Add half to the pot with the wine or water and the soy sauce and stir well.

10. Add the tomatoes and simmer 5-10 minutes, uncovered. Add a little water and cook another 5 to 10 minutes.

11. Add coconut milk and more water to make a thin sauce; cook 10 minutes. Check for seasoning and add salt and pepper.

12. Peel potatoes and cut into 1-inch cubes.

13. Peel carrots and cut into large chunks.

14. Add potatoes and carrots. Bring back to a boil and reduce heat to simmer until potatoes and carrots are done, about 10-15 minutes.

15. When potatoes are done, mash 1 potato to thicken the sauce.

16. Add the rest of the coriander and lime juice. Press in the rest of the garlic. Stir well.

17. Cut fish into 6 pieces and place gently on top. Cover pot and cook until fish is done, about 5-10 minutes.

Serve over rice by carefully taking out fish fillets and surrounding with vegetables and sauce.

TOSTONES

This recipe also came from Consuelo, but is the universal Dominican-American favorite, and also much loved by other Caribbean immigrants. (If your plantains start turning yellow or black, cut them into long strips and fry them only once. Those make soft, sweet French fries Dominican-Americans call "maduros.") Hispanic grocery stores sell a hinged wooden press called a "tostonera" to crush the plantains for the second frying.

CAUTION: Hot oil used.

2 green plantains
1 cup oil

Equipment: Deep-fry thermometer, skimmer or long slotted spoon, paper towels or wire racks, heavy pot

1. To skin plantains, cut off the ends and cut a shallow slit down the side. Peel around horizontally, the opposite way a banana peels.

2. Cut into 1-inch pieces.

3. Heat oil to 330-350 degrees.

4. Fry plantains, in batches, until light golden brown.

5. Drain plantains and cool somewhat on paper towels or wire cake racks.

6. When plantains are cool, smash them flat with a heavy pot.

7. Increase oil temperature to 350-370 degrees. Fry plantains a second time until golden-brown and crisp.

8. Drain again on paper towels or a wire rack.

Serve hot with salt as a side dish.

DUTCH-AMERICANS

P eople have come from the Netherlands in all four major periods of European settlement and immigration, with some 6.2 million Americans reporting Dutch ancestry on the 1990 census. Most of the "founding stock" Dutch-Americans were descended from settlers in the colony of New Netherland before the British takeover (and renamed as New York) in 1664. By 1790, they numbered 100,000 in New York and New Jersey. Some moved to German-speaking areas of Pennsylvania and helped form the **Pennsylvania Dutch** ethnic group, which is "Dutch" in the sense of "Deutsch"—meaning German. But most Dutch settlers had already learned English, although they certainly remembered the Dutch names for their coleslaws, doughnuts, waffles, and Christmas cookies, even as these ethnic foods were becoming all-American favorites.

The second wave of about 400,000 Dutch immigrants came between 1845 (when there was a potato famine in Holland) and 1930, when new laws limited the number of immigrants. Although some settled in New York City and New Jersey, most moved to farms and factories in the Midwest. These Dutch-Americans were able to learn English and give up much of their ethnic identity in a few generations, though a few prominent settlements can still be found in Grand Rapids and Holland, Michigan, and Pella, Iowa. The latter two communities still hold tulip festivals with Dutch costumes and foods.

A third group of Dutch-Americans, about 80,000, immigrated to the U.S. after World War II to escape the hardship and destruction caused by the war and the lengthy German occupation. They were joined in the mid-1950s by 18,000 Dutch Indonesians, who left Indonesia after that country gained independence from Holland in 1949. Both groups contribute Dutch food to community cookbooks all over the United States without forming a visible ethnic concentration anywhere.

The early Dutch influence on American food was substantial but is hard to trace. Coleslaw comes from Dutch "kool slaa," and cookies and crullers are also taken from Dutch words and foods of New Netherland. The first doughnuts were New Netherland "olykoeks" and "krullen." These are easier to trace because English colonial cookery had no raw cabbage salads or fried dough desserts, and the British terms for what we Americans call "cookies" were and are "cakes" or "biscuits."

Most other American recipes with the word "Dutch" in them are Pennsylvania Dutch, and it is hard to tell whether a given pea soup, wilted salad, coffee cake, scrapple, or pepperpot is **Anglo-American, German-American,** or Dutch-American. A recent book about seventeenth-century Dutch and Dutch-American food is Peter Rose's 142-page *The Sensible Cook: Dutch Foodways in the Old and the New World* (Syracuse University Press, 1989). The book includes a translation of a 1683 cookbook found in the library of an old Hudson Valley family.

ANIJSMELK (ANISE MILK)

This recipe appeared in *Eat Smakelijk: A Collection of Recipes by Members and Friends of the Junior Welfare League of Holland, Michigan,* which was first published in 1964 as the *Official Cookbook of Holland, Michigan.* Holland was founded as a Dutch settlement in 1867.

1 quart milk
1 tablespoon sugar
1 teaspoon anise seed

Yield: 4 cups hot anise milk

Equipment: Aluminum foil, hammer, candy/deep-fry thermometer (optional)

1. Heat milk to boiling point, but don't let it boil.

2. Crush anise seed by wrapping in aluminum foil and tapping with a hammer.

3. Add sugar and anise to hot milk. Stir to blend well. You can filter out the anise seeds, but most will sink to the bottom of the pot.

Serve hot or cold.

KRULLERS

This recipe from *Harmony Circle Cookbook,* an early twentieth-century fund-raiser in Syracuse, New York, was contributed by Mrs. Ten Eyck. It makes a plain, crisp, eggy fritter that is a lot like the crullers eaten in Dutch colonial America. Only the shape is similar to our cakey crullers of today. Older Dutch-American recipes add a pinch of nutmeg. I have reduced the quantities and filled in details of how to shape the crullers from Peter Rose's book.

CAUTION: Hot oil used.

Yield: 16 krullers
  2 eggs
  3 tablespoons sugar
  3/4 cup flour (packed down)
  oil for deep frying

Equipment: Whisk, board to knead flour, rolling pin, zigzag pie cutter (or see alternate method), deep-fry thermometer, skimmer

1. Beat eggs to a froth.

2. Stir in sugar.

3. Sift in flour, stirring with a wooden spoon.

4. When dough comes together, turn it out onto the floured board and knead like a bread dough.

5. When it is smooth, flour the rolling pin and roll out the dough 1/4-inch thick. (Alternate method: Instead of Steps 5-7, when dough is smooth, cut into 16 pieces. Roll each into a 6-inch rope. Fold each rope in half, and twist the ends in opposite directions to create a more familiar-looking spiral cruller. Proceed with Steps 8-10.)

6. With the pie cutter ("jaggered iron"), cut into strips 1/2-inch wide and 3 inches long.

7. Twist 2 strips together to form each spiraled cruller.

8. Heat the oil to 350 degrees and deep fry the crullers until golden brown.

9. Take them out carefully, and put them on a large dry platter.

10. Sprinkle pulverized sugar over them while hot.

Serve hot.

COLE SLAW

Also from *Eet Smakelijk,* this interesting cole slaw uses an old-fashioned hot dressing. The recipe was contributed by Mrs. Paul Heyboer and Cecilia Guss. I would guess that this recipe has been halved or quartered for the book.

NOTE: Make two hours ahead, or the previous night.

Yield: serves 4-6
  cabbage to make 2 cups shredded
  1 tablespoon grated onion
  1/2 teaspoon salt
  1/2 cup sugar
  1/2 cup vinegar
  1/2 cup water
  1 tablespoon celery seed
  2 tablespoons celery
  2 tablespoons cucumber
  2 tablespoons green pepper
  1 tomato

Equipment: box grater, cabbage cutter or chef's knife, or food processor with shredding and grating blades, saucepan.

1. Shred cabbage to make 2 cups.

2. Grate on "a little onion for flavoring"

3. Combine the next 5 ingredients in a saucepan and bring to a boil.

4. Pour dressing over shredded cabbage and onion.

5. Slice celery, cucumber, and green pepper into fine slices, and mix in with cabbage.

6. "Let stand overnight, or at least a couple hours."

7. Slice tomato and add when ready to serve.

Dutch Appel Koek

This is an adaptation of a contemporary Dutch quick bread by Mrs. Adrian Schagen of Pella, Iowa, for the book, *How Iowa Cooks*, compiled by the Tipton Women's Club in 1964. Mrs. Schagen describes her cake as "one that is always on hand in a Dutch home. A homey sort of every-day cake, it is a little tough, quite chewy, and not very sweet. It is delicious." Despite a number of different flavors, this recipe comes out as a mild spice cake similar to some banana breads. In Holland and elsewhere in the American Midwest, this cake is apt to be lighter, with nuts and chopped apples as well as raisins.

Yield: a large 9 by 13 sheet cake, or 2 large loaves
  2 cups hot applesauce
  1/2 cup shortening (I used margarine)
  2 cups sugar
  1 1/2 teaspoons baking soda
  1 tablespoon hot water
  3 tablespoons cocoa
  1 teaspoon cinnamon
  1 teaspoon ground cloves
  1/2 teaspoon nutmeg
  1/2 teaspoon baking powder
  3 1/2 cups flour
  1 cup raisins
  shortening to grease baking pan(s)

Equipment: Pastry blender or large fork to cream shortening and sugar, a 9 by 13 cake pan or 2 large loaf pans, toothpick or wire cake-tester

1. Grease baking pan or loaf pans.

2. Combine sifted dry ingredients except for sugar and baking soda in one bowl.

3. Cream sugar and shortening together with a large fork until fluffy and well mixed. (Leave margarine or butter out to soften, or microwave on defrost setting to soften.)

4. Dissolve baking soda in hot water and mix into applesauce.

5. Stir applesauce into sugar mixture.

6. Stir dry ingredients into sugar-applesauce mixture, and mix well.

7. Mix in raisins.

8. Bake at 325 degrees for 40 minutes in cake pan, 10 minutes longer in loaf pans.

9. Test with a cake-tester or toothpick, which should come out clean when cake is done.

Serve in slices without frosting.

St. Nickolas Koekjes

We must have a recipe for Dutch cookies. These are again from Mrs. Schagen, and are a somewhat richer and less spicy version of the Dutch "speculaas" that are pressed into wooden forms to make windmills and little St. Nicks for the December 6 celebration of St. Nicholas Day. What is American about them is that Mrs. Schagen makes them "the easy way," as refrigerator cookies, so now they are every-day cookies. Many recipes have almond slivers worked into the dough before baking.

Yield: about 40 slices of refrigerator cookies, more if you roll them out, or use a speculaas mold
  2 cups shortening
  2 1/2 cups sugar
  1 cup sour cream
  6 cups flour
  2 teaspoons baking soda
  4 teaspoons cinnamon
  1/2 teaspoon cloves
  1 teaspoon nutmeg

Equipment: Pastry blender or large fork, waxed paper, cookie sheets, cookie molds (if using), rolling pin and cookie cutters (if rolling out)

1. Cream shortening and sugar.

2. Sift together dry ingredients.

3. Add sour cream alternately with sifted dry ingredients to make a stiff dough.

4. Form into 2 rolls, each 12 inches long and 3 inches in diameter.

5. Roll in waxed paper and chill.

6. Slice 1/4-inch slices, or a little fatter, and lay out well-spaced onto a cookie sheet.

7. Bake 10-20 minutes at 350 degrees. They will spread and seem soft even when they are done, but they will crisp up as they cool down.

8. If using speculaas molds, take chilled dough, but instead of Step 6, flour the molds and press dough carefully into the forms. Cut away the excess dough. Knock out the cookies in one piece. Resume at Step 7.

9. If rolling out the cookies, roll thinly and cut with cookie cutters. Bake as Step 7.

Serve with milk.

DUTCH CARROTS

The family of William J. Beukema submitted this recipe to *The Shaw House Cookbook: A Collection of Choice Receipts from a Golden Era of St. Louis Living* (1963) by Marian Maeve O'Brien. It is another case of a subtle balance of spices.

    4 medium-sized carrots
    2 tablespoons butter
    1/2 teaspoon salt
    1/8 teaspoon white pepper
    1/4 teaspoon cinnamon
    1/2 teaspoon sugar

Equipment: Carrot peeler, food processor with slicing disk (optional)

1. "Remove the outer skin of the carrots by scraping (with a paring knife, or peel with peeler)—this is important to retain the full flavor of the carrots."

2. Slice "not thicker than 1/4 inch" (or use food processor with a slicing disk that cuts 1/4-inch slices) into the saucepan full of cold water.

3. Bring to a boil and cook "until tender" (about 5 minutes coming to the boil, and 5 more minutes for somewhat old carrots).

4. Drain off all the water and add the butter at once while the carrots are still hot.

5. "Scatter the seasoning ingredients into the vegetables in the order given, so that the butter may carry them down through the vegetables."

6. "When ready to place in the serving dish, give the whole a couple of quick stirs to assure that the seasoning is well mixed."

Serve as a side dish.

ECUADORIAN-AMERICANS

Most Ecuadorians in the U.S. are recent arrivals, although the 1990 census estimated 190,000 persons claiming Ecuadorian ancestry. The real number may be twice as high, with about half living in greater New York City, where Ecuadorians have some visibility as street vendors. Ecuador has a Pacific coast with a tropical climate, and an Amazonian jungle interior, but is mostly high Andes with an Indian culture like that of Peru. Ecuadorian-American dishes include ceviche (raw seafood in lime juice), fried pork with hominy, clear soups, stews with garlic and chile sauce, tamales, and steamed corn cakes called quimbolitos.

LLAPINGACHOS

These stuffed potato tortillas are popular street snacks in Ecuador and New York City. This recipe is from the personal Web site of Jorge Andrade Tapia, a University of New Mexico faculty member who attributes the recipe to his friend Marcelo Villacrés. I have translated from Spanish and added substitutions. As a street snack, llapingachos are usually colored with achiote (see Locro recipe, below) and served with a peanut butter sauce.

Yield: serves 6 to 8
    2 pounds potatoes (waxy red potatoes best)
    1/2 pound "queso fresco" (substitute
        mozzarella, muenster, or Monterey jack)

2 eggs
2 tablespoons margarine
1/4 cup lard or olive oil to fry potato cakes

Equipment: Skillet

1. Peel potatoes and boil in salted water until fork tender.

2. Drain and mash.

3. Grate cheese and mix well with the margarine.

4. Beat the eggs and mix with the potatoes.

5. Make 12 potato balls.

6. Poke a hole in each one with your thumb and fill it with a heaping tablespoon of the cheese mixture.

7. Close up the hole and flatten the potato ball into a patty.

8. Let it rest for 15 minutes.

9. Melt a little lard or olive oil in a skillet, and fry the patties over medium heat until they are golden brown on both sides, about 6 minutes. Add oil by tablespoonfuls as it is used up.

10. Drain on paper towels.

Serve with a roast or steak, with a lettuce salad, and slices of avocado, or for breakfast with fried eggs and sausage.

EL LOCRO GRINGO

Locro is a soupy potato or vegetable stew with a rich cheese sauce. Like llapingachos, locro is an important food for Ecuadoran immigrants because it can be made with potatoes available in the United States, whereas much Ecuadoran cuisine requires special potatoes or other high-altitude produce. This recipe comes from David Chiriboga, a second-generation Ecuadoran-American who grew up in suburban Boston, where his family began using sharp cheddar cheese instead of the mild white cheese of Ecuador. The recipe was published in *Latin American Cooking Across the U.S.A.* by Himilce Novas and Rosemary Silva.

2 medium yellow onions

1 large garlic clove
1 1/2 tablespoons olive oil
1 teaspoon ground achiote seeds (or paprika)
3 pounds russet potatoes (Idaho baking type)
1 quart chicken stock or water
1 cup milk
1 cup grated white cheddar cheese (or about 1/4 pound of cheese)
1/2 cup minced fresh cilantro

Equipment: Saucepan, mortor-and-pestle or coffee grinder, slotted spoon

1. Halve, peel, and mince onion.

2. Peel and mince garlic clove.

3. Heat the olive oil in a saucepan and sauté the onions and garlic until limp, about 10 minutes.

4. If using achiote seeds, boil 5 minutes to soften, drain, and grind in a mortar-and-pestle or a coffee grinder cleaned out with rice. Add achiote or paprika to onion mixture.

5. Peel potatoes and cut into 1-inch cubes.

6. Add potatoes and stock or water to onions, bring to a simmer, cover, reduce heat, and simmer for 25 to 30 minutes, until potatoes are fork tender.

7. With a slotted spoon, move half the cooked potatoes to a mixing bowl.

8. Mash the potatoes in the mixing bowl, and whisk in 1/2 cup of the cooking liquid.

9. Return this thickener to the saucepan, stir in the milk, and cook the soup over medium heat until hot but not boiling.

10. Stir in the grated cheese and remove the soup from the heat.

11. Season to taste with salt and pepper.

Serve in bowls garnished with cilantro or avocado. Chiriboga's children garnish with buttered popcorn!

Egyptian-Americans

A lmost all Egyptian-Americans are recent immigrants, and have arrived at a rate that is hard to count. The first notable groups were Coptic Christians arriving in the late 1960s and settling visibly in New Jersey and New York. The ancestry survey of the 1990 census projected 78,000 Egyptian Americans, but more recent estimates range from 200,000 to 2 million Egyptian-Americans, with visible communities in Houston and Florida, and across the American sunbelt.

Egyptian food is distinctive, and has a long heritage. Flatbreads and bean stews depicted in ancient paintings and inscriptions are still eaten, along with a variety of foods recognizable to most **Arab-Americans** and highly-spiced and sophisticated stews like those of North African countries.

FALAFEL (FRIED BEAN CAKES)

Falafel is the Egyptian version of deep-fried bean cakes (see Appendix 3, "They All Fried Bean Cakes") and one of the oldest fried foods known. Sandy Bateh contributed this recipe to *Friends of Barnett Favorite Recipes*, compiled in 1988 by the Barnett Bank of Jacksonville, Florida, to benefit Ronald McDonald House. Egyptians use a hot chile pepper, like a serrano or jalapeño, but you can get an idea of falafel with a mild frying pepper. Falafel in a slightly different form is also popular among Israeli-Americans.

CAUTION: Hot oil used.

    4 cups chick peas (dried)
    2 large onions
    1 whole head garlic
    2 bunches parsley
    hot green pepper (to suit taste)
    2 teaspoons cumin powder
    salt and pepper (to taste)
    1 teaspoon baking powder
    1/4 teaspoon baking soda
    oil for frying
    tomato slices and Arabic flatbread (pita) to
       make sandwiches

Equipment: Electric meat grinder or food processor, heavy pot with deep sides

1. Soak the chick peas overnight.

2. Halve and peel the onions.

3. Peel the garlic.

4. Chop the parsley roughly.

5. Stem and halve the green chile pepper. Scrape out the seeds and pith with a teaspoon. Cut into small pieces. Wash hands carefully and don't touch eyes or sensitive body parts after handling hot peppers!

6. Drain the chick peas, and combine with onions, garlic, parsley, and hot pepper.

7. If using electric meat grinder, grind twice. If using a food processor, process in batches to what looks like a thick cornmeal batter. Stir batches together in a large bowl.

8. Add salt, pepper, cumin, and baking powder; mix thoroughly.

9. When ready to fry the falafel, mix in baking soda.

10. Shape into patties 1 1/2 inches in diameter and 1/2-inch thick.

11. Heat an inch of oil in a deep-sided, heavy pan.

12. Dip skimmer in oil, put on a bean patty, and lower carefully into the hot oil to avoid splashing.

13. Fry in deep, hot oil until light brown and crisp.

14. Drain on paper towels well away from the stove.

Serve hot with tomato slices in Arabic bread in the form of a sandwich.

Eggplant and Zucchini Salad

This eastern Mediterranean classic comes from Shafik Rifaat of Houston via *A Taste of the Gulf Coast* by Jessie Tirsch. The **Greek-American** version of this dish uses just zucchini and a related garlic sauce called skordalia. This recipe works best with fresh, rock-hard vegetables. Small Asian eggplants are good this way.

CAUTION: Hot oil used.

Yield: 2 or 3 lunch servings or 4 side servings
   1/2 cup plain nonfat yogurt
   1 tablespoon minced garlic (6 medium
      cloves)
   1 teaspoon chopped fresh mint leaves
   1/4 teaspoon salt
   1 medium eggplant (about 3/4 pound)
   2 small zucchini (about 1/2 pound)
   1 cup vegetable oil

Equipment: Small bowl, high-sided pan
   1. Peel and mince garlic to get a tablespoon.

2. Chop mint leaves.

3. Combine yogurt, mint, garlic, and salt in a small bowl. Cover and allow the flavors to mingle.

4. Rinse and dry eggplant and zucchini.

5. Slice eggplant in 1/4-inch-thick rounds.

6. Cut ends off zucchini and take a half-inch slice the long way from one side.

7. Roll zucchini onto the cut side, and slice into long half-inch thick slices.

8. Heat oil very hot in a high-sided pan.

9. Fry the vegetables in batches until light golden brown on both sides, 6-9 minutes.

10. Drain on paper towels.

11. "Mound eggplant slices in the center of a serving dish, and arrange the zucchini in spokes radiating out from the eggplant."

12. Spoon the dressing over the eggplant and zucchini.

El Salvadoran-Americans

See Salvadoran-Americans

English

See Anglo-Americans (English), Cornish-Americans, Welsh-Americans

English Canadian-Americans

About 500,000 Americans list English-Canadian ancestry, apart from more than 2 million Americans of French-Canadian background (see also **French Canadian-Americans**). The Immigration and Naturalization Service also estimated that 120,000 Canadians are in the United States without legal documents, the fourth largest such group. Because Canada itself is a nation of immigrants, and because the long border was barely policed until recent decades, many ethnic groups have come to the United States through Canada. Thus many immigrants from Newfoundland identi-fied with the **Irish-American** community, many from Nova Scotia and Ontario with the **Scottish-American** community, and other Canadian immigrants would probably list themselves now as **Jewish-American, Icelandic-American,** or **Asian Indian-American,** among many others. Many Cana-dians originally came from the United States, beginning with about 20,000 British loyalists who went to Nova Scotia during the American Revolution, and a number of **African-American** slaves who took the Underground Railway to freedom in Canada between 1830 and 1860. Some Native American groups with bands in both the U.S. and Canada include the **Eskimo, Tlingit, Haida, Sioux,** Blackfeet, **Ojibway, Potawatomi, Iroquois,** and Mi'kmaq.

NANAIMO BARS— CHOCOLATE SQUARES

These rich, no-bake, three-layered desserts are descended from "ribbon cake" and "refrigerator cake" recipes, but actually come from Nanaimo Island in British Columbia. A 1952 fund-raising cookbook from the island had three recipes for chocolate squares and chocolate slices that were reprinted under the name "Nanaimo Bars" in the Vancouver *Sun* newspaper. The recipes were then taken up by Canadian food companies, but cooks in western Canada keep making them and even have contests for the best new variations, including the use of cherries, peanut butter, al-monds, pistachio nuts, mint, and pina colada mix. English Canadians moving to the United States have figured out how to substitute instant vanilla pudding for the Bird's Custard Powder they would buy in Canada. This recipe comes mostly from *The Ahern Girls Family Cookbook* edited by Bernadette M. Giuffrida (Marblehead, Massachusetts, 1991).

CAUTION: Egg is not always fully cooked. Substitute pasteurized egg equivalent if at risk for infections.

Yield: 16 bars or about 60 squares
First layer:
1/2 cup butter (one stick)
1/3 cup cocoa
1 egg (or equivalent)
1 cup shredded coconut
1/3 cup chopped walnuts
1/4 cup sugar
1 teaspoon vanilla extract
3 cups graham cracker crumbs

Second layer:
1/2 cup butter (at room temperature for an hour)
3 tablespoons milk
2 cups confectioner's sugar
2 tablespoons instant vanilla pudding mix

Top layer:
4 ounces semi-sweet chocolate (or chocolate chips)
1 tablespoon butter

Equipment: 9 by 9-inch square brownie pan, heat-safe mixing bowl that fits into a pot (or double boiler), whisk, large fork or pastry blender to cream butter, microwave oven (optional), flexible spatula for spreading

1. For first layer, place butter, sugar, cocoa, egg, and vanilla in a mixing bowl. Stir well with whisk.

2. Set dish in boiling water and stir until but-ter has melted and mixture resembles thin cus-tard (or melted ice cream), at least 5 minutes.

3. Combine graham cracker crumbs, coco-nut, and walnuts and blend well.

4. Add to custard mixture, and stir well.

5. Butter the square pan, and pack the first layer evenly into it. Refrigerate 15 minutes to set.

6. To make second layer, cream butter with fork or pastry blender.

7. Combine milk and vanilla pudding mix. Add to creamed butter.

8. Blend in confectioner's sugar.

9. Spread over the first layer and refrigerate about 15 minutes or until firm.

10. To make top layer, melt chocolate and butter in cleaned out double boiler, or in microwave oven (medium setting, 3 minutes).

11. Spread over the second layer.

12. When set, put in refrigerator for at least 1 hour, or overnight.

Serve cut into bars or one-inch squares.

LEMON COOKIES

Lemon cookies have been popular in English Canada for at least 100 years. They can also be done as drop cookies, and cooked for 15-20 minutes. This recipe comes from *As the World Cooks: Recipes from Many Lands* (1938), published by the International Institute of Lowell, Massachusetts. The International Institute was a division of the YWCA that worked with immigrant women, and at this time published cookbooks in a number of cities, many with contributed recipes by both recent immigrants and leading members of ethnic communities.

4 cups flour
"1 teacupful of butter" (1/4 pound, or 1 stick)
3 eggs
1 tablespoon lemon juice
1 cup sugar
1/2 teaspoon baking soda
1 tablespoon milk
1 tablespoon lemon rind

Equipment: Round cookie cutter, grater or lemon zester, pastry blender or large fork, rolling pin and surface, baking sheet

1. Soften butter at room temperature for a half hour or more.

2. Work flour into butter.

3. Beat eggs until "very light."

4. Beat eggs into flour mixture.

5. Dribble on lemon juice and sugar, then mix them in well.

6. Grate lemon to get the tablespoon of rind, mix it with a little more sugar and set aside.

7. Grease a baking sheet.

8. Dissolve the baking soda in a tablespoon of milk.

9. Work that quickly into the dough. "Use no other liquid."

10. Flour board and rolling pin and roll out the dough very thin.

11. Cut out rounds with the cookie cutter or a large-mouthed glass jar.

12. Sprinkle each round with some of the lemon rind mixture.

13. Arrange on baking sheets.

14. Bake at 375 degrees for 5-8 minutes.

ESKIMOS (INUIT) AND ALEUTS

According to the 1990 census, 53,000 Eskimos live in the United States, almost all in Alaska. Because Eskimo means "raw meat eaters," the term Inuit ("the people") has become the preferred form in Canada. Alaskan Eskimos are divided linguistically into the Inupiak and Yu'pik subgroups. A few thousand Aleuts from the Aleutian Islands speak a related language. Most Eskimos live in a network of about 600 villages across north and west Alaska, but about 20 percent now live and work in Alaskan cities. Although traditional foods and lifestyles are available, and hunting and fishing are very much part of Eskimo identity, Eskimo villages now have electricity and modern conveniences, and Eskimo recipes are making more use of vegetables and spices from elsewhere. "Eskimo ice cream" is the best-known Native Alaskan dish, made from berries whipped with the fat rendered from certain fish or from seal oil or reindeer tallow, and frozen to make a high-calorie treat. The availability of canned fruit has brought new creativity to Eskimo ice cream. Eskimo doughnuts are much like other doughnuts, but fried in local fats. Eskimo cooks use a practical curved knife called an "ulu," which means "woman's knife." It resembles a European chopping knife or pizza cutter. I have also seen an Aleut recipe for a Russian-influenced fish pie similar to the **Tlingit** perok.

CHUGACH SALMON CHOWDER

Anthropologist Federica de Laguna collected this recipe from her Yu'pik interpreter, Ma Tiedeman, at Prince William Sound, Alaska, in 1933. Ma Tiedeman was the daughter of Chief Makari of the Chugash. Her chowder shows the influence of New England whaling ships, which visited Alaska and traded with Eskimos in the nineteenth century; the recipe also shows that items like onions, rice, and pasta were becoming more available. This recipe is from *The Anthropologists' Cookbook*.

Yield: serves 4 as a soup/stew
    1 pound fillets of salmon, cut in chunks
    4-5 strips fat bacon, cut in small pieces
    1 onion, finely sliced
    2-4 ounces elbow macaroni, spaghetti, or rice

Equipment: Kettle

1. Fry bacon in the kettle.

2. Add onion and cook until soft and yellow.

3. Add fish and macaroni (or rice or broken spaghetti) and water to cover.

4. Bring to a simmer, and add more water as the macaroni swells up.

Serve with "hard tack." (Nabisco Crown Pilot crackers are a supermarket substitute.)

CRANBERRIES (KEE-MEE-NACH)

This recipe and the next come from the 1952 *Eskimo Cookbook* by students of the Shishmaref Day School, Shishmaref, Alaska (1995 reprint by Southold Indian Museum, Southold, New York, 19 pages). Shishmaref is a seaside village in western Alaska with a current population of almost 500. To compile the book, students brought in family recipes to earn points in a school contest. Most of the other recipes in the book are for local plant and animal products, or for dishes like doughnuts fried in seal oil. However, non-Alaskan ingredients like flour, curry powder, catsup, and Campbell's soup were appearing in some families. These two recipes from student Agnes Kiyutelluk are dishes used by Inupiak Eskimo families that can be made from widely available ingredients.

    1 pound cranberries
    1 1/2 cups sugar
    1 tablespoon flour

1. Put the cranberries in a pan and add 2 cups of water.

2. Bring them to a boil.

3. Then mash them.

4. Mix flour and water, and add to the cranberries.

5. Also add sugar while they are boiling.

WHITE FISH SOUP

Most Eskimo recipes for fish are simply boiled, baked, or frozen raw. (Nellie Kigrook's family also made a fish soup with curry power and thickening.)

    2 pounds of whole or steaked white fish, such as flounder, cod, halibut, or freshwater whitefish or bass
    1 or more tablespoons curry powder
    2 tablespoons flour

1. Cut white fish into chunks and wash it.

2. Then put it into a pot and add 6 cups of water and salt to taste.

3. Boil it until it is just beginning to fall apart. Remove fish from soup.

4. Take fish off the bones. Make the fish into little pieces.

5. Mix flour and curry powder with a little water, and add this to the soup.

6. Simmer until thickened, then return fish to the soup to heat through.

Serve as soup.

ESTONIAN-AMERICANS

O
nly 27,000 Americans claimed Estonian ancestry on the 1990 census, although some estimate the group as high as 200,000. Estonia is one of the smallest countries in Europe, with
about 1.5 million people today. The Estonian language is closest to Finnish, but the country was conquered by Germans and then was in the Swedish and Russian empires for most of modern history. Many of the first Estonians to reach the United States, in the 1880s and 1890s, came
from other parts of Russia to which they had migrated to escape harsh treatment in Estonia. They
were joined by political refugees after the failed Russian Revolution of 1905. Estonia was independent from 1918 to 1940, but another 15,000 Estonian refugees were admitted to the United States
between 1940 and 1965; they were fleeing Nazism, Communism, or both. Estonia has been independent again since 1992, using the same constitution it wrote in the late 1930s.

About half of all Estonian-Americans are thought to live in the Washington-Boston corridor, with
many of the rest in the Midwest in Scandinavian and Lutheran communities. Traditional Estonian
foods emphasize seafood, dairy products, and salt, and are surprisingly devoid of seasonings like
pepper or even onions. Many **Lithuanian-American**, **Latvian-American**, and **Russian-American** dishes
will be familiar to Estonian-Americans. Another typical Estonian dish is sült, jellied cold veal or
pork.

ROSOLJE

Rosolje is a beet and potato salad that balances
the flavors of salted herring and fresh roast beef.
This recipe is from the *Mystic Seaport Global
Feast Cookbook*. The sauce will turn pink when
stirred up with the beets.

NOTE: The salted herring needs to be soaked
overnight.

  3 beets
  6 potatoes
  2 eggs
  1 cup sour cream
  1 teaspoon mustard
  1/2 teaspoon sugar
  1/4 teaspoon pepper
  1 tablespoon vinegar
  4 dill pickles
  2 apples
  2 cups cooked roast beef (or bologna)
  1/2 onion
  1 salted herring (soaked overnight) or
     pickled herring

1. Cut off roots and all but one inch of stem
on the beets. Boil until fork tender, as much as
an hour for large beets.

2. If potatoes show a lot of green, peel them.
Otherwise cook whole in another pot until fork
tender, about 30 minutes.

3. Hard boil eggs with potatoes, about 15
minutes.

4. In a small bowl, combine sour cream, vinegar, mustard, sugar, and pepper. Mix well and
set aside.

5. Peel and mince onion.

6. Chop roast beef or bologna into small
cubes.

7. Slice and chop dill pickles.

8. Slice and chop apples.

9. Cool eggs under cold running water. Shell
and chop.

10. Cool potatoes, and chop into 1/2-inch dice.

11. Cool beets under running water, rub off
skins, and cut into 1/2-inch dice.

12. Chop herring.

13. Combine all ingredients except dressing
in a large bowl.

14. Pour on sour cream dressing, mix gently.

Serve immediately, or chill overnight.

Pancakes

Estonian pancakes are thin, like Scandinavian and French pancakes (and unlike German or Russian pancakes). This recipe is from the personal Web page of Madis Rehepapp, a graduate assistant at Bentley College. The Estonian name for these is "pannkoogid."

  4 eggs
  1 quart milk
  about 2 cups wheat flour
  2 tablespoons sugar
  1 teaspoon salt
  2 ounces cooking oil or melted butter (and a little more to fry pancakes)

Equipment: Skillet, baking pan

  1. Beat eggs.

  2. Add milk, sugar, salt, and flour while stirring.

  3. Mix in the oil or butter. Let the mix stand for a half hour.

  4. Melt a little butter or flour in a skillet.

  5. Pour mix into hot pan, making thin cakes.

  6. Turn to brown on both sides.

Serve with jam, ice cream, honey, or whipped cream.

Ethiopian- and Eritrean-Americans

After a 30-year civil war, Eritrea became independent from Ethiopia in 1993. Fighting still occasionally breaks out between the two countries and some hard feelings linger among immigrant groups in the United States even though most Ethiopian-Americans were refugees from the Ethiopian Communist dictatorship (1974-1991) that did most of the fighting. In the 1990 census, there were only about 35,000 Ethiopians and Eritreans, but a 1995 estimate put the number closer to 100,000, the second-largest group of recent black African immigrants in the U.S.

Few Ethiopians came to the United States as slaves, in part because Ethiopia was never colonized by European countries, other than a brief Italian occupation in the 1930s and 1940s. Besides Amhara-speaking Ethiopians and Eritreans, the former Kingdom of Ethiopia contained hundreds of ethnic and language groups, including an ancient Jewish community that has mostly emigrated to Israel since the 1980s. Ethiopian and Eritrean food is based on sourdough pancakes called injera, which are used to enfold smaller amounts of stew so that people can eat with the right hand. Complicated spice mixtures are typical, and a lot of Ethiopian food is very hot, even as served in restaurants in Washington D.C., New York, Boston, and Toronto.

Injera

The large Ethiopian community in Washington, D.C., has developed bakeries for injera. This recipe is a reliable counterfeit by Wube Kumsa of Portsmouth, New Hampshire.

Yield: 5 9-inch pancakes
  1 cup buckwheat pancake mix
  1 cup biscuit mix
  1 egg
  2 tablespoons oil

Equipment: Clean brush, oven-proof skillet, 15-inch tray (optional)

  1. Preheat oven to 325 degrees. Mix together the mixes.

  2. Beat egg with one tablespoon of the oil and 1 1/2 to 2 cups of water to get "easy pouring consistency."

  3. Bring a 10-inch skillet or a handled griddle pan to a medium heat uniformly over the flame. Do not let the pan get too hot.

4. Spread 1/2 teaspoon of oil over the pan with a brush.

5. Fill a measuring cup (with spout) or a large cream pitcher with batter.

6. Pour the mixture on the hot pan or griddle in a thin stream starting from the outside and going in a circle to the center from left to right. Pancakes should be 9 inches in diameter.

7. As soon as it bubbles uniformly all over remove from heat.

8. Place the pan in the oven for about 1 minute until the top is dry but not brown.

9. Repeat until 5 pancakes are done.

To serve, "arrange the five pancakes overlapping each other so as to completely cover a fifteen-inch tray." Heaps of stews and other foods are arranged on the injera tray. Diners tear off pieces of injera with the right hand, and use it to scoop some of the stews.

ATAKELTE

Atakelte is a vegetable dish eaten by Ethiopian Coptic Christians during Lent, and as a side dish. This recipe comes from Ms. Bennet Yohannes, a student member of the International Food Club at the Piney Woods Country Life School, via the book *Soul and Spice: African Cooking in the Americas* by Heidi Haughy Cusick. The technique of steaming before frying appears in several Ethiopian recipes.

Yield: serves 6
  1/2 head green cabbage
  1 yellow onion
  2-3 tablespoons vegetable oil
  1 cup canned tomato sauce
  2 carrots
  2 potatoes (optional)
  cayenne pepper or ground red chile pepper
    (optional)

1. Cut the cabbage into 3 sections, and shred by cutting thin slices across each section.

2. Put the cabbage in a saucepan that just fits with a little water and cook tightly covered, stirring frequently, "until soft," about 5 minutes.

3. Halve, peel, and chop the onion.

4. Put the onion in a skillet with a little water, and cook until the water evaporates, about 5 minutes.

5. Reduce the heat to medium, stir in the oil, and cook until the onions are just beginning to brown, about 4-5 minutes longer.

6. Peel and chop carrots and potatoes, if using.

7. Add tomato sauce, a half cup water, and the optional carrots and potatoes to the onions.

8. Simmer to blend flavors and cook vegetables, 10-15 minutes

9. Add the steamed cabbage. Sprinkle with salt and cayenne to taste. (Ethiopian taste can be very hot, but this dish is often not spicy to make a contrast.) Mix well, cover, and simmer 10 minutes.

Serve hot in a pile on a tray of injera "or inauthentic pita bread."

AZIFA

This recipe for a mashed lentil salad with spices is from *Exotic Ethiopian Cooking* (1987) compiled by Daniel Jote Mesfin for Ethiopian Cookbook Enterprise in Virginia.

Yield: 6 to 8 servings
  1 1/2 cups green lentils
  3 medium limes
  5 medium green peppers or Anaheim chiles
  3 medium red onions
  1/2 teaspoon black pepper
  1/2 teaspoon powdered ginger
  1 cup cooking oil
  1 tablespoon mustard powder

Equipment: Juicer for limes

1. Pour out lentils on a plate and pick out any random seeds or rocks.

2. Wash lentils in a sieve.

3. Boil lentils in water to cover until they are soft.

4. Remove seeds from peppers with a spoon and cut them into small pieces.

5. Halve, peel, and chop onions into small pieces.

6. Juice limes.

7. Mix all ingredients together and refrigerate.

Serve cold in scoops with injera, or with lettuce, tomatoes, and cottage cheese for a light, diet snack.

FILIPINO-AMERICANS

More than 1.4 million Filipino-Americans, the 10th largest immigrant group by nation of origin, live in the U.S.; they are one of the largest Asian-American immigrant groups, and certainly the fastest growing. Early immigration began in 1899, when the United States took possession of the Philippines from Spain after the Spanish-American War. For 35 years, Filipinos traveled under American passports and came to the United States without restrictions, this at a time when Chinese immigration was banned and Japanese immigrants were increasingly prevented from becoming citizens or buying land. However, anti-Asian attitudes also extended to Filipinos, and half of the 133,000 Filipino contract workers in Hawaii during this period returned home (sometimes with amounts of money that made them substantial landowners back in the Philippines). The mainland population grew later and more slowly; they were mostly agricultural and cannery workers in California and Alaska, with a small but important group of college students and another of Navy employees in Chicago and other shipyard ports.

In 1934, the United States granted the Philippines commonwealth status, and effectively ended large-scale immigration until the 1965 immigration reform acts. The Hawaiian community remained predominantly plantation workers through the 1950s. About 169,000 Filipino-Americans live in Hawaii, the second-largest Asian-American minority. On the mainland, Filipino-American farm workers in California organized the first grape strikes, and united with **Mexican-Americans** in the 1960s United Farm Workers' Organizing Committee. When Filipino immigration expanded in the 1960s, professional employment opened up. English-speaking Filipino nurses who had trained in an American curriculum were able to get licensed for nursing in the U.S., and appeared on the staffs of big city hospitals.

Prior to Spanish and American colonization, the 7,000 islands of the Philippines were already home to a multi-ethnic society, with perhaps 60 dialects. Tagalog has been the national language since independence in 1948, and is also the home language of people from around Manila. Ilocanos from northern Luzon are thought to be the majority of Filipino-Americans, and Visayan-speakers from the central islands are the next-largest ethnic sub-group. Filipino Americans have sometimes settled by language groups, so regional cooking differences may appear in American cities.

Filipino-American cooking partakes of many influences, with some Chinese-Spanish dishes that are the original "Pacific Rim fusion food." So far, the most apparent Americanization has been the emphasis of chicken and pork adobo over the other 11 variations in *The Philippine Cookbook* by Reynaldo Alejandro! Some other common Filipino-American dishes are pansit (a noodle dish), lumpia (egg rolls), and beef pochero.

Adobo Manok (Chicken)

Adobo is the national dish of the Philippines. The Spanish word "adobo" means "marinade," but many Filipino-American recipes shorten that step. This one, which does require marinating, was contributed by Mrs. Ken Pinckney (Maria Muribus) to the *St. Louis Cookbook: Bicentennial Issue* by the Women's Association of the St. Louis Symphony (1964). Mrs. Pinckney notes that "Adobo, made with chicken or pork, or both, was always served at the Filipino gatherings I attended as a child in San Francisco." This is the author's favorite chicken recipe, and our family has had adobo hundreds of times since my sister-in-law, Judith Music, learned it from a Filipina neighbor in 1978. You can multiply it, remove the skin from the chicken, or omit the browning in Steps 9 through 12.

Yield: serves 4
    1/2 cup vinegar
    1 tablespoon soy sauce
    2 teaspoons salt
    1/2 teaspoon whole black peppercorns
    6 cloves garlic
    2 celery stalks and leaves
    2 bay leaves
    2 1/2- to 3-pound cut-up frying chicken
    about 3 tablespoons flour
    2 tablespoons salad oil

Equipment: Deep pot, frying pan

1. Peel and chop garlic.

2. Chop celery stalks and leaves.

3. Mix the first 6 ingredients in a deep pot.

4. Crumble in the bay leaves.

5. Add chicken pieces, turning to coat well.

6. Let stand for 2 hours, turning now and then.

7. Cover and bring to a boil.

8. Reduce heat to simmer and cook until chicken is barely tender, 30-40 minutes.

9. Take chicken from pan, saving marinade.

10. After chicken has cooled somewhat, coat each piece lightly with flour.

11. Heat oil in a frying pan, and brown chicken pieces on both sides, starting with the thighs and drumsticks.

12. When all the chicken is browned, pour marinade back over chicken.

13. Cook over low heat, uncovered, until sauce is reduced by half, about 40 minutes.

Serve with sauce over white rice.

Cirio's Pork Adobo

This is a rather different adobo from Hawaii, where it seems to have absorbed additional Chinese influence in the use of ginger, and Japanese influence in the use of MSG. The recipe was submitted by Eloise Tungpalan to the 1986 revised edition of *We, the Women of Hawaii Cookbook*, edited by Jean Keys and Adele Davis.

    2 pound pork
    1/3 cup vinegar
    1 tablespoon minced garlic
    1 tablespoon minced ginger
    4 bay leaves
    1/4 teaspoon monosodium glutamate
        (Accent)
    1/4 teaspoon black pepper (coarsely ground)

Equipment: Heavy, covered skillet

1. Peel and mince garlic to make up the tablespoon.

2. Peel an inch section of ginger, cut thin slices, and mince for the tablespoon of ginger.

3. Mix ginger and garlic with vinegar, monosodium glutamate, and black pepper in a plastic container.

4. Crumble in the bay leaves and add some salt.

5. Cut pork into 1-inch cubes.

6. Toss pork cubes in marinade and refrigerate overnight.

7. Place everything in a heavy skillet, and heat over a medium flame, with a cover. Cook slowly, stirring occasionally, until pork is browned on all sides and tender. "Meat will be crispy on out-

side and all the liquid in the pan will be absorbed."

"Serve hot with rice."

"BIBINKA ROYALE" BY ANA

Bibinka is a rich coconut sweet in the Philippines that has become popular among Hawaiians of all backgrounds. It is a common street food in the Philippines. But this version, by Ana Del Mundo, contributed to the 1994 *BAC Bites: A Savory Collection of Northwest Favorites* by the BankAmerica Club Washington, has lost the coconut and become more like cheesecake.

Yield: serves 24
  2 cups Bisquick baking mix
  2 cups sugar
  2 cups milk
  2 tablespoons freshly grated parmesan
    cheese
  1 tablespoon baking powder
  4 eggs
  1 8-ounce package of cream cheese
  1 teaspoon butter
  sugar and parmesan cheese to sprinkle on
    top

Equipment: 13 by 9 baking pan

  1. Mix first 6 ingredients in a bowl until the mixture is free of lumps.

  2. Level off in the baking pan.

  3. Cut the cream cheese into dice.

  4. Scatter cream cheese over the mixture in the pan.

  5. Bake at 350 degrees for 25-30 minutes or until golden brown.

  6. While still warm, spread a teaspoon of butter or margarine on top.

  7. Sprinkle on a bit of sugar and fresh parmesan cheese.

Serve warm in brownie-size squares.

FINNISH-AMERICANS

Although a few Finns were among early American settlers, major immigration did not begin until after the Civil War, and peaked between 1899 and 1917, when Finland became independent after centuries of Swedish and then Russian domination. Finns followed Swedish and Norwegian immigrants into the upper Midwest, and ended up in the northernmost parts of those states as farmers or miners. Later groups moved into industrial work, including a local concentration in the textile industries of central Massachusetts. Some moved to retirement areas around Lantana, Florida, west of Palm Beach, and have been joined by recent immigrants from Finland and Karelia (an eastern province which became part of Russia in 1940) to make up a warm-weather Finnish-American community of about 30,000.

As relative latecomers among Scandanavian immigrants, Finnish-Americans were sometimes the subject of jokes or discrimination, but also have held on to more of their original cooking, which also includes many dairy products, rutabaga and fish puddings, and pickled fish and vegetables. As you will see, two prominent newspaper food editors are of Finnish-American background.

ILMAPUURO (AIR PUDDING)

This dish was immediately popular as soon as Finnish immigrant families discovered the similarity of American cranberries to their lingonberries from home. The lengthy whisking is necessary for what develops into a marshmallow-like foam. As it chills, it becomes like pudding, although it is one of the few Finnish recipes that has no milk or cream in it. Canned and bottled cranberry juice cocktail has since simplified preparation, and raspberry, strawberry, and apple juice versions have developed in Minnesota. As a Finnish-American from Massachusetts recalled for *Folk Foods of Fitchburg* (1964), "In Finland the whipping was done with a beater made of small twigs. . . . The porridge was taken outside and often placed in the snow and whipped for a half hour of so until light and fluffy. Before the days of electric mixers in Fitchburg, one could often see a mother or more often a grandmother sitting on a porch beating away, and we always knew what that family was having for their meal." The Fitchburg community called it "puolukka puuroa," which translates as "lingonberry porridge" or "cranberry whip."

CAUTION: Hot syrupy liquid burns and sticks to skin.

Yield: 18-20 half-cup servings
   2 cups cranberries, or 4 cups cranberry juice cocktail
   1 1/4 cups sugar
   1/2 cup farina or Cream of Wheat

Equipment: Sieve or food mill to strain cranberries, whisk or hand-held mixer or standing mixer

1. If using cranberry juice cocktail, reduce sugar to 3/4 cup and go to Step 4. If using whole cranberries, cook cranberries in 3 cups of water over high heat until the berries pop.

2. Strain berries through a sieve or food mill, measure result, and add water to make up 4 cups.

3. Return to saucepan and add sugar, bringing to a boil and stirring to dissolve sugar.

4. When sugar is dissolved, add farina slowly while stirring with a whisk to avoid lumps.

5. Bring back to a simmer, lower heat, and simmer for 15 minutes, stirring occasionally. Mixture should thicken slightly.

6. Remove mixture from heat and carefully pour into a large mixing bowl (it will triple in volume). Beat with a whisk, hand-held mixer, or

standing mixer at least 20 minutes so that mixture is opaque, light, and foamy.

7. Refrigerate.

Serve cold with cream or whipped cream.

MOIJAKKA

Moijakka is a beef stew that can also be made with fish. The name is unknown in Finland, where a soupy beef stew would be called "lihakeitto." Finnish-American food writer Beatrice Ojakangas suggests that moijakka (also spelled "mojakka" and pronounced "moy-a-ca") may be a Finnish pronunciation of Mulligan Stew! Another Finnish-American food writer, Eleanor Ostman, thinks it "may be the 'Finnglish' way of asking for more of the meat version of the stew served in north woods logging camps, cooked on the back of a wood stove for so long that it looked like something unprintable in a family newspaper." One difference is that moijakka is a clear-broth soup where Mulligan stew usually has a thick gravy. This recipe is a combination of Ojakangas's (in *Country Tastes*), that of Elma Salmi (in Ostman's *Always on Sunday*), and one by John K. Bispala posted on the Internet recipe page of the Camden, Minnesota, *Community News*.

Yield: serves 8
   2 pounds beef stew meat
   shin beef soup bone (optional)
   12 allspice berries
   4 medium potatoes
   4 medium carrots
   4 small onions
   1 small (1/2 pound) rutabaga or turnip (optional)
   1 cup chopped celery
   2 teaspoons salt
   1/4 teaspoon pepper

Equipment: 8-quart spaghetti pot

1. Cut beef stew meat into 1-inch cubes.

2. Add water halfway up the pot, so there is enough room over the meat to skim.

3. Bring to a boil, reduce heat, and begin skimming foam off the surface so the broth will be clear.

4. Quarter potatoes and onions.

5. Peel carrots and cut into 2-inch pieces.

6. Cut celery into 1-inch pieces.

7. If using rutabaga or turnip, cut into 1-inch dice.

8. Add salt and allspice, then vegetables.

9. Cover pot and reduce heat to a simmer for 2-4 hours, until meat is tender.

PULLA

This coffee bread (also called "nisu") is cherished by Finnish-Americans. I have never seen a baking powder quick-bread version, as has happened with so many immigrant yeast-risen coffee breads. This recipe is based on that of St. Paul food editor Eleanor Ostman, who grew up in Hibbing. "My mother didn't need directions to make pulla or "biscuitia" as it was called by northern Minnesota Finns speaking 'Finnglish.' . . . My mother always shelled whole cardamom, then pounded the black seeds in the corner of a dish towel to release their pungent flavor. . . . Powdered cardamom will never produce the flavor of the flecks that make Finnish pulla perfect." Pulla is traditionally braided before baking, but is also sometimes made in plain loaf pans, or into individual knotted pastries.

Yield: 1 large braided bread, 3 smaller braids, or 2 loaf-pan loaves
  4 1/2 to 5 1/2 cups unsifted flour
  1/2 cup sugar
  1/2 teaspoon salt
  2 teaspoons grated lemon peel (optional)
  1 package active dry yeast
  2/3 cup milk
  1/2 cup (1 stick) margarine
  1 teaspoon powdered cardamom (or one tablespoon white or green cardamom pods, or one teaspoon whole cardamom seed)
  3 eggs

solid shortening to grease bowl and baking sheet
milk to brush over completed loaf
2 tablespoons sugar
slivered blanched almonds to sprinkle on top (optional)

Equipment: Saucepan, dish towel and solid rolling pin to crush cardamom by the Ellen Ostman method (or mortar and pestle), sieve for hand-crushed cardamom, baking sheet or 2 loaf pans, electric mixer, rubber spatula, board to knead dough, grater or lemon zester, pastry brush or clean natural paint brush, cake tester or toothpick, wire cooling rack

1. Grate lemon peel or remove it with a lemon zester and cut up fine.

2. In a large bowl, mix 1 1/2 cups flour, 1/2 cup sugar, salt, lemon peel, and undissolved yeast.

3. In the saucepan, combine milk, margarine, and 1/4 cup water. Heat over low heat until liquids are warm (margarine does not need to melt).

4. If you are starting from cardamom pods (Finnish-Americans would use the white ones), shell to get a enough for a teaspoon of black seeds, roll into a clean dish towel, and pound with a solid rolling pin to break them up. Add a teaspoon of ground cardamom (fresh or store bought) to the dry ingredients.

5. Stir warmed liquids into the dry ingredients.

6. With an electric mixer, beat for 2 minutes at medium speed, scraping down sides of bowl a few times.

7. Add eggs and 1/2 cup flour, or enough to make a thick batter.

8. Beat at high speed for 2 minutes, scraping down bowl a few times.

9. Stir in enough additional flour to make a soft bread dough.

10. Turn out onto a lightly floured board and knead (see Appendix 1) for 8-10 minutes by folding dough, pushing through it with both hands,

turning, folding, and pushing again. Dough should become smooth and elastic and lose its stickiness. Roll into a ball.

11. Grease large mixing bowl with shortening, and put in the ball of dough, turning to grease all sides.

12. Cover bowl with a dish towel or other cover and let bread rise in a warm place, free from draft, for about one hour, or until doubled in bulk.

13. Punch dough down to remove large air bubbles.

14. Grease either baking pans or large baking sheet (if braiding).

15. If baking in loaf pans, divide dough in half, shape into loafs, and place in greased pans. (Go on to Step 18.) If baking as one braided loaf, divide dough into fourths, and set one piece aside. If baking as 3 braided loaves, divide dough into thirds.

16. If baking as 1 braid, roll 3 pieces into 20-inch ropes. Braid ropes together. Pinch ends to square off and seal. Place braid on greased cookie sheet. (If baking as 3 braids, divide each third of the dough in three. Roll 3 of the dough parts into 16-inch ropes, pinch together one end, braid into an even loaf, pinch the other end, and turn both ends under. Set on greased cookie sheet. Repeat to make 2 more long braids. Go on to Step 18.)

17. If baking as one braid, divide fourth piece of dough in half again, and roll each half into a 12-inch rope. Twist together, pinch the ends to seal, and place on top of the braid.

18. Brush loaf or loaves with milk, sprinkle with 2 tablespoons sugar and optional almonds.

19. Cover loaf or loaves and let rise for an hour, or until doubled in bulk.

20. Bake large braid or loaf pans in a 350-degree oven for 40-45 minutes, or until done (test with cake tester or toothpick). Bake small braids at 375 degrees for 25 minutes or until golden brown.

21. Remove from pans or cookie sheet and cool on a wire rack.

Serve as coffee cake or dessert.

FRANCO-AMERICANS

The largest Franco-American ethnic groups—**French Canadian-Americans**, Louisiana Creoles, and **Acadians (Cajuns)**—had already become detached from European France before they became residents of the United States. At the same time, French cooking has been an ideal for wealthy Americans throughout the history of the United States, and had influenced the cooking of Great Britain for many centuries before 1776. It is therefore difficult to sort out how much many American or **Anglo-American** dishes—chowders, pot roasts, boiled dinners, cakes, tarts, "French Fries," or "French Toast"—represent Franco-American cooking. In addition, a stream of French chefs have immigrated to the United States since the 1790s, specifically to run restaurants, adding to a culinary influence that is not really ethnic cooking in the usual sense.

Nevertheless, the distinctive cooking of Louisiana Creoles was one of the first American ethnic cuisines to become widely popular, and late-nineteenth-century cookbooks from all over the United States have recipes for jambalaya and gumbo. Because the Louisiana Creole recipes in this book are those most used by groups of Afro-French Americans who are most often called Creoles today, this section contains some other Creole recipes that are less identified with the African-American side of Louisiana French cooking. In fact, Louisianans of all backgrounds are apt to claim as family recipes the dishes assigned in this book to Franco-Americans, Louisiana Creoles, Cajuns (Acadians), **Cane River Creoles**, and **Chitimacha Indians**.

The most notable French immigrants who came directly to the English colonies were Huguenots, Protestant refugees who fled France after the 1685 revocation of the Edict of Nantes, which had promised them religious freedom. They settled all over the East Coast, and generally had learned English and cut ties to French culture by the early 1700s. The prominent Huguenot families in Charleston, South Carolina, and New Paltz, New York, kept up their French lifestyles until and beyond the American Revolution.

HUGUENOT TORTE

This is a Huguenot dish still in general use in the Carolinas and Virginia, and I have seen a **Gullah** recipe for it as well. This recipe from *Charleston Receipts*, edited by Mary Vereen Huguenin and Anne Montague Stoney, was collected by the Junior League of Charleston in 1950 and attributed to "Mrs. Cornelius Huguenin (Evelyn Anderson)." This recipe can be halved, or multiplied. Some modern cooks cut squares and stack two to make something that looks like a brownie.

Yield: serves 16
  4 eggs
  2 cups chopped tart cooking apples
  3 cups sugar
  8 tablespoons flour
  2 cups chopped pecans or walnuts
  5 teaspoons baking powder
  1/2 teaspoon salt
  2 teaspoons vanilla
  whipped cream for serving

Equipment: Two 8 by 12-inch baking pans, spatula, pancake turner, electric mixer or rotary beater

1. Beat whole eggs in electric mixer or with rotary beater until very frothy and lemon-colored. Peel and chop apples.

2. Add other ingredients in above order.

3. Butter baking pans well.

4. Pour batter into baking pans and spread evenly.

5. Bake in 325-degree oven about 45 minutes or until crusty and brown.

6. To serve, slice into squares, scoop up with pancake turner (keeping crusty part on top), pile

on large plate, and cover with whipped cream and a sprinkling of the chopped nuts, or make 16 individual servings.

Serve with whipped cream.

SHRIMP A LA CREOLE

This is the best known Creole recipe, adapted all over the United States for more than 100 years. This recipe is from the *New Orleans Restaurant Cookbook* (1967) by Deirdre Stanforth, who got the recipe from Jimmy Plauché, a seventh-generation French Creole descendent of Haitian refugees and owner of Corinne Dunbar's restaurant.

Yield: serves 6
  3 pounds shrimp
  1 tablespoon shortening
  1 medium-sized onion
  2 strips celery
  1 pod garlic
  1 small bell (green) pepper
  1/2 can tomatoes
  1/2 can tomato paste
  3 sprigs thyme
  1 bay leaf
  1 tablespoon chopped parsley
  1/2 tablespoon sugar
  salt and pepper to taste
  boiled rice

Equipment: Skillet, shrimp peeler (optional)

1. Boil shrimp in water to cover approximately 10 minutes. (This varies with the size of the shrimp. The boiling should be enough to firm them up for cleaning.)

2. Drain, cool, peel, and clean out black vein if desired.

3. Halve, peel, and chop onion.

4. Wash and chop celery.

5. Peel and mince garlic.

6. Remove pith and seeds from green pepper and chop.

7. Melt shortening in a skillet and add onion, celery, garlic, and bell pepper.

8. Sauté 5 minutes and add tomatoes, tomato paste, thyme, bay leaf, parsley, sugar, and salt and pepper.

9. Mix well and add shrimp.

10. Cook rice according to package directions.

11. Simmer 1/2 hour.

Serve in a circle of boiled rice.

PECAN PRALINES

Pralines are candy that looks like a cookie; they were developed in Louisiana more than 200 years ago. Their manufacture and sale became a business for Creoles of color for about 100 years, but I am including them in this section because they were originally identified with French settlers and are Creole in the original sense. This recipe was submitted by the Alcée-Hymel family to *Legends of Louisiana Cookbook* (1987) by Sheila Ainbinder. Directions given are for sea level and a sunny day.

CAUTION: Hot candy sticks and burns.

Yield: approximately 24 pralines
  1 cup white sugar
  1 cup brown sugar
  1/2 cup evaporated milk
  2 tablespoons butter
  1 cup pecan halves
  1/4 teaspoon pure vanilla (extract)
  solid shortening to grease cooling surface

Equipment: Candy thermometer, marble slab or cookie sheets or stoneware plates or foil muffin cups

1. Combine the sugars and milk and bring to a boil, stirring occasionally.

2. Add butter and pecans and cook until syrup reaches 238 degrees.

3. Stir in vanilla and "cool without disturbing until it is somewhat thickened, but not until it loses its gloss."

4. "Drop by tablespoons onto a well-greased flat surface. (A piece of marble is best for this.)" You can use a baking sheet or some stoneware (oven-proof) plates, or foil muffin cups on a baking sheet. "The candy will flatten out into large pralines."

FRENCH

See FRANCO-AMERICANS

FRENCH CANADIAN-AMERICANS

French Canadian-Americans are different from most other American ethnic groups in that most of their ancestors had already come to North America by 1750—long before the United States or Canada became independent. The first large group of French Canadians to arrive in what became the United States were the deported **Acadians (Cajuns)** in 1755. Some French-speaking Canadians have come to the United States in every decade, but the bulk of migration was between 1845 and 1895, with another surge in the 1920s, and mostly to French-Canadian enclaves in New England mill towns. Large communities also exist around Detroit and Miami. **Franco-Americans** have always regarded Quebec, rather than France, as their homeland, despite 200 years of opposition to their economic advancement from English and Canadian governments. Only in the 1970s did French Canadians secure political control of Quebec. French Canadian-Americans were much slower than other immigrants to marry outside their own group, or to give up their language, maintaining separate newspapers and Catholic parochial schools in New England into the 1950s. More than 2 million Americans listed French Canadian ancestry on the 1990 census. Perhaps one-fourth are most comfortable speaking French.

SOUPE AUX POIS

This yellow pea soup is the best-known French Canadian recipe in New England, so popular that a canned brand is sold in supermarkets. This recipe, from Mrs. Emma Tourangeau of Portland, Maine, appeared in the 1985 *Yankee Magazine More Great New England Recipes*. Mrs. Tourangeau indicates that a bay leaf or finely diced carrots or turnip were later additions. Yellow split peas were used because they break up to thicken the soup more quickly.

NOTE: Split peas need to be soaked overnight.

    1 pound yellow split peas
    1/2 pound meaty salt pork
    1 onion
    1-2 cloves garlic (optional)

Equipment: Large pot

1. Soak split peas in water overnight, or at least 10 hours.

2. Drain and rinse.

3. Put split peas in a large pot with salt pork (traditionally in one piece), onion, and garlic.

4. Cover with 3 quarts cold water, and bring to a boil.

5. Reduce to a bare simmer for 2 or 3 hours.

Serve with some of the salt pork in each bowl.

FRENCH CANADIAN RAGOUT

This dish of meatballs in thick gravy is still popular in French Canada, and became a Christmas tradition for the Forget and Archambault families, whose grandparents and great-grandparents settled west of Ft. Pierce, Florida, in 1913. The recipe seems to combine two peasant stews from France. It appears with some other rather old-fashioned Quebecois recipes in *Cracker Cuisine*, compiled by the Saint Lucie Historical Society about 1993. I have checked quantities against New England recipes for "Ragoût de Pieds de Cochon" and "Ragout aux Boulettes."

Yield: serves 8-10
    1 1/2 pounds plain ground pork
    1 large onion
    dash salt
    2-3 tablespoons cinnamon, or to taste
    1/4-1/2 cup flour
    1 1/2 pounds lean ground beef
    2 pigs feet or fresh pork hocks
    dash pepper
    nutmeg, season to taste

Equipment: Heavy skillet

1. Halve and peel onion.

2. Simmer onions and hocks or pig's feet with about 2 quarts of water until meat is tender.

3. Meanwhile, toast flour in a heavy skillet over medium heat or in the oven until it is somewhat browned.

4. Remove meat and onions from stock.

5. Mix pepper and nutmeg with flour.

6. Mix ground beef and pork, cinnamon, and salt together and form into meatballs the size of a large egg.

7. Make the browned flour into a slurry with cold water, and stir rapidly into the hot stock to make "a semi-thick gravy."

8. "Gently add meatballs to the gravy. Stir carefully with long-handled spoon until meatballs are perfectly cooked."

9. Simmer for 15 minutes.

Serve with French bread.

Pork Pie

This recipe was traditional after Midnight Mass on Christmas Eve. French Canadians in the United States began mixing in ground beef and serving the pie at Easter and other family gatherings. It is usually called "tourtière," which might imply a pigeon pie, but probably refers to an oblong dish. The pie is now round in Quebec and everywhere that French Canadians have settled in the United States. The recipe was contributed by Jackie Roy to A *Taste of New Hampshire*, published in 1981 by the New Hampshire Division of the American Cancer Society. It is more usual to add a top crust, which doesn't change the cooking times because the filling is already cooked.

1 1/2 pounds ground pork
1 pound ground beef
1/2 teaspoon allspice
1/2 teaspoon cinnamon
1/4 teaspoon salt
1/4 teaspoon pepper
2 medium potatoes
2 (8-inch) unbaked pie shells

Equipment: Heavy kettle

1. Put ground pork in a large, heavy kettle. Add water to cover and boil 30 minutes, covered, over medium heat. Stir to break up pork and occasionally to keep it from sticking and burning.

2. Add ground beef and seasonings. Continue boiling 1 hour.

3. Peel potatoes and cut into large dice.

4. Add potatoes to the pot, lower heat to a simmer, and cook 20 minutes or until potatoes are soft. Add water if necessary.

5. "Mash all ingredients together."

6. Spoon into pie shells. (If you use a top crust, cut slits for steam to escape.)

7. Bake at 400 degrees for 30 minutes.

Serve hot, or freeze and reheat.

GARIFUNA

See HONDURAN- AND GARIFUNA-AMERICANS

GEECHEE

See GULLAH (GEECHEE AND SEA ISLANDERS)

GERMAN-AMERICANS

The 1990 census projected 58 million Americans claiming German ancestry. This figure took a large jump from previous surveys, which can mostly be attributed to the passage of another decade since World War II and the post-war revelations of Nazi crimes. More people from German-speaking ethnic groups that had viewed themselves as distinct, such as **Pennsylvania Dutch** and **Germans from Russia**, probably just listed "German" as their ancestry, because the figures for those groups were considerably lower than might be expected. Many **Jewish-Americans, Czech-Americans, Swiss-Americans,** and others were originally counted as German immigrants.

German-Americans are the largest immigrant group in the United States, having made up one-seventh of all immigrants between 1820 and 1970. In the early years of the twentieth century, more than 10 percent of all Americans spoke German, and there was a lively German-language press and theater. There was a higher proportion of students in German bilingual education in 1905 than in all such programs in the 1990s. German-Americans settled every part of the United States, married into most other immigrant groups, and thus are part of almost every ethnic food tradition.

Because Germany did not become a united country until 1870, many Germans arrived without strong national loyalties, and were eager to become Americanized. Although groups supported Germany before each of the World Wars, German-Americans generally were willing to fight "the Kaiser" and Hitler, and there was little spying or sabotage. Nevertheless, during much of the twentieth century, an enduring shame over Germany's role in both wars muted expressions of German ethnic pride that had been commonplace during previous periods of U.S. history.

German-Americans contributed such American cultural symbols as Christmas trees and the Easter Bunny, and German cooking had a part in the development of American cheesecakes, hot dogs, hamburgers, meat loaf, potato salad, casseroles, and numerous cakes and cookies.

SAUERBRATEN

Sauerbraten, the best-known German-American recipe, has been widely enjoyed by all Americans for more than 100 years. The long marinating made a flavorful, tender roast from tough cuts of beef. Today's beef is much more tender. This recipe, from the firehouse repertoire of Rich Frenzel, specifies brisket and reduces the amount of vinegar in the marinade relative to older recipes. It also simplifies the traditional gingersnap sauce, but increases the number of gingersnaps. The recipe appeared in the May 19, 1999, issue of the *Daily Southtown* newspaper, and is archived on the paper's Web site. The wine is traditional but can be replaced by water or more salad dressing.

NOTE: Meat needs to marinade for 3 days.

Yield: serves 6-8 Midway Airport firemen
　5 pounds beef brisket or equivalent cut of
　　meat
　1 16-ounce bottle of Italian dressing
　1 cup of your favorite red wine (no cooking
　　wine)(substitute water or more salad
　　dressing)
　4 fresh garlic cloves
　3 tablespoons brown sugar
　10 to 12 gingersnap cookies
　Gravy Master or Kitchen Bouquet

Equipment: Glass or plastic dish deep enough to fit beef roast for marinating, metal roasting pan with cover

1. Place beef roast on the dish and pour Italian dressing and wine over it and marinate for 3 days, turning beef once every day to let beef absorb marinade.

2. After 3 days, remove roast from dish and place in a roasting pan together with garlic and half of the marinade. Cover tightly and cook for 3 hours at 300 degrees.

3. When roast is finished cooking, remove and place on cutting board to cool.

4. Crush gingersnaps to make crumbs.

5. Put roasting pan on top of stove, add 1 cup water, and adjust burner to medium heat. Scrape the bottom of the pan with a spoon to get all the crusty parts into the gravy.

6. Smash the gingersnaps into drippings to make gravy. Whisk gravy until thickened and remove any oil from top of gravy.

7. Add small amount of Gravy Master or Kitchen Bouquet to gravy.

Serve sliced thin with potato pancakes and sautéed red cabbage, or more traditionally with dumplings or noodles.

STEWED RED CABBAGE

This recipe by Mrs. Lina Meier is from *The Art of German Cooking and Baking*, which was first published in 1909 in Milwaukee—the most German large city in the U.S. By the eighth edition in 1946, the book had survived two World Wars and Prohibition, and thus all the recipes had English or French names, but this recipe is still known to many Americans as "Rotkohl."

Yield: 12 one-cup servings
1 head of red cabbage, 4 pounds
half stick butter or "good drippings"
1/2 glass red wine or red wine vinegar
2 tablespoons vinegar
1 tablespoon sugar
2 apples
2 cloves
1 pinch pepper
salt to taste (try 2 teaspoons)
1 tablespoon flour

Equipment: Large soup pot

1. "The bad leaves are cut off, the cabbage cut into half, the heart cut out and the cabbage sliced."

2. Boil 2 cups water in a large soup pot.

3. Add the cabbage and butter or drippings, cover and simmer-steam 1 hour.

4. Add all the other ingredients. Cook 1-2 hours longer, stirring occasionally

5. Ten minutes before serving, add flour, mix well, and stew 10 minutes longer.

6. "Taste the cabbage so that it is neither too sweet nor too sour." Correct with more sugar or vinegar.

LEBKUCHEN

Lebkuchen is a popular German-American spice cake with many local variations. This recipe from my mother-in-law, Helen Vogel, is based on one first set down in a family manuscript cookbook begun in the 1890s. Over four generations in a prominent German-Jewish-American family, the cakes/cookies became lighter, less spicy, and easier to make. Earlier versions contained chocolate, lemon peel, and candied citron.

Yield: 150 or more small cakes
4 eggs
1 pound light brown sugar
1 teaspoon allspice
1/4 pound ground almonds (1/2 cup)
1 teaspoon cinnamon
1 3/4 cups flour
1 1/2 teaspoon baking powder
2 cups confectioner's sugar
a little milk
solid shortening to grease pans

Equipment: Food processor if needed to grind almonds, two 9 by 9 or larger cake pans, 2 mixing bowls, large fork or whisk, flexible spatula to spread icing

1. If unable to purchase ground almonds, process whole or slivered almonds in food processor to a coarse grind.

2. Beat eggs thoroughly in mixing bowl.

3. Add brown sugar and beat.

4. Stir in allspice, ground almonds, cinnamon.

5. Sift together flour and baking powder, and stir into the rest.

6. Grease pans with solid shortening and dust lightly with flour.

7. Pour and spread dough evenly about 1/4-inch thick.

8. Bake 15 minutes in a 350-degree oven.

9. As soon as lebkuchen are baked, add milk by spoonfuls to the powdered sugar, just enough to wet it (which is very little) and stir.

10. Pour this icing over the top of the hot cakes and spread to cover.

11. Cool and cut into small squares

Serve with cookies.

HOPPEL-POPPEL

Ghana-born food writer Dorinda Hafner collected this recipe for her television series and book, *United Tastes of America*. She got the recipe from the German-American community of New Ulm, Minnesota. This hearty farmer's breakfast is also known as hoppel-poppel in Germany.

Yield: serves 6-8

1/2 cup corn or other vegetable oil
8 small potatoes
6 tablespoons butter
1 large onion
2 large green bell peppers
6 ounces mushrooms
8 ounces all-beef salami, preferably German
10 large eggs, well beaten
2 tablespoons milk
2 tablespoons fresh parsley
8 ounces cheddar cheese
salt and pepper

Equipment: Grater, large skillet or frying pan

1. Peel and slice potatoes into thick slices.

2. Heat oil in a large skillet or frying pan and fry the potato slices over medium heat until they turn brown.

3. Halve and peel onion. Cut into thin slices the long way, and across the slices to make fine dice.

4. Core, seed, and de-pith the green peppers, and cut into fine dice.

5. Brush dirt off mushrooms with a damp cloth, and slice them thickly.

6. Slice salami.

7. To half-cooked potatoes, add half the butter, onion, and green pepper, and fry for about 2 minutes over medium heat.

8. Add the mushrooms and salami and continue cooking and stirring until the vegetables become limp, the salami crusty, and the potatoes crisp.

9. Grate the cheese and chop the parsley.

10. Whisk together the eggs, milk, and parsley.

11. Melt the rest of the butter and whisk it quickly into the eggs, milk, and parsley. Pour mixture over the potatoes.

12. Continue cooking and, as eggs start to set, sprinkle the top with cheese.

13. Cover and cook, without stirring for 5-6 minutes or until the eggs are well set but still soft. "Be careful not to overcook and dry out the eggs."

Serve immediately, with muffins, bagels, or buttered toast and a hot drink.

Schman

Taken from *The Shaw House Cookbook* (1963), this St. Louis dish is made from a pancake batter, scrambled like eggs. The concept somewhat resembles that of Creole or Cajun coush-coush, but is probably an American simplification of "schmarren," a group of southern German egg dishes that food historian William Woys Weaver describes as "slashed or torn apart with forks into large pieces right before it is served." Compare to stirrum in the **Germans from Russia** section.

1 egg
2 tablespoons melted shortening or butter
1/2 teaspoon salt
2 teaspoons baking powder
1 cup flour
1 cup milk

Equipment: Heavy skillet

1. Mix all ingredients together as you would for pancakes.

2. Melt a little lard or butter in a heavy skillet, and turn in the batter.

3. Cook at a fairly high heat, and be sure to stir steadily so it doesn't burn on the bottom.

4. Cook until it resembles scrambled eggs and is dry.

Serve with molasses or syrup.

Dampfnudeln (Steam Buns)

Unlike France or England, Germany has sent emigrants to the United States in all periods of our history. In 1990 it was still the fifth-largest source of foreign-born residents, the third-largest origin of naturalized citizens, and, in 1996, the fourth-largest source of temporary workers.

When Parry Betts, of Caney, Kansas, recently won the Dinner Rolls Championship of the Kansas Festival of Breads with this recipe, she described it as developed in Germany by her great-grandmother to deal with the fuel shortages of World War II (see <www.wheatmania.com>). Dampfnudeln are known to all German-American groups, but more usually as dumplings, and the electric skillet is, of course, one way the recipe has changed since the 1940s.

Yield: 8 buns
  4 teaspoons active dry yeast
  1/4 cup granulated sugar
  1 cup 1% milk
  2 large eggs
  2 tablespoons vegetable oil
  1 teaspoon salt
  3 1/2 to 3 3/4 cups bread flour (or unbleached flour, or "high protein" flour)
  2 tablespoons solid shortening, plus enough to grease bowl and waxed paper

Equipment: Waxed paper, non-stick frying-pan or electric skillet with lid, standing mixer with dough hook (optional), bread machine (optional)

1. Warm milk to lukewarm (105-115 degrees). (If using bread machine to make dough, check size of recipe, and follow machine instructions on adding ingredients through Step 5.)

2. In a medium bowl, dissolve yeast and sugar in milk.

3. Stir in eggs, oil, salt, and 2 cups flour. Beat 2 minutes.

4. Add enough remaining flour to make a soft dough.

5. Knead 10-12 minutes by hand or with a dough hook.

6. Place in lightly greased bowl, turning once to grease the surface of the bread.

7. Cover and let rise in a warm (80 degrees) place until doubled.

8. Punch down bread to remove large air bubbles.

9. Cover and let rest 10 minutes.

10. Divide dough into 8 equal pieces. Grease a long sheet of waxed paper.

11. Shape each piece into a bun. Place on a greased piece of waxed paper, then cover and let rise 15-20 minutes.

12. In a large non-stick electric skillet or frying pan with lid, heat 1/2 cup water, one tablespoon of the shortening, and a dash of salt to a boil on high heat.

13. Place 4 buns in boiling mixture. Cover with lid and reduce temperature setting to medium-low, or 250 degrees.

14. Cook for 10-15 minutes without removing lid. "Listen and you can hear them fry. At this point, the majority of the water will be evaporated."

15. Remove lid and increase temperature to 375 degrees. Brown both sides of buns.

16. Repeat Steps 12 through 15 to cook the other 4 buns in the same manner.

Serve warm. "Patty said her husband likes to eat them with butter and jelly."

GERMANS FROM RUSSIA

The 1990 census estimated only 10,000 Americans claiming German/Russian descent. Because the actual number is estimated at about one million, the 1990 figure suggests that the wording of the ancestry survey steered Germans from Russia to list either their German or Russian origins, or that this distinct group of prairie-state pioneers has come to see itself simply as **German-American** after more than a century of aloofness from other German-Americans.

Germans began settling the interior steppes of Russia in the second half of the eighteenth century with the encouragement of Catherine the Great. The offer included military exemption and religious tolerance, and was especially attractive in the same Protestant and southwestern German provinces from which came the founding stock of the **Pennsylvania Dutch** at about the same time. Villages along the Volga River, and in southern and western Ukraine (and the present countries of Moldova and Romania) were generally German-speaking and of one religious denomination, which might be Lutheran, Catholic, Hutterite, or Mennonite. In the 1870s, reform-minded Russian governments began to push the German settlements to learn Russian and perform military service. Whole villages picked up stakes and moved to the United States, western Canada, and South America, a migration that ended with World War I and the Russian Revolution. German settlers from Russia bypassed the Pennsylvania Dutch areas and the established German-American communities in the Midwest and set up farm villages in Kansas and the Dakotas, eventually spreading west to Colorado and Oregon, and south to Oklahoma. They kept to their religious and Russian regional identities, thus Black Sea Mennonites had a concentration in central Kansas. Because Germany was the enemy of the United States in two World Wars, Germans from Russia either Americanized their names or developed the identity of "Germans from Russia" (Russia being an American ally during the wars).

The Germans from Russia Heritage Society, based in North Dakota, has published several cookbooks, and characteristic Russian-German recipes can also be found in Mennonite cookbooks.

KRAUT BEERUCKS OR CABBAGE BUSTERS

Beerucks (also called bierocks, bieruchs, or bierochen) are the most characteristic food of Germans from Russia. The word comes from the Russian and Ukrainian word "perog," for a stuffed pie of any kind. Beerucks are also called "runzas" or "kraut runzas," which are the German words for buns or cabbage buns. Mrs. Carol Scherzer of Hemlock, Michigan, contributed this recipe to *Seasonal Samplings: A Culinary Look at the Seasons of Michigan* (1981), a fund-raiser for the American Cancer Society. Frozen bread dough has kept a lot of ethnic dishes going in the United States, from frybreads to pizza. Mrs. Scherzer's shape is traditional, although some people make half-moon turnovers. Not everyone bakes them upside down, however.

Yield: 20 buns

2 loaves frozen bread dough
1 medium head cabbage
3 medium onions, chopped
1 tablespoon shortening
salt and pepper to taste
11/2 pounds ground beef
solid shortening to grease baking sheets

Equipment: Rolling pin, 2 baking sheets, large pot, saucepan, skillet

1. Thaw bread dough.

2. Quarter and core cabbage. Make fine slices across each segment to shred.

3. Halve, peel, and chop the onions. (Wear swim goggles to avoid tears.)

4. Melt shortening in a large pot.

5. Add onions, cabbage, salt, and pepper in a saucepan. Stir around to coat cabbage. Cover and cook over low heat until cabbage is tender.

6. Meanwhile, brown meat in a skillet; drain off oil.

7. When cabbage is tender, drain it as well.

8. Stir cooked beef into cabbage and set aside.

9. Grease baking sheets. Cut bread dough and roll out 1/4-inch thick. Cut into 5-inch squares.

10. Gather up scraps and roll out in next batch.

11. Put 2 to 3 tablespoons cabbage mixture on each square.

12. Pick up the 4 corners and pinch together to seal. (It's fine if you can see a little of the filling through the seams, but you should pinch together any big gaps.)

13. Place dough squares upside down on a greased cookie sheet or cake pan.

14. Let rise in a warm place for 15 minutes.

15. Bake at 400 degrees for 15 to 20 minutes, or until browned.

16. Melt butter and brush tops of buns as they come out of the oven.

Serve with a cucumber salad in summer, or with pickles in winter.

DILL PICKLES

Germans from Russia found this common no-vinegar pickling method from Russia and Ukraine useful on the American Great Plains, where winter vegetables were just as hard to find. Table salt and iodized salt have additives that darken pickles; canning salt, sea salt, and kosher salt do not. These pickles should be refrigerated. "Well water works better for the contributor than city water." This recipe is from *Food'n Folklore*, published by the Germans from Russia Heritage Society of Bismarck, North Dakota.

NOTE: Pickles need to be stored for 6 weeks before they are ready to eat.

fresh clean slender medium cucumbers
1 head of fresh dill
1/4 onion
1 clove garlic
1 tablespoon canning salt (substitute 1 1/2 tablespoons kosher salt)
1 grape leave or pinch of alum

Equipment: 1 clean quart jar, tight cover

1. Put dill into a clean quart jar.

2. Fill jar with cucumbers.

3. Add remaining ingredients.

4. Fill jar with old water and seal.

5. Store in a very cool place (or refrigerator) and check periodically for spoilage.

6. "Should be ready to eat in six weeks."

SHTIRUM

Shtirum (or steerum or stirrum) is a pancake batter stirred like scrambled eggs, or cut into pieces as it cooks. It is eaten as a breakfast dish like the **German-American** schman, but Germans from Russia also like it with spring lettuce in a sour-cream dressing. This is the most detailed of three recipes in *Food'n Folklore*.

2 eggs
1 tablespoon sugar
1/2 teaspoon salt
1/4 cup milk
1/2 teaspoon baking powder
3/4 cup flour
2 teaspoons butter or stick margarine
1 head of lettuce
3 scallions
3/4 cup sour cream
1 tablespoon vinegar

Equipment: Salad spinner to wash and dry lettuce, large bowl, skillet

1. For shtirum without the salad, go to Step 4. Chop lettuce, then wash and dry.

2. Chop scallions, and mix with lettuce in a large bowl.

3. Add a pinch of salt to the sour cream and stir in the vinegar. "[I]f too sour, add remaining 1/4 cup of sour cream." Add salt if necessary.

4. Mix flour, salt, sugar, and baking powder.

5. Bring milk to room temperature.

6. Beat eggs and blend with milk.

7. Work milk mixture into flour mixture to make a pancake batter.

8. Heat butter or margarine in a large skillet. Turn skillet to coat pan.

9. Pour all batter into skillet and fry like a pancake on low heat.

10. When a crust has formed, flip over the other side.

11. With a table knife and fork, cut the pancake into "small pieces (as large as your thumb nail)."

12. Keep stirring until pieces are no longer sticky (moist) but crisp. "Don't fry too much that it will be hard—just starting to get crisp."

13. Pour dressing over lettuce and toss.

Serve in large bowls. Shtirum can also be topped with "syrup, honey, jelly, anything sweet."

GREEK-AMERICANS

The 1.1 million Greek-Americans are descended mostly from people who came to the United States between 1890 and 1924, and since 1965. The original group emigrated after 1891 when crop failures and threats of Turkish military conscription and relocation emptied Greek villages. So many young men left Greece that the government became alarmed, although by then it had become dependent on the remitted wages of Greek-Americans and other émigrés. As many as half the original immigrants returned to Greece for military service in the successful Balkan wars before World War I and the failed invasion of Asia Minor in the early 1920s. In the United States, Greek immigrants concentrated in large cities, and early became involved in the food business, although they did not generally serve Greek food. Greek men learned to cook continental dishes in restaurants and ran diners, ice cream parlors, candy stores, groceries, and fruit stands. Greek-style food was stereotyped at that time as all garlic, squid, and grape leaves, and was thought to have little appeal outside the community. An interesting exception is the Greek-American community in Tarpon Springs, Florida, which was founded by sponge divers recruited in the Greek islands. Many southerners tasted their first Greek salad or pastitsio in a restaurant while passing through Tarpon Springs. In the northeast, Greek-owned pizzerias began introducing Greek salad, souvlaki, and gyros only in the 1960s. However, Greek home cooking and Orthodox church fairs preserved traditional flavors until the ethnic revivals of the 1970s and 1980s prepared Middle America for Mediterranean food. Since then, almost every community cookbook has a distinctively Greek-American recipe or two.

As relatively late immigrants, Greek-Americans suffered considerable discrimination through the first half of the twentieth century. Although the community had internal political differences over events in Greece, the institutions that kept them together and, initially, somewhat apart from other Americans—the Greek Orthodox Church, Greek-language schools, and communal credit organizations—also enabled them to succeed in business and move up in American society without losing their cultural distinction and language.

STUFFED GRAPE LEAVES (ATHENIAN)

This characteristically Greek-American dish is so easy and fun to make, I don't know why it hasn't spread faster. I got this recipe from Demetra Levrakas in the 1970s. She has since moved from Boston to Alaska. I've added the method for fresh vine leaves from several Greek community cookbooks. You can omit the egg-lemon sauce, but it's a classic part of the dish that you won't experience in canned versions or in most Greek restaurants.

1/2 pound jar grapevine leaves in brine (or 50 or more fresh vine leaves).
1 pound hamburger
3 eggs
1 tablespoon finely chopped onion (or more if you wish)
2 tablespoons uncooked rice
1/2 teaspoon salt
1/4 teaspoon pepper
1 teaspoon parsley flakes
2 tablespoons butter
2 cups stock or bouillon
1 to 1 1/2 lemons

Equipment: Juicer for lemons, stoneware plate that fits inside saucepan to use as a weight, tongs to remove cooked leaves, heat-proof serving dish

1. If using fresh vine leaves, cut off stems with a sharp knife; wash, and dip in boiling water for a minute to soften. For brined grape leaves, take them out of the jar and rinse thoroughly to remove salt.

2. Mix hamburger, one egg, onion, rice, salt, pepper, and parsley in a bowl.

3. Use a few of the smallest leaves to line a saucepan.

4. Take a large vine leaf, and set it down in front of you, stem side up, stem end toward you.

5. Put a heaping teaspoon of meat mixture on the side of the leaf closest to you. Roll the leaf from the near edge toward the middle like a cigar, fold in the sides, and finish rolling. See illustrations.

6. Put the stuffed leaf in the pot, with the loose end underneath so it doesn't unroll.

7. Repeat, arranging the stuffed leaves in a neat pattern. You may need several layers.

8. Save any leaves that tear or the smallest ones to put on top.

9. Cut the butter into thin slices and put them on top of the stuffed grape leaves.

10. Pour on bouillon or stock to cover.

11. Put the stoneware plate on top to keep the vine leaves under a weight.

12. Bring to simmer and cook until a fork penetrates easily and the rice is done, about 45 minutes.

13. Carefully, so they don't tear, move the cooked leaves with tongs to a heat-proof serving dish so they can be kept warm in an oven while you make the egg-lemon sauce. Reserve the hot stock they were cooked in.

14. To make the egg-lemon sauce, juice the lemons and strain out any seeds and pulp.

15. Beat the 2 eggs very well.

16. Beat in the lemon juice.

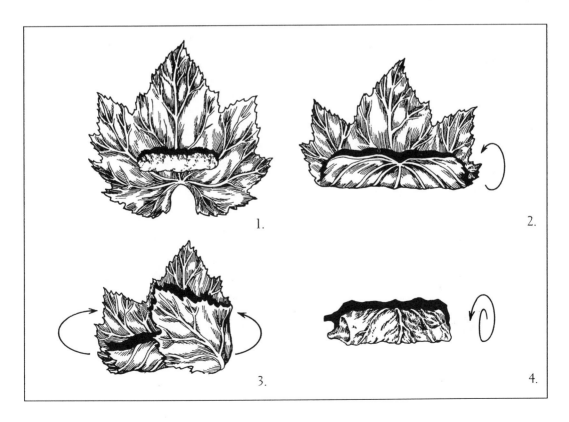

1.

2.

3.

4.

17. Dip out 1/2 cup of the hot stock and slowly beat it into the egg-lemon mix.

18. Take the serving dish out of the oven, and pour the egg-lemon sauce over the top. Shake dish to distribute the sauce well.

Serve hot as an entree or appetizer. Stuffed grape leaves without sauce may be chilled and eaten cold.

PECAN CRESCENTS
(KARITHATA)

As you might suspect, these were walnut or almond cookies in Greece, but were made over with American pecans and simplified for *Hellenic Cuisine* (1959), which was edited by Mary Pyrros Karay for the Sts. Constantine and Helen Parent-Teacher Association of Detroit.

Yield: about 3 1/2 dozen
  1/2 pound butter
  1 cup confectioner's sugar
  1 1/2 teaspoons vanilla
  2 cups flour
  1 cup chopped pecans

Equipment: Pastry blender, baking sheets

1. Soften and cream butter with a pastry blender or large fork.

2. Work in 1/2 cup of the confectioner's sugar, the flour, the pecans, and the vanilla.

3. Mix well.

4. Pinch off pieces of dough and form into 2-inch-long, finger-shaped pieces.

5. Turn ends in slightly to form crescents. Arrange on ungreased baking sheets.

6. Bake at 325 degrees for about a half hour.

7. Sprinkle the rest of the confectioner's sugar on a large pan.

8. Place warm crescents on sugar, and sprinkle tops with additional sugar.

TOURLOU

Former Massachusetts Governor Michael S. Dukakis submitted this recipe to *What's Cooking Under the Dome?*, a fund-raising cookbook compiled by Representative Thomas Finneran of Boston. This healthful dish of roasted vegetables is in the style of northeastern Greece and Macedonia, the place of origin of many Greek-American families in New England.

  1 large eggplant (slender)
  3 green peppers
  2 or 3 large zucchini
  3 large onions
  1 cup chopped parsley (Italian flat-leaf is best), from one bunch
  1 can whole tomatoes
  1/2 small can tomato sauce
  1 cup olive oil

Equipment: Blender, baking pan about 12 by 16 inches

1. Cut eggplant into large cubes.

2. Core green peppers and remove seeds and pith. Cut into strips.

3. Cut zucchini into large pieces.

4. Peel onions and cut into thin slices. (Wear swim goggles to avoid tears.)

5. Chop parsley.

6. Puree tomatoes in blender.

7. Oil pan, and spread out all ingredients except remaining olive oil.

8. "Pour olive oil over all. Add dash of salt and pepper."

9. Bake at 350 degrees until bubbly. Stir every so often while baking.

10. Once it bubbles, turn oven down to 300 degrees, and bake until vegetables are fork tender. Should be fairly dry, not watery.

Serve hot or cold.

GUAMIANS (CHAMOROS)

About 35,000 to 50,000 Americans had ancestors who came from Guam or Saipan in Micronesia, and who are also identified by their home language as Chamoros. The United States acquired these islands after World War II, and extended citizenship to Guamians in 1950, setting off the migration of almost half the population of the islands to Hawaii. Guamian men joined the U.S. armed forces or secured work in naval base and shipyard cities in Hawaii and California, especially San Diego, Los Angeles, and San Francisco. Guamian food shows a strong Spanish influence via the Philippines. For example, a dish called eskabechi is similar to the Spanish and Caribbean escaveche—fried fish in a vinegar pickle or sauce—except that many vegetables and fresh ginger have found their way into the fancier Guamian versions.

KELAGUEN (CHICKEN SALAD FROM GUAM)

Judi Gutierrez contributed this recipe to *Give Us This Day: Recipes from Reseda II Ward Relief Society, Church of Jesus Christ of Latter-day Saints*, published in 1978 in Chatsworth Stake, California. The Mormons were active missionaries in the Pacific Islands. You can sometimes buy coconut graters in Asian grocery stores. Ms. Gutierrez adds that Kelaguen can also be made with shrimp.

Yield: serves about 8 as a main dish salad
1 chicken, cut up
1 fresh coconut
1 bunch scallions
1/2 cup lemon juice
3/4 teaspoon salt

Equipment: Clean screwdriver, hammer, coconut grater or very dull old knife, meat grinder or food processor

1. Buy a coconut in which the water can be heard when you shake it.

2. Drain and discard the coconut water by piercing shell at the three "eyes" with the screwdriver.

3. Preheat oven to 400 degrees and bake coconut for 15 minutes.

4. Broil chicken pieces about 15 minutes per side to cook through.

5. Wrap hot coconut in a towel and crack coconut shell with hammer by tapping all the way around "the equator."

6. Carefully remove coconut meat from shell with a coconut grater or a very dull old knife. Don't force anything, because the knife can slip and hurt you. If the meat won't give way, bake it a little more.

7. Grate coconut meat with a box grater or the grating blade of a food processor.

8. When chicken is done, cool and take meat off bones.

9. Run chicken meat through meat grinder, or mince in food processor.

10. Chop scallions.

11. Dissolve salt in lemon juice.

12. Combine all ingredients and chill.

Serve cold, with hot sauce (see below) on the side.

HOT SAUCE (GUAM)

Mrs. Helen Salas of Quantico, Virginia, contributed this recipe to *Recipes on Parade Foreign Foods: 1000 World Wide Favorites of Military Officers' Wives* (1970), which was edited by Mary Ann Richards. This sauce is known as "finadene" in Chamoro.

5 hot peppers
1 large onion
1/2 cup soy sauce
juice of one lemon

Equipment: Long tongs to handle roasting peppers

1. "Burn peppers on a hot stove until black in spots." (If you have an electric stove, broil for a few minutes, turning them with tongs to roast evenly.)

2. Place in glass bowl and crush with fork.

3. Halve, peel, and slice onion into half-round slices.

4. Add onion, soy sauce, 1/4 cup water, and lemon juice.

5. Let stand for several hours before using.

Serve sprinkled on rice or meat dishes. "Will keep for 2 weeks."

GUATEMALAN-AMERICANS

Most Guatemalan-Americans are recent immigrants who came to the United States after the late 1970s. Many were fleeing civil war and intense government repression, especially of the Mayan Indians. According to the 1990 census, about 241,000 people of Guatemalan ancestry live in the U.S. An estimated (1996) 165,000 Guatemalan refugees or migrants are in the U.S. without documentation, the third-largest such group after Mexicans and El Salvadorans. There are visible Guatemalan neighborhoods in Los Angeles, and communities of some size in Houston, New York, Chicago, San Francisco, and Washington, D.C. Guatemala has the largest Indian population in Central America; most of these Native peoples are speakers of Mayan and other Indian languages and are famous for brilliant weaving. Guatemalan food has more complexity than other Central American cuisines, in part because of the Indian community, and in part because there is such a variety of climates—from the tropical Atlantic coast to the cool highlands. Some Guatemalan specialties are refried black beans, black tamales colored with chocolate, and "black rice" cooked with the juice of black beans. Since most Guatemalans are recent immigrants, few Guatemalan-American recipes have developed, so Guatemalan-American cooking consists of dishes from Guatemala with some ingredients necessarily changed, and often dishes that don't take so much time to make.

RADISH SALAD

This salad intensifies flavors by chopping the vegetables into flecks of color. The recipe is from Alba Santizo, as told to Sheryl Julian for a column in the *Boston Sunday Globe Magazine.* "At home Santizo would use a bitter Spanish orange for this salad; here she uses lime."

Yield: serves 4
  2 bunches radishes
  2 tomatoes
  3 scallions
  3 tablespoons chopped fresh mint
  1 fresh green chile pepper (optional)
  1/4 cup fresh lime juice
  salt

Equipment: Large chef's knife

1. Trim and thinly slice the radishes. Cut the slices into match sticks. Cut the match sticks into tiny dice.

2. Chop scallions very fine, rocking a large chef's knife over them to mince.

3. Chop mint leaves very fine.

4. If using chile pepper, cut off top, slit down one side, and remove pith and seeds with a teaspoon. Cut into long match sticks and cut the match sticks into fine dice.

5. Slice and chop tomatoes into small chunks.

6. Stir everything thoroughly, add lime juice and salt.

7. Cover tightly and refrigerate before serving.

Pollo Guisado

Salomon Vides Collao of Leucadia, California, contributed this recipe for chicken stew to "Recetas Chapinas," an online collection of Guatemalan recipes in Spanish at <www.quetzalnet.com>. While relatively few Guatemalan-Americans have computer access, some that do are using the Internet to swap recipes in a way that lets outsiders see how Guatemalan-American cuisine is developing. In Guatemala, this dish might be made with a roasted tomato sauce called chirmol and colored with achiote paste. As the Guatemalan-American community develops, these things may be more widely imported or produced in the United States, and such dishes may become "more authentic." I have translated from the Spanish.

Yield: 4 or 5 portions
  1 chicken, 3 or 4 pounds
  7 cloves garlic
  1 cinnamon stick
  2 tablespoons olive oil
  1 onion
  10 Roma (plum) tomatoes
  1 1/2 soup spoons of sugar
  1 pinch of salt or to taste
  8 small potatoes
  2 ounces vinegar
  2 chicken bouillon cubes
  6 bay leaves
  "a little thyme, better in fresh sprigs (4 or 5 sprigs)" (1/2 to 1 teaspoon)
  4 carrots

Equipment: Large skillet with a tight cover

1. Cut chicken into serving pieces.

2. Break the cinnamon stick into pieces.

3. Peel the 7 cloves of garlic.

4. Heat the olive oil in the skillet, and put in the chicken, garlic cloves, pieces of cinnamon stick, bay leaves, and sprigs of thyme.

5. Cover and cook for about 5 minutes, stirring a little bit so the chicken doesn't stick.

6. Cut up the tomatoes, not too fine.

7. Peel the carrots and cut into large pieces, perhaps halves.

8. Peel the onions and cut into rings.

9. Peel and quarter the potatoes.

10. Add one cup of water, the salt, the bouillon cubes, the tomatoes, the carrots, the potatoes, and the onions.

11. Lower the heat, cover, and cook about 15 to 20 minutes, until the chicken is almost done.

12. Add the vinegar and sugar for the last 5 minutes.

Serve with fresh tortillas and avocado slices.

GULLAH (GEECHEE AND SEA ISLANDERS)

None of these names are entirely satisfactory to describe the distinctive cooking of an area around Charleston, South Carolina, and the **African-American** ethnic group that developed it. As in Louisiana, African-American cooks developed a group of dishes that were also influenced by wealthy white planter families, and which later became general regional dishes. But it is much clearer with Gullah cooking which dishes came from Africa because the higher proportion of African-American population in the region was able to keep more African names for okra, sesame seeds ("benne"), peanuts ("goober" from "nguba"), and, possibly, hoppin' john (rice pilaf with beans).

"Gullah" was originally a derogatory term for a black English dialect now more properly called Sea Island Creole, and for African-Americans who spoke this dialect. In slavery times, the Gullah dialect was probably the main form of black English all along the Atlantic coast, and words from more than 20 African languages have been found in Gullah. More than 100 years ago, Gullah speakers in the sea islands off the Carolinas, Georgia, and Florida were known to have retained many African customs, and recently certain songs have been identified as traditional with African ethnic groups living in what is now Sierre Leone. About 100,000 speakers of Sea Island Creole still live on the islands and the "low country" of the tidewater Carolinas and Georgia. "Geechee" was another derogatory regional term for African-Americans, possibly derived from the Ogechee River in Georgia.

In the 1990s, Gullah and Geechee became terms of ethnic pride for some Carolina and Georgia African-Americans who had migrated north, but still enjoyed dishes like benne cookies, hoppin' john, red rice, and breakfast shrimp. It is in that spirit that I include these recipes here. If you would like to read some recipes in easy Gullah, the Gullah instructor and translator Virginia Mixson Geraty has written *Bittle en' T'ing: Gullah Cooking with Maum Crish'*. A more recent Gullah invention is Frogmore stew.

AUNT GERTIE'S RED RICE

Red rice is called "Spanish Rice" in much of the rest of the U.S. South Carolina was an important center of American rice farming, but African slaves were much more familiar with rice and rice cookery than their English or French Huguenot masters. This recipe comes from the Web site of film-maker Julie Dash and her Geechee Girls Productions, Inc., and is attributed to Gertrude Prunella Dash Banks (1895-1995). Because only a little rice is grown in South Carolina today, you can use any long-grain white rice in the recipe. In Georgia and Florida, "white bacon" (lean salt pork) replaces smoked bacon.

1 cup of South Carolina white rice (do not use converted rice)
2 cups water
1 clove garlic
5 strips of bacon (or smoked turkey)
1/2 cup chopped onions
1/2 cup chopped bell peppers
1 6-ounce can of tomato paste
1/4 cup vegetable oil

Equipment: Heavy pot with a tight lid, brown paper bag to seal pot

1. Place the rice in a large bowl of water and scrub the rice between your hands. (Don't rub so hard as to break the rice.)

2. Keep changing the water until it is clear of starch. Pour off water.

3. Use a deep, heavy pot with a lid. Cook the bacon, or if you prefer, smoked turkey, with 1/4 cup of vegetable oil in the bottom of the pot.

4. Halve, peel, slice, and chop a medium onion. Peel and chop garlic. Core and chop a large pepper.

5. Add your onions, peppers, garlic, and cook until they are done (onions translucent).

6. Add the tomato paste and 2 cups water. Bring to a boil.

7. When the sauce begins to boil, add the rice. Use a fork to make sure the rice is evenly distributed in the tomato sauce. "Never stir the rice once it begins to boil. Never put a spoon in rice that's cooking. . . ." (You may shake the pot, however.)

8. When the rice begins to boil, lower the heat. Wrap a wet brown paper bag around the lid of the pot and cover.

9. Slow-cook until the rice absorbs all the sauce. "Every grain must stand on its own. Every grain must be red."

Serve as a side dish or light supper. "Red rice tastes even better the next day."

PROPER GEECHEE RICE

Vertamae Grosvenor included this recipe in *Vertamae Cooks in the Americas' Family Kitchen*. It slightly adjusts her earlier recipe in *Vibration Cooking, or the Travel Notes of a Geechee Girl*. Grosvenor does not salt her rice. I have adjusted quantities to fit the hoppin' john recipe that follows.

1 1/2 cups long grain white rice
3 cups cold water

Equipment: Heavy saucepan with a tight lid

1. "Rinse the rice until the water runs clear (or as Grandma Sula used to say, 'rinse it three times, and then once more.'") Rub it together in the palms of your hands and make sure you get all the grains washed.

2. In a heavy saucepan, combine rice and water. Turn the heat high and put the lid ajar.

3. Bring the water to a boil, shut the lid so that it covers the pan tightly, turn down the heat to very low, and cook for 20 minutes, or until the rice is tender and the liquid is absorbed.

4. "Never, never, never stir the rice during this time. Don't even think about uncovering the pot to peek."

5. Remove from heat and let rest for 10 minutes before serving. (Still no peeking.)

Serve with every meal.

HOPPIN' JOHN

Hoppin' john is an African-style dish of rice and beans, now served throughout the South on New Year's Day for good luck. This recipe is from Mary Sheppard and recorded by Jean Anderson for *The Grass Roots Cookbook* (1977). Hoppin' john is often a bean pilaf, but some cooks, like Ms. Sheppard, make the rice separately. The likeliest theory of the name is that Gullah speakers made it out of the French phrase, "pois de pigeon." The food historian Karen Hess, in *The Carolina Rice Kitchen*, has proposed a Hindi-Arabic phrase "bhatta cajan." I have doubled the recipe given, and worked in Ms. Sheppard's instructions for steamed rice. (You can make rice according to package directions.)

1 pound (2 cups) dried cowpeas or black-eyed peas
1/2 pound lean slab bacon
1/4 teaspoon cayenne pepper
1/4 teaspoon black pepper
2 1/2 teaspoons salt
1 1/2 cups rice to make 6 cups cooked rice

Equipment: Medium-sized heavy kettle

1. Wash cowpeas or black-eyed peas and remove any dirt or stones.

2. Cut bacon into 1/2-inch cubes. (This task is easier if you put the bacon in the freezer for an hour before cutting.)

3. Place dried peas, bacon, and 5 cups water in a medium-sized heavy kettle, and bring to a boil.

4. Reduce heat and simmer until the peas are just "firm-tender"—20 minutes for cowpeas, 40-45 minutes for black-eyed peas.

5. Make proper Geechee rice, (see recipe above), or cook rice according to package directions.

6. Drain peas, reserving liquid for soup or another use. (Some Carolina recipes measure the liquid and use it to cook the rice.)

7. Add cayenne, black pepper, and salt to peas. Toss lightly with forks to mix.

8. Add rice and toss lightly again.

9. Taste for salt and add more if needed.

Serve hot on its own or with pork chops. "You eat it with greens. They're s'posed to be good luck, too."

GUYANESE-AMERICANS (AND INDO-CARIBBEANS)

The history and ethnic make-up of Guyana, a small country in northeastern South America, are similar to that of Trinidad and Tobago. Until independence in 1966, Guyana was a British colony with a plantation economy. After the end of slavery in 1834-38, Asian-Indian contract laborers were employed until the end of the indenture system in 1917. About half of today's Guyanese are descended from Asian-Indians, and about 30 percent are African-American. Up to 1924, only about 800 Guyanese had come to the United States, mostly **African-Americans** who joined the West Indian black community in New York City. African-American Guyanese came in greater numbers in the 1950s and 1960s, many of them women working as nurse's aides and domestics in greater New York. More recently, Asian-Indian Guyanese have come to the United States, forming a visible neighborhood alongside **Trinidadian-American** Indo-Caribbeans in Queens.

The 1990 census estimated 82,000 Guyanese-Americans, more than two-thirds in greater New York City, where they were among the five largest Caribbean immigrant communities.

SEA TROUT SALAD

Gladys Benn contributed this handsome salad to *The Brooklyn Cookbook* by Lynn Stallworth and Rod Kennedy, Jr. Sea trout is an ocean species that holds together well when cooked, but you can get a similar result with codfish.

NOTE: Fish must be chilled overnight.

Yield: serves 4 as a main dish
 1 pound center-cut sea trout
 salt and pepper to taste
 1 large lime or lemon
 1 pound yams
 1 tablespoon minced parsley
 6 tablespoons mayonnaise
 1/2 pound cabbage
 1 medium cucumber
 2 large firm tomatoes
 1 head lettuce, leaves separated, washed and
   chilled

1. Steam the fish in a little water until the flesh turns milky white.

2. Drain it and let it cool. Remove any bones or skin. Flake the flesh, and season it with salt and pepper and lime juice.

3. Cover the fish with plastic wrap and chill overnight.

4. The following day, peel the yams and cut them into neat "cubes the size of croutons."

5. Steam the yam cubes, "and don't cook them too long. They should be firm, not mushy."

6. When they are cool, add them to the flaked fish with the parsley and 3 tablespoons mayonnaise. Blend carefully with a fork. Do not crush the yam cubes.

7. Slice the cabbage into fine shreds.

8. Peel the cucumber and cut it into cubes, and cut the tomatoes into neat chunks.

9. Toss the vegetables with the remaining 3 tablespoons of mayonnaise.

10. Arrange the lettuce leaves on a platter. Heap the fish salad in the center and arrange the tossed vegetables around it.

JUNE BOBB'S GARLIC PORK

Mrs. Bobb lives in Brooklyn, but gave this recipe to Molly O'Neill for *The New York Cookbook*. This tropical dish originally used long marinating as a preservative. The recipe is generally attributed to Portuguese contract laborers who came to Guyana (and Trinidad and Hawaii) somewhat later than the East Indians. Compare the dish to African-American marinated pork and **Filipino-American** adobo. Mrs. Bobb warns that, if not closed, "your closet doors or your clothes will reek of the wonderful aroma of garlic pork for days." For the chiles, you can substitute any tiny red chiles, or a single red hot pepper, or a tablespoon of red pepper sauce.

Yield: serves 3 as a main dish
 2 cups cider vinegar
 6 thick, center-cut pork chops
 15 large cloves garlic
 10 "wiri-wiri" chiles (see substitutions
   above) or other small non-red chiles; if
   they are more than the size of a dime in
   circumference, use only 5)
 1/4 cup plus 1 tablespoon dried thyme
 salt to taste
 6 whole cloves
 2 tablespoons vegetable oil

Equipment: Plastic storage container with a tight lid, blender or food processor

1. Bone the pork chops and cut off any fat. Cut each chop into 4 pieces.

2. In a medium bowl, mix the vinegar with 2 cups water.

3. Add the pork and mix so that each piece of pork is washed in the mixtures.

4. Transfer the pork to plastic storage container.

5. In a blender or food processor, grind up the chiles, garlic, and thyme with 1 cup of the vinegar mixture.

6. Pour the mixture over the pork, and add enough of the original vinegar-water mixture to cover the pork completely.

7. Add the cloves and salt, and stir to taste.

8. Refrigerate tightly covered for 4 days.

9. Heat the oil in a large heavy skillet over medium heat.

10. Remove the pork from the marinade and pat dry with paper towels. (Reserve the marinade.)

11. Brown the pork in batches in the skillet, about 3 minutes per side.

12. Set each batch aside while browning the remaining pork.

13. Pour 1/4 cup marinade into the skillet, pick out any cloves, and boil over high heat 1 or 2 minutes to concentrate by half.

14. Return the pork to the skillet and stir so the pieces absorb the reduced marinade.

15. Remove from heat.

Serve hot with slices of homemade bread.

GYPSY-AMERICANS (ROMANICHALS, TRAVELLERS, AND ROMA)

Gypsy-Americans have been uniquely misunderstood, stereotyped, and persecuted in the United States. Because their traditional culture is closed to outsiders, it is difficult to find reliable information. For example, estimates of the number of Gypsies in the U.S. range from 50,000 to 2 million. The higher number may be more accurate, for many Gypsies do not admit to being Gypsies when asked. The first Gypsies to arrive in the American colonies were deported from throughout Europe as slaves or indentured servants. They assimilated into American society, including into the **African-American** community. A functioning community of Romanichal Gypsies from England were horse traders in New England by 1840, and Eastern European Gypsies immigrated to the U.S. with other Eastern Europeans between 1880 and 1920. Unlike the colonial deportees, these later immigrants came in groups and retained their language and customs. Gypsies today are somewhat less migratory and rural, and more settled in large cities like Los Angeles and Chicago, and in many southern states.

Many Gypsies who speak the Romani language now prefer to be called "Roma." Groups that do not speak Romani, but with some Romani customs, such as Irish Tinkers and the Travellers of the British Isles, may also be regarded as Gypsies. Many Roma still prefer the names of their "nations" as they developed over the centuries in Europe, such as Kaldarash, Boyash, Louvari, or Romanichals. These names refer to national origins in Europe, dialects, clans, or types of work (e.g., the Kaldarash were copper workers).

About 150 years ago, linguists noticed that the Romani language is similar to modern Hindi and Urdu. It is now widely accepted that the ancestors of the Roma came from India and started west in one or more large migrations or deportations, beginning about 1,500 years ago. In India, they may have been a soldier caste taken as prisoners, or a caste of wandering entertainers or metal workers.

One likely remnant of their Indian culture is a complex series of rules about how to live and avoid contamination, in which individual mistakes or violations can bring misfortune on the entire family or clan. There are even more complex rules about water. Fear of contamination makes physical contact with outsiders hazardous, especially at meal times. Because kitchen counters and other household furniture can be contaminated, Gypsies often prefer to own mobile homes or use apartments previously used by related Gypsies.

Many Roma have their own plates and tableware (and it is always safest to eat with the fingers), and both men and women learn to cook early. Some Romani families have a designated chair and separate dishes for non-Romani visitors. Traditionally, meals are served on a large tray on a cloth on the ground, or on a low table. Politeness requires that one leave a little bit on the plate to show that more than enough food was served. Romani guests must eat something, even a cup of coffee, or it will imply that the host is "unclean." Two meals are held each day, breakfast and a meal in the late afternoon.

Some foods, called baxtaló xabé, are considered to be beneficial and healthful; these items include such strong-tasting foods as chile peppers, black pepper, garlic, lemon, pickles, vinegar, and salt. Bright colored spices and vegetables are also lucky and even curative. This use of expensive spices is notable in a group that has often been poor and on the move, and may be another retention from India.

Because Gypsies arrived in the Balkan countries in the fifteenth century, shortly before the Ottoman conquests, it is possible that they introduced such Middle Eastern foods as stuffed cabbage, noodle pudding, and certain pastries to Eastern Europe, and then to modern European cooking. Gypsies today seldom eat with outsiders or run restaurants, and thus there are few published Gypsy recipes, although pseudo-Gypsy recipes abound.

SAX SUKLÓ

This Vlax (or Vlach) Romani recipe is from Professor Ian Hancock, author of "Romani Foodways: Gypsy Culinary Culture" (*The World & I*, June 1991, p. 666). I estimated the quantities below, and found a surprisingly light, lively stew with a tang of vinegar, one of the strong flavors in traditional Romani cooking.

Yield: serves 8
  1 small chicken (broiler-fryer)
  1 pound pork chops or pork shoulder
    (optional)
  1/2 cup rice
  2 tablespoons paprika (Hungarian is best)
  1 teaspoon salt
  1/2 teaspoon pepper
  1/2 cup vinegar
  3 tablespoons rendered lard
  3 tablespoons flour
  1 small head of green cabbage

Equipment: Skimmer to remove meat from soup, flat whisk to make thickening roux, soup pot, saucepan

1. Cut chicken in quarters or serving pieces.

2. Put chicken and pork (if using) in soup pot with water to cover, and bring to a boil.

3. Reduce heat and simmer until chicken is almost done, about 15 minutes.

4. Add rice, paprika, salt, pepper, and vinegar.

5. Remove cabbage core, and chop cabbage into inch squares.

6. When chicken is beginning to leave the bone, remove it and optional pork from soup with the skimmer, and place in a bowl to cool.

7. Add cabbage to the pot.

8. When chicken and optional pork are cool enough to handle, remove all bones and skin and cut meat roughly into inch squares.

9. In small saucepan, melt lard and blend in the flour with a whisk.

10. Cook flour-lard paste for a few minutes, stirring with the whisk so it doesn't burn, until it is just golden.

11. Add a ladle of hot broth from the soup pot to the paste (roux), and whisk over heat to make a thick gravy.

12. Repeat with a second ladle of broth.

13. Return gravy to the soup pot, add the meat, stir once, and let cook on gentle heat for another 15 minutes.

Serve in soup bowls.

PIROGO (GYPSY CAKE OR PUDDING)

This is the only published American Gypsy recipe I have found; it appeared in a database of recipes from Fundcraft, a large publisher of community cookbooks, at <www.cookbooks.com>. Unfortunately, the database does not include any information about where this recipe was published. The dish is a rich noodle pudding, probably the ancestor of many East European noodle puddings, such as the **Jewish-American** lokshen kugel. You may recognize the similarity to the word "pirogy" for **Polish-American** stuffed noodles. In Dr. Hancock's family, the dish is called pirógo le strugurlása; the yellow color comes from saffron, and the cheese is cream cheese. You can halve this recipe.

2 dozen eggs
1 large box raisins
handful crushed walnuts (optional)
2 cans crushed pineapple
1 pound sugar (white)
1 quart cottage cheese
1 1/2 pounds butter, melted
2 large bags egg noodles

Equipment: Large roasting pan, or lasagna pan for halved recipe

1. Beat the eggs.

2. Melt the butter slowly, and allow to cool slightly.

3. Beat sugar and butter into the eggs

4. Mix in cottage cheese and pineapple.

5. Add raisins and optional noodles.

6. Start egg noodles cooking in boiling water according to package directions, but drain them when they are only half cooked, about 5 minutes.

7. "Mix everything and put in some kind of roasting pan, greased."

8. Bake at 350 degrees for about 45 minutes or until golden brown. The halved recipe will cook more quickly, but check that the center is almost firm before removing from the oven.

9. Let set about 20 minutes to complete cooking before cutting into squares.

Serve at room temperature. The recipe direction of "Needs no refrigeration," may refer to the Romani custom of giving or throwing away leftovers.

IRISH SCONES

This is one of a group of Irish Traveller recipes collected by Richard J. Waters of Texas (who uses the British spelling of Traveler) and posted on his Web site about Travellers in the U.S. As he explained in an e-mail, "While the following are authentic Irish Traveller family recipes, they are not presented as typical or characteristic of Irish Traveller 'cuisine.' In truth, over the one to one hundred and fifty years that we have traveled over these United States as migratory citizens and craftsmen, many of the more superficial parts of our lifestyle have been readily adapted to local conditions as we encountered them." As this recipe shows, the group has kept an Irish hearth bread, but now fry it on both sides in a frying pan, which suits both migration and southern U.S. food styles.

Yield: 5-6 small cakes
2 cups flour
3 teaspoons baking powder
1/2 cup whole milk
3 tablespoons butter
1/2 cup raisins

Equipment: frying pan

1. In a large bowl, mix flour and baking powder evenly.

2. Add raisins and mix to coat with flour.

3. Pour in milk and mix to make a firm dough. ("If a little dry or wet, adjust milk/flour ratio.")

4. Pat into 5 or 6 flat, round cakes.

5. Melt butter in frying pan on medium heat.

6. Slide in cakes to fit, and let them brown.

7. Turn once and brown on the other side.

Serve hot, with butter and jam.

HAIDA

See TLINGIT AND HAIDA

HAITIAN-AMERICANS

Almost all of the 600,000 to 800,000 Haitian-Americans now in the United States emigrated from Haiti since 1965, fleeing poverty and political conflict. They are most visible in New York, Miami, and other East Coast cities, but a high proportion are undocumented and fear deportation. After Spanish, Haitian Creole (a language distinct from French) is now the most widely used language by bilingual students in New York City.

An early and important group of Haitian immigrants fled the slave revolts of the 1780s; this group included French planters, their slaves, and some free people of color. They introduced a number of foods to U.S. cities from New Orleans to Philadelphia, took leadership in the free **African-American** communities, and influenced the culture of New Orleans at all levels—from neo-African Voudon ("Voodoo") religion to white Creole French dialects.

RIZ ET POIS ROUGES

This recipe is adapted from one posted on the Web site of Haitian-American computer programmer Kathleen Abrahams-Holley. Although this American version is much simplified, it is a typical Haitian recipe for red beans and rice, with the cooking liquor from the beans used to give the rice extra richness and color without much oil. Cooks in Haiti might flavor with meat, onion, cloves, or herbs, and might enrich it with coconut milk. Typical Haitian red beans are small. You can substitute red kidney beans, and you may need more water. Your choice of hot pepper determines the flavor of the dish. For a bland dish, use an Italian frying pepper. The Creole name for this dish is diri ak pwa.

Yield: 6 dinner portions or 12 side-dish portions

1 cup dry red beans (or a can of cooked red beans)
2 tablespoons oil
1 hot pepper (or a few drops hot pepper sauce), seeded and chopped
1/2 cup chopped parsley
4-5 cloves chopped garlic
1 teaspoon salt
1 tablespoon tomato paste (optional)
2 cups rice

1. If using canned red beans, start at Step 3, reserving the bean liquid for part of the 4 cups of liquid in Step 4. Boil dried red beans in 10 cups of water for an hour, or until the beans become tender.

2. Separate the beans from water but do not discard cooking liquid.

3. Put oil in a separate pot and heat a little. Add drained beans, chopped hot pepper, garlic, parsley, salt, and optional tomato paste. Fry until the beans are dried.

4. Add 4 cups liquid (use the cooking liquid from the beans and add water if necessary) and bring to a boil.

5. Add the rice, mix in, and let water boil a second time. Reduce the fire, cover, and cook for one-half hour.

Serve with griots, see recipe below.

GRIOTS

Griots (from the French "grillades") is a popular dish of cubed pork that is boiled, then fried. The recipe is from Hubert Montas as posted on the Web site of the Purdue University Haitian Student Association, with some details from another online recipe contributed by Alexandra Desgranges to the Suffern (NY) High School Youth Against Racism. In the older, African-influenced recipes, the pork was merely washed with lemon juice, blanched quickly with boiling water, and then deep fried to resemble grilled meats. Ms. Desgranges omits the shallots and onions, and most of the marinating.

NOTE: Meat needs to marinade overnight.

3 pounds meat from shoulder of pork (from half pork shoulder)
1 large onion
1/2 cup chopped shallots (2 small packages)
1 cup bitter orange juice (or lemon juice)
1 green hot pepper, chopped
half cup vegetable oil
salt, pepper, and a little thyme
1 1/2 tablespoons tomato paste for optional sauce

Equipment: Non-metallic container

1. Halve, peel, and chop onion.

2. Halve, peel, and chop shallots.

3. Cut off top of hot pepper, slit one side, and use a teaspoon to scrape out seeds and pith. Cut into strips, and across the strips to make fine dice. Wash hands carefully after handling even one hot pepper.

4. Combine spices, juice, pepper, shallots, and onions in a non-metallic container.

5. Cut all skin and fat from pork shoulder.

6. Cut meat into cubes from 1 to 2 inches on a side.

7. Marinate overnight.

8. The next day, place the marinated pork in a pot with water to cover, and simmer for 90 minutes.

9. Drain the mixture.

10. Heat oil in the pot and fry the pork until brown and crusty on the outside.

11. Alexandre Desgranges makes a sauce for griots by stirring the tomato paste into a cup of water, and simmering with a teaspoon of oil and spices (perhaps a clove). You could also flavor the tomato sauce with some of the marinade.

Serve topped with tomato sauce or sliced onions, along with riz et pois rouges (see recipe above), fried plantains, and ti-malice sauce (see recipe below).

HAITIAN SAUCE TI-MALICE

This is Hubert Montas' version of hot sauce. "This extra-hot sauce brings out the flavor of meat and fish dishes but can also bring tears to the eyes of the diners!"

Yield: makes about 2 cups, "use with caution"
2 teaspoons of hot yellow pepper (cayenne or red chile pepper)
1 large onion
1/2 cup shallots
2 cloves of garlic
1/2 cup lemon or lime juice
1/4 cup olive oil
salt and pepper

1. Halve, peel, and chop fine the onion.

2. Halve, peel, and chop 2 packages of shallots to get about 1/2 cup.

3. Marinate onions and shallots in lime juice for 2 hours.

4. Peel and chop garlic.

5. Bring all ingredients to a boil.

6. Allow to cool and store in a glass jar in the refrigerator. Shake periodically.

Shake and serve with main dishes.

HAITIAN CAKE

Marie Lourdes Joseph submitted this recipe to *We're Cooking: The City Mission Society Real People's Cookbook*, which was published in Boston in 1988.

1/2 pound butter
2 cups sugar
1/2 teaspoon salt
2 eggs
2 cups flour
1 1/2 cups water or coffee
1 teaspoon vanilla extract
2 teaspoons baking powder
solid shortening to grease tube pan

Equipment: Tube pan, pastry blender or large fork

1. Cream the butter and sugar together with a pastry blender or large fork.

2. Add the eggs and salt, beating until light.

3. Add the water or coffee 1/2 cup at a time, alternating with flour and beating well after each addition.

4. Fold in the vanilla and baking powder last.

5. Grease tube pan.

6. Pour in cake, and bake for 1 hour at 375 degrees.

HAWAIIANS

The first Hawaiians probably reached the islands almost 2,000 years ago, and there were probably more arrivals and perhaps some trade with Polynesia after that. By the time Captain James Cook "discovered" the islands in 1788, about 300,000 native Hawaiians had a highly evolved society and cuisine. Today, the population has declined to a core group of about 20,000, although more than 250,000 people claim some native Hawaiian ancestry, including 30,000 in California. Hawaii remained an independent kingdom until 1893, when the monarchy was overthrown by a group eager to join the U.S., which was already investing in Hawaiian plantation agriculture. The U.S. government acquired 37 percent of the land of the islands in the 1890s, and formally annexed Hawaii in 1898. It became a state in 1959. In the late 1970s, the "Sovereignty Movement" among Native Hawaiians began demanding restoration of native land claims (including the 1890s transfers) and control of endangered wild areas.

Native Hawaiians brought chickens, pigs, and taro to the islands, and Hawaiian foods are eaten by all groups in Hawaii. The earth-oven feast called lu'au has been a tourist event for more than 100 years. Thus, the identity of these dishes as ethnic foods has blurred, but all groups on Hawaii still list them as such. Other Native Hawaiian dishes include poi, chicken long rice (with noodles), pipikaula (beef jerky), taro cakes, fish baked in taro leaves, poké (raw or cooked seafood with chopped seaweed salad), kalua pig, and laulaus.

HAUPIA

This coconut pudding was originally steamed in leaves and thickened with a native arrowroot plant. This recipe is from Jane Goo of Anahola, as cooked at the 1989 Smithsonian Festival of American Folklife and posted on the Internet as a 1996 "virtual festival." This pudding is rich, so you could cut 49 smaller, one-inch squares.

Yield: serves 36

3 cups frozen coconut milk, thawed (or 2 cups fresh coconut milk mixed with 1 cup water, or 2 cans coconut milk)

1/2 cup sugar

1/2 cup cornstarch

1/2 teaspoon vanilla

pinch of salt

oil to coat baking pan

Equipment: 8- or 9-inch square brownie pan, saucepan

1. In a cold saucepan, combine coconut milk and sugar.

2. Gradually mix in cornstarch. Add vanilla and salt.

3. Stir and cook on medium heat until thickened.

4. Oil baking pan and pour in coconut mixture.

5. Chill for at least 1 hour.

6. Cut into 36 squares.

Serve as dessert on squares cut from taro or banana leaves.

Lomi Salmon

Lomi means "massage" in Hawaiian. There are no salmon in Hawaii, but Native Hawaiians picked up a taste for salted salmon working on ships that brought it back from the Pacific Northwest. Since the development of canning and freezing, salt salmon is now produced almost entirely for the Hawaiian market, and Hawaiians on the mainland have learned to make their own salt salmon for lomi salmon. The recipe is a composite of many Internet recipes from Texas, Georgia, Ohio, Washington State, California, and Hawaii.

NOTE: Salmon needs to be refrigerated overnight.

1 pound fresh salmon filet

6 tablespoons Hawaiian salt or rock salt (kosher salt)

5 tomatoes or 1/2 pound cherry tomatoes

1 round onion

1 bunch green onions (scallions)

1 12-ounce can tomato juice (optional)

crushed ice (optional)

Equipment: 1 gallon reclosable heavy plastic bag

1. Rub salmon with Hawaiian salt until completely covered. Put in baggy over night in refrigerator.

2. Wash off salt. Shred salmon with a spoon or 2 forks.

3. Chop tomatoes.

4. Halve, peel, and chop onion.

5. Clean and chop green onions.

6. Mix all ingredients except ice in a bowl.

7. Chill until ready to serve.

Serve under a layer of crushed ice, or with poi.

Hmong-Americans

The Hmong are an ethnic minority in the mountains of Laos and Vietnam. They were heavily involved in the American war effort in those countries between 1962 and 1975. After the United States withdrew from Southeast Asia, about 110,000 Hmong came to the United States as refugees, and there are about 200,000 in the U.S. today. They initially were settled in 20 states, but reconcentrated with about one-fourth now living around Fresno, California; almost as many around St. Paul, Minnesota; and a third concentration in eight cities of Wisconsin. Clan relationships are important, and much of the resettling was done to reunite clans. Certain clans have individual food taboos. Hmong women are often seen at craft fairs, selling their characteristic embroidery and appliqué (quilting).

Hmong-Americans are sometimes described as **Laotian-Americans,** but they do not identify with the lowland Lao people. Hmong cooking became more like Laotian cooking as the Indochina wars brought more Hmong to Laotian cities; thus, most of the Laotian dishes in this book, and especially the hot pepper paste, would be familiar foods to the Hmong. Hmong extended families sit down to eat together, with everyone eating from dishes in the center of the table. Spoons and forks, rather than chopsticks, are used. White rice is a staple, and there are few snacks or desserts, other than fruit. Breakfast might be a rice soup; lunch is eaten fairly early, and dinner late in the evening.

TOMSUM—A HMONG SALAD

This recipe in *Fresh Market Wisconsin* (1993) by Terese Allen came from Kathy Khamphouy of Madison, who was then working for United Refugee Services. "She and her colleague, Xai Voung, often prepare tomsum for their co-workers at staff meetings." Tomsum was originally made with unripe papaya. It is supposed to be spicy. According to Xai, "Every time we eat, we must have something hot, or we cannot eat!" You can reduce or eliminate the hot peppers and dried shrimp, but try to use enough hot sauce or pepper to get the idea of a refreshing spicy slaw.

CAUTION: Hot peppers used. Do not rub eyes. Wash hands thoroughly after handling hot peppers.

Yield: 4 servings

5-6 cups shredded carrot, cucumber, turnip, or unripe papaya
2 teaspoons minced garlic
2-5 chopped red or green Thai chile peppers ("two will make it very hot, five will light you on fire!")
1/2 cup roasted, lightly salted peanuts, ground
2 tablespoons dried shrimp, ground
3-4 thin slices tomato
3 thin slices fresh lime, plus additional lime juice to taste
2 teaspoons bottled Thai fish sauce ("nam pla")
2 teaspoons sugar (or more to taste)

Equipment: Food processor with shredding blade (optional), blender or mini-chop

1. Peel and shred vegetable(s).

2. Peel and mince garlic.

3. Halve hot peppers and remove inner pith and seeds with a spoon. Mince peppers.

4. Grind peanuts to a coarse meal. (Don't make peanut butter.)

5. Grind shrimp.

6. "In a large bowl or wooden mortar, combine 2 cups shredded vegetable of your choice with garlic and peppers. With a wooden pestle or large, sturdy spoon, smash and press until garlic and peppers are somewhat mashed. This will take several minutes; you'll be able to 'hear' the moisture in the dish after a while."

7. Slice lime and tomato.

8. Add remaining ingredients to salad mixture, along with the remaining shredded vegetable. Continue to smash and press mixture against the sides and bottom of bowl for 5-10 minutes, until vegetables are limp and juicy and ingredients are well combined.

9. Add more sugar or lime juice to taste.

Serve at room temperature with rice and grilled meats.

WATERCRESS AND BEEF

This recipe is one of 12 in *The Minnesota Ethnic Food Book*, by Anne Kaplan, Marjorie Hoover, and Willard Moore, which is still the most detailed discussion of Hmong-American cooking in English, although it was published in 1986. The authors note that "Watercress comes close in taste to a kind of greens the Hmong traditionally used. Cooks are pleased to find cress in the stores, but are dismayed at the price."

3 pounds beef top round
1/2 cup oil

2 cups sliced onions (2 large onions)

3 tablespoons minced garlic (large head of garlic)

2 quarts (8 cups) watercress

1 tablespoon salt

Equipment: Food processor to mince garlic (optional), oversized frying pan (optional)

1. Halve and peel onions. Cut thin slices the long way to get long shreds of onion.

2. Peel garlic and mince fine (easier in food processor). Slit cress stalks in half lengthwise.

3. Cut beef into 1/4-inch strips about 2 inches long. Remove all fat from beef. (This is easier to do if the beef is half-frozen.)

4. Heat oil in an oversized heavy frying pan (or 2 frying pans) over moderate heat.

5. Add beef to hot oil and cook for 2 minutes, stirring constantly.

6. Add onions and garlic and stir-fry for 2 more minutes.

7. Stir watercress into meat mixture.

8. Add salt and stir only until watercress is slightly cooked but still crisp and bright green.

Serve in bowls accompanied by rice and hot chile paste.

HONDURAN- AND GARIFUNA-AMERICANS

The 1990 census counted 116,000 Honduran-Americans, and the Immigration and Naturalization Service believes that there are 90,000 Honduran illegal aliens, making them the seventh-largest undocumented group. The majority of Honduran immigrants are in fact Garifuna, Afro-Carib Indians who are a small minority in Honduras (as well as Belize, Guatemala, and Nicaragua), but who began coming to New Orleans and other U.S. port cities after World War II. The Garifuna became more visible after 87 died in the 1990 Happyland social club fire in Brooklyn, New York. Newspaper stories indicated that as many as 100,000 Garifuna lived in the New York City area.

Non-Garifuna Honduran-Americans come from the same Spanish and Native-American roots as other Central Americans. Their food is generally less spicy than North Americans expect, especially the large tamales, but also the rice-and-beans and the casseroles.

Garifuna history is very specific. Around 1635, a raiding party of Carib Indians (who called themselves "Kalipuna," or cassava-eaters) defeated the Taino Indians on the island we now call St. Vincent, taking Taino wives. Two Spanish slave ships were wrecked on St. Vincent in 1635, and, after some fighting, the Africans (from Nigeria) and survivors of the Spanish crew joined the Carib Indians. British colonists were unable to subdue these "Black Caribs," and in 1796 and 1797 deported them to the coast of Central America, where the Garifuna flourished. They preserved their Indian language and traditional ways of making cassava bread, alongside some African cultural survivals, including dishes based on plantains and coconut palm. They developed a reputation as seafarers, and were often employed as translators between English and Spanish colonists and coastal Indians. An estimated 500,000 Garifuna now live in Central America and the U.S.

Garifuna seamen advanced in the American merchant marine and were employed as dock-workers in New Orleans during World War II. Many stayed over, forming the first Honduran and Garifuna communities. There is also a community of 20,000 to 30,000 Garifuna in Los Angeles, most of whom are from Belize. Garifuna are comfortable describing themselves as Garifuna, as **African-Americans**, as Hispanics, or as Honduran- or Belizan-Americans, and are developing Internet links with Native American groups as well.

Garifuna cooking emphasizes African staples such as coconut milk and plantains, as well as fresh seafood and wafers and sweets made from cassava meal. The Garifuna and other Hondurans also share the styles of tamales, tortillas, and beans used by other Central Americans.

RICE AND BEANS

This Garifuna recipe is my reconstruction of one I ate at the quincanera (15th birthday celebration) of Taisha David-Guity in Cambridge, Massachusetts, as cooked by her Garifuna aunts from Brooklyn. Garifuna cooks usually make their own coconut milk for this recipe, sometimes using the bean liquid with the grated coconut meat to make the rich coconut milk.

NOTE: Beans should be soaked for several hours or overnight.

Yield: serves 16-24
  1 pound dried red beans
  2 teaspoons salt
  4 cans coconut milk
  1 small onion
  4 cloves garlic
  1 small red bell pepper
  2 tablespoons oil
  4 cups rice
  1 teaspoon dried thyme

  1. Bring 2 1/2 quarts of water to a boil.

  2. Add the beans and cook 4 minutes.

  3. Let soak several hours or overnight.

  4. Add salt to water and cook beans until done, 45 minutes to an hour.

  5. Halve, peel, and chop the onion.

  6. Peel and chop the garlic.

  7. Cut off the ends of the bell pepper, remove pith and seeds, and cut into fine dice.

  8. Heat the oil in a soup pot and add the onion, green pepper, and garlic.

  9. Stir fry for a few minutes until the onion is translucent, then add the rice.

  10. Stir fry until all the rice is coated with oil and beginning to turn white, another few minutes.

  11. Drain the beans over a bowl so you still have the bean liquid.

  12. Add the coconut milk, 2 cups of the bean liquid, the drained beans, and the thyme to the rice pot.

  13. Bring almost to a boil, reduce heat, and cover the pan to simmer for 20 minutes or until rice is done.

Serve as a side dish.

HONDURAN CABBAGE SALAD

This recipe from Lorena Simon of New Orleans was collected by Jessie Tirsch in A *Taste of the Gulf Coast.* The recipe makes a fresh, light salad that goes well with the bland, starchy Honduran tamales.

Yield: 10 large side servings
  1 large head green cabbage (about 4 pounds)
  2 large tomatoes
  1 large bunch fresh cilantro
  1/2 cup fresh lemon juice (about 2 medium lemons)
  2 1/2 teaspoons salt
  3/4 teaspoon ground cumin
  6 turns freshly ground black pepper

Equipment: Lemon squeezer

  1. Shred cabbage by cutting into sixths, removing the core, and slicing thin slices across each section.

  2. Chop the tomatoes to get about 2 cups.

  3. Chop up the cilantro to get about 1 cup.

  4. Toss together the chopped ingredients.

  5. Sprinkle on salt, cumin, and pepper.

  6. Sprinkle on lemon juice and toss again.

7. Let the salad sit for about 15 minutes, then toss again.

Serve in small bowls.

CHICKEN WITH RICE

This Honduran version of arroz con pollo or paella was contributed by Lila Lanza to the *Cookbook 1991* of the Intergenerational Literacy Project in Chelsea, Massachusetts.

    1 whole chicken
    1/2 pound (1 cup) rice
    1 small onion
    1 teaspoon green olives (6 olives)
    2 packages of Latin American seasoning
        with cilantro, or 4 tablespoons chopped
        fresh cilantro
    salt and pepper to taste
    2 large tomatoes
    1 bell pepper
    1 large carrot
    2 cups string beans (or 1 pound frozen)

1. Wash chicken and cut into small pieces. Cut the breast into 6 pieces, each wing into 2 pieces, and so on.

2. Put in pot with 2 or 3 cups water to cover. Add salt, pepper, and cilantro or seasoning.

3. Bring to a boil and simmer about 20 minutes.

4. Scrape and slice the carrot into small pieces. If using fresh string beans, cut off ends and stems and slice into 1-inch lengths.

5. Cut off the top and bottom of the bell pepper, remove seeds and pith, and cut into small squares.

6. Put the rice and vegetables with about 1 1/2 cups water in a tightly covered pan. Cook 15 minutes and remove from heat to steam for another 15 minutes.

7. When chicken is done, add it to the rice and "stir slightly so that it is mixed."

8. Add a little of the chicken broth, cover the rice, and put on low heat to finish cooking.

Serve with a salad as a one-pot supper.

HOPI

Many of the 11,700 Hopi live in settlements atop mesas in northern Arizona; some of the adobe buildings in these settlements have been dated by tree rings to be at least 500 years old. The Hopi are the largest single group of Pueblo Indians in the Southwest; they are descended from the Anasazi, who, about 1,000 years ago, lived to the north of the present Hopi lands in pueblos and kivas (underground ceremonial rooms) that were similar to those of the Hopi. Hopi culture involves a complicated yearly schedule of ceremonies. The Hopi have been successful in resisting European and American cultural influences, as well as the very different Navajo culture which completely surrounds the 1.5-million-acre Hopi reservation. The Hopi participated in the 1680 Pueblo revolt, and essentially never let Spanish missionaries return.

The Hopi have evolved a considerable cuisine, and have learned to use about 200 species of wild and domestic plants in their high desert environment. Blue food is considered important, and Hopi blue corn tortillas became a gourmet fad in the 1980s. They also use the ashes from burning the chamisa shrub to make the blue corn dishes more blue. Their cooking has been well recorded in *Hopi Cookery* by Juanita Tiger Kavenna (University of Arizona Press, 1980).

WHOLE WHEAT STEW

The Hopi were able to grow Spanish wheat, and logically tried it out as a replacement for hominy in their usual stew. Although Mrs. Kavenna doesn't say so, the use of whole wheat may have later been encouraged by Mormon missionaries, who had some early success among the Hopi.

You can get whole wheat in health food stores.

NOTE: Wheat should be soaked overnight.

3 cups whole wheat, or hulled whole wheat berries
1 pound stew meat
1/4 cup chopped onions (1 small onion)
1 tablespoon salt

Equipment: Large cooking pot

1. If using whole wheat in the hull, wash well and cover with lukewarm water. Soak overnight to soften. Drain and grind on a stone to remove hulls. (See **Zuni** method for hulling hominy corn.) If using whole wheat berries without hulls, start at Step 2.

2. Put hulled wheat in a large cooking pot and cover with water. Bring to a boil.

3. Halve, peel, and chop onion.

4. Add meat, onion, and salt to whole wheat.

5. Return to a boil, lower heat to a simmer, and cover pot. Cook 3 hours, or until meat is tender and wheat has softened. Stir occasionally and add water as needed.

Serve with your favorite bread and a green salad.

HOPI PINTO BEANS

This recipe is considered a traditional food by the Hopi, who were growing 14 kinds of beans by the 1970s. Mrs. Kavenna reports that the beans were originally made in pottery pots, but the bottoms tended to wear out. The pots were then used as chimneys. Since Mrs. Kavenna originally came to the Hopi reservation as a home extension agent, she helpfully provides a pressure cooker method adjusted to the altitude of the Hopi reservation.

2 1/2 cups dried pinto beans
1 cup bacon, or an 8-ounce piece of ham
salt to taste
4 tablespoons oil if using pressure cooker

Equipment: Large pressure cooker (optional), bean or soup pot

1. Wash and sort beans carefully.

2. Put beans in a bean or soup pot and add bacon or ham and 7 cups water.

3. Bring to a boil and simmer for 3 hours, or until beans are tender, stirring occasionally and adding hot water as needed. If using pressure cooking, add oil and pressure cook 45 minutes at 15 pounds pressure (at sea level, 25 minutes); let pressure drop naturally to zero, remove lid and simmer an additional 12 minutes.

4. Taste for salt, which will depend on the saltiness of the meal and individual preference.

"Serve as a main meal with tortillas and a green vegetable, or as a light meal with fried bread."

HUNGARIAN-AMERICANS

The 1990 census estimated 1,582,000 Americans claiming Hungarian descent. Although immigration records indicate that a total of 1,674,000 Hungarians arrived in the U.S. between 1820 and 1996, Hungary was part of the much larger Austro-Hungarian Empire before World War I, and included many Eastern European emigrants who now see themselves as **Jewish-Americans, German-Americans, Slovak-Americans, Carpatho-Rusyn-Americans,** and others. The Hungarian people are descended from the Magyars, one of a number of tribes that migrated into the region from Asia in the ninth century. They speak a language that is unrelated to the languages spoken in surrounding nations, and this difference in language and ethnic origins has been an important factor in establishing Hungarian ethnic identity.

Nonetheless, even the smaller Hungary of today is a country of ethnic and religious diversity. One consequence of this diversity is that Hungarian immigrants were both more internally cohesive and more ready to Americanize than many other East European groups. The earliest Hungarian groups were political refugees from an 1848 revolt against the Austrian empire; about 800 served in the Union army during the Civil War. Poverty drove a much larger group from Hungary beginning in 1880, but , until 1902, most were not Hungarian Magyars.Hungarian immigrants arrived with a high rate of literacy, and many were able to find or move to better jobs in large cities. After 1924, U.S. immigration quotas limited Hungarian immigration, although Hungary's fascist government drove many people to the U.S. in the 1930s and 1940s. Another 24,000 refugees reached the United States after World War II, and more than 35,000 refugees came to the U.S. after Soviet tanks crushed the Hungarian anti-Communist revolt of 1956. Hungary was one of the first countries in Eastern Europe to move away from Soviet domination in the late 1980s, and business opportunities there have since attracted some Hungarian-Americans.

Hungarian food is a classic European cuisine; it is well described in English by such Hungarian-American restaurant chefs as Paul Kovi, George Lang, and Louis Szathmáry (who has also been a major collector and writer about American food history). The characteristic strong flavors of paprika, caraway, and sautéed peppers and onions have influenced the cuisines of surrounding countries. Other Hungarian-American dishes include goulash of several kinds, stuffed cabbage, sour cherry soup, and noodle puddings with poppy seeds.

POGACHELS

This recipe is from my Hungarian-Jewish grandmother, Malvina Kurtz, who emigrated from Transylvania as a young teenager. It was written down in two variations for my Aunt Helen, her daughter-in-law, in the late 1940s. The Hungarian spelling is "pogácsa," but "pogachels" is how Grandma Kurtz pronounced it and wrote it. All her baking involved a lot of butter and cream, but these butter cookies are the richest and most delicate of all.

4 cups flour
1 cup butter
1/2 pint sour cream
2 egg yolks
1 whole egg
1/2 cup sugar, plus 1/4 cup to make cinnamon sugar topping
1 teaspoon baking powder
1 teaspoon vanilla
1 teaspoon cinnamon for topping
butter to grease baking sheets

Equipment: 2 baking sheets, pastry blender or food processor, rolling pin, 2 1/2-inch round cookie cutter (or a glass jar)

1. Cream together butter and 1/2 cup of the sugar with pastry blender or food processor.

2. Separate eggs by pouring back and forth from shell to shell over a cup to catch the white.

3. Whisk eggs into butter mixture.

4. Mix vanilla into sour cream.

5. Mix baking powder with flour in a bowl.

6. Work flour mixture and sour cream mixture into butter-sugar mixture, alternating between them.

7. When dough is finished, refrigerate.

8. Butter baking sheets. Flour board and rolling pin.

9. Roll out dough about 1/4-inch thick.

10. Mix cinnamon and sugar. Sprinkle on dough.

11. Cut out rounds with a 2-inch cookie cutter or glass jar with a narrow mouth.

12. Roll up the scraps and roll out again.

13. Bake at 350 degrees for 15-20 minutes.

14. Remove from baking sheets carefully with a spatula and cool on wire racks.

Serve cooled to room temperature. Can be frozen and reheated at 200 degrees.

CHICKEN PAPRIKA

This recipe for one of the best-known Hungarian dishes comes from *Jolie Gabor's Family Cookbook*, which was written in 1962 with Ted and Jean Kaufman. Mrs. Gabor, the mother of Zsa-Zsa and TV actress Eva, departs from the usual only in the substitution of chicken fat for lard. My Jewish-Hungarian grandmother also made this with chicken fat, and omitted the sour cream. You will also hear and see "paprikash" and "paprikas," which are the Hungarian pronunciation and spelling, respectively.

Yield: serves 6
   2 large onions
   4 tablespoons chicken fat
   1 tablespoon paprika
   4 pounds chicken
   1/2 clove garlic
   1 cup chicken stock
   1 large tomato, fresh or canned
   1 cup sour cream

Equipment: Garlic press, large skillet with a cover

1. Halve, peel, and mince the onions. (Use swim goggles to avoid tears.)

2. In a large skillet with a cover, sauté onions in chicken fat until soft and light golden.

3. Add paprika and stir to fry the paprika along with the onions.

4. Cut chicken into serving pieces.

5. Remove onions, increase heat, and brown chicken pieces on all sides for about 10 minutes.

6. Sprinkle with salt and pepper.

7. Peel garlic and press onto chicken.

8. Return onions to pan and add chicken stock.

9. Stir carefully to get any browned and stuck material into the sauce.

10. Cut the tomato into small pieces and add it to the chicken.

11. Cover pot, reduce heat, and cook slowly for 1 to 1 1/2 hours, or until chicken is tender.

12. Remove chicken, skim off fat, and add sour cream to the sauce, a little at a time, stirring constantly until the sauce is well blended.

13. Return chicken to the pot and spoon sour cream sauce over it.

14. Simmer gently over very low heat for 5 minutes or until thoroughly heated. Do not boil.

Serve with noodles or dumplings.

PAPRIKA POTATOES

This is the kind of ethnic recipe that is often forgotten once an immigrant group can afford regular meat, but paprika potatoes have persisted in Hungarian-American families because they are so good. This recipe appeared in the May 13, 1999, *Pittsburgh Post-Gazette*, and is archived on the paper's Web site.

Yield: serves 6
   2 medium onions, peeled and chopped
   2 garlic cloves, crushed
   3 tablespoons lard or fat
   1/4 teaspoon caraway seeds
   1 to 2 tablespoons Hungarian paprika
   salt and pepper to taste
   6 medium potatoes, peeled and cubed
   1 cup sour cream, at room temperature

Equipment: Garlic press, large saucepan

1. Remove sour cream from refrigerator so it can come to room temperature.

2. Halve, peel, and chop the onions. (Use swim goggles to avoid tears.)

3. In a large saucepan, heat the lard or fat, and sauté onions.

4. Peel garlic and press into the fat. Cook until the onions are tender.

5. Peel the potatoes and cut into small cubes.

6. When onions are light golden brown, stir in caraway seeds, paprika, salt, and pepper and cook for 1 minute.

7. Add potatoes and enough water to barely cover. Cook slowly, covered, for 20 minutes or until potatoes are cooked.

8. Stir in sour cream (or shake the saucepan to avoid breaking up potatoes) and leave on low heat until hot.

KÖRÖZÖT LIPTAUR CHEESE SPREAD

This recipe, the mother of all cheese appetizers, comes from *By Special Request*, which was published by Rachel R. Isserow in Brookline, Massachusetts in 1978. She has somewhat scrambled her languages, since "Körözöt" is Hungarian for cheese spread, but "Liptaur" is the German name for the cheese named after a region in Slovakia (formerly part of the Austro-Hungarian Empire). Known in Hungarian as "Lipto," the cheese is a sharp sheep's milk product, so I sometimes use imported feta in this recipe.

1/2 pound farmer cheese
1/4 pound cream cheese
1/8 pound (1/2 stick) butter
3 tablespoons sour cream
1 teaspoon prepared mustard
1 teaspoon capers (optional)
2 anchovy fillets (optional)
2 scallions (or one small onion)
1 1/2 teaspoons paprika
2 teaspoons caraway seeds
1/4 teaspoon sharp Hungarian paprika or cayenne pepper, "which you may increase if you get used to the flavor"

parsley, capers, or rolled anchovies to garnish

Equipment: Blender or food processor, large bowl, potato masher

1. Take out butter to soften. Chop the green parts of the scallions, or halve, peel, and chop the onion.

2. If using capers or anchovies, mash them up with a fork.

3. Mash all ingredients but the hot pepper and garnishes in a large, wide bowl using a potato masher or fork. "This spread may be prepared in a blender or processor but elbow grease is the secret flavor."

4. Add salt and pepper to taste.

5. Mound blended mixture on a plate.

6. Garnish with parsley, capers, or rolled anchovies.

7. "It is customary to use the tines of a fork to decorate the top of the mound. Eva taught me a little trick. She 'spilled' a bit of sharp paprika on some wax paper and repeatedly dipped a teaspoon in it, each time inserting the spoon in the cheese spread to create a scalloped design."

Serve as an appetizer with crackers or wedges of pumpernickel bread.

ICELANDIC-AMERICANS

Since Leif Ericsson, born in Iceland, was the first European known to reach North America, Icelanders could have been the first immigrants to the United States. But so far archeologists have confirmed only one ancient Viking settlement, and that one is on Newfoundland, in Canada. As the Viking sagas record, Icelanders left North America and did not return until the 1850s, when small groups joined the Mormons settling around Spanish Fork, Utah, which still celebrates its Icelandic heritage with an annual parade. Between an 1870 volcanic eruption and 1900, about 15,000 Icelanders came to the U.S. and Canada. Although not a large number, it was about one-third of the island's population at that time. About 50,000 Icelandic immigrants and their descendants live in the U.S. now, with notable groups around Mountain, North Dakota, and in western Minnesota. Immigration is hard to estimate because Iceland was part of Denmark from 1397 until July 17, 1944. Icelander immigrants were thus often counted as Danes. Icelandic-Americans celebrate "August the Deuce," the anniversary of the king of Denmark granting Iceland an improved constitution on August 2, 1874, although this has never been a legal holiday in Iceland.

Iceland is on the Arctic circle, though warmed by ocean currents and geothermal activity. One immigrant now living in Charlotte, North Carolina, describes her childhood food as "Lamb and potatoes, fish and potatoes. Very little beef and less pork. And salmon to die for. Atlantic salmon, to me, is God's Food! Nirvana! As for creative potato cooking—the first time I had anything but boiled potatoes was when I moved to Canada from Iceland. I don't honestly remember even having baked potatoes before then." Some other Icelandic-American foods include boiled fish, fish balls, mutton soup, rolled pancakes, and caramel potatoes.

VÍNARTERTA

This is a stack cake, rather like the **Scotch-Irish** and **Melungeon** apple stack cakes. The name means "Viennese Torte," so it may have been a homemade response to something like a multi-layer Hungarian dobos torte. Diana Raphael Schlesser contributed the recipe to *Recipes from Around the Pond*, published by the First Church Unitarian Universalist in Jamaica Plain, Massachusetts, in the early 1990s. Ms. Schlesser visited Iceland and decided that her North Dakota grandmother substituted prunes for rhubarb, and dropped the traditional cardamom. I think the rhubarb may have reached Iceland after her ancestors left; I have seen other Icelandic-American recipes that include a half teaspoon of cardamom seeds in the prune filling.

3/4 cup solid shortening
1 cup sugar
2 eggs
2 teaspoons vanilla
3 1/3-4 cups flour (approximately)
1 teaspoon salt
2 teaspoons baking powder
1/4 cup milk
2 (one-pound) boxes pitted prunes

1 lemon
almond extract, vanilla extract, or 2 tablespoons cardamom (optional)

Equipment: Pastry blender or large fork, rolling pin, one or more cast iron skillets or 9-inch round cake pans or cookie sheets, wire racks to cool layers, knife or spatula to spread filling, aluminum foil, blender or food processor to puree filling, lemon zester or box grater, lemon juicer

1. Cream together shortening and sugar with pastry blender or large fork.

2. Stir in eggs and vanilla.

3. Mix together flour, salt, and baking powder.

4. Add dry ingredients and milk alternately to shortening mixture.

5. Knead dough (see Appendix 1).

6. Divide dough into 6 equal parts.

7. Grease and flour cake pans, skillet, or cookie sheets.

8. Flour hands (remove jewelry first) and pat dough into skillet or round cake pan. Or roll each portion of dough to fit a 9-inch round cake pan. (*Hint:* You can use the cake pans or the top to a skillet to cut precisely round sheets, and add the trimmings to the next ball of dough. Or you can put dough on the bottom of a round cake pan, trim off the excess, and bake on the upside-down pan.)

9. Bake each layer at 400 degrees for 12-15 minutes.

10. Cool a few minutes, and remove from skillet or cake pans to cool on a wire rack.

11. Bake additional layers in the skillet or cake pans as needed until all 6 layers are baked.

12. Simmer prunes in water to cover until soft.

13. Remove rind of lemon with zester or grater.

14. Juice lemon.

15. Puree prunes. Add rind and juice of lemon and other optional flavorings.

16. Set aside the neatest looking cake layer for the top.

17. Take the ugliest layer, and put it on a plate.

18. Spread with 1/5 of the filling, and top with another cake layer.

19. Repeat until you put on the top layer, which is not covered with filling.

20. Try to arrange layers so that you have a reasonably neat and level cake.

21. Wrap in plastic wrap for at least several hours, "allowing prune spread to moisten cake layers."

Serve plain or with whipped cream.

CREAMED POTATOES

This recipe from Gayle Swanson of North Carolina is so familiar to her that I had to provide quantities. It is usually made from leftover boiled potatoes, reheated in the cream sauce. **Danish-Americans** will also recognize this dish.

2 tablespoons butter, and a little more for garnish
3 tablespoons flour
1 cup milk
2 large potatoes
1 tablespoon chopped parsley

1. Peel and dice potatoes to 1/2-inch cubes. Boil in water to cover.

2. Melt butter in a small pan and stir in flour.

3. Cook for 3 minutes.

4. Warm milk separately.

5. Whisk warm milk into butter and flour so that the mixture makes a thick cream sauce.

6. When potatoes are fork tender, drain.

7. Combine potatoes and cream sauce.

8. Chop parsley.

Serve with fish or as a snack, garnished with dots of butter and chopped parsley.

INDIANS (AMERICAN)

See UNDER NAMES OF INDIVIDUAL TRIBAL NATIONS

INDIANS (ASIAN)

See ASIAN INDIAN-AMERICANS

INDO-CARIBBEANS

See GUYANESE-AMERICANS, TRINIDADIAN-AMERICANS (AND INDO-CARIBBEANS)

INUIT

See ESKIMOS (INUIT) AND ALEUTS

IRANIAN-AMERICANS

See PERSIAN-AMERICANS (IRANIANS)

IRISH-AMERICANS

Almost 39 million Americans claim Irish ancestry. The most visible wave of Irish immigration came between 1820 and 1860 when Ireland produced more than one-third of all immigration to the U.S. The **Scotch-Irish** and other Protestants from Ireland who had arrived earlier began at this time to be differentiated from the flood of impoverished Irish Catholics. In the Potato Famine decade of the 1840s, Irish immigration was almost half of total immigration to the U.S. This influx of Irish was the first really mass migration to the United States, and the first arrival of a large Roman Catholic group. Despite coming from about 80 percent rural backgrounds, the Irish-Americans were also the first immigrant group to remain about 90 percent in cities. One reason was that the early generations sent most of their earnings home to desperately poor relations, and thus could not save to buy farmland. Because the Irish immigrants arrived speaking English, even the relatively unskilled were able to begin work in factories, mines, railroads, or in private homes as maids or coachmen. Rural backgrounds and discrimination held back many Irish immigrants from advancing as far as other European groups, but the second generation did much better. By the 1900s, Irish-Americans were a large fraction of all policemen, teachers, and longshoreman, and were moving forward in politics. Full acceptance was marked for many by the election of a Catholic Irish-American, John F. Kennedy, to the presidency in 1960.

Irish immigration resumed somewhat in the 1980s and 1990s as the expanding American economy drew Irish immigrants, not all with legal documentation, to eastern cities to work in construction and service industries. This recent immigration has brought a welcome renewal to the "Irish food" served in restaurants and pubs, adding seafood dishes to meat-and-potatoes staples like "Irish stew," corned beef and cabbage, and colcannon. Creamy clam chowder is also on many Irish-American menus; while it is not usually described as Irish food, the milk and potatoes were not often recorded before the arrival of Irish cooks in the 1840s. Today's clam chowder more resembles traditional Irish soups than the New England fish chowders of the nineteenth century. A tiny sub-group of Irish-Americans are the Tinkers and Travellers discussed under **Gypsy-Americans**, with a recipe for Irish scones.

MAYOR CURLEY'S FAVORITE IRISH BREAD

This fairly recent version of Irish bread was brought over from County Mayo by Helen McDonough, maid to James Michael Curley, Boston's "Last Hurrah" Irish-American mayor in the 1940s. These breads were originally plain with special sweetened ones for holidays, but only the sweet ones have remained in use in the U.S., and often only appear on St. Patrick's Day. Mrs. McDonough made these for Sunday night suppers. Irish breads were originally yeast breads, then became "soda bread," leavened with baking soda and buttermilk, from the early 1800s. The recipe was produced by Mrs. McDonough's son John for *Recipes from Around the Pond*, which was published by the First Church Unitarian Universalist in Jamaica Plain, Massachusetts, in the early 1990s. John E. McDonough was then a state representative, and retains the additional and supreme qualification, as Major Curley used to say, of being my friend.

1/2 stick softened butter
2 cups flour
3 teaspoons baking powder
1/4 to 1/3 cup sugar
pinch salt
1 egg
1/2 cup milk
1 cup currants
solid shortening to grease cake pan or baking sheet

Equipment: Round cake pan or baking sheet, pastry blender

1. Mix dry ingredients.

2. Mix butter through flour with a pastry blender or large fork.

3. Beat egg and mix with milk.

4. Mix all ingredients together with a spoon. You may need a bit more milk.

5. Flour a board and roll mixture onto it to knead (see Appendix 1).

6. Grease and flour pan or baking sheet.

7. Pat into cake pan evenly, or flatten to about 1 1/2 inches and put on the middle of baking sheet.

8. Slash an "X" or plus-sign fully across the top.

9. Bake at 400 degrees for 30-40 minutes.

10. Test for doneness with a toothpick or wire cake tester.

11. Cool on a wire rack.

12. A safe way to cut a round bread is to half it, put the cut sides down, and cut straight slices. You can get more even slices by halving the bread and cutting on the diagonal.

Serve with hot tea or cold buttermilk.

COLCANNON

I have added quantities to this recipe from Mrs. Mike O'Callaghan, whose husband was governor of Nevada in the early 1970s. The recipe appeared in *The Democratic Caucus Cookbook*, which was edited by Myrna B. Shevin and published by the Democratic Women's Club of Florida. In Ireland, colcannon was traditional at Halloween. Mrs. O'Callaghan has made the dish richer and the fortunes more optimistic than they were in Ireland, where the finder of a button or thimble was destined to be a bachelor or spinster.

Yield: 12-16 servings
  3 pounds potatoes (9-12 medium potatoes)
  1 cup cream
  1 large leek or 3 small leeks
  3 stalks celery

1 large onion
1-3 pounds green cabbage
2-10 tablespoons butter
2 tablespoons parsley
finger ring (optional)
silver coin (optional)
button (optional)

Equipment: Potato ricer or sieve, wax paper to wrap fortunes

1. Peel and boil potatoes until soft.

2. Halve, peel, and chop the onion.

3. Halve, core, and chop the cabbage.

4. Cut off dried green leaves on the leek, wash carefully under outer leaves, and slice thinly the white part and some of the green. Slice celery.

5. Simmer green vegetables in water to cover until tender, about 7-12 minutes, and drain. ("Stock may be preserved for soup.")

6. Drain potatoes, return to the pot, and dry over heat.

7. Rice potatoes through a sieve or strainer. Mix in butter and cream (or milk) until fluffy.

8. Add vegetable to potatoes and mix together.

9. Chop parsley and melt more butter for serving.

Serve hot or reheated on plate in a mound. "Press in middle to form a well and fill with melted butter. Garnish with parsley. If you are feeling traditionally Irish, you might want to hide fortune symbols in the colcannon. These symbols will be meaningful to the person who finds them. The finder of a button will be blessed with good fortune of the day. A ring means early marriage, and a silver coin will bring its finder wealth and riches. The fortunes should be wrapped in paper so that the guests will find them before breaking a tooth."

CONAN O'BRIEN'S IRISH STYLE POTATO-CHIVE PANCAKES

The Irish-American comedian and late-night host had some help from the Milk Processor

Education Program in working out this low-fat version of traditional Irish pancakes called "boxty." The method of drying out boiled potatoes in the empty pot is called "stoving" in Ireland, and the potatoes at that stage are "stovies." This recipe appeared in the Detroit *News* of March 17, 1998.

Yield: 12 patties, or 4 main-dish servings

    2 pounds potatoes (6-8 medium potatoes)
    1 cup fat-free or 1-percent low-fat milk
    1 bunch chives to make 1/3 cup chopped
    3/4 teaspoon salt
    1/4 teaspoon freshly ground black pepper
    3 teaspoons butter or margarine
    1/2 cup fat-free or low-fat sour cream

Equipment: Potato masher, non-stick skillet, large saucepan

1. Peel potatoes and cut into 1-inch cubes.

2. Place potatoes in a large saucepan; cover with cold water, and bring to a boil over high heat.

3. Reduce heat; simmer uncovered until potatoes are tender, 15 to 20 minutes.

4. Chop chives.

5. Drain potatoes; return to saucepan. Turn heat under saucepan to medium-low. Cook potatoes until dry, about 2 minutes, stirring occasionally.

6. Add milk. Using potato masher, mash potato mixture until fairly smooth.

7. Remove from heat; stir in chives and salt and pepper.

8. Transfer to a medium bowl; cover and refrigerate until cold. Potatoes will thicken as they cool.

9. Form potato mixture into 12 patties about 3 1/2 inches in diameter and 1/2-inch thick.

10. Melt 1 teaspoon butter in a large nonstick skillet over medium heat until hot and sizzling.

11. Add 3 or 4 patties to skillet; cook until golden brown, about 2 minutes per side. Keep warm in a 200-degree oven while cooking remaining patties in remaining butter.

Serve warm with sour cream.

CORNED BEEF AND CABBAGE

Corned beef and cabbage was an Easter dish in Ireland. In the United States, it became the official dish of St. Patrick's Day and then weekly fare as immigrants took advantage of cheaper beef. Recent immigrants from Ireland are surprised at how often corned beef and cabbage is served by Irish-Americans, and how the beef and potatoes have pushed traditional carrots and turnips out of the pot. This 1997 recipe is by Meghan K., who was then in the fourth grade at St. Patrick School in Smithtown, New York. It is posted as part of an Internet e-mail cookbook project at <http://www.otan.dni.us/webfarm/emailproject/cook.htm>. Meghan's family uses different pots to cook the vegetables, but this is usually a one-pot boiled dinner.

    1 corned beef brisket
    1 garlic clove
    pepper
    5-pound cabbage
    5-pound bag of potatoes
    1 loaf rye bread

Equipment: 8-quart pot

1. Peel garlic clove.

2. In an 8-quart pot, bring beef brisket, garlic clove, pepper, and water (to cover) to a boil. Reduce heat to simmer for 3 1/2 hours.

3. Scrub potatoes and peel around the equator.

4. In a separate pot, boil potatoes until fork tender, starting about 40 minutes before brisket is done.

5. Halve cabbage and cut into wedges.

6. In a separate pot, boil cabbage until done, starting about 15 minutes before brisket is done.

7. Remove meat from broth and slice.

Serve sliced meat with cabbage, a potato, and slices of fresh rye bread and butter.

IROQUOIS

As with many Native Americans, the Iroquois, whose main territory was in what is now central New York State, were first named to Europeans by other Indians, eastern enemies who called them "snakes" in their Algonkian language. Another possible derivation is from the word "Ierokawa," meaning "they who smoke." Recently, the Iroquois, like many other tribes, have revived their own term for themselves— Hodenosaunee (Hoo-deno-SHAW-nee), meaning "people of the longhouse." Until the sixteenth century, the people known as Iroquois had been five separate and warring tribes—the Mohawk, Oneida, Onondaga, Cayuga, and Seneca. In the late sixteenth century, a Mohawk named Hiawatha convinced the individual tribes to unite, thereby creating a federation with a form of representative government that in the eighteenth century may have influenced the U.S. Constitution. By 1650, the five federated tribes controlled a larger territory than many European countries and could put thousands of warriors into the field. Caught in the wars of the European colonial powers, the Iroquois tried to remain neutral, though most of the federated tribes backed the British during the American Revolution. Today, the Iroquois lands have been reduced to small reservations in upstate New York and neighboring Canada. Confrontations with whites over land and water rights continue to this day. In 1712, the Iroquoian-speaking Tuscaroras became the sixth member of the federation, which currently is the largest Indian group east of the Mississippi, with about 50,000 enrolled members in the U.S. and at least 5,000 more in Canada. Some groups of Iroquois live in Oklahoma.

Iroquoian people in New York State and neighboring parts of Canada retain much of their language and culture. The sports and games they pioneered continue to bring them together, especially for lacrosse leagues. In addition to the corn and bean dishes each group of European settlers learned from various Indian tribes, the Iroquois in particular passed along techniques of large-scale maple syrup production. Popcorn with maple syrup was probably the inspiration for Crackerjack. The Iroquois also made a roasted-corn coffee that must have been rather like Postum.

ROAST CORN SOUP
('O' NANH-DAH)

Corn soup, the most popular Iroquois recipe, is in wide use at tribal and social events. This Seneca recipe by Miriam Lee was published on the Internet site of the Center for World Indigenous Studies at <ftp.halcyon.com /pub/FWDP/ CWIS>. When fresh corn is not in season, the Iroquois use hominy or dried sweet corn.

NOTE: Beans need to be soaked overnight.

12 ears white corn in milky stage (or two 15 1/2-ounce cans hominy)
1 pound salt pork (lean and fat)
1 pound dried pinto or kidney beans

Equipment: Large griddle, cookie sheet, aluminum foil, large soup pot

1. Pick over beans, wash twice, and soak overnight.

2. In a large soup pot, bring beans to a boil with 4 quarts of water for 30-40 minutes.

3. Cut salt pork into small pieces. (It is easier to do this if the pork is partially frozen.)

4. Husk corn and roast on top of range (using built-in griddle if your stove is equipped with one) over low heat. Grease griddle with a fat piece of salt pork and keep rotating corn until ears are golden brown.

5. After the corn is roasted, take ears and put on foil-covered cookie sheet until cool enough to handle.

6. After beans have cooked 30-40 minutes, drain and rinse well in tepid water.

7. Put beans and diced salt pork in a large soup pot with 4 quarts of water. Bring to a boil.

8. Scrape each ear once or twice with a sharp knife.

9. Add corn to soup and cook about 1 hour, or until beans are done.

Serve with salt and pepper, and bread and butter; the bread could be white bread, biscuits, "scoon" (Iroquois fry bread), or ghost bread (see below).

ONONDAGA GHOST BREAD

Mrs. Louella Derrick of Nedrow, New York, contributed this recipe to Anita Borghese's *Foods from Harvest Festivals and Folk Fairs*. This recipe is called ghost bread because it was historically used in ceremonies for the dead, which required serving a meal. Mrs. Derrick did not usually cook with measurements, but the measures given produce a biscuit-like loaf similar to **Wampanoag** bannock.

Yield: small loaf
   4 cups flour
   1/4 teaspoon salt
   4 teaspoons baking powder
   1/4 cup lard or margarine
   1 cup water or milk

Equipment: Food processor (optional, see below), pastry blender or large fork, small loaf pan

   1. Grease the small loaf pan.

   2. Preheat the oven to 375 degrees.

   3. Combine dry ingredients in the mixing bowl.

   4. Cut in the lard or shortening with pastry cutter or large form until the mixture resembles coarse meal.

   5. Add liquid gradually, stirring constantly.

   6. When it gets too hard to stir with a spoon, flour your hands, and knead by hand (see Appendix 1).

   7. Shape into a small loaf and pat down into the loaf pan.

8. Bake about 35 minutes until the loaf sounds hollow when turned out of the baking pan and rapped on the bottom.

9. Cool slightly on a wire rack.

Serve warm with butter.

OGWISSIMANABO (YELLOW SQUASH SOUP)

This Tuscarora recipe is posted on the Web site at <www.wisdomkeepers.org>, which belongs to a Tennessee-based youth group for girls. "Soups were the mainstay of many American Indian diets. It was common to find a pot of soup simmering on the fire all day long. . . . 'pot luck' was the bill of fair, and creativity was the key to a successful soup."

Yield: serves 6
   1 medium yellow squash
   4 shallots or scallions (with tops)
   2 tablespoons maple syrup (real, not imitation)
   1 medium cucumber
   1 tablespoon salt
   1/4 teaspoon black pepper

Equipment: Potato masher

   1. Dice squash.

   2. Chop shallots or scallions

   3. Put vegetables and maple syrup in soup pot with 4 cups of water, and simmer for 40 minutes or until squash is tender.

   4. Slice cucumber into 1/2-inch slices.

   5. Add cucumber slices to soup.

   6. "Pour everything into a large mixing bowl and 'mash' until it forms a thick, creamy paste."

   7. Pour the paste back into the soup pot, season with salt and pepper, and simmer for another 5-10 minutes.

ITALIAN-AMERICANS

A bout 14.7 million Americans claimed Italian ancestry in 1990, up from 12.1 million in 1980. This increase reflects the increasing pride and success of the group more than an actual increase. Although Columbus, Cabot, Verrazzano, and Vespucci were early explorers of North America, most Italian immigration occurred in the "New Immigration" period of 1876 to 1924, and peaked relatively late, with 2 million coming between 1900 and 1910. Thus, many Italian-Americans suffered by being late arrivals who seemed more foreign than members of other immigrant groups. Discrimination against Italians as well as against Jews and Eastern Europeans was a major factor in the literacy testing of immigrants after 1917 and the restrictive quota system of 1924-65. Stereotypes about Italian-Americans persisted into the 1990s, even as the group progressed economically and politically, and "Italian food" became universally popular in the U.S.

More than most immigrants, Italians arrived with a sense of attachment to their village or province rather than to Italy as a whole. This occurred because Italy did not become a unified country until the 1860s, and there was little agreement on a nationwide standard dialect until well into the twentieth century. Although most came from rural backgrounds, more than 90 percent of Italian-Americans remained in American cities because they arrived after most farmland was taken and when farm areas were already in decline. Only in the "Little Italies" of American cities did most Italian immigrants first encounter such regional dishes as pizza (from Naples) or pesto sauce (from Genoa). Even factory pasta had been an expensive luxury in southern Italy.

About 75 percent of the immigrants came from southern Italy and Sicily, although significant groups from northern Italy came early to California and became involved in farming and wine-making. Many Italian foods have come into general use in the United States, and no one really thinks of spaghetti or large cold-cut sandwiches as ethnic foods today. Like many immigrants, Italian-Americans tried to keep Sunday dinners, Christmas, and Easter for ethnic foods. They succeeded better than many other groups, although the present generations are more likely to need restaurants and visits to city neighborhoods to reinforce their memories.

BONELESS CHICKEN CACCIATORE

Italian country life allowed for long hours of simmering. One of the first changes to Italian food in American immigrant neighborhoods was the emphasis on dishes that could be assembled more quickly. The Italian names indicate that these dishes had been associated with hasty cooking by men or people in situations isolated from farm families—hunter's chicken, sailor's sauce (i.e., marinara, a quick tomato sauce), and pasta putanesca (prostitute's spaghetti). This recipe for chicken cacciatore is from *The Mayor's Cookbook* (1987), by Mayor Marilyn Catino Porreca of Medford, Massachusetts. It shows changes from the immigrants' dish in that the mayor has increased the proportion of meat, combined the usual chicken stew with the spa-

ghetti course that would have been a separate course in Italy, and used boneless chicken breasts that make it faster to eat.

Yield: 6-8 servings
   4-6 pounds boneless chicken breasts
   1/4 cup oil
   4 cloves garlic
   2 28-ounce cans crushed Italian tomatoes
   1/2 teaspoon basil
   4 green peppers
   1/2 pound fresh mushrooms
   2 pounds spaghetti

Equipment: Soup pot, skillet

   1. Put on a large pot of water for spaghetti. Cut chicken breasts in quarters.

2. Heat 2 tablespoons of the oil in a soup pot and brown the chicken breasts "slightly" in batches. Add oil as needed.

3. Peel and mince the garlic into fine dice.

4. Put remaining oil in skillet and brown garlic.

5. Remove garlic and add tomatoes and 1 can water. Add salt and pepper and "small amount of basil to taste."

6. Core peppers and cut into long vertical slices. Brush any dirt off mushrooms.

7. Salt the pot of boiling water and add spaghetti; break up with a fork.

8. Add peppers and mushrooms to sauce. Simmer on low heat, and add chicken.

9. Continue cooking until peppers and mushrooms are soft.

"Serve with hot Italian bread or over spaghetti."

Greens and Beans

Immigrants from southern Italy were accustomed to foraging weeds, nuts, and mushrooms. In smaller cities, they surprised their neighbors and school classmates by picking and eating dandelions. This recipe is from Tommy Lasorda, longtime manager of baseball's Los Angeles Dodgers. It appeared in the May 15, 1988, issue of the *New York Times* via the May/June 1996 issue of *Simple Cooking* newsletter. It developed from a family dish Lasorda's mother would make from dandelion greens picked by Tommy or his four brothers when he was growing up in Rochester, New York. If you pick dandelion greens for the dish, get them before they flower, and avoid lead pollution by picking them more than 10 feet from old houses and more than 70 feet from major highways.

Yield: serves 6
   4 heads escarole (about 3 pounds) or same
      weight of Swiss chard, dandelion greens,
      or chicory
   1/4 cup olive oil
   4-6 cloves garlic

1/4 pound pepperoni
1/2 teaspoon dried oregano
salt and freshly ground pepper
2 19-ounce cans of cannellini (white kidney)
   beans, drained

Equipment: Salad spinner (optional), large pot

1. Wash greens thoroughly.

2. Bring a large pot of salted water to a boil.

3. Blanche greens for 3 minutes.

4. Drain greens and press out surplus water.

5. Chop greens coarsely (1-inch lengths).

6. Slice pepperoni very thin, then cut each slice in half.

7. Peel the garlic and chop by cutting thin slices, thin sticks, and thin dice.

8. Heat the olive oil in a large pot over medium heat.

9. Add garlic and sauté until golden.

10. Add the pepperoni and oregano and sauté for 1 minute.

11. Add the greens and 3/4 cup water. Cook at a bare simmer for 20 minutes, stirring to cook the greens evenly.

12. Drain the canned cannellini beans, add to the greens, and bring back to a simmer for a few more minutes, until the beans are heated through.

Serve with a fresh loaf of Italian bread for sopping up the liquid.

Pasta and Bean Soup (Pasta e Fagioli)

This is the famous "pasta fazool," here in a somewhat improved version from Nancy Verde Barr's *We Called It Macaroni*, which was based on her background in the Federal Hill neighborhood of Providence, Rhode Island.

Yield: serves 6
   2 ounces pancetta (fresh bacon) optional

2 tablespoons extra-virgin olive oil

1/2 small hot red pepper or 1/8 teaspoon hot pepper flakes

1 small onion

1 small rib celery

1 carrot

2 garlic cloves

1 1/4 pounds fresh tomatoes (or equivalent Italian style whole plum tomatoes)

1 1/2 pounds unshelled fresh cranberry beans, or 2 1/2 cups canned beans, drained (2 cans pinto beans)

4 cups meat broth or water

3/4 cup "assorted short macaroni" (generally ditalini or elbows)

freshly grated pecorino cheese (or parmesan)

1. Mince the pancetta, if using, and put it with the olive oil in a big pot and cook over gentle heat until the pancetta renders fat but does not brown, about 4 minutes.

2. Halve, peel, and chop the onion.

3. Peel the carrot and chop into fine dice.

4. Chop celery.

5. Peel garlic and mince.

6. Add hot pepper, onion, carrot, celery, and garlic to the hot oil and cook gently 10 minutes, or until the vegetables are soft.

7. Peel fresh tomatoes by dipping in boiling water for a minute, and plunging into cold water. The skins will loosen. With either fresh tomatoes or the skinned canned tomatoes, remove seeds by cutting each tomato in half along the equator. Squeeze out seeds and clear liquid over the sink.

8. Add tomatoes and salt to taste to the olive oil mixture and cook another 10 minutes.

9. If using fresh beans, shell, rinse, add to tomatoes and cook together 3 more minutes. Add the hot broth or water and cook until the beans are tender, 45 minutes to 1 hour. If using canned beans, add to the tomatoes, cook 3 minutes, add the broth, and cook 15 minutes.

10. Add the macaroni to the soup and continue cooking until the pasta is "al dente" (slightly resists the teeth in the middle).

11. Remove the soup from heat and let rest 10 minutes before serving.

Serve with freshly grated pecorino cheese.

NONNIE'S MEATBALLS (OR SHRIMPBALLS) AND SPAGHETTI

Spaghetti and meatballs is not an Italian food. In Italy, the pasta course was small and came before the meat course. Meatballs might be cooked in tomato sauce, which was then called "gravy" (many Italian-Americans still call it gravy). And the gravy makes a good spaghetti sauce. Italian restaurants in the United States began serving spaghetti and meatballs together to suit customers who were used to starch and meat on the same platter, and to save time. However, this recipe from the Italian-American shrimp-fishing community in Amelia Island, Florida, is one of the few home recipes I have seen in which the meatballs are actually served at the same time as spaghetti. The shrimpballs seem to be a local variation. Mrs. Joanna Litrico contributed the recipe to Helen Gordon Litrico's *Recipes from Amelia Now* (1991).

1 pound ground chuck (or 1 1/2 pounds raw shrimp)

1/3 cup plain bread crumbs (increase to 1 cup with shrimp)

3 sprigs parsley

1 medium clove garlic

2 eggs

1/4 cup grated Romano cheese

1 tablespoon water or milk

about 1/2 cup oil for frying (Mazola preferred)

1 medium onion

6-ounce can tomato paste

8-ounce can tomato sauce

1/2 stick butter

Equipment: Heavy skillet, 2 bowls

1. Peel and mince garlic.

2. Chop parsley.

3. If using shrimp, shell, devein, and chop very fine or grind in a meat grinder or food processor. Combine shrimp or meat with parsley and garlic in a bowl.

4. In a second bowl, combine bread crumbs, salt and pepper to taste, and add grated cheese.

5. Beat eggs, and mix with bread-crumb mixture.

6. Combine bread mixture into meat mixture. Mix well by hand.

7. Add a little water or milk and mix more.

8. "Dipping hands in water between times, shape meat balls, reserving a little loose meat for the sauce." (They are more cylindrical than round.)

9. Heat about a half-inch of Mazola in a heavy skillet.

10. "Sprinkle in a little salt to reduce sticking."

11. Over medium high heat, brown meatballs well on all sides.

12. Drain off and strain oil, discarding crumbs left in skillet.

13. Put 3 tablespoons of clear oil back in the skillet to start the sauce.

14. Halve and peel the onion, and cut into thin half-moon slices.

15. Over medium heat, sauté onion until limp.

16. Add reserved loose meat mixture and brown well.

17. Add tomato paste, stir and brown.

18. Add tomato sauce, stir and brown.

19. Add salt and pepper, and taste for seasoning.

20. Stir and cook about 5 minutes, then add water equal to 2 tomato paste cans (1 1/2 cups).

21. Reduce heat and cook down, stirring occasionally, about 20 minutes.

22. When sauce has thickened to a good consistency, add meatballs and allow to cook about 5 minutes.

23. Just before serving, remove meatballs, add butter to the sauce, and stir until it melts.

24. "To serve, place a little sauce on platter, then add cooked, drained spaghetti, then more sauce, and mix in with two forks."

"Serve meatballs or shrimpballs around edge of platter or in separate bowl"

RISOTTO

Risotto has become such a gourmet item that it is important to remember that this was unfussy, daily food for thousands of North Italian immigrants. This recipe, from the Viviani family of Wisconsin, is included in *Grandmothers of Greenbush* by Catherine Tripalin Murray. The constant stirring sets up a creamy, pudding-like starch gel. Imported short-grain rice works best, but my friend Steve Bodio uses inexpensive medium-grain rice successfully. If no creaminess is developing, you can cheat a little with a tablespoon of rice flour toward the end. I have given pressure-cooker directions because this device makes excellent risotto without much stirring, if you use the instant pressure release.

Yield: serves 4-6 as a main dish, 6-8 as an appetizer
  2 tablespoons oil
  1/2 cup chopped onion
  2 cups rice ("not instant")
  7 or 8 cups fresh chicken broth, or canned
  3 envelopes of saffron (3/8 gram or .0132 ounces in all)
  1/2 cup grated parmesan cheese
  2 tablespoons butter

Equipment: Pressure cooker with instant release valve for optional pressure-cooker method

1. Chop onion into small dice by halving the long way, slicing the long way, and then slicing across.

2. Dissolve saffron in 1/2 cup boiling water.

3. Pour oil, onion, and rice into a deep pan and brown slightly.

4. Add 2 cups of broth and stir constantly until broth is almost gone. (If using pressure cooker, add 6 cups broth, lock top of pressure cooker and bring up to high pressure. Cook 3 minutes and use the quick release. Open pot carefully to avoid being burned by steam. Add saffron water, and complete Steps 7 and 8, using the rest of the chicken broth before starting on water.)

5. Repeat until all the broth is gone, or rice is cooked with a slight hard spot at the center of each grain. If the rice is too soupy, stir and cook a few minutes longer.

6. Add saffron water. (Rice should turn a nice yellow color).

7. If rice is not fully cooked (or a little hard at the center), add water a cup at a time and keep stirring.

8. Add cheese and butter and mix well.

Serve soon, but, as Bodio has written, "It stays hot for a while, and you'll burn your mouth if you are tempted to start too soon. Every Northern Italian kid I know remembers making little troughs in it and pushing it up against the sides of the dish to thin and cool."

RED AND WHITE HERB ROASTED POTATOES

Oven roasted potatoes are one northern Italian answer to pasta. They are often made along with a pork roast. This recipe is from a family cookbook, *Recipes from the Heart*, published in 1994 in Glastonbury, Connecticut, by Joy Smith.

14 new potatoes (1/2 red, 1/2 white)
1 teaspoon salt
1/2 teaspoon rosemary
1/4 teaspoon fennel seed
1/2 teaspoon pepper
1/2 teaspoon paprika
4 tablespoons olive oil

Equipment: Large bowl, shallow roasting pan

1. Scrub potatoes well, but leave skin on. Cut into quarters.

2. Mix spices and olive oil in a large bowl.

3. Add potatoes and shake or stir until potatoes are well coated with oil mixture.

4. In a shallow roasting pan, arrange potatoes in a single layer.

5. Bake at 425 degrees for 30-40 minutes, or until potatoes are crispy and brown on the outside and soft in the middle. Turn the potatoes over with a spatula once or twice during cooking.

JAMAICAN-AMERICANS

Jamaica has about half the population of the British West Indies, and Jamaican-Americans have been the largest and most distinctive group of voluntary **African-American** immigrants. About 323,000 Jamaican-Americans have immigrated to the U.S. since 1981. Arriving since 1834, earlier Jamaican immigrants have provided significant leadership to the African-American community. The resistance of escaped slaves on Jamaica, called Maroons, was an inspiration to American abolitionists. The Jamaican community is concentrated in New York City (especially Brooklyn), Miami, and New Jersey. Because there are also significant numbers of undocumented Jamaican workers and of legally admitted migrant farm workers, the total number of Jamaican-Americans is estimated at 600,000 or more.

Jamaican food and music have become internationally popular, with jerk chicken and Jamaican meat pies commercially available in many U.S. cities, and ackee fruit and other Caribbean ingredients available in import stores. Many typical Afro-Caribbean dishes have colorful names in Jamaica, like "Jamaican coat of arms" for peas and rice, "bammies" for cassava bread, "bust-up shut" for a stew with torn flat-bread, and "stamp-and-go" for codfish fritters.

OXTAIL STEW WITH VEGETABLES

Shima Carter, wife of St. Louis Rams defensive end Kevin Carter, submitted this recipe to the 1997 *NFL Family Cookbook*, edited by Jim Natal. Frozen lima beans and simplified seasoning are the apparent changes in the recipe of Mrs. Carter's grandmother, who now lives in Florida.

2 pounds oxtail
2 tablespoons soy sauce
2 medium onions
2 medium cloves garlic
1 10-ounce package, frozen lima beans
12-16 baby carrots

Equipment: Garlic press, large bowl

1. Cut oxtail into 3/4-inch to 1-inch sections. Trim as much fat as possible.

2. Halve, peel, and chop the smaller onion.

3. Peel garlic cloves.

4. In a large bowl, combine soy sauce, the chopped onion, and salt (perhaps 1/2 teaspoon) and pepper to taste (start with 1 teaspoon). Some Jamaican-Americans would also add allspice or curry powder to this marinade.

5. Crush garlic into the marinade and stir well.

6. Marinate the oxtail in the mixture for at least an hour.

7. In a deep frying pan (2- to 2 1/2-inch sides), pour 1 cup of water and add the oxtail sections. Cook over medium heat, turning the sections occasionally to cook evenly. "Do not allow the water to cook away; keep adding to it as needed through the entire cooking process."

8. Simmer the meat until tender, 3 hours or longer, occasionally skimming off the fat.

9. About 30 minutes before the meat is done, add the lima beans and carrots to the pan.

10. Halve and peel the larger onion. Cut into half-moon slices, and add to the pan.

11. Continue cooking, adding small amounts of water as needed, until the vegetables are tender. The idea is to end up with a small amount of thick gravy.

Serve hot with dumplings or rice and peas.

CURRY GOAT/CHICKEN

An early stereotype of Jamaican immigrants involved curried goat meat, although people in many different foreign countries eat goat meat. As you can see by this Internet recipe posted by Richard L. Dennison, president of the Caribbean Club at Adelphi College, curry goat is apt to be lamb or chicken these days. His recipe implies that the meat is boneless, which shows the effect of relative prosperity on this immigrant dish.

2 pounds mutton or chicken
1 clove garlic
2 tomatoes
2 onions
1 scallion
1 hot pepper (*warning:* Jamaican "Scotch bonnet" chiles are very, very hot!)
3 tablespoons curry powder
2 tablespoons butter
2 ounces oil

Equipment: Garlic press, large bowl, heavy skillet

1. Cut meat into small cubes.

2. Peel garlic and press into a large bowl.

3. Slice tomatoes.

4. Halve, peel, and chop onions.

5. Trim and chop scallion.

6. Cut top off hot pepper, slit down side, and scrape out seeds and pith with a teaspoon. Cut into tiny pieces.

7. Mix vegetables, seasonings, and salt and pepper with the garlic in the bowl. Add the meat and toss to cover. Allow to rest for 1/2 hour.

8. "Separate meat from seasoning." (Scrape off most of the seasonings and reserve.)

9. Heat the butter and oil in a heavy skillet and brown meat on all sides.

10. Meanwhile, heat up 2 to 3 cups water in a teapot.

11. When meat is lightly browned, add back the seasonings and water to cover.

12. Simmer, covered, until meat is tender.

"Serve with rice or roti (Indian flat bread)."

JAPANESE-AMERICANS

Japanese immigration to the United States began in the 1860s, and most Japanese-Americans are descended from an "Issei" (first generation) of 300,000 immigrants who came between 1890 and 1924. In the West Coast states, the Issei were laborers and successful farmers, many owning their own farms despite legal barriers. In Hawaii, they were the largest group of sugar workers, and are still the largest Asian-American minority in that multi-ethnic state. Of about 1.1 million Japanese-Americans today, about half live in California, and one-quarter in Hawaii.

During World War II, 110,000 Japanese-Americans were forced to leave their West Coast homes and farms and were held for up to four years in internment camps. Although the "relocation" was found to be unconstitutional in 1944, many people lost leased farms and businesses they had been legally prohibited from buying, and issues of restitution lingered into the 1990s. In Hawaii, where Japanese settlers were about one-third of the population in the 1940s, there was almost no internment; however, Japanese-language schools and some Buddhist institutions were banned under martial law.

After World War II, the U.S. military occupation of Japan gave many other Americans a more favorable view of Japanese culture, and some servicemen returned with Japanese wives. Japanese restaurants became popular, and, by the 1990s, sushi, sukiyaki, and tempura were popular foods in most American cities.

Because the Japanese community on the mainland preserved its Japanese lifestyles and was isolated by discriminatory laws into the 1950s, its cooking did not change greatly from Japanese cooking. The community organized to provide itself with familiar kinds of rice, vegetables, and soy products, although quicker preparations like sukiyaki and peasant fast-foods like mitsuba (rice balls) were emphasized to fit into American lifestyles.

In Hawaii, the story was different. Japanese dishes were swapped with other Asian and local influences, leading to multi-ethnic inventions like "spam sushi," watermelon shave ice, tofu fish patties, and butter mochi (a pounded rice dessert). Other Japanese-American dishes include ozoni (New Year's chicken soup), nishime (a mixed vegetable stew), various pickles, tempura (fried shrimp and vegetables), and miso soup.

OBACHAN'S SPECIAL TERIYAKI SAUCE

Okoto Gotan contributed this recipe to Mindy Martin's *The Secret to Tender Pie: America's Grandmothers Share Their Favorite Recipes.* "Obachan" means "grandmother." Mrs. Gotan immigrated to the Sacramento Valley in the 1920s, and her family was able to return to their farm in Florin, California, after internment in Arkansas. She notes that the recipe is special "because only on special occasions, such as holidays, are the onion, ginger and garlic added to the sauce." In traditional Japanese cooking, teriyaki sauce is not so sweet and lacks the special ingredients, which may reflect Chinese influence, either in California and Hawaii or in the parts of Japan from which emigrants came to the United States.

Yield: enough marinade for chicken, beef, or vegetables for 6
  1 piece ginger root
  1 yellow onion (to make 3 tablespoons grated)
  3-4 garlic cloves
  1 cup soy sauce
  1 cup sugar
  1/2 cup mirin (Japanese cooking wine, or substitute 3 more tablespoons sugar)

Equipment: Grater, broiling pan or charcoal grill

1. Peel 1/2 inch of the ginger.

2. Using the narrowest openings on the grater, grate the peeled portion of the ginger into a bowl.

3. Halve and peel the onion.

4. Grate about an inch of onion into the bowl, to make 3 tablespoons.

5. Peel garlic cloves and grate into the bowl.

6. Combine with liquid ingredients to make sauce. (If necessary, bring to a boil in a small pot to dissolve sugar.)

7. Pour over chicken, beef, or vegetables (Mrs. Gotan does not mention fish) and let marinade for at least 1 hour before cooking.

8. Grill or broil. Because the sugar in the marinade will burn easily, lower temperature (or move farther from hot spots on the grill) if the food is browning too rapidly.

Serve with rice.

PAN SUSHI

Restaurant sushi is fancy and exotic, and often involves raw fish. This homemade version, contributed to an Internet list of Hawaiian recipes by Colorado college student Robert Matsuo, is a common picnic dish for Japanese-Americans in Hawaii. I have added some details from a pan sushi recipe in Rachel Laudan's *The Food of Para-*

dise: Exploring Hawaii's Culinary Heritage. Laudan's recipe doesn't use nori, but adds strips of egg, shrimp flakes, and pickled ginger to the topping. However, her topping flavors twice as much rice.

Yield: serves 10-12
  2 cups Calrose (or other short- or medium-grain rice)
  2 cans tuna
  4 tablespoons shoyu (soy sauce)
  4 tablespoons sugar
  2 tablespoons mirin (or substitute 2 more teaspoons sugar)
  1/2 cup Japanese (rice) vinegar (or use 1/4 cup white vinegar and 1/4 cup water)
  1/2 cup sugar
  1 1/2 teaspoons salt
  4 large sheets of nori (seaweed paper, optional)

Equipment: Rice cooker or large pot, 2 saucepans for topping and sushi sauce, large shallow bowl to make sushi rice, 9 by 13 cake pan, fan for sushi rice, waxed paper, pancake turner or other flat implement, slicing knife

1. Wash rice in several changes of water until water runs clear.

2. Put rice and 2 1/2 cups water in rice cooker or heavy pot. Cover and let soak for 20 minutes.

3. Turn on rice cooker or bring heavy pot to a boil; reduce heat and cook about 5 minutes until the sound changes, indicating that all the water is absorbed.

4. Remove covered pot from heat and let the rice steam for 10 minutes; rice cooker will reduce heat and steam rice automatically.

5. Drain canned tuna and combine with next 3 ingredients to make topping.

6. Cook topping ingredients together for 1 or 2 minutes, stirring constantly. Set aside to cool.

7. Combine vinegar, sugar, and salt for sushi sauce and heat until the sugar and salt have dissolved. Set aside to cool.

8. Line the 9 by 13 cake pan with waxed paper, and then with nori, if using.

9. When rice is done, but still hot, turn it into the large shallow bowl.

10. Toss the rice with the sushi sauce, fanning to cool it quickly.

11. Pour half of vinegared rice in bottom of pan, spreading it out.

12. Pour tuna mixture over that, and even it out.

13. Layer rest of rice over tuna.

14. Lay 2 more sheets of nori over rice and press firmly with something flat, such as a pancake turner.

15. Invert onto a cutting board.

16. Wet slicing knife and cut into even, bite-sized squares.

17. Cover until ready to serve, but do not refrigerate, which hardens the rice.

Serve arranged on a tray.

CHICKEN HEKKA— NABEMONO, PAN-COOKED FOOD

Beef hekka is usually the name for sukiyaki in Hawaii. This one-pot dish with chicken is probably what Japanese farmers made in the fields before beef came to Japan in the 1860s. The recipe comes from the *Kauai Cookbook*, compiled in 1954 by the Kekaha Parent-Teacher's Association. In Hawaii, as in Japan, it is often cooked at the table on a small charcoal stove or hibachi. Don't try that in cold climates where the windows have to be closed!

Yield: serves 4-6
  4 tablespoons Nucoa (a brand of margarine) or butter
  2 1/2 pounds chicken or chicken parts
  6 tablespoons shoyu (soy sauce)
  4 tablespoons sugar
  1/4 cup chicken stock
  1/2 pound mushrooms (canned)
  1 can bamboo shoots, "2 1/2 size" (28 ounces)
  1 block tofu
  2 tablespoons sake (rice wine, may omit)
  1/2 bunch watercress (or substitute other greens)
  8 stalks green onions (scallions)

Equipment: Large skillet or two
  1. Cut chicken parts into small sections.

  2. Cut watercress or other greens into 2-inch lengths.

  3. Cut green onions into 1 1/2-inch lengths.

  4. Heat skillet to melt margarine or butter.

  5. Add chicken pieces and brown on all sides.

  6. Add stock, soy sauce, and sugar; simmer until chicken is nearly done.

  7. Drain canned vegetables. Add all vegetables to pan and toss lightly "until all vegetables are partially cooked and soaked in gravy."

  8. Cut tofu into 1 1/2-inch cubes, and add near the end so that it just warms and firms slightly.

Serve hot with rice.

JEWISH-AMERICANS

The 5.8 million Jewish Americans are perhaps the clearest example of how immigrants who were ethnically divided elsewhere became a single ethnic group in the United States. The Jews had no homeland for almost 2,000 years until the establishment of the state of Israel in 1948. Jews were a small, oppressed minority in many countries of Europe, North Africa, and the Middle East. Jewish food was the food of the surrounding country, minus shellfish and pork products, and without mixing meat and dairy products. This book includes some recipes from American Jews who also consider themselves to be **Hungarian-American, Romanian-American, German-American,** and so on. Eggs, which could be used in either meat or dairy meals, have always been emphasized in Jewish cookery, but the only universally Jewish foods are those associated with religious observances and festivals, such as unleavened bread for Passover. Small differences of ritual and custom separated North European Jews (known as "Ashkenazim" after the Hebrew word for Germany) from Mediterranean Jews and communities in the Arab world (known as "Sephardim" after the Hebrew word for Spain).

Small groups of Sephardim were present in Dutch New Amsterdam from 1654, and a few more Jews were permitted in several British colonies, but the first large group of Jewish immigrants came from Germany in the 1840s and 1850s. Many had participated in liberal German society until the 1848 revolutionary disorders, and were able to fit in with the larger community of German-American "Forty-Eighters." In New York and Cincinnati, German Jewish-Americans were established and relatively prosperous by the time the much larger group of Eastern European Jews arrived between 1880 and 1925. Over the peak decade of 1900 to 1910, almost one million Jews came to the U.S., representing more than half of all immigrants during the period. Jewish immigrants were thus relatively late arrivals, and settled in urban neighborhoods, often nearest the docks or the railroad depot. At first, the East Europeans formed synagogues and associations by country of origin: Polish, Ukrainian, Latvian, Lithuanian, Russian, Galician (from southern Poland), Austrian, Hungarian, Romanian, and more. They spoke at least four distinct dialects of Yiddish, the Judeo-German lingua franca. But in the U.S., and especially in New York City, they became a single ethnic group. Cooks exchanged recipes for Lithuanian-style kugel, sweet-and-sour Polish stuffed cabbage, Russian borscht, and German-American cheesecakes. Baltic salt-salmon and German-American cream cheese went onto Polish bagels to make the most famous Jewish-American dish, bagels and lox.

Today's Jewish community is increasingly defined by the Jewish religion, although "cultural Jews" persist. There are still Sephardic communities, Chassidic denominations based on specific European origins, some Reform Jewish temples with a strong German-Jewish flavor, and a distinctive community of immigrants born in Israel. Many of the recent immigrants from the former Soviet Union are Jewish, but because the Jewish religion was repressed there, it is unclear how many will identify as Jewish-Americans and how many as **Russian-Americans.** Social acceptance and intermarriage have allowed many Jewish descendants to "volunteer out" of the group, or retain only a casual relationship with the Jewish community. As with other ethnic groups and ethno-religious groups, special foods like knishes or pastrami are usually among the last ties to hold on. At the same time, some Jewish-American foods, such as bagels, have become universally American and are losing their ethnic identity.

Matzo Kloese

Matzo balls are lighter than other dumplings because they are made from cooked meal, and have been recognized as a Jewish food in general American cookbooks since the 1870s. I have seen recipes for Jewish-Cajun matzo balls. These Dutch-style matzo balls are from *Tilly Draisen's Campaign Cookbook*, which was published in the 1990s to support her son's campaign for state representative in Brookline, Massachusetts.

2 matzos

2 tablespoons fat (chicken fat preferred)
2 eggs
1 small onion
1 teaspoon chopped parsley
1/2 cup matzo meal
1 teaspoon salt
1/8 teaspoon pepper
1/4 teaspoon ginger
1/8 teaspoon nutmeg

Equipment: Rolling pin or glass jar, frying pan

1. If you cannot obtain matzo meal in a store, crumble 1 or 2 on a large board with a rolling pin or glass jar to make pieces no larger than kernels of corn.

2. Soak whole matzos in cold water for a few minutes.

3. Halve, peel, and mince the onion.

4. Mince the parsley.

5. If you have made chicken soup from scratch, you can use fat skimmed from the soup. Heat fat in frying pan, and sauté onion to golden brown.

6. Drain matzos and squeeze dry. Add to frying pan and stir "until it leaves the frying pan clean."

7. Remove from heat.

8. Crack eggs individually into a cup, then beat them together in a large bowl.

9. Mix seasonings and parsley into egg mixture.

10. Mix soaked matzos into egg mixture.

11. Finally, mix in the matzo meal.

12. Let mixture stand 2 or 3 hours.

13. With wet hands, shape mixture into balls the size of walnuts.

14. Drop into boiling soup 15 minutes before serving. Cover until ready to serve.

Serve 1 or 2 matzo balls in clear chicken soup with onion and carrot.

MATZA BRIE

This omelet is the typical Passover breakfast. "Brie" is Yiddish for scalded or boiled. This recipe is from *The Jewish Festival Cookbook* by Fannie Engle and Gertrude Blair.

Yield: 4-5 portions
  4 matzoth (matzos)
  4 eggs
  dash of pepper
  1/2 teaspoon salt

cinnamon sugar or honey (optional)
  2 tablespoons butter or margarine

Equipment: Large pot, colander, large bowl, frying pan

1. Bring several quarts of water to a boil in a large pot.

2. Break each matzo into 2-inch pieces and place in a colander.

3. Break the eggs individually into a cup, then beat with salt and pepper in a large bowl.

4. Pour boiling water over the matzos. "Drain quickly to prevent sogginess."

5. Heat butter or margarine in a large frying pan.

6. Mix matzos into eggs, and turn the mixture into the frying pan.

7. Cook over low heat to golden brown on one side.

8. Turn carefully to brown on the other side.

Serve on a hot platter as a large family-size pancake. Sprinkle with sugar that has been mixed with a dash of cinnamon, or with honey.

HUEVOS HAMINADOES

These long-cooked eggs develop a unique flavor and texture. The recipe is common to all Mediterranean Jewish cultures, and was written down by Jodi Kassoria for *The Sephardic Gourmet Cookbook*, which was compiled in 1999 by the Sisterhood of the Magen David Sephardic Congregation in Rockville, Maryland. Sephardic Jews also cook eggs like this in slow-cooked meat stews. The oil slows evaporation so the pot does not run dry.

  1 dozen eggs
  6-10 onion skins
  1 teaspoon salt
  1/4 cup olive oil
  1 teaspoon pepper
  1 lemon

Equipment: Crockpot (optional)

1. Place onion skins, oil, salt, and pepper in a 6-quart pan (or crockpot).

2. Add eggs, carefully so they do not crack.

3. Add water to cover by at least an inch.

4. Bring to a boil, reduce heat to simmer, and cover pot.

5. Cook over low heat approximately 4-6 hours.

6. Slice lemon.

Serve with lemon and black pepper.

CARROT-SWEET POTATO TZIMMES

Tzimmes is a combination of vegetables, often with meat, in a sweet and sour sauce. The word is also a Yiddish expression for a mixed-up situation. This American recipe adds sweet potatoes to the traditional carrots, and uses a lot of sugar because the dish would be made for Jewish New Year. Richard Tucker, a fine operatic tenor who was also known in the Jewish-American community for performances and recordings of Jewish ritual music, submitted this recipe to *What Aria Cooking: The San Francisco Opera Cookbook* (1974).

Yield: serves 6-8

1 pound soup meat (beef shank or brisket)
7 large carrots
2 large sweet potatoes
8 prunes
1 tablespoon finely cut onion
1 pinch ginger
1/2 tablespoon cornstarch
1/2 cup brown sugar
1/2 cup honey
1 tablespoon salt

1. Cover meat with boiling water and bring to a simmer.

2. Cut up onion and add to stew. Simmer 45 minutes.

3. Peel carrots and cut into 3/4-inch rounds.

4. Peel sweet potatoes and cut into large chunks.

5. Add carrots and potatoes to stew with sugar, ginger, prunes, honey, and 1/2 glass of water. Cook until meat and potatoes and carrots are fork tender. (It is traditional not to stir tzimmes.)

6. Mix cornstarch with a little "carrot water" until smooth.

7. Mix in and cook until really soft, about another 15 minutes.

JORDANIAN-AMERICANS

See ARAB-AMERICANS (LEBANESE AND SYRIANS)

KOREAN-AMERICANS

Korea was the third largest source of U.S. immigrants in the 1980s, and about 70 percent of the million Korean-Americans came to this country between 1970 and 1993. The first Korean immigrants were fewer than 10,000 sugar workers who came to Hawaii in the early 1900s. Asian immigration was banned by the Immigration Act of 1924, although the U.S. presence in Korea since the Korean War of the early 1950s brought some military wives, refugees, adopted orphans, and students to the mainland. About 200,000 Korean-Americans now live in Los Angeles County, including a 25-square-mile "Koreatown." Midtown Manhattan has become a Korean-American center in New York City. But many Korean immigrants have started restaurants, convenience stores, fruit stands, and flower shops throughout the United States. Korean cooking is an important strand of the multi-ethnic mix in Hawaii, and Korean restaurants have popularized traditional Korean dishes in many American cities. Korean food is a lively fusion cuisine with many North Chinese and Japanese influences; Korea was under Japanese rule from 1910 to 1945. The food suits Asian fusion restaurants, and the barbecued beef and tasty vegetable stir-fries are likely to develop Americanized versions quickly. Kim chee (or kimchi), a form of spicy sauerkraut, is the universal Korean condiment, but few non-Koreans like it the first time they try it. It's also smelly to make at home, so Korean-Americans often prefer to buy it in jars.

MARINATED CHICKEN WINGS

Haekyung Kim Weir of Andover, Massachusetts, contributed this recipe to *Cook It in Massachusetts* (1981), an American Cancer Society fundraiser. Toasted sesame oil can be found among the Asian foods in many supermarkets, or in Asian or Middle Eastern markets. A possible substitute is the oil that accumulates on the top of jars of natural peanut butter.

NOTE: Recipe needs to marinade overnight.

Yield: 30 pieces for a snack or appetizer
   3 pounds chicken wings
   6 tablespoons soy sauce
   2 tablespoons sugar
   1 tablespoon sesame oil
   1 teaspoon garlic powder or 1 teaspoon fresh
      minced garlic
   1 teaspoon ground ginger or 1 teaspoon
      fresh minced ginger root
   1/2 teaspoon pepper

Equipment: Garlic press, broiler pan and rack, long tongs or chopsticks, rounded chef's knife or cleaver

1. If using fresh garlic, peel a large clove by rubbing between hands. Press in garlic press or mince by slicing into thin flakes, thin sticks, and tiny dice. You can rock a rounded chef's knife or cleaver through the diced garlic to get finer mince.

2. If using fresh ginger root, peel about a half inch; slice first across the grain into thin slices, then mince as above.

3. Combine all ingredients except chicken wings in large bowl to make the marinade.

4. Wash chicken wings and remove any residual pin feathers and excess fat.

5. Cut off wing tips and discard or save for soup stock.

6. Cut each wing across the joint to make 2 pieces.

7. Mix wings well with marinade, cover bowl or casserole, and marinate overnight in refrigerator. Turn a few times.

8. Remove chicken from marinade, set on rack of broiler pan (so fat drains and wings cook evenly), and broil at 500 degrees or "broil" setting until tops are brown.

9. Turn over wings with tongs and brown the other side.

Serve hot, or broil ahead and reheat in a 250-degree oven.

BUL-KOGI
(KOREAN BARBECUE)

Barbecued beef is an easy introduction to Korean food for North Americans. This fairly traditional version comes from Myunghee Reimann, who submitted it to *Cooking Is Our Bag*, which was published in 1980 by the Overlook Hospital Auxiliary in Summit, New Jersey.

Yield: serves 4
   1 to 1 1/2 pounds beef flank steak
   3 tablespoons sugar
   5 tablespoons soy sauce
   2 scallions
   1 garlic clove
   2 teaspoons minced ginger
   4 tablespoons rice wine (may omit and add
      pepper
   3 tablespoons sesame oil (may substitute
      salad oil)

1. Slice beef on the diagonal, 1/4-inch thick. (Optional: Partially freeze steak to make it easier to slice.)

2. Sprinkle beef with sugar a half hour before cooking.

3. Peel, slice, and mince ginger and garlic; mince scallions.

4. Combine soy sauce, scallions, garlic, ginger, wine, and pepper.

5. Mix with beef.

6. Stir in sesame oil. Broil or cook over charcoal using a fine rack. Don't over cook.

"Serve with rice and Kimchi."

SPINACH SALAD

Here the same sesame-soy-sugar flavors are applied to a well-known vegetable in a common Korean-American side dish, or part of a bi-bim-bop (noodle platter). The recipe is from *The Hawaii Cookbook & Backyard Luau* by Korean-American food writer Elizabeth Anh Toupin.

Yield: serves 8-16
  2 pounds fresh spinach
  1 1/2 tablespoons soy sauce

1 1/2 tablespoons sesame oil (or salad oil)
1 1/2 teaspoons sugar
1 1/2 tablespoons vinegar
1/2 teaspoon monosodium glutamate (may omit)
1/2 teaspoon salt
2 tablespoons toasted sesame seeds
1/8 teaspoon minced garlic (optional)

Equipment: Garlic press, heavy skillet

1. Toast sesame seeds briefly in a heavy skillet.

2. Bring 2 quarts of water to a boil, add spinach, and cook for 1 minute.

3. Drain well, squeeze moisture out, and cut into 1 1/2-inch lengths.

4. Mince garlic or put a peeled clove into a garlic press.

5. Combine dressing ingredients and pour over spinach.

6. Toss until spinach is well-coated with dressing.

7. Chill.

Serve in small bowls, decorated with sesame seeds.

LAKHOTA

See SIOUX (DAKOTA, LAKHOTA, AND NAKOTA)

LAOTIAN-AMERICANS

Almost all the 250,000 Laotian Americans arrived as refugees after the 1975 Communist takeover of Laos. They were initially settled in scattered locations, but many have since relocated to larger concentrations. Ethnic Lao are only about half the population of Laos, which has some 40 other ethnic groups, many represented in small communities in the United States. The largest Laotian minority are the **Hmong,** who are usually counted separately but sometimes as Laotian-Americans and **Vietnamese-Americans.** Mien, Khmu, Lahu, Thai Phu, and Thai Dam people also came to the United States. The lowland Lao are related to the Thai, but their food is different. Like the mountain-dwelling minorities, they use many more herbs and fewer spices than in other Southeast Asian cuisines. Several of these herbs still have no English names, but you can sometimes find lemongrass, Asian basil, and lemon basil in Asian supermarkets. Some other Laotian foods that may become Laotian-American foods are spicy meatballs and meatloaf, chicken noodle soups, and several kinds of spring rolls.

BOILED CHICKEN WITH JAEW SOM

Ana Kondo Corum collected this recipe for *Ethnic Foods of Hawai'i* (1983). The jaew som hot sauce is served at every meal by many Laotian-Americans, but on the side so you can add it to suit your individual taste. Many children do not use any at all.

2 tablespoons fish sauce
4 dried red chile peppers
10 cloves garlic
1 teaspoon coriander leaves
1 chicken, about 3 pounds
1/2 teaspoon salt
3 stalks coriander
1 onion
1 pound carrots
1 daikon (Japanese radish) or substitute 2 white turnips
2 bulbs kohlrabi
2 stalks celery
4 stalks green onions (scallions)
1 small head cauliflower
finely chopped cilantro and green onion for garnish

Equipment: Mortar and pestle to make hot sauce, deep serving platter, soup pot

1. To make the jaew som, toast chiles for 1 or 2 minutes under the broiler or in a toaster oven.

2. Cool and discard stems and seeds.

3. Peel and chop garlic.

4. Chop coriander leaves.

5. Combine these ingredients in mortar and pestle and pound until it reaches a paste-like consistency. Refrigerate until ready to serve.

6. Heat 3 cups water to boiling in a soup pot.

7. Add whole chicken and salt.

8. Cover and simmer 20 minutes, turning once.

9. Peel carrots and cut in half.

10. Peel daikon or turnip and cut into lengthwise wedges like the sections of an orange.

11. Pare stems off kohlrabi and cut each bulb into quarters.

12. Add the above ingredients to chicken soup and simmer, covered, another 15 minutes.

13. Wash celery and cut into 2-inch lengths.

14. Separate cauliflower into florets.

15. Halve and peel onion and cut lengthwise into wedges.

16. Trim and chop green onions.

17. Add next 4 ingredients to chicken soup. Simmer for another 15 minutes, or until chicken and vegetables are tender.

18. With a slotted spoon, moved cooked vegetables to the outside edges of a deep platter.

19. Carefully remove chicken to a cutting board and cut into serving pieces. Arrange chicken pieces in the center of the platter.

20. Sprinkle with black pepper and garnish with coriander and green onion.

Serve chicken and vegetables in individual soup bowls with a small amount of broth ladled on, and with hot sauce in tiny bowls or ramekins on the side.

LAOTIAN SALAD

This salad was created by Bounhang, Savannallay, and Khaysa Phrasavath, three sisters in a Brooklyn language program called CAMBA, and reprinted in *The Brooklyn Cookbook* by Lyn Stallworth and Rod Kennedy, Jr. It is a typical Laotian beef salad with herbs and many eggs, stretched out with some American salad ingredients.

Yield: serves 12 or more as part of a buffet
12 eggs
1 cup peanuts

1/2 head garlic

2 1/2 bunches scallions

3 bunches cilantro

3 small heads romaine lettuce

4 ripe tomatoes

5 cucumbers

3 tablespoons sugar

1/2 teaspoon plus 3 1/2 tablespoons corn oil

1 pound beef

2 teaspoons fish sauce

1/4 cup fresh lemon juice

Equipment: Juicer, mortar and pestle or food processor, small saucepan, large skillet

1. Hard boil the eggs for 15 minutes and let them cool under running cold water.

2. Crush the peanuts with a mortar and pestle or chop them in the bowl of the food processor (but don't make peanut butter!)

3. Peel and mince the garlic cloves.

4. Trim the scallions and cut each crosswise into 5 pieces. Slice the pieces into thin strips.

5. Cut off most of the cilantro stems (save for Asian soups). Break each sprig into 3 pieces.

6. Break the romaine leaves in half, or 4 pieces if they are large.

7. Slice the tomatoes.

8. Peel and slice the cucumbers into rounds.

9. Boil 1/4 cup water in a very small saucepan and add the sugar. Stir to dissolve and add 1/2 teaspoon of the oil. Set aside.

10. Heat one tablespoon of the oil in a large skillet and sauté the garlic until it becomes lightly golden. Remove from heat and spoon browned garlic into a small saucer.

11. Cut the beef into small cubes.

12. In the same skillet, heat the remaining 2 1/2 tablespoons of corn oil and brown the beef cubes.

13. Add fish sauce and cook 5-7 minutes, stirring.

14. Shell eggs and cut into small chunks.

15. Place all ingredients except eggs and lemon juice in a large serving bowl. Mix gently.

16. Add the eggs and mix.

17. Add the lemon juice and mix again.

MIXIENSUI (MIEN NOODLE SALAD)

This salad is like the one above in some ways, but goes farther in using American ingredients. Although the jalapeño peppers have a quick bite, Laotians in California usually prefer the hotter chile de arbol. The recipe comes from an adult literacy project in Visalia, California, and was posted on the Internet with several such projects at <www.otan.dni.us/webfarm/emailproject/cook.htm>. This salad was described for Steve Winston's beginning English as a Second Language class by Chio Kwang Saechao and Lai Choi Saelee, who are Mien, and Tai Kue Moua and May Chang, who are Hmong. They write, "We eat this salad in celebrations. It's a special food. We buy the ingredients at supermarkets and Lao food stores. The ingredients are not the same as in our country. The ingredients here cost $37." The largest Mien communities are in the Pacific Northwest.

2 packages Chinese rice noodles

12 eggs

10 jalapeño peppers

2 bell peppers

3 bunches cilantro

some Laotian mint (substitute fresh spearmint)

2 green onions (scallions)

6 carrots

2 heads lettuce

2 tablespoons thousand island dressing

4 tomatoes

2 packs Italian dressing

2 teaspoons MSG (Accent, optional)

Salt to taste

1. Boil rice noodles until soft. (Only a few minutes, depending on shape.)

2. Drain noodles and set aside.

3. Boil eggs until hard (15 minutes). Cool under running cold water.

4. Peel carrots and cucumbers.

5. Peel eggs.

6. Wash lettuce.

7. Slice off top and bottom of each bell pepper. Remove stems and cores, and slice off pith and seeds. Cut into thin strips.

8. Slice cucumbers into thin strips.

9. Slice carrots into thin strips.

10. Slice tomatoes lengthwise.

11. Chop lettuce into small pieces.

12. Chop cilantro, using only the leaves.

13. Put noodles into a large bowl.

14. Add chopped vegetables, eggs, and spices.

15. Add Italian dressing packages and thousand island dressing. Mix thoroughly.

16. Add the MSG and salt to taste.

Serve with rice.

LATVIAN-AMERICANS

The 1990 census estimated about 102,000 Americans of Latvian ancestry. This number is hard to check against immigration and census statistics because Latvia was divided between Sweden, Poland, and Russia for much of modern history, and because Latvian immigrants were sometimes counted as Lithuanians, Russians, or Germans. Some people who emigrated from Latvia were not ethnic Latvians, and affiliated themselves with **Jewish-American, Russian-American,** or **German-American** communities. Latvian immigrants have been present since the Swedish colonization of New Jersey in the 1640s, but most came between 1900 and 1918, when Latvia became independent. Another 40,000 refugees fled the Nazi and then Soviet occupations of Latvia between 1939 and 1951. Latvian-Americans tended to remain in the port cities where they arrived, such as Boston, Philadelphia, and Baltimore, and in the Pacific Northwest. Some other Latvian foods include mixed salads, herring salads, and a variety of breads.

BALTIC BACONETTES (PIRAGI)

Piragi are the most common Latvian-American recipe, so the main reason to pick Mrs. Anton Kromas' version from *Favorite Recipes of Harvard Church Woman's Guild Brookline, Massachusetts* (about 1960) was the wonderful name. The alternate method of making the turnovers is illustrated in Jeff Smith's *The Frugal Gourmet on Our Immigrant Ancestors: Recipes You Should Have Gotten from Your Grandmother*, which has a group of good Latvian-American recipes.

Yield: 20 turnovers

4 cups sifted flour
1 cake yeast (or 1 envelope dry yeast)
1 cup milk
3/8 cup butter
1 teaspoon salt

1/2 pound lean smoked bacon
1 onion
dash pepper
1/2 teaspoon sugar
caraway seeds (as desired)
1 egg
solid shortening to grease baking sheets

Equipment: Baking sheets, pastry brush, water glass or glass jar with a 3-inch rim, skillet

1. Melt butter in the milk in a saucepan (or microwave).

2. Let cook to lukewarm, and mix in salt, yeast, and flour to make a dough.

3. Turn it out onto a floured board and knead (see Appendix 1) for a few minutes to make it smooth.

4. Put back into a bowl, cover, and set in a warm place to rise.

5. When dough has risen, "push it back" (down by working out the large bubbles), and let it rise again.

6. To make filling, cook the bacon crisp in a skillet.

7. Halve, peel, and chop the onion. (Wear swim goggles to avoid tears.)

8. Cut bacon into small pieces, mix with chopped onion and seasonings.

9. When dough has again doubled in bulk, punch down, and divide the dough into 20 small pieces. Or go to alternate method, Step 11, below.

10. Grease baking sheets.

11. Flatten each piece of dough into a 3-inch disk.

12. Leaving 3/4 inch at the margins, spread a spoonful of filling in the middle of each disk. Be careful not to get the oil on the margins, or the turnover won't stay closed.

13. Close to form a half-moon and crimp edges well so filling doesn't "smile out" during baking. Go on to Step 14.

14. For the alternative method, take all the dough in a lump, and pull some of the dough toward you and flatten it with your fingers to make a thin part at least 3 inches in diameter.

15. Put a rounded teaspoon of filling on the middle of the thin area, and roll the outer edge of the dough back over it to form a turnover.

16. Crimp the edges a little so the turnover holds together, and cut it off the main body of the dough with a glass or jar. Finish crimping the edges. Repeat to make about 20 turnovers.

17. Put completed buns on the baking sheets and let them rise once more.

18. Beat egg with a tablespoon of water to make a thin wash.

19. Shortly before putting buns in the oven, brush each one lightly with beaten egg.

20. Bake at 375 degrees for about 12 minutes, or until brown.

"Serve hot or cold with a clear soup, or as a canapé [appetizer], or with Sunday supper."

KIMENMAIZITES (CARAWAY ROLLS)

These useful little morsels of bread, probably devised to use up leftover dough, were contributed by Mrs. Emma Kitners to the 1976 *Global Gourmet*, published by the International Institute of Boston. She suggests an alternate sprinkle of poppy seeds and sugar, making these less like breadsticks and more like sweet rolls.

1 order of piragi dough (see above)
1 egg
cold butter
caraway seeds (optional)
coarse salt (optional)

Equipment: Cookie sheet

1. Make dough as in recipe, above.

2. Form into very small round balls.

3. Grease cookie sheet, and set balls on sheet with enough room to double in size.

4. When they have risen, brush with beaten egg.

5. Cut cold butter into small cubes.

6. Press a little butter into the center of each bun. Sprinkle with caraway and coarse salt, if desired.

7. Preheat oven to 450 degrees.

8. Bake 10 minutes, or until golden brown.

Serve as breakfast or snacks.

LEBANESE-AMERICANS

See ARAB-AMERICANS

LEMKIANS

See CARPATHO-RUSYN-AMERICANS (RUSKINS, RUSNYAKS, RUTHINIANS, AND LEMKIANS)

LITHUANIAN-AMERICANS

The 1990 census ancestry survey projected 811,000 Lithuanian-Americans, by far the largest of the Balkan groups. The figure may include some Lithuanian Jews who would consider themselves more **Jewish-American** than Lithuanian-American. However, the Census Bureau is prohibited by law from counting people by religion. The relatively low profile of such a large immigrant group could be for several reasons: nineteenth-century Lithuanians often identified with the **Polish-American** community and attended Catholic churches in Polish parishes; early immigrants were mostly men who moved from job to job; Lithuanian-American politics focused on the independent Lithuania between the two World Wars; and Lithuanian immigration was steady over a long period (1860-1914), thus forming few identifiable Lithuanian neighborhoods outside the coal mining districts or the multi-ethnic cities of Chicago, Boston, New York, and Philadelphia. Another group of immigrants came as refugees from the Soviet takeover of Lithuania after World War II, but the independence of Lithuania since the breakup of the Soviet Union in 1991 has so far been so successful that it has not provoked much emigration to the U.S.

KUGELIS (POTATO CASSEROLE)

Kugelis is the most common Lithuanian-American recipe. This one was submitted by then-U.S. Representative Richard J. Durbin of Illinois to the 1986 *American Sampler Cookbook* collected by Linda Bauer. One kugelis tip is to use old potatoes.

10 large red potatoes
1 large onion
5 strips bacon
1/2 cup hot milk or evaporated milk
3 eggs
2 teaspoons salt
1/4 teaspoon black pepper

Equipment: Grater or food processor with grating disk, 9 by 13-inch baking pan, large bowl

1. Dice bacon and fry until crisp. Use a little of the grease to oil baking pan.

2. Peel and grate potatoes. Halve, peel, and grate onion. (If not using food processor, wear swim goggles to avoid tears.)

3. Preheat oven to 400 degrees.

4. Mix onion and potatoes in a large bowl.

5. Pour bacon and grease over potatoes.

6. Add hot milk.

7. Beat eggs and add one-third at a time.

8. Add salt and pepper and mix well.

9. Pour into greased baking pan. Bake in 400-degree oven for 15 minutes.

10. Reduce heat to 375 and bake for 45 minutes, or until firm when tested by inserting a knife in center.

Serve hot with sour cream.

LITHUANIAN HOT DISH

This recipe appears in *Eat! Eat! Wonderful Recipes from the Old Country Like My Mother Used to Make* by Ruth Kanin. Although Ms. Kanin is of Lithuanian-Jewish background, the dish was contributed by Dena Lisovskis, "a young salesgirl we met in a gift shop. She learned it from her aunt—a true heirloom recipe, since she was a second-generation Lithuanian." The Lithuanian name for the dish is kepta varske. Some recipes substitute a teaspoon of caraway seeds or minced onion for the chives.

Yield: serves 6
  1 pint low-fat, small-curd cottage cheese
  4 extra-large eggs
  2 tablespoons minced chives
  butter to grease baking dish

Equipment: Small baking dish

  1. Preheat the oven to 325 degrees.

  2. Butter baking dish.

  3. Mince chives.

  4. Beat eggs and mix with cottage cheese and chives.

  5. Pour mixture in baking dish. Bake uncovered at 325 degrees for 45 minutes.

Serve as a snack or Lenten lunch.

COOKIE SLICES (SAUSAINIAI)

This unusual cookie recipe appears in *Popular Lithuanian Recipes* (1955) by Josephine J. Dauzvardis. The technique of baking the dough in a loaf, then cutting into cookies and baking again, is like that of Italian biscotti and Central European almond rusks.

Yield: about 100 cookies
  6 eggs
  1 cup butter (2 sticks) and a little more to grease baking sheets
  1 1/2 cups sugar
  7 cups flour
  3 teaspoons baking powder
  1 teaspoon vanilla
  1 cup chopped nuts
  1/2 teaspoon cardamom seeds

Equipment: Pastry blender, baking sheets, large bowl

  1. Cream butter and sugar with pastry blender or a large fork.

  2. Beat eggs, and stir into the butter mixture 1/6 at a time.

  3. Sift together flour and baking powder.

  4. Blend flour mixture with butter mixture in a large bowl.

  5. Add vanilla, cardamom seeds, and nuts.

  6. Blend thoroughly.

  7. Divide dough into 4 sections.

  8. Roll each section in a long, round, thin loaf an inch in diameter.

  9. Set loaves well apart on baking sheets and bake a half hour in a 400-degree oven.

  10. Remove from oven, and put loaves on a cutting board.

  11. "While still warm, cut into 1/2-inch slices." If you cut at a 45-degree angle, the slices will be longer.

  12. Reduce heat to 250 degrees.

  13. Arrange slices on baking sheets and continue baking "until dry and light" (about 30-40 minutes).

Lumbee Indians of North Carolina

T he Lumbee are one of the largest tribes of Native Americans remaining east of the Missis-sippi. About 40,000 still live in Robeson County, North Carolina, in and around Lumberton and the Lumber River, which they call the Lumbee River, as they have since the early 1700s. Thousands more work in Baltimore, Philadelphia, and Chicago, and in other parts of North Carolina. The Lumbee converted early to Christianity, lost most of their language, and took on many escaped and freed **African-American** slaves, so there have been centuries of confusion about their Indian origins. After the Tuscarora War of 1711-13, the Lumbee absorbed Tuscarora refugees from South Carolina and black and white military deserters. Similar things happened after the Civil War. The Lumbee have always insisted that they were Indians, and demanded their own schools during the period of racial segregation. At different times, the State of North Carolina and different Lumbee factions have designated them as Croatoan Indians (and possible descendants of the lost English colony of Roanoke), Cherokees, and Lumbee. A movement is now afoot for federal recognition of the tribe as Tuscaroras, while the dominant academic theory is that their ancestors spoke a Souian language such as Cheraw. (The Cheraw were a small band of South Carolina Indians in the 1500s and 1600s who were driven north and probably absorbed by other tribes in the early 1700s.)

The Lumbee have always known they were Lumbee, and have fought for recognition as an Indian tribe. The Lumbee hero is Henry Berry Lowrie, a Robin Hood-like guerrilla fighter who lead a 10-year armed resistance in the 1860s and 1870s. In the eventual settlement of the "Lowrie War," the Lumbee won back the right to vote in the 1880s. When segregation returned to North Carolina, the Lumbee kept the vote, and built up their own school system, neither white nor black, including a teacher's college which is now the University of North Carolina at Pembroke. In early 1958, the Ku Klux Klan burned a cross in front of a home where Lumbee students lived with white students, and shortly thereafter the Klan called a rally in the town of Maxon. A crowd of armed Lumbee broke up the Klan rally with gunshots and tear gas grenades while the county sheriff looked on. The Klan did not return.

The Lumbee are strong church-goers with a special style of gospel singing. The following recipes are from a church cookbook published in Fairmount, North Carolina, and sent to me by Mary Chitwood, who recently retired from the Indian Studies Department at UNC Pembroke. Some other dishes popular at Lumbee gatherings are fried chicken, frybread, pecan pie, and homemade ice cream.

Sweet Potato Bread

This recipe from Loelear Eddings is known throughout the South and some Caribbean countries as sweet potato pone, from the Algonk-ian word "pone" or "apan," meaning "baked"; the term is often applied to corn breads. The list of ingredients suggests influence from all parts of the Lumbee's tri-racial background: Native American sweet potatoes, African coco-nut, and Western European cake making. But it is more likely that this recipe has been exchanged and redeveloped several times among the eth-nic kitchens in North Carolina, a process that continues with Mary Chitwood's notations on Ms. Eddings recipe to reduce the butter and in-crease the oven temperature. Baking in a skillet is an old technique.

Yield: serves 6 as a side dish
  2-pound, 8-ounce can sweet potatoes
  3 eggs
  1/2 teaspoon vanilla
  1/2 teaspoon ground allspice
  1 stick butter
  2 cups sugar
  1/2 cup grated coconut
  1/2 teaspoon cinnamon

1/2 cup self-rising flour (or 1/2 cup all-purpose flour and 3/4 teaspoon baking powder)

margarine to grease pan and a little more flour

Equipment: 9 by 9 cake pan or 10-inch cast-iron skillet, mixing bowl, small saucepan or microwave-safe dish to melt butter, colander to drain sweet potatoes

1. Grease pan or skillet with margarine. Dust with a little flour.

2. Melt butter in small saucepan over low heat, or in microwave on low-defrost.

3. Drain canned sweet potatoes in colander.

4. Combine all ingredients in a mixing bowl and blend well.

5. Pour into the pan and smooth top.

6. Bake at 350 degrees for 1 hour. It should be well browned on top.

Cut into squares (or pie-shaped wedges, if skillet is used) and serve as a side dish with simple meat dishes.

Mom Chavis' Ginger Bread

This is a nice, old fashioned sheet cake from the family of Wilma Chavis.

Yield: 30 squares of cake
  3 eggs
  1 cup self-rising flour (or 1 cup all-purpose flour and 1 1/2 teaspoons baking powder)
  2 cups plain flour
  2 sticks softened butter
  1 1/2 teaspoons powdered ginger
  2/3 cup molasses
  1 tablespoon vanilla
  2 cups sugar ("fill measuring cup to top")
  solid shortening

Equipment: Pastry blender or large fork, flexible spatula to spread batter, 9 by 13 cake pan or two 8 1/2-inch round pans, cake tester or toothpicks

1. Cream butter and sugar together.

2. Open each egg into a cup, then beat into the butter-sugar mixture one at a time.

3. Beat in molasses.

4. Mix together the 2 flours (or baking powder and 3 cups all-purpose flour).

5. Beat the flour into the egg-butter-sugar batter a little at a time.

6. Beat in vanilla and ginger.

7. Grease the pan or pans with solid shortening, and sprinkle flour over the grease.

8. Pour in the batter and level it with the spatula, or by shaking the pan(s).

9. Bake at 350 degrees for 40 minutes; test that a toothpick or wire cake tester comes out clean.

Cut into squares to serve.

Blueberry Sheet Cake

This cake from Roberta Oxendine uses a native fruit to make a large cake ideal for group events like pow-wows, church suppers, or wild game festivals. Compare to **Cherokee** huckleberry bread. If you live in an area where you can gather wild nuts (such as hickory nuts in the Lumber River area), that would also be popular at Indian events.

Yield: 30 squares of cake
  2 cups sugar
  1 cup Crisco oil
  1 pint blueberries (frozen)
  3 eggs
  1 cup chopped nuts
  1 teaspoon vanilla
  2 cups self-rising flour (or 2 cups all-purpose flour and 3 teaspoons baking powder)
  solid shortening to grease pan(s)

Equipment: Mixing bowl, large fork or spoon to blend, flexible spatula to spread batter, 9 by 13 cake pan or two 8 1/2-inch round pans, cake tester or toothpicks

1. Mix together dry ingredients (except blueberries).

2. Add all other ingredients (except blueberries) and mix well.

3. Mixture will be rather thick. "This keeps blueberries from falling to the bottom." Add blueberries last and mix lightly.

4. Grease pans with solid shortening. Dust with flour.

5. Pour in batter and smooth out.

6. Bake at 350 degrees for 1 hour or less. Test for doneness with toothpick or wire cake tester.

Serve cut into large squares.

Macedonian-Americans

See Bulgarian-Americans, Macedonian-Americans, and Vlachs (Arumanians)

Melungeons

The Melungeons were a dark-skinned, light-eyed people who have lived in the Appalachian mountains at the meeting point of Tennessee, Kentucky, Virginia, and North Carolina for more than 200 years. The name possibly comes from the French term "melange" meaning "mix," and may have been applied by French speakers in the Carolinas. Much of Melungeon history and culture has been lost because of restrictive racial laws and attitudes, and the efforts of Melungeons themselves to conceal their background and to avoid being classified as **African-American** in schools and workplaces. Today a group of Melungeon descendants is actively researching genealogy and history to find out more about their background, and have held two reunions in Hancock County, Tennessee, where Melungeon families persisted as an identifiable ethnic group well into the 1950s. One study estimated that there were more than 20,000 in 1950. A recent estimate is 70,000. The end of segregated schools in the late 1950s and early 1960s was probably also the end of most identifiable Melungeon communities. Many Melungeon descendants have spread out into West Virginia, southern Ohio, and Indiana.

Ancestors of the Melungeons were among the first non-Indian settlers in the Appalachians, and came from Virginia and the Carolinas. When they were encountered by **Scotch-Irish** settlers in the late eighteenth century, the Melungeons said they were "Portyghee." Some other Melungeon families have a tradition of being Turkish. Recent research suggests that a core group may have been North African Berbers who remained in Portugal and northern Spain after 1492, converted to Christianity, but came under pressure during the Inquisition, particularly between 1568 and 1582. Such people were heavily recruited for the lost Spanish colony of Santa Elena, which existed near present-day Beaufort, South Carolina, in the sixteenth and seventeenth centuries, and for possible exploratory settlements as far inland as Tennessee. Hundreds of Iberian Berbers also emigrated to Brazil, where they intermarried with Indians and were known as "melungos." Others were deported as servants or slaves to Central or South America. Several hundred such slaves were captured by Sir Francis Drake in 1586, and possibly off-loaded on the coast of North Carolina when Drake agreed to bring back most of the Roanoke settlers back to England. This would place the Melungeon ancestors in America before Jamestown or Plymouth.

Another theory is that "Melun jinn" or "Melun can" means "cursed soul" in Turkish and Arabic, and the terms were used by Muslims forced to convert to Christianity who felt abandoned by their God. This would fit the Portuguese origin, but also possible links to Turkish and Armenian weavers who were brought to the Americas by the English in the sixteenth century, or to shipwrecked Turkish or Portuguese sailors.

Today's Melungeon descendants often learn about the Melungeons while researching the genealogy of their Scotch-Irish ancestors. They also find early ancestors who were recorded as American Indians or as "Free People of Color." The latter were mostly freed slaves, some of whom were freed because they were mixed-race descendants of relationships between owners and slaves.

In the past, some scholars classified the Melungeons with more than 200 groups (in the 1970 census) of "tri-racial isolates," people of mixed Indian-African-European descent. However, genealogical research suggests that while most such groups (including the Melungeons) are more or less tri-racial, they may not always have been isolated from each other. Thus, some Melungeon descendants have common ancestors with **Lumbee** Indians, smaller multi-racial groups, and **Creole** communities. (See the discussion of race and ethnicity in the Introduction.)

For more information on the Melungeons, the newest book by a Melungeon descendent is N. Brent Kennedy's *The Melungeons: The Resurrection of a Proud People* (Mercer University Press, 1999). The *Appalachian Melungeon Heritage Cookbook* is available from compiler Wilma Wireman, 21 North Kniffin Street, Greenwich, Ohio 44837. The recipes treasured by Melungeon descendants are common to other mountain dwellers, such as **Cherokees** and Scotch-Irish, but little known outside the Appalachians.

TOMATO GRAVY

Fran Powell posted this recipe on an Internet mailing list of Melungeon descendants. I have added approximate quantities, since Ms. Powell cooks "by eyeballin'." Some versions of tomato gravy begin by frying round steak, rabbit, or other meats, or chopped onions, and use 4 or 5 cut up, fresh tomatoes instead of canned.

3 tablespoons bacon fat (from 5 rashers of bacon)
3 tablespoons flour
1 can pureed tomatoes
salt and pepper

Equipment: Skillet with a tight lid

1. Fry bacon. Remove for another purpose (perhaps a bacon, lettuce, and tomato sandwich for the cook).

2. Pour off grease, measure, and return 3 tablespoons to the frying pan.

3. Stir in the flour, breaking up any crusted bacon bits from the pan.

4. Cook slowly for at least 2 minutes until the flour browns to somewhere between a golden brown and "the color of a cigar." Be careful not to burn the flour, which will ruin the gravy.

5. Stir in the tomatoes and salt and pepper to taste, blending until the sauce is smooth and beginning to thicken.

6. "If too thick, add water; if too thin, thicken a bit with flour and water mixed well."

Serve "over some biscuits, hoecake, or some rice, yummm."

SARAH'S CHOCOLATE GRAVY

Chocolate gravy is a thin pudding served hot with biscuits for breakfast. The only places outside the Appalachians where people eat something like this for breakfast are Spain and Mexico, where a thick hot chocolate pudding is the dip for corn crullers called "churros." This recipe was contributed to the Melungeon cookbook by Madge Parker Ray, niece of Sarah Elizabeth Tackett, who was born in Pike County, Kentucky. Mrs. Ray prefers this with canned biscuits, for it "just doesn't taste the same with home made biscuits. When cooked just right, this is a delicious, smooth Milk Chocolate dream. It is not a pudding or a sauce, but something in between."

1 cup sugar

3 tablespoons flour

1/4 cup cocoa

2 cups milk

Equipment: Heavy kettle

1. Combine cocoa and flour.

2. Stir in milk.

3. Bring to a boil in a heavy kettle.

4. Reduce heat and boil about 5-7 minutes.

Serve over fresh-baked biscuits.

STACK CAKE

Stack cakes provide a way for people without a lot of pots and pans to make a cheap (few eggs), high, layer cake. One story is that these were baked cooperatively by several families as a wedding cake, with each guest bringing a layer or two to the wedding. Although there are a lot of steps, this is not a hard cake to make. In this recipe, the layers are made of gingerbread; see the Scotch-Irish apple stack cake for one based on a plainer bannock dough. Both types of stack cake are made by all groups in the Appalachians. However, in light of the Melungeon traditions about Portuguese origin, compare it to the **Portuguese-American** bolo de filho and the **Icelandic-American** vinartera. This recipe came to the Melungeon cookbook from Tera McKenzie Sparks of Kentucky via her granddaughter Mary Katherine Goodyear. An optional filling is "sweetened blackberries, mixed with blackberry jam; or blackberry jam, alone."

NOTE: Cake needs to sit wrapped in aluminum foil for at least 24 hours.

4 cups flour

1 teaspoon salt

2 teaspoons ginger

2 teaspoons baking powder

2 eggs

2 cups molasses or sorghum

1/2 cup lard or shortening

1/2 cup butter

buttermilk to make a soft dough, start with a few tablespoons

2 cups dried apples

1/3 cup sugar

2 cups apple butter (or start with 4 cups dried apples and double sugar)

powdered sugar for decoration

Equipment: 1 or more cast iron skillets or round cake pans or cookie sheets, wire racks to cool layers, knife or spatula to spread filling, aluminum foil, paper doily for decoration

1. Simmer dried apples in 3 cups water in a covered saucepan until tender.

2. Add sugar and mash apples (or use a food processor or blender).

3. Stir in apple butter, and let filling cool while you make cake layers (or overnight in refrigerator).

4. Preheat oven to 450 degrees.

5. Sift together flour, salt, ginger, and baking powder.

6. Beat eggs in small mixing bowl.

7. Stir in molasses.

8. Mix shortening mixture, buttermilk, and most of the dry ingredients in the large bowl.

9. Beat in the buttermilk and the rest of the dry ingredients to form a firm and slightly sticky dough.

10. Turn out on a floured surface and knead (see Appendix 1) in additional flour until the dough is "smooth, firm, and no longer sticky."

11. Divide dough into 8 equal parts.

12. Grease and flour cake pans, skillet, or cookie sheets.

13. Flour hands (remove jewelry first) and pat dough into skillet or round cake pan. Or roll each portion of dough to fit a 9-inch round cake pan. (*Hint:* You can use the cake pans or the top to a skillet to get precisely round sheets, and add the trimmings to the next ball of dough.)

14. Bake each layer until brown, about 15 minutes.

15. Cool a few minutes, and remove from skillet or cake pans to cool on a wire rack.

16. Bake additional layers in the skillet or cake pans as needed until all 8 layers are baked.

17. Set aside the neatest looking layer for the top.

18. Take the ugliest layer, and put it on the plate.

19. Spread with 1/7 of the filling, and top with another layer.

20. Repeat until you put on the top layer, which is not covered with filling.

21. Try to arrange layers so that you have a reasonably neat and level cake.

22. Wrap in aluminum foil for at least 24 hours. "This cake is better the second or third day, because it gives the filling time to soak into the cake layers."

23. You can decorate the top layer by putting a paper doily on it, sifting on powdered sugar, and removing the doily to reveal a pattern.

Serve in thin slices to show off the layers.

MESOPOTAMIAN-AMERICANS

See ASSYRIAN- AND CHALDEAN-AMERICANS (MESOPOTAMIANS)

MEXICAN-AMERICANS (CHICANOS)

Because parts of eight U.S. states belonged to Mexico when it became independent in 1821, it can be said that Mexican-Americans are a founding-stock group, as well as perhaps the second-largest immigrant group, and clearly the leading source of "recent immigrants," being almost one-fourth of legal immigration between 1981 and 1996. The 1990 census recorded 11.5 million Americans claiming Mexican descent, but the census is thought to undercount Mexican-Americans by as much as 15 percent. The census lists 4.2 million Mexican-Americans as the largest foreign-born community in the U.S., with just under a million of those comprising the largest group of naturalized citizens and 3.3 million of them comprising the largest group of legally resident aliens. In 1996, Mexicans were an estimated half or more of an illegal alien population estimated at 5 million.

At least one group of Mexican-Americans, the **New Mexico Hispanics,** who became U.S. citizens after the American conquest of the Southwest in the 1840s, have become a distinct ethnic group. In the 1990s, civil strife in Mexico underlined the amount of ethnic and regional division there, but Mexico has been a unitary country since 1821 and the Mexican-American community has been held together by external prejudice as well as common history.

One consequence of the recent immigration has been a series of demographic changes. In 1900, Mexican-Americans were the most rural major immigrant group; they are now one of the most urban. In perhaps 40 years, they have moved from a concentration in the Southwest to major communities in Denver and Chicago and notable groups in every major U.S. city. Recent immigrants come from every part of Mexico, where earlier groups were primarily from northern and border regions.

More than most immigrants, Mexican-Americans have enjoyed the cultural support of home visits and easy access to Spanish-language media and religious services. On the negative side, the group as a whole has faced significant segregation and lingering discrimination, and has remained poor, relative to other immigrant groups.

Mexican-American food and music have been regionally popular for almost 200 years, and Mexican-American vaqueros contributed much to the American cowboy myth. A succession of border foods has passed into general American use, beginning with "hot tamales" and chili con carne, and continuing to the fajita fad of the 1990s. Many recent immigrants from Mexico have never heard of these foods, or eat very different styles of tacos and enchiladas. Individual Mexican chefs invented nachos, fried corn chips, and Caesar salad directly for American customers, just as Chinese chefs developed chow mein and shrimp toast. The large size of the community and nearness of Mexico have meant that recent immigrants from Mexico have been able to keep some of their traditional foods intact. In this section, I have concentrated on some recipes that show how Mexican-American food has changed to help families express their ethnic identity while adapting to American lifestyles. If you collect Mexican-American recipes, ask about tamales, which are so time consuming that they are usually made in the United States by groups of women for holidays.

EASY MIGAS

Migas means crumbs. It is a favorite way to use up tortillas and stretch eggs in Mexican-American communities across the U.S. This 15-minute version with commercial tortilla chips is from María Gonzáles de Herrera of Santa Ana, California; it was described in *Cocina de la Familia: More than 200 Authentic Recipes from Mexican-American Home Kitchens* by Marilyn Tausend with Miguel Ravago.

    8 eggs
    50 unsalted tortilla chips (about a 10-ounce
        bag)
    2 tablespoons unsalted butter
    1/4 cup shredded queso añejo or parmesan
        cheese
    1 cup salsa

Equipment: Heavy skillet, large bowl

1. Open the eggs over a cup one at a time so you can easily remove bits of shell with the empty shells.

2. Beat the eggs together in a large bowl.

3. Break up the tortilla chips "slightly."

4. "Carefully fold in the tortilla chips."

5. Melt the butter over medium heat in a large heavy skillet.

6. Pour in the egg mixture and cook very briefly, stirring constantly, so all the eggs are set, but not dry.

7. Remove from heat and fold in the salsa.

8. Taste for salt and pepper.

9. Scatter the cheese over the top before serving.

Serve with beans and more salsa.

FRIJOLES FRITOS (FRIED BEANS)

These are usually known as refried beans. The recipe is from Mrs. Louise DeLeon and Mrs. Dolores Torres, sisters whose family grew up in one of 25 boxcars turned into living quarters by the Burlington Railroad in Edgemont, South Dakota, in the 1920s. When they contributed the recipe to Mary S. Colgan's *Friendly Cookerie from Edgemont* in 1968, Mrs. DeLeon was the postmaster in Provo, South Dakota, and Mrs. Torres had become a nurse's aide at Edgemont Hospital.

    1 pound dry pinto beans
    3 or 4 slices bacon
    1 tablespoon flour

Equipment: Potato masher

1. Wash beans and pick out any stones or dirt.

2. Cook in salted water to cover "until done—about three hours." (Time will be shorter at sea level. This Mexican method makes somewhat tastier beans, but they can be hard to digest. If you don't eat beans every day, bring dry beans

to a boil for a few minutes in a half pot of water, drain, and soak in fresh water for an hour or more. Discard the water before cooking.)

3. Keep adding water as needed.

4. Cut bacon in small pieces and fry.

5. When bacon is done, add flour to bacon and grease and stir well.

6. Drain beans and empty into the bacon mixture.

7. Keep stirring over heat to mix well.

8. "Mash beans with potato masher while frying."

9. Stir often until almost dry.

"Delicious served with Chili Con Carne; also can be used for Taco filling."

GRILLED CORN

This kind of roasted corn is sold in the streets all over Latin America and also in the Maxwell Street Market in Chicago, which has a large Mexican-American community. The basic grilled corn is also frequently served at Native American pow-wows. This recipe was noted by author and restaurateur Rick Bayless in an article on "Chicago Mexican" in the July/August 1999 issue of *Saveur* magazine. The chile arbol powder is hot, so substitute milder pure chile powders if you have to. Some other condiments used with chile powder by Mexican Americans are sour cream and cheese, and lime juice.

    6 ears corn in husk
    3 tablespoons butter, melted
    1/2 cup mayonnaise
    1/3 cup grated queso añejo, or parmesan
    1 tablespoon powdered arbol chile (or a
        milder pure chile pepper powder or
        paprika)

Equipment: Cheese grater if not using pre-grated cheese, charcoal or gas grill, plate that fits into the pot or bowl, long tongs, watering can or spayer to put out any flare ups, pastry brush or clean natural paint brush

1. Half-fill large pot or bowl with water, add ears of corn, and weight down with a plate and food jars or stones so that all the ears are held under water. Soak for 30 minutes while preparing charcoal grill (if using).

2. If using charcoal grill, arrange charcoal and build fire so as to have a wide area of medium heat. Arrange ears, still in the husks, so that they are 5 inches above the flames.

3. Grill 15-20 minutes, turning ears so that all sides are cooked until the husks are dried and blackened at the edges (but don't catch fire).

4. Remove from heat, let cool.

5. When ears are cool enough to handle, peel off husks and remove silk.

6. Brush ears with the melted butter, put back on the grill to brown.

7. Turn ears frequently for about 10 minutes so that they brown but do not burn on all sides.

8. Remove again from heat.

9. Grate cheese if using whole cheese. Spread grated cheese out on a clean plate

10. Spread ears with mayonnaise.

11. Roll ears in cheese.

12. Spread ears with powdered chile.

Serve as a hot snack, with paper towels or napkins to hold ears of corn.

KIKA'S CHILI BEANS

This is actually chili con carne, which developed in south Texas in the nineteenth century. Although meat, chiles, and beans went into many Native American and Mexican stews, the cumin—a little used spice in Mexico—is the distinctive feature of Texas chili. The spice may have come from early Spanish settlers from the Canary Islands, or from later German immigrants. The combination was served by colorfully dressed Mexican-American women street vendors in San Antonio, and began to appear in English-language cookbooks in the 1890s. After it was included in army messes in World War I, chili con carne became nationally popular outside the Mexican-American community. Chili cook-offs have been a kind of sport since the early 1960s, but again, few Mexican-Americans are involved, because, outside southern Texas, this food is now regarded as being "not really Mexican." This recipe was given by Texas Congressman E. (Kika) de la Garza to the *VIP Cookbook* (1976), which was published by the American Cancer Society, Virginia Division. Another version of his recipe, from 1986, added more chile powder and garlic.

NOTE: Beans must be soaked overnight.

Yield: serves 4-6
   1 pound dry pinto beans (or 2 cans)
   1 pound lean ground beef
   1 large onion
   1 8-ounce can tomato sauce
   1 16-ounce can stewed tomatoes, chopped
   5 tablespoons chili powder
   1 1/2 teaspoons ground cumin
   1 clove garlic
   salt to taste
   hot chiles or tabasco sauce to taste

Equipment: Large pot, frying pan

   1. Clean and wash beans. Place in large pot and cover with cold water. Let soak overnight.

   2. Next day, drain beans, cover with fresh water, and heat pot to boiling. Reduce heat and simmer, covered, for 30 minutes.

   3. Brown beef in frying pan and drain.

   4. Halve, peel, and chop onion.

   5. Peel and chop garlic.

   6. Add remaining ingredients to meat and mix.

   7. Then add mixture to beans and cook over low heat until beans are tender, about 1 hour longer.

Serve in bowls with bottled hot sauce on the side.

Chicken Pozole

Irene Mendez of the Taylor House Day Care contributed this recipe to the 1990 *Ethnic Food Festival Cookbook: Favorite Recipes Title XX and Head Start Child Care Sites,* prepared by the City of Chicago Department of Human Services. This is really a large recipe for a typical central Mexican stew.

Yield: serves 80-100
   20 pounds chicken
   4-6 medium white onions
   1 head garlic
   3 63-ounce cans hominy (15-16 12-ounce cans)
   1/2 pound dried ancho chile (about 16 dried peppers, or substitute 3/4 cup mild chile powder)
   6 8-ounce packages radishes
   2 pounds lemons
   20 dozen tostadas (tortilla chips)

Equipment: One or more very large pots, blender

   1. Halve, peel, and chop onions. (Wear swim goggles to avoid tears.)

   2. Peel and chop garlic.

   3. Remove skin and cut chicken into chunks.

   4. Boil chicken chunks, onion, and garlic in water to cover for 10 minutes.

   5. Wash hominy and add to chicken.

   6. Simmer ancho chiles in a little water until you can remove seeds and stems.

   7. Blend chiles or chile powder to make a slurry. Add to stew.

   8. Add 1 to 1 1/2 gallons water to the pots to make a soupier stew.

   9. "Cook until done" (about 40 minutes).

   10. Shred lettuces.

   11. Cut thin slices of radishes and lemons.

Serve in bowls topped with shredded lettuce and slices of radishes, with bowls of tostadas and dishes of lemons on the side.

Chicken Enchilada Casserole

Nikki Fresquez of the Interlibrary Loan Department contributed this recipe to the online recipe book of the University of California at Santa Cruz's library diversity committee. Her explanation speaks to changing family roles, which now include working mothers and children who are full-time students: "We used to make enchiladas, but, the larger our family became, the harder they were to make. This recipe is quick and easy!!" Cream of mushroom soup often appears in Mexican-American cooking as a replacement for sour cream.

    1 cup diced onions (optional)
    1 pound cooked shredded chicken
    1 large can enchilada sauce
    2 cans cream of mushroom soup
    corn tortillas cut into bite size pieces
    1-2 cups grated cheese
    1 can sliced olives
    shortening to grease baking pan

Equipment: Large baking pan, saucepan

1. Boil chicken or chicken parts 40 minutes in salted water to cover.

2. Remove chicken. Reserve broth for soup.

3. When chicken is cool, remove meat from bones and cut into shreds.

4. Grease baking pan and cover the entire bottom with a layer of tortillas.

5. If using onion, halve, peel, and dice 1 large onion to get a cup of diced onion.

6. Bring enchilada sauce and mushroom soup to a boil in a saucepan, stirring constantly.

7. Layer chicken and optional onions into baking pan.

8. Pour hot sauce over chicken.

9. Sprinkle on cheese to taste, and olives on top for garnish.

10. Bake at 325 degrees for a half hour.

Mohawk

See Iroquois

Montenegrin-Americans

See Serbian-Americans (including Montenegrins)

Moravians

Originally identified as an ethnic group living in the eastern provinces of what is now the Czech Republic, the Moravians are today an ethno-religious group, identified with the Protestant denomination founded there in 1457. In Europe, the group spoke German, and were the official church of Bohemia and Moravia, with 150,000 to 200,000 members in the 1520s. However, the Catholic Counter-Reformation drove a few hundred leaders to move to Saxony in what is now eastern Germany in 1722, to take refuge on the estate of Count Ludwig von Zinzendorf. The count helped revive and reorganize the Moravian Church, and encouraged pioneering in the colonies of Pennsylvania and North Carolina in the mid-1700s. Their communities around Bethlehem, Pennsylvania, were and are part of the **Pennsylvania Dutch** ethnic group, but their "Southern Province," in Winston-Salem, North Carolina (founded 1753), has been a notable center of **German-American** culture and cooking in the American South. Bakeries in North Carolina now send very thin rolled Moravian cookies all over the United States. The Moravian Church has been more interested in missionary and ecumenical work than most other German-American sects, and thus American Moravians today come from many backgrounds, and their ethnic foods are primarily the dishes that are prescribed for church ceremonies, such as the frequent thanksgiving "Love Feasts." The Moravian Church has about 60,000 members in the United States, and a worldwide membership of about 450,000.

LOVE FEAST BUNS

This recipe comes from *North Carolina and Old Salem Cookery*, by Elizabeth Hedgecock Sparks, who was a Moravian from Salem. Love Feasts are held in connection with Christmas, New Year's, and Easter, but also to honor missionaries or for the anniversaries of a particular church. Because the menu for these events was set by central authority, it has since the 1700s consisted of a large flat yeast bun and a cup of coffee with cream and sugar. Miss Ella Stewart was the "old time bun maker" consulted for this recipe; I have halved her quantities. Coffee replaced tea in 1789. Some congregations served lemonade in the summer.

Yield: 22 buns
  2 eggs
  2 cups sugar
  1/2 cup soft butter and lard (mixed)
  1 tablespoon salt
  1/2 cup warm mashed potatoes
  1 1/2 cakes yeast (or 1 envelope of dry yeast)
  1 gallon flour (16 cups)
  solid shortening to grease baking sheets
  cream or another stick of butter, melted to
    brush finished buns

Equipment: Two baking sheets, pastry brush or clean, new paintbrush

1. Beat eggs.

2. Dissolve yeast in a half cup warm water with a pinch of sugar.

3. Stir the sugar into the egg mixture, then the butter and lard mixture, the salt, and the mashed potatoes.

4. Check to see that the yeast has foamed up a little, then mix with 2 more cups warm water.

5. Stir in the flour to the egg mixture as much as possible, then add the yeast/water mixture and as much more water as you need to make a soft dough.

6. Turn out onto a lightly floured board and knead (see Appendix 1) until smooth.

7. Roll dough up into a floured bowl, cover, and set in a warm place until "light."

8. Punch down dough to break the large bubbles, knead a few times, and cut into 22 pieces.

9. Grease baking sheets with solid shortening.

10. Form each piece of dough into a bun about 4 inches in diameter. Place on greased sheets so they don't touch and let rise again until light.

11. Preheat oven to 375 degrees. "Bake until golden brown." (Look after 15-20 minutes.)

12. Brush with cream or melted butter just after removing from stove.

"At love feasts, the buns are served cold."

MORAVIAN SUGAR CAKE

This recipe from the early 1700s is used by Moravians in both Pennsylvania and North Carolina. The recipe is from Gwyneth Peischl of Nazareth, Pennsylvania, and appeared in Mary Gubser's 1985 *America's Bread Book*

  2 cups sugar
  1 cup mashed potatoes (from 2 medium
    potatoes)
  2 sticks butter, plus enough to grease cake
    pans
  1/2 cup lard or vegetable shortening
  2 eggs
  1 teaspoon salt

1 cup milk
2 packages active dry yeast
1 cup warm potato water
6 cups flour, plus one tablespoon for topping
1 pound brown sugar
2 teaspoons cinnamon

Equipment: Four 8- or 9-inch round cake pans, sieve

1. Peel potatoes and cut into large dice.

2. Boil in 3 cups water until potatoes are soft, about 20-25 minutes.

3. Push potatoes through sieve over a bowl using a wooden spoon to mash them through. Reserve one cup of mashed potatoes. Add enough of the potato cooking water to make a cup of "thick potato water."

4. Combine the cup of mashed potatoes with 2 cups white sugar in a large mixing bowl, stirring thoroughly.

5. Melt 1 stick of butter and the lard or vegetable shortening over low heat.

6. Beat the eggs. Add to the mashed potato mixture. Stir in the melted butter and lard or shortening, salt, and milk.

7. In another bowl, dissolve the yeast in the cup of warm potato water. (If too hot, it will kill the yeast.)

8. Add yeast mixture to the potato mixture.

9. Beat in sufficient flour to make a stiff batter (not a kneaded dough).

10. Cover loosely with plastic wrap and a towel, and let rise until doubled, about 1 hour.

11. Butter the cake pans.

12. Stir the dough, and divide into the 4 pans, spreading evenly. Cover with a light cloth and let rise until doubled, an hour or a little less.

13. Preheat the oven to 350 degrees.

14. Melt 2 tablespoons of butter and combine with brown sugar and 1 tablespoon flour to make the topping.

15. Sprinkle topping over the cakes.

16. Cut the remaining butter into pieces the size of a lima bean.

17. At about 1-inch intervals, punch a deep hole in the dough with a chopstick or your smallest finger.

18. Push a nugget of butter into each hole.

19. Sprinkle the cakes lightly with cinnamon.

20. Bake 20 to 30 minutes, until golden brown.

Serve cut into squares warm or at room temperature.

MORMONS

The Mormons first formed in the United States as a religious movement in the 1830s. Although the Church of Jesus Christ of Latter-day Saints has grown to more than 8 million members internationally, there is a core identity as an American ethnic group, based on the early community's experience of persecution and migration across the U.S. in the late 1840s to what is now the state of Utah. About one-eighth of all Mormons now live in Utah, but the group sets a high value on having its members visit and perform ceremonies in the Salt Lake City Temple.

Mormon cuisine starts with the plain, hearty cooking of the American West, but has been affected by church teachings and the experience of pioneering and farming Utah. Although almost all Mormon men and some women serve as missionaries, many in foreign countries, and although groups of converted immigrants have settled in particular towns in Utah, surprisingly little international food is seen as "Mormon cooking."

Members are required to maintain a year's supply of four staple foods: wheat, powdered milk, sugar or honey, and salt, and to rotate these stocks to keep them fresh. Recommended amounts are 200 to 365 pounds of wheat and 60 to 100 pounds of powdered milk per person. Thus Mormons work a lot of whole wheat, honey, and milk into their baked goods, and do a lot of canning and preserving with the salt and sugar. Certain recipes are treasured as church supper dishes, or because they cook slowly and are ready to eat when the family returns from lengthy weekly services and study sessions. Many Mormon recipes feature potatoes, cheese, and honey because these are produced in Utah.

HONEY BUTTER

Donna Hook contributed this no-cook recipe to *Give Us This Day: Recipes from Reseda II Ward Relief Society Church of Jesus Christ of Latter-day Saints* (1978) in Chatsworth Stake, California. If you are concerned about the safety of uncooked egg, you can use egg substitutes or pasteurized egg products.

1 cube margarine, left out to soften
2 cups honey
2 eggs
dash of salt
2 teaspoons vanilla

Equipment: Whisk or electric hand beater

1. Beat margarine, eggs, and vanilla until smooth.

2. Add honey and salt and beat again until smooth.

"Serve on nut bread, toast, rolls, corn bread, pancakes, waffles, etc."

ADELE MILCZARK'S POTATO SALAD

New York food writer Clementine Paddleford attended a Mormon church potluck supper in Utah, and worked through seven versions of potato salad. She picked this one for her 1960 book, *How America Eats.* Although this recipe looks long and complicated, the only hard part is the double-boiler dressing, which is a version of the "boiled dressing" most Americans used for salad dressing before the development of commercial mayonnaise. The details of the recipe—such as dressing the hot potatoes with one kind of salad dressing, and then again with another, thicker dressing when they are cold—are what made Mrs. Milczark's potato salad memorable.

Yield: 12 large portions
    12 cups diced, cooked new potatoes
    18 hard-boiled eggs
    1 onion, finely chopped
    1/3 cup bottled French dressing
    4 tablespoons cornstarch
    1 cup water
    1 uncooked egg
    3/4 cup vegetable oil
    1/4 cup vinegar
    2 teaspoons prepared mustard
    2 tablespoons sugar
    3 teaspoons salt
    1/4 teaspoon paprika
    1 cup evaporated milk

Equipment: Double boiler, whisk, large serving bowl, colander

1. Bring water for potatoes to a boil.

2. Put 18 eggs in a second pot and cover with cold water; bring to a boil and cook 15 minutes.

3. When potato water is boiling, add salt and whole new potatoes (older russet potatoes will be mealy).

4. Bring potatoes back to a boil and cook 15-25 minutes, or until a fork goes in easily.

5. When eggs are cooked, cool them under cold running water.

6. Peel eggs, and cut 12 of them into half-inch dice.

7. Peel the onion and chop by cutting in half the long way, cutting each half into slices the long way, and slicing across the slices to make fine dice.

8. When the potatoes are done, cool them in a colander until they can be handled.

9. Peel the potatoes, and cut into half-inch dice.

10. In a large mixing bowl, combine onions, French dressing, potatoes, and eggs.

11. Stir quickly so potatoes can absorb the dressing and chill.

12. In a bowl, beat together the uncooked egg, oil, vinegar, mustard, 1 tablespoon of the sugar, 1 teaspoon of the salt, and the paprika.

13. In the top of the double boiler, combine cornstarch and water.

14. Boil water in bottom of double boiler and whisk the cornstarch mixture constantly over the boiling water until it clears and thickens.

15. Whisk in the egg mixture gradually until smooth.

16. Whisk in the evaporated milk, and the remaining sugar and salt.

17. Beat until smooth.

18. Cool this dressing, taste for seasoning, and combine with potatoes.

19. Peel the other 6 hard-boiled eggs.

20. Put half the potato salad in the large serving bowl.

21. Layer on thin slices of 3 of the remaining hard boiled eggs.

22. Put in the other half of the potato salad.

23. Garnish the top with the other 3 hard-boiled eggs cut into wedges.

Serve chilled.

BLENDER PANCAKES

Here's a way to use up stored whole wheat "berries" from *Whole Kernel and Bulgur Wheat Preparation and Usage , 1992 Revision by the Utah State University Extension Service*. This recipe is popular because most recipes for whole wheat require lengthy cooking, even with a pressure cooker. It makes a pancake with something of the heavy, gritty texture of cornbread. Outside Utah, you can get whole wheat berries in health food stores, or substitute a little less cracked wheat with some unprocessed bran.

Yield: 8 servings
  1 cup uncooked whole wheat berries
  1 egg
  2 tablespoons sugar
  3 teaspoons baking powder
  1 1/2 cups milk
  1/4 cup vegetable oil
  1 teaspoon salt

Equipment: Blender, griddle or frying pan

1. Combine whole wheat and 1 cup milk in blender. Blend at high speed for 3 minutes.

2. Add remaining milk and blend for 1 minute more.

3. Add remaining ingredients and blend until smooth.

4. Adjust with a little milk or flour to get a batter a little thinner than your usual pancake batter.

5. Cook on a hot griddle, or thick frying pan.

Serve with butter, syrup, or jam.

BERRIE GOOD WAFFLES (DIET WHOLE WHEAT WAFFLES)

This low-fat spin on the pancakes comes from *The Mormon Diet Cookbook* (1992). The soy milk shows a long-standing Mormon interest in health foods and alternative medicine, and also gets a vanilla flavor without using alcohol-based vanilla extract. It takes a little practice to get these to cook through without sticking.

Yield: 3 or 4 waffles, depending on iron

  1 cup wheat berries, (whole kernels)
  1 cup Edensoy Vanilla Soy Milk
  2 tablespoons unsweetened applesauce
  1 tablespoon egg replacer (mixed with 6 tablespoons water)

1/2 teaspoon salt (optional)
4 teaspoons baking powder
1 tablespoon sugar

Equipment: Blender, waffle iron

1. Blend wheat berries and soy milk "until smooth" (at least 3 minutes).

2. Mix remaining ingredients and add to blender and process briefly to combine.

3. You should have about 3 cups. Waffle batter is thicker than most pancake batters.

4. An electric waffle iron will cook these about right. If you are using a manual waffle iron, cook on high for 6 to 7 minutes. "Cooking longer will add crispness, but can burn."

Serve with a dusting of sugar or jam.

NAKOTA

See Sioux (Dakota, Lakhota, and Nakota)

NARRAGANSETT

The Narragansett Indians who befriended the Rhode Island Colony of Roger Williams in the seventeenth century still live in and around a 1900-acre reservation in Charlestown near the Connecticut border. Their name is an English attempt to pronounce "Nanhigganeuck," which means "people of the small point." The Narragansett attempted to remain neutral in King Philip's War (1675-82) but were attacked by the English settlers for harboring women and children of the combatant **Wampanoag** tribes. Their present reservation land had been broken into individual allotments for almost 100 years when the Narragansetts won a 1978 land settlement with the state. They won federal recognition in 1983, and have built up their tribal enrollment to more than 2,400 members. Narragansett White Cap Flint Corn is still grown and ground in Rhode Island, which is the only northern state that prefers white cornmeal. Some other Narragansett recipes you may find are for popcorn, fish chowders, herbal teas, cranberry sauces, and johnny cakes with strawberries or blueberries.

DOVECREST QUAHOG CHOWDER

This recipe is from Eleanore Dove, who founded the Dovecrest Restaurant in Arcadia Village, South Kingston, Rhode Island. The Dovecrest is also a trading post and Narragansett museum. Clear-broth chowder is eaten all over Rhode Island, but since it uses neither milk nor tomato, it is probably closest to the original Indian style. The recipe appears in Jane and Michael Stern's *Real American Food.*

1/2 pound salt pork
1 large onion
2 large potatoes (2 cups diced)
2 cups shucked quahog clams (from 4 quarts whole cherrystone clams, or 2 cans chopped clams, drained)
2 cups clam juice (bottled if using canned clams)
2 tablespoons butter

Equipment: 4-quart or larger soup pot

1. Dice salt pork into fine dice (This is easier if you partially freeze it first).

2. Fry salt pork over low heat to render out the fat.

3. If using whole clams, steam over a little water to open, cool, remove meats, and reserve

juice. Dice up meats. If using canned clams, don't use their canning liquid in the soup.

4. Dice onions and potatoes.

5. Add onions to salt pork and fry until light brown.

6. Add potatoes and water to cover, up to 2 cups.

7. Bring to a boil and cook until potatoes can be easily pierced with a fork.

8. Add clams, clam juice, butter, and a little more water.

9. Simmer 15-20 minutes.

Serve with oyster crackers.

RHODE ISLAND JOHNNY CAKES OR JOURNEY CAKES

This recipe from "'Nakomis' of the tribe of Narragansett" appeared in the 1935 *Nationality Recipes* compiled by Eleanor F. Wills for the YWCA of Providence, Rhode Island. As discussed with **Anglo-American** recipes for Johnny cake, "journey cakes" is probably not the original term. More recent Narragansett recipes are a little richer.

Yield: 8-10 pancakes as a breakfast or side dish
1 cup fine white cornmeal
1 teaspoon salt
2 teaspoons sugar
2 tablespoons milk
vegetable shortening to grease the griddle
butter

Equipment: Food processor or blender, fine sieve

1. If you cannot obtain Rhode Island Johnny Cake meal, whirl coarse white cornmeal in a blender or food processor propped up with a book, then sift it through a fine sieve. Bring 1 1/2 cups water to a boil.

2. Blend dry ingredients.

3. "Scald with boiling water" but only enough water to make a stiff mush that "will stand without spreading."

4. Grease griddle with shortening. Turn on at medium heat.

5. The batter will absorb more fluid and become stiffer as it sits, so stir in milk to maintain a workable texture.

6. Drop by heaping tablespoons. Flatten each patty with a spoon, leaving them about 1/2-inch high.

7. Cook 15 minutes to brown.

8. Turn and cook 15 minutes more.

9. Butter between johnny cakes if you stack them before serving.

Serve as a side dish or breakfast pancakes.

CORN MEAL PORRIDGE

This unusual recipe comes from a small pamphlet, *Narragansett Indian Recipes Traditional and Contemporary* by Ella Thomas Sekatu. Dr. Sekatu is the daughter of a medicine man and herself a medicine woman of the Narragansetts.

1 cup johnny cake meal (fine white cornmeal)
1 cup cold water
3 cups shellfish juice (substitute bottled clam juice)

1. Place cornmeal in thick-bottomed pan with 1 cup cold water.

2. Place on medium heat, and begin stirring constantly.

3. Add shell-fish juice 1 cup at a time, until it comes to a bubbling boil.

4. After the final cup of shellfish juice has been added, reduce heat and simmer for at least 10 minutes.

"This nutritious porridge can be eaten right away or allowed to set and fried later."

NATIVE AMERICANS

See UNDER NAMES OF INDIVIDUAL TRIBAL NATIONS. *See also* ESKIMOS (INUIT) AND ALEUTS; HAWAIIANS; HONDURAN- AND GARIFUNA-AMERICANS

NATIVE HAWAIIANS

See HAWAIIANS

NAVAJO (DINÉ OR DINEH)

The Navajo are the largest Indian nation living on one reservation, with more than 200,000 residents on a space larger than the state of West Virginia. The reservation gives the Navajo Nation a true feeling of being a separate country, with its own police, time zone, and road system. The name Navajo comes from Pueblo Indian words for "cultivated field" and "canyon mouth," and was first used by the Spanish explorers as "Apaches de Navaju" because the Navajo language is related to the **Apache** language (and to the languages of Alaska coastal Indians like the **Tlingit and Haida**). Although Navajo history holds that they have always lived where they do now, linguistic evidence suggests that they arrived with the Apache in the Southwest about 600 to 800 years ago. They have been uniquely successful as a tribe due to a remarkable mixture of flexibility and cultural conservatism. They were able to learn settled farming from the **Pueblo** Indians; herding, weaving, and silversmithing from the Spanish; and jewelry techniques from the **Zuni**. At the same time, the Navajo have preserved their language and religious system.

The Navajo took in refugees from the Pueblo Revolt of 1680, but generally avoided foreign domination until the 1860s, when Kit Carson forced them to surrender by destroying their sheep and crops, including their peach orchards. In 1864, the Navajo were forced to march 800 miles in winter to a concentration camp at Fort Sumner, New Mexico. Many died on this bitterly remembered "Long Walk." After four years of internment in a wasteland where corn would not grow, the Navajo were allowed to return to a reservation in their homeland. During World War II, Navajo "Code Talkers" were used as radio operators who employed the Navajo language to keep transmissions secret from the Japanese.

Navajo food includes the posoles and blue-corn dishes of the Pueblos, peaches, tamales called "kneel-down bread," roast corn, some reservation traditions like spam-and-eggs and macaroni-and-cheese, and a variety of lamb and mutton stews spiced with chiles. The Navajo have a special feeling for local wild foods, such as pine nuts and juniper tea. Some traditionalists will not eat seafood because they believe that sea creatures are relatives from the Fourth World of creation before the Navajo emerged into the present world.

FRY BREAD

The Navajo fry bread may be the original Indian fry bread because it is usually dated from the Fort Sumner days when people could not get corn. A **New Mexico Hispanic** fry bread, known as sopaipillas, is also found in the Southwest.

This recipe is from the personal Web page of Roberta Goh of Tuba City, Arizona, a 1999 high school graduate. Navajo fry breads are often enriched with dry milk powder or fats such as mayonnaise.

CAUTION: Hot oil used.

Yield: three 8-inch breads
   2 cups unsifted flour
   1/2 cup dry milk solids
   2 teaspoons double-acting baking powder
   1/2 teaspoon salt
   2 tablespoons lard, plus 1 pound lard for
      deep frying
   1/2 cup ice water

Equipment: High-sided heavy 10-inch pot, long tongs, paper towels

1. Make a glass of ice water.

2. Combine the flour, dry milk solids, baking powder, and salt, and sift them into a deep bowl.

3. Cut 2 tablespoons of the lard into 1/2-inch cubes.

4. Add the lard bits to the flour mixture. "With your fingertips, rub the flour and fat together until the mixture resembles flakes of coarse meal."

5. Pour in a half cup of ice water and toss the ingredients together until the dough can be gathered into a ball.

6. Drape the bowl with a kitchen towel and let the dough rest at room temperature for about 2 hours.

7. After the resting period, cut the dough into 3 equal pieces.

8. Flour a board and rolling pin, and roll each piece into a rough circle about 8 inches in diameter and 1/4 inch thick.

9. With a small sharp knife, cut two 4- to 5-inch-long parallel slits completely through the dough down the center of each round, spacing the slits about 1 inch apart.

10. "In a heavy 10-inch skillet, melt the remaining pound of lard over moderate heat until it is very hot but not smoking." (For safety, I recommend that inexperienced fry-bread makers use a high-sided spaghetti pot or heavy saucepan.) "The melted fat should be about 1 inch deep; add more lard if necessary."

11. Fry the breads one at a time for about 2 minutes on each side, turning them once with tongs or a slotted spatula. The bread will puff slightly and become crisp and brown.

12. Drain the Navajo fry bread on paper towels.

Serve hot with stew or make a Navajo taco (see below).

KNEEL DOWN BREAD

This is the Navajo version of fresh-corn tamales, probably the third-most common Native American way to eat corn, after dried-corn soups and roasted fresh corn. The name probably comes from the way the Navajo women kneel down to place these breads in an earth oven to cook them. Another possibility is that the folded corn shucks look like kneeling corn-shuck dolls. This recipe from Ella Tsinnie appeared in Carolyn Neithammer's *American Indian Food and Lore*. Out-of-season sweet corn is more like the fresh flour corn used by the Navajo.

Yield: 12-14 servings
   10 ears of corn in the husk

Equipment: Blender, sharp knife or corn cutter

1. Peel the corn, saving the husks and discarding the silks. Put the husks in a plastic bag to keep them from drying out. (If you steam the ears briefly, the husks will be more flexible.)

2. Grind the kernels into a mush in a food grinder, blender, or food processor.

3. Take 1 large piece of corn husk, or overlap 2 smaller pieces. Kneel facing the pointed end of the husk.

4. Put 2 or 3 tablespoons of the corn mixture toward the top and one side of the corn husk(s).

5. Roll into a long tube to enclose the mush.

6. Fold up the bottom (pointed) side of the husk in half, but entirely over the mush, so it is enclosed on 3 sides. (If your husks have "tails," you can tie the breads as illustrated.)

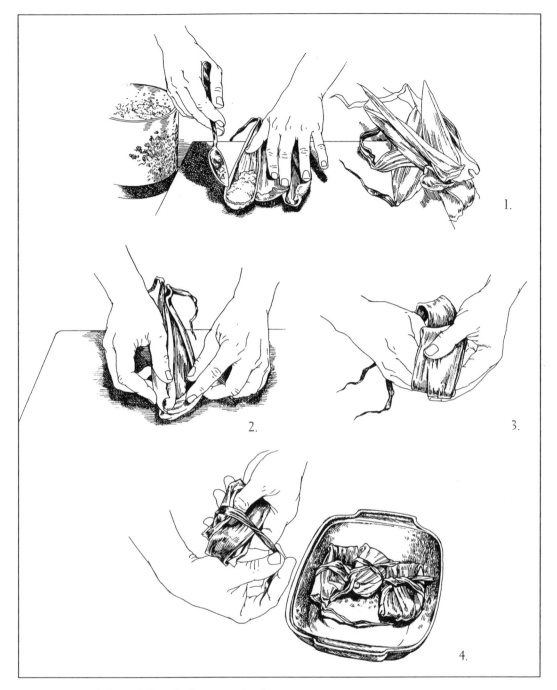

7. Put into a baking dish with the empty husk down, so it doesn't unfold.

8. When you have all the husks in the dish, bake for 1 hour in a 350-degree oven.

Serve hot with mutton stew, or dry and preserve for the winter.

NAVAJO TACO

Another argument for Navajo fry bread being one of the oldest is that this is the best-known way to serve fry bread, which is sold from trailers at every pow-wow across the United States. This recipe is by Roberta Goh.

6 rounds of fry bread
1 tablespoon lard
1 head lettuce
3 tomatoes
1 onion
1 1/2 pounds ground lamb
1/2 pound cheddar cheese
small can green chiles

Equipment: Grater or food processor with grating disk

1. Brown lamb in lard.

2. Grate cheese.

3. Shred lettuce.

4. Chop tomatoes and chiles.

5. Divide lamb onto 6 fry bread rounds.

6. Top with cheese, lettuce, tomatoes, chiles, and onions.

Serve with salsa!

MUTTON STEW

This recipe is from a cookbook published by the Navajo Curriculum Center, Rough Rock Community School, and posted on the Internet as part of Web page nutrition project by Pam Chihak of Kayenta (Arizona) Middle School.

The original recipe is rather vague, but has been in wide use by Navajo families for hundreds of years. I have added some specifics and quantities following a recipe in *Spirit of the Harvest* by Beverly Cox and Martin Jacobs.

Yield: serves 8

4 cups diced mutton (or 3 pounds lamb stew neck with bones)
2 large potatoes
2 large carrots
1 head celery
2 cloves of garlic
3 tablespoons chili powder

1. "To make mutton stew any part of the meat can be used. The backbone, neck, or the hind leg are often put in the stew. Sometimes bones are cut in half and added. The meat is put into a pot of water (6-8 cups) and boiled for at least 30 minutes."

2. Peel potatoes and cut into 6 pieces each.

3. Peel carrots and cut into large chunks.

4. Pull apart celery stalks and wash and chop.

5. Add vegetables and spices to the stew and simmer until the vegetables are done.

"Serve with coffee and fry bread."

NEW MEXICO HISPANICS

Many families in the Rio Grande Valley of New Mexico, especially the country north of Santa Fe, do not describe themselves as **Mexican-Americans** because their ancestors only lived in Mexico for 24 years, from Mexican independence in 1821 to the U.S. conquest in 1845. For most of the Spanish colonial period, the New Mexico settlements were a six-month journey on mules from Mexico City, so some families retain some very old Spanish customs. The first Spanish settlements in New Mexico were established in the 1590s, and with a brief departure after the Pueblo revolt of 1680, have remained to this day. New Mexico Hispanics are still known for growing apples and chile peppers, and for traditional carvings and weavings in the towns along the Rio Grande. New Mexico Hispanic food has some old **Spanish-American** and Mexican-American qualities, but also shares many dishes with the Eastern **Pueblo Indians**. The altitude and isolation of the area meant that there were no avocados and only seasonal tomatoes until the coming of the railroads. Some other oddities are enchiladas that are stacked rather than rolled, bread pudding without eggs, and chile peppers in almost everything. It is hard to estimate the size of this community because they are counted by the census as Hispanics along with Mexican-Americans whose families migrated to New Mexico after 1845. In the 1980s, a few families realized that their customs of lighting candles on Friday nights and avoiding pork meant that they were descended from Jewish converts to Christianity at the time of the Spanish Inquisition—an indication of the isolation and continuity of this old Spanish-American ethnic group.

Bizcochitos

These Christmas cookies became favorites for all occasions among the old Hispanic families of northern New Mexico. They are also made by Eastern Pueblo Indians. The recipe is from the 1982 revised edition of *The Good Life, New Mexico Traditions and Food* by Fabiola Cabeza de Baca Gilbert.

Yield: 60 cookies
  1 cup sugar
  2 cups lard or shortening, plus a little to grease baking sheets
  1 teaspoon anise seed
  4 cups white flour
  2 cups whole wheat flour
  1 teaspoon salt
  2 teaspoons baking powder
  granulated sugar to dip cookies

Equipment: 2 baking sheets

1. "Cream lard with hand" (or pastry blender or large fork).

2. Add sugar and beat until light and fluffy.

3. Sift flour with salt and baking powder.

4. Add anise seed and flour mixture to the lard mixture.

5. Add enough water (about 3/4 cup) to make the mixture hold together.

6. Flour a board and rolling pin and roll out dough 1/2-inch thick and cut into "fancy shapes." (Fleur-de-lis and floral irises were two traditional shapes, but rounds are common.)

7. Grease two baking sheets.

8. Dip cut-out cookies in sugar on one side; arrange sugar-side-up on baking sheets.

9. Bake at 350 degrees for 15 minutes. They will be slightly browned but still a little soft in the middle.

Sopaipillas

Sopaipillas are the likely ancestors of Indian fry bread. The name is unique to New Mexico. They would be called bunuelos in Mexico or Spain. Earlier recipes were made with yeast dough, which works rapidly at the 7,000-foot elevations of northern New Mexico. Sopaipillas are served in New Mexico with a plastic squeeze bottle of honey. This recipe from Anna Paiz appeared in the online version of *Indian Country Dining Guide*, edited by Lance Begaye.

CAUTION: Hot oil used.

  2 cups flour
  2 teaspoons baking powder
  1 teaspoon salt
  2 tablespoons lard
  2 cups water
  about 1 pound shortening for frying

Equipment: Deep-fry thermometer, high-sided pan

1. Sift dry ingredients together.

2. Work in lard and about 2 cups of lukewarm water to make a soft dough.

3. Chill in refrigerator.

4. Roll out dough on a floured surface to about 1/4-inch thickness. Cut into 3-inch squares.

5. Heat lard or vegetable shortening in a high-sided pan to almost 400 degrees, but stop before it smokes, a sign that the oil is about to catch fire!

6. Deep fry squares of dough a few at a time. Brown on each side and drain on paper towels.

Serve piping hot. To eat, poke open (or tear off a corner) and put in honey or slather with honey butter. Sopaipillas offset the hot chile sauces of much New Mexico cooking.

QUICK CHOCOLATE

This is the easiest of three hot chocolate recipes in the 1934 edition of Erna Fergusson's *Mexican Cookbook*, which has been republished ever since by the University of New Mexico Press. It may be the first recipe to use marshmallows in hot chocolate. Unlike the sopaipillas (see above), this recipe will go faster at sea level.

Yield: serves 4-6
  4 cups milk
  1 1/2 squares Mexican chocolate (or sweet baking chocolate)
  2 tablespoons sugar
  1/4 teaspoon cinnamon
  1/2 teaspoon nutmeg
  1/4 teaspoon almond extract or 1/2 teaspoon vanilla
  5 marshmallows

Equipment: Grater or food processor with grating disk, egg beater or hand mixer or Mexican chocolate beater

1. Heat milk in a pot (or microwave oven) almost to boiling.

2. Grate chocolate.

3. Boil chocolate, sugar, spices, and a pinch of salt in a half cup water for 5 minutes.

4. Add hot milk and marshmallows and beat until the marshmallows are dissolved.

5. Reheat and add extract.

6. Beat until foamy.

Ms. Fergusson's sources served hot chocolate with sopaipillas at 4 p.m.

CAPIROTADA

New Mexico bread pudding differs from other Hispanic bread puddings in that it is made from cheese and without eggs or milk. (The New Mexico version of custard, natillas, economizes by using both the white and yolk of eggs.) This recipe is from *The Rancho de Chimayo Cookbook* by Cheryl Alters Jamison and Bill Jamison. The substitution for pine nuts and some details of technique are from *The Feast of Santa Fe* by Huntley Dent.

CAUTION: Hot syrup sticks to skin and burns.

  1 cup brown sugar
  2 cloves
  1 stick cinnamon
  8 slices white bread
  1 cup grated mild cheddar cheese
  1/2 cup raisins
  1/2 cup piñon nuts (or slivered almonds)
  butter to grease baking dish

Equipment: Baking sheet, long tongs, grater or food processor with grating disk, shallow baking pan, ladle, aluminum foil

1. In a small saucepan, heat the brown sugar with 2 1/2 cups water, the cloves, and the cinnamon. Simmer about 15 minutes, until the mixture has cooked down by about one quarter.

2. Remove the spices, and set the syrup aside to cool.

3. Butter a medium-sized baking dish.

4. Tear the bread into bite-size pieces, and spread the pieces on a baking sheet.

5. Toast in a 350-degree over for 10-15 minutes, turning occasionally with tongs, until dry and lightly browned.

6. In the baking dish, layer half the toast pieces.

7. Sprinkle on half the cheese, raisins, and nuts.

8. Repeat for the second layer.

9. Slowly ladle the syrup over the layers, making sure the toast pieces are soaked well.

10. Press the toast pieces gently into the syrup with the bottom of the ladle.

11. Cover the dish with aluminum foil and bake at 350 degrees for 30 minutes, or until the syrup is absorbed and the capirotada has a creamy, almost custard-like consistency.

NICARAGUAN-AMERICANS

T he 1990 census recorded 177,000 Nicaraguan-Americans. In 1996, the Immigration and Naturalization Service estimated that there were also about 70,000 illegal aliens from Nicaragua
in the United States. Nicaragua's history has long been tangled with that of the United
States, but large-scale immigration began only in the final years of the Samoza dictatorship in the
1960s and 1970s, with Nicaraguans fleeing mostly to Los Angeles and San Francisco. The Sandanista
revolution from 1972 to 1980 brought some political exiles home, but also sent a wealthier population loyal to the conservative elite to the U.S., predominantly to Miami but also to the West Coast
communities. With the United States supporting the "contra" rebels, Nicaraguan refugees were
somewhat more likely than other Central Americans to receive political asylum, but the civil war
and chaos also sent many poor Nicaraguans and young males north without legal papers or political
credentials. Nicaragua again reversed directions with the contra electoral victory of 1990, but many
Nicaraguans have settled into successful careers in Miami, and poorer Nicaraguans are still working
in the restaurants and laundries of major U.S. American cities. Nicaraguan governments since 1990
have lobbied against deportations from the United States to reduce the impact on the still-fragile
Nicaraguan economy.

Nicaraguan food is typical of Central American food in that it is not very spicy, relies on rice and
(small red) beans, and has some very sweet desserts designed to go with coffee. Tres leches cake is a
sweetened cake of fresh milk, evaporated milk, and sweetened condensed milk that has become
popular with **Cuban-Americans** as well as with Nicaraguan-Americans in Miami. Nicaraguan food is
surprisingly diverse, reflecting the wide class divisions within the country and also the ethnic differences between the Afro-Caribbean east coast and the relatively Hispanic Pacific side where most of
the population lives. Steak houses are popular in Nicaragua, and an Argentine green sauce, chimichurri,
has become the favorite condiment.

GALLO PINTO

The Nicaraguan version of rice and beans is
made with red beans, and the beans and rice are
fried together at the end. The recipe is from
Steven Raichlen's *Miami Spice.*

NOTE: Beans need to be soaked overnight.

Yield: serves 6 to 8
    1 cup small red beans
    1 bay leaf
    2 onions
    1 whole clove
    2 cloves garlic
    salt
    1 1/2 cups converted long-grain white rice
    3 tablespoons lard or olive oil

Equipment: Large pot, large saucepan, colander,
large frying pan

1. Soak beans overnight in cold water to cover
by 3 inches.

2. Drain the beans and place in a large pot
with 2 quarts salted water.

3. Peel the smaller onion. Pin the bay leaf to
the onion with the clove. (This makes it easier
to discard these spices when the beans are done.)

4. Add the garlic and bring the beans to a
boil. Skim off any foam that rises to the surface.

5. Reduce heat and simmer the beans, uncovered, for 1 to 1 1/2 hours or until tender.

6. Bring 2 1/2 cups water and 1 teaspoon salt
to a boil in a large, heavy saucepan. Add the rice,
return to a boil, then reduce heat, cover, and cook
the rice about 18 minutes, until tender.

7. Drain the beans in a colander and wash
with cold water. Discard the onion with clove
and bay leaf.

8. When the rice is done, let it sit covered for 5 minutes.

9. Fluff the rice with a fork.

10. Halve, peel, and chop the larger onion.

11. Heat the oil in a large frying pan. Add the chopped onion and thoroughly brown over medium heat, about 5 minutes.

12. Add the beans and rice, and cook over medium heat until the rice is lightly browned and the mixture is very aromatic, about 5 minutes. "The longer the mixture fries, the more flavorful it becomes."

13. Taste for salt and add black pepper to taste.

Serve as a side dish with steak.

SOPA DE FRIJOLES AL ESTILO NICARAGUENSE

Patricia Molina De Blackmon posted this family recipe on an Internet exchange of Nicaraguan recipes. I have translated from the Spanish. Most of the beans are reserved for another use, either in gallo pinto (see above) or for refried beans.

NOTE: Beans need to be soaked overnight.

2 pounds dry beans (small red beans or black beans)
1 large onion
2 medium tomatoes
1 large green pepper
1 scallion or green onion
1 stick margarine
1 1/2 cups buttermilk or sour cream (or a mixture of both)
1 dozen eggs (9 optional)
salt, pepper, and garlic to taste
2 or 3 tablespoons of vinegar

Equipment: Food processor (optional), blender, 6-quart pot

1. Soak the beans in 6 quarts of water overnight.

2. Discard the water and bring the beans to a boil in 6 quarts of fresh cold water.

3. Lower the heat and simmer, partly covered, until the beans are soft. If the water runs low, add more as necessary.

4. Cut off the top and bottom of the green pepper. Remove core and pith.

5. Cut off roots and any dry leaves of the scallion and cut into 2-inch lengths.

6. If using a food processor, process green pepper chunks and scallion to get pieces as fine as you can. If not, cut pepper into thin strips and very fine dice. Slice tomatoes into small chunks. Slice scallion into fine rings.

7. Melt margarine in a 6-quart (or larger) pot. Add vegetables and sauté until they are golden, and the tomatoes are just beginning to fall apart.

8. Add all the liquid from the beans to the fried vegetables. Reserve beans for another use.

9. For a thicker soup, put one cup of beans in a blender and blend until you have a thick liquid, which you can mix into the soup.

10. In a saucepan, bring the buttermilk or sour cream (or a mixture of both) to a boil with salt, pepper, and garlic (or garlic salt) added to your personal taste.

11. Add sour cream mixture to the soup and bring back to a simmer.

12. Beat 3 eggs in a bowl.

13. Add the eggs to the soup, stirring as you go so that they mix in without lumps.

14. Break the other 9 eggs, if using, one-by-one into the soup. Try not to put any on top of other ones, so that they poach evenly.

15. When the soup is back to a boil and the eggs are completely cooked, add the vinegar, 2 or 3 tablespoons according to taste, and cook 5 more minutes before serving.

Serve on rice or by itself with tortilla or bread.

NIGERIAN-AMERICANS

Nigeria, the most populous country in Africa, has more than 200 ethnic groups. Most people who describe themselves as Nigerian-Americans are recent immigrants, with communities in New York and Washington, D.C., and a large group, perhaps more than 100,000, in Houston. Of the three largest ethnic groupings in Nigeria, the Igbo (or Ibo) people predominate in Houston, and there are also many Yoruba in the U.S. Because about one-eighth to one-fourth of the Africans brought to North America as slaves were taken from ports in what is now Nigeria, millions of **African-Americans** must be of Nigerian descent. Two boatloads of shipwrecked slaves from ports in Nigeria are ancestors to most of the Garifuna (see **Honduran- and Garifuna-Americans**) in Central America and the U.S., and specifically Yoruba religious practices have survived as "Santeria" among **Cuban-Americans**. Yoruba food and religion are also influential among **Brazilian-Americans**.

Nigerian food today is the product of a long history of exchanges, dating back before the great trading empire of Mali, which existed during the European Middle Ages, and continuing into modern dishes like curry spaghetti and jolof rice (from Senegal). Some African-American families like to try Nigerian dishes as part of the December Kwanzaa feast. A recent Nigerian-American cookbook is *Cooking Nigerian Style: Recipes of the Motherland*, written by J. Imoisi and sold by Gamosi Enterprise, 8045 Antoine St., Suite 368, Houston, Texas 77088, or on their Web site at <http://www.cookingwithstyle.com>.

A MOI MOI

A moi moi (the Yoruba spelling is a moyen moyen) is a kind of steamed tamale made from cowpeas in Nigeria, and from closely related black-eyed peas in the U.S. Nigerian-Americans in some cities can obtain imported cowpeas called "African beans." The same tamales are called abará in the strongly Afro-Brazilian areas of Bahia, Brazil. The hard part of the recipe is skinning all the black-eyed peas. If you leave on the skins with their black markings, the tamales are good but grey and coarse next to the real creamy white ones. In Africa, the tamales would be steamed in leaves. This recipe comes from *Cooking Nigerian Style*, with some details from *Soul and Spice* by Heidi Haughy Cusick. You could substitute weaker or hotter peppers for the caribe chiles, or 1 1/2 teaspoons of cayenne or other ground red pepper. But try to use some kind of fresh hot pepper—bean tamales are extremely bland without the hot pepper, and hot sauce does not seem to help as much as it does with corn tamales.

CAUTION: Hot pepper used. Wash hands thoroughly after handling hot pepper. Do not rub eyes with hands even after washing.

NOTE: Peas need to be soaked overnight.

Yield: serves 4 to 6 as a main course

    1 pound (2 1/2 cups) dried black-eyed peas
    1 small tomato
    1 tablespoon oil
    1 bouillon cube
    1 teaspoon salt (optional)
    2 small red (caribe) peppers
    1/2 can of corned beef (optional)
    1 onion

Equipment: Aluminum foil, blender or food processor, potato masher (optional), tongs to remove tamales from boiling water

1. Soak black-eyed peas overnight in a large pot of water.

2. Drain and add water to cover.

3. Loosen skins by rubbing beans between your hands, mashing with potato masher, or putting batches with water in the food processor with the plastic blade. There is no easy way to do this, and it takes most of an hour no matter how you do it. The last 20 or 30 beans always have to have their skins pinched off by hand. When you have discarded the skins, you should have all cream-colored beans.

4. Drain the remaining beans, and transfer 2 cups of beans to a blender or food processor with the metal blade.

5. Add a half cup water.

6. Puree until "smooth and creamy." If the beans do not blend well, you may need to add a little more water.

7. Repeat until all the beans are done.

8. Halve and peel the onion, and cut into large chunks.

9. Slice open the peppers, and remove the seeds and pith with a spoon. Cut into small pieces.

10. Blend or process the onion, bouillon cube, and pepper (or dried pepper) with the tomato and enough of the bean puree to make a paste.

11. Mix thoroughly with the bean puree. "Stir very well with a large spoon for three minutes" to make sure the hot pepper is evenly distributed through all the mixture.

12. Next, add salt, optional corned beef, and vegetable oil, and stir everything together with a large spoon.

13. Take aluminum foil and make 5 by 7-inch pockets to hold the mixture. (Make 8 to 10 pockets.) Make sure that the sides are folded so that no liquids can escape. Leave an opening at the top to spoon in the mixture.

14. Spoon mixture into square pockets until they are half full. Fold down the tops tightly. Continue to do this until all the mixture has been placed into the square foil pockets. (Set all aside.)

15. Fold edges of foil at least twice to seal.

16. In a large pot, bring half a pot of water to a rolling boil.

17. Add all the foil pockets to the pot of boiling water and cover the pot.

18. Boil for 25 to 30 minutes. Remove with tongs, and let cool for 10 minutes.

Serve with stew and rice, or cut up as an appetizer.

AKARA

Akara is the Nigerian fried bean cake. (See Appendix 3: "They All Fried Bean Cakes" for other ethnic bean cakes.) This recipe from Mary Olandu appeared in *The Griots Cookbook* (1985) by Alice McGill, Mary Carter Smith, and Eleanora M. Washington. I have doubled the recipe.

CAUTION: Hot oil used.

NOTE: Peas need to soak overnight.

Yield: appetizers for 12
  2 cups black-eyed peas
  fresh chopped red pepper to taste (start with one hot chile)
  2 medium sweet green peppers
  1/2 teaspoon "salt and seasonings of your choice"
  2 small onions
  oil for frying

Equipment: Deep-fry thermometer, large potato masher or food processor, heavy pan with high sides, bowl, frying pan

1. Soak black-eyed peas overnight in a large pot of water.

2. Drain and add water to cover.

3. Loosen skins by rubbing beans between your hands, mashing with potato masher, or putting batches with water in the food processor with the plastic blade. There is no easy way to do this, and it takes most of an hour no matter how you do it. The last 20 or 30 beans always have to have their skins pinched off by hand. When you have discarded the skins, you should have all cream-colored beans.

4. Drain the remaining beans, and transfer 2 cups beans to a blender or food processor with the metal blade.

5. Add a half cup water.

6. Puree until "smooth and creamy." If the beans do not blend well, you may need to add a little more water. Try not to add too much water.

7. Halve and peel onions and put in blender or food processor.

8. Core green peppers and remove pith. Cut into pieces and add to blender or food processor.

9. Cut off stem of red pepper, slit one side, and scrape out seeds and pith with a teaspoon. Cut into small pieces and add to blender or food processor.

10. Add beans to blender and repeat Steps 5 and 6 until all the beans are done.

11. Put all bean paste in a bowl and mix well. Season to taste and mix again.

12. In a heavy pan with high sides, heat an inch of vegetable oil to 360 to 375 degrees.

13. "Form balls of paste with hands or spoon it into frying pan." Fritters should contain 4-6 tablespoons of bean mixture.

14. Fry until browned evenly on all sides.

15. Drain on paper towels or a wire rack.

Serve at breakfast or as an appetizer or snack.

BLACK-EYED PEAS, NIGERIAN STYLE

This is the third major style of Nigerian cowpea cuisine. Susan Eroraha contributed this recipe to *What's Cookin'* (1991), which was compiled by Arlene Luskin for the Montgomery County [Maryland] Humane Society.

2 cups uncooked black-eyed peas
1 onion chopped
1 green pepper, chopped
red pepper, salt, and pepper to taste
1/2 of a 6-ounce can tomato paste

1. Wash black-eyed peas. Drain and cook in 4 to 6 cups water for 45 minutes, or until tender but not mushy.

2. Halve, peel, and chop onion.

3. Remove stem and core of green pepper, and slice off white pith. Cut into small dice.

4. When beans are soft, add onion, green pepper, seasoning, and tomato paste. Cook about 15-20 minutes. "It should be relatively thick."

Serve with rice.

PEPPER SOUP (STEW OR SAUCE)

This Yoruba version of one of the best-known Nigerian dishes comes from the Smithsonian Institution's 1996 "virtual festival" on its World Wide Web. Try to use all the red pepper and remember that a little "sauce" goes on a lot of rice.

Yield: serves 4 to 6
3 pounds stewing beef (or goat meat or fish)
1 medium onion, chopped or ground in blender
1 teaspoon dried red pepper, crushed or ground
4 fresh red tomatoes, chopped or ground in blender (or one 6-oz can tomato paste)
2 tablespoons cooking oil
1 teaspoon salt
1 teaspoon curry powder (optional)
2 bouillon cubes (optional)
1 teaspoon thyme leaves (optional)
1 cup water

Equipment: Mortar and pestle, food processor or blender

1. Halve, peel, and chop onion, or cut into large chunks and grind in food processor or blender.

2. Cut up beef (or goat meat or fish) in small pieces and place in stewing pot with salt and water to cover.

3. Boil until meat is tender.

4. Remove meat from pot and save soup in a bowl.

5. Heat oil in stewing pot; add onion and brown.

6. Add meat and ground tomatoes (or tomato paste diluted with another cup of water).

7. Stir in the remaining ingredients one by one, with an additional cup of water if needed.

8. Simmer for 10 minutes.

Serve over white rice.

NORWEGIAN-AMERICANS

T he 1990 census found 3.8 million Americans claiming Norwegian ancestry, the second-largest of the Scandinavian groups, after **Swedish-Americans**. Norwegians arrived over a relatively long period (1820-1910), with large numbers coming as early as the 1860s, but they still have strong concentrations in the farming areas of Minnesota, Wisconsin, and North and South Dakota, and in the cities of Minneapolis and greater Chicago. Norwegian-Americans were generally well assimilated into American life by the time of the ethnic revival of the 1970s and 1980s. Since then, the radio commentaries of Garrison Keilor have brought a humorous view of Norwegian-American life to the general public. A recent memoir-with-recipes of Norwegian-American farm life in North Dakota is *Prairie Cooks* by Carrie Young with Felicia Young (HarperPerennial, 1997).

One of the most interesting developments in Norwegian-American cooking is the use of lutefisk, wind-dried codfish revived by soaking in lye. This dish was an important winter food in Norway and Sweden, but is seldom eaten there now that fresh fish can be flown in. Norwegian-Americans, however, have stuck with lutefisk as a kind of test of ethnic solidarity, since the fishy aroma and unusual texture are off-putting even for some Norwegian-Americans. Lutefisk suppers became an important social event in the Scandinavian community, with men cooking the lutefisk, and women making lefse (see below) and a cottage cheese pudding called ostakaka (see recipe in Swedish-American section.) Both recipes have been somewhat simplified because you can now buy pre-soaked lutefisk in stores in the Midwest. Ostakaka once required gallons of fresh milk and rennet tablets, but recipes have developed using commercial cottage cheese. Carrie Young also has a lot to say about lefse, a kind of potato tortilla that is eaten with lutefisk and is tricky to make. With some Norwegian-American recipes, either the cooking or the eating is a test of character.

MICROWAVE ROMMEGROT

Rommegrot, a porridge of cream and flour, can be made in a surprising number of ways. This recipe from Winona, Minnesota, is posted on the Web site of the Lutheran Brotherhood insurance co-operative at <www.lutheranbrotherhood.com>. The microwave cuts about 30 percent off the time of a dish that has always been something to make for unexpected but valued guests.

Yield: serves 6 to 8
1/2 cup margarine or butter
1/2 cup all-purpose flour
1/4 cup sugar, plus 1 tablespoon for topping
1/2 teaspoon salt
4 cups whole or 2% milk
1 tablespoon cinnamon

Equipment: 2-quart casserole, microwave oven, whisk, 4-cup Pyrex measuring cup

1. In a 2-quart casserole, melt margarine on high (1 to 1 1/2 minutes).

2. Stir in flour, 1/4 cup sugar, and salt.

3. In a 4-cup measuring cup, microwave milk on high until hot (4 to 5 minutes).

4. Whisk hot milk into flour mixture; mix well.

5. Microwave on high, stopping to whisk every 2 minutes, until thickened (8 to 11 minutes).

6. Mix remaining sugar and cinnamon for topping.

Serve in deep dinner plates, with cinnamon and sugar sprinkled on top.

NORWEGIAN KRINGLES

These shaped cookies are not to be confused with the pastry-like Danish kringle. This recipe by Phyllis Hegdahl appeared in the *Hawarden [Iowa] American-Lutheran Church 1961-1986 25th Anniversary Cookbook*. The pretzel shape described by Ms. Hegdahl is associated with Christmas cookies. You can also make these in figure eights or circles. I've seen a recipe that just says, "make into kringle shapes," which are probably the figure eights.

2 cups whole milk
3/4 cup lard or shortening
1 cup white sugar plus a teaspoon to proof yeast
1 teaspoon salt
6-7 cups flour
2 eggs
2 packages yeast
1 teaspoon sugar
solid shortening to grease bowl and cookie sheet

1. Mix yeast with a half cup water and a teaspoon of sugar. It should foam up by the time you use it.

2. Heat milk and shortening to melt shortening. Add sugar and salt, and cool to lukewarm.

3. Add 1 cup flour and mix well.

4. Beat eggs, and add to flour mixture.

5. Add the yeast mixture, and mix well.

6. Slowly add the rest of the flour.

7. Grease bowl, and turn dough into it.

8. Cover and let rise in a warm place until doubled in size.

9. Knead down (see Appendix 1) and let rise again.

10. Grease baking sheets.

11. Cut small portions of dough (golf balls or a little larger) and roll in hand to make thin ropes, "then form letter 'O' with a knot."

12. Let rise 1 hour.

13. Bake at 375 degrees for 6-7 minutes. Don't overbake.

LEFSE

Lefse is a mashed potato flatbread rather like a large tortilla. Norwegian-American women used to be judged on the quality of their lefse, and many have inherited special grooved rolling pins, oversize round griddles, and long spatulas to move the breads onto the stove. Lefse used to be eaten as a snack, or wrapped around pieces of meat or fish. It is now most often made in quantities for lutefisk suppers. I have taken the most modernized recipe from the 1979 *Minnesota Heritage Cookbook* and added details from a very old-fashioned recipe in Felicia Young's *Prairie Cooks*. The most obvious ways lefse has changed is that the breads have gotten thicker and smaller as skills and patience have declined. The use of instant potatoes for a smoother batter is now fairly widespread.

Yield: 32 rounds
1 pound instant potatoes
3/4 cup margarine (1 1/2 sticks)
1 cup cream
1 tablespoon sugar
1 tablespoon salt
4 cups flour

Equipment: Rolling pin and board, wide metal spatula or "lefse stick," large seasoned griddle or oversize cast-iron frying pan, clean dry dish towels

1. Bring 6 1/2 cups water to a boil.

2. Mix potatoes, boiling water, margarine, sugar, and salt.

3. Let stand until cold. (Carrie Young refrigerates 2-4 hours.)

4. Add flour. Work in well with your hands. (Young: "Do not add flour before you refrigerate. Lefse must be made immediately after flour is added.")

5. Divide dough into 4 sections, then divide each of these into 8 pieces.

6. Flour the rolling pin and board. "Roll out one at a time, paper-thin, on a floured board." (Young: "It will be much easier to roll lefse if you use a pastry cloth and stocking on your rolling pin which have been well seasoned with flour from previous use.") If dough is sticky and comes

apart, work it back together, flour all surfaces and try again. But the less you handle it, the more tender it will be.

7. Heat up the grill with low-medium heat and carry over the lefse with the spatula or lefse stick and your other hand to keep it from sticking to itself.

8. Bake on a dry griddle over low heat until little brown spots appear on the surface. (Young: "Prick the dough in four or five places with spatula. Let it bake for about a minute or until it bubbles in the middle. If the heat is correct, it will still be very pale, with just a few flecks of brown."

9. Turn with the spatula and bake the other side. (Young cooks 45 seconds on the other side,

turns again and keeps turning in an accelerating rhythm until she is turning every 5 seconds, for a total of about 3 minutes. "When done it should be dry on both sides but still tender and pliable.")

10. Move cooked lefse to a dry dish towel and cover with another to let cool.

11. When cool, the circles can be piled up on each other, or stored overnight in a covered tin.

12. To serve, halve them, spread with softened butter, and roll into cone-shaped rolls.

Serve on a platter as bread, or sprinkled with cinnamon sugar.

Ojibway (Chippewa, Ojibwe, and Ojibwa)

The names for this large tribe are all variant pronunciations of an Algonkian word, "otchipwa," which referred to the puckered seams on the traditional moccasins of people who called themselves "Anishinabe" ("original people"). Chippewa is the legal term in the United States. Ojibway, which seems to be the favored term today, is the Canadian version, and Ojibwe is the French spelling. Some groups now use Anishinabe, and the nickname "Shinobs." More than 100,000 Chippewa live in the United States, 60,000 Ojibwa live in Canada, and there are also many uncounted descendants.

Ojibway history begins on the shores of a "great salt sea" to the East, which may have been the Atlantic Ocean or Hudson's Bay. They were then one people with the **Potawatomi** and Ottawa tribes, who share their language. Around 1400, when the climate grew colder, they moved south and west, parting with the Potawatomi in northern Michigan. The Ojibway met French traders in Upper Michigan as early as 1623, and began acquiring the guns that enabled them to push the Dakota **Sioux** out of the rich wild-rice and beaver lakes of Wisconsin and Minnesota by the early nineteenth century. They established themselves as traders with the French so early that their language became the language of the Great Lakes fur trade. In 1800, they lived in seven states and three Canadian provinces, arguably the largest territory ever controlled by a single Indian tribe north of Mexico. Although most of their lands were taken for settlement, the Ojibway have never left their homeland, nor suffered a major military defeat. They participated in French-British conflicts and the British-Indian alliance in the Ohio Valley until 1815, but managed to avoid fighting the United States after that. One unusual feature of this powerful tribe is that it never had centralized leadership, so the United States has more than 50 separate treaties with 22 federally recognized groups, and the three historic governments of Canada made another 30 treaties with Ojibway groups.

Another unusual feature of Ojibway culture is that the epidemics of European diseases actually strengthened the development of the secret medicine society, which kept written records on birch bark scrolls and united members of many bands. Ojibway tribes had the monopoly on wild rice production for many decades, and tribal enterprises still produce much rice. **French Canadian** dishes like pea soup are a heritage from the fur-trading days. Harvesting wild rice and tapping maple trees for syrup and sugar are family activities with traditional religious content for many Ojibway today, and traditional foods include many dishes based on wild fish and deer meat, as well as oatmeal, macaroni, salt pork, and bacon from reservation allotments.

SPINACH-RICE CASSEROLE

This is the creation of the late Paula Giese, whose Web pages about Native American foods are preserved by Fond du Lac Community College at <http://indy4.fdl.cc.mn.us/~isk>. Ms. Giese wrote a lot about the meaning of wild rice in Ojibway culture, and was also concerned with health and nutrition.

4 cups cooked wild rice (from 8 ounces uncooked)
2 pounds washed fresh spinach
4 eggs
2 big bunches green onions (or scallions)
1 teaspoon salt
1 cup shelled sunflower seeds
1/2 teaspoon pepper
4 tablespoons chopped parsley
1/2 pound cheese
2 tablespoons sesame seeds
4 tablespoons butter, and some more to grease casserole

Equipment: Grater or food processor with grating blade, large (2 1/2 quart) casserole dish or 2 casserole dishes, heavy skillet

1. Cook rice according to package directions. Cool.

2. Beat eggs with salt and pepper.

3. Stir eggs into rice.

4. Grate cheese on grater or grating wheel of food processor.

5. Chop parsley.

6. Stir cheese and parsley into egg-rice mixture.

7. Tear large stems from spinach and chop these tough stems very fine.

8. Chop scallions or green onions.

9. Melt 2 tablespoons butter in a heavy skillet, and fry spinach stems and green onions.

10. Tear up or chop coarsely the spinach leaves and stir them into the frying pan to wilt a little.

11. Then stir it all into the rice mix.

12. Stir in some sunflower seeds. Taste for seasoning.

13. Pack mixture into 1 or 2 greased heavy casseroles.

14. Melt remaining butter.

15. Top casserole(s) with sesame seeds and melted butter sprinkled around on top.

16. Bake uncovered at 350 degrees for 35 minutes.

Serve with sweet-baked squash, pumpkin, or candied sweet potatoes.

GAGOONZ—LITTLE PORCUPINES

This recipe from Olga Masica of Minneapolis was posted on the Web site of the late Paula Giese (see above). Commercial wild rice, which is almost black, cooks much more slowly than the lighter-colored rice parched by older Ojibway methods.

1 pound ground venison or fatless (extra lean) round steak
1/3 cup uncooked light brown wild rice
1 small onion minced very fine
1 seeded green pepper minced very fine
1 teaspoon salt
1/4 teaspoon pepper
1 can tomatoes
1 can tomato soup

Equipment: Frying pan with cover

1. If using commercial wild rice, cook about halfway according to package directions, then rinse and cool.

2. Halve, peel, and mince onion very fine.

3. Slice off top and bottom of green pepper. Remove stem, cut out core and pith, and cut into thin strips, then across the strips for fine dice.

4. Combine meat, rice, onion, green pepper, salt, and pepper. Mix thoroughly.

5. Shape into 17 firm meat balls.

6. Bring soup and tomatoes (and their liquid) to a boil in frying pan with tight cover; put in meat balls and reduce heat to very slow simmer.

7. Simmer tightly until done with rice popping out of balls like porcupine quills, about 40-45 minutes.

BREAD PUDDING

Anne R. Kaplan, Marjorie A. Hoover, and Willard B. Moore collected this recipe for their *Minnesota Ethnic Food Book*. They note: "Except for the maple syrup, this pudding does not contain any of the traditional Minnesota Ojibway ingredients; however, the dish is made by many families, and the recipe appears in the few cookbooks that are available." In my opinion, this note reflects a "melting pot" prejudice that ethnic cooking can only be about the past, which is most often expressed about Native Americans.

2 1/2 cups milk
1/4 cup cornmeal
2 1/2 cups stale white bread or a mix of
  white and whole-wheat bread
3 eggs

1/3 cup maple syrup
1/3 cup sugar
1 teaspoon ground cinnamon
1/4 teaspoon salt
1/2 teaspoon vanilla
1/4 cup butter (half stick), and some to
  butter baking dish
1/2 cup raisins
1/2 cup chopped apple (optional)
1 teaspoon flour

Equipment: 2-quart baking dish and a larger pan that can hold the baking dish and water, small saucepan

1. In a small saucepan, heat milk to warm.

2. Stir in cornmeal.

3. Tear or cut bread into small cubes and add to milk. Set aside to soak.

4. In a bowl, beat eggs well. Blend in syrup, sugar, cinnamon, salt, and vanilla.

5. Melt butter, and blend into egg mixture.

6. Preheat oven to 350 degrees.

7. Butter 2-quart baking dish.

8. Place an inch or so of water in pan larger than baking dish, and put pan in the oven.

9. Toss raisins in a small bowl with flour.

10. Combine egg mixture, bread mixture, and raisins. Pour into baking dish.

11. Put baking dish into the pan of hot water, and bake for 1 hour, or until custard is firm.

Serve plain or with cream or ice cream.

OKINAWAN-AMERICANS

Okinawan-Americans came to California in the 1890s among other emigrants from Japan, but the 25,000 who went to Hawaii between 1900 and 1924 felt excluded by the already established **Japanese-American** community. As a result, Okinawan-Americans have a distinct identity in Hawaii, but generally identify as Japanese-Americans in California and the other 48 states. When the U.S. military occupation of Okinawa ended in 1972, Okinawan-Americans in Hawaii generally opposed the return of Okinawa to Japan, while a majority of Japanese-Americans with Okinawan ancestors elsewhere in the U.S. thought Okinawa should become part of Japan again. Although only 10,000 Okinawan-Americans were estimated by the 1990 census, there are likely many more descendants of California immigrants who consider themselves Japanese-American.

The 50 islands of Okinawa are 1,000 miles from Tokyo, and Okinawan kings originally paid tribute to China. The islands became a unified kingdom in 1429, but fell under increasing Japanese influence after an invasion in 1609. However, they were not finally incorporated into Japan until 1879. Okinawan cooking has more Chinese than Japanese influences, with a lot of pork, a special love for sweet potatoes, and hearty stir-fries. Another Okinawan dish that is popular in Hawaii is "Okinawan doughnuts," while older people remember pig foot soup and sparerib soup.

OKINAWAN SPARERIBS

This is a variation on an Okinawan dish of glazed pork called "rafute," which seems to have picked up some of the technique of **Filipino-American** adobo, which is also popular in Hawaii. I have combined a recipe submitted by Nate Lum to a recipe contest on <www.alohaworld.com> with a glazed pork recipe by Bea Shimabukuro that was demonstrated on the "Hawaiian Electric Kitchen" cable TV show in September 1995, and archived at <www.heco.com>.

Yield: serves 10-15 in a multi-course dinner
   3 pounds pork ribs
   2/3 cup sugar
   2-inch piece ginger root
   2/3 cup shoyu (soy sauce)

Equipment: Garlic press, saucepan

1. Have ribs cut into 2-inch squares, or sawed once or twice across the bones so that you can cut them into small pieces.

2. Place ribs in a saucepan with water to cover. Bring to a boil and simmer until ribs are tender.

3. Drain all but 1 1/2 cups of the cooking liquid (you can save the rest for a soup).

4. Add sugar and bring to a boil.

5. Peel ginger root, slice thinly across the grain, and crush slices. Add to pot.

6. When about half the liquid is gone, add soy sauce and cook until almost all the liquid is gone, turning ribs occasionally to glaze.

Serve with rice and chanpuru (see below).

CHANPURU

Chanpuru, the typical Okinawan stir-fry, is almost always based on tofu and scallions (replacing the Asian garlic chives), mixed vegetables, and optional eggs, meat, or fish. The recipe is from Rachel Laudan's *The Food of Paradise: Exploring Hawaii's Cultural Heritage*. Don't try to double this recipe, but you could use 2 teams and 2 skillets, or do all the preparation steps for 2 recipes, and cook them quickly one after the other.

Yield: serves 4
   2 tablespoons oil
   1 pound block (firm) tofu
   2 teaspoons salt
   2 green onions (scallions)
   4 cups shredded vegetables, such as bean
      sprouts, Chinese cabbage, carrots, grated
      green papaya, bitter melon, daikon
      (Japanese radish, substitute white turnip),
      or chives

Equipment: Stiff spatula to stir-fry vegetables and tofu, large pot, large skillet

1. If using bitter melon, slice thinly and cook briefly in a large pot of boiling water to remove some of the bitterness. Peel carrots and daikon or turnip, if using. Peel and seed papaya, if using. Cut all vegetables into thin shreds that will cook quickly. Slice scallions into 1-inch shreds or fine rings.

2. Dry tofu with paper towels. Cut or break tofu into bite-sized pieces.

3. Heat oil in a large skillet.

4. Toss in tofu, and sprinkle on salt.

5. When tofu is browned on bottom, flip over to brown the other side if possible.

6. Add scallions, then other vegetables and toss briefly to coat them with oil and warm them up.

Serve immediately with rice.

OKINAWAN FRIED SOMEN

This recipe was demonstrated in August 1999 by Chef Jason Kina on the "Hawaiian Electric Kitchen" and archived at <www.heco.com>.

Yield: serves 4

1 package (9-ounce) somen (fine wheat
    flour noodles, substitute half-box angel-
    hair spaghetti)
2 tablespoons salad oil
1 can (3 3/4 ounces) sardines in oil
salt and pepper to taste
1/4 cup sliced green onions

1. Cook somen noodles according to package directions.

2. In a skillet, heat oil and sauté sardines.

3. Stir in somen. Season with salt and pepper.

4. Slice green onions into fine rounds.

Serve, garnished with green onions, with salad.

ONEIDA

See IROQUOIS

ONONDAGA

See IROQUOIS

PAKISTANI-AMERICANS

The 1990 census estimated almost exactly 100,000 Pakistani-Americans, and more have immigrated in the last decade. Probably few people from what is now Pakistan came to the United States before 1965, although some fraction of Indo-Caribbeans from the **Trinidadian-American** and **Guyanese-American** communities are Muslims whose ancestors may have been recruited from areas of British India that are now Pakistan.

Modern Pakistan was partitioned out of British India as a Muslim homeland in 1947, but the borders have never been well settled, and violent conflicts between Pakistan and India continue to the present. The present country of Bangladesh became independent of Pakistan in 1971, setting off another bitter civil war. Although Pakistan has generally been allied with the United States since independence, Pakistani-Americans keep a rather low profile. Their visible communities are in New York City and Los Angeles.

Pakistani food is somewhat like the North Indian menu of most Indian restaurants. The Arab-influenced meat dishes were popular with the British colonials. Because Muslims from various parts of India relocated to Pakistan after the partition, a variety of Indian cooking styles can be found in the Pakistani capital of Karachi.

BIRYANI

Mrs. Shaheen A. Lari contributed this recipe to *Global Gourmet* (1959), which was published for the International Institute of Boston. Mrs. Lari admits that this is an "elaborate rice pilaf." A biryani like this would be served at fancy occasions like a wedding.

1 1/2 pounds beef
2 1/2 cups rice
1 teaspoon salt
2 cloves garlic
1/2 teaspoon ginger
1/2 teaspoon paprika
1/2-inch stick of cinnamon
1/2 teaspoon cumin
1 large onion
3-4 tablespoons oil
1 lemon
pinch of nutmeg
pinch of mace
2 whole cardamoms
1/4 cup milk
2 heaping teaspoons plain yogurt
a little saffron

Equipment: Blender, deep pot, frying pan

1. In the blender, puree a little water with the ginger, peeled cloves of garlic, cinnamon stick broken in pieces, cumin, paprika, salt, and yogurt.

2. Halve, peel, and slice the onion.

3. Heat the oil in a deep pot, add onions and fry slowly to medium brown.

4. Remove onion from pot leaving oil behind. Reserve onion.

5. Cut beef into 1-inch cubes. Wash and drain beef.

6. Put beef into pot with onion-flavored oil.

7. As the bottom of the beef cubes brown, add blended spices plus enough water to cover beef.

8. Bring to a boil, then lower heat to simmer long enough to make the beef tender.

9. Very little water should remain in the pot. If there is more than about 1/4 cup, turn heat to medium to evaporate it.

10. Add cardamom, mace, and nutmeg. Set aside pot with beef and spices.

11. About 45 minutes before serving, boil rice in salted water until almost done.

12. Remove meat from pot, leaving as much oil as possible.

13. Drain rice.

14. Spread a 2-inch layer of rice in the bottom of the frying pot, a layer of meat on top of that, another layer of rice, "and so on till all the meat and rice are used up, with the last layer meat."

15. Juice lemon.

16. Sprinkle lemon juice, a little saffron, the milk, and the browned onions on top.

17. Cover pot and leave on the lowest heat for 15-20 minutes.

18. Shut off heat but leave on stove to steam until serving time.

Serve with a mild, rich curry, or on its own with salad.

CARROT HALVA

This recipe for a rich pudding comes from the 1979 *Minnesota Heritage Cookbook: Hand-Me-Down Recipes for the Benefit of the American Cancer Society, Minnesota Division, Inc.* It is a Punjabi dish known as gajjar halva in Urdu.

Yield: serves 4
1/4 cup raisins
few strands Spanish saffron
1 pound carrots
5 cups milk
1 cup sugar
1/4 cup butter, and a little more to grease dish
1/4 cup sliced almonds
cardamom powder

Equipment: Grater or food processor with grating disk

1. Wash and dry raisins.

2. Soak saffron in 2 teaspoons hot water.

3. Peel carrots and grate "as finely as possible."

4. Bring milk to a boil and add grated carrots. Simmer about 2 hours, stirring occasionally, until mixture is thick and creamy. The stirring loosens any coagulated milk and thickens the evaporated milk in the pan, which is nearly gone.

5. Add the sugar and raisins and cook "a while longer" (about 30 minutes or until the carrots begin to stick).

6. Add butter and saffron and continue cooking until the halva is a rich, golden color.

7. Place in a greased bowl or dish and sprinkle with almond slices and cardamom.

Serve cold, cut into squares.

PALESTINIAN-AMERICANS

See ARAB-AMERICANS

PANAMANIAN-AMERICANS

The 1990 census estimates 86,000 Panamanian-Americans, but the real number is likely higher. Some early Panamanian immigrants affiliated with **African-American** communities, and many recent Panamanian immigrants are in this country without legal documents. Panamanian immigration began in earnest after the completion of the Panama Canal (1904-1914). Many of the workers were English-speaking West Indian blacks who still make up about 14 percent of the population of Panama, but who began moving to the United States in search of work, especially to New York City. In the early 1970s, as Panama's military governments became more unstable and threatening, a number of Hispanic Panamanians began coming to the U.S. as political exiles, notably to Miami. Other Panamanian communities began to develop in student areas of Miami, New Orleans, Boston, and the District of Columbia.

Panamanian food and culture include influences from native peoples and neighboring countries, but also seaborne influences from all the countries of the Caribbean and Latin America, as well as from the United States, which owned and operated the Panama Canal Zone until the end of 1999.

MOM'S FRIED CHICKEN

This recipe is from Enrique Antonio Riggs, a Panamanian-American whose parents came from Jamaica and Barbados to Panama to work on the Canal. It appears in the 1990 *Family of the Spirit Cookbook: Recipes and Remembrances from African-American Kitchens* by John Pinderhughes.

CAUTION: Hot oil used.

Yield: serves 4 as a main dish, makes 10-12 pieces

1 whole chicken
2 lemons
1 tablespoon Dijon mustard
1 tablespoon soy sauce
1 tablespoon vinegar
1 1/2 teaspoons salt
1 teaspoon freshly ground pepper
1 teaspoon crushed allspice
1 teaspoon paprika

1 cup flour
peanut oil for deep frying

Equipment: Juicer, skimmer, rubber mallet and cleaver, high-sided pot

1. Cut chicken into 10-12 pieces. You will have to cut the breast into 2 or 3 chunks, bones and all. You can do this with a sharp chef's knife, or a meat cleaver and rubber mallet. (Don't take wild swings with the meat cleaver.)

2. Place the chicken in a large bowl and cover with water.

3. Juice one of the lemons and add to the water, stir up the chicken pieces. Soak for 3 hours.

4. Drain chicken and pat dry.

5. Juice second lemon, and mix the juice with soy sauce, vinegar, 1 teaspoon salt, 1/2 teaspoon pepper, 1/2 teaspoon allspice, and the paprika.

6. Pour this marinade over the chicken, toss, and marinate for another 2-3 hours, turning occasionally.

7. In a plastic bag, mix the flour with the remaining 1/2 teaspoon each of salt, pepper, and allspice.

8. Put a few chicken pieces at a time into the bag, close the top, and toss around to coat the chicken pieces.

9. Set pieces on a clean dish or metal rack while you finish the rest.

10. Heat 2 inches of peanut oil in a high-sided pot.

11. Fry chicken pieces for 20 minutes, turning once, until the chicken is golden brown and crisp, but tender and juicy on the inside.

12. Drain on wire rack or paper towels.

Serve with hot pepper sauce, peas and rice, and salad.

PLATANOS EN TENTACION

Panamanian-Americans make twice-fried green plantains called "patacones" just like tostones, but thinner and crisper (see **Dominican-Ameri-**

cans). With yellow or black ripe plantains, they make sweet dishes like this one, which was donated by Dora L. de Dominguez to the 1989 *Celebrity Cookbook* of St. Peter's Child Development Centers, Inc. and McGinnis Sisters Special Food Stores in Pittsburgh.

3 ripe plantains
1/2 cup brown sugar
2 tablespoons butter
2 cloves
1 large stick cinnamon
1 slice lemon

Equipment: Heavy skillet

1. Peel plantains by cutting off the ends and slitting the skin down one side. Green plantains peel sidewise, just the opposite way of bananas.

2. Cut plantains into halves the long way, and then into 3-inch sections.

3. Place in a heavy skillet with all ingredients and 3/4 cup water and cook over low heat.

4. Turn often to coat with glaze.

5. Plantains are done when tender and golden brown.

Serve with roast meat or fish.

MILLIE'S FOO-FOO

This cousin of **Barbadan** coo-coo and **Creole** coush-coush is cooked by Millie Tynes, who immigrated to Key West in 1990. A number of her recipes are in Jessie Tirsch's *A Taste of the Gulf Coast* (1997).

Yield: about 8 side servings
1/3 pound salt pork
1 1/2 pounds okra (or two 10-ounce packages frozen)
6 medium garlic cloves
1 1/4 cups yellow cornmeal
1 1/2 teaspoons salt, or to taste

Equipment: Aluminum foil and paper towels (for optional refrying method), large pot, heavy pot with high sides

1. Cut salt pork into fine dice. (It is easier to do this if it is partially frozen.)

2. Put salt pork and 4 cups of water in a large pot and bring to a boil over high heat.

3. Cook pork about 5 minutes, until it is tender.

4. Drain pork (reserving water) and return the empty pot to the burner to dry out. When the pot is dry, return the salt pork and begin to render out the fat over medium-high heat.

5. Slice the okra in 1/4-inch slices.

6. When the fat begins to liquefy, add the okra to the pot and reduce the heat to medium. Cook, stirring frequently, for 4 minutes. Don't let the okra stick and burn.

7. Peel and mince the garlic to get a tablespoon. Add that to the pot and cook another 6 minutes until the okra is tender and has lost its slimy texture.

8. Bring water to a boil in another pot, and add to the okra.

9. When the okra mixture is back to a rolling boil, slowly stir in the cornmeal.

10. When all the cornmeal is in the mixture, reduce heat to low, and cook covered for about 15 minutes, until the okra has come apart and the cornmeal is a yellow mush. Open the pot often to stir and scrape the bottom, so the mush does not stick and burn.

11. Add salt and serve immediately, or cool slightly and mound on a large piece of aluminum foil.

12. Form a log, and roll the aluminum foil into a sausage shape to make a roll about 3 inches in diameter. Refrigerate overnight.

13. To reheat, heat an inch of vegetable oil or bacon fat in a heavy pot with high sides, over medium heat. Open the aluminum foil and slice the roll into 1/2-inch slices. Dry the slices until brown, 3 to 4 minutes per side. Drain on paper towels.

Serve straight from the pot in mounds, with a dollop of gravy or sauce from the main course. Serve the refried foo-foo cakes as a side dish with dinner, or as a breakfast with bacon and syrup.

PAPAGO

See PIMA AND PAPAGO (TOHONO O'ODHAM)

PENNSYLVANIA DUTCH

The Pennsylvania Dutch were an ethnic group distinct from their European origins before the American Revolution, and were speaking their unique dialect of Low German by the early 1700s. The founding stock were Protestants from what is now southern and western Germany, Eastern France, and Switzerland, who had suffered in religious wars and came to southeastern Pennsylvania between 1683 and the mid-1700s. Although the original group included some Netherlanders, the "Dutch" part refers to the "Deutsch" (German) language they spoke (which is today spelled "Deitsch" in proper "Pennsylfaanisch"). For many other Americans, the first image of the Pennsylvania Dutch are the **Amish,** with their old-fashioned dress and horse-drawn carriages, but the original Pennsylvania Dutch were mostly mainstream Protestants, and even now the Amish are only about 8 percent of the Pennsylvania Dutch community. Although the early community included many religious dissenters like the Amish and the **Moravians,** Pennsylvania Dutch were innovative and pioneering farmers who moved into the mountain areas beyond the English coastal settlements and developed their own culture. They introduced sauerkraut, pretzels, whoopie pies, hot salads, various forms of casseroles, scrapple, and apple pie to other Americans, and developed widely used forms of barns, rifles, and the Conastoga wagon.

Because this is a founding stock group, many millions of Americans have some Pennsylvania Dutch ancestry. However, the 1990 census recorded only about 300,000 "Pennsylvania Germans," which is about the number of speakers of the Pennsylfaanisch dialect. Some people who indicated they were of Dutch ancestry may have meant to write "Pennsylvania Dutch," or Pennsylvania Dutch descendants may now be more comfortable with a German-American designation than they were in the past. A reasonable guess would be that 800,000 to 1 million Americans are conscious of having a Pennsylvania Dutch background.

The Pennsylvania Dutch were an important support for the American Revolution because they had no special loyalty to England or any European country. Language differences kept them apart from most **German-Americans,** especially the large group of immigrants who came after the failure of the 1848 revolutions in Europe. Other than through the Mennonite Church, they also did not connect with **Germans from Russia,** who had left the same parts of Germany for the same reasons at the same times, but who had set up villages in Russia before coming to the prairie states in the late nineteenth century.

Pennsylvania Dutch food was one of the first American regional cuisines to be recognized as such, and visitors have commented since colonial times on rivel soup, shoo-fly pie, and the many pickles and condiments of the Pennsylvania Dutch table. Culinary historian William Woys Weaver has been studying the roots of this cuisine and has published several excellent books of historic and contemporary recipes.

PICKLED EGGS AND RED BEETS

Mrs. Fred H. Sitler contributed this recipe to *Heritage House Receipts* (1969), which was edited by Virginia O'Hara and published by the Association for the Preservation of Tennessee Antiquities, Memphis Chapter.

NOTE: Recipe requires several days to complete.

5 or 6 small fresh beets
small piece stick cinnamon
1/4 cup brown sugar
3 or 4 cloves
1/2 teaspoon salt
1/2 cup vinegar
3 eggs

1. Boil the beets in water to cover until tender, up to 45 minutes depending on the age of the beets.

2. Cool in cold running water. The skins will rub right off.

3. Boil 1/2 cup water with the vinegar; brown sugar, salt, and spice for 10 minutes.

4. Cool this liquid, and add the beets for several days.

5. Boil eggs 12 minutes in water to cover.

6. Cool eggs in cold water, and shell carefully.

7. Put the eggs in the now-pink pickling brine for several more days.

8. Store in refrigerator or cool place.

Serve as a side dish.

MRS. WEISSENBURG'S "DUTCH MARBLE" GOOSE EGGS

This is not exactly an ethnic *food* because the eggs come out as ordinary hard-boiled eggs. The distinctively Pennsylvania Dutch part of the recipe is the technique of painting the eggs in false marble, similar to a technique used for painting church columns. Mrs. Weissenburg tied her eggs with string and used goose eggs. Jonas Slonaker worked out the aluminum-foil technique and passed both to William Woys Weaver for his *Pennsylvania Dutch Cooking* (1993). If you use the vinegar and a cast iron pot, the dye will be olive green; if not, it will be red.

Yield: 13 eggs, if you are careful
  1 dozen white chicken eggs (or 4 goose eggs)
  1 white chicken egg to serve as a "control egg"
  36 large pieces of yellow onion skins
  1 cup broken pieces of yellow onion skins
  1/4 cup vinegar (optional)

Equipment: Deep and non-reactive saucepan or cast iron pot, aluminum foil, wire rack to dry eggs

  1. Put the onion skins in a bowl with cold water to cover for 1-2 minutes, just long enough to make them soft enough to wrap around the eggs.

  2. Wrap each egg in onion skins, using several pieces and layers to get an interesting pattern.

  3. Wrap the onion-skin-wrapped eggs in aluminum foil tightly enough to hold the onion skin to the egg surface. (It's okay if the aluminum foil leaks in the water or vinegar-water, however.)

  4. Put the wrapped eggs in a deep, non-reactive saucepan (or a cast iron pan) and cover with cold water. (Add the optional vinegar here if using.)

  5. Add the one unwrapped egg as a control, and the rest of the broken onion skins.

  6. Bring the water to a boil, and simmer until the control egg is dark brown, about 20-25 minutes.

  7. Remove the pan from heat and set aside, letting the eggs stay in the water for another 5 minutes.

  8. Remove the skins and wash the eggs with cold water.

  9. Set the eggs on a rack to dry.

Serve in a basket to show off the marble-like designs.

"SHOO-FLY PIE I"

Although all American colonists were noted for making pies, the Pennsylvania Dutch have kept up this tradition more than almost any group. According to Edna Eby Heller in *The Dutch Cookbook* (1953), this recipe is "the dry kind—good for dunking." Mrs. Heller was the food editor of *Pennsylvania Folklife Magazine*, and seems to be the first editor to distinguish clearly between dry and moist pie recipes and the all-crumb "shoo-fly cake," which is also baked in a pie shell. The dunking would be in morning coffee, which might be poured over a cold piece of the "wet bottom" pie.

Yield: "three 7-inch" pies, but only two of the 8-inch shells sold today
  2 unbaked pie shells
  1 cup molasses
  1 teaspoon baking soda
  4 cups flour (unsifted)
  1 cup brown sugar
  3/4 cup lard

Equipment: Pastry blender or large fork

  1. Mix the molasses with 1 cup boiling water and let cool slightly before adding baking soda.

  2. Mix the flour, brown sugar, and lard into crumbs with the pastry blender or a large fork.

  3. Pour the molasses mixture evenly into the pie shells, and put the crumbs on top.

  4. Bake 25-35 minutes at 350 degrees.

Serve for breakfast, or as a dessert.

ROSINA BOY

This old-fashioned raisin pie was sometimes called funeral pie because it was the kind of thing a cook could put together in a hurry from materials on hand to take over when a neighbor died. Some versions add sour cream. Amy Kerr contributed this recipe to Ruth Hutchison's *The New Pennsylvania Dutch Cookbook* (1958). The recipe calls for "seeded raisins" because raisins were made before the development of seedless grapes, and many Pennsylvania Dutch farmers dried their own. For cooking, seeds were usually removed, a chore often assigned to children.

Yield: two 8-inch pies
  two 8-inch prepared pie crusts and additional prepared crust or dough to make a lattice top
  1 cup "seeded raisins"
  1 egg
  1 1/2 cups sugar
  4 tablespoons sifted flour
  1 lemon

Equipment: Grater for lemon rind, juicer for lemon juice, double boiler

1. Soak raisins in 1 cup clean water until soft and plump.

2. Mix egg and sugar in a bowl.

3. Stir in flour, salt, raisins, and 2 cups water.

4. Juice lemon and add juice to the raisin mixture.

5. Bring water to a boil in the lower part of a double water, then put on the top part and pour the raisin mixture on the top. Cook gently for 15 minutes.

6. Grate lemon rind (not the white pith) and stir into the raisin mixture. Remove mixture from the heat and allow to cool.

7. Fill pie shells with the mixture.

8. Cut pie crust into strips and weave lattice tops as illustrated under Austrian Linzer Torte recipe in the **Austrian-Americans** section.

9. Bake in a 375-degree oven for about 40 minutes.

Serve as a winter dessert.

PERSIAN-AMERICANS (IRANIANS)

Most of the million Iranian-Americans have come to the United States since the 1979 revolution that overthrew the Shah and established an Islamic Republic in Iran. Most call themselves Persians to make clear their differences from the regime that held 52 American hostages for over a year. "Persia" was the name of the country until 1935; the term also denotes the core highland area, the non-Arab half of the population, and the classical civilization of the region. Although some Iranian immigrants to the U.S. are Bah'ai or Jews, the vast majority, as in Iran, are Shi'ite Muslims, observing the fast of Ramadan and avoiding pork products. One uniquely Persian observance is the ancient spring festival of Noruz, which involves an elaborate table display of certain foods. About 40 percent of all Iranian-Americans live in southern California.

PERSIAN CUTLET

Mrs. Nazan Saniee contributed this recipe to the *Diamond Jubilee Cookbook: Star of the Sea Academy, 1910-1985* from San Francisco. The word cutlet for a fried patty is French, but may have reached Iran via Russian cooking, which has a lot of "cutleti." The Americanization of a Persian "kotlet-e-goosht" is the substitution of oil for butter, the non-stick frying pan, and the paper towels. Even with the optional spices, this is a rather bland patty. You can get more of the idea of the tart stews of Persian cuisine by sim-

mering the fried patties in a thin tomato sauce with fresh lemon juice.

Yield: serves 6 as an entree, but the 25 patties can be used as individual appetizers
  1 pound potatoes
  1 pound lean ground beef
  1 medium onion
  1 teaspoon salt
  1/2 teaspoon pepper
  2 eggs
  pinch saffron (optional)

pinch turmeric (optional)
2 cups bread crumbs
oil for frying

Equipment: Skimmer, potato masher or ricer, food processor with grating disk or box grater, paper towels, non-stick frying pan

1. Peel and cook enough potatoes to make up a pound (2 cups) mashed.

2. Combine potatoes and next 5 ingredients and optional spices "and mix thoroughly with your hands until a dough-like consistency is achieved."

3. Spread the bread crumbs into a thin layer on a platter. Take 2 spoonful portions of the mixture each time and make a hamburger-like patty.

4. Heat a little oil in a non-stick frying pan.

5. Coat the patties with bread crumbs on both sides.

6. Fry on medium heat for 10 minutes on each side.

7. Drain the patties on a paper towel to get the oil out.

"You can serve hot or cold." You could also eat the leftovers in a pita bread with a sour Persian chutney called "torshi."

POTATO-TOMATO OMELET

Marylon Rahbar submitted this recipe to the *Treat Yourself to the Best Cookbook* (1984), compiled by the Junior League of Wheeling, Inc.

Yield: 4-6 servings
4 tablespoons margarine
1 large onion
2 tablespoons lemon juice
1 large potato
2 tomatoes
3/4 teaspoon salt
1/4 teaspoon pepper
4 eggs
1/4 teaspoon cinnamon

Equipment: Skillet with cover, paper towels

1. Halve, peel, and finely chop the onion.

2. In a skillet, melt margarine and sauté onions until golden.

3. Remove onions from skillet (reserving oil in skillet) and add lemon juice to onions; let stand.

4. Peel potato and slice 1/4 inch thick.

5. Rinse potato slices in cold water.

6. Dry potatoes with paper towels and fry them in the same skillet in which the onions were sautéed.

7. Fry potato slices until golden brown.

8. Core and slice tomatoes.

9. Arrange tomatoes over potato slices and top with onions.

10. Season with 1/2 teaspoon of salt and pepper

11. Beat eggs with the rest of the salt and the cinnamon. Pour over potato mixture.

12. Cover pot and let omelet cook over low heat another 10 minutes.

13. When top is set, work knife around the edges and invert onto a large plate.

Serve cut in wedges with toasted pita bread.

CHELO

Persians have a special way of cooking rice. Khalil Sharifzadeh, a public health veterinarian in Massachusetts, carefully recorded the technique in one of a group of recipes made up as a Christmas gift to friends in the 1970s. Imported Persian rice is extra long grain, and white basmati rice is also popular with Persian-Americans, but any long-grain white rice will work. The hard, buttery crust of potato and rice at the bottom of the pot is called the "tadiq," and is considered the best part.

1/2 cup salt
2 pounds long-grain white rice ("not parboiled")
2 potatoes
5 tablespoons butter
pinch saffron

Equipment: Large metal sieve, large pot with tight cover, clean dish towel to seal pot, skillet

1. Eight hours before serving, dissolve the salt in about 2 quarts water, and soak the rice.

2. Peel the potatoes and then slice into thin slices.

3. Heat 4 tablespoons of butter in a skillet and fry the potato slices. Put aside.

4. Dissolve the saffron in 4 tablespoons of water. Put aside.

5. An hour before serving time, bring a gallon of water to a boil.

6. Drain rice and put it into the boiling water. Stir once to prevent it from sticking to the bottom of the pan.

7. "Watch the rice constantly and skim off the white foam as it rises to the surface."

8. "Test the rice frequently until the grains are *almost* done."

9. Remove the pot from the heat and immediately pour the rice into the sieve.

10. Rinse the rice with cold water to get rid of the salty taste.

11. In a deep pot, melt the other tablespoon of butter.

12. Reduce the heat to a very low flame. Arrange the fried potatoes on the bottom of the pan.

13. "Either by hand, or with a large spoon, gently distribute the rice into the pot (*do not dump it in all at once*) so that it forms a large cone."

14. With the saffron liquid, "make your own initial (or the initial of the one you are thinking about) on top of the rice."

15. Cover the pot with a cloth so that the lid is tight, and cook on a very low flame for an hour. A crust should form on the bottom of the rice.

Serve with stew.

GORMEH SABZI

The best-know Persian stew is the rich fesanjoon with a sauce of walnuts and pomegranate syrup.

Here is another famous stew, again from Dr. Sharifzadeh's collection. I have added some precise quantities.

Yield: serves 6
  1/2 pound dry red kidney beans
  1 pound boneless lamb (or beef)
  1 medium onion
  3 tablespoons oil
  1 bunch parsley
  4 large scallions
  3 tablespoons chopped fresh mint, or 1 1/2 tablespoons dried
  3 tablespoons chopped fresh dill, or 1 1/2 tablespoons dried
  1/2 cup tomato sauce
  1 lime (or lemon)
  1/4 teaspoon turmeric

Equipment: Juicer for lime, skillet

1. Bring a pot of water to a boil and add the kidney beans. After 5 minutes, turn off heat and soak the beans from 1 hour to overnight.

2. Drain beans and bring to a boil in salted water to cover by 2 inches.

3. Cook until tender.

4. Halve, peel, and chop the onion.

5. Cut the meat into cubes.

6. Heat the oil in a skillet, sprinkle on the turmeric, and brown the onions and meat. Set aside, reserving the oil in the skillet.

7. Trim and chop the scallions.

8. Chop the parsley and fresh herbs.

9. Sauté the scallions and herbs in the skillet. Crumble in the dried herbs.

10. Add the meat, kidney beans, tomato sauce, and a glass of water. Add salt and pepper to taste, starting with about 1/4 teaspoon of each. Simmer for a half hour.

11. Juice the lime and add the juice to the stew. Simmer for another 5 minutes.

"Serve only with chelo" [see above].

PERUVIAN-AMERICANS

Although a few Peruvians came for the California Gold Rush in the 1840s, serious Peruvian immigration only began in the 1980s when economic changes moved more than half the country's population into squatter settlements in the capital city of Lima. At the same time, many Peruvians of middle- and upper-class backgrounds felt squeezed between the terrorist Sendero Luminoso movement and the military crackdown against the Senderos. The 1990 census estimated 83,000 Peruvian-Americans, but the numbers have increased in the 1990s, and there are probably at least as many undocumented immigrants. The largest community is thought to be 50,000 or more in greater New York, but the Los Angeles area may have surpassed that. Other centers of Peruvian settlement are Washington, D.C., and San Francisco, with some wealthy Peruvians relocating to Miami.

Peru has a large population of Native peoples who still speak the Inca language, Quechua, and still maintain traditional lifestyles and cooking, with many distinctive dishes that have developed using local varieties of fish, potatoes, and chile peppers. Because the Peruvian-American population is such a recent development, it is unclear how these foods are Americanizing. Peruvian-Americans share many dishes with **Ecuadorian-Americans,** although the two communities have not mixed much in the U.S.

CAUSA LIMEÑA

Causa is a mashed-potato salad with a variety of decorations. Mejia of Davie, Florida, posted this recipe in both English and Spanish on an Internet recipe exchange at <http://www.2000two.com/peru>, a site apparently sponsored by a Los Angeles real estate brokerage. The amount given fills a large soup bowl, but is a little tricky to unmold from a small Pyrex casserole. You can multiply the recipe to fit larger molds.

1 pound yellow potatoes (Yukon Gold),
   (about 2 large potatoes)
1/3 cup mayonnaise
1 1/2 lemons
1 chicken breast
salt and pepper to taste
2 eggs
12 black olives
parsley as garnish

Equipment: Lemon squeezer or juicer, 6-inch round mold or bowl, flexible spatula, food mill or potato ricer, egg slicer (optional)

1. In a pot, boil water and cook potatoes, eggs, and chicken at a medium temperature.

2. Juice the lemons, straining out any seeds.

3. When potatoes are done, remove skins if you have not already done so. Mash potatoes and cool down.

4. Add lemon juice to cooled potatoes and stir well. When the mixture is softened, let rest until cool.

5. Cool chicken breast and remove skin and bones.

6. Shred chicken meat, and mix with mayonnaise, salt, and pepper.

7. Press half the potatoes into the mold.

8. Add the chicken salad as a layer so that it shows around the edges.

9. Top with the second half of the potatoes. Set the mold in the refrigerator to chill.

10. Chill and shell the eggs. Slice the olives.

11. When ready to serve, run a spatula around the edge of the potatoes, and unmold the salad onto a plate by putting a plate on top of the bowl, holding them together, and flipping them upside down, then lifting off the bowl.

12. Slice the hard-boiled eggs and arrange on top of the molded potatoes, along with the black

olives and parsley. Season with salt and pepper or red chili powder.

Serve cold.

CHUPE DE CAMARONES (SHRIMP CHOWDER)

This hearty soup has become a company dish for Dolores Carver, a receptionist in Chicago who gave her recipe to Himilce Novas and Rosemary Silva for *Latin Cooking Across the U.S.A.* Ms. Carver told them that "If I'm serving it as a first course, I add less corn and potatoes. . . . If it's a main dish, I double up on the corn and potatoes for a stew."

Yield: serves 4 as a main dish and 6 as an appetizer
   2 tablespoons olive oil
   1 medium yellow onion
   2 medium cloves garlic
   1 large ripe tomato
   1/4 aji chile, or substitute 1/2 jalapeno chile, or hot sauce to taste
   1 teaspoon paprika
   1/2 teaspoon dried oregano
   1 1/2 quarts homemade or canned chicken broth
   2 medium red-skinned potatoes (about 3/4 pound), or 1/2 cup long-grain rice
   1/2 cup frozen whole kernel corn, or a medium ear fresh corn
   1 pound shrimp
   3/4 cup half-and-half
   3 tablespoons minced fresh cilantro or dill

Equipment: Saucepan

1. Halve, peel, and chop the onion. Peel and chop the garlic.

2. Heat the olive oil in a medium saucepan over medium heat, and sauté the chopped onions and garlic, stirring occasionally, until the onions are golden brown, about 10 minutes.

3. Dice the tomato.

4. Cut the top off the chile pepper, slit down the side, and remove seeds and pith with a teaspoon. Cut pepper into long strips, and across the strips to make fine dice.

5. Stir the tomato, chile pepper, paprika, and oregano in with the onions and cook for 3 minutes more.

6. Peel the potatoes and cut into 1/2-inch cubes. If using whole ear of corn, cut 1-inch slices.

7. Add chicken broth, potatoes, and corn rounds (if using). Bring to a boil, then reduce the heat, cover and simmer until potatoes are tender, about 25 minutes.

8. Peel and de-vein the shrimp by running a knife along the black line in back. (This is what Ms. Carver does, but you will not be harmed if you don't de-vein shrimp.)

9. Rinse the shrimp under cold running water, and add with frozen corn (if using), and cook until the shrimp turn bright pink, about 5 minutes.

10. Stir in the half-and-half and heat slowly until the soup is hot, but do not boil.

11. Taste for seasoning and add salt and pepper as needed

12. Mince fresh cilantro or dill.

Serve in large soup bowls, garnished with fresh herbs.

CEVICHE PERUANO

Probably the best-known Peruvian dish is ceviche—raw fish or scallops "cooked" with lime juice. Although the idea of raw fish is scary to some Americans, the method is safe and delicious when you start from fresh seafood. This recipe, from Boston Web designer Claudio Vero, is from his Web site at <www.blackbean.com>. He notes that this is a late-night breakfast in coastal Peru, but usually an appetizer in the U.S. In Peru, this is often an elaborate platter garnished with fresh cilantro, slices of corn on the cob, and fresh sweet potatoes.

Yield: "serves 6—or 15 if they're squeamish"

- 1 pound fresh bay scallops or white fish cut into 1/2-inch chunks
- 6 limes
- 1 red onion
- 1 teaspoon ají amarillo (or any hot pure chili powder)
- cracked black pepper
- salt, if needed

Equipment: Juicer for limes

1. Juice the limes.

2. If using fish, cut fillets into 1/2-inch chunks. Don't wash fish or scallops. Soak fish pieces or scallops in lime juice in a small bowl. (You'll only need enough juice to keep the seafood covered.)

3. Add the ají amarillo (Peruvian yellow peppers) or chili powder, cover with plastic wrap, and soak for about an hour, until the fish or scallops are "cooked" (turn solid white and firm up).

4. While the fish or scallops are soaking, slice the red onion into paper-thin rings with the sharpest knife you have. When the fish or scallops are done, stir the sliced red onions into the mixture.

5. Let sit briefly, and serve in small bowls.

Serve on leaves of lettuce.

PIMA AND PAPAGO (TOHONO O'ODHAM)

The Pima and Tohono O'odham are legally different tribes, but speak mutually intelligible dialects. They live in southern Arizona and the neighboring Mexican state of Sonora. They are descendants of the ancient civilization we now call Hohokam, and some Pima farmers still use a Gila River irrigation system that, in parts, is more than 2,000 years old. The Pima are the somewhat more settled and smaller half of the 30,000 Piman-speaking Indians in the U.S. The Tohono O'odham, who until 1986 were called Papago (from Spanish "papabotas," meaning "bean eaters"), have a more southerly range, and thousands of members in Mexico. "Tohono O'odham" is their phrase for "desert people"; the Pima could also be called "Akimel O'odham" ("river people"). The Tohono O'odham traditionally farmed corn, beans, and squash in summer villages and grew wheat or hunted from winter villages. By the 1940s, both tribes had lost much of their traditional land and lifestyle, and developed a high rate of adult-onset diabetes and other health problems. Since then, many traditional foods have been revived. Pima fry breads are known as popovers, and were earlier called "wamachida," meaning "something brown." You may also find Pima and Tohono O'odham recipes for several kinds of cactus, salsa, chili stews, and mesquite beans.

PIMA TORTILLAS

The Pima and Tohono O'odham were among the first Native Americans to grow wheat, which they used to replace corn in ash breads, tortillas, stews, and a kind of beer. This recipe is from *The Arizona Cookbook*, edited by Al and Mildred Fischer.

- 2 cups flour
- 1 teaspoon baking powder
- 1 teaspoon salt
- 1/2 cup lard

3/4 cup water
solid shortening to grease griddle

Equipment: Pastry blender, rolling pin, griddle or large, heavy frying pan

1. Mix together dry ingredients.

2. Cut in lard with a pastry blender or large fork until the mixture has the texture of coarse cornmeal.

3. Add water little by little to make a soft dough.

4. Flour a rolling pin and board, and roll out dough very thin.

5. Cut into cakes 6-inches across.

6. Bake on a lightly greased griddle, turning frequently to brown on both sides.

PAPAGO TEPARY BEAN SOUP

This much reprinted recipe appears on the The Peoples' Paths Web site at <http://www.yvwiiusdinvnohii.net/NAIFood/NAIrecipes.htm>. Tepary beans are small, high-protein beans that have been grown by Piman farmers for millennia. The name comes from the Piman "t'pawi" ("it is a bean"). The Piman peoples grow a variety of teparies, for which the nearest substitute is small white beans, although the Tohono O'odham also cook with pinto beans when they don't have teparies.

NOTE: Beans need to be soaked overnight.

Yield: serves 6
　　2 cups tepary beans
　　1 teaspoon mixed oregano and cumin
　　1 clove garlic, diced
　　1 medium onion, chopped
　　1 cup diced celery
　　3 cups canned tomatoes with juice
　　2 carrots, sliced
　　4 slices bacon, diced
　　red chili powder (optional)

Equipment: Large pot
　　1. Soak beans overnight.

2. Drain soaked beans and bring to boil with 6 cups of water in a big pot.

3. When beans are nearly tender, dice bacon and fry until limp.

4. Halve, peel, and chop onion. Peel and dice garlic.

5. Dice celery.

6. Peel and slice carrots.

7. Remove bacon and add onion, carrots, celery, and garlic to bacon grease and sauté.

8. Add bacon, tomatoes, juice, and the remaining spices. Cook 10 minutes.

9. Add sautéed vegetables to beans. Cook another hour until beans are mealy-tender. If using red chili powder, add during last 10 minutes.

Serve with flour tortillas or fresh fry bread.

PIMA POSHOL SOUP

This Pima version of posole (a word for hominy in many Native American languages that is now widely used in Mexico and New Mexico) substitutes wheat and beans for the usual hominy. It was originally made from freshly harvested cracked wheat, boiled with salt and cactus seed "fat," as well as with wild greens, corn, beans, or cabbage. Use small white beans or pea beans if you cannot get tepary beans.

　　2 cups white tepary beans
　　2 cups whole wheat kernels
　　1 large soup bone

Equipment: Large pot
　　1. Wash beans, wheat, and soup bone.

2. Put in large pot and cover with boiling water.

3. Cover and cook until beans are tender, about 4 hours. Add salt to taste the first hour. (Small white beans will cook more rapidly than teparies.)

"Serve with warm tortillas."

POLISH-AMERICANS

On the 1990 census, an estimated 9.3 million Americans claimed Polish descent, the largest of the Slavic groups. Most are descended from 2 million immigrants who arrived between 1860 and 1914. At that time, Poland was partitioned between three surrounding powers. The movement to the United States began with religious repression of Polish Catholics in Prussian (German) Poland, moved east and south to include the desperately poor peasants of Galicia (Austrian-controlled southern Poland), and ended with a migration generated by both poverty and language "Russification" in Russian-controlled "Congress Poland." Although land was important to Polish immigrants, only 10 percent were employed in agriculture by 1911. Three-quarters lived in urban neighborhoods in the Northeast and Midwest, generally in parishes served by Polish Catholic churches. Polish immigrants worked in mining and manufacturing, with a concentration in the meat-packing industries of the Midwest.

Poland was a great power in the 1600s, but gradually weakened until it was partitioned three times in the eighteenth century. After World War I, Poland was independent for 20 years until occupied by Nazi Germany in 1939. From 1945, Poland had a Russian-controlled Communist government. In 1980, a shipyard strike established the free trade union, Solidarity. In 1989, Russian troops left the country and the Polish army handed power to an elected government, making Poland the first country in Eastern Europe to break free of Russian domination. Migration both to and from the U.S. has been considerable at each political change.

Polish cooks have built up one of the world's great cuisines from hearty peasant food, early links to French and Italian chefs, and the best dishes of each conquering empire. Pierogy are now sold in supermarkets in many parts of the country, and everyone has heard of Polish stuffed cabbage (see Appendix 2, "They All Stuffed Cabbage").

FRIENDLY POLISH TEA

This is a modern variation of a tea with spices and fruit juice that has been known as Polish tea or Russian tea for many years. The recipe comes from *Traditional Polish Recipes*, edited by Sophia N. Wysocki-Fulton and published by the Polish American Club of Athens, Illinois. The club served this at the Illinois State Fair. The recipe is large, but you can reuse the dry mix at a later time. I have worked out quantities for the entire batch.

Yield: 120-180 glasses
  2 cups instant lemon tea (powder)
  3 cups Tang (powdered)
  2 cups fruit punch Kool-Aid (powder)
  1/2 cup sugar
  1 1/2 teaspoons cloves
  3 teaspoons cinnamon
  ice

7-Up, Sprite, or Ginger Ale (7-10 two-liter bottles)

Equipment: Airtight container

1. Mix powdered ingredients and spices and store in an airtight container.

2. In a tall glass, mix 2 or 3 teaspoons with a cup of water.

3. Add ice and top with soda.

STUFFED CABBAGE

Stuffed cabbage is the best-known Polish-American recipe, often under its Polish name, "Galumpke." This recipe from Sonya Kupchak, mother of Mitch Kupchak, basketball player and later coach, appeared in the *Los Angeles Lakers Are Cookin' Family Cookbook* (1985).

Yield: serves 6
  1 medium-large head cabbage

1 large and 1 small onion
1 16-ounce can tomato sauce
1 1/2 pounds ground beef
2 eggs
1/2 teaspoon basil
1 clove garlic
2 tablespoons butter
2 teaspoons light brown sugar
1 1/2 teaspoons Worcestershire sauce
1 1/2 cups cooked rice (from 3/4 cup raw
   rice)

Equipment: Large pot, skillet, large bowl

1. In a large pot, bring about half a pot of water to a boil.

2. Add cabbage without splashing, and boil for 10 minutes.

3. Drain and cool cabbage.

4. Halve, peel, and chop the large onion.

5. In a skillet, heat butter and sauté onion for a few minutes, stirring until tender.

6. Add tomato sauce, brown sugar, 1 teaspoon salt, and 1/4 teaspoon pepper. Mix well and set aside.

7. Halve, peel, and mince the small onion. Peel and mince garlic. In a large bowl, combine onion and garlic with the remaining ingredients plus another teaspoon salt and 1/4 teaspoon pepper. Mix well.

8. Lift off first 3 leaves of cabbage and line bottom of a large pot with the leaves.

9. Gently lift off the softened leaves of cabbage. Shave off some of the tough central stem.

10. Fill the center of each leaf with meat mixture, "folding sides to center and rolling, jelly-roll fashion" in the direction away from you. (See illustration. You can also use the method illustrated with Greek-American grape leaves.)

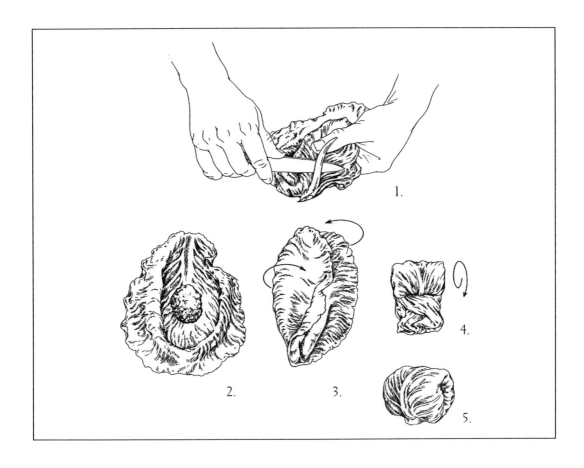

11. "Put seam side down on top of leaves in pot." Make a neat layer and add other layers as needed.

12. "As necessary when you reach tough leaves, reboil cabbage for a few minutes, lift out, drain, trim, and continue stuffing each leaf until the meat mixture is gone."

13. Pour 1/2 cup water over the rolls, then pour the tomato sauce mixture on top.

14. Heat sauce and filled rolls to a simmer. "Cover and simmer on low heat for one hour, or until cabbage leaves are tender to the touch."

Serve with sauce from the pot, crisp fried bacon and pickled beet salad, or hot kolbasi.

HUNTER'S STEW

Usually called by its Polish name, "bigos," this dish, like the Italian-American chicken cacciatore (which also means "hunter's stew"), became much more important to immigrant cooks as the rapid pace of urban American life pushed slow-cooked peasant dishes off the weekday table. Factory workers, like hunters, needed a dinner that could be assembled quickly from standard provisions or leftovers. This recipe from Illinois Congressman Edward J. Derwinski appeared in the 1972 *National Republican Heritage Groups Council World Cookbook*. Rep. Derwinski's version of bigos makes a more elaborate stew, and his mother's slow-oven technique is also somewhat unusual. He notes that "Bigos should be prepared at least 3 days in advance of serving, and reheated once or twice a day during this period. Refrigerate in a glass or nonmetal container." Some of the recipe probably gets eaten during these reheating episodes, because he describes this large stew as serving eight.

1 cup chopped onion
2 tablespoons butter
1 small head white cabbage
1 quart sauerkraut
6 large whole mushrooms
4 cups (2 pounds) diced Polish sausage and any combination of roast beef, veal, pork, or lamb

2 bouillon cubes or 1 cup gravy from roast
2 sour apples
1 tablespoon plum marmalade or 4 pitted prunes
1 cup tomato puree
1 bay leaf
1 teaspoon salt
1/2 teaspoon freshly ground black pepper
3/4 cup red wine (optional, substitute water or broth)
1 glove garlic

Equipment: Garlic press, 3-quart casserole or baking dish, heavy skillet

1. Halve, peel, and chop onions to get 1 cup. (Wear swim goggles to avoid tears.)

2. Heat butter in a heavy skillet and cook onions until golden brown.

3. Halve, core, and shred cabbage.

4. Wash and drain sauerkraut.

5. Clean mushrooms with a dish towel and slice.

6. Dice polish sausage and other meats.

7. If using bouillon cubes, dissolve in a cup of boiling water.

8. Peel, core, and dice apples. Preheat oven to 300 degrees.

9. Combine all ingredients as listed, except garlic and optional wine, in the casserole.

10. Put covered casserole in a preheated 300-degree oven and cook for 2 hours.

11. Peel and crush garlic and mix with wine, water, or broth. Add to bigos and continue cooking for 20 minutes.

Serve at lunch or dinner. In Poland, bigos was soupier but eaten before the main soup course, to warm up.

LAZY PIEROGI

The name is a literal translation from Polish for this quick noodle stew, since real pierogy would be carefully stuffed and sealed like large ravioli.

This dish is sometimes called "Polish lasagna." This recipe from State Representative William P. Nagle of Northampton, Massachusetts, appeared in *What's Cooking Under the Dome*, a fund-raiser from the 1980s. I've also seen lazy pierogy made with fresh cabbage, and served with a side dish of cottage cheese or a glass of buttermilk.

  1-pound box of flat noodles or other pasta
  1-pound can of sauerkraut
  1 large onion
  1 pound mushrooms
  1 stick butter
  1 pound cooked sausage, preferably Polish
    (kielbasa)
  black pepper
  caraway seeds (optional)

Equipment: Large pot, large skillet

  1. Bring a large pot of water to a boil

  2. Halve, peel, and chop onion.

  3. Brush any dirt off mushrooms and slice.

  4. Melt butter in a large skillet and add onions and mushrooms

  5. Wash and drain sauerkraut.

  6. Boil noodles or pasta according to package directions.

  7. Add sauerkraut to onion mixture and sauté until noodles are done.

  8. Dice sausage or kielbasa.

  9. Drain cooked noodles and combine with sauerkraut mixture.

  10. Add sausage and season with pepper and optional caraway seeds.

Serve with rye bread.

POLISH KLUSKI

Mrs. Jean Surowiec submitted this recipe (pronounced "klot-ski")to *Three Rivers Cookbook: The Good Taste of Pittsburgh*, published by the Child Health Association of Sewickley, Inc. I have added some details from a recipe for potato dumplings from *Our Best Home Cooking* (1997) by the Polish Hill Civic Association of Pittsburgh.

  2 cups grated raw potatoes
  1 egg
  1/2 teaspoon salt
  3/4 cup flour
  1 large onion
  1 stick butter or 1/2 pound bacon

Equipment: Grater or food processor with grating blade, slotted spoon or skimmer, skillet

  1. Peel and grate potatoes.

  2. Drain and squeeze the grated potatoes by handfuls.

  3. In another bowl, collect the squeezed potatoes. Add egg, salt, and flour and mix to make a soft dough.

  4. Boil a large pot of water. Salt the water.

  5. Form into small balls, or take teaspoonfuls and drop them into the boiling water (wetting the teaspoon with the boiling water so the dough doesn't stick), or put some of the dough on a plate and use the teaspoon to scrape off portions smaller than a teaspoon into the water.

  6. Cover, bring to a boil, and cook until they float, 10 to 15 minutes. Stir often to keep dough from sticking to bottom of pot.

  7. Halve, peel, and chop the onion.

  8. If using bacon, dice and fry to a crisp, and remove bacon from skillet. If using butter, melt it in skillet.

  9. Sauté onion until lightly browned.

  10. Transfer the dumplings with a slotted spoon onto a hot platter. Pour bacon or butter mixture over dumplings. (If making ahead, transfer dumplings to skillet, and reheat everything with a cup of the salted water in which the dumplings were cooked.)

"Serve these as an accompaniment to beef stew."

MAZUREK

These rich pastry cookies are usually cut into small rectangles, which is probably the source of the slang expression "mazorkas" for dollar bills. They are also called "mazurkas." The recipe is from *Treasured Polish Recipes for Americans* (1948), edited by Marie Sokolowski and Irene Jasinsky for the Polanie Club of Minneapolis. This book stayed in print for more than 30 years, and has six toppings for mazurek, as well as chocolate and almond versions without toppings. This is the apple mazurek.

3 cups sugar
12 apples
1 lemon (for rind)
1/2 cup butter
3 tablespoons cream
2 cups flour
1 egg
1/4 teaspoon salt
solid shortening to grease baking sheet

Equipment: Grater, food processor or pastry blender (optional), baking sheet, large bowl

1. Peel apples and cut into slices.

2. Bring 1 cup of water and 2 cups of sugar to a boil to make a thick syrup.

3. Add the apple slices and boil "until glossy."

4. Grate the rind of the lemon (yellow skin only) and add to the apples. Let cool.

5. Sift the remaining dry ingredients together in a large bowl. Cut butter into mixture "with knife" until crumbly. (I use a pastry blender or food processor and get the butter to nuggets the size of kernels of corn.)

6. Mix beaten egg with cream and add to flour. "Mix lightly with hand." (Avoid overblending this dough and developing tough gluten for what should be a tender pastry.)

7. Grease baking sheet.

8. Spread out dough into a rectangular shape.

9. Bake 20 minutes in a 350-degree oven.

10. Remove from oven and quickly cover with apple topping.

11. Bake 20 minutes longer.

12. Cut into small 1 by 2-inch pieces.

PORTUGUESE-AMERICANS

Although Portuguese sailors were involved in many voyages of exploration and settlement in the Americas, the Portuguese-American community of about 1.1 million is a fairly recent one, with more than half arriving since the 1958 earthquake in the Azores Islands. Recent immigrants have joined older seaside communities that grew up around the whaling ports of New England, the tuna fleet in southern California, dairy farms in northern California, and plantations in Hawaii.

For a possible Portuguese-American group that arrived before the *Mayflower*, see the **Melungeons**. For Portuguese-speaking groups, see **Cape Verdean-Americans** and **Brazilian-Americans.** In New England and Hawaii, the most popular Portuguese-American dishes include kale soup, eggy sweet breads, marinated fish dishes, combinations of shellfish and pork, and squid stew.

PORTUGUESE SOUP— FAIAL STYLE

Kale soups are so well known in New England that they are usually just called Portuguese soup.

This recipe is one of six in *Favorite Portuguese Recipes,* which was published about 1975 by the Portuguese American Federation, Inc., of Bristol, Rhode Island. What makes Maria E. Pinheiro's recipe faial-style are the Azorean touches of pureeing the kidney beans and adding chopped fennel at the end. Leave the beans whole, omit the fennel, and you have the typical southern New England Portuguese soup.

Yield: 8-10 servings
  1 can red kidney beans
  1 pound kale
  6 medium potatoes
  2 fresh tomatoes
  1 medium onion
  1/2 pound linguica (Portuguese garlic-pork sausage, substitute kielbasa and a pinch of paprika)
  2 heaping tablespoons solid vegetable shortening
  1 tablespoon salt (or to taste)
  1 teaspoon crushed red pepper
  1 tablespoon chopped fennel bulb

Equipment: Food mill or blender and sieve, soup pot

1. Drain beans and puree through a food mill, or puree them in a blender and press through a large sieve.

2. In a large soup pot, combine beans and 2 1/2 quarts water. Bring to a boil.

3. Chop kale into small pieces and add to soup.

4. Peel (or scrub and leave skin on) potatoes and cut into cubes. Add to soup.

5. Peel onion and add whole to soup.

6. Add vegetable shortening to soup.

7. Core tomatoes, cut into quarters, and add to soup.

8. Cut linguica into half-inch sections and add to soup.

9. Allow all to boil about 25 minutes, until potatoes are ready and kale is soft.

10. Mince a tablespoon of fennel bulb and the feathery leaves.

11. Add fennel to soup and turn off the fire.

Serve with crusty bread and butter.

BOLO DE FOLHA (LEAF CAKE)

Grace Goveia Collinson submitted this unusual recipe to *Food as Famous Folks Like It* (1947), published by the St. Mary's Guild of Provincetown, Massachusetts. The dough is so rich that Mary Alice Cook's *Traditional Portuguese Recipes from Provincetown* (1983) uses it for rolled up and sliced cookies called "boles de folha." I have modernized some directions.

NOTE: Dough needs to rise overnight.

Yield: a rich layer cake or 4 dozen cookies
  4 cups flour
  1/2 teaspoon salt
  2 sticks butter at room temperature or softened in a microwave
  1 cup Crisco
  1 tablespoon dry yeast
  1 tablespoon sugar
  juice of 3 oranges (a little more than 1 cup)
  extra melted butter
  cinnamon mixed with extra sugar

Equipment: Pastry blender or large fork, deep round baking pan such as a spring-form pan, rolling pin, dough scraper, small bowl, ungreased baking sheet (for cookies)

1. Mix yeast, sugar, and a little warm water in a small bowl.

2. Mix flour and salt in a mixing bowl.

3. Blend in softened butter and Crisco to the consistency of pie crust (lumps like corn kernels).

4. Check yeast mixture to see that a lot of small bubbles have formed and it is beginning to smell like yeast. (This is called "proofing" the yeast.) If not, you may need fresh yeast, or to wait a while longer.

5. Stir in yeast mixture and orange juice with a large spoon. You should get a sticky dough. If necessary, stir in a little more orange juice or flour to correct.

6. Turn the dough out onto a floured surface and knead (see Appendix 1) with floured hands until nearly smooth. Don't work it too much because dots of butter keep the cake light and flaky.

7. Return dough to large bowl. Cut off pieces and roll out thin, perhaps 1/4-inch.

8. Cut rounds of dough to fit the cake pan. Save scraps and add to dough to roll out.

9. Brush each round of dough with butter and sprinkle on cinnamon-sugar mixture.

10. Repeat for 4-6 layers.

11. Cover and leave overnight to rise.

12. In the morning, bake at 350 degrees until brown, "making sure to turn it over at least once."

13. For Mrs. Cook's cookies, go through Step 6, but roll out larger rectangles of dough. Coat them with melted butter and cinnamon sugar and roll up "like a jelly roll."

14. Cut off 1-inch slices, and set them on an ungreased baking sheet, close together. "Tuck any loose ends under the roll."

15. Let the dough rise until soft to touch.

16. Preheat oven to 325 degrees and bake until lightly colored, about 25 minutes.

17. Remove cookies from baking pan at once so the sugar doesn't stick. Turn upside down to cool on wire racks.

VINHA D'ALHOS

This recipe is distributed by the Residential Services Division of the Hawaiian Electric Company. The garlic vinegar marinade is also used for certain fish. In Massachusetts, similar sautéed pork is sold as "rojoes" or "pork trimmings" in Azorean restaurants.

NOTE: Recipe needs to be refrigerated overnight.

Yield: serves 6
> 3 pounds boneless pork
> 1 1/2 cups vinegar
> 2 cloves garlic, crushed
> 6 Hawaiian red peppers or other mild red
>   hot peppers
> 1 bay leaf
> 2 teaspoons salt
> 6 whole cloves
> 1/4 teaspoon thyme
> 1/8 teaspoon sage
> 2 tablespoons salad oil

Equipment: Garlic press, skillet

1. Cut pork into 2 by 1 1/2-inch pieces.

2. Peel garlic and press into vinegar.

3. Stem and core peppers. Slit one side and use a teaspoon to strip out pith and seeds. Slice and cut into fine dice.

4. Add red peppers, bay leaf, salt, cloves, thyme, and sage to vinegar. Mix well and pour over pork and let stand overnight in refrigerator.

5. Cook pork in marinade for 20 minutes. Drain and pat dry with paper towels

6. Heat oil in skillet; add pork and sauté slowly for 10 to 15 minutes until browned.

Serve with fried sliced potatoes or rice, and salad.

POTAWATOMI

The 1990 census counted almost 17,000 Potawatomi. They are one of the most dispersed Native American tribes, with 2,000 descendants in Canada and some in Mexico, although most now live in Oklahoma. According to their traditional history, they came from what is now eastern Canada with the Ottawa and **Ojibway** to the eastern shore of Lake Huron in about 1400. In the early 1600s, the Potawatomi were relatively settled farmers in Michigan, but were gradually driven west to Wisconsin and then south into Illinois and Indiana by the "Beaver Wars" of 1630-1700 with the **Iroquois**. Over much of the eighteenth century, the Potawatomi were allied with French traders against the Iroquois and English settlers. They focused more on farming and trapping around European settlements, including Detroit, although they were using horses to hunt buffalo in northern Indiana and Illinois by the 1760s. During and after the American Revolution, the Potawatomi sought British help against American settlement in the Ohio Valley, and many fought alongside the great **Shawnee** war chief Tecumseh, who died in the War of 1812.

Most Potawatomi were "removed" to Iowa and Kansas starting in 1834. An 1838 "March of Death" is remembered with some anger by the Kansas group. From 1846 to 1867, the two groups lived on a single reservation in Kansas, but divided acrimoniously. The conservative "Prairie Potowatomi" remained in Kansas, while the "Citizen Potowatomi" (favoring assimilation into U.S. society) moved to Oklahoma and settled near the Shawnee, and in the town of Shawnee, Oklahoma, where members of the largest group are still successful farmers. There are also three groups in Michigan, one in Wisconsin, and descendants on three reserves in Ontario, Canada, and among the Kickapoo in Coachila, Mexico. The word Potawatomi may mean "people of the place of fire." Some modern Potawatomi are reviving their language, especially in the Great Lakes groups, and calling themselves Nishnabek, "the people."

BAKED CORN

This recipe retains the flavor of corn-harvest puddings from the Native American past, yet uses commonly available ingredients. It was submitted by Dorothy L. Singleton for a group of Potawatomi recipes published by Potawatomi descendent Kenneth Power at <http://www.bakingmasters.com/power/native.htm>. Ms. Singleton's father, Charles Henry Anderson, said this recipe "was real close to what he had as a child on special occasions. . . . We always had this at Thanksgiving, Christmas or any special day in the family."

    1 can cream style corn
    1 can whole kernel corn
    1 egg
    1 tablespoon butter
    1/2 cup milk
    1 teaspoon sugar
    1/4 teaspoon salt
    1 stack of saltine crackers
    solid shortening to grease dish

Equipment: Casserole dish

1. Melt butter.
2. Mix first 7 ingredients well.
3. Crush saltines and stir most into the corn mixture. (Save a little for topping.)
4. "Let set for about 15 minutes till crackers absorb some of the liquid."
5. Grease the casserole dish.
6. Fill the casserole dish and top with cracker crumbs.
7. Bake at 350 degrees for about 35 minutes or until all liquid is gone and top is toasty brown.

SWEET POTATO BISCUITS

This is one of a group of recipes found written on pieces of paper and stuck inside an old book that Kenneth Power bought at an antique shop in Shawnee, Oklahoma. "Each piece of paper had 'Potawatomi Recipe' at the top of the page." This would appear to be a recipe acquired by Potawatomi in Oklahoma, perhaps from one of the Five Civilized Tribes of Indians that came originally from the southern states.

    2 cups all-purpose flour
    4 teaspoons baking powder
    1 teaspoon salt
    1 sweet potato
    2 tablespoons bacon fat or shortening, plus
        some to grease baking sheet

2/3 cup milk

4 tablespoons granulated sugar

Equipment: Baking sheet, grater or food processor, biscuit or cookie cutter (optional)

1. Half-cook a sweet potato (3 minutes in a microwave oven might be about right).

2. Mix the dry ingredients in a bowl.

3. Grate the sweet potato on a grater or the grating blade of a food processor.

4. Melt bacon fat or shortening.

5. Add the sweet potato and milk to the dry ingredients and mix well.

6. Pat out onto a board. Cut into biscuits

7. Grease the baking sheet with melted bacon fat.

8. Place the biscuits on the fat and then turn them over.

9. Bake at about 400 degrees for about 20-30 minutes or until the top is a golden brown.

CORN DUMPLINGS

Roscoe "Rocky" Baptiste of Gervais, Oregon, likes these corn dumplings with "chili stew." This is one of a group of recipes he has posted at <http://redrival.com/nishnabek/foods.html> as part of his pages as regional representative of the Citizen Potawatomi (the large Oklahoma group) for Oregon and Washington.

1 cup flour

1 teaspoon baking powder

1/4 cup cornmeal

1 cup fresh corn (or canned whole kernel corn)

salt to taste

Equipment: Blender (optional)

1. Mash corn thoroughly or grate in blender.

2. Mix with other ingredients until well blended.

3. Add water if necessary, but keep dough stiff.

4. Drop by tablespoonfuls onto the top of soup stew about 15 minutes before serving.

5. Cover the stew tightly until ready to serve.

Serve with any meaty soup or stew, or chili con carne.

PUEBLO INDIANS (EASTERN)

Government statistics count more than 55,000 Pueblo Indians in all, about half of whom live in 19 eastern communities, mostly along the Rio Grande in New Mexico and Texas. (Western Pueblo Indians include the **Hopi, Zuni,** Acoma, and Arizona Tewa.) There were 70 to 100 Pueblo communities when the Spanish settlers arrived in 1598, but most were destroyed or moved in the ensuing conflicts. The western pueblos were larger and the Spanish settlements in Arizona smaller, so the Western pueblo Indians preserved their languages and cultures longer. The coordinated Pueblo revolt in 1680 drove the Spanish out for 14 years, but they returned, and the Pueblo Indians began to ally with the Spanish against the **Apache.** In 1820, the Pueblo Indians became Mexican citizens, and in 1848 U.S. citizens, although the great majority of Indians in the Southwest did not become voting citizens until 1924.

The Eastern Pueblos speak languages from several different families, and retain some old traditions, but most became Catholic over the centuries of Spanish settlement in New Mexico. They also exchanged foods with **New Mexico Hispanic** neighbors, including posole (hominy stew), biscochitos (cookies), and wheat breads baked in large adobe ovens. Their pueblos are the oldest continuously occupied towns in the United States. Some of the Eastern Pueblo Indians have one home in the pueblo, and another in farming areas off the small reservations or in town. Taos Pueblo, one of the oldest, is famous for making drums.

WILD SAGE BREAD

This flat round bread, like the **Wampanoag** bannock, is popular in most of the Eastern Pueblos, sometimes as a baking powder bread. The source for the recipe is <www.cookingpost.com>, a tribal enterprise based at the Santa Ana Pueblo, which sells blue cornmeal, posole corn, and other ingredients. If you can't get wild sage, start with a half teaspoon of dried sage.

Yield: serves 6 as an appetizer
  1 package dry yeast
  1 cup cottage cheese
  1 egg
  2 tablespoons shortening
  1 tablespoon sugar
  2 teaspoons crushed dried sage
  1/2 teaspoon salt
  1/4 teaspoon baking soda
  2 1/2 cups flour
  coarse salt (optional)
  2 tablespoons pine nuts (optional)

Equipment: 10-inch pie plate, pizza pan, quiche pan, or clay baking dish

1. Combine sugar, sage, salt, baking soda, and flour.

2. Dissolve yeast in 1/4 cup warm water.

3. Beat egg and cottage cheese together until smooth.

4. Melt 1 tablespoon of the shortening, allow to cool a little, and add to egg mixture.

5. Add yeast to egg mixture and mix well.

6. Add flour mixture slowly to egg mixture, beating well after each addition until a stiff dough is formed.

7. Cover dough with cloth and put in warm place until double in bulk (about 1 hour).

8. Punch dough down to work out the large bubbles, knead (see Appendix 1) for 1 minute and place in a well-greased pan.

9. Cover and let rise for 40 minutes.

10. Bake in a 350-degree oven for 50 minutes.

11. Melt the remaining shortening and brush on the bread.

12. If using pine nuts, toast briefly in an oven or in a heavy pan on top of the stove. Crush nuts with a heavy cup or mortar and pestle. Sprinkle nuts or salt over the bread.

Serve hot.

POJOAQUE CREAM SOUP

This recipe from the small Pojoaque Pueblo was reprinted in a pamphlet of "Native American Recipes" by the Smithsonian Institution Festival of American Folklife.

  4 cups home-cooked pinto beans (or 3 cans)
  1 cup bean juice
  1 clove garlic
  1 tablespoon minced onion
  3/4 teaspoon salt
  1 cup undiluted evaporated milk
  pinch oregano
  1 tablespoon red chili powder (not chili con carne spice)

Equipment: Blender (optional)

1. Cook pinto beans according to package directions, or open cans. Mash beans thoroughly and mix in bean juice, or put both in blender until smooth.

2. If using blender, blend in all other ingredients gradually while blending. If not, mix them in slowly while beating.

3. Heat beans to a simmer, stirring frequently so the soup does not stick to the bottom.

4. Simmer soup for 10 minutes.

Serve hot, or cold with a dollop of sour cream.

JOHN'S FAVORITE RECIPE

This dish of spam and potatoes reminds us that Native American food continues to grow and change. The recipe from John Gonzales, an MIT graduate and one of several generations of brilliant potters at the San Ildefonso Pueblo, appeared in *Artistic Tastes: Favorite Recipes of Native American Artists*. A tortilla wrapped around spam and potatoes is a popular Indian breakfast throughout the Southwest; here it is made more healthful with traditional squash and chile pepper.

1 can Spam Lite
3 to 4 potatoes
1 zucchini
1 yellow squash
1 onion
1 green chile
1 tablespoon oil
salt, pepper, and garlic powder to taste

Equipment: Large skillet

1. Peel potatoes.

2. Microwave potatoes about 5 minutes.

3. Wash and slice zucchini and yellow squash.

4. Slice potatoes.

5. Heat oil in a large skillet, and sauté zucchini, potatoes, and squash for several minutes.

6. Halve, peel, and slice onion.

7. Remove seeds, stem, and pith from green chile and slice.

8. Cut Spam into 1-inch cubes.

9. Add the rest of the ingredients to the skillet and cook until the potatoes are golden brown.

"Serve with warm tortillas."

PUERTO RICANS

Puerto Rico was taken over by the United States at the conclusion of the Spanish-American War in 1898, and its people were granted citizenship in 1917, just in time for the World War I military draft, although they could not elect even their own governor until 1948. By 1930, some 52,000 Puerto Ricans lived in New York, forming the first large Hispanic community in the Northeast. After World War II, the world's first major airborne migration brought 900,000 Puerto Ricans to the mainland, perhaps half to greater New York City, which passed San Juan as the largest Puerto Rican city. The lagging Puerto Rican economy was the major reason for migration. Puerto Ricans return to the island for frequent visits, send their children home to stay with relatives and renew their Spanish, and often plan to retire back home.

Nevertheless, the mainland community continues to grow, and is now more than 2.7 million, compared to 3.5 million residents of Puerto Rico itself. New York continues to be the major center. In the 1950s and 1960s, Puerto Rican migrant farm workers often remained in New England cities after their picking seasons ended, and Chicago became a second center, with smaller, older, and more established groups in Hawaii, Los Angeles, and San Francisco. One of the most characteristic Puerto Rican foods is rice with fresh pigeon peas, a cousin of the **Gullah** hoppin' john. Puerto Ricans did not grow much corn until the early twentieth century, so the characteristic tamale is a pork "pastel" made of plantains and starchy roots. Many fried snacks in Puerto Rico are unknown on other Caribbean islands, and the island boasts an African-style mash of plantains and lard called "mofongo."

HABICHUELAS

This recipe from Mrs. Roberto Clemente was published in the *Pirate Wives' Cookbook* and reprinted in the *Three Rivers Cookbook* (1973). It's a typical Puerto Rican recipe for beans, Americanized by the use of canned beans and green pepper. The initial sauté of onion, ham, garlic, and green paper makes what is called a "sofrito," the savory base of most Latin American sauces and stews. The Italian term is "batuto."

Yield: serves 8

1 teaspoon olive oil
1 medium onion
1/4 pound ham
1 clove garlic
1/2 green pepper
1/4 teaspoon salt
1 teaspoon stuffed olives
1 teaspoon capers
1 8-ounce can tomato sauce
2 17-ounce cans red kidney beans

Equipment: Saucepan, knife and cutting board

1. Mince onion by halving it the long way, peeling, cutting thin slices the long way, and cutting thin slices across each half. To get finer mince, rock a chef's knife or Chinese cleaver across the pile of minced onion a few times.

2. Dice ham to fine dice.

3. Mince the garlic by slicing thinly 3 ways.

4. Mince green pepper by cutting off top and bottom, removing seeds and white pith, cutting into long thin slices, and slicing across groups of slices.

5. Put oil in saucepan and slowly sauté onion, ham, garlic, green pepper, and salt.

6. When onion is transparent, add olives, capers, and tomato sauce. Simmer over low heat 5 minutes.

7. Add beans to a half cup water. Cover and cook 8-10 minutes until sauce becomes thickened.

Serve over rice as a light supper or side dish.

ASOPAO DE CAMARONES ("SHRIMP ASOPAO")

Asopaos are soupy rice stews like the Cape Verdean and Brazilian canja, but unknown elsewhere in the Caribbean. Carmen Valdes submitted this version to the *Bicentennial Cookery Book* (1976) published by the General Services Agency Bicentennial Committee of Region One (New England). When my wife was an English-Spanish bilingual teacher in Boston, her Puerto Rican colleagues would make a chicken asopao for parties, generally serving it around midnight. This recipe substitutes paprika for the red-colored achiote oil that would be used in Puerto Rico, itself probably an old substitution for the red dende palm oil used in Africa.

1/2 pound fresh or frozen shrimp
2 big potatoes
1 cup rice
1 clove garlic
1 small onion
1 teaspoon parsley
1 teaspoon oregano
1/2 small can of tomato sauce (optional)
1 teaspoon paprika
1/4 cup oil
1/2 cup of mixed capers and olives (sold in Hispanic food sections as alcaparrada, or substitute 1 part capers to 4 parts green olives with pits)

Equipment: Medium soup pot

1. Halve, peel, and chop the onion.

2. Peel and mince the garlic.

3. In a medium soup pot, combine the oil, garlic, and onion and cook for 5 minutes.

4. Add the tomato sauce, if using, and let it cook on low heat for 10 minutes.

5. Add about 2 quarts of water and the rice, parsley, oregano, salt, pepper, paprika, capers, and olives. Simmer for 10 minutes.

6. Peel potatoes and cut into small pieces.

7. Add potatoes to soup and simmer for another 10-15 minutes (potatoes should be not quite tender).

8. Add in shrimp and lower heat to a simmer. Cook for 5 more minutes.

Serve in soup bowls.

Pernil Al Horno (Roast Pork Shoulder)

This kind of slow-roasted pork is a traditional Christmas-week dish in Puerto Rico. Families drive into the countryside to restaurants that serve "lechon" (fresh ham) and "pavon" (ham-style roast turkey). Samantha L. S., a fourth grader, contributed this recipe to an Internet cookbook at St. Patrick School in Smithtown, New York; the cookbook is archived at <http://www.otan.dni.us/webfarm/emailproject/cook.htm>.

NOTE: Recipe needs to be refrigerated overnight.

> 4-to-6-pound pork shoulder
> juice of one whole lemon
> 3 cloves garlic
> salt and ground black pepper to taste
> 1 tablespoon dried oregano

Equipment: Roasting pan

1. Remove skin and most of the fat from the pork roast with a sharp knife. (Some cooks reserve the skin to add body to bean soups.)

2. "Cut the lemon in half and sprinkle lemon juice over the entire pork shoulder. This will rid the meat of its 'swinish' odor."

3. Wash pork thoroughly under cold running water. Pat dry with paper towels.

4. Peel cloves of garlic and cut into slivers.

5. With a sharp knife make slits in the fat and meat of the pork shoulder. Stud the slits with garlic slivers.

6. Sprinkle the shoulder with salt, pepper, and oregano.

7. Rub seasoning into the surface.

8. Place meat in a large pot or kettle. Cover and refrigerate for at least 4 hours, preferably overnight.

9. After marinating, arrange pork shoulder in greased, shallow roasting pan.

10. Preheat an oven to 300 degrees.

11. Bake pork roast at 300 for about 1 hour. The meat should have a golden brown color.

12. Raise oven temperature to 350 degrees and bake for another 2 hours. Roast is done when pork is tender.

Serve with rice and pigeon peas.

ROMA

See Gypsy-Americans (Romanichals, Travellers, Roma)

ROMANIAN-AMERICANS

About 400,000 Americans claim Romanian descent, probably including some minority Gypsy-Americans, Jewish-Americans, Hungarian-Americans, and Germans from Russia from the border area of Bessarabia. The largest concentration of Romanian-Americans is around Cleveland and Detroit. The major immigration was from 1895 to 1920, with another large group coming since the 1989 revolution.

MAMALIGA WITH CHEESE

Mary Ann Suciu contributed this version of the best-known Romanian dish to *Cuisine International* (1979), which was published by the International Institute of Metropolitan Detroit. In Romania, this dish would be made with sharp or aged cheeses, so the mild cheese here makes something more like **African-American** cheese grits, a possible influence in Detroit!

1/4 pound bacon
11/2 cups yellow cornmeal
1 tablespoon salt
grated cheese (mild) (start with a cup)
solid shortening to grease ovenproof dish

Equipment: Ovenproof dish or casserole, large pot

1. Cut bacon into small pieces and fry.

2. Mix the cornmeal with 1 cup cold water.

3. Bring 3 cups water to a fast boil in a large pot.

4. Add the salt and slowly add the cornmeal mixture, "stirring constantly with a large wooden spoon."

5. Lower the heat when it begins to boil again. Cook until "rather soft."

6. Grease the ovenproof dish.

7. Spread a layer of cornmeal mush in the dish.

8. Sprinkle with cheese.

9. Continue forming these layers, ending with a layer of cheese on top.

10. Add pieces of fried bacon to the top layer.

11. Place in 350-degree oven "for a few minutes," until cheese is melted.

Serve hot. "Mamaliga is delicious served by itself or as a side dish."

"PHELAJEL" (EGGPLANT SALAD)

This recipe comes from a collection dictated by my late father, Martin Zanger. It is a recreation of the Romanian-Jewish-American cooking of his mother's family, and includes many optional techniques he used at different times. The usual Romanian term is "Patlagele," so "Phelajel" may have been a dialect pronunciation, or a child's effort at patlagele. Many Romanian-Americans char eggplants by turning them over a gas burner like giant marshmallows, but we never had a gas stove. Carbon steel knives discolor eggplants and give them a metallic flavor, so many old recipes specify all wood utensils, although stainless steel, glass, or ceramics are also fine.

1 large eggplant
few drops liquid smoke seasoning (optional)
half sweet onion (red or Vidalia)
2-4 tablespoons olive oil
1 teaspoon salt
black pepper

Equipment: Colander, charcoal grill (optional), food processor (optional), broiler pan with rack (for oven), whisk

1. Select firm, relatively heavy eggplant.

2. "Pierce it all over with a fork so that it doesn't explode."

3. If using charcoal grill, make fire with briquettes on one side to make hotter and cooler areas. If using oven, preheat to 350 degrees.

4. Set eggplant in oven for 30 minutes, or on cooler side of charcoal grill for 15 minutes.

5. Turn eggplant and cook 30 minutes more (15-20 minutes on charcoal grill), until "nice and soft and mushy."

6. If skin is not mostly charred, grill briefly under the broiler or on the hot side of the charcoal grill, turning to get most of the skin lightly burned.

7. "Put it in a colander and slash it in a few places, and let it drain and cool until it's cool enough to handle."

8. When it is completely cool, peel off all the skin and cut the eggplant up. (It's okay if a little charred skin gets mixed in.)

9. If using a food processor, use plastic blade and add a few drops of liquid smoke seasoning,

especially if the eggplant was cooked in the oven. If not using food processor, chop with a large knife until a smooth paste develops

10. Chop onion into fine dice. Mix in with eggplant.

11. Whip in olive oil to taste. "Eggplant will absorb tons of olive oil." The best flavor is obtained by using just enough olive oil to "calm the onions down."

12. Add salt and pepper.

Serve as an appetizer with flatbread, or chilled as a small salad garnished with black olives, tomatoes, or roast red peppers.

PAPANASH

Romanian-American conductor and music educator Sergiu Comissiona contributed this recipe to *Star Recipes from the Maryland Science Center* (1982). In Romania, "papanasi" are fried cookies, while these are more like pancakes. This recipe can be increased, which makes it easier to beat the egg whites.

1 package farmer's cheese
2 eggs
3 tablespoons Cream of Wheat (or farina, uncooked)
3 tablespoons flour
pinch of salt
butter for frying

Equipment: Whisk or electric hand beater to beat egg whites, pancake turner, frying pan

1. Break and separate eggs. (One technique is to pour the yolk back and forth between the halves of the egg shell, catching the white in a small bowl beneath. A little white in the yolks will not change this recipe, but any yolk in the whites will make it much harder to beat in air.)

2. Mix cheese with egg yolks.

3. Mix in Cream of Wheat, flour, and salt.

4. In a small bowl, beat egg whites until they form soft peaks, if possible.

5. Add to the yolk-cheese mixture.

6. Melt butter in frying pan, and drop spoonfuls of the mixture into the hot pan to brown on both sides.

"Serve with sour cream or preserves."

ROMANICHALS

See GYPSY-AMERICANS (ROMANICHALS, TRAVELLERS, ROMA)

RUSKINS, RUSNYAKS

See CARPATHO-RUSYN-AMERICANS (RUSKINS, RUSNYAKS, RUTHENIANS, AND LEMKIANS)

RUSSIAN-AMERICANS

The present Russian Republic, which is considerably smaller than the former Soviet Union, still has more than 100 ethnic groups. Recent immigrants from Russia also include many people from elsewhere in the former Soviet Union whose families had migrated to large Russian cities or been forced to relocate in Siberia. Although the 1990 census estimated only 3 million Americans of Russian descent, 3.5 million immigrants had come to the U.S. from Russia through 1990. Most of the descendants of those immigrants may regard themselves more as **Jewish-Americans** (an estimated 60 percent of Russian immigration from 1900 to 1930), **Polish-Americans, Ukrainian-Americans, Germans from Russia, Armenian-Americans, Belorussian-Americans,** Molokans (an ethno-religious sect with 20,000 members in California), or members of some other ethnic group.

The first Russian-Americans were settlers and traders in Alaska and northern California from the 1760s to 1867, when Alaska was sold to the United States. (See the **Tlingit** fish perok for a Russian food that stayed with Native Alaskans.) Some remnant of Russian churches and communities remain in both states. Russians immigrating to the U.S. between 1880 and 1920 were often rural people in search of land. Since 1967, recent immigrants from Russia have again been mostly Jews and religious dissidents, and have settled in Eastern and Midwestern cities, with a notable concentration around Coney Island in New York City, and in Greater Boston. Russian food has a core of pickled snacks, hearty soups, stuffed breads, and dumplings. There is also a nostalgia for the upper-class dishes of imperial Russia, like beef stroganoff and chicken Kiev, which remained status symbols during the Soviet era, and a list of Soviet regional dishes that were served in restaurants in Russia, such as Georgian chicken.

PILAF

Pilafs came into modern Russian cooking because the Soviet Union included many Turkish-speaking peoples from the Caucasus and Central Asia. A recent immigrant, Ilya M., contributed this recipe to *The New Lincoln School Cookbook*, which was published in 1998 in Brookline, Massachusetts. Brookline is home to the largest Russian-American community in greater Boston.

1 pound rice (2 cups)
1 pound meat (stew beef)
1 green pepper
5 carrots
5 cloves garlic
1 onion
1/2 cup oil

Equipment: Large ovenproof pot with a cover, knife, mixing spoon

1. Preheat oven to 325 degrees.

2. Using a large pot with a cover, fry meat in oil until "half done."

3. Peel and slice carrots.

4. Remove stem, seeds, and pith from green pepper. Cut into small squares.

5. Add carrots and pepper to the pot and cook about 10-15 minutes.

6. Halve, peel, and chop the onion.

7. Add onions and rice to the pot and sauté until rice has turned white.

8. Peel garlic and put cloves into "five different places" in the rice mixture.

9. Add 6 cups of water and cover pot. Bring to a boil.

10. Move to a 325-degree oven, and bake for 1 1/2 hours.

MARINATED MUSHROOMS (GRIBY MARINOVANNYE)

This typical Russian recipe from Natasha Gavrilina appeared in the online cookbook of the University of Pittsburgh Summer Languages Institute.

NOTE: Recipe should marinate overnight.

1 pound mushrooms
1/2 cup lemon juice
1/2 cup olive oil (or olive and corn mixed)
2 green onions
1/4 cup chopped parsley
1 decent-sized clove garlic
3/4 teaspoon salt
1/4 teaspoon black pepper

1/4 teaspoon paprika

2-3 bay leaves

Equipment: Knife, large mixing bowl, mixing spoon

1. Use small mushrooms or cut larger ones into thickish slices.

2. Trim and slice green onions. Chop parsley.

3. Peel and chop garlic clove.

4. Mix everything together except the paprika, which should be added at the end.

5. Mix up with mushrooms. "Turn the mushrooms around every few hours—leave overnight in the refrigerator, or at least leave them to marinate for about 3 hours. (The longer the better.)"

6. Before serving, keep at room temperature for a few minutes and stir for the oil to melt.

Serve as an appetizer or with meat, fish, or boiled potatos.

ELENA VALERIANOVNA VOLKOVA'S "SIMPLE PASHTET"

What has been simplified here is a pate of liver, butter, carrots, and onions that is the inspiration of **Jewish-American** chopped liver. This "quick alternative" was developed by a friend of Siberia-born George G. Vitt of Los Angeles, whose 1988 collection of Russian recipes is periodically reposted around the Internet.

8-oz. Braunschweiger sausage (Oscar Meyer is fine)

4 ounces butter

Equipment: Large mixing bowl, mixing spoon, small skillet, two-cup plastic freezer container

1. Place contents of braunschweiger sausage in large mixing bowl and break up well.

2. Melt butter in small skillet and add to the sausage, stirring.

3. Place in a plastic container and refrigerate overnight.

4. To remove the contents in one piece, for serving, place container upside-down on dish, dip in hot water and separate.

Serve with thin slices of dark rye bread.

VINEGRET (COOKED VEGETABLE SALAD)

Known as "Russian salad" all over Europe and Latin America, this salad is on the menu of virtually every Russian-American restaurant. The recipe is from *Contemporary Russian Cuisine* (1988) by Irina Chernomordik. The author, who had come to the United States 11 years earlier, was careful not to give any information about where she lived or where the book was published. I bought it in a Russian grocery in suburban Boston.

Yield: serves 6-9

5 medium potatoes

1/2 cup canned pinto or red kidney beans (optional, reduce potatoes to 2)

2 medium beets

2 medium carrots

2 teaspoons chopped parsley

2 teaspoons chopped fresh dill

2 medium pickled cucumbers

2 tablespoons pickled mushrooms (see above, optional, reduce pickled cucumbers to 1)

3/4 cup sauerkraut

1 large onion

3-4 tablespoons oil

2 tablespoons mayonnaise (optional, reduce oil to 2 tablespoons)

1 tablespoon prepared mustard

salt and pepper to taste

2 tablespoons chopped green onions (optional)

1 apple (optional)

Equipment: Colander, large bowl, mixing spoon, knife, small bowl

1. Trim all but the last inch of stem on the beets, put in a small pot with cold water to cover, and bring to a boil. Cook until fork-tender, about 45-50 minutes. Remove from heat and place in colander in sink.

2. Cook unpeeled carrots and potatoes the same way and add to colander with beets.

3. Peel the potatoes, carrots, and beets under cold running water. "It is easier to do when they are warm." When peeled, dice the vegetables.

4. Drain and chop the sauerkraut and add to beet mixture.

5. Dice pickles and optional picked mushrooms.

6. Halve, peel, and chop the onion.

7. Mix all vegetables together.

8. In a small bowl, combine mustard, oil, optional mayonnaise, and salt and pepper to make the dressing.

9. Season vegetables with dressing.

10. Wash, core, and dice the apple if using. Wash canned beans if using. Trim and chop green onions if using.

11. Add optional ingredients to salad. Refrigerate at least 35 minutes prior to serving.

Serve as an appetizer, or light lunch.

RUSYNS

See CARPATHO-RUSYN-AMERICANS

RUTHENIANS

See CARPATHO-RUSYN-AMERICANS

SALVADORAN-AMERICANS

Prior to the 1960s, few immigrants came to the United States from El Salvador, a small country on the Pacific side of Central America. The first 20,000 to 40,000 Salvadorans came to the United States after the "Soccer War" crisis with Honduras in 1965-67, with small communities establishing themselves in San Francisco and other coastal cities. The Salvadoran civil war that began in 1979 suddenly sent hundreds of thousands of Salvadorans into exile. Young males, who were caught between the conflicting demands of the government army, pro-government death squads, and the five guerrilla organizations, were sent to the United States by their families. The United States supported the Salvadoran government and refused political asylum to the vast majority of these refugees, thereby making Salvadorans the second-largest group of illegal aliens after Mexicans. (Many apprehended Salvadorans claimed to be Mexicans to prevent deportation to El Salvador.) By 1990, the economy of El Salvador had become dependent on the money sent home by Salvadorans working in the U.S., and the Salvadoran government began lobbying the U.S. government to allow all the refugees to stay. Immigration reform and an order by President George Bush to halt deportations of Central Americans (including Nicaraguans) allowed 400,000 Salvadorans to legalize their immigration status by 1990, although the Immigration and Naturalization Service estimated in 1996 that there were still 335,000 Salvadorans in the U.S. without legal status. In the late 1990s, the Salvadoran-American community was estimated at between 500,000 and one million.

Salvadoran-American neighborhoods now exist in Washington, D.C.; northern New Jersey; and Greater Boston, as well as in West Coast and Midwestern cities. Many Salvadoran refugees found restaurant work in the 1980s and 1990s, and some have advanced within the restaurant industry. However, restaurants owned by Salvadorans tend to be small neighborhood kitchens offering pupusas and inexpensive meals. A more common pattern is still the informal "pupuseria" in a private apartment, which provides not only a taste of home but some networking and counseling like the boardinghouses of earlier immigrants. Other Salvadoran-American foods include hot cornmeal drinks called "atole," cold drinks flavored with tamarind or almond, chicken in pineapple vinegar, and an eggy cheesecake topped with sesame seeds called "quesadilla."

MARIA'S GUACAMOLE

This recipe from Maria Avalos was published on the Internet at <http://www.otan.dni.us/webfarm/emailproject/res.htm>as part of a group of recipes written by adult students of English as a Second Language at the Baldwin Park Adult School in Baldwin Park, California. The chopped egg is the major difference between Salvadoran guacamole and Mexican guacamole. I have made the jalapeño peppers optional because I have another Salvadoran recipe from Massachusetts that does not use hot peppers.

> 6 ripe avocados
> 3 eggs
> 3 green onions
> 2 tomatoes
> 2 jalapeno peppers
> juice from 2 lemons
> 2 teaspoons salt

Equipment: Small saucepan, knife, potato masher, large mixing bowl, mixing spoon

1. Hard-boil eggs 15 minutes in small saucepan, shell under cold water, and chop.

2. "Peel the Avocados and smash them until they get soft." (You can also cut them in half, remove the seed, and scoop out the green flesh with a soup spoon, then smash them with a potato masher until they get soft.)

3. Trim and chop the green onions.

4. Core and chop the tomatoes.

5. Slice and chop the hard-boiled eggs.

6. In a large mixing bowl, "Mix everything with the avocados."

7. Add the lemon juice and a little salt to the guacamole and mix well.

Serve with tortilla chips.

PUPUSAS

Street food in El Salvador, pupusas are stuffed tortillas that serve as a taste of home for Salvadoran immigrants and refugees. They vary a lot. This recipe from Carmen Hernandez appeared in *Cookbook 1991*, which was published by the Intergenerational Literacy Project in Chelsea, Massachusetts. The recipe includes details from several other sources. The pork and potato filling is the most characteristic, but pupusas are also filled simply with grated mozzarella or Monterey jack cheese, refried red or black beans, and various combinations. As with many ethnic foods, the best are made by one's mother, and the pupusas of the wife or girlfriend are not so good, but few Salvadoran men—even after decades of kitchen work—make pupusas.

Yield: 7 snacks
> 1 small green cabbage (or 1/2 green and 1/2 red cabbage)
> 1 onion
> 1 large carrot
> 1 chile pepper (optional)
> 1 cup vinegar
> 3 cups corn tortilla flour ("Masa Harina")
> 1/2 pound pork
> 2 potatoes
> 4 tablespoons sour cream
> 1/2 cup grated mild cheese

Equipment: Knife, vegetable peeler, glass or ceramic bowl, mixing spoon, small pot with cover, food processor or meat grinder to grind pork and potato filling, large bowl, damp cloth, greased griddle, metal spatula

1. To make the "curtido" (cole slaw topping), trim, half, and core the cabbage. Cut into wedges, and then cut the wedges into fine shreds.

2. Peel and chop the carrot into fine pieces.

3. Halve, peel, and chop the onion. If using chile pepper, remove top, slit, and use a teaspoon to scrape out seeds and pith. Cut into fine shreds.

4. In a glass or ceramic bowl, combine the vegetables with the vinegar and salt and pepper (or optional hot chile). Mix well and let stand 3 hours or overnight.

5. To make filling, peel potatoes and cut into chunks. Put pork and potatoes in a small pot with salt to taste and water to cover. Bring to a boil over medium heat, then reduce heat to a rapid simmer. Cover pot and cook until pork is tender and water is almost gone, about 30 minutes. Remove cover and allow water to evaporate completely. If there is enough fat for pork to fry and brown a little, so much the better.

6. Using food processor or meat grinder, grind cooked pork and potatoes together. Add sour cream, grated cheese, and more salt if needed and mix well.

7. To make dough, combine tortilla flour with 2 cups water in a large bowl. Knead well (see Appendix 1), and roll into a thick rope. Divide dough into 14 pieces. Roll each piece into a ball, and roll out or pat each ball into a 3-inch mini-tortilla about 1/8 inch thick. Experienced pupusa makers can slap out these tortillas between their hands.

8. Cover completed tortillas with a damp cloth so they don't dry out.

9. Put a tablespoon of the filling on a tortilla, cover with another, and crimp the edges with a fork or pinch them together. Pat the completed pupusa into a flatter shape, about 3/8 inch thick.

10. Cook on a heated greased griddle over medium heat (or a non-stick griddle or a well-seasoned cast-iron griddle without grease) until flecked with brown, about 4-5 minutes.

11. Turn once with metal spatula and heat until speckled brown on both sides.

Serve topped with the curtido. Some Salvadoran-Americans add salsa or hot sauce.

CRAB SALAD

Reina Duran wrote down this recipe for Steve Winston's 1998 English as Second Language Class at the Visalia Adult School in Visalia, California. The recipe is archived on the Internet at <http://www.otan.dni.us/webfarm/emailproject/res.htm>. Although Mexican-Americans Guadalupe Flores, Genoveva Nuno, and Rafael Cortez helped write the recipe, they explain that this "is a Salvadoreno plate. And we eat crab salad in celebrations. The total cost of this dish is $15 with imitation crab. All Latin Americans eat this food, too. This is a healthy food, without fat." The healthfulness of the dish depends on whether you use real mayonnaise, but their training in writing recipes is very good—the instructions below are exactly as written by the students.

3 pounds imitation crab
2 heads lettuce
3 stalks celery
1 bunch cilantro
4 bunches green onions
1 cup mayonnaise
2 bags Frito chips
2 eggs
salt to taste

Equipment: Large saucepan, big bowl, knife, mixing spoon

1. In a large saucepan, "Boil eggs for ten minutes until hard. Cool under cold water."

2. "Shred the crab. Put in big bowl."

3. "Peel eggs. Chop and add to crab."

4. "Chop the cilantro, green onions, celery and lettuce fine."

5. "Add chopped vegetables to the crab."

6. "Add the mayonnaise and mix."

7. "Salt to taste."

"Serve with Frito chips."

SAMOAN-AMERICANS

About 63,000 Samoan-Americans live in the U.S., about half in California and one-fourth in Hawaii. Statistics are approximate because people from Western Samoa (an independent country that was formerly administered by New Zealand) must immigrate, but people from American Samoa are U.S. citizens and do not have to go through immigration. Leaving aside possible ancient explorations by this seafaring people, the first Samoans came to Hawaii in 1919 after the dedication there of a **Mormon** temple. Larger groups came to Hawaii and to the mainland states after military service in World War II. Like **Hawaiians**, Samoans have a Polynesian language and culture, and some of their food and cooking traditions are similar, including ways of eating salted raw fish and cooking in taro leaves ("lu'au" in both languages) and in earth ovens.

Other Samoan recipes include salt beef, corned beef and cabbage, fish or chicken baked in leaves, raw fish in coconut milk, and pani popo (sweet rolls baked with coconut milk).

BANANA POI

This rich sweet is made more so by the characteristic use of coconut cream. This recipe from Ann Kondo Corum's *Ethnic Foods of Hawaii* begins with one of her recipes for coconut cream. You can also use canned coconut milk by pouring off any liquid that has separated out.

Yield: serves 4

1 1/2 cups unsweetened dried coconut

1 cup half-and-half (or 1 cup coconut cream from Asian grocery)

2 cups very ripe bananas, mashed

2 tablespoons lemon juice

Equipment: Medium saucepan, medium mixing bowl, mixing spoon, fine sieve or colander with cheesecloth or clean dish towel

1. In medium saucepan, simmer dried coconut with half-and-half for 10 minutes. (Do not boil.)

2. Strain through a fine sieve, cheesecloth, or clean dishtowel into medium mixing bowl. Cool before use.

3. Mash bananas to a smooth paste and add to coconut mixture.

4. Add lemon juice.

5. Stirring constantly, gradually add the coconut cream.

6. Mix well and chill until thickened.

Serve in glasses.

SAPASUI (SAMOAN CHOP SUI)

This somewhat fancied-up version was demonstrated by caterer Iva Kinimaka on the "Hawaii's Kitchen" show broadcast on July 25, 1999. Older recipes use beef chuck or canned corned beef, of which a fattier New Zealand brand is preferred.

Yield: serves 6

1 8-ounce bundle long rice (bean thread or cellophane noodles)

1/2 cup oil

1 pound onions (four medium)

1 pound carrots

1/2 bunch watercress

2 pounds bean sprouts

1/2 head cabbage

6 cloves garlic

1 tablespoon salt
1 tablespoon black pepper
1 cup Kikoman shoyu (Japanese soy sauce)
1 pound celery

Equipment: Medium mixing bowl, spoon, knife, vegetable peeler, kitchen scissors, deep pot or skillet with high sides, garlic press

1. In medium mixing bowl, soak long rice in water until soft, about 15-20 minutes.

2. Halve the onions, peel, and slice thinly. (Wear swim goggles to avoid tears.)

3. Peel carrots and slice into thin rounds.

4. Slice celery into chunks. Chop cabbage.

5. Cut softened noodles into 2-inch pieces with scissors.

6. Slice pork thinly.

7. Heat oil in a deep pot or skillet with high sides and brown pork. Crush garlic with garlic press into the pot as you go.

8. Add onions, soy sauce, and salt and pepper.

9. Stir in all vegetables and long rice, and cook until vegetables are tender, about 15 minutes.

10. Add a little water as needed to keep vegetables from sticking to the pan.

Serve as a one-pot supper.

SCOTCH-IRISH

Terminology for this large and important ethnic group is confusing, but their story is well recorded. It begins with about 200,000 Scots, mostly from the lowlands, moving across the 20-mile channel to northern Ireland from about 1607 to 1698. They were initially encouraged by King James I of England (James VI in Scotland), who wanted more Protestants in Ireland. However, as Presbyterians, they (and all Scots) later suffered discrimination under the officially sanctioned Church of Ireland. In the eighteenth century, about 200,000 came to America. At the time, they were usually known as Irish, Ulster Irish, Ulster Scots, or Protestant Irish. At the time of the American Revolution, they were the largest non-English ethnic group in the British colonies, constituting 10-15 percent of the total population of the colonies. Their anti-British feelings made them important supporters of the American Revolution.

Because the Scotch-Irish arrived after the best lands were taken on the East Coast, they moved inland to pioneer the then-Indian territories in the Appalachian Mountains. They were joined by a second wave of people leaving all parts of Ireland after the 1842 potato famine. It was at that time that they adopted the name Scotch -Irish to distinguish themselves from the Irish Catholics crowding into eastern cities. With little nostalgia for either Scotland or Ireland, the group eagerly took up the identity of unhyphenated Americans. Thirteen of the first 42 U.S. presidents had some Scotch-Irish roots, beginning with Andrew Jackson. The Scotch-Irish remained subsistence farmers and pioneers, working their way west to Arkansas and Oklahoma.

In isolated areas of the mountains, Scotch-Irish descendants retained some old Scottish ways of talking, and especially their old folk songs and fiddle tunes, which became the basis of bluegrass and country music. When the Great Depression of the 1930s forced southern mountain families to migrate north and west in search of work, the change was so abrupt that they suffered many of the adjustment problems of immigrants recently come from Europe. Families kept strong links to their friends and relatives back home. Stereotypes of "hillbillies" and "Okies," which developed in the early twentieth century, referred in part to these internal migrations of the Scotch-Irish.

Not all Appalachian mountain people today are of Scotch-Irish background, and few would call their food "Scotch-Irish-American." Published recipes from the eastern mountains feature "Southern" or "Mountain" cooking, and few of these dishes would seem ethnic to any other group of southerners, white or black. Appalachian cooking has also shared dishes with several Indian nations, and with **Melungeon, German-American,** and **Pennsylvania Dutch** neighbors, as well as with diverse immigrants in mining towns.

Scotch-Irish immigrants introduced the "Irish" potato to most of the United States, and potatoes are still served at almost every meal in many mountain homes. Like the Highland Scots, Welsh, and Irish immigrants, Scotch-Irish also made oatcakes and oat breads, and knew how to cook and bake on an open fire with a "girdle" or griddle. The experience of pioneering and isolated country life has lead to many dishes using small game and wild plants, as well as simple and filling one-pot suppers and fruit desserts. The *Foxfire Appalachian Cookbook* is one of a series of books produced by students who interviewed older mountain people about old-time crafts and ways of life. Most of their recipes come from Georgia and the Carolinas. Walter N. Lambert's *Kinfolks and Custard Pie: Recollections and Recipes from an East Tennesseean* is another book I used, and you can find more recipes in collections from Kentucky and Ohio.

POTATO SOUP WITH CORNMEAL

This recipe—one of three in the *Foxfire Appalachian Cookbook*—is similar to several Scottish and Irish soups that also use a mixture of milk and water. Onion and cornmeal replace the leeks and oatmeal that were used in the old country. The cook, Belle Ledford, told students that "My mother used to make it, and she didn't have any recipe. When [my daughter] Mary Ann was a little girl, every time she got sick, she'd say, 'Grandmother, make me some potato soup.' And [Mary Ann] still cooks it. When I'm at her house, I say, 'Cook *me* some potato soup.'"

Yield: 8-10 bowls
  1 quart water
  1 quart milk
  6 large potatoes
  2 stalks celery
  1 medium onion (optional)
  1/2 cup fine cornmeal
  butter (optional)
  salt and pepper
  Equipment: Soup pot, potato peeler, jar with
    cover

1. Mix milk with a quart of water in a soup pot, and put on to boil.

2. Peel potatoes, and cut them up in thin slices.

3. Add potatoes to soup.

4. Slice up celery the same thickness as potatoes.

5. Add celery to soup.

6. Cut the onion in half the long way, and peel each half. Cut once or twice more the long way, then slice about as thickly as the celery and potatoes.

7. Add the onion to the soup.

8. When potatoes are tender through, put cornmeal in a jar with water or milk. Shake until well mixed, and add to soup.

9. Let mixture cook just below a boil a few minutes more to thicken. If it gets too thick, add milk or water.

Serve with a thin slice of optional butter floated on each bowl.

APPLE STACK CAKE

Walter Lambert describes this as "the best of all East Tennessee desserts," and gives a three-page recipe with variations. Compare this recipe with the **Melungeon** stack cake. Stack cakes have also been recorded in Kentucky, Virginia, and North Carolina, and among **Pennsylvania Dutch** and **Icelandic American** cooks. Lambert is adamant about using dried tart apples, but you can substitute applesauce or a mixture of applesauce and apple butter.

NOTE: This recipe takes 24 hours.

4 cups flour
1/4 teaspoon salt
1/2 teaspoon baking soda
1 teaspoon baking powder
1/2 cup shortening
1/2 cup buttermilk
1 1/2 cups sugar
1 egg
1 1/2 teaspoons vanilla extract
1 1/2 teaspoons lemon extract
1/2 teaspoon cinnamon

Equipment: large covered saucepan, large mixing bowl, potato masher or food processor/blender, 2 medium mixing bowls, sifter, pastry blender or large fork, rolling pin, one or more cast iron skillets or 9-inch round cake pans or cookie sheets, wire racks, knife or spatula, plate, aluminum foil.

1. Simmer dried apples with cinnamon in 5 cups of water in a large covered saucepan until tender.

2. Once tender, transfer apples to large mixing bowl, add 1/2 cup sugar, and mash apples with potato masher (or use a food processor or blender).

3. Let filling cool while you make cake layers (or overnight in refrigerator).

4. Preheat oven to 350 degrees

5. In medium mixing bowl, cream together the shortening and remaining 1 cup sugar with pastry blender or large fork. Add egg and mix well.

6. In second medium mixing bowl, sift together dry ingredients (flour, salt, baking soda, and baking powder).

7. Add all but a small portion of the dry ingredients to the shortening mixture, add buttermilk and extracts, and mix well.

8. Beat in the rest of the dry ingredients to form a firm and slightly sticky dough.

9. Turn out on a floured surface and knead (see Appendix 1) in additional flour until the dough is "smooth, firm, and no longer sticky."

10. Divide dough into 6 equal parts.

11. Grease and flour cake pans, skillet, or cookie sheets.

12. Roll each portion of dough to fit a 9-inch round cake pan. (Hint: You can use the cake pans or the top to a skillet to get precisely round sheets, and add the trimmings to the next ball of dough.

13. Bake each layer until brown, about 15 minutes.

14. Cool a few minutes, and remove from skillet or cake pans to cool on a wire rack.

15. Repeat until all layers are baked.

16. Set aside the neatest looking layer for the top. Take the ugliest layer, and put it on the plate.

17. Using knife or spatula, spread bottom (ugliest) layer with 1/5 of the filling, and top with another cake layer.

18. Repeat until you put on the top (neatest) layer, which is not covered with filling. Try to arrange layers so that you have a reasonably neat and level cake.

19. Wrap in aluminum foil for at least 24 hours.

Serve in thin slices to show off the layers.

IRISH SHORTBREAD

Dorinda Monteith contributed these buttery cookies to *Recipes from Our House to Yours: The Mountain Cooker II*, which was sponsored by Living Water Ministries of Bryson City, North Carolina. I've seen another Appalachian version that added ground nuts and was cut into squares. Neither are as sweet as **Scottish-American** shortbreads, nor do they use cornstarch or rice flour to soften the texture.

Yield: 40-80 cookies
1 cup (2 sticks) butter or margarine
1/2 cup sugar
2 1/2 cups all-purpose flour

Equipment: Large mixing bowl, mixing spoon, pastry blender or large fork, 9 by 13-inch cake pan, knife

1. Preheat oven to 350 degrees.

2. In large mixing bowl, cream together butter or margarine and sugar until it is a smooth, light paste.

3. "Cut in flour with a pastry blender or fork until the consistency of fine crumbs."

4. Press lightly into ungreased cake pan.

5. Bake for 35 minutes, or until edges are lightly browned. ("These cookies will not brown on top.")

6. While still warm, cut into diamond shapes by cutting 1 1/2-inch strips the short way, then slicing diagonally, again in 1 1/2-inch intervals.

SCOTTISH-AMERICANS

About 5.4 million Americans claim Scottish descent, probably a low figure given that about 1.5 million Scots have come to America since the seventeenth century. Although early figures included **Scotch-Irish,** probably 150,000 Scots lived in the U.S. in 1785 after tens of thousands of Scots who were loyal to the British Crown (unlike the Scotch-Irish) had left for Canada. In the 1790 census, the 221,000 Scots were the second largest group of foreign-born Americans, ahead of both the Germans and the Dutch. Immigration increased in the 1840s, which lesser versions of the Irish potato famine made "the hungry forties" across northern Europe. Scottish immigration peaked in the Scottish depression of 1921-1930. Some of the latecomers worked in stone quarries, making small but visible communities in small towns in Vermont and Minnesota. A number of Scottish immigrants came to the United States via Canada, and may think of themselves as **English Canadian-Americans.**

Scottish contributions to American culture are old but not always recognized, e.g., the customs around Halloween or many plaid cloth patterns. Our breakfast oatmeal, hard candies, marmalades, and many cookies and cakes come from Scotland, as does the lamb-and-barley soup often called "Scotch Broth." We think of scones as Scottish, although there are also Welsh, Irish, and English scones. The Celtic griddle is the basis of our stovetop grill—the way modern Americans make pancakes, breakfast bacon and eggs, hamburgers and grilled-cheese sandwiches. Most Presbyterian churches are still Scottish and Scotch-Irish in membership, and there are public displays of kilt wearing and bagpiping on St. Andrew's Day (November 30) and the birthday of Robert Burns (January 25).

MRS. BOWEN'S SCOTCH SHORTBREAD

This recipe was brought to New Hampshire from Canada by Blanche Pearson and printed in Hayden Pearson's *Country Flavor Cookbook* in 1946. As compared to traditional recipes, it is much less fussy about lightening the flour with cornstarch or rice flour, and about working the butter with cool hands. The egg yolk is an Americanism, as is the word "Scotch," which in Scotland is only applied to whiskey.

Yield: 48-60 cookies
   2 cups butter (one pound, or 4 sticks), softened
   1 cup light brown sugar, firmly packed
   1 egg yolk
   pinch of salt
   4 cups sifted flour
   solid shortening to grease cookie sheets

Equipment: Large mixing bowl, pastry blender or large fork, small cup, rolling pin, cookie cutters or molds, cookie sheets, metal spatula

1. Take out the butter to soften. Preheat oven to 325 degrees.

2. Grease cookie sheet or sheets.

3. In large mixing bowl, cream the butter with a pastry blender or large fork. Add sugar and cream thoroughly.

4. Separate the egg, and beat the yolk in a small cup.

5. Cream the egg yolk and salt into the butter-sugar mixture.

6. Now add the flour and work it in. Knead (see Appendix 1) only until the flour is evenly mixed.

7. Roll out to about 3/8 inch thickness.

8. Cut into squares or fancy shapes. (Some recipes suggest pressing the dough into buttered and floured cookie molds, or making decorated edges with the fingers.)

9. Place dough shapes on greased cookie sheets.

10. Place cookie sheets in oven and bake at 325 degrees for about 30 minutes. These don't turn brown except at the edges.

Serve with home-canned fruit or afternoon tea. Can bake ahead and keep in tins.

Oatcakes

Mrs. George Lehrke, the American-born wife of a Scottish quarryman of St. Cloud, Minnesota, contributed this recipe to the *Minnesota Centennial Cook Book: 100 Years of Good Cooking* (1958), which was edited by Virginia Huck and Ann H. Anderson. These traditional Scottish oatcakes are a kind of cracker. Mrs. Lehrke's big change is to use wheat flour, which makes them a little easier to roll, but tougher once baked. (I'd recommend "quick oats" and cake flour.) Although some people in Scotland cook oatcakes in the oven like this, the traditional way to make them was on an iron griddle over a stove top. Stovetop oatcakes were generally rolled out the size of dinner plates, and cut into quarters called "farls" before cooking. Ironically, many of the traditional techniques and equipment for mak-

ing oatcakes are similar to those used by Scandinavian-Americans in Minnesota to make a potato bread called lefse (see **Norwegian-Americans**).

Yield: 30-40 rounds
   4 cups oatmeal
   1 scant cup flour
   1 teaspoon salt
   1 1/2 teaspoons baking powder
   1 heaping tablespoon lard

Equipment: Large mixing bowl, mixing spoon, small frying pan, rolling pin, rolling board or work surface, cookie cutter, 2 baking sheets

1. Measure the oatmeal and flour into a large mixing bowl, and mix in the salt and baking powder. Make a little hole in the center of the mixture.

2. Place lard in small frying pan and melt over medium-high heat. Dribble the melted lard into the hole in the oatmeal mixture.

3. Pour on a cup of warm water and stir to make a stiff paste. This tends to harden as the oatmeal absorbs the water, so you may have to add more water as you go along.

4. Dust rolling board or work surface with flour or oatmeal, and turn out the mixture. Roll it into a ball. (You're not really kneading, just mashing all the ingredients together.)

5. Flour a rolling pin and roll out "very thin" (about 1/4 inch).

6. Using a cookie cutter, cut out the cookies and lay out on *ungreased* cookie sheets.

7. Place in oven and bake at 350 degrees for about 15-20 minutes, until the edges curl slightly. (They may still look floury and uncooked.)

Serve with soups or with fried fish for breakfast, or warmed up and buttered and sweetened with honey and cheese. Oat cakes can be stored in a tight tin, and toasted or reheated in a low oven to crisp them again.

Scotch Pancakes (Bannocks)

Here's a fancied-up bannock, still cooked on a stovetop griddle, but with a typically American substitution of cornmeal for part of the oats and a cake's worth of sweetening. The recipe was contributed by Elsie Seaton of Whitehorn, California, to the 1975 *National Grange Bicentennial Year Cookbook.*

1 cup quick-cooking oatmeal
1 cup cornmeal
1/3 cup toasted diced almonds
1/2 teaspoon salt
1/2 teaspoon ground ginger
1 tablespoon brown sugar
2 cups buttermilk
1 tablespoon molasses
1 teaspoon grated lemon peel
2 eggs
2 tablespoons melted butter
more butter and jelly to spread on finished
    pancakes

Equipment: Large mixing bowl, mixing spoon, medium mixing bowl, heavy frying pan or griddle, spatula

1. Combine oatmeal, cornmeal, almonds, salt, ginger, and brown sugar in a large mixing bowl.

2. Combine buttermilk and molasses in a medium mixing bowl.

3. Grate lemon peel and add to buttermilk mixture.

4. Beat eggs and add to buttermilk mixture.

5. Melt butter and add to buttermilk mixture.

6. Add buttermilk mixture to oatmeal mixture and mix well.

7. Grease a heavy frying pan or griddle and place on oven burner.

8. When pan is hot, spoon on small rounds of batter about 1/4 inch thick.

9. Fry each round for about 10 minutes on one side, then turn with spatula.

10. Fry each pancake 5 minutes longer on other side, or until done.

11. Remove cakes from pan, cut or fold in half, and spread with butter and jelly.

"May be served with creamed chipped beef, shredded ham, or slivered chicken."

The Highlander's Soup

Jim Warren submitted this recipe to an online "International Cookbook" developed by "Youth Against Racism" at Suffern, New York, High School. Warren wrote that "The recipe below was brought from the Scottish Highlands by my mother's parents when they arrived in America sometime between 1900 and 1910. My grandfather arrived as an indentured worker—his employer paid for his boat passage to the USA in exchange for his labor at low wages for seven years. He lived in western Massachusetts in a company-owned boarding house and saved his wages. At the end of three years, he paid the boat passage for my grandmother and her sister to the USA."

NOTE: This recipe takes two days.

2 cups dried lentils or peas
3 pounds ham or beef bone ("whatever was
    cheaper")
1/2 cup chopped dandelion greens (or diced
    celery, if available)
1 cup carrots
1 small onion
1 tablespoon oil
2 tablespoons flour
2 teaspoons salt
1/4 teaspoon pepper

Equipment: Small bowl, large stock pot, knife, medium skillet, spatula

1. Wash lentils or peas and soak in small bowl overnight in cold water.

2. Drain lentils or peas and place in large stock pot. Add the bones and 3 or 4 quarts of water.

3. Bring to a boil, reduce heat, and simmer 2 hours.

4. After the 2 hours, chop greens or celery and add to soup.

5. Peel and chop carrots and add to soup.

6. Remove bones from soup, cut off any meat, dice it, and return diced meat to the soup without bones.

7. Halve, peel, and chop onion.

8. Heat oil in medium skillet and sauté onions.

9. Add flour, salt, and pepper. Mix well with spatula.

10. Slowly add 1 cup hot soup stock to onion mixture, stirring over heat until the mixture becomes thick and smooth.

11. Return thickened mixture to rest of hot soup and mix well.

SEA ISLAND CREOLES

See GULLAH (GEECHEE, SEA ISLANDERS)

SEMINOLE AND MICCOSUKEE

These two different tribes share many events and cultures in Florida. Most of the approximately 16,000 Seminoles now live in Oklahoma, with a few more in Mexico. The Florida Seminole and Miccosukee number perhaps 1,500 together, but they have an important history and presence. Although most history books claim that neither tribe entered Florida until after Spanish settlement, more recent evidence links the present Seminole and Miccosukee to ancestral Florida Indians. Both tribes were originally part of the loose **Creek** federation, but split off to become separate tribes. The Seminoles speak a Muskogean language like most of the Creek tribes, but the word "Seminole" may come from the Spanish "cimarrón," which was used both for escaped African slaves who joined the tribe and in the general sense of "pioneers" or "frontiersmen." Between 1817 and 1860, the U.S. government fought three wars with the Florida Seminoles, primarily because they harbored escaped slaves. After each war, thousands of Seminoles were deported to Oklahoma, but the remaining Florida Seminoles can justly claim never to have been defeated by the United States in war.

The Miccosukee Indians speak a Hitchiti language. They are known for brilliantly colored patchwork clothing and run a restaurant on the Tamiami Trail (U.S. 41). The popularity of fried foods and the use of sweet potatoes and black-eyed peas are part of the African-American heritage of these tribes. You may also find Seminole and Miccosukee recipes for fried meat pies, black-bean fritters that may be related to **Nigerian-American** accra, wild plants, and fish and game.

SOFKEE

Sofkee was originally a soupy version of hominy grits served among all the **Creek** tribes as a social drink like tea or coffee. It is still a part of Seminole daily life in Florida and Oklahoma. This unusual recipe comes from the letters column of the online version of the *Seminole Tribune* at <www.seminoletribe.com>. "Other variations (instead of rice) could be quick grits, oatmeal, cracked corn, or coarse grits. Cooking times would vary according to the size of grains being used." In my testing, the proportions below work best for instant rice. Long-grain rice required more water and longer cooking times.

2 cups rice
1 teaspoon baking soda

Equipment: Large stock pot, spoon

1. In large stock pot, boil 5 quarts of water and stir in 2 cups of white rice.

2. Cook for 10 minutes with constant stirring.

3. Add a teaspoon of baking soda and continue to cook for another 5 minutes.

Serve in mugs.

PUMPKIN BREAD

This Seminole recipe appears in *Jane Nickerson's Florida Cookbook*. Use the small sugar pumpkins for the best flavor, and allow time to cook and cool the pumpkin beforehand, and to let the cake set overnight before slicing.

NOTE: This recipe takes 2 days.

Yield: one loaf of 8 thick slices
    solid shortening to grease pan
    2 cups flour
    3/4 cup sugar
    1 tablespoon baking powder
    1 teaspoon salt
    1/4 teaspoon mace or nutmeg
    1/2 cup chopped pecans
    2 eggs
    1 cup mashed, cooked pumpkin or sweet
        potatoes
    1/2 cup milk
    3 tablespoons oil

Equipment: Medium mixing bowl, mixing spoon, whisk, small bowl, 4 1/2 by 8 1/2-inch baking pan, paring knife, foil or plastic wrap

1. Preheat oven to 350 degrees.

2. Grease baking pan.

3. Stir together dry ingredients (flour, sugar, baking powder, salt, mace or nutmeg, and pecans) in a medium mixing bowl.

4. Using whisk, beat the eggs in a small bowl, and blend in pumpkin, milk, and oil.

5. Add this mixture, all at one time, to the dry ingredients. Stir only enough to blend the ingredients.

6. Pour into the greased pan.

7. Place baking pan in oven and "bake 70 to 75 minutes, or until a paring knife inserted in the center comes out clean."

8. Remove from oven, cool 10 minutes in the pan, then remove and cool completely.

9. Wrap in foil or plastic wrap and store overnight before slicing.

INDIAN FRIED PUMPKIN BREAD

This is a sweet fry bread served at the Miccosukee Restaurant, and also at the Florida Folk Festival The recipe comes from *Famous Florida Cracker Cookin' and Other Favorites* by B.J. Altshul, with some changes from online recipes at <www.seminoletribe.com> and <www.miccosukeetribe.com/recipes.html>, and from a Miccosukee recipe from *Native Peoples* magazine (Winter, 1997). This bread also used to be made with sweet potatoes.

Yield: 24 cakes

CAUTION: HOT OIL USED.

    4 cups self-rising flour
    1 tablespoon baking powder (if using regular
        flour)
    1 16-ounce can pumpkin "not pumpkin pie
        filling"
    1 teaspoon salt
    1 cup white or brown sugar
    2 cups corn oil

Equipment: Large mixing bowl, mixing spoon, rolling pin, deep heavy frying pan, long-handled skimmer, screen to cover pan, paper towels

1. In large mixing bowl, combine 3 1/2 cups of flour with the baking powder, pumpkin, and sugar.

2. Blend well and knead briefly (see Appendix I), forking in the rest of the flour if needed to make a smooth dough. Refrigerate for 2 hours to firm up the dough.

3. Divide dough into fourths and knead each portion on a floured board or cloth for a few minutes.

4. Using floured rolling pin, roll each portion into a cylinder 8 to 10 inches long.

5. Cut each cylinder into 6 slices.

6. Flour each slice and form into a cake no more than 1/2 inch thick. Dough cooks faster if thinner.

7. Heat 3/4-inch of oil in a deep, heavy frying pan until a bit of dough begins to bubble immediately.

8. Fry the cakes in hot oil. Turn after 2 or 3 minutes, when bottom side is brown. You can reduce spattering by covering the pan with a screen.

9. When both sides are brown, remove from pan with skimmer, drain on paper towels, and serve.

Serve immediately with butter, honey, or maple syrup.

SENECA

See IROQUOIS

SERBIAN-AMERICANS (INCLUDING MONTENEGRINS)

After years of civil wars following the breakup of Yugoslavia in the early 1990s, Serbian-Americans are today somewhat on the defensive, especially since the 1999 NATO bombing of Serbia by American planes and crews. This was not always the case. The first large numbers of Serbs to immigrate to the U.S. came from homes in what is now Croatia, and settled among **Croatian-Americans**, with whom they shared a common language (though Serbo-Croatian is written with a Cyrillic alphabet like Russian, and Croato-Serbian is written with a Roman alphabet, like Italian or English). In the large group that came from 1880 to 1910, most were rural people and worked initially as miners and steel workers. Probably the first distinctly Serbian neighborhoods were in Pittsburgh. Tensions with Croatian-Americans increased in response to events in Europe and old religious differences. Serbian immigration resumed after World War II, when refugees from the war and the Communist take-over of Yugoslavia fled to this country.

The 1990 U.S. census estimated only 117,000 Serbian-Americans, but probably most of the 258,000 who gave their ancestry as Yugoslavian were Serbian-Americans as well. Thus there are probably 300,000 to 400,000 Serbian-Americans, most of whom would recognize the dishes listed in this book under **Albanian-Americans,** Croatian-Americans, **Slovene-Americans,** and **Macedonian-Americans.** Serbian-Americans enjoy many desserts that are in common use from Greece and Turkey to the Czech Republic. One of the most characteristic desserts is a difficult rolled walnut strudel known as potica or povitica. This is dish is made by groups of women, who stretch out the dough on a floured bedsheet over a dining room table. Other Serbian-American recipes include lamb sausages, mousaka with potatoes, cheesy casseroles (some baked in pastry shells), and rolled pastry desserts.

CUCUMBER SALAD

Darlene Gakovich of Madison, Wisconsin, submitted this recipe to *Ethnic Cooking Wisconsin Style* (1982). This kind of cucumber-yogurt salad defines the widest boundaries of the historic Turkish empires, from India to Serbia, with the garlic and hot pepper being the distinctly Serbian accent. Ms. Gakovich says that oil and vinegar may be substituted for sour half-and-half as a dressing.

Yield: 4-6 servings

3-4 medium cucumbers, young, without
   large seeds
salt
1 clove garlic
pepper to taste
1 small green hot pepper (optional)
1 1/2 cups sour half-and-half or whole milk
   yogurt
fresh chopped dill

Equipment: Vegetable peeler, knife, medium mixing bowl, mixing spoon

1. Peel cucumbers and slice thinly.

2. Sprinkle cucumbers with salt and let stand 15 minutes.

3. Peel and mince garlic.

4. If using hot pepper, cut off the top, slit down one side, and strip out the pith and seeds.

5. Mince hot pepper. (After handling hot pepper, wash hands carefully and avoid touching eyes or sensitive areas.)

6. Press cucumbers with hands to squeeze out liquid.

7. Add garlic, pepper to taste, and optional hot pepper to medium mixing bowl and mix well.

8. Chop dill.

9. Mix in sour half-and-half or yogurt and fresh dill and mix well to blend all ingredients.

Serve chilled as a side dish or salad.

JUVECH

You will also see recipes for "djuvéc" and "gjuwetsch," all versions of juvech that resulted from attempts to write down a word in English that is normally written in a Cyrillic (Russian) alphabet. This rice casserole is common across the Balkan countries, but has served Serbian-Americans especially well. Desanka Knezevic of Madison and Nikola Svircev of Middleton separately submitted this recipe to *Ethnic Cooking Wisconsin Style* (1982), an American Cancer Society fund-raiser. This recipe has been Ameri-

canized by precooking the meat and vegetables on top of the stove, which makes for much shorter baking times. Traditional recipes might be baked for hours, with a layer of sour cream slathered on for the final baking.

2 pounds pork shoulder meat roast, cut into
   large cubes
1/2 cup vegetable oil
1 pound onions (4 large)
5-6 large green peppers
1 medium eggplant
2 heaping tablespoons chopped parsley
paprika
3 pounds tomatoes
1/2 cup uncooked rice
salt and pepper to taste
1 pint sour cream

Equipment: Knife, large skillet, metal spoon, large casserole dish with cover

1. Cut meat into 2-inch pieces, place in large skillet with a small amount of oil and cook until brown. Once browned, remove pork from skillet and set aside.

2. Halve, peel, and dice onions. (Wear swim goggles to avoid tears.)

3. Remove pork from pan. Add onions to skillet and sauté until soft, about 5-7 minutes.

4. Cut tops and bottoms from green peppers. Remove cores, slit down one side and slice off pith. Remove stems and cut peppers into strips.

5. Cube eggplant.

6. Add green peppers to onion and sauté slightly.

7. Chop parsley.

8. Add eggplant, parsley, and paprika to taste, mixing well after each addition.

9. Oil a large casserole dish.

10. Slice tomatoes.

11. Layer the bottom of the casserole dish with 1/3 of the tomato slices. Salt and pepper lightly the tomatoes and each succeeding layer.

12. Layer on half the mixed vegetables.

13. Layer on the meat.

14. Then add another 1/3 of the tomato slices.

15. Pour on the rice as evenly as possible.

16. Cover with the remainder of the mixed vegetables.

17. Top with the remaining tomatoes.

18. Pour 3/4 cup water over the whole pot.

19. Drizzle on the remaining oil.

20. Bake covered at 450 degrees for 30 minutes.

21. Turn down to 325 degrees for 15–20 minutes, or until done.

Serve with sour cream as a garnish.

SHAWNEE

The U.S. Census Bureau estimates that about 6,600 Shawnee live in the U.S., as well as almost 1,000 "Cherokee Shawnee." Many other Indian people also have Shawnee ancestors. Over the many dislocations of this much-moved tribe, Shawnee people made lives and families with neighboring tribes, especially the Delaware (who spoke a related language), Seneca, **Cherokee**, and **Creek**.

The Shawnee appear briefly in textbooks as the tribe of Tecumseh, the brilliant organizer who tried to unite Indian tribes from Florida to Canada to resist American expansion after the American Revolution. The plan fell apart when his brother, Tenskwatawa, a spiritual leader and prophet, prematurely attacked United States troops at Tippecanoe, Indiana, in 1811. Tecumseh died in battle as a British brigadier general in 1813.

As with many Indian tribes, the history of the Shawnee began thousands of years earlier. By about 1600, the Shawnee were a relatively small tribe in the Ohio Valley, with an Algonkian language related to that of the Delaware. As they were squeezed between the more powerful **Iroquois** and Cherokee, they broke up into three subgroups that scattered as far as Florida, and had to move often. Tecumseh's plans grew from the experience of a small tribe losing its land many times, and the pattern continued until all three bands of Shawnee were finally forced to Oklahoma in the 1870s.

CHEEMEE

Cheemee is one of the best recipes in this book! This traditional treat for kids is made today by Stands Alone in the Moon Wilson-McSwain of Cincinnati for her grandchildren; she wrote it up in the April 3, 1999, issue of "Turtle Tracks," an online magazine for Native American youth at < http://www.radparker.com/tamakoce/ turtletracks > (the site is now being moved to < www.turtletrack.org >). "Cheemee" is a child's mispronunciation of "Ah-Gee Chim Buh-Gee," the recipe Ms. Wilson-McSwain adapted from the journal of her Shawnee-Cherokee great-great-grandmother, Morning Light.

Yield: about 16 brownie-like squares

1 1/4 cups flour
1/4 cup extra fine cornmeal
1/3 cup brown sugar
1/2 cup white sugar
1 stick butter (1/2 cup)
8 tablespoons honey or maple syrup
1 egg
1/2 cup coarse chopped nuts (walnut, hickory, or pecan)
1/2 cup golden raisins
1/2 cup chopped dates (optional: dried berries or cherries)

Equipment: Square brownie pan or round cake pan, blender if needed to regrind cornmeal, spoon, spatula, toothpick, knife

1. If you can't buy extra-fine cornmeal, run white cornmeal through a blender for a few minutes.

2. Preheat oven to 350 degrees.

3. Butter the bottom only of a cake pan or brownie pan.

4. Mix all ingredients with a spoon until the batter is thicker than a brownie batter.

5. Pour evenly into pan. Level dough with a spatula.

6. Bake for 35-40 minutes until golden brown and a toothpick inserted in the center comes out clean.

7. Cut into small bars and remove from pan while still warm.

Serve like a brownie when cooled down and chewy.

FRIED CORN SOUP

This is another recipe from Stands Alone in the Moon Wilson-McSwain; she e-mailed it to me after I asked about the Cheemee (see above). Compare this recipe to the **Chitimacha** macque choux.

Yield: serves 6
2 cups fresh corn
2 onions
hot peppers to taste (optional)
2-3 tablespoons butter
3-4 boiling potatoes
3 cups milk
salt and pepper

1. Chop the bacon or pork into small pieces.

2. Fry until browned on all sides.

3. Cut corn off ears with a sharp knife.

4. Halve, peel, and chop onions. (Wear swim goggles to avoid tears.) If using hot peppers, cut off tops, slit down the side, remove pith and seeds with a teaspoon, and cut into fine dice.

5. Add butter to pan, then add corn, onions, and peppers, if using. Cook slowly until onions are transparent or lightly golden.

6. Peel and dice potatoes to small cubes.

7. Add the potatoes and 2 cups boiling water.

8. Heat milk near to boiling in a separate pot.

9. When the potatoes are "fork soft," stir in the hot milk, salt, and pepper.

SIOUX (DAKOTA, LAKHOTA, AND NAKOTA)

The Sioux include at least 10 subgroups and have rights on 13 different reservations in 5 states. They are the third or fourth largest tribe in the United States, with more than 100,000 members, and some bands also live in Canada. About half the U.S. Sioux have migrated to cities. They are perhaps the most widely stereotyped of American Indians, being well known for their victory over General George Custer at the Little Big Horn in 1876; the massacre of 153 Dakotas at Wounded Knee Creek in 1889; and their takeover of the town of Wounded Knee, South Dakota, in 1973, which led to the killings of an Indian and two FBI agents in 1975 and to the conviction and incarceration of Leonard Peltier. The characteristic feathered "war bonnet" of certain Sioux war chiefs is the stereotypical Indian headdress, adopted briefly by many other tribes during the pan-Indian movement of the 1910s and 1920s, but enduringly by politicians and cartoonists.

The name "Sioux" is a French version of the **Ojibway** term "nadouessioux," meaning "poisonous snakes." This term has been generally replaced by their own name for themselves, a word meaning "the Allies," which is pronounced as "Lakhota," "Nakota," or "Dakota" in the eastern, middle, and western dialects, respectively. The Lakhota are the largest group, including four of the original seven sub-groups, the "seven council fires" ("Oceti Sakowin"). Other Siouan languages are spoken all over

North America, suggesting that the group has a long and complicated history. Despite the stereotype of the Sioux as warriors of the plains, most were settled farmers in the Midwest at the time of European settlement. They were pushed onto the plains by the Ojibway, who had traded earlier for firearms with the Europeans, and only gradually developed the horsemanship, buffalo hunting, and moveable teepees they needed to live off the buffalo herds of the plains, a lifestyle from which they were removed in the 1870s.

BILLY MILLS' SIOUX FRY BREAD

Billy Mills, who won the gold medal in the 10,000 meter run at the 1964 Olympics, gave this recipe to the *Olympic Cookbook from Mazola Corn Oil* (1987). While all Native Americans have enjoyed fry bread since it spread along with inter-tribal pow-wow movement of the early 1900s, the Sioux apparently had it several generations earlier. Fry bread can also be cut into squares, diamonds, or doughnut shapes.

CAUTION: Hot oil used.

Yield: 16 frybreads, serves 8
  2 cups unsifted flour
  2 teaspoons baking powder
  1/2 teaspoon salt
  3/4 cup milk
  1 quart (approximately) Mazola corn oil

Equipment: Heavy skillet or saucepan with sides at least 3-4 inches high, deep-fry thermometer, tongs, paper towels, large bowl

1. In a large bowl, stir together flour, baking powder, and salt.

2. With fork, gradually stir in milk and 1 tablespoon corn oil to form a soft dough.

3. On lightly floured surface, knead dough about 5 minutes or until smooth (see Appendix 1).

4. Roll out dough into a thin rope. Cut dough into 16 pieces; shape each into a ball.

5. Flour surface, and hands or a rolling pin, and pat or roll each ball to a 4-inch round, about 1/8-inch thick. (Rounds will be uneven.)

6. Pour corn oil into deep, heavy 10-inch skillet or saucepan, to a depth of about 1 inch, filling no more than 1/3 full.

7. Heat over medium heat to 375 degrees.

8. Carefully add 2 dough rounds at a time, pressing down sections of dough with tongs or slotted spoon to submerge.

9. Fry 1 to 2 minutes on each side or until puffed and golden brown.

10. Drain on paper towels.

Serve immediately with jam, stew, or berry topping.

WOJAPI PUDDING

Wojapi is a traditional Lakhota whipped berry treat that has become a popular topping for fry bread. It was originally made with wild berries or chokecherries, but now can involve strawberries or peaches. Elaine Kelty of the Northside YWCA Child Development Center submitted this version to the *Ethnic Food Festival Cookbook: Favorite Recipes of Title XX and Head Start Child Care Sites* (1990), prepared by the City of Chicago Department of Human Services. Indians of almost 100 tribes have migrated to Chicago.

Yield: serves 20
  1 Number 10 can purple plums (104 ounces) or about 7 15-ounce cans)
  3 tablespoons cornstarch

Equipment: Blender

1. Blend purple plums in blender until smooth.

2. Add a little water to cornstarch to make a paste.

3. Stir into plum puree.

4. Heat until mixture is thick.

5. Cool.

BOILED MEAT

Jeweler Nelda Schrupp contributed this Nakota recipe to *Artistic Tastes: Favorite Recipes of Native American Artists*. It has the mild flavors of much traditional Native American cooking, which took its subtlety from the variations of the animals hunted and the plants gathered.

1 1/2 pounds chuck roast
6 medium potatoes, peeled and quartered
half a large onion
salt and pepper

1. Cut meat into 1- to 2-inch cubes.

2. Peel and quarter potatoes.

3. Halve and peel the onion.

4. Boil meat, salt, pepper, and onion until the meat is tender.

5. Add potatoes, then boil until done.

"Serve the meat and potatoes on a plate with the meat juice. Mash the potatoes on your plate and mix the meat juice in like gravy. Serve with fry bread and enjoy."

INDIAN POPOVERS

Another fry-bread variation popular at the Pine Ridge Oglala (Lakhota) Reservation pow-wows is this turnover recipe which was posted on an Internet site by Liz Cornelius.

1 recipe fry bread dough (see Step 4 of the
   fry bread recipe given above)
1 pound coarse-ground beef
1 jalapeño pepper
1 onion
1 package taco seasoning
1 can green enchilada sauce
1 can pinto beans, drained
taco sauce (store bought), as desired.
oil for frying, about a quart

Equipment: Skillet

1. In a skillet, brown the ground beef, then drain off the grease.

2. Chop the jalapeño pepper, first removing pith and seeds if you don't like too much heat.

3. Halve and peel the onion, slice the long way, then across the mince.

4. Add the jalapeño, onion, taco seasoning, enchilada sauce, and a half can (6 ounces) of water.

5. Cook this mixture according to the instructions on the taco seasoning package.

6. Add the pinto beans and heat through.

7. Remove from heat and allow to cool.

8. Portion out the fry bread dough so that you end up with 8-inch-diameter circles of rolled dough 1/4- to 1/2-inch thick. (Probably dividing Billy Mills' recipe, above, into about 8 pieces.)

9. Spoon some of the meat mixture onto half a rolled-out piece of dough, leaving a good margin to seal; sprinkle with the shredded cheese (if desired), and fold the other half over to form a half-moon-shaped turnover.

10. Seal the edges by crimping with the tines of a fork.

11. Deep fry the popover as you would the fry bread (until golden brown).

12. Drain on paper towels.

Serve with lettuce, tomatoes, more onions, and taco sauce.

STUFFED PUMPKIN

Amythest Otis contributed this contemporary Lakota recipe to *Red Beans & Rice and Other Rock 'n' Roll Recipes* by Johnny Otis. Amythest says that the Lakhota people remembered wild rice from their origins near the Great Lakes, and traded for it after migrating to the plains.

1 5-pound pumpkin
2 teaspoons salt
1/2 teaspoon dry mustard
2 tablespoons vegetable oil or rendered fat
1 pound venison, buffalo, or beef (optional)
1 chopped onion
1 cup wild rice, cooked

3 eggs, beaten
1 tablespoon dried sage, crushed
1 teaspoon black pepper

Equipment: Roasting pan, large skillet

1. Cook wild rice according to package directions. It doesn't take much wild rice to make up a cup cooked.

2. Preheat oven to 350 degrees.

3. Cut off top of pumpkin and remove the seeds.

4. Run a fork over the entire inside surface of pumpkin, creating grooves in the flesh.

5. Rub 1 teaspoon salt and mustard into the grooves.

6. Heat oil in a large skillet. Add meat and onions, and cook over medium heat until brown.

7. Take skillet off heat, and stir in rice, eggs, remaining salt, sage, and pepper.

8. Stuff mixture into pumpkin.

9. Put a little water in a shallow baking pan, and place pumpkin in pan.

10. Bake 1 1/2 hours, adding water to pan as needed to avoid scorching.

11. Remove from oven, cut in wedges, and serve.

CORN BALLS (WAHUWAPA WASNA)

This dish is a kind of vegetarian pemmican, combining corn, fat, and dried fruit into something like a modern power bar—easy to carry, packing a lot of nutrition in a few bites, and durable enough for storage or trade. The recipe is a Dakota version posted by Louis Garcia on the Native Technology Internet Web site, with details from a Lakota version called "wagmiza wasna."

ground dried flour corn kernels (to make 2 cups yellow cornmeal)
dried chokecherries or juneberries (saskatoons) (or 1 cup raisins)

tallow or lard (or substitute water) or 1 cup melted suet or butter
1/2 cup sugar, optional

Equipment: Hand grinder (if using dried flour corn), large skillet or shallow pan

1. Soak dried berries or raisins

2. If starting from dried corn, grind the kernels in a hand grinder.

3. Toast cornmeal in a large skillet or a shallow pan in a 350-degree oven, stirring so it won't burn, for about 30 minutes. Cool.

4. You can grind the dried berries or raisins in a blender, or use them whole.

5. "Mix the corn and berries together at a ratio of 4 corn to 1 berry."

6. Put fat in a frying pan and lightly brown the mixture. "*Note:* The old timers at this point would put more tallow/lard in the pan."

7. Add sugar if using. Cool until the fat begins to congeal.

8. Dig into the corn mixture with fingers to form an elongated (4 fingers wide) mass. "That's why they call it in Dakota Wahuwapa (corn cob)." You can also work them into 3-inch disks, or press them into an 8 by 8 cake pan, freeze, and cut into squares.

9. Dry them in the sun for later storage, or refrigerate or freeze.

Serve as a snack or candy-like dessert.

BEANS 'N BACON

Terry and David Graywolf of the Pine Ridge Oglala Lakota Reservation described this recipe as a "Good ol' Rez' staple"; they posted it on the Native American Technology and Art Web site. Beans cooked without soaking give many people gas. As the Greywolfs note, "You may want to purchase some air freshener when you are out buying the beans and the bacon."

Yield: serves 5-10, or "feeds my husband, who is 6'2, 240 pounds, for a good 3–4 days."

2 bags pinto beans
1 pound bacon

1. Rinse the beans.

2. Boil the beans in water to cover by several inches for 45-60 minutes, "until nearly done. . . just taste 'em."

3. Add bacon and boil about another half hour or so, more or less.

Serve with fry bread. "If you make enough, you won't have to cook again for a month."

SLAVONIANS

See CROATIAN-AMERICANS

SLOVAK-AMERICANS

The 1990 census estimates 1.9 million Americans claiming Slovak descent, mostly from the 500,000 immigrants who came to the U.S. between 1880 and 1920. Although Slovak and Czech are mutually intelligible dialects, Slovaks and Czechs have been separated politically in Europe for most of the last 1,000 years. In 1918, a unified Czechoslovakia was set up, and Slovak-Americans generally supported it. During World War II, the Germans again divided the two countries. Czechoslovakia's brief post-war democracy was ended by a Communist coup in 1948. Democracy returned with the peaceful "velvet revolution" of 1989. In 1992, the Slovaks voted to secede and an independent Slovak Republic was established.

Slovak-Americans are the second-largest Slavic group (after Polish-Americans), but are not very visible outside the industrial and mining areas where they first settled, especially in Pennsylvania. As immigrants, they were lumped with **Hungarian-Americans** as "hunkies," and later with **Czech-Americans**. Some joined churches or organizations with **Carpatho-Rusyn-Americans** or **Ukrainian-Americans**. Slovak-American food partakes of all the cuisines of the countries surrounding the Slovak Republic, although probably least of Hungarian-style dishes. This probably reflects lingering resentment of the forced use of the Hungarian language after 1848, which gave rise to more Slovak national feeling. Slovak-American food has a heartiness suitable to hard-working people, leading one recent cookbook author to call it "Soul Food." However, Slovak-Americans also have equal claims on Czech-American kolaches, **Polish-American** pierogi (which they call pirohy), Ukrainian-American stuffed breads, and soups from all over. Complicated Easter and Christmas dishes are a big part of the Slovak-American heritage.

SNITCHLEH (OLD FASHIONED HAMBURGERS)

Yield: serves 4 as a main dish

June Paola submitted these simple cutlets to the *St. Mary of Carmel Ethnic Cookbook* (1984), which was published in Dunmore, Pennsylvania.

1 pound ground beef
1 small onion
1 cup bread crumbs
1 egg
flour to coat patties, about 1 cup
shortening to fry patties, about 1/4 cup

Equipment: Grater or food processor with grating blade, heavy skillet with high sides, waxed paper

1. Halve, peel, and grate onion. (Wear swim goggles to avoid tears.)

2. Mix onion, 1/4 cup water, salt and pepper to taste, and all other ingredients, except flour and shortening.

3. Form into patties.

4. Spread flour on waxed paper and flour patties on both sides, patting between your hands to remove excess flour.

5. Heat shortening over medium heat in a heavy skillet with high sides.

6. Fry patties slowly in shortening till lightly brown.

"Serve with home fries or scalloped potatoes and a vegetable."

SLOVAK COOKIES

This recipe is from the "Ethnic Dishes" section of *St. Elizabeth Seton Presents Treasured Recipes* (1981), which was published by the St. Elizabeth Seton Church in North Huntington, Pennsylvania.

Yield: 25 squares
    1 cup margarine
    1 cup sugar
    2 egg yolks
    1 teaspoon vanilla
    1/4 teaspoon allspice
    2 cups sifted flour
    1 cup walnuts (broken pieces)
    1/2 cup strawberry jam
    shortening to grease pan

Equipment: Pastry blender or large fork, 8-inch square brownie pan, small bowl

1. Soften margarine almost to room temperature and cream with sugar until light and fluffy.

2. Separate egg yolks by pouring from shell to shell over a cup to catch the whites.

3. Beat the egg yolks and vanilla in a small bowl, then beat into the sugar mixture.

4. Beat in flour and allspice.

5. Stir in walnuts.

6. Spoon half the dough into the pan and spread evenly.

7. Spread with the strawberry jam, and top with the remaining dough.

8. Bake in a 325-degree oven for 1 hour, until lightly browned.

9. Cool in the pan, then cut into 1 1/2-inch squares.

SLOVAKIAN NUT CANDY

This simple, delicious recipe is from *Homemade Candy by the Food Editors of Farm Journal*. It cooks quickly, then hardens quickly as well, so read the recipe a few times before you make it.

CAUTION: Melted sugar burns and sticks to skin.

Yield: 1/2 pound of candies, about 16 pieces (more if you cut them smaller)
    1 cup ground nuts (or somewhat more to grind)
    1 cup sugar
    butter to grease cutting board, rolling pin, and spatula

Equipment: Rolling pin, large sharp knife to cut candy, cutting board, spatula, heavy skillet

1. If starting from whole nutmeats, put through food chopper or cut with the steel blade of a food processor and measure 1 cup. Butter spatula, rolling pin, and cutting board.

2. Place sugar in a heavy 10-inch skillet and stir over medium heat until sugar melts and turns a light golden brown. (This can be as soon as all the sugar is melted.)

3. Remove from heat at once.

4. Stir in nuts and pour onto buttered board.

5. Being careful not to touch the hot candy, roll with buttered rolling pin until very thin, about 17 by 6 inches if you can. The candy tends

to stick and ride up the rolling pin. Don't use your hands to push it down; use the spatula. Rolled out, the candy will be 1/8 inch thick. If it cools down and hardens before fully rolled out, don't worry.

6. Cut at once into strips 2 inches wide.

7. Loosen strips from board with buttered spatula and cut with sharp knife on the diagonal to make diamonds.

Serve from candy dish, or as vertical decorations on pies or cakes.

HALUSKY

Betty Cerrone submitted this recipe to the *St. Mary of Carmel Ethnic Cookbook* (1984), which was published in Dunmore, Pennsylvania. This dish reminds us how a recipe is really only a blueprint. Although it lists only three ingredients, it requires two hours of semi-attentive cooking. Haluski was originally the name of the noodles, and traditional recipes were made from scratch. The original name of the dish with cabbage is "halusky kaposta."

3-pound green cabbage
1 1/2 pounds butter or margarine
1 pound wide noodles

Equipment: Large pot

1. Halve, core, and chop or shred cabbage.

2. Melt butter or margarine in a large pot, add cabbage, and cook slowly for about 1 1/2 to 2 hours. Cover so the cabbage steams and fries, but stir often to keep from burning.

3. Cook noodles according to package directions.

4. Combine drained noodles with cabbage mixture.

Serve as a side dish with roast meat.

BABA

Helen Burdej Jones submitted this recipe to the Internet Web site at <www.Iarelative.com>, which has many recipes and links for Slovak, Czech, and Carpatho-Rusyn genealogy.

3 large potatoes, grated
1/4 pound of bacon, cut in small pieces
1/2 large onion, diced
1 egg
1 cup barley, cooked in salt water and drained
1/2 teaspoon salt
1/8 teaspoon pepper

Equipment: Grater or food processor with grating disk, 9 by 13-inch pan, soup pot

1. Put barley in a soup pot with 4 cups water and simmer 45 minutes.

2. Peel and dice onion.

3. Fry bacon and onion until brown.

4. Drain and cool barley.

5. Peel and grate potatoes.

6. Mix barley with potatoes. Add egg, then add this mixture to the bacon and onions and stir well.

7. Spread in baking pan. Bake at 375 degrees approximately 35 minutes or until edges are golden brown.

Serve warm "in place of potatoes." Leftovers can be sliced, broiled, or fried, and buttered like bread.

SLOVENE-AMERICANS

Slovenia, which seceded from the former Yugoslavia in 1991, borders on Croatia, Hungary, Austria, and Italy. Like Croatians, Slovenes are mostly Roman Catholic, but their language is distinct from Serbo-Croatian. The 1990 census recorded 124,000 Slovene-Americans, but this figure is probably low because Slovene immigration has been estimated at 300,000-400,000, and was most extensive from 1850 to 1914. At that time, the Slovenian homeland was ruled by Austria, and some Slovene immigrants came from areas that are in the present-day countries of Austria and Hungary. Some Hungarian Slovenes still identify themselves as "Windish" from the German "wenden," meaning "strangers," the same word applied to the German-Slavic **Texas Wends**. Another possible confusion is with Slavonia, a province of Croatia.

Like **Croatian-** and **Serbian-Americans**, Slovene-Americans came to the United States from rural areas and found work at unskilled jobs in mining. They came somewhat later than other Yugoslav groups, and initially worked in northern Michigan and the Minnesota iron range, with some moving westward to Montana. Most planned to return to Slovenia with their earnings. But after World War I, Slovenia became part of a Yugoslavian Kingdom that increasingly became a Serbian dictatorship until Slovenia was again divided by Germany, Italy, and Hungary during World War II. Refugees continued to arrive with bad news about conditions in Slovenia, and the Slovene-American communities began to concentrate in Midwestern cities, especially Cleveland. Postwar Yugoslavia, a Communist-led federation, also turned gradually against the Slovenian minority. Slovenia was the first part of Yugoslavia to declare independence in the 1990s, and had to fight a 10-day war with Yugoslavia, in which 64 people were killed, a small preview of the civil wars in Croatia and Bosnia and of the 1999 international crisis over Kosovo.

Slovenian-American food shares many dishes with Croatian-American and Serbian-American cuisine, and also has an extra large repertoire of pastries that resemble those made by **Austrian-** and **Hungarian-Americans**.

SLOVENIAN POTATO SALAD

This recipe from a community cookbook shows some of the influence of Austrian potato salad.

- 6 medium potatoes
- 1 medium onion, sliced thin
- 1/4 cup cider vinegar
- 3 tablespoons salad oil
- 1/2 teaspoon salt
- 1/8 teaspoon pepper

1. Boil potatoes in jackets until cooked.
2. Drain and let stand until cool.
3. Halve, peel, and slice the onion into thin half-rounds.
4. Remove potato skins.
5. Slice potatoes thin into a salad bowl.
6. Stir together onions, oil, vinegar, salt, and pepper.
7. Pour over potatoes, and toss gently.

Serve immediately.

SLOVENIAN ICEBOX POTICA

This recipe from Lillian Hlabse of Cleveland appeared in the *Cleveland Plain Dealer*, and in *Food Editor's Hometown Favorites Cookbook*, to which it was submitted by food editor Janet Beighie French. The recipe is not as hard as it looks, and makes a good group project over two days. In older recipes, the dough was made in one piece, pulled to stretch over a floured tablecloth by groups of women. Found among all the Southern Slavic ethnic groups, the dish appears under the names Potica, Povitica, or Orhanica (which means "walnut"). The Slovene versions in Europe used a ceramic pot with a central chimney like our angel-cake pans to get a taller coffeecake. A quick-bread version with no rolling is found in the Midwest, but I cannot attach it to any particular ethnic group.

NOTE: Recipe requires 2 days to complete.

- 1 package dry yeast
- 1 2/3 cups granulated sugar
- 4 1/2 cups unbleached hard-wheat bread flour
- 1 cup (2 sticks) butter or margarine
- 1 1/2 teaspoons salt
- 5 eggs
- 1 pint dairy sour cream
- 1 cup milk

2 1/2 pounds walnuts

2 tablespoons honey

2 tablespoons orange zest or lemon zest (optional)

1 1/2 cups golden raisins

solid shortening to grease pans and bowl

Equipment: Pastry blender or large fork, food processor, electric mixer or whisk to beat egg whites, three angel cake pans or six 9 by 5 by 3-inch "Pullman loaf" pans, rolling pin

1. Take out 1 stick of butter to soften. Add yeast and a teaspoon of sugar to 1/4 cup warm water, and let stand until foamy.

2. Sift flour with 3 tablespoons of sugar and the salt into a mixing bowl.

3. With a pastry blender or a large fork, cut in the butter until the chunks are no larger than kernels of sweet corn.

4. Separate 3 egg yolks by pouring back and forth between the shells over a cup to catch the whites. Reserve the whites in a tightly covered cup or jar in the refrigerator.

5. Beat the yolks with 1 cup of sour cream, then beat in the yeast mixture.

6. Stir the liquid mixture into the flour mixture to make a dough.

7. Turn out on a floured board and knead (see Appendix 1), about 5 minutes, or until smooth and somewhat sticky.

8. Grease a bowl. Turn the ball of dough to grease top, cover, and refrigerate overnight.

9. The next day, remove dough from refrigerator and let stand an hour to come to room temperature and rise.

10. Meanwhile, start the filling by combining the milk and the other stick of butter in a saucepan and heating to melt the butter.

11. Remove from heat and allow to cool.

12. Grind the nuts in a food processor in batches. Ms. Hlabse has found that home-ground nuts have more oil than commercially ground nuts.

13. Separate another egg and reserve the white with the others.

14. Stir together the ground nuts and the milk mixture, then stir in the other cup of sour cream, 1 1/2 cups sugar, the honey, and 1 egg yolk.

15. Separate the last egg and reserve the yolk. Beat the 5 egg whites until they form stiff peaks when you lift the beaters.

16. Mix stiff egg whites thoroughly into the filling mixture. Stir in zest, if using.

17. Divide dough into 6 parts.

18. Work each piece into a rectangle.

19. Grease angel cake pans or loaf pans.

20. Flour board, rolling pin, and dough, and roll out each piece to a rectangle 9 inches wide and 14 to 18 inches long. Pull and trim to get an even shape.

21. After each piece of dough is rolled out, spread with 1/6 of the filling. Sprinkle on one-sixth of the raisins.

22. Roll from the smallest side to the other narrow side, stopping at intervals to prick a few fork holes to keep the bread from cracking. (Do not prick the top of the roll.)

23. Tuck under the ends of a roll and put in a loaf pan, or put in an angel cake pan and work the ends together.

24. If you are using angel cake pans, put a second roll on top of the first one. They will come together into one cake with a double spiral.

25. Set completed rolls aside to rise, covered, for 1 1/2 hours.

26. Preheat an oven to 325 degrees.

27. Mix the last egg yolk with a teaspoon of water. Brush the tops of the rolls with this wash.

28. Bake loaves 1 hour and round cakes 1 1/4 hours, or until a toothpick comes out clean.

29. Cool loaves in pans for 10 minutes, then take out and cool on wire racks.

Serve as a coffeecake or dessert. Potica freezes well. Mrs. Hlabse includes one in her Easter basket of good things that she takes to church for blessing.

Slovenian Kifles (Yugoslavia Nut Horns)

My Hungarian-Jewish grandmother also called these kifles, although most **Jewish-Americans** know them as rugelach. This recipe has a lot of steps, but it's really easy and somewhat foolproof. You can make the dough a week ahead of actually making and baking the cookies. You can also make this dough into simple butter cookies like the **Hungarian-American** pogachels. Susie Godish submitted the recipe to *Treat Yourself to the Best Cookbook* (1984) by the Junior League of Wheeling, West Virginia. It was her mother-in-law's old family recipe.

Yield: 3 dozen cookies

2 cups flour
1 cake compressed yeast or 1 package dry
   yeast
1/2 cup (1 stick) margarine plus 3 tablespoons to melt
2 eggs
1/2 cup sour cream
1/4 cup powdered sugar
1/2 cup sugar for the filling
1 cup ground walnuts
1 teaspoon vanilla

Equipment: Pastry blender or food processor to mix dough, electric hand beater or whisk for egg whites, rolling pin, dough scraper or spatula to lift sticky dough, 2 baking sheets

1. In a large mixing bowl, crumble or sift yeast over flour.

2. Cut in margarine until mixture is crumbly.

3. Separate egg yolks by pouring back and forth between shells over a cup to catch whites. Reserve whites for walnut filling.

4. Add egg yolks and sour cream to flour mixture, mixing well.

5. Form dough into a ball and knead on floured board for 5-10 minutes until smooth.

6. Divide dough into 3 equal balls. Cover with plastic wrap and refrigerate for 1 hour to 1 week.

7. Beat egg whites until stiff.

8. Combine walnuts, 1/2 cup sugar, and vanilla

9. Mix in egg whites.

10. Grease baking sheets. Flour rolling pin and a board, and roll each portion of dough into a 10-inch circle. It will be quite thin.

11. Cut each circle into 12 wedges.

12. Spread each wedge with a well-rounded teaspoon of walnut filling. (If you want to spread 4 tablespoons of the filling on a whole circle and then cut it, I won't tell.)

13. Roll from wide end to point. (You can try a few the other way, if you want to see the difference.)

14. Place on baking sheets and bake at 350 degrees for 20 minutes or until light golden brown.

15. When they come out of the oven, set on wire rack to roll and dust with powdered sugar.

Serve when cooled with tea or milk. I personally like them better after a day or two. These cookies freeze well.

Spanish-Americans

Before Jamestown or Plymouth, the Spanish had a settlement called Santa Elena in South Carolina, and Spain also colonized the present states of Florida, Louisiana, Texas, New Mexico, Arizona, and California before the establishment of the United States. An identifiable group of Canary Islands descendants still lives in Louisiana, and a few dishes are associated with Minorcans who settled around St. Augustine, Florida. Many **New Mexico Hispanic** families in the Southwest do not describe themselves as Mexicans because their ancestors north of the Rio Grande only lived in Mexico for 25 years, from Mexican Independence in 1821 to the U.S. conquest in 1845. An estimated 900,000 Americans of Spanish descent come from families that lived in what is now the U.S. prior to 1776, and perhaps 250,000 Spanish immigrants have come since, most arriving via Cuba and other Latin American countries.

The largest Spanish settlements in 1845 were in northern New Mexico and southern Arizona, and on the vast ranches of inland California. There are also old and new settlements of Sephardic **Jewish-Americans** who preserve Spanish cooking from before their exile in 1492. The first large group of "old immigrant" Spaniards came via Cuba to the cigar factories of Tampa, Florida, in the 1890s. Many were originally from Asturias and Gallegos in northwestern Spain. New York was the next magnet for Spanish-American immigration. **Basque-Americans** from Spain came to California and the Rocky Mountain states as shepherds.

SPANISH EGGS

The Spanish families who owned large ranch lands in California retained their culinary traditions into the early twentieth century. A descendant of Senora Benicia Vallejo gave this recipe to Clarence E. Edwords for his 1914 book, *Bohemian San Francisco*. I have specified some quantities.

    16-ounce can whole tomatoes
    3 tablespoons bread crumbs
    2 or 3 small green peppers
    1 small onion
    1 teaspoon butter
    6 eggs

Equipment: Frying pan

1. Halve and peel the onion; cut into thin half-moon slices.

2. Cut off the tops of the peppers and core and remove seeds and pith. Cut into small dice.

3. "Empty a can of tomatoes in a frying pan; thicken with bread and add two or three small green peppers and an onion sliced fine. Add a little butter and salt to taste. Let this simmer gently."

4. When the onions and peppers are well cooked, break the eggs one-by-one into a cup, and pour whole eggs onto the simmering tomato sauce. Arrange the eggs around a central egg.

5. "Dip the simmering tomato mixture over the eggs until they are cooked."

ARROZ GUISADO CON TOMATE

We still call this dish "Spanish rice." The recipe is from a pamphlet by Señora Teresa Ynez Pinto, which was reprinted in *Sumptuous Dining in Gaslight San Francisco* by Frances de Talavera Berger and John Parke Custis.

Yield: serves 4-6
    2 tablespoons butter
    1 1/2 cups long-grain white rice
    1 onion
    1 large tomato

Equipment: Skillet with a cover

1. Halve, peel, and chop the onion.

2. Dice the tomato.

3. In a deep skillet with a cover, melt the butter.

4. Pour rice into pan, and add onions. "Fry together until rice is light brown."

5. Add the tomatoes. Sauté together.

6. Bring 4 cups of water to a boil. Add boiling water carefully to hot rice mixture.

7. Cover and reduce heat to simmer until rice is tender, about 20 minutes. More water may be added if needed.

FLORIDA GISPACHI

This version of gaspacho is widely traced to Spanish sailors settling in Pensacola, Florida, at the turn of the twentieth century. The pilot cracker was originally the hardtack cracker from ship's stores, softened in the cool salad. This recipe is from Cora, Rose, and Bob Brown's *America Cooks: Favorite Recipes of the 48 States* (1940).

Yield: serves 3 or 4

1 cucumber
1 tomato
1 medium onion
1 sweet red pepper (or canned pimento)
3 tablespoons vinegar
1 garlic clove
1 1/2 tablespoons olive oil
1 egg
1 pilot cracker

Equipment: Strainer, large bowl

1. Hard boil the egg (about 15 minutes).

2. Slice cucumber and sprinkle with salt. Let it stand and drain.

3. Halve and peel the onion; slice into thin half-rounds.

4. Core the pepper, remove pith and seeds, and cut into fine dice.

5. Mince tomato.

6. Peel and mince garlic and mix with vinegar in a small cup.

7. Cool and shell egg under cold water.

8. Halve the egg and remove yolk.

9. Chop egg white.

10. In a large bowl, mash the egg yolk with the olive oil.

11. Strain in the vinegar.

12. Add and mix the cucumber, onion, tomato, and egg white.

13. Add salt and pepper and let stand.

14. When ready to serve, crumble in the cracker and add.

Serve cold as an appetizer.

CALDO—SPANISH SOUP

This recipe from the southern Louisiana Isleño community was submitted by Louise Perez to Sheila Ainbinder's *Legends of Louisiana Cookbook* (1987). Mrs. Perez is herself **Italian-American**, and learned these soups from her husband's grandmother. Although the community is more than 200 years old, the recipe has obviously expanded to include many local vegetables.

Yield: serves 10-12

1 pound white beans
3 medium onions
1 16-ounce can stewed tomatoes
1 15-ounce can tomato sauce
5 pieces 1-inch-thick pickled pork (or 1 pound lean salt pork, soaked to remove salt)
1 package (10 ounces) frozen lima beans
1 pound fresh snap beans (or two 8-ounce packages frozen snap beans)
1 large turnip
6 carrots
1 large package (20 ounces) frozen mixed vegetables
1 can (15 ounces) white corn
1 can (15 ounces) green peas
6 pieces corn on the cob
6 red-skinned potatoes
1 small head cabbage
1/2 package frozen mustard greens (5 ounces total)
6 sweet potatoes

Equipment: Large pot

1. Wash white beans and put in a large pot half full of water. Bring to boil.

2. Halve, peel, and chop onions and add to soup.

3. When beans are half-tender, cut pickled pork into pieces and add to beans.

4. When meat is tender, add lima beans, snap beans, and frozen mixed vegetables.

5. Peel turnip and cut into pieces. Add to soup.

6. Peel and cut up carrots. Add to soup.

7. After it comes to a full boil again, add a can of whole corn, and a can of peas.

8. Scrub and add potatoes.

9. Shuck corn, cut into pieces, and add to soup.

10. Cut cabbage into small pieces and add with mustard greens.

11. When beans are almost tender, add tomatoes and tomato sauce.

12. Peel sweet potatoes and cook separately in some of the stock from the soup, or just enough water to cover. "The reason for that is that if you put sweet potatoes with soup, they tend to break apart."

13. When everything is tender, turn off heat. Add sweet potatoes to soup pot.

14. "If soup gets too thick, add some water because it is supposed to be a little soupy."

15. Taste for salt and pepper.

SWEDISH-AMERICANS

About 4.6 million Americans claim Swedish descent. Community cookbooks probably contain more Swedish-American recipes than recipes from any other ethnic group. This fact suggests a relative comfort with Swedish-American identity, as shown by both the rapid Americanization and dispersion of Swedish immigrants, and their unusually low rate of marriage outside the group.

Sweden had a small American colony around Wilmington, Delaware, from 1638 to 1655, but these founding stock Swedes left few enduring traces. Sweden was the first European country to recognize the United States in 1783, and was an important trading partner through the early nineteenth century. The vast majority of immigrants arrived between 1860 and 1930, with about one-fourth the population of Sweden coming to North America. A potato famine in the 1860s sent many poor farmers to states in the Midwest, while later groups were single men and women seeking work in American cities, especially Chicago and Minneapolis. By 1920, Swedish-Americans owned more farmland than there was in all of Sweden. Lutheran churches continue to be important to the Swedish-American community, as is the observation of St. Lucia Day on December 13.

Swedish-American cooking has most in common with **Norwegian-American** cooking, a fact that is perhaps explained by the relatively high rate of intermarriage between the two groups.

SWEDISH MEATBALLS

U.S. Representative Charles W. Stenholm of Texas contributed this recipe to the *American Sampler Cookbook* (1986) collected by Linda Bauer. This spicing of ginger, pepper, and nutmeg is probably what most often came over from Sweden. In the U.S., many Swedish-American families substituted allspice. As the dish became popular in the larger community, the spice has often disappeared entirely. The mixture of pork and beef was typical of many American ground-meat dishes a century ago—beef alone is more typical today, and ground turkey may be the next wave.

Yield: about 36 meatballs to serve 10 as a main dish

1 1/4 pounds ground beef
1/4 pound ground pork
1 1/2 cups soft bread crumbs (about 3 slices bread)
1 cup light cream or half-and-half
1 medium onion
3 tablespoons butter or margarine, divided
1 egg
1/4 teaspoon ground ginger
Dash ground nutmeg
salt to taste

black pepper to taste

3 tablespoons all-purpose white flour

3/4 cup canned condensed beef broth (do not dilute)

1/4 cup water

1/4 teaspoon instant coffee (regular or decaf)

Equipment: Electric mixer or food processor, skillet

1. Mix meats together.

2. Soak bread crumbs in cream about 5 minutes.

3. Halve, peel, and chop onion to get a half cup.

4. Cook onion in 1 tablespoon butter until tender.

5. Combine meat, crumb mixture, egg, onion, and seasonings.

6. Beat vigorously with electric mixer until fluffy.

7. Form in 1 1/2-inch balls. (Mixture will be soft.)

8. Brown meatballs in remaining 2 tablespoons butter, shaking skillet to keep balls round.

9. Remove meatballs. Stir flour into drippings in skillet.

10. Add broth, water, and coffee. Heat and stir until gravy thickens.

11. Return meatballs to gravy. Cover and cook slowly about 30 minutes, basting occasionally.

OVEN PANCAKES

This recipe was submitted "in memory of Austrid Hanson by Winetta Hanson Hayes" to the *Hawarden* [Iowa] *American-Lutheran Church 1961-1986 25th Anniversary Cookbook.* Mrs. Hanson's recipe is a typical oven pancake that would not surprise anyone in northern Europe, and might be called a "big Dutch baby" in parts of the U.S. ("Swedish pancakes" are thin and eggy, like French crepes.) Along with yellow pea soup, these pancakes were traditional on Thursday nights in many Swedish-American homes.

3 eggs

3 cups milk

1 1/2 cups flour (about)

2 tablespoons sugar

1/2 teaspoon baking powder (optional)

1/2 teaspoon salt

2 tablespoons butter or bacon drippings

Equipment: 2 large (4 1/2 by 9-inch) loaf pans. (The recipe can also be increased by 1/3 again to fit a 9 by 13 cake pan.)

1. Beat eggs and salt.

2. Gradually mix in remaining ingredients (except butter or bacon drippings).

3. Preheat oven to 400 degrees.

4. Put pans in oven with butter or bacon drippings in them; let them get hot, but don't brown butter.

5. Add the egg mixture and bake on lower rack for 15 minutes (until they rise up in "bubbles").

6. Then move up to the upper rack for 15 minutes or until lightly brown.

Serve hot. (Other recipes suggest cranberry sauce, fruit syrup, or jam on top.)

RISGRYNSGRÖT (SWEDISH RICE PORRIDGE)

This is a good example of a Christmas dish becoming everyday food, and of a recipe being reduced for a less-extended family. The recipe comes from a 1990 cookbook by the Eureka (Oregon) Learning Center. The story of this recipe, contributed by Sam Hayes and "mamma" Barbro, is that "Sam loves this porridge and would eat it all the time if he could. However it takes a while to make, so he gets it for supper some evenings. In many Swedish homes this rice porridge is served at the end of the traditional Christmas meal on Christmas Eve. The porridge is then made special with cream and sugar. A blanched almond is mixed in, and the person who gets the almond will be the first one to marry." There is a similar **Danish-American** rice porridge called Ris a La'Mande. The Norwegian porridge is called Risgraut. You can multiply the recipe, but it will take longer to boil the water and somewhat longer to cook.

Yield: 2-3 servings
  1/2 cup white rice ("round" [short grain] preferred but long grain is okay)
  1 teaspoon salt
  3 1/2 cups milk (or milk and cream)
  1 tablespoon (or less) sugar (optional)

Equipment: Sieve to rinse rice, wooden spoon, saucepan

  1. Boil 1 1/2 cups water in saucepan. Add salt.

  2. Rinse rice, add to boiling water.

  3. Cook uncovered on medium heat until water is absorbed (about 5 minutes).

  4. Add milk and cover pot, reduce heat, and simmer about an hour.

  5. Stir now and then to prevent burning.

  6. When pudding is smooth, add sugar.

"Serve with sugar, cinnamon, and milk. Leftover porridge can be mixed with whipped cream and orange bits and served as dessert."

OSTA KAKA

Osta kaka (or Ostkaka) is a delicate cheesecake from the rural eastern provinces of Sweden from which came most early Swedish immigrants. Old recipes usually start with a gallon of milk and rennet tablet. Make the cottage cheese from scratch. This one from the 1961 *Congressional Club Cookbook* is one of the first to use supermarket cottage cheese. It was submitted by the wife of Minnesota Congressman Odin Langer. Osta kaka was a winter dish, and is still served at Swedish lutefisk suppers. In Sweden it is now sold in stores.

Yield: serves 9
  2 8-ounce packages cottage cheese
  3 eggs
  1 cup sugar
  2 cups sweet cream

butter to grease pan

Equipment: 10-inch fluted pie pan or 8-inch brownie pan, larger pan to contain pie pan or brownie pan, clean dish cloth

  1. Stir cottage cheese until granular.

  2. Stir in remaining ingredients and mix well.

  3. Grease pan.

  4. Pour in mixture.

  5. Put clean dish cloth in larger pan and add enough hot water to cover, but not so that it will overflow when pie pan or brownie pan goes in.

  6. Put the pan of water in the oven, then put on the pie pan or brownie pan.

  7. Bake at 350 degrees for 1 to 1 1/2 hours, or until a knife inserted in the center comes out clean.

To serve, cut into nine squares and top with heavy cream, cranberry sauce, fruit preserves, or chopped toasted almonds.

SWEDISH APPLE PIE

This dish looks like a pie, but it has no bottom crust and is really more like a cobbler. The recipe is from the Web site of the Lutheran Brotherhood, a cooperative organization that began by providing insurance to immigrant farmers. Several Swedish-American recipes are included in the "heritage recipes" at <www. lutheranbrotherhood. com>. The recipe was submitted by the Pony Express Branch #8731 of Waterville, Kansas.

Yield: serves 8
  6 cups sliced tart cooking apples (from about 10 apples)
  1 cup plus 1 tablespoon sugar
  1 teaspoon cinnamon
  1/2 cup margarine or butter, softened, plus some to grease pie pan
  1 egg
  1 cup all-purpose flour
  1/2 cup chopped walnuts, if desired
  ice cream

Equipment: 10-inch pie pan, hand mixer or light standing mixer, small mixer bowl

1. Preheat oven to 350 degrees. Set butter or margarine out to soften.

2. Peel apples and cut into 1/4-inch slices until you have 6 cups.

3. Grease pie pan and add apples.

4. Sprinkle with 1 tablespoon of the sugar and the cinnamon.

5. In small mixer bowl, beat remaining sugar and margarine at medium speed, scraping bowl often, until well mixed (2 to 3 minutes).

6. Beat in egg; stir in flour.

7. Spread batter over apples.

8. Bake for 45 to 55 minutes or until golden brown and apples are tender.

Serve warm with ice cream.

OLD FASHIONED PEPPARKAKOR

These hard gingerbread cookies are cut into various shapes with cookie cutters. The dough is always refrigerated overnight, and sometimes over two nights. Miss Clara Berg of Polk County submitted this recipe to *100 Years of Good Cooking: Minnesota Centennial Cookbook* (1958). The blanched almond halves are not typical, but either a local custom or a fancification. The dough can be made ahead and refrigerated for about a week before baking.

NOTE: Recipe needs to chill overnight.

Yield: 7-8 dozen cookies
   3 1/2 cups sifted flour
   1 teaspoon baking soda
   1 1/2 teaspoons ginger
   1 1/2 teaspoons cinnamon
   1 teaspoon ground cloves
   1/4 teaspoon ground cardamom (optional)
   1/2 cup butter
   3/4 cup sugar
   1 egg
   3/4 cup molasses
   2 teaspoons grated orange rind
   1 pound blanched almond halves (optional)
   solid shortening to grease baking sheets

Equipment: Pastry blender or large fork, grater for orange rind, pastry cloth or board, rolling pin, cookie cutters, baking sheets, large bowl

1. Sift together flour, baking soda, and spices.

2. In a large bowl, cream butter with pastry blender.

3. Gradually add sugar, creaming until light and fluffy.

4. Grate orange rind.

5. Cream in unbeaten egg, molasses, and orange rind; beat well.

6. Gradually stir in dry ingredients, mixing until well blended.

7. Cover and chill overnight.

8. Flour a pastry board or cloth and rolling pin. Grease baking sheets

9. Cut off 1/4 or less of the dough and roll out to 1/8-inch thickness.

10. "Cut into various shapes with cookie cutters."

11. Place on baking sheets. "If desired, place a blanched almond half in the center of each cookie."

12. Bake in a 375-degree oven for 8 to 10 minutes. These cookies don't brown except at the edges, so don't overbake them.

Swiss-Americans

Switzerland is itself a multi-ethnic country, and many Swiss immigrants to the United States identified with **German-American, Franco-American, Italian-American,** or **Pennsylvania Dutch** communities. The projection of one million Swiss descendants in the 1990 census is probably somewhat low. About 400,000 Swiss have immigrated to the United States, including some of the original core of the **Amish,** Mennonite, and Brethren communities. Relatively few Swiss-Americans are concerned with their ethnic background, although Swiss-German farmers have introduced such distinctive foods as chipped beef and Swiss cheese. Swiss Germans have formed somewhat visible communities in Texas and Wisconsin, and Italian-Swiss were notable settlers in northern California.

Swiss Cheese Pie

Marie Inderbitzen contributed this recipe to a cookbook compiled by the St. Anne's Altar Society of Immaculate Conception Church of Sacramento, California, in about 1962 or 1963. It is an entirely traditional Swiss recipe, except for the California additions of green pepper and olives.

Yield: 1 pie, 6-8 wedges
  1 9-inch unbaked pie shell
  4 eggs
  1 1/2 cups milk (or part half-and-half)
  1/2 teaspoon salt
  1/2 teaspoon prepared mustard
  1 cup shredded Swiss cheese (about 1/4 pound)
  1/2 cup ripe olive wedges
  1/4 cup finely diced green pepper

1. Chill the unbaked pie shell thoroughly in the refrigerator or freezer.

2. Preheat the oven to 375 degrees.

3. Break the eggs into the mixing bowl, remove any bits of shell, and beat well.

4. Add the milk, salt, and mustard.

5. Grate or shred the cheese, unless using purchased shredded Swiss cheese.

6. Cut up olives.

7. Cut the top and bottom from a small green pepper, core and remove pith, and cut into fine dice.

8. Stir pepper, olives, and cheese into egg mixture.

9. Pour filling mixture into the pie shell.

10. Bake 10 minutes in the middle of the oven, then reduce heat to 350 degrees.

11 Bake about 30-40 minutes longer, until pie is well set. (If center is slightly soft, it will finish cooking when removed from the oven.)

12. Allow to cool for at least 5 minutes before cutting.

Swiss Style Pork Chops

Miss Mary E. Mahoney of Omaha, Nebraska, contributed this recipe to *The Time Readers Book of Recipes* (1952) with the note, "This recipe was a favorite of my maternal grandmother, who was a native of Willerzell, Switzerland, about a hundred years ago." You can see why the common American dish of steak braised in tomato sauce is called "Swiss steak."

Yield: serves 6
  6 pork chops, 3/4 to 1 inch thick
  3 tablespoons flour
  1/2 teaspoon salt
  1 small onion
  1/8 teaspoon cinnamon

Equipment: Large frying pan

1. Halve, peel, and dice the onion.

2. "Trim excess fat from chops."

3. Melt fat from chops in a large frying pan.

4. Sprinkle chops with flour.

5. Brown lightly on each side.

6. Remove excess fat. Add salt, onion, and water. Cover pot.

7. Simmer for 35 minutes or until the meat is tender.

8. Add the cinnamon to the gravy.

SWISS TEA

This tea is made at the Ohio Relief Sale by the Swiss-German Mennonite community around Kidron, Ohio. The recipe is from *More Treasured Mennonite Recipes: Food, Fun, and Fellowship from the Mennonite Relief Sales* (1996).

1/2 cup green Tenderleaf tea (or any loose green tea)
2 sticks cinnamon
1/2 teaspoon (or big pinch) saffron
1 1/2 cups sugar ("more or less to taste")

1. Break cinnamon into pieces.

2. Add saffron, cinnamon, and tea to 1 quart boiling water. Simmer 15-20 minutes.

3. Bring 3 1/2 quarts of water to a boil in another pot.

4. Strain tea.

5. Add enough hot water to make 1 gallon of tea.

6. Stir in the sugar until dissolved.

SYRIAN-AMERICANS

See ARAB-AMERICANS (LEBANESE AND SYRIANS)

TAIWANESE-AMERICANS

See CHINESE-AMERICANS

TEXAS WENDS

The Texas Wends are a few thousand descendants of a Slavic people in eastern Germany known there as Lusatian Sorbs. ("Wend" is a German-language term for "foreigner.") In the early nineteenth century their lands were confiscated and they were forced to change language and religion by the Prussian state. Under the leadership of Rev. Jan Killian, the Wends came to Texas just before the Civil War, and pioneered an area around Serbin, which still has many Wendish families and the historic St. Paul's Lutheran church (completed 1871). Originally, the men sat in the balcony, while the women sat in pews at the floor level. Sermons were preached in Wendish, German, and English. Communities elsewhere in Texas and in Missouri gradually lost their distinctive Wendish character, but the group around Serbin has kept a little of the language and many Wendish customs.

SLAVIC OVEN STEW

Mrs. Mary Schimank of Houston published this recipe in *The Melting Pot: Ethnic Cuisine in Texas* (1977), by the Institute of Texan Cultures at the University of Texas. Compare to **Serbian-American** Juvech. Despite some Texas vegetables, this casserole shows how the Slavic culture of the Texas Wends has resisted both Germanization and Americanization.

Yield: serves 10

10 medium onions
8-10 large tomatoes
1/2 cup rice
6-8 potatoes
5 lamb chops
5 pork chops
1 eggplant
6 green peppers
1 cup diced okra (from one can, frozen
  package, or 1/2 pound fresh)
2 tablespoons butter

Equipment: Large roasting pan with cover

1. Halve, peel, slice, and mince onions. (Wear swim goggles to avoid tears.) Spread out on bottom of roasting pan.

2. Core and slice half the tomatoes. Layer over the onions.

3. Spread rice over tomatoes.

4. Peel and slice potatoes. Layer over rice.

5. Alternate lamb and pork chops for the next layer.

6. Pare and dice eggplant. Core peppers and cut into rings. Layer eggplant and peppers onto the meat.

7. Core and slice the rest of the tomatoes for the next layer.

8. If using frozen okra, defrost. If using canned okra, drain. If using fresh okra, slice off stems and tips.

9. Dice okra, and layer on top of everything else.

10. Cut the butter into small pieces and dot on top. Sprinkle with salt and pepper.

11. Cover roaster and bake at 450 degrees for one hour.

12. Remove cover and continue cooking at 350 degrees for 30 minutes, or until chops are cooked through and the dish is browned on top.

Serve as a one-pot supper, or with noodles.

WENDISH SAUERBRATEN

Also from *The Melting Pot,* this is less like the typical **German-American** sauerbraten than like some yogurt-marinated dishes of the southern Slav groups. Since the Wendish homeland is well to the north of the Balkans, this may reflect ancient kinship or Texas contact with Serbian or **Croatian-Americans.**

NOTE: Recipe takes two days

Yield: 14-15 servings
  6 pounds choice roast beef
  1 quart buttermilk
  2 large onions
  2 bay leaves
  6 whole cloves
  1-1/2 teaspoons salt
  1/2 teaspoon pepper
  4 tablespoons butter
  2 tablespoons mustard
  1 tablespoon brown sugar
  4 tablespoons flour
  1 smoked ham hock

Equipment: Roasting pan with cover, large non-metallic bowl for marinating

1. Wipe meat with a damp cloth.

2. Put in deep non-metallic pan or dish and cover with butter milk.

3. Halve, peel, and slice the onions. Scatter onto the meat.

4. Add bay leaves, cloves, salt, and pepper. Roll the meat around to coat.

5. Let stand in a cool place for 24 hours, turning often.

6. When ready to cook, remove one cup of buttermilk for baking.

7. Remove meat from spiced buttermilk and wipe dry.

8. Rub the meat with butter and mustard.

9. Place meat in roasting pan. Spread brown sugar on top and sprinkle with flour.

10. Add the reserved cup of buttermilk and one cup of water to the pan.

11. Cover roaster and bake one hour at 400 degrees.

12. Add ham hock and another cup of water to pan. Bake at 350 degrees until meat is tender enough to slice.

13. Pour gravy into a serving dish.

Serve with wilted-lettuce salad and noodles.

THAI-AMERICANS

The 1990 ancestry survey projected more than 90,000 Thai-Americans, almost all of whom have immigrated since 1965, when the national quota system for U.S. immigration ended. Thailand was an important U.S. ally in the Vietnam War, and relations between the two countries remain close. This is one immigrant group for which the restaurant business has been important. It sometimes seems like all 90,000 Thai-Americans work in Thai restaurants. Thai food is so popular in some U.S. cities that immigrants from elsewhere in Southeast Asia also open Thai restaurants. Most Thai-Americans live on the West Coast, and there are Thai neighborhoods in Hollywood, California, and Queens, New York. But the popularity of Thai restaurants has made Thai-Americans both more visible and more scattered than other recent immigrants.

The popularity of Thai restaurants has brought Thai ingredients into some supermarkets, and American hobby cooks try to duplicate their favorite restaurant dishes. Ironically, it is difficult to find printed recipes for Thai home cooking because almost all the Thai people who contribute to community cookbooks or newspaper food pages are male restaurant chefs!

THAI SPICY BEEF WITH MINT LEAVES

This typical Southeast Asian salad was submitted by the Thai-Am Association for the Milwaukee Holiday Folk Fair cookbook, and reprinted in the 1990 A *Feast of Festivals* by the International Festivals Association.

1 1/2 cups ground beef
1 tablespoon chopped red onion
3 cloves garlic
1 tablespoon nampla (fish sauce)
1 teaspoon salt
2 tablespoons lemon or lime juice
1 teaspoon powdered coriander
1 tablespoon rice powder, browned
1 teaspoon chili powder (not mixed chili con carne spice)
3 small green onions
10 fresh mint leaves
lettuce, long green beans, and celery stalks

Equipment: Skillet, coffee grinder or food processor

1. Brown ground beef, without oil, in a skillet.

2. Place in a mixing bowl and let cool for 5 minutes.

3. Peel and chop garlic and mince red onion.

4. Wrap the onion and garlic in 2 layers of aluminum foil and cook in a hot oven "until it is almost burned."

5. Unwrap it and add onion and garlic to the beef.

6. To make rice powder, toast uncooked white rice in a dry heavy skillet or in the oven until it is fragrant and slightly browned. Pound in a mortar or grind in a cleaned out coffee grinder or a food processor with one side propped up.

7. Season the beef with nampla, salt, lemon or lime juice, coriander, rice powder, and chili powder.

8. Trim and chop green onions and mix into the beef.

9. Pour the mixture into a serving dish.

Serve with leaves of lettuce, trimmed raw green beans, or celery stalks.

KAI YAT SAI

These pork-stuffed omelets use the roots of fresh coriander in a spice paste. You'll have to find cilantro sold with the roots to get the full effect. The recipe is from *Ethnic Foods of Hawai'i* (1983) by Ann Kondo Corum, a school librarian who researched her book to help students complete assignments about the food customs of Hawaiian ethnic groups. Good idea, Mrs. Corum!

Yield: serves 4-6
    2 teaspoons chopped coriander roots
    3 cloves garlic
    8 peppercorns
    4 tablespoons vegetable oil
    1/2 cup ground pork
    1 small onion
    1 teaspoon sugar
    8 eggs
    1/2 cup Chinese peas (snow peas)
    1 medium tomato
    1 tablespoon fish sauce (nampla)
    2 tablespoons coriander leaves (cilantro)

Equipment: Mortar and pestle, spatula for stir-frying, omelet pan (optional), heavy skillet

1. Scrub and chop enough coriander roots to make up the 2 teaspoonfuls. (They're too small to peel.)

2. Peel and chop the garlic.

3. Break up the peppercorns in the mortar. Add the coriander root and garlic, and grind together into a paste.

4. Halve, peel, and chop the onion.

5. Wash and chop enough snow peas to make up the half cup.

6. Chop the tomato.

7. Heat half the oil in a heavy skillet and fry the garlic-coriander paste for 2 minutes.

8. Add the pork and stir-fry until all the pork is brown.

9. Add the onion, peas, and tomato, and stir-fry about 1 minute.

10. Stir in the sugar and remove from heat.

11. Beat the eggs with the fish sauce.

12. Heat one tablespoon of the oil in an omelet pan or frying pan.

13. Coat the pan with oil, then pour in half the egg mixture.

14. Spoon half the pork mixture onto the center of the omelet.

15. Allow eggs to set, and fold omelet over.

16. Turn over to brown both sides.

17. Slide the cooked omelet onto a plate and repeat the process with the remaining oil, egg, and pork mixture.

18. Cut omelets into serving pieces.

Serve garnished with coriander leaves.

TLINGIT AND HAIDA

The U.S. census estimates almost 17,000 Tlingit and 2,000 Haida in the United States, mostly in coastal Alaska. The Tlingit won many rights through the Alaska Native Brotherhood and Sisterhood, twin organizations founded in 1912. However, these organizations also began with a program of assimilating Native Americans into American culture and reducing the use and influence of the Tlingit language (related to Navajo) and religion. Early leaders of the organizations were Presbyterian converts. In 1966, the groups expanded to include **Eskimos** and inland Athapaskan tribes, and are now The Alaska Federation of Natives. The Tlingit and Haida had one of the most elaborate cultures of any non-farming peoples, and quickly took up potato and vegetable gardening. Elaborate carving of wood and stone was common to both tribes. Since the 1960s, there have been a number of revivals of traditional Tlingit and Haida culture, including the active use of totem poles and traditional hunts of sea mammals.

Some other Tlingit recipes are for fry bread, pilot crackers, and a surprising number of rice dishes, reportedly influenced by **Filipino-American** co-workers in the canneries (but see also the Russian-influenced fish perok with rice, below).

RAINY DAY FISH CHOWDER

"Laura" of Olympia, Washington, posted this recipe on the Native Tech Internet site. She learned the recipe from her mother, Pearl, who came from Klawock, Alaska, west of Ketchikan. Her background is Tlingit and Haida. This recipe can be made from fresh salmon heads and bones and from fresh fish fillets. The recipe is precisely written in a modern style, yet embodies millennia of Tlingit fishing, the name "chowder" from New England whalers and missionaries, and recent adaptations to city life with canned chicken broth and rosemary.

Yield: 16 cups, which Laura describes as serving 2 or 3

leftover skin, bones, head, or tail "of whole fish you ate the day before," or 4 quarts chicken broth

1 pound left-over cooked fish such as halibut, salmon, cod, ling cod

2 large onions

3 or 4 stalks celery

a twig of rosemary ("for the Martha Stewart-influenced")

1 1/2 cups milk

1 head garlic

2 carrots

2 cups fresh or frozen (thaw first) chopped greens of your choice

1/2 cup flour

1. If using leftover fish, remove at least a pound of cooked fish from all bones. If using chicken broth, go ahead to Step 6.

2. Halve, peel, and chop one of the onions.

3. Chop the celery.

4. Simmer fish parts, onions, celery, and optional rosemary in 6 quarts of water for 2 hours. (If using bluefish, flounder, or other small fish, simmer only 30-40 minutes.)

5. Strain carefully to remove all bones and scales. You can do this part ahead and refrigerate the stock overnight.

6. If using frozen greens, thaw or microwave briefly. Halve, peel, and chop the other onion.

7. Peel and chop the carrots.

8. In a deep pot, sauté onions and carrots in a bit of canola oil until vegetables are translucent.

9. Peel and chop the garlic. Add to the onion/carrot mixture.

10. Add the broth. Bring to a boil and reduce heat to simmer for about 20 minutes. Broth will reduce slightly.

11. If using fresh greens, wash carefully, remove stems, and chop.

12. Mix a bit of the milk into the flour and stir until you get a smooth paste.

13. Gradually add all the milk to the mixture.

14. Stir milk mixture into the simmering broth.

15. "Throw in the fish and greens."

16. Cook until fish is heated through.

Serve with salt and pepper, or add "crumbled-up smoked fish, dried seaweed, even bacos. . . . I like to eat this soup with some homemade bread, or biscuits. It's best on those evenings when it's raining so hard you can hear it bounce off the roof!"

Fish Perok

This recipe is similar to the special "pirog" (oblong pie) served by Russians on their name days. Before the United States purchased Alaska from Russia in 1867, the Tlingit had been trading furs with Russians for more than 100 years. This recipe from The Alaska Federation of Natives (reprinted in a pamphlet of "Native American Recipes" by the Smithsonian Institution Festival of American Folklife) does not specify the pie crust, so I am guessing that the tough yeast-dough used by Russians for their free-form pies has given way to American-style pastry.

Yield: 12 three-inch-square servings, or 36 slices from pie pans

    pie crust for top and bottom of a 13 by 9 by
       2-inch pan or 6 frozen 2-crust pie shells
    2 cans salmon or fresh salmon (2-3 pounds)
    4 cups cooked rice (from 1 cup rice)
    5 eggs
    2 onions
    2 sticks margarine
    salt and pepper to taste

Equipment: 13 by 9 baking pan, or 6 pie pans

1. If using a large pan, make pie crust with any standard pie crust recipe, multiplied by 5. If you use pre-baked pie shells, they are shallower (unless you can find deep-dish ones) and the filling will go farther.

2. Cook rice according to package directions.

3. Hard boil the eggs.

4. Halve, peel, and chop the onions.

5. Sauté onions in both sticks of margarine until tender.

6. Cool, shell, and chop the eggs.

7. In a bowl, combine onions, rice, eggs and seasoning.

8. If using canned salmon, pick out any bones or skin and flake. If using salmon fillets, dice.

9. Line the pan with pie crust.

10. Put half the rice mixture in the bottom of the pan.

11. Distribute the fish on top of the rice and season with a little more salt and pepper.

12. Put the rest of the rice on, then the top crust.

13. Crimp the edges of the crust together, and cut some vent slits with a knife.

14. Bake one hour at 400 degrees.

Serve with lemon wedges and butter.

Tohono O'Odham

See Pima and Papago (Tohono O'Odham)

Travellers

See Gypsy-Americans

Trinidadian-Americans (and Indo-Caribbeans)

The 1990 census estimated only 76,000 Americans claiming ancestors from Trinidad or Tobago, but the real size of the group is probably about 325,000, including perhaps 50,000 undocumented aliens. One reason for the difference is that the two ethnic groups on Trinidad, African-Americans and Indo-Caribbeans, each with about 40 percent of the population, have tended to identify with the U.S. **African-American** and **Asian-Indian-American** communities, respectively. The groups have different histories and some tensions on Trinidad and Tobago, although there is a common Trinidadian food, which is too good not to share.

Africans came to Trinidad as slaves, and worked on sugar plantations. When slavery ended there in 1838, most refused to continue in the sugar industry, and were replaced by "East Indian" indentured workers. Descendants of the freed slaves began coming to New York City before the Civil War, and the number increased in the early twentieth century. However, this migration shifted toward England when the U.S. began restricting immigration in 1925, and set up low quotas on European colonies in 1952 specifically to restrict immigration from the British West Indies. In 1962, Great Britain began restricting immigration, and the fairer 1965 U.S. Immigration Act brought a new influx from Trinidad, in particular to Brooklyn. African-Americans are thought to be about two-thirds of Trinidadian-Americans now, and have provided such African-American leaders as civil rights activist Kwame Touré (Stokely Carmichael) and former U.S. Representative and California Lieutenant Governor Mervyn Dimally. Indo-Caribbeans worked in Trinidad under a series of indentures that ended only with World War I. Most were Hindus from southern India. Their most visible community, in Queens, New York, adjoins that of Indo-Caribbean **Guyanese-Americans**. Indo-Caribbeans may form a separate ethnic group in the United States, or may reconnect with Asian-Indians, or may have their connections to Trinidad restored by political changes on the island.

TRINIDAD CURRIED CHICKEN

This recipe was contributed by Mrs. Alice Dymally to *Red Beans & Rice and other Rock 'n' Roll Recipes* by Johnny Otis, the musician who served as Lieutenant Governor Dymally's chief-of-staff. Bone the chicken or cut it into smaller pieces to wrap in fried flatbread to make Trinidadian roti.

2 tablespoons vegetable oil
1 whole chicken, cut up
2 teaspoons salt, plus a little extra
3 tablespoons curry powder, plus a little extra
1 large onion, chopped
2 cloves garlic, chopped
2 tablespoons celery, chopped
1 bay leaf

Equipment: Large skillet

1. Season chicken with a little salt and pepper and pat with a little curry powder

2. Halve, peel, and chop onion.

3. Peel and mince garlic.

4. Slice finely a few inches of celery to get 2 tablespoons.

5. Heat oil in a large skillet and brown chicken evenly on all sides without burning.

6. Transfer chicken to a plate, and add onions to the pan.

7. Cook onions slowly for about 5 minutes or until soft and transparent.

8. Dissolve remaining curry powder in 1 cup water, and add to skillet along with garlic, celery, and salt and pepper, stirring constantly.

9. Return chicken and any juices that have accumulated to the skillet.

10. Add another cup of water and bay leaf and bring to a boil.

11. Reduce heat to low, cover tightly, and simmer about an hour.

Remove bay leaf before serving.

POTATO BREAD

This is a variation on a kind of fried bread called "floats" in Trinidad. The recipe from Joycelyn Villarael appeared in the *Dorchester* [Massachusetts] *International Cookbook* (1979).

CAUTION: Hot oil used.

1 pound potatoes
2 cups flour
1 package yeast

1 tablespoon sugar
1/2 cup oil

Equipment: Skimmer, wire rack or paper towels to drain fried breads, high-sided heavy pot

1. Peel, cube, and boil potatoes until soft.

2. Drain potatoes, reserving 1 3/4 cups of the liquid.

3. Mash potatoes and set aside.

4. Cool the potato cooking liquid to lukewarm, and dissolve the yeast and sugar in 1 cup of the liquid.

5. Add the yeast mixture to the mashed potatoes.

6. Stir in the flour.

7. Stir in the rest of the potato cooking liquid.

8. Place batter in a warm place to rise.

9. When batter is fluffy, stir down the bubbles and form into 1-inch rounds.

10. Let rounds rise about 20 minutes.

11. Heat oil in a high-sided, heavy pot.

12. Dip skimmer in oil, then use it to gently lower in the rounds of dough. (You can also drop the risen batter by tablespoonfuls.)

13. Turn fry breads to brown all sides, then drain on a wire rack or paper towels.

"Serve with fish or meat."

TURKISH-AMERICANS

The 1990 census estimated 83,000 Americans of Turkish ancestry, far fewer than the 360,000 immigrants from the Ottoman Turkish Empire. The Turkish-American community today consists of people who are or were Muslims and speak Turkish, and some of their descendants. Many hold dual citizenship with the Turkish Republic, which was declared in 1923. At times, speakers of Turkish languages from the former Soviet Union, China, and elsewhere in the Middle East affiliate with the Turkish-American community.

Although Turkey is a NATO ally of the United States and a trading partner with Israel, Turkish-Americans keep a low political profile because events in Turkey have led to conflicts with larger immigrant groups in the United States. A large proportion of **Armenian-Americans** are descended from Armenians who fled the Turkish genocide of 1915. A large fraction of **Greek-Americans** are descended from Greeks who fled modern Turkey in the 1920s, and have strong opinions about the ongoing civil strife in Cyprus. In the 1990s, Middle East politics often separated Turkish-Americans from the small Kurdish-American community.

Turkish food is a mother cuisine of much Arab-American cooking, and of many dishes in the Balkan countries and those surrounding the Black Sea. A belt of Turkish languages and cultures stretches across the former Soviet Union to Muslim minorities in China; historians call this belt the "Silk Road," although some political scientists describe it as "Greater Turkistan."

SIS KEBAB

Aydan Kalyoncu contributed this original "shish kebab" to a booklet of *Creative Recipes from Famous People and Friends* that was distributed by A.H.M. Graves Realtors of Indianapolis in the late 1970s.

NOTE: Recipe must be refrigerated overnight.

1 1/2 pounds lamb or beef (round steak)
2 onions
1/4 cup olive oil
1/2 cup lemon juice
1 teaspoon salt
1/2 teaspoon black pepper
1/8 teaspoon allspice

3 cloves garlic (or 1/4 teaspoon garlic
   powder)
2 green peppers
2 firm tomatoes

Equipment: Garlic press, skewers, deep bowl

1. Peel the larger onion, slice across "the equator," and separate the slices into rings.

2. Put onion rings into a deep bowl with the olive oil, lemon juice, salt, pepper, and allspice.

3. If using whole garlic cloves, peel them and crush them into the marinade. If using garlic powder, stir that into the marinade.

4. Cut the meat into 2-inch cubes and add to the marinade, turning to coat all the pieces.

5. Cover and refrigerate overnight.

6. Halve and peel the smaller onion, and cut into quarters.

7. Quarter the tomatoes.

8. Seed and core the peppers and cut into 2-inch squares.

9. Remove meat from marinade and thread onto skewers, alternating with onion pieces.

10. Thread the tomato slices and green pepper pieces alternately onto separate skewers.

11. Broil 4 inches from heat, turning occasionally. The vegetable skewers cook faster, and should be removed sooner, or cooked on cooler parts of the grill.

Serve with rice.

COBAN SALATASL (SHEPHERD'S SALAD)

This recipe makes a typical Middle Eastern salad with the one irresistible direction to toss the salad with your hands, so as not to break up the tomato and cucumber. Ziya Ahmed submitted the recipe to *Cuisine International* (1979), which was published by the International Institute of Metropolitan Detroit. Because the recipe does not include instructions on how to uncurl pars-

ley, you will have to start with the Italian, flat-leaf parsley.

Yield: serves 6
   1 large tomato
   1 medium-sized sweet white onion
   1 green pepper
   1 medium-sized cucumber
   salt to taste
   3 tablespoons snipped parsley, "uncurled"
   3 tablespoons fresh mint leaves, snipped
   1 1/2 to 2 tablespoons olive oil
   1 1/2 to 2 tablespoons fresh lemon juice or
      vinegar

Equipment: Kitchen scissors to snip fresh herbs, large bowl

1. Halve, peel, and dice onion.

2. Core green pepper and remove white pith. Cut into small dice.

3. Peel cucumber if waxed, remove seeds, and dice the flesh.

4. Put tomato, onion, pepper, and cucumber in a large bowl.

5. Add salt and snip in mint leaves and parsley.

6. "Mix ingredients with your hands."

7. In a small bowl, stir together the olive oil and lemon juice or vinegar.

8. Pour over the salad ingredients.

"Must be served in small individual bowls."

SPICY RICE (IC PILAV)

Also in the Detroit *Cuisine International* cookbook is this slightly sweet version of the original pilaf. Contributed by Kemale Ahmed, this recipe "can also be used as a stuffing for lamb, chicken, Cornish Rock hens and turkey."

Yield: serves 8 as a side dish
   2 cups uncooked rice
   4 cups chicken broth (or water)

1 stick butter
1/2 cup pine nuts
1/2 cup currants (or white raisins)
1 small onion
1/2 teaspoon cinnamon
1/2 teaspoon sugar

Equipment: Clean dish towel or a "clean Turkish hand towel," saucepan

1. Melt butter in saucepan.

2. Add nuts and cook until they are pinkish.

3. Halve, peel, and dice the onion.

4. Add onion to butter and nuts and cook until the onion is soft.

5. Add currants, stirring well.

6. Add rice, mixing with a fork until each grain is coated with butter.

7. Pour in chicken broth and add salt and pepper, cinnamon, and sugar.

8. Bring to a boil, then stir well and reduce heat, simmering uncovered until all the liquid is absorbed.

9. Stir once again and remove from heat, covering saucepan with a clean Turkish towel until mixture is fluffy, about 10 to 15 minutes. (You can also use the lid of the saucepan to hold the towel in place, or the towel to make a tight seal with the lid.)

TUSCARORA

See IROQUOIS; LUMBEE INDIANS OF NORTH CAROLINA

UKRAINIAN-AMERICANS

For the 1990 census, 740,000 Americans listed Ukrainian ancestry. This figure probably includes many descendants of Carpatho-Rusyns and Ukrainians from areas that are now in Poland and Slovakia, and some from Moldova and Romania. It probably doesn't include many **Jewish-Americans** and some **Russian-Americans, Germans from Russia, Armenian-Americans,** and **Polish-Americans** who originally emigrated from regions now in the country of Ukraine. In fact, when most Ukrainians came to the United States, between 1880 and 1914, the Ukrainian homelands were split between the Hungarian and Russian empires, and immigrants only adopted the term Ukrainian in the 1920s and 1930s. A second group of immigrants, perhaps 85,000, arrived as refugees after World War II. The earlier Ukrainian community came from rural areas, predominantly in Galicia (southern Poland), and were mostly Eastern Rite Catholics. Their descendants in Pennsylvania often think of themselves as **Carpatho-Rusyn-Americans,** while those in Chicago view themselves as Ukrainian-Americans. Some converted in the U.S. to join Russian Orthodox churches, leading to a more even division in the group, and periodic tensions in Ukrainian-American social organizations. Religious ties and parochial schools and colleges remain important in this ethnic group, as does music, food, crafts, and folk dancing. The independence of Ukraine under a more liberal government since the breakup of the former Soviet Union has re-opened communications for Ukrainian-Americans who have kept up their language.

Traditional Ukrainian cooking is rich in dumplings, vegetarian dishes for the many religious fast days, fruit purees, pickles, and soups. Many dishes are similar to Polish, Russian, or Slovak cooking. The cuisine has many versions of borsch and potato pancakes, which are sometimes known under their Ukrainian name of "kartoplyanky," sometimes (as in Pennsylvania) under their Russian name of "bleenie," and sometimes under the Yiddish "latkes."

Svikly

Mrs. John Lewicki submitted this recipe to *Three Rivers Cookbook II: The Good Taste of Pittsburgh*, which was published in 1981 by the Child Health Association of Sewickley, Inc. Svikly is a traditional Easter dish.

Yield: 3 cups as a side dish or condiment
  3 cups beets
  1/2 cup horseradish (small root)
  1 tablespoon vinegar
  1 tablespoon brown sugar

Equipment: Grater or food processor with grating or shredding disk

1. Boil beets in water to cover until tender to an inserted fork, 45 minutes or more depending on size.

2. Peel horseradish and grate.

3. Mix vinegar with horseradish.

4. Drain beets and cool.

5. Rub skins off beets under cold running water.

6. Shred beets finely, and mix with horseradish.

7. Add sugar and mix well.

8. "Put in jar and refrigerate at least several days before serving."

Serve as a garnish with hot or cold meat.

Borsch

Various kinds of borsch are the best-known Ukrainian-American recipes, and there are also Polish, Russian, and Jewish-American versions. This one is from a group of Ukrainian-American recipes on the personal Web site of Joanne Pryhorocki Potter, and credited to her mother, Stacia Kabanuk Pryhorocki of Milton-Freewater, Oregon. "Some Ukrainian folks call this Red Borsch because of the beets in it. I grew up on this soup recipe and still make it almost weekly." Sometimes she starts with a beef soup bone or adds meat at the end.

  1 cup chopped fresh beets (2 medium beets)
  1 cup chopped fresh carrots (2 large carrots)
  2 cups green beans
  3 or 4 medium potatoes
  1 quart chopped or shredded cabbage (from half a large cabbage)
  1 pint fresh tomatoes or a 16-ounce can of tomatoes
  1/2 cup chopped onion (1 small onion)
  1/2 cup fresh dill weed, chopped
  salt to taste
  2 tablespoons finely chopped onion
  2 tablespoons oil
  2 tablespoons flour
  1 cup cream, or more to taste
  minced garlic to taste

Equipment: Carrot peeler, small frying pan

1. Slice off the top of each beet to make a flat side. Peel with a carrot peeler, and dice, using the flat side down so the beet doesn't roll while you are cutting it.

2. Peel and chop the carrots.

3. Wash the green beans and drain, cut off the stem and tip, and cut them into 1-inch lengths.

4. Put the chopped beets, carrots, and green beans into a 6-quart kettle with about 2 quarts of water and cook a little while.

5. Peel and cube the potatoes. Cut up fresh or canned tomatoes.

6. Halve the cabbage, cut out the core, and chop.

7. Chop the fresh dill.

8. Add cabbage, potatoes, tomatoes, and dill to the soup.

9. Taste for salt, and cook until vegetables are tender, adding more water for the desired consistency.

10. Halve, peel, and mince the onion.

11. Sauté onion in oil in a small frying pan and add flour. Stir until smooth.

12. When vegetables are cooked, stir in the onion-flour mixture as a thickener.

13. Peel and chop very fine as many garlic cloves as you like, and add to the soup with some cream. Cook about 5 minutes more to heat thoroughly.

14. Taste and add more salt if necessary.

"Serve with warm bread and butter and you have a very good meal."

KAPUSNYAK

Stacia Kabanuk Pryhorocki used this recipe for a somewhat unusually thickened version of the well-known Ukrainian sauerkraut soup. In Ukraine, the cereal would be served on the side.

1 package oxtail pieces (about 2 to 3 pounds)
1 quart sauerkraut
1 quart cabbage (1 medium cabbage)
1 cup carrots (2 medium carrots)
2 to 3 cups cooked potatoes (2 large potatoes)
1 teaspoon salt
1/2 cup Cream of Wheat cereal
2 to 3 cloves garlic, minced

1. Wash oxtail and put in cold water in a 6-quart kettle.

2. Bring to a boil and then turn down to simmer.

3. Spoon off the scum or foam until no more appears.

4. Cook the oxtail until it is almost done.

5. Drain the sauerkraut and squeeze out remaining liquid from it, reserving the juice.

6. Cut the cabbage into quarters, core, and chop well.

7. Chop the sauerkraut.

8. Peel the carrot and cut into cube-like chunks.

9. Add sauerkraut, cabbage, and carrots to the kettle and cook until vegetables are tender.

10. Peel and boil potatoes in a separate pan.

11. When they are done, mash them in their own liquid. Add this to the soup kettle.

12. Cook together until flavors are blended.

13. When almost done, stir in Cream of Wheat to thicken the soup. Stir frequently because Cream of Wheat tends to stick easily.

14. Peel and mince garlic, add to soup, and cook a few minutes more.

15. If the soup isn't sour enough, add some of the reserved sauerkraut brine. If it isn't salty enough, add salt.

VIETNAMESE-AMERICANS

Almost all of the 900,000 Vietnamese-Americans have come to the U.S. since the fall of South Vietnam to the Communist North in 1975. The immigration continues as Vietnamese refugees from other countries rejoin relatives in the United States—42,000 in 1996, for example, making the Vietnamese the fourth-largest group of legal immigrants that year. In some ways, the first group of more than 110,000, who had been connected with the American war effort, were best equipped for life in the United States. As with the Cuban refugees of the 1960s, the U.S. government attempted to scatter the Vietnamese in different parts of the United States, with more than half going to states where there would be less than 3,000 Indochinese. As with the Cuban refugees, the Vietnamese eventually relocated themselves to large communities and familiar climates in southern California and Houston, Texas. Substantial urban communities remain in Boston, Denver, and the Pacific Northwest. Somewhat more than 100,000 ethnic Chinese, sometimes called "Chinese-Vietnamese," who faced heavy discrimination from the new government, were among the first "boat people" and arrived with some commercial skills and contacts with other overseas Chinese in Malaysia, Indonesia, Hong Kong, and Singapore. Later arrivals are sometimes the survivors of traumatic escapes, lengthy stays in refugee camps, or prolonged imprisonment in Vietnam, but have the advantage of finding an established community life in the U.S.

Vietnamese restaurants appeared in the late 1970s, and became popular with Americans because Vietnamese cooking has both exotic flavors and familiar elements, including extensive use of beef and lively salads. Because of the French colonial influence, Vietnamese cooking already had "fusion food" before it became fashionable. Some Vietnamese foods that have adapted well to Vietnamese-American lifestyles are "fresh spring rolls" made and eaten at the table, grilled pork sandwiches, and pho (beef noodle soup.)

VIETNAMESE CHICKEN NOODLE SOUP

The Vietnamese name for this is "pho ga." Pho usually refers to a beef soup that developed in Hanoi, the French colonial capital, among the Catholic Vietnamese upper class, and the name is thought to come from the French "pot au feu." When one million North Vietnamese moved south in the 1956 partition of Vietnam, many were Catholics who worked with the pro-American government of South Vietnam, and thus brought this soup first to Saigon and then to the United States. In Vietnam, beef soup was thought to be healthful, enjoying a reputation similar to that of Jewish-American chicken soup. However, chicken pho is easier to make at home. Robin Nguyen posted this recipe on the Internet newsgroup at <rec.food.recipes>.

1 whole chicken (about 3 pounds, with or
   without skin)
1 large onion
2 carrots
2 celery stalks
1 teaspoon coriander seeds
3 star anise (substitute 2 teaspoons anise
   seed)
1/2 teaspoon black peppercorns
1 stick of cinnamon (about 3 inches long)
1 small piece of ginger (size of a teaspoon)
2 cans chicken stock
salt to taste
1 tablespoon sugar
Oriental rice noodles
Vietnamese fish sauce to taste
1/4 large onion, thinly sliced

1/2 cup chopped scallions
1/2 cup chopped cilantro
1/2 cup chopped basil leaves (Asian anise
   basil is best)
2 cups bean sprouts
1 large lime
dash of pepper
freshly sliced jalapeno peppers (optional)
chili paste (optional)

Equipment: Tea ball or small cheesecloth sack for spices, large stock pot

1. Wash chicken, remove large pockets of fat from openings, and place in a large stock pot with water to cover.

2. Bring to a boil, skimming off scum on top.

3. Peel onion and add to soup.

4. Peel and trim carrots and add to soup.

5. Wash and trim celery and add to soup.

6. Reduce heat to a simmer and cook for 1 hour uncovered, until chicken is fully cooked.

7. "Pour stock through strainer and remove breast meat and any other part of the chicken you would like at this time." (You can also cook additional chicken to serve with the soup, which will have more flavor.)

8. Place coriander seeds, peppercorns, and star anise in a tea ball or a seasoning bag and drop it into the strained chicken stock.

9. Slice a piece of ginger root and smash lightly with the handle of a knife. Add to soup with cinnamon stick and 2 cans of chicken stock and cook for about 20 minutes more.

10. Remove spices, cinnamon stick, and ginger.

11. Add sugar, salt, and fish sauce to taste. (You can refrigerate stock at this point to reheat, or to solidify and remove grease.)

12. When ready to serve, cook the rice noodles in salted water like pasta.

13. When they are done (more quickly than spaghetti), rinse with hot water to remove starch.

14. Cut 1/4 onion into thin slices. Chop scallions, cilantro, basil leaves, and chili peppers, if using.

15. Bring stock back to a boil.

16. To serve, put about a cup of noodles in each bowl, add some cooked chicken and a teaspoon each of scallions and cilantro, then a couple of slices of onion. Ladle on enough broth to fully cover the toppings.

Serve with a platter of bean sprouts, lime slices, basil leaves, chile peppers, hot sauce, or chile paste. Each diner selects mix-ins or a grind of fresh black pepper.

ARHAT'S FEAST

This Chinese-Vietnamese dish was posted on <rec.food.recipes> by "Vietgirl," apparently in response to a request for a Vietnamese dish for an adopted child. The name of the dish would be the same in Chinese as the Chinese restaurant dish of mixed vegetables, "Buddha's Delight." The great majority of Vietnamese are Buddhists, and I tasted similar dishes at a fundraising dinner to build a Vietnamese Buddhist temple in Boston.

1/4 cup raw cashew nuts
1/2 cup oil for deep-frying
2 slices ginger
2 green onions (scallions)
1/4 cup bamboo shoots
1/4 cup red bell pepper
8 whole water chestnuts
1/4 cup carrots
1/4 cup asparagus tips or broccoli spears

salt to taste
1 tablespoon soy sauce
1 tablespoon sugar
1 tablespoon rice vinegar
1/2 teaspoon cornstarch

Equipment: Wok or large skillet, spatula with curved or straight end to fit wok or skillet, deep-fry thermometer, skimmer, small saucepan

1. Heat oil to 325 degrees in a small saucepan.

2. Deep-fry the cashew nuts over a moderate heat until they are golden brown, lift out, and drain well.

3. In a small cup, mix together soy sauce, sugar, rice vinegar, and a tablespoon of water.

4. In another small cup, mix the cornstarch with a teaspoon of water.

5. Trim and chop the scallions.

6. Peel a section of ginger root and make 2 slices. Mince ginger.

7. Cut bamboo shoots into 3/4-inch pieces.

8. Core pepper and cut into 3/4-inch squares.

9. Slice each water chestnut in half around the "equator."

10. Peel carrots and cut into 3/4-inch pieces, rolling between cuts so the pieces are like pyramids.

11. Slice asparagus or broccoli spears into similar pieces.

12. Boil a small pot of water and plunge in carrots and broccoli spears (if using).

13. Drain and cool under running cold water.

14. In a wok or large frying pan, heat 1 tablespoon of oil and stir-fry the ginger and green onions for 15 seconds.

15. Add the bamboo, red pepper, water chestnuts, and carrots and stir-fry for 2 minutes.

16. Mix in the soy-sauce mixture and bring to a boil.

17. Add fried cashew nuts and asparagus tips (or broccoli) and season to taste with salt.

18. Stir up cornstarch mix and add to wok.

19. Toss a few times until sauce is thickened and coats vegetables; turn out immediately onto a warm serving platter.

Serve with rice and sprinkled with a little toasted sesame oil.

VIETNAMESE CABBAGE AND GRAPEFRUIT SALAD

Vietnamese cuisine encourages the blending of fresh and cooked flavors in each mouthful, and uses a number of salads blending meat, vegetables, and fruits. This unusual recipe was written out by Loan Ly for the online cookbook of the Pittsburgh Dinner Co-op.

Yield: serves 6-8
   1/2 head of Chinese green cabbage (thinly sliced like coleslaw)
   1/2 head red cabbage (thinly sliced like cole slaw)
   3 sweet red grapefruits (peeled so only fruit parts remain)
   1/2 cup grapefruit juice
   2 tablespoons salt
   1/2 tablespoon ground black pepper
   1/4 cup sugar

Equipment: Medium bowl, large salad bowl

1. In a medium bowl, combine grapefruit juice, salt, pepper, and sugar.

2. Core cabbages and slice into thin shreds as for cole slaw.

3. Peel grapefruits with a sharp knife "so only fruit parts remain."

4. Halve the grapefruits and remove any seeds.

5. Take half of a grapefruit and squeeze the juice into the bowl. Mix in the grapefruit pulp and set the sauce aside.

6. In a large salad bowl, combine the cabbages, add the sauce, "and massage the sauce into the cabbage for about 2-5 minutes."

7. Cut the grapefruit halves into sections and arrange on top of the salad, or divide into portions.

NUOC CHAM

Nuoc Cham is the dipping sauce made from "nuoc mam," the fermented fish sauce that is basic to all Vietnamese cooking. Nuoc cham has no fishy taste, but is enticingly sweet, salty, sour, and hot with a fruity aroma. This recipe comes from Phan Huang of Maryland via Joan Nathan's 1984 *An American Folklife Cookbook.*

   1/4 cup Vietnamese or Thai fish sauce
   2 tablespoons white vinegar
   2 tablespoons sugar
   1 small dried red hot pepper (or crushed red pepper to taste)
   1 clove garlic
   1 tablespoon fresh lime juice
   1/4 carrot

1. In a small bowl, crush red pepper and add vinegar.

2. Peel carrot and take a slice off one side.

3. Roll the carrot onto the flat side, and take thin lengthwise slices until the carrot is too thin to slice.

4. Turn the last slice on its side and cut very thin sticks. Repeat for the other slices.

5. Add carrot, a half cup water, and all other ingredients to the bowl.

Serve as a dipping sauce with spring rolls or rice rolls.

COM NAM (RICE ROLLS)

These rice rolls were used in Vietnam for cold meals away from home during busy farm seasons. Dipped in nuoc cham (see above) or soy sauce, they were a staple food for poor people, and still serve well at picnics or buffets. This recipe is also from Phan Huang via Joan Nathan.

   2 cups long-grain rice

Equipment: Piece of thread or clean unscented dental floss, clean kitchen towels, kitchen twine

1. Cook rice in 4 cups water according to package directions, but do not salt.

2. When cooked, remove pot from heat and let stand, covered, until rice is cool enough to hold in your hands.

3. Remove rice to a bowl.

4. "Knead it as you would bread, to break up the grains of rice." (See Appendix 1.)

5. Place rice dough on damp towels, forming a cylinder about 12 inches long (see illustrations).

6. Wrap the rice in the towels like a sausage, twisting the ends as tightly as possible.

7. Tie the ends with twine. Set aside until completely cooled, several hours or overnight. (Don't refrigerate, which makes rice unpleasantly hard.)

8. When ready to serve, unfold the towel.

9. Wrap a piece of thread or floss all the way around the circumference of the roll, about 3/4 inches from the end.

10. Cross the ends of the thread and pull through. This will make a clean, round cut.

Serve the rice rounds on a platter with Hmong or Laotian or Cambodian salads, or with any cold meat dish, or plain with nuoc cham.

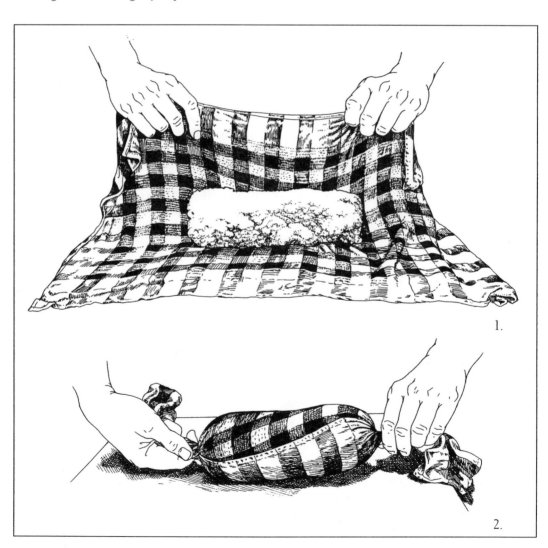

1.

2.

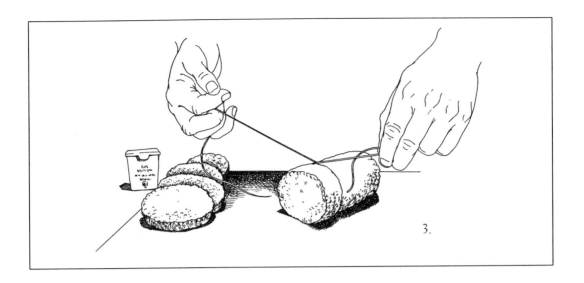

3.

VLACHS

See BULGARIAN-AMERICANS, MACEDONIAN-AMERICANS, AND VLACHS (ARUMANIANS)

WAMPANOAG

Although many books view the Wampanoag Indians who met the Pilgrims as extinct, some 1,500-2,000 people around southern Massachusetts disagree. They are the survivors of 20 bands of Wampanoag who once farmed and hunted most of eastern Massachusetts. The two largest groups are the federally recognized (since 1987) Aquinnah Wampanoag, on Martha's Vineyard, and the Mashpee Wampanoag, around the old Indian town of Mashpee on Cape Cod. The Mashpee Wampanoag are again seeking recognition despite losing federal land cases in 1977 and 1983. Young Wampanoags are relearning their language, which is well documented—it was the language of the first book printed in English North America, a Bible translation. The Wampanoag had lost the spoken language, but still sing it in ceremonial songs.

Like many present-day American Indians, the Wampanoags have a variety of foods to express their ethnicity: the wild plants and animals they still hunt and gather; the clambakes that have become tribal events; a body of old Cape Cod recipes their ancestors developed, influenced, or preserved; and the occasional buffalo burger or Navaho taco at inter-tribal pow-wows. Mashpee Chief Earl Mills recalls hunting for skunks as a boy, so that the meat could be salted and preserved for the winter. Although The Flume restaurant that he co-owns serves excellent versions of New England chowders and fried fish, it serves no skunk.

BANNOCK

Cynthia Akins contributed this recipe to a collection of Mashpee Wampanoag recipes that was part of their 1977 land and recognition court case. Federal Judge Walter Skinner ruled that recipes like this one were early American, but not distinctively Wampanoag. Certainly the wheat flour and the frying pan are European, as is the English name "bannock," which probably derives from the Latin "panicum" for wheat. However, the cooking method, suitable for a campfire or open fireplace, had not been used by Anglo-Americans in eastern Massachusetts for more than 100 years. As an Indian recipe, bannock probably predates the Pilgrims, because the Wampanoags traded for iron pots with some of the hundreds of fishing ships that visited New England between 1500 and 1620. It almost certainly predates the registration of Indian land claims to Mashpee in 1685.

Yield: 8 pie-shaped wedges
  2 cups flour
  2 teaspoons baking powder
  1/2 teaspoon salt
  "enough water to make a medium soft batter" (see below)
  a little shortening or oil for frying

Equipment: Frying pan (black cast iron is best), toothpick or wire cake tester to test

1. Mix ingredients to make a soft batter. Start with about 1 cup water to get a dough that leaves the sides of the bowl, but can be barely kneaded with floured hands. (See Appendix 1.)

2. The softer the dough, the moister the eventual flatbread, so don't use too much flour, and don't overknead.

3. Grease the frying pan, and pat out the dough into a flat round, like a giant English muffin.

4. Cook over medium heat for 20-30 minutes, until the bread is rubbery and a toothpick or cake tester comes out clean.

5. For a browned surface, you can pop an oven-safe frying pan (like cast iron) into a 350-degree or hotter oven for a few minutes at the end of cooking. This kind of dough doesn't brown or burn easily, which is important in open-fire cooking. Before stoves and home ovens became common in the nineteenth century, a bannock might be tilted in the pan (or on a plank or flat stone) for radiant heat.

Serve sliced into wedges with jam, or with chowder or succotash.

THREE SISTERS RICE

This dish is made by Joan Avant Tavares (Owamaskqua) for Mashpee Wampanoag events. The recipe comes from her 1993 booklet, "A Prelude to the soon-to-be published book *Wampanoag Foods & Legends.*" The three sisters are the corn, beans, and squash that grew together in Indian fields. The colors are those of the four directions in the culture of many Native American tribes. The combination of cinnamon and pepper leads people to think there is curry powder in this dish, perhaps a nod to the Wampanoag ancestors who were sailors on the clipper ships.

Yield: serves 6 to 10 portions
  1 pound rice ("good results with Uncle Ben's")
  1 8-ounce can whole kernel corn
  1 8-ounce can dark kidney beans
  1 medium zucchini squash
  1 medium yellow summer squash
  1 teaspoon cinnamon
  1 medium onion
  salt and pepper "to taste" (Mrs. Tavares uses a lot of pepper)
  Equipment: Frying pan (black cast iron is best) with cover

1. Boil rice according to package directions.

2. Let rice cool.

3. Drain corn and beans, and stir into rice.

4. Dice the green and yellow squash rather fine.

5. Combine all ingredients and sauté in frying pan or on a griddle.

6. Briefly cover the frying pan to finish cooking the squash.

Serve hot. Leftovers reheat well in a microwave.

CRANBERRY SAUCE

This is one of the things Earl Mills makes for Thanksgiving, according to an article by Molly O'Neill in the November 21, 1999, issue of the

New York Times. The family usually begins the day, which some Native Americans take as a day of mourning or protest, with a sweat lodge, burning tobacco to purify themselves, and traditional drumming and singing all day long. They eat turkey, winter squash, stuffing, and succotash (with corn cobs for extra flavor), but may also have fry bread, buffalo, fresh skunk or raccoon, or clam chowder or eels. Cranberries are native to the area, and many Mashpee Wampanoags of older generations worked as pickers in the commercial cranberry industry.

Yield: 2 cups
   4 cups whole cranberries
   2 cups water
   6 tablespoons sugar
   pinch of salt

1. In a medium saucepan, combine all ingredients, bring to a boil, lower to a simmer and cook, uncovered, for 10 minutes. (Or until cranberries burst).

2. Cool.

WELSH-AMERICANS

About 2 million Americans claim Welsh descent, almost half of whom list it on the census as their second ancestry. This unusually high figure shows both pride in ancestors from Wales, and the relative ease with which Welsh-Americans have intermarried and assimilated among other immigrant groups from the British Isles. Wales industrialized early, and so experienced Welsh miners and steel workers came to the United States for higher wages before the Civil War, but relatively few in the peak immigrations of 1880 to 1920. Welsh-language cultural festivals of poetry and song peaked between 1875 and 1915. Even in the Welsh farm areas of Ohio, Wisconsin, and Pennsylvania, Welsh-American recipes have a historical feeling. The popular "Welsh Rarebit" is related to a real Welsh dish of toasted cheese named, "caws-wedi-pobi," but came to the U.S. as a universal British Isles dish called "Welsh Rabbit," a negative ethnic joke about Welsh thrift.

WELSH TEA CAKES

Welsh Cakes, a specialty of South Wales, are the one recipe that every Welsh-American seems to know and treasure. This recipe was contributed to the Web site of the Weirton (West Virginia) Library. They are "pice ar y maen" in Welsh, and also pics, pix, South Wales cakes, tish and cluck ones, and bakestones. They are rolled out anywhere from 1/8 to 1/2 inch thick, and almost always cooked on a griddle on top of the stove. A number of Welsh-Americans now use electric skillets set at 350 degrees, and some dip the completed cakes in sugar or cinnamon sugar.

Yield: 30 or 40 cookies if you roll them out 1/4 inch thick
   2 cups sifted all-purpose flour
   2 eggs
   1 teaspoon baking powder
   1 cup shortening (a mixture of margarine and Crisco may be used)
   1/4 teaspoon salt
   1/2 cup black currants (raisins may be substituted, but either should be soaked in hot water)
   1/2 teaspoon nutmeg
   2/3 cup white sugar

Equipment: Pastry blender

1. Soak currants or raisins in hot water.

2. Mix all dry ingredients

3. Cut in shortening until you have a mixture that will cling together when pressed in your hand.

4. Beat eggs and mix thoroughly.

5. Drain fruit and add to the mixture. Divide the mixture into 3 or 4, and roll into balls. Refrigerate until ready to roll.

6. Flour a rolling pin and board, roll out 1/3 of the mixture and cut with cookie cutter. "My mother used a water glass." Save scraps, roll into a ball, and roll it out as well.

7. Grease skillet or grill and cook cookies "over medium-low heat if using electric stove." Cook on one side about 4 or 4 1/2 minutes, turn, and cook on other side.

WELSH RAISIN BREAD

This recipe from a Fundcraft community cookbook at <www.cookbooks.com> was "served at the Welsh Booth, Folk Fair '85," likely a folk fair in Wisconsin or Illinois. The Welsh name is "Bara Brith" or "Barragh Briegh."

1 cup raisins
1 egg
3/4 cup sugar
2 1/4 cups sifted flour
1 teaspoon baking soda
1 teaspoon baking powder
1/2 teaspoon salt

1/2 cup chopped nuts
1 tablespoon shortening for bread and solid shortening to grease loaf pan
1 teaspoon vanilla

Equipment: Large loaf pan

1. Pour 1 1/2 cups boiling water over raisins and let stand while preparing other ingredients.

2. Beat egg lightly.

3. Add sugar gradually while beating egg.

4. Sift together flour, soda, baking powder, and salt.

5. Add dry ingredients alternately with raisins to egg mixture.

6. Add nuts.

7. Melt the tablespoon of shortening. Stir in with vanilla.

8. Grease large loaf pan.

9. Bake at 350 degrees for 1 hour.

Serve with butter and jam for tea.

ZUNI

Most of the 8,000 Zuni still live in the same pueblo built by their ancestors many centuries ago south of what is now Gallup, New Mexico. They remember by name ruins of several other pueblos that may have made up the "seven cities of Cibola" reported by Spanish explorers in the 1530s. Their language is unrelated to that of the **Hopi** or that of the **Eastern Pueblo Indians**, and has only had a written form since the 1970s. They preserve the kivas and kachinas of the ancient Pueblo religion, with a special emphasis on altars and carved "fetishes."

At the time they first encountered Europeans, the Zuni had effective methods of growing many types of corn, beans, and squash on the high desert, and may have had domesticated turkeys. They quickly learned how to grow wheat and developed dwarf fruit trees. Like the Hopi, they preferred blue cornmeal and used the ashes of certain plants and ground limestone to keep the blue color in cooked foods, including a version of piki bread. Two well-known Zuni foods are a wheat bread baked in large batches in communal ovens, and fried squash blossoms. The recipes below come from Rita Edaakie's *Idonapshe (Let's Eat): Traditional Zuni Foods*, which was published in 1999 by the University of New Mexico Press and the A:shiwi A:wan Museum and Heritage Center.

CHULEYA:WE (POSOLE STEW)

The Zuni grow corn in six colors, of which blue corn is their favorite. This hominy stew is one of

their uses for white corn. Note that everyday Zuni cooking is not very spicy, although they do grow and use chile peppers and sometimes mix chile stews with posole. The colon in the middle of the word "Chuleya:we" means that the preceding vowel sound is held for twice the usual amount of time. The name "posole" comes from the Aztecan languages of Mexico.

Yield: serves 15 with a 2-cup serving each
  1 pound dry white corn for posole (or whole hominy or samp, or use 1 pound frozen white hominy or 4 cans white hominy)
  2 pounds beef or mutton stew meat
  1 pound meat bones
  1 teaspoon salt

Equipment: Grinding stone (if using dry white corn) or "an unpainted, rough-surfaced patio tile" (cleaned and soaked), willow basket or colander, stock pot

1. If using dry corn for posole, soak corn in warm bowl for 5 minutes the night before. Test that you can easily peel off the outer shell with a fingernail. If so, drain corn, roll on grinding stone until hulls peel off, and sift clean in a willow basket or colander. If using other kinds of hominy that have already been hulled, go on to Step 2.

2. Cut the meat into bite-sized cubes.

3. Bring 2 gallons of water to a boil in a large stock pot, and add meat, bones, and prepared corn.

4. Add salt "so it won't boil over."

5. "The way you can tell it's ready is when the corn looks like popcorn." Dried whole hominy cooks in 2 to 2 1/2 hours; frozen hominy is somewhat faster; and canned hominy stew is done when the meat is tender, about 40 minutes, although it gets better if it cooks longer.

Serve in bowls with hot chile sauce on the side.

ME:MO'LE (PUMPKIN AND PUMPKIN SEEDS)

Try to get a "sugar pumpkin," which has more flavor, like the three kinds of pumpkins grown by the Zuni. The flesh of the orange pumpkins grown for Halloween is very bland, although the seeds will work in this recipe. In Zuni, the pumpkins are often baked overnight in the leftover heat of adobe bread ovens.

Yield: serves 30 or more
  1 large pumpkin
  butter
  honey or sugar
  salt
  chili powder (for seeds)
  oil for baking sheet

Equipment: Cake pan to hold pumpkin, aluminum foil, baking sheet

1. Place the whole pumpkin in a cake pan and cover with foil.

2. If cooking in a conventional oven, bake at 350 degrees until tender. Check after 45 minutes with a fork. "If the pumpkin is tender and smells good, it's cooked."

3. Remove from oven, and cautiously remove foil.

4. Cut around the top, and spoon out seeds. Reserve seeds for roasted pumpkin seeds in Step 6.

5. Add butter, honey, or sugar to sweeten the baked pumpkin.

6. Oil a baking sheet.

7. Clean flesh off the pumpkin seeds.

8. Spread the seeds on the baking sheet and bake an hour at 250 degrees, turning them occasionally.

9. Add salt, chili, or spices to seeds as they are roasting.

Serve pumpkin as a vegetable side dish, and the seeds as a snack.

APPENDIX 1: HOW TO KNEAD

Several recipes for yeast breads contain the instruction "knead dough until smooth and elastic." Kneading is a process of pressing and stretching dough whereby the protein fibers, called gluten, are lined up to make sheets that trap the yeast bubbles so a wheat or rye bread will rise. "Quick breads," made with baking powder, don't need this structure. (Many ethnic breads and cakes started with yeast dough, and have been reformulated for baking powder in the United States, where women have less time to bake.) Experienced cooks can feel the gluten develop as they knead because the texture of the dough changes from clay-like and crumbly to relatively rubbery and smooth.

Different cooks do this in somewhat different ways, and standing mixers with a dough hook or bread machines also do the job. But here is the way I do it. Because I am right-handed, you may want to reverse some of these directions if you are left-handed.

1. I begin stirring the liquid and flour together in a large, heavy bowl, using a wooden spoon.
2. After this gets too hard, I take off any rings, flour my hands lightly, and finish mixing the dough in the bowl with my fingers.
3. I flour a wooden board on top of the kitchen table. (Countertops are higher, and I want to get some weight on top of the actual kneading.)
4. I turn the dough out onto the board, and scrape off large scraps from the bowl. I put some flour on top of the dough, and push it down to a fat disk like a stack of two or three Frisbees.

5. I fold this over in half, right-to-left. (This is the right-handed part.) Sometimes I fold it again, from the edge nearest to me, over and away from me.
6. With both hands, I push down and away from me, flattening the dough in a somewhat rolling motion over the top. It should end up as a flatter oblong, with the long way running from nearest me to farthest.

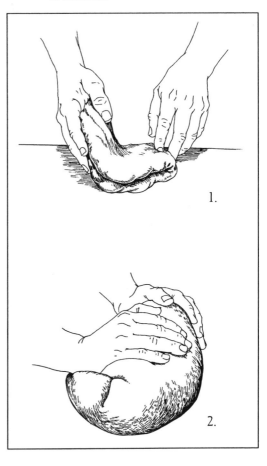

7. I then turn the oblong one-quarter turn, and again fold it over right-to-left, and again maybe near-to-far.
8. Then I push down and away from me again.
9. As the dough is kneaded, it stretches less, and doesn't get as flat, and I only have to fold it once. I may have to add more flour to my hands, the board, or the dough, but not much. I can also punch the dough, pick it up and throw it down, or pound it with a rolling pin. (You can get out some aggression at this stage.)
10. When the dough is getting so smooth and elastic that it barely flattens out enough to fold, and it isn't sticky anymore, kneading is done. If you are using a two-rise method, you dust it with flour or oil and put it in a bowl to rise. If your recipe doesn't call for two rises, or you've already done the first, you shape it for the eventual bread or buns or coffeecake, and let it rise in the baking pans.
11. If you are using two rises, you wait until the dough is about doubled, and a finger poke leaves a big dent. Then you "punch down" the dough to get rid of the first round of air bubbles. You can do this with fists, karate chops, fingers, or flat handed—anything to push the air bubbles out. When that's about done, you finish the job with a couple of kneads, and shape the dough for the second rise or the baking pans.

Appendix 2: They All Stuffed Cabbage

Although the Polish-American "galumpki" are the best-known, similar dishes of cabbage leaves stuffed with meat and rice are found among many immigrant groups. The rice stuffing suggests that the dish originated in the Middle East, and spread into Europe with the expanding Turkish Empire. The dish may also have been introduced into the Balkan countries by Gypsies prior to the Turkish invasions. Some Pennsylvanian slang expressions for stuffed-cabbage recipes are "pigs in a blanket" and "blind pigeons."

Ethnic Origin	Name(s)	Features
Armenian	gaghamp patat	some with dried fruit sauce
Assyrian (from Iraq)	dolmas	folded into triangles
Austrian	kohlwürstchen	
Bulgarian	sarmi	variations with cubed meat, sauerkraut leaves, New Year's dish.
Bulgarian Sephardic Jewish	yaprakes di kol dulce/agra	fresh cabbage/sauerkraut leaves
Carpatho-Rusyn	haluski	
Croatian	sarma	ham or bacon in filling, Christmas dish
Czech	hulopki	
Dutch	gevulde kool	no rice, wrapped in cheesecloth
Finnish	kaali pullia	
French	chou farcie, dolmas de chou	
German	gefullt krautroladen, kohlrouladen	German names mean "rolled cabbage"
Germans from Russia (Volga, Ukraine, Moldova)	halupsy, gefulltes sauerkraut	some with sauerkraut leaves
Greek	sarmathes, lehanadolmathes	
Hungarian	toltoot kaposztja	many variations, some with sour cream

Ethnic Origin	Name(s)	Features
Iranian	dolmeh kalam	rice and lamb filling, or lentil stew
Italian	cavioli ripieni, cavolo ripieno	
Jewish	holishkes, kalumpkes, prokes, gefulte kraut	names derive from the Galician, Polish, Russian, and German dialects of Yiddush
Lebanese	yebrak malfoof (malfoof mehshi, warak malfoof)	some thin as cigars
Norwegian	Kaalruletter golumpki	sometimes no rice
Polish	**galumpky**	**name means "little pigeons"; many variations**
Provençal (southern France)	sou fassum	
Romanian	sarmale	
Russian	golubtsi	
Serbian	sarmele	
Slovak	holupki, polena kapusta	
Spanish	col relleno, lombarda rellena	the later is red cabbage leaves stuffed for Christmas
Swedish	kaldomar, kaldalmiar	sometimes tied with string
Turkish	lahana sarma	
Ukrainian	galubtzi	many variations, including mushroom barley

Appendix 3: They All Fried Bean Cakes

The distribution for fried bean cakes is both wider and more southerly than that for stuffed cabbage (see Appendix 2). Note the similarity of names, which suggests a common origin in India and a diffusion to West Africa and then via the slave trade to the Americas. Unless otherwise noted, most of these dishes are made from members of the black-eyed pea family with the skins removed. I have included a few non-bean fritters of the same names. **Boldface type** denotes recipes that appear in this book.

Ethnic Origin	Name of Dish	Features
Bahamas	acaras	
Barbados	pumpkin accra	pumpkin fritters
Benin	akkra funfun	
Brazil	acarajés	bean tamales are "abarás"
Burkina Faso	akara	
Cuban (Key West)	bollos, bollitos de carita	
Curacao, Aruba	callas	"callas" are rice fritters in New Orleans
Egyptian	**Felafel,** Falafel	ground chick peas
Florida Seminole	black-eyed pea fritters	may be an African survival via runaway slaves who joined the tribe
Ghana	kose, akla	
Guadeloupe, Martinique	acras de zieu nois	
Haiti	acras, acrats	applied to other fried foods
Jamaica	akkra, accra	
Nigerian	**akara**	steamed mixture is called "**moin moin**"
Northern Indian	pakora	fritters in bean flour
Sierre Leone	binch akara	
Trinidad	accra, accras	salt-cod fritters

APPENDIX 4: THEY ALL FRIED DOUGH

It seems like every ethnic group in America has at least one form of fried dough, and many have several, ranging from crisp sweet cookies to doughnuts, crullers, and fry breads. Shapes vary, but many involve cutting slits and pulling part of the dough through the slit to make knots or bows. **Boldface type** denotes recipes that appear in this book.

Ethnic Group	Name of Fried Dough	Notes on Shapes
Asian Indian	poori, shanker-para	puffed fry bread, sweet diamonds
Colombian	hojuelas	diamonds
Croatian	flancats, hrstule	strips
Czech	listy, borshe milluste ("angel's kisses")	"vanities" knots, squares
Dutch	**krullers**, ollie koeks, ollie bollen	double spirals, bread balls
Eskimo	uqsrukuaqtaq	round doughnuts with holes
Ethiopian	dabo kolo	wheat nuts
French	beginets, corasse	square doughnuts
German	grebble	twisted squares
Germans from Russia	schlitz kuechla	squares or slit squares
Greek	theples	"honey curls"
Hungarian	csöröge	slit knots
Icelandic	kleinur	slit strips pulled into knots
Indo-Caribbean (Trinidadian and Guyanese)	roti	fry bread like Asian Indian poori
Iroquois	scoon	fry bread
Israeli	sufganyot	jelly doughnuts
Italian	strufoli	knotted strips

Ethnic Group	Name of Fried Dough	Notes on Shapes
Lithuanian	sausainiai, zagareliai, ausukes, kruzdys	"cookies," "little twigs," "little ears," and "lover's knots," respectively; slit diamonds and slit strips
Maltese	xkunvat ("lovers' knots")	bows
Mexican	bunuelos	
Moravian	strumbbundles, tanglebritches, heifta cakels, tanglejackets	slit strips
Native American	**fry bread,** squaw bread	various shapes
New Mexico Hispanics	**sopaipillas**	square or triangular pillows
Norwegian	smultboller	sour cream doughnuts
Norwegian	fattigman	crullers
Pennsylvania Dutch	krebel	slit strips
Polish	chrusciki	knots
Portuguese	sonhos ("dreams"), malassadas	fritters, doughnuts
Romanian	Minciunele ("little lies")	slit strips
Russian	harushee, xvorost	slit bow ties
Serbian	gagoules tulumbe	doughnut holes
Slovak	ceregy	diamonds or slit diamonds
Slovene	flancati	slit rectangles
Spanish	suspiros de monja	"nun's sighs"
Swedish	klenatur	knotted crullers
Swiss	kuchli, schenckeli, pfeuserli	diamonds, strips, respectively
Swiss-Mennonite	knie blatza ("knee patches")	flat rounds
Trinidadian	**potato bread,** floats	fry breads

ANNOTATED BIBLIOGRAPHY

Listed below are the best of hundreds of sources used for this book.

ETHNIC ENCYCLOPEDIAS

Barer-Stein, Thelma. *You Eat What You Are: People, Culture and Food Traditions*. 2nd ed. Ontario, Canada: Firefly Books, 1999; first published in 1979.

> Packed with food facts, but weak on generalizations. Written from a Canadian perspective, and focusing mainly on the foods of foreign countries rather than those used by ethnic groups in Canada. No recipes. Surprisingly little on Asians and West Indians, but does have some information on Canadian "First Nations" and Canadian cooking per se.

Gaines, Judy, Anna Sheets, and Robyn V. Young, eds. *The Gale Encyclopedia of Multicultural America*. New York: Gale Research, 1995.

> Updates the *Harvard Encyclopedia of American Ethnic Groups* (Thernstrom et al.) with articles on many recent immigrants, some individual Indian tribes, and some sub-ethnic groups from India. Most articles have a brief culinary section and a list of prominent representatives of the ethnic group. Has 1990 census ancestry survey summary as an appendix.

Levinson, David, and Milton Ember, eds. *American Immigrant Cultures: Builders of a Nation*. New York: Macmillan Reference, 1997.

> Updates the *Harvard Encyclopedia of American Ethnic Groups* (Thernstrom et al.) with newer census data, and recent immigrant groups, but omits Native Americans and ethnic groups that formed in the United States. Immigration focus tends to emphasize national origins more than other aspects of ethnicity.

Thernstrom, Stephan, Ann Orlov, Oscar Handlin, eds. *Harvard Encyclopedia of American Ethnic Groups*. Cambridge, MA: Harvard University Press, 1980.

> Groundbreaking and still definitive, although very much a work of its period in that it emphasizes European immigrant groups and passes quickly over African-American subgroups and recent immigrants from Latin America and the Caribbean. The article on "Tri-Racial Isolates" is negative in tone, but none of the newer books deal with tri-racial ethnic groups at all.

MULTI-ETHNIC NATIONAL COOKBOOKS

Bauer, Linda. *The American Sampler Cookbook: America's Leading Statesmen and Their Families Share Their Favorite Recipes*. Kuttawa, KY: McClanahan Publishing House, 1986.

> Recipes contributed by U.S. congresspeople and senators at the height of the ethnic revival.

Borghese, Anita. *Foods from Harvest Festivals and Folk Fairs: The Best Recipes from and a Guide to Food Happenings Across the Nation*. New York: Thomas Y. Crowell, 1997.

Recipes and notes from fairs, many of them ethnic, across the United States and southern Canada.

Cordova, Regina, with Emma Carrasco. *Celebración: Recipes & Traditions Celebrating Latino Family Life.* New York: Doubleday Mainstreet Books, 1996, 214 pages.

Published for the Mexican-American organization, National Council of La Raza, this book is a good complement for the Novas and Silva book, *Latin Cooking Across the U.S.A.* (see below). Many of the cooks are named and interviewed, and there is a brief introduction about Hispanic and Caribbean cultures and holidays.

Estes, Annice, ed. *Global Feast Cookbook.* Mystic, CT: Mystic Seaport Museum Stores, 1994.

Mystic Seaport is a historical museum in eastern Connecticut. The book is organized by regions of the world and has many foreign recipes, but also has a good Native American chapter by tribes, and some American ethnic recipes that were apparently contributed by museum staff.

Gubser, Mary. *America's Bread Book: 300 Authentic Recipes for America's Favorite Homemade Breads Collected on a 65,000-Mile Journey Through the Fifty United States.* New York: Morrow, 1985.

Although organized by states, the book's index has 59 recipes under "Ethnic Breads," most with individual attributions. Some recipes are the author's reconstructions, but many come from local cooks and commercial bakeries.

Harjo, Barbara (collector), with text by Julie Pearson-Little Thunder. *Artistic Tastes: Favorite Recipes of Native American Artists.* Walnut, CA: Kiva Publishing, 1998.

A useful collection of recipes from the traditional to the individually eccentric, reminding the reader that many Native Americans are today of mixed ethnicity and cook all kinds of food.

Kirlin, Katherine S., and Thomas M. Kirlin. *Smithsonian Folklife Cookbook.* Washington, D.C.: Smithsonian Institute Press, 1991.

Recipes drawn from summer festivals from 1968–1990. Organized regionally, but many ethnic recipes provide specific information. Besides the book in your hand, the Kirlin volume is the best primary resource on contemporary American ethnic cooking. For the ten festivals since this book was written, only scattered publications have appeared in pamphlets and on the Internet.

McClimon, Thomas L. *The Mayor's Cookbook: The Favorite Recipes of over 300 Mayors Across the U.S.A.* Washington, D.C.: Acropolis Books, 1987.

Published by the United States Conference of Mayors at the height of the ethnic revivals as more politicians—this time mayors—were emphasizing roots or local ethnic voting blocks.

Neithammer, Carolyn. *American Indian Food and Lore.* New York: Collier Macmillan, 1974. Reissued in 1999 as *The Southwest Indian Cookbook.*

Organized by plant species with many wild plants, but well-researched. Primarily covers southwestern tribes.

Nelsen, Peter J. T. *National Republican Heritage Groups Council World Cookbook.* Washington, D.C.: Atland Publishing, 1972.

An impressively broad, if badly dated, concept of ethnicity. Recipes representing 32 groups organized to support the Republican national campaign, and elected officials eager to show their ethnic roots. Also contains an unusual selection of foreign recipes, possibly from Washington embassies.

Novas, Himilce, and Rosemary Silva. *Latin Cooking Across the U.S.A.* New York: Knopf, 1997.

The Cuban-American authors collect food from named individuals of many recent immigrant groups, including some non-Hispanic Caribbean immigrants, and only sometimes make their own adaptations, which they confusingly describe as Colombian-American, etc.

Otis, Johnny. *Red Beans & Rice: and Other Rock 'n' Roll Recipes.* Rohnert Park, CA: Pomegranate Art Books, 1997.

As a Greek-American in the world of black music, Johnny "hand-jive" Otis must have learned early to explore the foods of other cultures, and apparently never quit, since he gets authentic recipes from family, musicians, and ethnic politicians of many backgrounds.

Paddleford, Clementine. *How America Eats.* New York: Scribner's, 1960.

Organized by regions and full of details about people and recipes. Some later versions edit out the stories. Not focused on ethnic cooking, but the author inquires about the background of her sources, local cooks, food editors, and some producers. Material about African-American and Native American cooks shows much less interest.

Smith, Jeff. *The Frugal Gourmet on Our Immigrant Ancestors: Recipes You Should Have Gotten from Your Grandmother.* New York: William Morrow, 1990.

An enthusiastic look at the foods of 35 ethnic groups. Smith generally "fixes" the recipes and often includes foreign food the ancestors "should have brought over" or ancestors you should have had but didn't—i.e., Smith favorites that aren't American ethnic recipes at all. Authentic and useful on some cuisines where he had good contacts, such as Latvian-Americans.

Stern, Jane, and Michael Stern. *Real American Food.* New York: Alfred Knopf, 1986.

The authors include some ethnic recipes in their survey of regional specialties from the roadside restaurants they review in other books and magazines.

Tirsch, Jessie. *A Taste of the Gulf Coast: The Art and Soul of Southern Cooking.* New York: Macmillan, 1997.

Almost all the recipes are from named individuals, and the author has a real nose for ethnic cooking from Galveston to Key West.

Tracy, Marion, ed. *Favorite Regional Recipes of America: By America's Newspaper Food Editors.* New York: Grosset & Dunlap, n.d. (Reprint of *Coast to Coast Cookery*, Indiana University Press, 1952.)

Regional favorites of the then-48 states, Canada, and Hawaii; contains some ethnic recipes.

Williamson, Darcy, and Lisa Railsback. *Cooking with Spirit: North American Indian Food and Fact.* Bend, OR: Maverick Publications, 1987.

Few individual attributions, but many recipes are attributed by tribes, and were collected by Railsback at pow-wows. Includes traditional and contemporary reservation recipes.

MULTICULTURAL STATE COOKBOOKS

American Cancer Society, Massachusetts Division, Inc. *Cook It in Massachusetts.* Memphis: Wimmer Brothers, 1981.

Contributed by patients and families, but apparently part of a national series with some ethnic focus.

American Cancer Society, Michigan Division, Inc. *Seasonal Samplings: A Culinary Look at the Seasons of Michigan.* Memphis: Wimmer Brothers, 1981.

Has an ethnic chapter.

American Cancer Society, Minnesota Division, Inc. *Minnesota Heritage Cookbook: Hand-Me-Down Recipes.* Eden Prairie, MN: Bolger Publications, 1979, 170 pages.

Early and completely ethnic book in this series; recipe contributors are listed at the end of the book in one block.

American Cancer Society, Wisconsin Division, Inc. *Ethnic Cooking Wisconsin Style.* Memphis: Wimmer Brothers, 1982.

The most explicitly ethnic of the series in my collection of seven, but if you see any more of these, please let me know about it.

Corum, Anna Kondo. *Ethnic Foods of Hawai'i.* Honolulu: Bess Press, 1983.

A school librarian assembled these foods of nine ethnic groups.

Eberly, Carole. *Our Michigan: Ethnic Tales & Recipes.* East Lansing, MI: Shoestring Press, 1979.

I obtained this book too late to include recipes. However, it has 21 ethnic groups, including Cornish, Irish, Canadian, and Dutch, with recipes generally attributed to one cook.

Kaplan, Anne R., Marjorie A. Hoover, and Willard B. Moore. *The Minnesota Ethnic Food Book.* Minneapolis: Minnesota Historical Society Press, 1986.

Usefully illustrated and well researched for 14 ethnic groups in Minnesota, from the Ojibway and the British to the Hmong. Unfortunately, all ethnic groups from the former Yugoslavia are listed together as "South Slavs."

Kekaha Parent-Teachers' Association. *Kauai Cookbook*. Lihue, HI: Garden Island Publishing Company, 1954.

Organized by nine ethnic groups, including dishes of an otherwise little-known Spanish community that arrived in 1906.

Laudan, Rachel. *The Food of Paradise: Exploring Hawaii's Culinary Heritage*. Honolulu: University of Hawai'i Press, 1986.

More interested in shared "local food" than ethnic dishes per se, but has a recipe index by 11 ethnicities, including "local" and "Kakaaina," which applies to longtime Anglo residents.

MULTICULTURAL CITY COOKBOOKS

Dorchester Community News. Introduction by Sue Ennis. *Dorchester International Cookbook*. Dorchester, MA: Circulation Service, c. 1979–81.

An impressive by-product of a left-liberal community newspaper in Boston's largest neighborhood.

Fitchburg Historical Society. *Folk Foods of Fitchburg: A Culinary Heritage in Recipes from Many Lands*. Fitchburg, MA, 1961.

A truly remarkable work published for the bicentennial of a small industrial city, with more than 14 ethnic groups represented.

International Institute of Metropolitan Detroit. *Cuisine International*. Detroit, 1979.

The International Institutes were founded as settlement houses for immigrants by the YWCA in the 1920s, and began almost immediately to produce cookbooks with recipes contributed by their clients. They dropped the YWCA affiliation in 1945, but several have continued as independent agencies. If you ever run across the 1930s St. Louis book, I'd like to see that one. This is the most recent International Institute cookbook in my collection, and contains many ethnic groups, including hard-to-find recipes from Turkish, Bulgarian, and Rumanian immigrants.

O'Brien, Marian Maeve, ed. *The Shaw House Cook Book*. St. Louis: The Historical Committee and The Women's Association of Missouri Botanical Garden, 1963.

A wonderful collection of family recipes from Victorian St. Louis.

O'Neill, Molly. *New York Cookbook*. New York: Workman, 1992.

A recent culinary portrait of America's most multi-ethnic city, with some information about the cooks, although it leans toward restaurateurs and cooking teachers.

Raichlin, Steven. *Miami Spice: Latin America, Cuba, & the Caribbean Meet in the Tropical Heart of America*. New York: Workman, 1993.

Raichlin is an innovative cook and knows young chefs in Miami, but he also knows enough to leave good ethnic recipes as he finds them in this city with many recent immigrants.

Stallworth, Lyn, and Rod Kennedy. *The Brooklyn Cookbook*. New York: Knopf, 1994.

Impeccable and beautifully illustrated history and portrait of the Dutch farm settlement that grew to be a city of immigrant neighborhoods. Second only to the *Smithsonian Folklife Cookbook* as a resource on American ethnic cooking, and especially strong on recent immigrants. The authors write recipes very well.

COOKBOOKS ABOUT INDIVIDUAL GROUPS

Densmore, Frances. *Indian Uses of Wild Plants for Crafts, Food, Medicine, and Charms*. (Originally in *Forty-fourth Annual Report of the Bureau of American Ethnology, 1926–1927.*) Reprinted Ontario, Canada: Iroqcrafts Iroquois Reprints, 1987.

Classic study of Ojibway/Chippewa uses of wild foods and traditional recipes for wild rice.

Geraty, Virginia Mixon. *Bittle en' T'ing: Gullah Cooking with Maum Crish*. Orangeburg, SC: Sandlapper Publishing,1992.

I did not use recipes from this book because Maum Crish is a fictional character developed by Geraty, a Gullah language instructor and translator who is not African-American herself. However, the recipes are well observed and given "bilingually" in English and easy Gullah.

Hom, Ken. *Easy Family Recipes from a Chinese-American Childhood*. New York: Knopf, 1997.

Most recipes revised by this well-known chef. Introduction discusses slow development of Chinese-American food.

Parker, Arthur C. *Iroquois Uses of Maize and Other Food Plants*. Ontario, Canada: Iroqcrafts Iroquois Reprints, 1983. (Originally *New York State Museum Bulletin 144*, November 1, 1910. Reprinted with some additional material by William Guy Spittal.)

Classic source for Iroquois foodways and recipes, with recent comments on green corn soup.

Pinderhughes, John. *Family of the Spirit Cookbook: Recipes and Remembrances from African-American Kitchens*. New York: Simon and Schuster, 1990.

Organized by individual cooks, but covers a variety of African-American regional and ethnic styles, including one cook of Jamaican-Barbadian-Panamanian background.

Prudhomme, Paul. *The Prudhomme Family Cookbook: Old-Time Louisiana Recipes by the Eleven Prudhomme Brothers and Sisters and Chef Paul Prudhomme*. New York: William Morrow, 1987.

Cajun home cooking including rare hard-times recipes from the 1930s.

Sekatu, Ella Thomas. *Narragansett Indian Recipes*. n.p., n.d.

Self-published tribal recipes and lore from the medicine woman and daughter of the previous medicine man of the Rhode Island tribe.

Wampanoag Cookery. Boston: American Science and Engineering Education Division, copyright by the Children's Museum of Boston, 1972.

Dishes gathered primarily by Mashpee Wampanoags as part of their federal recognition and land case.

Warda, David Benjamin. *Assyrian Cookery*. Cincinnati: Self-published, 1992.

Lavishly illustrated with photos of family life in Flint, Michigan, and ancient Assyrian reliefs. Available for $25 at P.O. Box 23157, Cincinnati, OH 45223.

Young, Carrie, with Felicia Young, *Prairie Cooks: Glorified Rice, Three-Day Buns, and Other Recipes and Reminiscences*. Reprint ed.

Chicago: HarperPerennial, 1997. (Originally published by University of Iowa Press, 1993.)

Food of the author's mother, who was born in Norway in 1879, grew up in Minnesota, and moved to a farm in western North Dakota.

Internet World Wide Web Sites

Bawarchi, Your Indian Cook, Contributions. <http://www.bawarchi.com/contribution/index.html>, April 6, 2000.

Commercial Asian Indian-American site with lively exchange of reader recipes from all regions of India and some Chinese recipes. The page is large and crashes some browsers.

Cookbook Committee of St. Gregory's Armenian Apostolic Church (Shirley Setian, Chair). *Adventures in Armenian Cooking.* <http://www.cilicia.com/armo_cookbook.html>, April 7, 2000, (Raffi Kojian, Webmaster).

Complete text of 200-recipe cookbook, originally published in 1973 by the church in Indian Orchard, Massachusetts, as a fund raiser. The site as a whole is an excellent source for Armenia and Armenian-American information.

Cookbooks On/Line, Inc. *Cookbooks On/Line: One Million Plus Recipes Database.* <http://www.cook-books.com>, April 7, 2000.

Although some recipes are duplicates, this site has a large searchable database of recipes contributed to community and church cookbooks published by Fundcraft, Inc., one of the largest do-it-yourself cookbook publishers. Brief registration required. The recipes are not sourced, but some have background information attached, and can be searched by words like "Polish," "sauerkraut," "gingersnaps," or "stack cake." Perhaps most useful in collecting multiple versions of popular recipes to compare the variations.

Giese, Paula. *Native American Indian Art, Culture, Education, History, Science.* March 21, 1997. <http://indy4.fdl.cc.mn.us/~isk>, April 2, 2000.

Individual and thoughtful pages by Paula Giese, an Ojibway woman, with many Native American recipes from her own and other traditions. Ms. Giese died in July 1997, but the Web pages are preserved by Fond du Lac Community College. Recipes from several tribes collected and used by Ms. Giese, including a lot of wild rice and health food information.

Hawaiian Electric Company. *The Electric Kitchen.* <http://www.heco.com/ekitchen/history.htm> April 3, 2000.

The Hawaiian Electric Company has archived cooking recipes from cooking demonstrations it has sponsored since 1995, including presentations by ethnic cooks (and some professional chefs) of Japanese-American, Okinawan-American, Chinese-American, Filipino-American, Puerto Rican, Portuguese-American, Sri Lankan-American, Vietnamese-American, and Thai-American backgrounds. A wonderful resource.

Lutheran Brotherhood Potluck Recipes, Heritage Recipes. <http://www.luthbro.com/potluck/Recipes/Heritage.htm>, April 7, 2000.

A collection of ethnic recipes from the Lutheran Brotherhood, a 60-year-old cooperative insurance venture and fraternal charity serving many Scandinavian-American and German-American communities.

Staff Development Institute (SDI) and the Outreach Technical Assistance Network (OTAN), (Susan Gaer, Webmaster). Completed Projects. September 29, 1996. <http://www.otan.dni.us/webfarm/emailproject/com.htm>, March 10, 2000.

1995 and 1996 cookbook projects of adult literacy programs, featuring many recipes written by recent immigrants and gathered by the Outreach and Technical Assistance Network of California, but also including recipes from an elementary school in New York and adult literacy projects in England and Italy. The 1997 and 1998 recipes are at <http://www.otan.dni.us/webfarm/emailproject/cook.htm>.

Sultzman, Lee. *First Nations Histories.* February 9, 2000. <http://www.dickshovel.com/Compacts.html>, April 2, 2000.

Detailed tribal histories, mostly of tribes east of the Mississippi, as part of an ongoing book project. The site as a whole has many political links. No recipes.

Wilson, Darlene, Webmaster. A *Melungeon Homepage.* <http://www.melungeons.org>, April 7, 2000.

Site maintained by Melungeon descendents with current developments and speculations on this little-known ethnic group.

INDEX OF RECIPES BY STATES

by Mark Zanger

ALABAMA

African-American Neck Bones and Rice, 8

ALASKA

Eskimo Chugash Salmon Chowder, 102; Cranberries (kee-mee-nach), 102; White Fish Stew, 102
Tlingit Fish Perok, 274

ARIZONA

Apache Acorn Stew, 15–16; Acorn Bread, 16; Black Walnut Corn Bread, 16–17
Hopi Whole Wheat Stew, 141–42; Pinto Beans, 142
Navajo Fry Bread, 189–90; Kneel Down Bread, 190–91 (ill. 191); Navajo Taco, 191–92; Mutton Stew, 192
Pima and Papago Pima Tortillas, 218–19; Papago Tepary Bean Soup, 219; Pima Poshol Soup, 219

ARKANSAS

African-American White Potato Pie, 8

CALIFORNIA

African-American Guilt-Free Collard Greens (and Pot Likker), 7
Assyrian-American Zazich, 26; Booshala, 26–27
Belorussian-American Milk Soup, 41; Apples Baked with Honey, 41–42
Bulgarian-American Meatball Soup, 48–49
Chinese-American Iceberg Lettuce-Egg Drop Soup, 64–65
Creole (Louisiana) Turnips and Pork Ribs Etouffée, 78–79
Croatian-American Dalmatian Baked Fish, 80

Filipino-American Adobo Manok (Chicken), 107
Guamian Kelaguen Chicken Salad, 125
Guatemalan-American Pollo Guisada, 127
Japanese-American Obachan's Special Teriyaki Sauce, 159–60
Jewish-American Carrot-Sweet Potato Tzimmes, 164
Laotian-American Mixiensui (Mien Noodle Salad), 168–69
Mexican-American Easy Migas, 179; Chicken Enchilada Casserole, 182
Mormon Honey Butter, 185
Persian (Iranian)-American Persian Cutlet, 213–14
Peruvian-American Causa Limeña, 216–17
Russian-American "Simple Pashtet," 236
Salvadoran-American Maria's Guacamole, 238; Crab Salad, 239–40
Scottish-American Scotch Pancakes (Bannocks), 246
Sioux Stuffed Pumpkin, 255–56
Spanish-American Spanish Eggs, 262; Arroz Guisado con Tomates, 262
Swiss-American Cheese Pie, 268
Trinidadian-American Curried Chicken, 275

COLORADO

Colombian-American Short-Cut Arequipe, 71
Japanese-American Pan Sushi, 160–61

CONNECTICUT

Anglo-American Connecticut Kedgeree, 14
Arab-American Tabouli, 18–19
Bulgarian-American Vlach Cheese Corn Bread (Pispilita), 47
Italian-American Red and White Herb Roasted Potatoes, 157

DELAWARE

Armenian-American Nutmeg Cake, 21

DISTRICT OF COLUMBIA

Haitian-American Rix et Pois Rouges, 134–35
Nigerian-American Black-Eyed Peas, Nigerian
    Style, 199; Pepper Soup, 199

FLORIDA

African-American Sweet Potato Pie, 7–8
Bahamian-American Old Sour, 33
Cuban-American Black Bean Soup, 82–83; Puffed
    Wheat Batido, 83–84
Egyptian-American Felafel, 98
French Canadian-American Ragout, 114
Italian-American Meatballs (or Shrimpballs) and
    Spaghetti, 155–56
Nicaraguan-American Gallo Pinto, 195–96
Panamanian-American Foo-Foo, 209–10
Seminole and Miccosukee, Sofkee, 247–48;
    Pumpkin Bread, 248; Indian Fried Pumpkin
    Bread, 248–49
Spanish-American Florida Gispachi, 262–63

GEORGIA

Austrian-American Salzburger Raisin Bread, 29–30
Scotch-Irish Potato Soup, 242

HAWAII

Chinese-American Turkey Bones and Rice Chow-
    der, 66; Shoyu Chicken, 66–67
Filipino-American Cirio's Pork Adobo, 107–08
Native Hawaiian, Haupia, 136–37; Lomi Salmon,
    137
Japanese-American Nabemono (Hekka)— Pan
    Cooked Food, 161
Korean-American Spinach Salad, 166
Laotian-American Boiled Chicken with Jaew Som,
    167
Okinawan-American Spareribs, 205; Chanpuru,
    205–06; Fried Somen, 206
Portuguese-American Vinha D'alhos, 226
Samoan-American Banana Poi, 240; Sapasui, 240–
    41
Thai-American Kai Yat Sai, 272

IDAHO

Basque-American Walnut Pudding, 37

ILLINOIS

Asian Indian-American Peanut Potatoes, 23–24
Belgian-American Beef and Beer Stew, 40–41
Black Muslim Muhammad Supreme Bean Soup,
    43–44
Chinese-American Quick and Easy Corn and Egg,
    65
German-American Saurbraten, 116
Hungarian-American Pogachels, 143
Lithuanian-American Kugelis, 171; Cookie Slices
    (Sausainiai), 172
Mexican-American Grilled Corn, 180; Chicken
    Pozole, 181
Peruvian-American Chupe de Camarones (Shrimp
    Chowder), 217
Polish-American Friendly Tea, 220; Hunter's Stew,
    222
Sioux Wojapi Pudding, 253–54

INDIANA

Brazilian-American Canja (Chicken Soup), 45
Bulgarian-American Macedonian Style Peppers,
    46–47
Haitian-American Griots, 135; Sauce Ti-Malice,
    135–36
Turkish-American Sis Kebab, 276-77

IOWA

Amish Yummasetti, 11–12
Dutch-American Apple Koek, 95; St. Nicholas
    Koekjes, 95–96
Norwegian-American Kringles, 200–01
Swedish-American Oven Pancake, 265

KANSAS

German-American Dampfnudeln (Steam Buns),
    118–19
Swedish-American Swedish Apple Pie, 266–67

KENTUCKY

Melungeon Chocolate Gravy, 176–77; Stack Cake,
    177–78

LOUISIANA

Acadian (Cajun) Shrimp Jumbalaya, 2–3; Catfish
    Courtbouillon, 3; Smothered Potatoes, 4–5
Cane River Creole Meat Pies, 52; Tea Cakes, 52–
    53; Okra Gumbo, 53; Cinnamon Pecan
    Pralines, 54

Chitimacha Macque Choux, 67–68; Baked Duck, 68; Corn Soup, 68
Creole (Louisiana), Gumbo Z'Herbes, 77; Coush-Coush, Red Beans (Mrs. Olivier's), 78
Franco-American Shrimp a La Creole, 112–13; Pecan Pralines, 113
Honduran-American Cabbage Salad, 140–141
Spanish-American Caldo, 263

MAINE

Acadian (Cajun) Plogue (Ployes), 4
French Canadian-American Soup aux Pois, 114

MARYLAND

Asian Indian-American Baked Yogurt, 24
Australian-American Anzacs, 28
Cape Verdean-American Cachupa, 54–55; Canja, 56
Jewish-American Huevos Haminadoes, 163–64
Nigerian-American Akara, 198–99
Romanian-American Papanash, 235
Vietnamese-American Nuoc Cham, 283; Com Nam (Rice Rolls), 283–84

MASSACHUSETTS

African-American Marinated Pork Chops, 6–7
Albanian-American Hamburg with Potato (Moussaka), 9
Anglo-American Custard Johnnycake, 13–14; Yorkshire Pudding, 15
Arab-American Tiny Kibbee Balls, 18
Armenian-American Bean Salad, 20; Lemon-Yogurt Cake, 20; Tan, 21; Prinzov Pilaf, 21–22
Austrian-American Oatmeal Soup, 30–31
Brazilian-American Couve à Mineira, 45
Cambodian-American Ngiom, 49–50; B'baw Poat (Corn Pudding), 50
Cape Verdean-American Jag (Jagacida), 55
Chinese-American Cucumber Salad, 66
Cuban-American Picadillo, 83
Dominican-American Coconut Fish Stew, 91–92; Tostones, 92
English Canadian-American Nanaimo Bars, 100–01; Lemon Cookies, 101
Estonian-American Pancakes, 104
Greek-American Stuffed Grape Leaves (Athenian), 122–24 (ill. 123); Tourlou, 124
Guatemalan-American Radish Salad, 126
Haitian-American Haitian Cake, 136
Honduran-American Chicken with Rice, 141
Hungarian-American Liptaur Cheese Spread, 145
Irish-American Mayor Curley's Favorite Irish Bread, 148–49

Italian-American Boneless Chicken Cacciatore, 153–54
Jewish-American Matzoh Kloese, 162–63
Korean-American Marinated Chicken Wings, 165
Latvian-American Baltic Baconettes (Piragi), 169–70; Kimenmaizites (Caraway Rolls), 170
Pakistani-American Biryani, 207
Persian-American (Iranian) Chelo, 214–15; Gormeh Sabzi, 215
Peruvian-American Ceviche Peruano, 217–18
Polish-American Lazy Pierogi, 22–23
Portuguese-American Bolo de Filho (Leaf Cake), 225
Puerto Rican Asopao de Camarones, 231
Romanian-American Phelagel (Eggplant Salad), 234–35
Russian-American Pilaf, 235; Vinegret (Cooked Vegetable Salad), 236–37
Salvadoran-American Pupusas, 238–39
Trinidadian-American Potato Bread, 275–76
Wampanoag Bannock, 285–86; Three Sisters Rice, 286; Cranberry Sauce, 286–87

MICHIGAN

Assyrian-American Lettuce Leaves with Honey, Vinegar, and Mint Dip, 25; Flat Egg and Fresh Herb Pancakes, 26
Cornish-American Saffron Bread, 74
Dutch-American Anijsmelk (Anise Milk), 93; Coleslaw, 94–95
Germans from Russia Kraut Beerucks or Cabbage Busters, 120
Greek-American Pecan Crescents (Karithata), 124
Romanian-American Mamaliga with Cheese, 233
Turkish-American Coban Salatasl (Shepherd's Salad), 277; Spicy Rice (Ic Pilav), 277–78

MINNESOTA

Danish-American Kringle, 89
Finnish-American Ilmapuuro (Air Pudding), 108–09; Moijakka, 109–10; Pulla, 110–11
German-American Hoppel Poppel, 117–18
Hmong-American Watercress and Beef, 138–39
Norwegian-American Microwave Rommegrot, 200; Lefse, 201–02
Ojibway Gagoonz—Little Porcupines, 203–04; Bread Pudding, 204
Pakistani-American Carrot Halwa, 207–08
Polish-American Mazurek, 224
Scottish-American Oatcakes, 245
Swedish-American Osta Kaka, 266; Old-Fashioned Pepperkakor, 267

MISSISSIPPI

Arab-American Kibbee, 18
Choctaw Bananha, 69–70
Ethiopian-American Atakelte, 105

MISSOURI

Dutch-American Carrots, 96
German-American Schman, 118
Jamaican-American Oxtail Stew, 158

MONTANA

Cornish-American Pasties, 72–73

NEBRASKA

Cherokee Succotash, 60
Czech-American Poppyseed Cake, 87
Swiss-American Pork Chops, 268–69

NEVADA

New Zealander-American Bacon and Egg Pie, 28
Basque-American Soup, 36; Basque Beans, 36–37
Irish-American Colcannon, 149

NEW HAMPSHIRE

Ethiopian-American Injera, 104–05
French Canadian-American Pork Pie, 115
Scottish-American Shortbread, 244–45

NEW JERSEY

Korean-American Bul-Kogi (Korean Barbecue),
    165–66

NEW MEXICO

Ecuadoran-American Llapingachos, 96–97
New Mexico Hispanic Biszcochitos, 193;
    Sopaipillas, 193; Capirotada, 194; Quick
    Chocolate, 194
Pueblo Indians (Eastern) Pojoaque Cream Soup,
    229; Wild Sage Bread, 229; John's Favorite
    Recipe, 229–30
Zuni Chuleya:we (Posole Stew), 288–89; Me:mo'le
    (Pumpkin and Pumpkin Seeds), 289

NEW YORK

Barbadan-American Cou Cou or Turn Corn, 34;
    Codfish Cakes, 34–35
Carpatho-Rusyn-American Pagach, 58

Colombian-American, Arepas, 70–71; Coconut
    Rice, 71–72
Dominican-American Chicharrones de Pollo, 90–91
Dutch-American Krullers, 94
German-American Lebkuchen, 117
Guyanese-American Sea Trout Salad, 130; Garlic
    Pork, 130–31
Honduran- and Garifuna-American Rice and Red
    Beans, 140
Hungarian-American Chicken Paprika, 144
Irish-American Conan O'Brien's Irish Style Potato-
    Chive Pancakes, 149–50; Corned Beef and
    Cabbage, 150
Iroquois Roast Corn Soup ('o' nanh-dah), 151–52;
    Ghost Bread, 152
Italian-American Greens and Beans, 154
Jamaican-American Curry Goat/Chicken, 158–59
Laotian-American Laotian Salad, 167–68
New Zealander-American Pikelets, 28–29
Panamanian-American Fried Chicken, 208–09
Polish-American Stuffed Cabbage, 220–22
Puerto Rican Pernil Al Horno, 232
Scottish-American Highlander's Soup, 246

NORTH CAROLINA

African-American Baked Grits, 6
Cherokee Huckleberry Bread, 60–61
Icelandic-American Creamed Potatoes, 147
Lumbee Sweet Potato Bread, 173–74; Ginger
    Bread, 174; Blueberry Sheet Cake, 174–75
Moravian Love Feast Buns, 183
Scotch-Irish Shortbread, 243–44

NORTH DAKOTA

Germans from Russia Dill Pickles, 119; Shtirum,
    121–22
Icelandic-American Vinarterta, 146–47
Sioux Boiled Meat, 254

OHIO

Amish Church Peanut Butter Spread, 11
Shawnee Chimee, 250–52; Fried Corn Soup, 252
Slovene-American Icebox Potica, 259–60
Swiss-American Tea, 269

OKLAHOMA

Cherokee, Blue Dumplings, 59–60; Wild Onions
    and Eggs, 61
Chickasaw Pashofa, 62; Pumpkin Cookies, 62–63
Choctaw Tonshla Bona, 69
Creek Osafkee, 75; Green Corn Pudding, 75–76
Czech-American Varmuza, 85

Iroquois Ogwissimanabo (Yellow Squash Soup),
152
Potawatomi Sweet Potato Biscuits, 227–28

OREGON

Potawatomi Corn Dumplings, 228
Swedish-American Risgrynsgröt, 265–66
Ukrainian-American Borsch, 279–80; Kapusnyak,
280

PENNSYLVANIA

Asian Indian-American Nuked Rice, 24–25
Black Muslim Bean Pie, 43
Bulgarian-American Cucumber Soup, 48
Carpatho-Rusyn-American Machanka, 57; Easy
Bake Pierogy, 67–58
Croatian-American Spinach Pie, 80–81; Ajvar, 81;
Zgance, 81–82
Hungarian-American Paprika Potatoes, 144–45
Moravian Sugar Cake, 183–84
Panamanian-American Platanos en Tentacion, 209
Pennsylvania Dutch, "Marble" Goose Eggs, 211–
12; Shoo-Fly Pie I, 212; Rosina Boy, 212–13
Polish-American Kluski, 223
Puerto Rican Habichuelas, 230–31
Russian-American Marinated Mushrooms, 235–36
Slovak-American Snitchleh (Old Fashioned
Hamburgers), 256–57; Slovak Cookies, 257;
Halusky, 258
Ukrainian-American Svikly, 279
Vietnamese-American Cabbage and Grapefruit
Salad, 283

RHODE ISLAND

Anglo-American Jonnycakes, 13
Estonian-American Rosolje, 103
Italian-American Pasta and Bean Soup (Pasta e
Fagioli), 154–55
Narragansett Dovecrest Quahog Chowder, 187–88;
Johnny Cakes, 188; Corn Meal Porridge, 188–
89
Portuguese-American Soup—Faial Style, 224–25

SOUTH CAROLINA

Franco-American Huguenot Torte, 112
Gullah Red Rice, 128; Proper Geechee Rice, 128–
29; Hoppin' John, 129

SOUTH DAKOTA

Danish-American Sweet Soup, 88–89
Mexican-American Frijoles Fritos, 179–80

Sioux Fry Bread, 253; Indian Popovers, 254; Beans
'n' Bacon 255; Corn Balls (Wahuwapa Wasna),
255–56

TENNESEE

Pennsylvania Dutch Pickled Eggs and Red Beets,
211
Scotch-Irish Apple Stack Cake, 242–43

TEXAS

Bahamian-American Crab and Rice, 33
Czech-American Kolaches, 85–86; Molasses
Cookies (Melasové Cukroví), 86–87
Ecuadoran-American El Locro Gringo, 97
Egyptian-American Eggplant and Zucchini Salad,
99
Gypsy (Rom, Romani) Sax Sukló, 132–33
Irish Traveller Scones, 133–34
Mexican-American Chili Beans, 180–81
Nigerian-American A Moi Moi, 197–98
Swedish-American Meatballs, 264–65
Texas Wend Slavic Oven Stew, 269–70; Wendish
Saurbraten, 270–71

UTAH

Mormon Potato Salad, 185–86; Blender Pancakes,
186; Berrie Good Waffles, 186–87

VIRGINIA

Anglo-American Quick Sally Lunn, 14–15
Ethiopian-American Azifa, 105–06
Guamian Hot Sauce, 125–26

VERMONT

Asian Indian-American Stuffed Green Peppers, 22–
23, Sheera, 23
Austrian-American Linzer Torte, 31-32
Brazilian-American Quindim, 44–45

WASHINGTON

Danish-American Ris a la Mande (Rice Dessert),
88
Filipino-American Bibinka Royale by Ana, 108
Tlingit Rainy Day Fish Chowder, 273

WEST VIRGINIA

Persian (Iranian)-American Potato Tomato Omelet,
214–15
Slovene-American Potato Salad, 259; Kifles, 261
Welsh-American Tea Cakes, 287–88

WISCONSIN

Austrian-American Goulash Soup, 30
Belgian-American Chicken Booyah, 38–39; Belgian
  Pies, 39–40
German-American Sauteed Red Cabbage, 116–17
Hmong-American Tomsum, 138
Italian-American Risotto, 156–57

Ojibway Spinach-Rice Casserole, 203
Serbian-American Cucumber Salad, 249–50;
  Juvech, 250–51
Thai-American Spicy Beef with Mint Leaves, 271–72

WYOMING

Basque-American Basque Potatoes, 37

INDEX

by Mark Zanger

A Moi Moi, 197–98
Abureshe. *See* Albanian-Americans, 9; Italian-Americans, 153
Acorn Bread, 16
Acorn Stew, 15–16
Adele Milczark's Potato Salad, 185–86
Adobo Manok (chicken), 107
African-Americans, Development of Ethnic Foods, xi, xiii
Ajvar, 81
Akara, 198–99
Aleuts. *See* Eskimos (Inuit) and Aleuts, 101
Almonds, in Danish-American, Ris a la Mande, 88
American Indians. *See* under names of individual tribal nations
Americanization of Recipes, 10 steps, ix
Anijsmelk, 93
Anise Seed, in
    Dutch-American Anijsmelk, 93
    New Mexico Hispanic Biszcochitos, 193
Anzacs, 28
Appel Koek, 95
Appetizers and Snacks
    Arab-American Tiny Kibbee Balls, 18
    Assyrian-American Zazich, 26
    Ecuadoran-American Llapingachos, 96–97
    Hungarian-American Liptaur Cheese Spread, 145
    Korean-American Marinated Chicken Wings, 165
    Mexican-American Grilled Corn, 180
    Nigerian-American Akara, 198–99
    Romanian-American, Phelagel (Eggplant Salad), 234–35
    Russian-American Pashtet, 236
    Salvadoran-American Guacamole, 238
    Salvadoran-American Pupusas, 238–39
    Sioux Wahuwapa Wasna (corn balls), 255–56
Apple Sauce, in Dutch-American Appel Koek, 95

Apple Stack Cake, 242–43
Apples, in
    Franco-American Huguenot Torte, 112
    German-American Sauteed Red Cabbage, 116–17
    Polish-American Mazurek, 224
Apples Baked with Honey, 41–42
Apples, Dried, in
    Melungeon Stack Cake, 177–78
    Scotch-Irish Apple Stack Cake, 242–43
Applesauce, in Dutch-American St. Nicholas Koekjes, 95–96
Arepas, 70–71
Arequipe, Short-Cut, 71
Arhat's Feast, 282–83
Arroz Guisado con Tomates, 262
Arumanians. *See* Bulgarian-Americans, Macedonian-Americans, and Vlachs, 46
Asian-Americans, Development of Ethnic Foods, xii
Asopao de Camarones, 231
Atakelte, 105
Aunt Gertie's Red Rice, 128
Azifa, 105–06

B'baw Poat (Corn Pudding), 50
Baba, 258
Bacon, in
    Creole (Louisiana) Red Beans, 78
    Hopi Pinto Beans, 142
    Latvian-American Baltic Baconettes (Piragi), 169–70
    Mexican-American Frijoles Fritos, 179–80
    Romanian-American Mamaliga with Cheese, 233
    Sioux Beans 'n' Bacon, 255–56
Bacon and Egg Pie, 28
Bagels, Changes in as Example of Americanization, ix

Baked Corn, Potawatomi, 227
Baked Grits, African-American, 6
Baked Yogurt, Asian Indian-American, 24
Baltic Baconettes (Piragi), 169–70
Banana Poi, 240
Bananha, 69–70
Bannock, Wampanoag, 285–86
Bannock, Scottish-American, 246
Bean Cake, Black Muslim, 43
Bean Cakes, Fried, As Made by 17 Ethnic Groups, 295
Bean Dishes
    Basque-American Beans, 36–37
    Black Muslim Muhammad Supreme Bean Soup, 43–44
    Cape Verdean-American Jag (Jagacida), 55
    Creole (Louisiana) Red Beans, 78
    Cuban-American Black Bean Soup, 82–83
    Egyptian-American Felafel, 98
    Gullah Hoppin' John, 129
    Haitian-American Rix et Pois Rouges, 134–35
    Hopi Pinto Beans, 142
    Kika's Chili Beans, 180–81
    Mexican-American Frijoles Fritos, 179–80
    Nigerian-American A Moi Moi, 197–98
    Nigerian-American Black-Eyed Peas, 199
    Papago Tepary Bean Soup, 219
    Pima Poshol Soup, 219
    Puerto Rican Habichuelas, 230–31
    Sioux Beans 'n' Bacon, 255–56
Bean Salad, 20
Beans, in
    Iroquois, Roast Corn Soup ('o' nanh-dah), 151–52
    Italian-American Pasta and Bean Soup (Pasta e Fagioli), 154–55
    Haitian-American Rix et Pois Rouges, 134–35
    Wampanoag Three Sisters Rice, 286
Beef Dishes
    Albanian-American Moussaka, 9
    Apache Acorn Stew, 15–16
    Cuban-American Picadillo, 83
    German-American Saurbraten, 11
    Greek-American Stuffed Grape Leaves, 122–24 (ill. 123)
    Hmong-American Watercress and Beef, 138–39
    Irish-American Corned Beef and Cabbage, 150
    Korean-American Bul-Kogi, 165–66
    Mexican-American Chili Beans, 180–81
    Persian (Iranian)-American Cutlet, 213–14
    Polish-American Hunter's Stew, 222
    Stuffed Cabbage, 220–22 (ill. 221)
    Slovak-American Snitchleh, 256–57
    Texas Wendish Saurbraten, 270–71
    Thai-American Thai Spicy Beef with Mint Leaves, 271–72

Beerucks or Cabbage Busters, 120
Beets, in
    Estonian-American Rosolje, 103
    Pennsylvania Dutch Pickled Eggs and Red Beets, 211
    Russian-American, Vinegret (Cooked Vegetable Salad), 236–37
    Ukrainian-American Borsch, 279–80
    Ukrainian-American Svikly, 279
Belgian Pies, 39–40
Belorussian Milk Soup, 41
Berrie Good Waffles, 186–87
Beverages
    African-American Pot Likker, 7
    Armenian-American Tan, 21
    Creek Osafkee, 75
    Cuban-American Puffed Wheat Batido, 83–84
    Dutch-American Anijsmelk (Anise Milk), 93
    New Mexico Hispanic Quick Chocolate, 194
    Seminole Sofkee, 247–48
    Polish-American Friendly Polish Tea, 220
    Swiss-American Swiss Tea, 269
Bibinka Royale by Ana, 108
Billy Mills' Sioux Fry Bread, 253
Biryani, Pakistani-American, 207
Biscuits. See also Breads
    Potawatomi Sweet Potato Biscuits, 227–28
Biszcochitos, New Mexico Hispanic, 193
Black Bean Soup, Cuban-American, 82–83
Black-Eyed Peas, in
    Gullah Hoppin' John, 129
    Nigerian-American, A Moi Moi, 197–98
    Nigerian-American Akara, 198–99
    Nigerian-American Black-Eyed Peas, 199
Black Walnut Corn Bread, Apache, 16–17
Blender Pancakes, 186
Blue Dumplings, 59–60
Blueberries, in Cherokee Huckleberry Bread, 60–61
Blueberry Sheet Cake, 174–75
Boat, 9–10
Boiled Chicken with Jaew Som, 167
Boiled Meat, Sioux, 254
Bolo de Filho (Leaf Cake), 225
Boneless Chicken Cacciatore, 153–54
Booshala, 26–27
Booyah, 38–39
Borsch, 279–80
Bread, in
    New Mexico Hispanic Capirotada, 194
    Ojibway Bread Pudding, 204
Bread, Kneading Technique (ill.), 291–92
Breads. See also Corn Breads; Flatbreads; Fry Breads; Pancakes; Rolls; Stuffed Breads; Sweet Breads
    Cornish-American Saffron Bread, 74
    Iroquois Onondaga Ghost Bread, 152
    Pueblo Wild Sage Bread, 229

Breakfast Dishes
    African-American, Baked Grits, 6
    Anglo-American Connecticut Kedgeree, 14
    Assyrian-American Flat Egg and Fresh Herb
        Pancakes, 26
    Creole (Louisiana) Coush-Coush, 78
    German-American Hoppel Poppel, 117–18
    German-American Schman, 118
    Jewish-American Matza Brie, 163
    Melungeon Chocolate Gravy, 176–77
    Mormon Berrie Good Waffles, 186–87
    Mormon Blender Pancakes, 186
British-Americans. *See* Anglo-Americans, 12;
    Cornish-Americans, 72; Scotch-Irish, 241;
    Scottish-Americans, 244; Welsh-Americans,
    287
Bul-Kogi, 165–66
Burn Safety, xvi
Burned Food, How to Avoid, xvii
Butter, in
    Hungarian Pogachels, 143
    Pakistani-American Carrot Halwa, 207–08
    Scottish-American Mrs. Bowen's Scotch
        Shortbread, 244–45

Cabbage Dishes
    Cambodian-American Ngiom, 49–50
    Dutch-American Coleslaw, 94–95
    Ethiopian-American Atakelte, 105
    Germans from Russia Kraut Beerucks, 120
    Gypsy (Roma)-American Sax Sukló, 132–33
    Honduran-American Cabbage Salad, 140–41
    Irish-American Colcannon, 149
    Polish-American Hunter's Stew, 222
    Slovak-American Halusky, 258
Cabbage and Grapefruit Salad (Vietnamese-
    American), 283
Cabbage, Stuffed, As Made by 29 Ethnic Groups,
    293–94
Cachupa, 54–55
Cajuns. *See* Acadians, 1
Cakes. *See also* Desserts
    Armenian-American Lemon-Yogurt Cake, 20
    Armenian-American Nutmeg Cake, 21
    Cherokee Huckleberry Bread, 60–61
    Czech-American Poppyseed Cake, 87
    Franco-American Huguenot Torte, 112
    Haitian-American Haitian Cake, 136
    Lumbee Blueberry Sheet Cake, 174–75
    Lumbee Mom Chavis' Ginger Bread, 174
    Portuguese-American Bolo de Filho (Leaf
        Cake), 225
    Seminole and Miccosukee Pumpkin Bread, 248
    Slovene-American Icebox Potica, 259–60
Caldo—Spanish Soup, 263

Canadian-Americans. *See* English Canadian-
    Americans, 99; French Canadian-Americans,
    113
Candy
    Cane River Creole Cinnamon Pecan Pralines, 54
    Franco-American Pecan Pralines, 113
    Slovakian Nut Candy, 257–58
Canja (Brazilian-American), 45
Canja (Cape Verdean-American), 56
Capirotada, 194
Cardamom, in
    Finnish-American Pulla, 110–11
    Lithuanian-American Cookie Slices
        (Sausainiai), 172
Carrot Halwa, 207–08
Carrots, in
    Dutch-American Dutch Carrots, 96
    Hmong-American Tomsum, 138
Carrot-Sweet Potato Tzimmes, 164
Casseroles
    Creek Green Corn Pudding, 75–76
    Lithuanian-American Hot Dish, 172
    Mexican-American Chicken Enchilada
        Casserole, 182
    Norwegian-American Microwave Rommegrot,
        200
    Serbian-American Juvech, 250–51
    Sioux Stuffed Pumpkin, 255–256
    Texas Wends Slavic Oven Stew, 269–70
Catfish Courtbouillon, 3
Causa Limeña, 216–17
Cayuga. *See* Iroquois, 151
Ceci's Coconut Fish Stew, 91–92
Census, U.S.
    Ethnic Ancestry Survey, xiii–xiv
    Problems Counting Ethnic Groups, xiv
Ceviche Peruano, 217–18
Chaldean-Americans. *See* Assyrian- and Chaldean-
    Americans, 25
Chanpuru, 205–06
Chard, in
    Assyrian-American Booshala, 26–27
    Italian-American Greens and Beans, 154
Cheese Dishes
    African-American Baked Grits, 6
    Carpatho-Rusyn-American Easy Bake Pierogy,
        67–58
    Colombian-American Arepas, 70–71
    Ecuadoran-American Llapingachos, 96–97
    Ecuadoran-American Locro Gringo, 97
    Filipino-American Bibinka Royale by Ana, 108
    Gypsy (Roma)-American Pirogo, 133
    Lithuanian-American Hot Dish, 172
    Mexican-American Grilled Corn, 180
    Swiss-American Swiss Cheese Pie, 268
    Vlach Cheese Corn Bread (Pispilita), 47

Chelo, 214–15
Chicanos. *See* Mexican-Americans, 178
Chicharrones de Pollo, Dominican-American, 90–91(ill. 91)
Chicken Dishes
    Cambodian-American Ngiom, 49–50
    Cape Verdean-American Canja, 56
    Chinese-American Shoyu Chicken, 66–67
    Dominican-American Chicharrones de Pollo, 90–91(ill. 91)
    Filipino-American Adobo Manok, 107
    Guatemalan-American Pollo Guisada, 127
    Gypsy (Roma)-American Sax Sukló, 132–33
    Honduran-American Chicken with Rice, 141
    Hungarian-American Chicken Paprika, 144
    Italian-American Boneless Chicken Cacciatore, 153–54
    Japanese-American Nabemono (Hekka) 161
    Korean-American Marinated Chicken Wings, 165
    Laotian-American Boiled Chicken with Jaew Som, 167
    Mexican-American Chicken Enchilada Casserole, 182
    Mexican-American Pozole, 181
    Panamanian-American Fried Chicken, 208–09
    Peruvian-American Causa Limeña, 216–17
    Trinidadian-American Curried Chicken, 275
    Vietnamese-American Chicken Noodle Soup, 281–82
Chili Beans, Kika's, 180–81
Chili Pepper Safety, xvii
Chimee, 250–52
Chippewa. *See* Ojibway, 202
Chitimacha Baked Duck, 68
Chocolate Gravy, 176–77
Chocolate, Quick, 194
Chugash Salmon Chowder, 102
Chuleya:we (Posole Stew), 288–89
Chupe de Camarones (Shrimp Chowder), 217
Cinnamon, in
    Moravian Sugar Cake, 183–84
    Swiss-American Swiss Style Pork Chops, 268–69
    Swiss-American Swiss Tea, 269
    Vietnamese-American Chicken Noodle Soup, 281–82
Cinnamon Pecan Pralines, 54
Cirios Pork Adobo, 107–08
Coban Salatasl (Shepherd's Salad), 277
Coca Cola, in Colombian-American Coconut Rice, 71–72
Coconut, in
    Australian-New Zealander-American Anzacs, 28
    Brazilian-American, Quindim, 44–45
    Cambodian-American B'baw Poat (Corn Pudding), 50

    Guamian Kelaguen Chicken Salad, 125
    Garifuna-American Rice and Red Beans, 140
    Lumbee Sweet Potato Bread, 173–74
Coconut Cream, in Samoan-American Banana Poi, 240
Coconut Fish Stew, Ceci's 91–92
Coconut Milk, in Hawaiian Haupia, 136–37
Coconut Rice, 71–72
Codfish Cakes, 34–35
Coffee Cakes. *See also* Breads; Desserts; Sweet Breads
    Dutch-American Appel Koek, 95
    Finnish-American Pulla, 110–11
    Welsh-American Raisin Bread, 288
Colcannon, 149
Coleslaw, 94–95
Collard Greens, in
    African-American Guilt-Free Collard Greens, 7
    Brazilian-American Couve à Mineira, 45
Com Nam (Rice Rolls), 283–84 (ill. 284–85)
Conan O'Brien's Irish Style Potato-Chive Pancakes, 149–50
Condiments
    Bahamian-American Old Sour, 33
    Carpatho-Rusyn-American Machanka, 57
    Guamian Hot Sauce, 125–26
    Haitian-American Sauce Ti-Malice, 135–36
    Melungeon Tomato Gravy, 176
    Mormon Honey Butter, 185
    Ukrainian-American Svikly, 279
    Vietnamese-American Nuoc Cham, 283
    Wampanoag Cranberry Sauce, 286–87
Connecticut Kedgeree, 14
Cookbooks, Bibliography of, 299–303
Cookies. *See also* Desserts
    Australian-New Zealander-American Anzacs, 28
    Cane River Creole Tea Cakes, 52–53
    Chickasaw Pumpkin Cookies, 62–63
    Czech-American Molasses Cookies, 86–87
    Dutch-American St. Nicholas Koekjes, 95–96
    English-Canadian-American Lemon Cookies, 101
    English-American Nanaimo Bars, 100–01
    German-American Lebkuchen, 117
    Greek-American Pecan Crescents, 124
    Hungarian-American Pogachels, 143
    Lithuanian-American Cookie Slices, 172
    Moravian Sugar Cake, 183–84
    New Mexico Hispanic Biszcochitos, 193
    Norwegian-American Kringles, 200–01
    Scotch-Irish Shortbread, 243–44
    Scottish-American Shortbread, 244–45
    Slovak-American Cookies, 257
    Slovene-American Kifles, 261
    Swedish-American Old-Fashioned Pepperkakor, 267
    Welsh-American Tea Cakes, 287–88

Corn and Egg, Quick and Easy, 65
Corn Balls (Wahuwapa Wasna), 255–56
Corn Breads. *See also* Breads; Flatbreads; Fry
    Breads; Pancakes; Rolls; Stuffed Breads; Sweet
    Breads
    Anglo-American Custard Johnnycake, 13–14
    Apache Acorn Bread, 16
    Black Walnut Corn Bread, 16–17
    Choctaw Bananha, 69–70
    Colombian-American Arepas, 70–71
    Navajo Kneel Down Bread, 190–91 (ill. 191)
    Pima Tortillas, 218–19
    Vlach Cheese Corn Bread (Pispilita), 47
Corn Dumplings, 228
Corn Meal Porridge, 188–89
Corn Soup, 68
Corned Beef and Cabbage, 150
Cottage Cheese, in
    Lithuanian-American Hot Dish, 172
    Croatian-American Spinach Pie, 80–81
    Pueblo Wild Sage Bread, 229
    Swedish-American Osta Kaka, 266
Cou Cou or Turn Corn, 34
Coush-Coush, 78
    Bahamian-American Esther's American Crab
        and Rice, 33
    Brazilian-American Couve à Mineira, 45
    Crab Salad, 239–40
Cranberries, in
    Eskimo Cranberries (kee-mee-nach), 102
    Finnish-American Ilmapuuro (Air Pudding),
        108–09
    Wampanoag Cranberry Sauce, 286–87
Cream Cheese, in
    Assyrian-American Zazich, 26
    Filipino-American Bibinka Royale, 108
    Hungarian-American Liptaur Cheese Spread,
        145
Creamed potatoes, 147
Cucumber, in
    Bulgarian-American Cucumber Soup, 48
    Chinese-American Cucumber Salad, 66
    Germans from Russia Dill Pickles, 119
    Serbian-American Cucumber Salad, 249–50
    Spanish-American Florida Gispachi, 262–63
    Turkish-American Coban Salatasl (Shepherd's
        Salad), 277
Curried Chicken, Trinidadian-American, 275
Curry Goat/Chicken, Jamaican-American, 158–59
Custard Johnnycake, 13–14

Dakota. *See* Sioux, 252
Dalmatian Baked Fish, 80
Dalmatians. *See* Croatian-Americans, 79
Dampfnudeln (Steam Buns), 118–19
Dandelions, in Italian-American Greens and Beans,
    154

Danish Sweet Soup, 88–89
Democrats, Recipes by
    Greek-American Tourlou, 124
    Irish-American Colcannon, 149
    Irish-American Mayor Curley's Favorite Irish
        Bread, 148–49
    Jewish-American Matzoh Kloese, 160
    Mexican-American Chili Beans, 180–81
    Swedish-American Osta Kaka, 266
    Trinidadian-American Curried Chicken, 275
Desserts. *See also* Breads; Cakes; Candy; Coffee
    Cakes; Cookies; Pastries; Pies and Tarts;
    Puddings; Stack Cakes; Sweet Breads
    Belorussian-American, Apples Baked with
        Honey, 41–42
    Cherokee Blue Dumplings, 59–60
    Danish-American Sweet Soup, 88–89
    Dutch-American Krullers, 94
    Filipino-American Bibinka Royale, 108
    Shawnee Chimee, 250–52
    Sioux Wojapi Pudding, 253–54
Dill Pickles, 119
Dineh. *See* Navajo, 189
Dovecrest Quahog Chowder, Narragansett, 187–88
Duck, Chitimacha Baked, 68
Dumplings
    Jewish-American Matzoh Kloese, 162–63
    Polish-American Kluski, 223
    Potawatomi Corn Dumplings, 228
"Dutch Marble" Goose Eggs, 211–12

Easy Bake Pierogy, 67–58
Easy Migas, 179
Egg Dishes
    Anglo-American Yorkshire Pudding, 15
    Cherokee Wild Onions and Eggs, 61
    Chinese-American Quick and Easy Corn and
        Egg, 65
    Czech-American Varmuza, 85
    German-American Hoppel Poppel 117–18
    Germans from Russia Shtirum, 121–22
    Jewish-American Huevos Haminadoes, 163–64
    Mexican-American Easy Migas, 179
    Pennsylvania Dutch "Dutch Marble" Goose
        Eggs, 211–12
    Pennsylvania Dutch Pickled Eggs and Red
        Beets, 211
    Persian (Iranian)-American Potato Tomato
        Omelet, 214–15
    Swedish-American Oven Pancake, 265
    Swiss-American Swiss Cheese Pie, 268
    Thai-American Kai Yat Sai, 272
Eggplant, in
    Croatian-American Ajvar, 81
    Romanian-American Phelagel, 234–35
    Greek-American Tourlou, 124

Eggplant and Zucchini Salad, Egyptian-American, 99

El Salvadoran-Americans. *See* Salvadoran-Americans, 237

E-mail, The Author, mark@ethnicook.com, xv

English. *See* Anglo-Americans, 12; Cornish-Americans, 72; Welsh-Americans, 287

Esther's American Crab and Rice, 33

Ethnic Encyclopedias, Bibliography of, 299

Ethnic Groups
    Census, xiii–xiv
    Census, Problems of, xiv
    Defined, vii
    Give Up Mainstreamed Foods, xi
    How Selected, viii
    Multiracial, xii
    "Nationalization Process" in U.S., xi

Ethnic Identity, xiv–xv
    Having None, xiii, xiv–xv
    Multi-Ethnic, xiii
    Multi-Racial, xiii

Ethnography, xiv–xvi
    Ethnic Identity, xiv–xvi
    Exchanging Information, xv–xvi
    Facts, Verifying, xv
    Field Notes, xv
    Opinions, xv
    Sample Questions to Ask, xv
    Talking about Politics or Religion, xv

Felafel, 98

Field Notes in Ethnography, xv

Fire Safety, xvi

Fish Dishes
    Acadian (Cajun) Catfish Courtbouillon, 3
    Anglo-American Connecticut Kedgeree, 14
    Barbadan-American Codfish Cakes, 34–35
    Dalmatian Baked Fish, 80
    Dominican-American Coconut Fish Stew, 91–92
    Eskimo Chugash Salmon Chowder, 102
    Eskimo White Fish Soup, 102
    Guyanese-American Sea Trout Salad, 130
    Hawaiian Lomi Salmon, 137
    Italian-American Nonnie's Meatballs (or Shrimpballs) and Spaghetti, 155–56
    Okinawan-American Okinawan Fried Somen, 206
    Peruvian-American Ceviche Peruano, 217–18
    Tlingit Fish Perok, 274

Fish Sauce, Vietnamese-American, Nuoc Cham, 283

Flat Egg and Fresh Herb Pancakes, Assyrian-American, 26

Flatbreads. *See also* Breads; Corn Breads; Fry Breads; Pancakes; Rolls; Stuffed Breads; Sweet Breads

Colombian-American Arepas, 70–71
Norwegian-American Lefse, 201–02
Pima Tortillas, 218–19
Scottish-American Oatcakes, 245
Wampanoag Bannock, 285–86

Flemish Beef and Beer Stew, 40–41

Florida Gispachi, 262–63

Food-Borne Illness, xvii

Foo-Foo, 209–10

French. *See* Franco-Americans, 111

Fried Bean Cakes, As Made by 17 Ethnic Groups, 295

Fried Chicken (Panamanian-American), 208–09

Fried Corn Soup, Shawnee, 252

Fried Dough, As Made by 37 Ethnic Groups, 296–97

Fried Pumpkin Bread, 248–49

Fried Somen, 206

Friendly Polish Tea, 220

Frijoles Fritos, 179–80

Fry Breads. *See also* Breads; Corn Breads; Flatbreads; Pancakes; Rolls; Stuffed Breads; Sweet Breads
    Gypsy (Irish Traveller) Irish Scones, 133–34
    Navajo Fry Bread, 189–90
    New Mexico Hispanic Sopaipillas, 193
    Trinidadian-American Potato Bread, 275–76
    Seminole and Miccosukee Indian Fried Pumpkin Bread, 248–49
    Sioux Bill Mills' Fry Bread, 253

Gagoonz—Little Porcupines, 203–04

Gallo Pinto, 195–96

Garifana. *See* Honduran- and Garifana-Americans, 139

Garlic Pork, 130–31

Geechee. *See* Gullah, 127

Getting Started in Ethnology, xiv–xvi

Getting Started in the Kitchen, xvi–xviii

Ghost Bread, 152

Ginger, in
    Filipino-American Adobo Manok, 107
    Filipino-American Cirio's Pork Adobo, 107–08
    Korean-American Marinated Chicken Wings, 165
    Okinawan-American Okinawan Spareribs, 205

Ginger Bread, Mom Chavis', 174

Gingersnaps, in German-American Saurbraten, 116

Gispachi, Florida, 262–63

Gormeh Sabzi, 215

Goulash Soup, 30

Grape Leaves, Stuffed 122–24 (ill. 123)

Grapefruit, in Vietnamese Cabbage and Grapefruit Salad, 283

Green Corn Pudding, 75–76

Green Peppers, Stuffed , 22–23

Greens and Beans, 154
Grilled Corn, 180
Griots, 135
Guacamole, 238
Guilt-Free Collard Greens, 7
Gumbo Z'Herbes, 77
Gumbo, Okra, 53

Habichuelas, 230–31
Haida. See Tlingit and Haida, 272
Halusky, 258
Hamburger Dishes. See Beef Dishes
Hamburg with Potato (Albanian Moussaka), 9
Haupia, 136–37
Hekka, 161
Herring, in Estonian-American Rosolje, 103
Highlander's Soup, 246
Hominy, in
    Cape Verdean-American Cachupa, 54–55
    Chickasaw Pashofa, 62
    Choctaw Tonshla Bona, 69
    Creek Osafkee, 75
    Mexican-American Chicken Pozole, 181
    Zuni Chuleya:we (Posole Stew), 288–89
Honey, in
    Belorussian-American Apples Baked with Honey,
        41–42
    Shawnee, Chimee, 250–52
Honey Butter, 185
Hoppel Poppel, 117–18
Hoppin' John, 129
Hot Dish, Lithuanian-American, 172
Hot Pepper Safety, xvii
Hot Sauce, Guamian, 125–26. See also Condiments
How Large Are Ethnic Groups?, xiii–xiv
Huckleberry Bread, Cherokee, 60–61
Huevos Haminadoes, 163–64
Huguenot Torte, 112
Hunter's Stew, 222

Iceberg Lettuce-Egg Drop Soup, 64–65
Ilmapuuro (Air Pudding), 108–09
Imitation Crab Legs, in Bahamian-American Crab
    and Rice, 33
Immigrants
    "New Immigrants" (1880-1924), x
    "Old Immigrants" (1820-1860), x
    "Old Stock" (pre-1776), x
    "Recent Immigrants" (since 1965), x
    Cooking of First Generation, x
    Four Periods Defined, x
    Second Generation, x
    Third Generation, x–xi
Indian Popovers, 254
Indians (American). See under names of individual
    tribal nations
Indians (Asian). See Asian Indian-Americans, 22

Indo-Caribbeans. See Guyanese-Americans, 129;
    Trinidadian-Americans, 274
Injera, 104–05
Internet Web Sites
    Bibliography of, 302–03
    www.ethnicook.com (of this book), xviii
Inuit. See Eskimos (Inuit) and Aleuts, 101
Iranian-Americans. See Persian-Americans, 213

Jag (Jagacida), 55
John's Favorite Recipe (Pueblo), 229–30
Jordanian-Americans. See Arab-Americans, 17
Juvech, 250–51

Kai Yat Sai, 272
Kale, in Portuguese-American Soup—Faial Style,
    224–25
Kapusnyak, 280
Kedgeree, Connecticut, 14
Kelaguen Chicken Salad, Guamian, 125
Kibbee, 18
Kifles, 261
Kika's Chili Beans, 180–81
Kimenmaizites (Caraway Rolls), 170
Kitchen Safety, xvi–xvii
Kluski, 223
Kneading, Technique (ill, 291), Appendix 1, 291–
    92
Kneel Down Bread, Navajo, 190–91 (ill. 191)
Knife Safety, xvi–xvii
Kolaches, 85–86
Körözöt Liptaur Cheese Spread, 145
Kraut Beerucks or Cabbage Busters, 120
Kringle (Danish-American), 89
Kringles (Norwegian-American), 200–01
Krullers, 94
Kugelis, 171

Lakhota. See Sioux, 252
Lamb, in
    Arab-American Kibbee, 18
    Arab-American Tiny Kibbee Balls, 18
    Jamaican-American Curry Goat/Chicken, 158–59
    Navajo Mutton Stew, 192
    Navajo Taco, 191–92
    Persian (Iranian)-American Gormeh Sabzi, 215
    Texas Wends Slavic Oven Stew, 269–70
    Turkish-American Sis Kebab, 276-7
Large-Group, Recipes. See Recipes, For Large Groups
Lazy Pierogi, 22–23
Lebanese-Americans. See Arab-Americans, 17
Lebkuchen, 117
Leeks, in Dalmatian Baked Fish, 80
Lefse, 201–02
Lemkians. See Carpatho-Rusyn-Americans, 56
Lemon Cookies, 101
Lemon-Yogurt Cake, 20

Lentils, in
     Ethiopian-American Azifa, 105–06
     Scottish-American The Highlander's Soup, 246
Lettuce, in
     Chinese-American Iceberg Lettuce-Egg Drop
          Soup, 64–65
     Germans from Russia Shtirum, 121–22
Lettuce Leaves with Honey, Vinegar, and Mint Dip,
     25
Lima Beans, in
     Cherokee Succotash, 60
     Jamaican-American Oxtail Stew with
          Vegetables, 158
Lime Juice, in
     Bahamian-American Old Sour, 33
     Haitian-American Sauce Ti-Malice, 135–36
Linzer Torte, 31–32 (ill. 32)
Liptaur Cheese Spread, 145
Lithuanian Hot Dish, 172
Llapingachos, 96–97
Locro Gringo, El, 97
Lomi Salmon, 137
Love Feast Buns, 183

Macaroni, in Eskimo Chugash Salmon Chowder,
     102
Macedonian-Americans. See Bulgarian-Americans,
     Macedonian-Americans, and Vlachs, 46
Macedonian Style Peppers, 46–47
Machanka, 57
Macque Choux, 67–68
Mamaliga with Cheese, 233
Maple Syrup, in Ojibway Bread Pudding, 204
Marinated Chicken Wings, 165
Marinated Pork Chops, 6–7
Marshmallows, in New Mexico Hispanic Quick
     Chocolate, 194
Matza Brie, 163
Matzoh Kloese, 162–63
Mayor Curley's Favorite Irish Bread, 148–49
Mazurek, 224
Me:mo'le (Zuni Pumpkin and Pumpkin Seeds),
     289
Meat Pies, Mildred's Creole, 52
Meatballs
     Bulgarian-American Meatball Soup, 48–49
     French Canadian-American Ragout, 114
     Italian-American Meatballs (or Shrimpballs)
          and Spaghetti, 155–56
     Ojibway Gagoonz—Little Porcupines, 203–04
     Swedish-American Meatballs, 264–65
Men, Dishes Made by
     Acadian (Cajun) Catfish Courtbouillon, 3
     Arab-American Kibbee, 18
     Austrian-American Oatmeal Soup, 30–31
     Basque-American Basque Beans, 36–37

     Belgian-American Chicken Booyah, 38–39
     Chitimacha Macque Choux, 67–68
     Croatian-American Dalmatian Baked Fish, 80
     Cuban-American Black Bean Soup, 82–83
     Ecuadoran-American El Locro Gringo, 97
     Ethiopian-American Azifa, 105–06
     Ethiopian-American Injera, 104–05
     German-American Saurbraten, 116
     Haitian-American Griots, 135
     Irish-American Conan O'Brien's Irish Style
          Potato-Chive Pancakes, 149–50
     Jewish-American Carrot-Sweet Potato Tzimmes,
          164
     Lithuanian-American Kugelis, 171
     Mexican-American Kika's Chili Beans, 180–81
     Persian (Iranian)-American Chelo, 214–15
     Persian (Iranian)-American Gormeh Sabzi, 215
     Peruvian-American Ceviche Peruano, 217–18
     Potawatomi Corn Dumplings, 228
     Pueblo (Eastern) John's Favorite Recipe, 229–30
     Romanian-American Papanash, 235
     Romanian-American Phelagel (Eggplant Salad),
          234–35
     Russian-American Pilaf, 235
     Scotch-Irish Apple Stack Cake, 242–43
     Scottish-American The Highlander's Soup, 246
     Sioux Billy Mills' Sioux Fry Bread, 253
     Wampanoag Cranberry Sauce, 286–87
Mesopotamian-Americans. See Assyrian- and
     Chaldean-Americans, 25
Microwave Rommegrot, 200
Mien Noodle Salad, 168–69
Migas, Easy, 179
Mildred's Creole Meat Pies, 52
Milk, in
     Basque-American Walnut Pudding, 37
     Colombian-American Short-Cut Arequipe, 71
     Dutch-American Anijsmelk (Anise Milk), 93
     Norwegian-American Microwave Rommegrot,
          200
     Pueblo (Eastern) Pojoaque Cream Soup, 229
Milk Soup, Belorussian, 41
Mixiensui (Mien Noodle Salad), 168–69
Mohawk. See Iroquois, 151
Moijakka, 109–10
Molassas, in
     Chickasaw Pumpkin Cookies, 62–63
     Czech-American Molasses Cookies (Melasové
          Cukroví), 86–87
     Lumbee Ginger Bread, 174
     Pennsylvania Dutch Shoo-Fly Pie, 212
     Swedish-American Old-Fashioned Pepperkakor,
          267
Montenegrin-Americans. See Serbian-Americans,
     249

Moussaka, Albanian, 9
Moyen Moyen. *See* A Moi Moi
Mrs. Oliver's Red Beans, 78
Muhammad Supreme Bean Soup, Black Muslim, 43–44
Multi-Ethnic Identity, xiii
Multi-Racial Ethnic Groups, xii
Mushroom Soup, in Mexican-American Chicken Enchilada Casserole, 182
Mushrooms, Marinated, 235–36
Mutton Stew, 192

Nabemono (Hekka), 161
Nakota. *See* Sioux, 252
Nanaimo Bars, 100–01
Native Americans, Development of Ethnic Foods, xi–xii. *See also* Eskimos (Inuit) and Aleuts, 101; Hawaiians, 136; Honduran- and Garifana-Americans, 129; and under names of individual tribal nations
Native Hawaiians. *See* Hawaiians, 136
Navajo Taco, 191–92
Neck Bones and Rice, 8
"New Immigrants" (1880-1924), x
Ngiom, 49–50
No-Cook Recipes
    Amish Church Peanut Butter Spread, 11
    Armenian-American Bean Salad, 20
    Assyrian-American Lettuce Leaves with Honey, Vinegar, and Mint Dip, 25
    Bulgarian-American Cucumber Soup, 48
    Macedonian Style Peppers, 46–47
    Cuban-American Puffed Wheat Batido, 83–84
    Guatemalan-American Radish Salad, 126
    Hawaiian Lomi Salmon, 137
    Mormon Honey Butter, 185
    Peruvian-American Ceviche Peruano, 217–18
    Sioux Wojapi Pudding, 253–54
Noodles. *See* Pasta Dishes
Nuked Rice, 24–25
Nuoc Cham, 283
Nut Candy, Slovakian, 257–58
Nutmeg, in
    Armenian-American Nutmeg Cake, 21
    Cane River Creole Tea Cakes, 52–53

Oatcakes, 245
Oatmeal, in Australian-New Zealander Anzacs, 28
Oatmeal Soup, 30–31
Ogwissimanabo (Yellow Squash Soup), 152
Okinawan Spareribs, 205
Okra, in
    Cane River Creole Okra Gumbo, 53
    Barbadan-American Cou Cou or Turn Corn, 34
    Panamanian-American Foo-Foo, 209–10
"Old Immigrants" (1820-1860), x
Old Sour, 33

"Old Stock" Immigrants (Pre-1776), x
Oneida. *See* Iroquois, 151
Onondaga. *See* Iroquois, 151
Onondaga Ghost Bread, 152
Osafkee, 75. *See also* Sofkee, 247–48
Osta Kaka, 266
Oven Pancake, 265
Oxtail Stew with Vegetables, 158

Pagach, 58
Palestinian-Americans. *See* Arab-Americans, 17
Pan Sushi, 160–61
Pancakes. *See also* Breads; Corn Breads; Flatbreads; Fry Breads; Rolls; Stuffed Breads; Sweet Breads
    Acadian Plogue (Ployes), 4
    Anglo-American Rhode Island Jonnycakes, 13
    Australian-New Zealander-American Pikelets, 28–29
    Estonian-American Pancakes, 104
    Ethiopian-American Injera, 104–05
    Narragansett Johnny Cakes, 188
    Romanian-American Papanash, 235
    Scottish-American Pancakes (Bannocks), 246
Papago. *See* Pima and Papago, 218
Papanash, 235
Paprika Potatoes, 144–45
Pashofa, 62
Pashtet, Simple, 236
Pasta Dishes
    Amish Yummasetti, 11–12
    Italian-American Pasta and Bean Soup (Pasta e Fagioli), 154–55
    Italian-American Nonnie's Meatballs (or Shrimpballs) and Spaghetti, 155–56
    Polish-American Lazy Pierogi, 22–23
Pasties, Cornish 72–73 (ill. 73)
Pasties and Turnovers. *See also* Breads, Stuffed Breads
    Cane River Creole Meat Pies, 52
    Carpatho-Rusyn-American Easy Bake Pierogy, 67–58
    Cornish-American Pasties, 72–73 (ill. 73)
    Sioux Indian Popovers, 254
Pastries. *See also* Desserts
    Czech-American Kolaches, 85–86
    Danish-American Kringle, 89
    Polish-American Mazurek, 224
Peanut Butter Spread, Amish, 11
Peanut Potatoes, 23–24
Pecan Crescents (Karithata), 124
Pecan Pralines, 113
Pecans, in Cane River Creole Cinnamon Pecan Pralines, 54
Pepper Soup, 199
Pepperkakor, 267

Pernil Al Horno (Roast Pork Shoulder), 232
Perok, Fish, 274
Persian Cutlet, 213–14
Personal Taste, xvii–xviii
Phelagel (Eggplant Salad), 234–35
Picadillo, 83
Pickled Eggs and Red Beets, 211
Pickles, Dill, 119
Pie, Swiss Cheese, 268
Pierogi, Lazy, 22–23
Pierogy, Easy Bake, 67–58
Pies and Quiches
    New Zealander-American Bacon and Egg Pie,
        28
    Swiss-American Swiss Cheese Pie, 268
    Tlingit Fish Perok, 274
Pies and Tarts. See also Desserts
    African-American, Sweet Potato Pie, 7–8
    African-American White Potato Pie, 8
    Austrian-American Linzer Torte, 31–32 (ill. 32)
    Belgian-American Belgian Pies, 39–40
    Pennsylvania Dutch Rosina Boy, 212–13
    Pennsylvania Dutch Shoo-Fly Pie, 212
    Swedish-American Swedish Apple Pie, 266–67
Pikelets, 28–29
Pilaf, 235
Pine Nuts, in Turkish-American Spicy Rice (Ic
    Pilav), 277–78
Pineapple, in Gypsy (Roma)-American Pirogo, 133
Piragi. See Baltic Baconettes
Pirogo, 133
Plantains, in
    Dominican-American Tostones, 92
    Panamanian-American Platanos en Tentacion,
        209
Plogue (Ployes), 4
Plums, in Sioux Wojapi Pudding, 253–54
Pogachels, 143
Pojoaque Cream Soup, 229
Politics, Discussion of, xv, xviii
Pollo Guisada, 127
Poppyseed Cake, 87
Pork, in
    Serbian-American Juvech, 250–51
    Texas Wends Slavic Oven Stew, 269–70
    Thai-American Kai Yat Sai, 272
Pork Dishes
    African-American Marinated Pork Chops, 6–7
    African-American Neck Bones and Rice, 8
    Chickasaw Pashofa, 62
    Choctaw Tonshla Bona, 69
    Creole (Louisiana) Turnips and Pork Ribs
        Etouffée, 78–79
    Filipino-American Cirio's Pork Adobo, 107–08
    French Canadian-American Pork Pie, 115
    Guyanese-American Garlic Pork, 130–31

    Haitian-American Griots, 135
    Okinawan-American Spareribs, 205
    Portuguese-American Vinha D'alhos, 226
    Puerto Rican Pernil Al Horno, 232
    Samoan-American Sapasui (Samoan Chop Sui),
        240–41
    Swiss-American Swiss Style Pork Chops, 268–69
Pork Hocks, in French Canadian Ragout, 114
Portuguese Soup—Faial Style, 224–25
Poshol Soup, Pima, 219
Posole Stew, Zuni Chuleya:we, 288–89
Pot Likker (under Guilt-Free Collard Greens), 7
Potato Bread, 275–76
Potato Salad, 259
Potato Soup, 242
Potato Tomato Omelet, 214–15
Potatoes, in
    Asian Indian Peanut Potatoes, 23–24
    Estonian-American Rosolje, 10
    Slovak-American Baba, 258
Potatoes, Sweet. See Sweet Potatoes,
Potica, Slovenian Ice-Box, 259–60
Powdered Milk, in Navajo Fry bread, 189–90
Pozole, Chicken, 181
Pralines, Cinnamon Pecan, 54
Pralines, Pecan, 113
Prinzov Pilaf, 21–22
Proper Geechee Rice, 128–29
Prunes, in
    Belgian-American Belgian Pies, 39–40
    Czech-American Kolaches, 85–86
    Danish-American Danish Sweet Soup, 88–89
    Icelandic-American Vinarterta, 146–47
    Jewish-American, Carrot-Sweet Potato
        Tzimmes, 164
Puddings. See also Desserts
    Asian Indian-American Baked Yogurt, 24
    Asian Indian-American Sheera, 23
    Basque-American Walnut Pudding, 37
    Brazilian-American Quindim, 44–45
    Cambodian-American, B'baw Poat (Corn
        Pudding), 50
    Colombian-American Short-Cut Arequipe, 71
    Danish-American Ris a la Mande, 88
    Eskimo Cranberries, 102
    Finnish-American Ilmapuuro, 108–09
    Hawaiian Haupia, 136–37
    New Mexico Hispanic Capirotada, 194
    Ojibway Bread Pudding, 204
    Pakistani-American Carrot Halwa, 207–08
    Samoan-American Banana Poi, 240
    Swedish-American Osta Kaka, 266
    Risgrynsgröt, 265–66
Puffed Wheat Batido, 83–84
Pulla, 110–11
Pumpkin, in Seminole and Miccosukee Indian
    Fried Pumpkin Bread, 248–49

Pumpkin and Pumpkin Seeds (Me:mo'le), 289
Pumpkin Bread, 248
Pumpkin Cookies, 62–63
Pumpkin, Stuffed, 255–256
Pupusas, 238–39

Questions for Student Research, xiv, xv–xvi
Quiches. *See* Pies and Quiches
Quick and Easy Corn and Egg, 65
Quick Chocolate, 194
Quick Sally Lunn, 14–15
Quindim, 44–45

Race in Ethnicity, xiii, xiv
Radish Salad, 126
Ragout, French Canadian, 114
Rainy Day Fish Chowder, 273
Raisins, in
    Austrian-American Salzburger Raisin Bread, 29–
       30
    Gypsy (Irish Traveller) Irish Scones, 133–34
    Pennsylvania Dutch Rosina Boy, 212–13
    Sioux Corn Balls (Wahuwapa Wasna), 255–56
    Welsh-American Raisin Bread, 288
"Recent Immigrants" (since 1965), x
Recipes
    Americanization of, ix–xi
    Field Notes, xv
    First Generation, x
    Not Ethnic, xii–xiii
    Personal Tastes in, xvii–xviii
    Warning to Good Cooks, xvii
Recipes, For Large Groups
    Belgian-American Chicken Booyah, 38–39
    Cane River Creole Meat Pies, 52
    Cape Verdean-American Cachupa, 54–55
    Chinese-American Turkey Bones and Rice
       Chowder, 66
    Czech-American Kolaches, 85–86
    Dutch-American St. Nicholas Koekjes, 95–96
    Greek-American Stuffed Grape Leaves, 122–24
       (ill. 123)
    Mexican-American Chicken Pozole, 181
    Moravian Love Feast Buns, 183
    Polish-American Friendly Tea, 220
    Sioux Wojapi Pudding, 253–54
    Spanish-American Caldo, 263
    Tlingit Fish Perok, 274
    Wampanoag Three Sisters Rice, 286
Red and White Herb Roasted Potatoes, 157
Red Beans, in
    Nicaraguan-American Gallo Pinto, 195–96
    Persian (Iranian)-American Gormeh Sabzi, 215
Red Beans, Mrs. Olivier's, 78
Red Rice, Aunt Gerties', 128

Religion, Food Rules, xviii. *See also* Black Muslims,
    Jewish-Americans, Gypsy-Americans, Mor-
    mons
    Discussion of, xv, xviii
Republicans, Recipes by Office Holders
    Basque Soup, 36
    Belorussian-American Saurkraut Soup, 42
    Bulgarian Cucumber Soup, 48
    Lithuanian-American Kugelis, 171
    Polish-American Hunter's Stew, 222
    Swedish Meatballs, 264–65
Rhode Island Johnny Cakes or Journey Cakes
    (Narragansett), 188
Rhode Island Jonnycakes (Anglo-American), 13
Rice, in
    African-American Neck Bones and Rice, 8
    Brazilian-American Canja (Chicken Soup), 45
    Bulgarian-American Bulgarian Meatball Soup,
       48–49
    Cape Verdean-American Canja, 56
    Chinese-American Turkey Bones and Rice
       Chowder, 66
    Danish-American Ris a la Mande (Rice
       Dessert), 88
    Franco-American Shrimp a La Creole, 112–13
    Honduran-American Chicken with Rice, 141
    Polish-American Stuffed Cabbage, 220–22 (ill.
       221)
    Seminole and Miccosukee Sofkee, 247–48
    Serbian-American Juvech, 250–51
    Swedish-American Risgrynsgröt (Swedish Rice
       Pudding), 265–66
Rice Dishes
    Acadian (Cajun) Shrimp Jumbalaya, 2–3
    Armenian-American Prinzov Pilaf, 21–22
    Asian Indian-American Nuked Rice, 24–25
    Bahamian-American Esther's American Crab
       and Rice, 33
    Cape Verdean-American, Jag (Jagacida), 55
    Colombian-American Coconut Rice, 71–72
    Gullah Red Rice, 128
    Gullah Hoppin' John, 129
    Gullah Proper Geechee Rice, 128–29
    Haitian-American Rix et Pois Rouges, 134–35
    Honduran- and Garifuna-American Rice and
       Red Beans, 140
    Italian-American Risotto, 156–57
    Japanese-American Pan Sushi, 160–61
    Nicaraguan-American Gallo Pinto, 195–96
    Pakistani-American Biryani, 207
    Persian (Iranian)-American Chelo, 214–15
    Puerto Rican Asopao de Camarones, 231
    Russian-American Pilaf, 235
    Spanish-American Arroz Guisado con Tomates,
       262
    Turkish-American Spicy Rice (Ic Pilav), 277–78

Rice Dishes *(continued)*
    Vietnamese-American Com Nam (Rice Rolls),
        283–84 (ill. 284–85)
    Wampanoag Three Sisters Rice, 286
Rice Noodles, in Samoan Chop Sui, 240–41
Ris a la Mande (Rice Dessert), 88
Risgrynsgröt (Swedish Rice Pudding), 265–66
Risotto, 156–57
Rix et Pois Rouges, 134–35
Roast Corn Soup ('o' nanh-dah), 151–52
Rolls. *See also* Breads; Corn Breads; Flatbreads; Fry
        Breads; Pancakes; Stuffed Breads; Sweet
        Breads
    German-American Dampfnudeln (Steam Buns),
        118–19
    Latvian-American Kimenmaizites (Caraway
        Rolls), 170
Roma. *See* Gypsy-Americans, 131
Romanichals. *See* Gypsy-Americans, 131
Rommegrot, Microwave, 200
Rosemary, in Italian-American Red and White
        Herb Roasted Potatoes, 157
Rosina Boy, 212–13
Rosolje, 103
Runzas. *See* Beerucks, 120
Ruskins. *See* Carpatho-Rusyn-Americans, 56
Rusnyaks. *See* Carpatho-Rusyn-Americans, 56
Rusyns. *See* Carpatho-Rusyn-Americans, 56
Ruthenians. *See* Carpatho-Rusyn-Americans, 56

Safety in the Kitchen, xvi–xvii
Saffron, in Asian Indian-American Sheera, 23
Saffron Bread, 74
St. Nicholas Koekjes, 95–96
Salads
    Arab-American Tabouli, 18–19
    Armenian-American Bean Salad, 20
    Assyrian-American Lettuce Leaves with Honey,
        Vinegar, and Mint Dip, 25
    Bulgarian-American Macedonian Style Peppers,
        46–47
    Cambodian-American Ngiom, 49–50
    Chinese-American Cucumber Salad, 66
    Egyptian-American Eggplant and Zucchini
        Salad, 99
    Estonian-American Rosolje, 103
    Guamian Kelaguen Chicken Salad, 125
    Guatemalan-American Radish Salad, 126
    Guyanese-American Sea Trout Salad, 130
    Hmong-American Tomsum, 138
    Honduran-American Honduran Cabbage Salad,
        140–41
    Laotian-American Laotian Salad, 167–68
    Laotian-American Mixiensui (Mien Noodle
        Salad), 168–69
    Peruvian-American Causa Limeña, 216–17

Russian-American Vinegret (Cooked Vegetable
        Salad), 236–37
    Salvadoran-American Crab Salad, 239–40
    Serbian-American Cucumber Salad, 249–50
    Spanish-American Florida Gispachi, 262–63
    Turkish-American Coban Salatasl (Shepherd's
        Salad), 277
    Vietnamese-American Cabbage and Grapefruit
        Salad, 283
Sally Lunn, Quick, 14–15
Salmon, in
    Eskimo Chugash Salmon Chowder, 102
    Hawaiian Lomi Salmon, 137
    Tlingit Fish Perok, 274
    Tlingit Rainy Day Fish Chowder, 273
Salt Cod, in Barbadan-American Codfish Cakes,
        34–35
Salzburger Raisin Bread, 29–30
Sandwiches
    Albanian-American Boat, 9–10
    Amish Peanut Butter Spread, 11
Sapasui (Samoan Chop Sui), 240–41
Sauce Ti-Malice, 135–36
Sauerkraut, in
    Belorussian-American Saurkraut Soup, 42
    Polish-American Hunter's Stew, 222
    Polish-American Lazy Pierogi, 222–23
    Ukrainian-American Kapusnyak, 280
Saurbraten, German-American, 116
Saurbraten, Wendish, 270–71
Sauteed Red Cabbage, 116–17
Sax Sukló, 132–33
Schman, 118
Scones, Irish Traveller, 133–34
Sea Island Creoles. *See* Gullah, 127
Sea Trout Salad, 130
Second-Generation Immigrants, x
Seneca. *See* Iroquois, 151
Sesame Seeds, in Korean-American Spinach Salad,
        166
Sheera, 23
Shoo-Fly Pie, 212
Shortbread (Scotch-Irish), 243–44
Shortbread (Scottish-American), 244–45
Short-Cut Arequipe, 71
Shoyu Chicken, 66–67
Shrimp Dishes
    Acadian (Cajun) Shrimp Jumbalaya, 2–3
    Cane River Creole Okra Gumbo, 53
    Franco-American Shrimp a La Creole, 112–13
    Italian-American Shrimpballs and Spaghetti,
        155–56
    Puerto Rican Asopao de Camarones, 231
Shtirum, 121–22
Side Dishes
    Barbadan-American Cou Cou or Turn Corn, 34

Basque-American Wyoming Basque Potatoes, 3
Icelandic-American Creamed Potatoes, 147
Narragansett Corn Meal Porridge, 188–89
Romanian-American Mamaliga with Cheese, 233
Simple Pashtet, 236
Sis Kebab, 276-7
Slavic Oven Stew, 269–70
Slavonians. See Croatian-Americans, 79
Smoked Turkey, in African-American Guilt-Free Collard Greens, 7
Smothered Potatoes, 4–5
Snitchleh (Old Fashioned Hamburgers), 256–57
Sofkee, 247–48. See also Osafkee, 75
Sopa de Frijoles Estilo Nicaraguense, 196
Sopaipillas, 193
Soup aux Pois, 114
Soups. See also Beef Dishes; Chicken Dishes; Pork Dishes; Stews
    Austrian-American Goulash Soup, 30
    Austrian-American Oatmeal Soup, 30–31
    Basque Soup, 36
    Belorussian-American Milk Soup, 41
    Belorussian-American Saurkraut Soup, 42
    Black Muslim Muhammad Supreme Bean Soup, 43–44
    Brazilian-American Canja (Chicken Soup), 45
    Bulgarian-American Cucumber Soup, 48
    Bulgarian-American Meatball Soup, 48–49
    Cape Verdean-American Cachupa, 54–55
    Cape Verdean-American Canja, 56
    Chinese-American Iceberg Lettuce-Egg Drop Soup, 64–65
    Chinese-American Turkey Bones and Rice Chowder, 66
    Chitimacha Corn Soup, 68
    Creole (Louisiana) Gumbo Z'Herbes, 77
    Cuban-American Black Bean Soup, 82–83
    Danish-American Sweet Soup, 88–89
    French Canadian-American Soup aux Pois, 114
    Iroquois Ogwissimanabo (Yellow Squash Soup), 152
    Iroquois Roast Corn Soup ('o' nanh-dah), 151–52
    Italian-American Pasta and Bean Soup (Pasta e Fagioli), 154–55
    Narragansett Dovecrest Quahog Chowder, 187–88
    Nicaraguan-American Sopa de Frijoles, 196
    Nigerian-American Pepper Soup, 199
    Papago Tepary Bean Soup, 219
    Peruvian-American Chupe de Camarones (Shrimp Chowder), 217
    Pima Poshol Soup, 219; Portuguese-American Soup—Faial Style, 224–25
    Pueblo (Eastern) Pojoaque Cream Soup, 229
    Scotch-Irish Potato Soup, 242
    Scottish-American The Highlander's Soup, 246
    Shawnee Fried Corn Soup, 252
    Tlingit Rainy Day Fish Chowder, 273
    Ukrainian-American Borsch, 279–80
    Ukrainian-American Kapusnyak, 280
    Vietnamese-American Chicken Noodle Soup, 281–82.
Spanish Eggs, 262
Spareribs, Okinawan, 205
Spicy Beef with Mint Leaves, 271–72
Spicy Rice (Ic Pilav), 277–78
Spinach Pie, 80–81
Spinach Salad, Korean-American, 166
Spinach-Rice Casserole, Ojibway, 203
Split Peas, in French Canadian Soup aux Pois, 114
Stack Cakes. See also Cakes; Desserts
    Icelandic-American Vinarterta, 146–47
    Melungeon Stack Cake, 177–78
    Scotch-Irish Apple Stack Cake, 242–43
Stews. See also Beef Dishes; Chicken Dishes; Lamb Dishes; Pork Dishes; Soups
    Assyrian-American Booshala, 26–27
    Belgian-American Chicken Booyah, 38–39
    Belgian-American Flemish Beef and Beer Stew, 40–41
    Cane River Creole Okra Gumbo, 53
    Choctaw Tonshla Bona, 69
    Ecuadoran-American El Locro Gringo, 97
    Filipino-American Adobo Manok (Chicken), 107
    Filipino-American Cirio's Pork Adobo, 107–08
    Finnish-American Moijakka, 109–10
    Hopi Whole Wheat Stew, 141–42
    Jamaican-American Oxtail Stew with Vegetables, 158
    Mexican-American Chicken Pozole, 181
    Mexican-American Kika's Chili Beans, 180–81
    Polish-American Hunter's Stew, 222
    Sioux Boiled Meat, 254
    Zuni Chuleya:we (Posole Stew), 288–89
Stuffed Breads, See also Breads; Corn Breads; Flatbreads; Fry Breads; Pancakes; Pasties and Turnovers; Rolls; Sweet Breads
    Latvian-American Baltic Baconettes (Piragi), 169–70
    Germans from Russia Kraut Beerucks or Cabbage Busters, 120
    Carpatho-Rusyn-American Pagach, 58
    Salvadoran-American Pupusas, 238–39
Stuffed Cabbage (Polish-American), 220–22 (ill. 221)
Stuffed Cabbage, As Made by 29 Ethnic Groups, 293–94
Stuffed Grape Leaves (Athenian), 122–24 (ill. 123)
Stuffed Green Peppers, 22–23

Stuffed Pumpkin, 255–256
Succotash, Cherokee, 60
Sugar Cake, Moravian, 183–84
Svikly, 279
Swedish Meatballs, 264–65
Sweet Breads. *See also* Breads; Corn Breads;
    Flatbreads; Fry Breads; Pancakes; Rolls;
    Stuffed Breads
    Anglo-American Quick Sally Lunn, 14–15
    Austrian-American Salzburger Raisin Bread, 29–
    30
    Irish-American, Curley's Favorite Irish Bread,
    148–49
    Moravian Love Feast Buns, 183
Sweet Potato Biscuits, 227–28
Sweet Potato Bread, 173–74
Sweet Potato Pie, 7–8
Sweet Potatoes, in
    Guyanese-American Sea Trout Salad, 130
    Seminole and Miccosukee Pumpkin Bread, 248
Swiss Tea, 269
Syrian-Americans. *See* Arab-Americans, 17

Taboos, Religious or Personal, xviii
Tabouli, 18–19
Taiwanese-Americans. *See* Chinese-Americans, 63
Tan, 21
Tarts. *See* Pies and Tarts
Tea Cakes, Mildred's Creole, 52–53
Tea Cakes, Welsh, 287–88
Tea, Friendly Polish, 220
Tea, Swiss, 269
Tepary Bean Soup, 219
Teriyaki Sauce, Obachan's Special, 159–60
Third Generation Immigrants, x–xi
Three Sisters Rice, 286
Tiny Kibbee Balls, 18
Tohono O'Odham. *See* Pima and Papago, 218
Tomatoes, in
    Acadian-Cajun Catfish Courtbouillon, 3
    Acadian-Cajun Shrimp Jumbalaya, 2–3
    Arab-American Tabouli, 18–19
    Asian Indian-American Stuffed Green Peppers,
    22–23
    Bulgarian-American Macedonian Style Peppers,
    46–47
    Carpatho-Rusyn-American Machanka, 57
    Franco-American Shrimp a La Creole, 112–13
    Guatemalan-American Radish Salad, 126
    Melungeon Tomato Gravy, 176
    Nigerian-American Black-Eyed Peas, 199
    Persian (Iranian)-American Potato Tomato
    Omelet, 214–15
    Papago Tepary Bean Soup, 219
    Spanish-American Arroz Guisado con Tomates,
    262

Tomato Sauce, in Aunt Gertie's Red Rice, 128
Tomsum, 138
Tonshla Bona, 69
Tortillas, 218–19
Tostones, 92
Tourlou, 124
Travellers. *See* Gypsy-Americans, 131
Turkey Bones and Rice Chowder, 66
Turn Corn (Cou-Cou), 34
Turnips and Pork Ribs Etouffée, 78–79
Turnovers. *See also* Breads; Pasties and Turnovers;
    Stuffed Breads
Tuscarora. *See* Iroquis, 151; Lumbee Indians of
    North Carolina, 173

Varmuza, 85
Vegetable Dishes
    Acadian-Cajun Smothered Potatoes, 4–5
    African-American Guilt-Free Collard Greens, 7
    Asian Indian-American Stuffed Green Peppers,
    22–23
    Brazilian-American Couve à Mineira, 45
    Cherokee Succotash, 60
    Chitimacha Macque Choux, 67–68
    Croatian-American Spinach Pie, 80–81
    Croatian-American Zgance, 81–82
    Dominican-American Tostones, 92
    Dutch-American Coleslaw, 94–95
    Dutch-American Dutch Carrots, 96
    German-American Sauteed Red Cabbage, 116–
    17
    Greek-American Tourlou, 124
    Hungarian-American Paprika Potatoes, 144–45
    Irish-American Colcannon, 149
    Irish-American Potato-Chive Pancakes, 149–50
    Iroquois Ogwissimanabo (Yellow Squash Soup),
    152
    Italian-American Greens and Beans, 154
    Italian-American Red and White Herb Roasted
    Potatoes, 157
    Jewish-American Carrot-Sweet Potato Tzimmes,
    164
    Korean-American Spinach Salad, 166
    Lithuanian-American Kugelis, 171
    Lumbee Sweet Potato Bread, 173–74
    Mormon Potato Salad, 185–86
    Ojibway Spinach-Rice Casserole, 203
    Okinawan-American Chanpuru, 205–06
    Panamanian-American Foo-Foo, 209–10
    Panamanian-American Platanos en Tentacion,
    209
    Potawatomi Baked Corn, 227
    Russian-American Marinated Mushrooms, 235–
    36
    Slovak-American Baba, 258
    Slovak-American Halusky, 258

Spanish-American Caldo, 263
Zuni Me:mo'le (Pumpkin and Pumpkin Seeds),
    289
Vegetarian Dishes
    Asian Indian Peanut Potatoes, 23–24
    Austrian-American Oatmeal Soup, 30–31
    Basque-American Basque Soup, 36
    Black Muslim Bean Cake, 43
    Croatian-American Ajvar, 81
    Cuban-American Black Bean Soup, 82–83
    Ethiopian-American Atakelte, 105
    Ethiopian-American Azifa, 105–06
    Iroquois Ogwissimanabo (Yellow Squash Soup),
        152
    Pueblo (Eastern) Pojoaque Cream Soup, 229
    Ukrainian-American Borsch, 279–80
    Vietnamese-American Arhat's Feast, 282–83
Vinarterta, 146–47
Vinegret (Cooked Vegetable Salad), 236–37
Vinha D'alhos, 226
Vlach Cheese Corn Bread (Pispilita), 47
Vlachs. *See* Bulgarian-Americans, Macedonian-
    Americans, and Vlachs, 46

Waffles, Berrie Good, 186–87
Walnut Pudding, 37
Walnuts, in
    English Canadian-American Nanaimo Bars,
        100–01
    Franco-American Huguenot Torte, 112
    Slovak-American Cookies, 257
    Slovak-American Slovakian Nut Candy, 257–58
    Slovene-American Icebox Potica, 259–60, Kifles,
        261
Watercress and Beef, 138–39

Wendish Saurbraten, 270–71
Wheat Berries, in
    Hopi Whole Wheat Stew, 141–42
    Mormon Berrie Good Waffles, 186–87
    Mormon Blender Pancakes, 186
    Pima Poshol Soup, 219
White Beans, in Spanish-American Caldo, 263
White Fish Stew, 102
White Potato Pie, 8
Whitebread Americans, xiv–xv
Wild Onions and Eggs, 61
Wild Rice, in
    Ojibway Gagoonz —Little Porcupines, 203–04
    Ojibway Spinach-Rice Casserole, 203
    Sioux Stuffed Pumpkin, 255–256
Wild Sage Bread, 229
Wojapi Pudding, 253–54
World Wide Web Sites
    Bibliography of, 302–03
    For This Book, www.ethnicook.com, xvi, xviii
Wyoming Basque Potatoes, 37

Yogurt, in
    Armenian-American Lemon-Yogurt Cake, 20
    Armenian-American Nutmeg Cake, 21
    Armenian-American Tan, 21
    Assyrian-American Booshala, 26–27
    Egyptian-American Eggplant and Zucchini
        Salad, 99
    Serbian-American Cucumber Salad, 249–50
Yorkshire Pudding, 15
Yummasetti, 11–12

Zazich, 26

Mark H. Zanger is a longtime restaurant critic for the *Boston Phoenix* under the name "Robert Nadeau," and a veteran Boston journalist. He is a former executive editor of *Cook's Illustrated* magazine. He has written and edited for various newspapers, online services, and magazines. Zanger is the author of *Robert Nadeau's Guide to Boston Restaurants* and of a chapter on Boston restaurants in *Fodor's 98*.